T0100133

Introduction to Computational Thinking

Problem Solving, Algorithms, Data Structures, and More

Thomas Mailund

Apress®

Introduction to Computational Thinking: Problem Solving, Algorithms, Data Structures, and More

Thomas Mailund
Aarhus N, Denmark

ISBN-13 (pbk): 978-1-4842-7076-9   ISBN-13 (electronic): 978-1-4842-7077-6
https://doi.org/10.1007/978-1-4842-7077-6

Managing Director, Apress Media LLC: Welmoed Spahr
Acquisitions Editor: Steve Anglin
Development Editor: Matthew Moodie
Coordinating Editor: Mark Powers

Cover designed by eStudioCalamar

Cover image by Engin Akyurt on Unsplash (www.unsplash.com)

Distributed to the book trade worldwide by Apress Media, LLC, 1 New York Plaza, New York, NY 10004, U.S.A. Phone 1-800-SPRINGER, fax (201) 348-4505, e-mail orders-ny@springer-sbm.com, or visit www.springeronline.com. Apress Media, LLC is a California LLC and the sole member (owner) is Springer Science + Business Media Finance Inc (SSBM Finance Inc). SSBM Finance Inc is a **Delaware** corporation.

For information on translations, please e-mail booktranslations@springernature.com; for reprint, paperback, or audio rights, please e-mail bookpermissions@springernature.com.

Apress titles may be purchased in bulk for academic, corporate, or promotional use. eBook versions and licenses are also available for most titles. For more information, reference our Print and eBook Bulk Sales web page at http://www.apress.com/bulk-sales.

Any source code or other supplementary material referenced by the author in this book is available to readers on GitHub via the book's product page, located at www.apress.com/9781484270769. For more detailed information, please visit http://www.apress.com/source-code.

Printed on acid-free paper

Table of Contents

About the Author

Thomas Mailund is an associate professor in bioinformatics at Aarhus University, Denmark. He has a background in math and computer science. For the past decade, his main focus has been on genetics and evolutionary studies, particularly comparative genomics, speciation, and gene flow between emerging species. He has published *String Algorithms in C*, *R Data Science Quick Reference*, *The Joys of Hashing*, *Domain-Specific Languages in R*, *Beginning Data Science in R*, *Functional Programming in R*, and *Metaprogramming in R*, all from Apress, as well as other books.

About the Technical Reviewer

Troels Bjerre Lund is an associate professor of computer science at the IT University of Copenhagen. He is an expert in computational game theory and has been teaching programming and software development for the past seven years.

CHAPTER 1

Introduction

Using computers as more than glorified typewriters or calculators is an increasingly important aspect of any scientific or technological field, and knowing how to program a computer to solve new problems has become as essential a skill as mathematics. Learning how to program can be a frustrating experience at times since computers require a level of precision and rigor in how we express our ideas, which we rarely encounter elsewhere in life. While occasionally infuriating, programming can also be very rewarding. Programs are created out of pure thought, and it is a special feeling when you make a computer transform your ideas into actions and see it solve your problems for you.

Solving any kind of problem, on a computer or otherwise, requires a certain level of precision. To address the right question, we must first understand what the problem *is*. We also need to have a precise idea about what an adequate *solution* to the problem would be—or at the very least some way of distinguishing between two solutions to judge if one is better than the other. These are concerns we will need to address in any problem-solving task, but where everyday life might forgive some fuzzy thinking in problem solving, computers are far less forgiving. To solve a problem on a computer, you must first specify with mathematical clarity what the problem is and what a solution is and, after that, how you will go about deriving a solution. And only then can you write a program and put the computer to work.

For the novice programmer, the last step—implementing a solution in a computer language—is often the most frustrating. Computer programs do not allow any ambiguities, and that means that if you do not abide by the computer language's rules—if you get the grammar wrong in the slightest—the computer will refuse even to consider your program. Learning how to write programs the computer will even attempt to run is the first hurdle to overcome.

Many good books can teach you different programming languages, and it is worth your while getting a few of these about the programming languages you plan to use in your future work. This book is not only about programming, however, but about how

1

© Thomas Mailund 2021
T. Mailund, *Introduction to Computational Thinking*, https://doi.org/10.1007/978-1-4842-7077-6_1

computation is done and how you can make computation efficient. Still, from time to time, I will show you tricks for making your programming efficient as well, meaning speeding up how fast you can write your programs, which is a separate issue from how efficient your programs are once you have implemented them. These tricks are generally applicable, provided your programming language supports the features we use, and for a working programmer, efficient *programming* is as important as efficient *programs*. I won't cover these tricks as separate topics, but show them when we study topics where they are useful.

For the programming we do in the book, we will use the Python programming language. The Python language is generally considered an excellent first language to learn because of its high-level yet intuitive features, and at the same time, Python is one of the most popular programming languages for scientific programs. It is one of the most frequently used languages for data science. It is number one on the Kaggle machine learning platform (www.kaggle.com). It has powerful libraries for machine learning, data analysis, and scientific computing through various software modules. It is also one of the most popular languages for scripting workflows of data analysis and for administrating computer systems.

We will not explore the full language, however, as the book is already long without discussing all the powerful features in Python. But I will show you how the code we write would look if you implemented it like a "real" Python programmer, with the features of the language you would need to get there. You can safely ignore those parts if you only want to learn the aspects of programming that generalize to other languages and if you are only interested in how to write effective and efficient code. In any language you use regularly, however, it is worth knowing the programming style and idioms for that language. Styles do not directly translate from one language to another, since what is easy to do in one might be hard in another and vice versa. Spend the time to learn how experienced programmers use a language when you learn it, if you want to be effective.

We use Python to illustrate ideas and for exercising topics we cover, but the focus of the book is not on Python programming. The focus is how to think about problem solving in a disciplined way, to consider problems as computational tasks, and how to plan solutions in ways that are computationally efficient. Along the way, we will see different programming paradigms that will show you how you can think about programming in different ways. Primarily, these will be *functional programming* and *object-oriented programming*, both of which are supported by Python. Thinking about structuring data, about how to efficiently manipulate data to solve problems, and how to structure your code so it is easy to write, easy to extend, and easy to maintain is what we mean by *computational thinking*.

Models of the World and Formalizing Problems

Our goal is to learn how to *formalize objectives* in such a way that we can specify *mathematically and objectively* what solutions to our goals are. This also means formalizing what data we have and how we should interpret it. Formalizing a problem might reveal that we do not have sufficient data for the issue at hand. It might also show that we do not truly understand our problem. If we cannot clearly define what we want, we won't be able to formalize how to get it. We might, with some luck, be able to fudge it a bit and get *something* and then use subjective opinion to judge if what we get is what we wanted. This is far from optimal, though. If you and I disagree on whether one solution is better than another or not, we have no way of resolving the issue.

Formalizing problems and formalizing what data we have to work with is what you do in all natural sciences. You might not have thought about it this way before—depending on which science you have a background in—but when we derive theories (or laws) about the natural world, we are making formal statements about how the world works. For some theories there are exceptions—the world is breaking a natural law—which tells us we do not have a comprehensive theory. But any theory worth its salt can be falsified, which is another way of saying that we can judge if a data point matches the formalization of the theory or not.

In the hard sciences, like physics and chemistry, these theories are described in the language of mathematics, often in somewhat complex equations. In sciences describing very complex systems, such as biology that tries to explain life in general, we often have much simpler mathematics, and the rules almost always have exceptions. Biology is more complicated than particle physics, so it is harder to formalize, and thus we stick with simpler equations. There is no point in using very complex mathematics to describe something we do not understand—simple mathematics suffices for that. Any quantitative evaluation of the natural world requires some mathematics and some formalization of scientific theories—even if the mathematics is as simple as counting to see if some quantity is more abundant in some situations than others. All quantitative data analysis involves formalizing our thoughts about reality and reducing data to the relevant aspects for those formal descriptions.

Abstracting the complex natural world to something more manageable is called *modeling*. We build models of the real world—usually mathematical models. We aim at making the models simple enough to understand, yet sophisticated enough to describe the aspects of the world we are interested in. In principle, we could model molecular evolution as a physical system at the level of particles. We don't, because this would be

3

much too complex for us to work with and probably wouldn't help us answer most of the questions about evolution we are interested in. Instead, we model molecular evolution as random mutations in strings of DNA, abstracting the three-dimensional DNA molecules into one-dimensional strings over the four letters A, C, G, and T. We abstract away aspects of the world that are not relevant for the models, and we abstract away features about the data that are not modeled.

Building models of the natural world is the goal of all the sciences and much too broad a topic for this book. The models are relevant for computational thinking, however. When we formalize how to solve problems, we do so within a model of the world. This model will affect how we can formalize problems and at which level of detail we consider our data. Sometimes, changing the model of reality can change what can be efficiently computed—or make an easy problem intractable. Of course, we should not pick scientific theories based on what we can efficiently calculate, but sometimes, abstracting away aspects of the world that are not essential for the problem at hand will not qualitatively change solutions but might make an otherwise impossible problem easy.

This book is not about modeling the world. We will generally assume that we have some formal models to work with within whatever scientific field we find ourselves. You are rarely in the situation where you can pick your theories at random to satisfy your computational needs, but keep in mind that formalizing the *problem* you want to solve might give you some wiggle room within those formal scientific theories. When, for example, we study genome evolution or population genetics, we abstract complex DNA molecules to the level of strings or reduce populations to gene frequencies. These abstractions are there to simplify the subject matter to something that can be attacked computationally.

What Is Computational Thinking?

Computational thinking is what you do when you take a problem and formalize it, when you distil it into something where you can objectively determine if something is a solution to it or not. For example, given a sequence of numbers, are all positive? Easy to check, and either all the numbers are positive or they are not. Or perhaps the problem is not a yes-no question but an optimization issue. Finding the shortest route to get from points A to B is an optimization problem. It might be easy for us to determine if one path is shorter than another, which would be a yes-no problem, but actually coming up with short routes might be a harder problem. It is still a computational problem, as long as we can formalize what a path is and how we measure distance.

Computational thinking is also what happens after you have formalized the problem, when you figure out how to solve it. A formal description for how to solve a problem is called an *algorithm*, after the ninth-century mathematician Muhammad ibn Musa al'Khwarizmi who is also responsible for the term algebra. To qualify as an algorithm, a description of how to solve a problem must be in sufficient detail that we can follow it without having to involve any guesswork. If you implement it on a computer, I guarantee you that you do not want to leave any room for guessing. The description must always get to a solution in a finite number of steps—we don't want to keep computing forever—and the description must always lead to a valid solution—we don't want to follow all the steps and end up with something we cannot use anyway.[1]

Designing algorithms is part science and part art. There are general guidelines we can use to approach a computational problem to develop algorithms and general approaches to organizing data such that we can manipulate it efficiently, but you will almost always have to adapt the general ideas to your specific problem. Here, sparks of insight cannot be underestimated—sometimes, just looking at a problem in different ways will open entirely new ways of approaching it. The general approaches can be taught and learned and are the main topic of this book. The art of designing algorithms comes with practice, and as with all skills, the more you practice, the better you get.

Most of the algorithms we will see in this book are used in almost all software that runs on your computer (with the exceptions of some toy examples found in the exercises that are never used in the wild). Sorting and searching in data and arranging data for fast retrieval or fast update is part of almost all computations. The models behind such algorithms are often exceedingly abstract, much more so than any model we would use to describe real-world phenomena. A sorting algorithm might work in a world where the only thing you can do with objects is to determine which of two objects is smaller.

---

[1]There are exceptions to the requirement that an algorithm should always complete in a finite number of steps. When we implement something like a web service or an operating system, we don't want our programs to terminate after a finite number of calculations, but instead want them to run, and be responsive, indefinitely. In those cases, we relax the requirement and require that they can respond to all events in a finite number of steps. We also have exceptions to always getting correct answers. Sometimes, we can accept that we get the right answer with high probability—if we can quickly test if the answer is correct and maybe rerun the algorithm for another solution and continue this until we get lucky. These are unusual cases, however, and we do not consider them in this book.

Or maybe the algorithm works in a model that allows more structure to data, and this structure can be exploited to make the algorithm more efficient. In any case, what we can do with data depends on our models, and for computation, these models are often remarkably abstract. Such abstract models can feel far from the world your problem originates in, but it is because the models are so very theoretical that we can apply the algorithmic solutions to so many varied problems.

Some people spend their entire lives developing new algorithms for general problems. Those people would be professional computer science academics. Most people who solve problems on computers are not doing this, even if they develop algorithms on a daily basis. When we deal with concrete issues, we can usually do so by combining existing algorithms in the right ways. Having a toolbox of algorithms to pick from and knowing their strengths and weaknesses is more important in day-to-day computational work than being able to design algorithms entirely from scratch—although that can be important as well, of course, on the rare occasions when your toolbox does not suffice.

Whether you can get where you want to go by combining existing algorithms or you have to design new ones, the general approach is the same. You have to break apart big tasks that you do not know how to solve (yet) into smaller tasks that, when all done, will have completed the larger tasks. Steps to a job, such as "find the largest number in a sequence," can be broken into smaller steps such as "compare the first two numbers and remember the largest," "compare the largest of the first two to the third and remember the largest," and so on. You start out with one big task—the problem you want to solve—and you keep breaking down the problem into smaller tasks until they all are tasks you know how to handle—either because they are trivial or because you have an algorithm in your toolbox that can solve them. The practice of breaking down tasks until you can resolve them all is at the heart of computational thinking.

Developing and combining algorithms is a vital part of computational thinking, but algorithms alone do not solve any problems. Algorithms need to be executed to solve concrete problems; we need to follow the instructions they provide on actual data to get actual solutions. Since we rarely want to do this by hand or with pen and paper, we wish to instruct computers how to run algorithms, which means that we have to translate a high-level description of an algorithm to a lower-level description that can be put into a computer program that the machine will then slavishly execute. This task is called *implementing* the algorithm.

Designing an algorithm and implementing it as a computer program are two separate tasks, although tightly linked. The first task involves understanding the problem you want to solve in sufficient detail that you can break it down into pieces that you know how to address. The second task consists in breaking those pieces into even smaller ones that the computer can solve; this is where the algorithm design task meets the programming task.

The abstraction level at which you can implement an algorithm depends intimately on the programming language and the libraries of functionality you have access to. At the most basic level—the hardware of your computer—the instructions available do little more than move bits around and do basic arithmetic.[2] A modern CPU is a very sophisticated machine for doing this, with many optimizations implemented in hardware, but the basic operations you have at this level are still pretty primitive. This is the level of abstraction where you can get the highest performance out of your CPU, but we practically never program at this level, because it is also the level of abstraction where you get the lowest performance out of a programmer. Basic arithmetic is just too low a level of abstraction for us to think about algorithms constructively.

Programming languages provide higher levels of abstraction to the programmer. They can do this because someone has written a program that can translate the high-level operations in the programming language into the right sequence of lower-level operations that the computer can actually execute.[3] Which abstractions are available varies tremendously between programming languages, but they all need to describe programs that are eventually run at the low level of the computer's CPU. The programming language abstractions are just an interface between the programmer and

---

[2]Okay, at a more fundamental level, a computer is a rock you can communicate with through electricity, but from a computational perspective, basic arithmetic operations are as primitive as they come.

[3]If you think about it, there is an interesting question on how programs that translate high-level instructions into low-level instructions are written. It is hard enough to write a program that works correctly in a high-level programming language; it is substantially harder to do in the language the machine understands. You want to write the programs for dealing with high-level abstractions in programming languages that support these abstractions. But to support the abstractions, you need a program that implements them. That is a circular dependency, and that is problematic. You can solve it by first writing primitive programs that support some abstractions. Now you can use these abstractions to write a *better* program that can handle more abstractions. This, in turn, lets you write even better programs with better abstractions. At this point, you can throw away the most primitive programs because you have implemented a programming language that you can use to implement the programming language itself. This process is known as *bootstrapping*, named after the phrase *"to pull oneself up by one's bootstraps."*

the machine, and the language's implementers have handled how these abstractions are executed at the lower layers of the computer.

We sometimes talk about high-level and low-level programming languages, but there isn't a real dichotomy. There are merely differences in the higher-level abstractions provided by all programming languages. Some programming languages provide an environment for programming very close to the hardware, where you can manipulate bits at the lowest level while still having some abstractions to control the steps taken by your program and some abstractions for representing data beyond merely bit patterns. These we would call low-level languages because they aim to be close to the lowest level of abstraction on the computer. Other languages, high-level languages, provide a programming environment that tries to hide the lower levels to protect the programmer from them. How data is actually represented at lower levels is hidden by abstractions in the language, and the programming environment guarantees that the mapping between language concepts and bits is handled correctly.

Computational Thinking in a Broader Context

To summarize, what we call computational thinking in this book refers to a broad range of activities vital for solving problems using a computer. For some of those activities, computational thinking is merely a tiny aspect. Making models of the real world in order to understand it is the entire goal of science; considering scientific theories in the light of how we can make computations using the equations that come out of the theories is a minute aspect of the scientific process, but an essential one if you want to use your computer to do science. Creating new algorithms to solve a particular problem is also almost entirely computational thinking in action; implementing these algorithms, on the other hand, can be an almost mechanical process once you have fleshed out the algorithm in sufficient detail.

One thing that sometimes complicates learning how to think about computations is that there is rarely a single right answer to any problem you consider. It shares this with natural sciences. While we usually believe that there is a unique natural world out there to explore, we generally do not attempt to model it in full detail; an accurate model of reality would be too complicated to be useful. Instead, we build models that simplify reality, and there is no "right" model to be found—only more or less valuable models. When we seek to solve a problem on a computer, we are in the same situation. We need to abstract a model of reality that is useful, and there may be many different choices we can reasonably make in doing this, all with different pros and cons.

For any of these models, we have a seemingly endless list of appropriate algorithms we can choose from to solve our problem. Some will be horrible choices for various reasons. They might not solve the problem at hand in all cases, or at all, or they might solve the problem but take so long to do this that in practical terms they never finish computing. Many of the choices, however, will solve the problem and in a reasonable time, but use different computational resources in doing so. Some run faster than others; some can exploit many CPUs in parallel, solving the problem faster but using more resources to do so; some might be fast but require much more memory to solve the problem and therefore might not be feasible solutions given the resources you have. It requires computational thinking to derive these algorithms, but it is also computational thinking to reason about the resources they need and to judge which algorithms can be used in practice and which cannot.

Once you have chosen an appropriate algorithm to solve your problem, you need to implement it to execute it. On itself, the algorithm is useless; only when it is executed does it have any value, and executing it on a computer means you have to implement it as a computer program first. At this step, you need to decide on a computer programming language and then how to flesh out the details the algorithm does not specify. For choosing the programming language, you once again have numerous choices, all with different strengths and weaknesses. Typically, the first choice is between the speed and speed—how fast can you implement the algorithm in a given language vs. how fast it will run once you have implemented it. Typically, high-level languages let you implement your ideas more swiftly, but often at the cost of slightly (or less slightly) slower programs. Low-level languages let you control your computer in greater detail, which allows you to implement faster programs, but at the cost of also having to specify details that high-level languages will shield you from. You shouldn't always go for making your programs as fast as possible; instead, you should go for solving your actual problem as speedy as possible. You can make your program very fast to run by spending a vast amount of time implementing it, or you can implement it quickly and let it run a little longer. You want to take the path that gets you to your solution the fastest. Here, of course, you should also take into account how often you expect to use your program. A program that is run often gains more from being faster than one that runs only for a specific project and only a few times there.

In reality, the choice of programming language is not between all possible languages, but between the languages you know how to write programs in. Learning a new programming language to implement an algorithm is rarely, if ever, worth the time. If you only know one language, the choice is made for you, but it is worthwhile to know a few, at least, and to know both a high-level and a low-level language with sufficient fluency that you can implement algorithms in them with comfortable fluency. This gives you some choice in what to choose when you have a program to write.

The choices aren't all made once you have decided on the programming language, though. There will always be details that are not addressed by your algorithm, but that must be addressed by your program. The algorithm might use different abstract data structures, such as "sets" or "queues" or "tables," and it might also specify how fast operations on these have to be, but when you have to make concrete implementations of these structures or choose existing implementations from software libraries, there are more options to consider. In high-level programming languages, there are fewer details you have to flesh out than in low-level languages, which is one of the reasons it is usually much faster to implement an algorithm in a high-level language than in a low-level language—but there will always be some choices to be made at this point in the process as well.

You might hope you are done when you have implemented your algorithm, but this is usually not the case. You need to feed data into the program and get the answer out, and here you have choices to make about data formats. Your program will not live in isolation from other programs, either, but communicate with the world, usually in the form of files and data formatted in different file formats. Again, there are choices to be made for how you wrap your algorithm in a program. If your algorithm is useful for more than a single project, you might also put it in a software library, and then there are choices to be made about how you provide an interface to it. If you build a whole library of different algorithms and data structures, constructing interfaces to the library is full of critical design decisions, and these decisions affect how other programs can use the algorithms and how efficiently, so this is also an aspect of computational thinking—but here only a part of the broader topic of software engineering.

What Is to Come

The purpose of this book is to introduce computational thinking as basic problem-solving approaches for designing algorithms and implementing them in a computer language, the Python language. We will focus on the design of algorithms more than the implementation of them and only use a subset of the Python programming language for exercises. We will use the Python features necessary so our code behaves the way a Python programmer would expect, with the idioms of the language, but we will mainly use a subset of Python for the core code that you will find in many other languages. This will make it easier to transfer what you learn to other programming languages, but keep in mind that it also means that the solutions we consider are not necessarily the solutions an experienced Python programmer would come up with. There are ways of expressing things in Python that can implement our algorithms more effectively, but those are Python specific and might not be found in other languages.

In many of the following chapters, I will explain how computation is done on an actual computer, not just in Python but on computers in general. General computers do not understand Python programs but do understand more primitive instructions that you can give a CPU, and I will try to put our Python programs in a context of these. I will also explain how computers store data, which they can only do using simple memory words consisting of ones and zeros. These explanations are far from comprehensive and are only intended to give you a feeling for how instructions in a high-level programming language such as Python will have to be translated into much lower-level concepts on actual hardware. When I do explain these concepts, I will not always be completely honest about how Python *actually* handles these issues. Since Python is a very high-level programming language, it supports features that are not found in lower-level languages, and this means that to run a Python program, you need a more complex model of both data and code than you will need in many other languages. I will explain general concepts, but I will give a simplified explanation of them. If you want to know the details of how your computer really deals with these concepts and how Python handles these and more complex features of the language, you will need to find this information elsewhere.

We use a real programming language to explain the algorithms in the book to make it easier for you to experiment with them. Many algorithmic textbooks will not, preferring to describe algorithms in pseudo-code where the abstractions can be fitted to the problem. This might make the description of algorithms slightly more accessible, but can also easily hide away the issues that you will have to resolve actually to implement them.

We prefer to use an actual language. It is a very high-level language, so some details that you will have to deal with in lower-level languages are still hidden from you, but what you can implement in Python you can actually run on your computer. And it is vital that you do take the code in this book and experiment with it.

To get the full benefit out of this book, or any book like it, you must practice. And practice a lot. Programming can look deceptively easy—at least for the complexity level we consider in this book—but it is substantially harder to write your own code than it is to read and understand code already written.[4] Without exercising the skills involved in computational thinking and algorithmic programming, at best you will get a superficial understanding. Watching the Olympics doesn't prepare you for athletics. Each chapter has an exercise set associated with it, and you should expect to use at least as much time doing exercises as you spend reading the chapters if you want the full benefit out of the book.

---

[4]An interesting thing is that to inexperienced programmers, and with simple programs, it is a lot easier to read a program than to write it. The opposite is the case for experienced programmers working in more extensive and more complex programs. Once programs reach a certain level of complexity, they get harder to read than to write, and a lot of software engineering aims at alleviating this.

CHAPTER 2

Introducing Python Programming

Many textbooks on algorithms will present the algorithms in so-called *pseudo-code*, something that looks like it is written in a real programming language while it is in fact written in an approximation to such a language but where the abstractions and programming constructs are chosen to make the algorithms look as simple as necessary. Since the goal of these books is to present the essentials of an algorithm and not distract the reader with unnecessary language artifacts, it is a sensible approach. It does, however, occasionally hide too many details from the reader, and since the pseudo-code cannot be run by a computer, it is not possible to experiment with it to test different approaches to how an algorithm could be implemented in practice. In this book, we will not use pseudo-code but present all algorithms in the Python programming language. Python is a very high-level language, and in many ways, Python implementations of common algorithms look very similar to pseudo-code versions of them, but with Python, you get a working implementation.

Python is a general-purpose programming language with many advanced features, and it scales well to constructing large software systems. At the same time, it has a very gentle learning curve and lets you implement small programs with minimal programming overhead. It is perfect for our purpose in this book. By knowing just a tiny subset of the language, you will be able to implement the algorithms we cover, and you will be able to experiment with them. Should you decide to make more of a career out of programming, then you can easily pick up the more advanced features of Python and use this language for larger projects as well.

Writing complete programs, especially more extensive applications, requires different skills than the computational thinking we cover in this book. It takes a different skill set to be able to engineer software such that it is scalable and maintainable than the skills that are needed to build efficient algorithms. Those software engineering skills are

13

© Thomas Mailund 2021
T. Mailund, *Introduction to Computational Thinking*, https://doi.org/10.1007/978-1-4842-7077-6_2

beyond the topics here. If you are interested in writing larger systems, there are many excellent textbooks on the market.

Obtaining Python

When you write programs in Python, you will usually do this in one or more plain-text files using a text editor. You cannot use word processors such as Microsoft Word since these do not save their documents as plain text. An excellent editor that supports Python and is available on Windows, macOS, and Linux is Visual Studio Code (`https://code.visualstudio.com`). When you save a file, give it the suffix `.py`. This is not necessary to have Python run your program, but it is the convention, and it makes it easier to recognize that a file contains a Python program.

You can download Python from `www.python.org/`. There are installers for Windows and macOS, and if you use Linux, then chances are that Python is already installed. If not, the package manager on your platform will be able to install it. The dialect of Python we will use in this book is Python 3.x (version numbers that start with 3). The differences between Python 2.x and 3.x, for the purpose of the algorithms we will explore here, are very minor, and all the algorithms in this book work equally well in either version. There are differences in the built-in functions, though, so you should download the installer for a Python 3.x to get exactly the behavior as described here.

In a few places, we will use additional functionality from what you get with a basic Python installation, however. We use a module called `Numpy` for tables when we cover dynamic programming in Chapter 9, and I show you plotting code for empirically validating the running time of algorithms in Chapter 4 where I use a module called `matplotlib`. You do not need either to follow the book, however. There are alternatives to `Numpy` for tables, and you can always plot running times in spreadsheets or other plotting programs. You can install these packages using a tool, `pip`, that is installed together with Python

```
pip install <package name>
```

but if you do not mind a larger installation—taking up more space on your disk—you can install Python together with many packages for scientific computing and data science from `www.anaconda.com`. We only use a tiny fraction of the software that is installed via Anaconda, but everything we do use will be available to you once you have installed Anaconda. If you continue programming in Python after you have read this book, chances are that you will find a good use for many of the other modules installed by Anaconda, especially if you want to continue your career using Python for data science.

Running Python

When you have installed Python, written a program, and saved it to a file, say `file.py`, then you can run your program by writing

```
python3 file.py
```

in your terminal. If you want to use Python interactively, you can write

```
python3
```

Press Ctrl+D to leave the Python terminal again.

This will give you a Python terminal where you can write instructions to Python and get its response back. For the next few sections, you can just do that. I suggest you type all the following examples into your Python terminal to test the results they give you.

Expressions in Python

Try writing some arithmetic expressions into the Python terminal, for example

```
2 + 4
```

or

```
2 * 3
```

You can write expressions as you know and love them from basic arithmetic. The arithmetic binary operators +, -, *, and / work as you would expect them to from the arithmetic you learned in school,[1] as does the unary -. That is,

```
-4
```

---

[1] If you have used other programming languages or if you use Python 2, division might work differently from what you expect. In some languages, including Python 2, / is integer division if you divide two integers, so, for example, 3/2 would be 1 since 2 divides 3 once, with a remainder of 1. In Python 3, / works as you learned in school and is called "true division." Integer division has a separate operator, //; see in the following.

is minus four.

```
2 * 2 + 3
```

is 7. Notice that we interpret 2 * 2 + 3 as you are familiar with in mathematical notation. First, we multiply two by two, and then you add three. Python knows the precedence rules that say that multiplication binds stronger than addition. If you want another precedence, you use parentheses as you would with a pen and paper.

```
(3 + 2) * 2
```

would be 10.

When you do not use parentheses and arithmetic precedence is taken into account, the evaluation proceeds from left to right for the preceding binary operators (for exponentiation, the order is right to left; see in the following). For example,

```
1 / 2 / 2
```

is interpreted as $(1/2)/2 = 1/4 = 0.25$ and not $1/(2/2) = 1.0$. To get right-to-left evaluation, you will need to add parentheses:

```
1 / (2 / 2)
```

If you have not noticed that in the usual arithmetic notation, then trust me it is how it works there as well. In expressions like this, however, I would use parentheses as well to make the order explicit.

You can always use parentheses to change the default evaluation order or simply to make explicit what you intend, even if it is already the default. Writing (2 * 2) + 3, while it is the default for 2 * 2 + 3, doesn't make the expression any harder to read, after all. I wouldn't use parentheses here, and you would probably not either, but you can if you want to.

There are more operations than addition, subtraction, multiplication, and divisions, for example, raising a number to a power. If you want to compute two to the power of four, $2^4 = 16$, you can use the ** operator: 2**4. This operator has higher precedence than multiplication and division, so 2 * 2**4 is $2 \cdot 24 = 32$ and not $(2 \cdot 2)^4 = 256$. This operator is not evaluated left to right but right to left, also following typical mathematical notation. This means that 2**3**4 is interpreted as $2^{3^4} \approx 2.4 \times 10^{24}$ and not $(2^3)^4 = 4086$. If you want to compute the latter, you must write (2**3)**4. The notation *is* the same as it would be in the usual mathematical notation, but if you find it hard to remember, you can always use parentheses to avoid any surprises, even when not strictly necessary.

Python 3 has two different division operators. When you use /, you get the division you are used to in mathematics; 1 / 3 gives you a third. However, it is often useful to guarantee that if you divide two integers, you get the integer result of the division. Remember that for division, n/m, you get an integer if m divides n. In general, you can write $n = a \cdot m + b$ where a is the integer number of times that m divides n and $b < m$ is the remainder. To get the integer part of the division, a in this example, you will use the // operator. So while 5 / 2 will give you 2.5, 5 // 2 will give you 2. To get the remainder, you use the modulus operator, %. Since $5 = 2 \cdot 2 + 1$, we would expect 5 % 2 to be one, and indeed it is. If you evaluate

```
(5 // 2) * 2 + (5 % 2)
```

the $a \cdot m + b$ form of this division, you get five, as expected. Another way to put this is that 5 // 2 is five divided by two, rounded down, or $\lfloor 5/2 \rfloor$.

The rules for integer division and remainder are always like these if we consider positive numbers n and m, but if n or m is negative, the result of the two operators is not necessarily as well defined, and different programming languages have made different choices.

An example might be the best way to illustrate this. Let's say we work on a program where we need to know what weekday any given day is. There are seven weekdays, and we can number them from Monday = 0 to Sunday = 6. If today is Tuesday, we would represent it as 1. If we want to know what day it is 10 days from now, we could do

```
today = 1 # Today is Tuesday
k = (today + 10) % 7 # Weekday 10 days from today
```

and we would find that k=4, so a Friday. All programming languages will agree on this. They will reason that you have moved forward 11 days, or 11//7=1 week, and then you have 4 days left, 11%7=4.

But what if we want to know what weekday it was 10 days ago? Then we could do

```
k = (today - 10) % 7 # Weekday 10 days ago
```

Here, we are evaluating -9 % 7, and different programming languages make equally valid, but different, choices on what the result should be. Some will say that you move one week back, so –1 times 7 days, so -9//7 should be –1, and then you have another –2 to go, so `-9%2` should be –2. There is nothing wrong with that reasoning, but for an application like our example, where the remainders should be numbers from 0 to 6, it means that we need to convert negative numbers to something in that range. It isn't hard; we can always add 7 if we get a negative number, and that is what you do in those languages, but Python has decided on a rule for remainders that makes it unnecessary. In Python, the rule is that n%m always has the same sign as m. That way, it works as the modular arithmetic you might have seen in algebra classes. For `-9%7`, you get 5, because m=7 is positive.

Moduli 7, –2, and 5 are the same remainder class, so it is the same result you get if you consider it as working in that modulus class, but it is more convenient if you always get numbers in the range 0–m. (However, if m is negative, the result will also be negative, but that is rarely something we have).

Because we want n = `(n//m)*m + (n%m)`, the decision for what n%m should be also affects what n//m is. For our "10 days ago" example, if `-9%7=5`, we have to have `-9//7=-2`. Now we are saying that to go 9 days back, we first go 2*7=14 backward and then 5 forward. So integer division, when you allow negative numbers, can get further negative than you might expect if you think about them as rounding toward zero, as we do for positive numbers.

It might sound complicated, but in most cases where we use integer division, we work with positive numbers, and in practically all applications where we use remainders, we want modulus classes, and that is what the % operator gives us, so it is rarely something you need to worry about in practice.

Some languages will say that you go back one times seven (so `-9 // 7` is –1) and then you have another.

Exercise: Evaluate the following expressions in Python. Check that they give you the expected result. If not, check if you can change that by inserting parentheses:

1. $2 \cdot 4 + 2$

2. $2^4 - 4^2$

3. $2 \cdot (1 + 2 + 3)$

4. $5/2$

5. $\lfloor 5/2 \rfloor$

6. $\dfrac{2}{1 + 2 + 3}$

7. $(1+2+3)^{1+2+3}$

8. $\dfrac{1+2+3}{2}$

Although it rarely happens with arithmetic expressions, once we write more complex Python, we will sometimes have very long lines. If that happens to you, you can terminate the expression you have so far on a line, add a backslash, and continue on the next line. This

```
2 * 5 \
+ 7 \
* 8
```

is equivalent to

```
2 * 5 + 7 * 8
```

Logical (or Boolean) Expressions

There are more than arithmetic expressions in Python, some of which you might be less familiar with. One such kind is logical expressions, also known as Boolean expressions. Those are expressions that have a true or false result rather than a numerical result. In Python, true and false are written True and False. Notice that these are capitalized. It is not true and false but True and False. They will be interpreted as 1 and 0 if you use them in an arithmetic expression, though.

You are probably familiar with the most common logical expressions—$a = b$, $a \neq b$, $a < b$, $a \leq b$, $a > b$, and $a \geq b$—which in Python are written as, in the same order, a == b, a != b, a < b, a <= b, a > b, and a >= b. Notice that equality is written with two equality signs. If you write a = b instead of a == b, you are not comparing a and b, but rather assigning b to a, as we shall see in the following. If both a and b are numbers, you will get an error if you use a single equality sign. When we start using variables, you will not get any error, but you will not be comparing two values.

You can string comparisons together, so if you want to say that b is between a and c, you can write a < b < c. You don't need to write such comparisons low to high, as in the preceding, or high to low as in c > b > a, but use any sequence of comparisons, for example, a > b < c to say that b should be less than both a and c, without making any claims about the order of a and c.

I mentioned in the preceding that something like `2 = 1 + 1` would be an error—to compare two vs. one plus one, you need to write `2 == 1 + 1`. Try evaluating the first of these expressions and see the result. You should get an error message that says

```
SyntaxError: can't assign to literal
```

There are many ways that you can get an error in Python when you are doing something Python doesn't understand, and a `SyntaxError` is what you get when you write an expression that Python cannot interpret as a valid expression. When you get an error, Python will tell you what went wrong, but unfortunately, it isn't always easy to see what the error is from the message you get. With experience, it gets easier to understand the error messages.

There are other logical operators that you might also be familiar with if you are familiar with basic logic, but might not be otherwise. The logical operators that Python supports are logical-not ($\neg$), logical-and ($\wedge$), and logical-or ($\vee$).

The logical-not operator, `not`, is the simplest. If a value `x` is `True`, then `not x` is `False`, and if `x` is `False`, then `not x` is `True`.

Logical-and of two expressions, written as `and` in Python, is `True` if and only if both expressions are true. For example,

```
2 == 1 + 1 and 3 == 2 + 1
```

evaluates to `True`, while

```
2 == 1 + 1 and 3 == 2
```

and

```
2 == 1 and 3 == 2 + 1
```

will be `False`.

In these expressions, you can see that we mix arithmetic and logical operators. When you do this, the arithmetic operators bind tighter than the logical ones, and the comparisons bind tighter than `and` (as well as logical-or), so

```
2 == 1 + 1 and 3 == 2 + 1
```

means

```
(2 == (1 + 1)) and (3 == (2 + 1))
```

and not, for example,

```
((2 == 1) + 1) and ((3 == 2) + 1)
```

As with arithmetic operators, you can use parentheses to evaluate in an order different from the default. The preceding expressions are all valid Python expressions; they just mean different things. If you wonder how you can possibly add 1 to the preceding comparison 2 == 1, you are right to wonder. Usually, it doesn't make sense to add a logical value to a number. In many programming languages, however, you are allowed to, and then False is interpreted as zero and True as one. So, while

```
2 == 1 + 1
```

is True,

```
(2 == 1 + 1) + 1
```

is two because (2 == 1 + 1) evaluates to True that, when we add one to it, is interpreted as one. Likewise,

```
(2 == 1) + 1
```

will be one, since (2 == 1) is False, which is interpreted as zero.

Logical-or, written a or b, is true if either a or b is True or both a and b are True. So all of the following expressions evaluate to True

```
2 == 1 + 1 or 3 == 1 + 2
2 == 1 or 3 == 1 + 2
2 == 1 + 1 or 3 == 1
```

but

```
2 == 1 or 3 == 1
```

will be False since both 2 == 1 and 3 == 1 are False.

Variables

You can give the result of an expression a name. For example, if you write

```
a = 2 + 2
```

in the terminal, then a will be a label that refers to four. If you then write

```
a
```

Python will show the value that a refers to.

Such labels are called *variables*, and when we tell Python that a variable should refer to a value, we call it an *assignment*. People sometimes say that a variable holds a value—and you will see this in other books—but it is slightly incorrect. Two variables can "hold" the same value, but the values are not distinct. They will both be names that refer to the same value. This has no consequence for the result of an arithmetic or a Boolean expression, but for more complex values, it is essential to keep in mind.

You can use a variable where you would put the value it refers to:

```
2 * a
```

However, these variables do not refer to the *expression* you assigned to them; they hold the result of evaluating the expression. For arithmetic and Boolean expressions, this means that you can think of them as implicitly having parentheses around the expression you assigned to them when you use them in a larger expression.

You can assign to more than one variable and later use as many as you want in an expression. If a holds the value 4 as in the preceding and then

```
b = 2
a * b
```

gives you eight.

You can reassign to a variable to change what value it will be a label for. After

```
a = 5
```

the variable a now refers to five instead of four.

You can assign to more than one variable at a time using this syntax:

```
c, d = a, b
```

If you do this, then Python will take hold of the right-hand-side values before it assigns to the left-hand-side variables. This means that you can write

```
a, b = b, a
```

to switch what a and b hold. If you tried to do this in two steps

```
a = b
b = a
```

then you would update a to b's value and then give b its own value back again. You would need three variables to switch a and b this way:

```
c = b
b = a
a = c
```

Using multiple assignments makes it easier to use variables on the right-hand side and not run into this problem.

Variables are used everywhere in programs; they save you typing expressions everywhere you need them, and because you can update them, they are essential for implementing algorithms as we will see in the rest of the book.

Working with Strings

You have more than numbers to work with in Python. One type of data you can use is strings. You create a string by putting a text in quotes, either double quotes

```
"hello, world!"
```

or single quotes

```
'hello, world!'
```

You can assign strings to variables

```
a = "hello,"
b = "world!"
```

and you can concatenate two or more strings using +:

```
a + " " + b
```

Although it looks like you can add strings, it is concatenation; you cannot, for example, add a string to a number. This will give you an error:

```
a + 5
```

You can concatenate a string with itself a number of times using the multiplication operator:

```
a * 5
```

If you want to insert a value into a string, you use a so-called *format string*. You put an f in front of the string, and then you can put expressions in curly brackets. Everywhere you do that, the value of an expression will be put into the resulting string:

```
f"the answer is {format(42)}"
```

This inserts 42 into the string at the expression indicated by {}.

You can insert values everywhere in a string and use any value, including other strings:

```
a = "hello"
b = "world!"
f"{a}, {b}"
```

There is also an alternative syntax for this that occasionally is useful when you write more complex string formatting. You can use a normal string and then add a dot (.) and then format(...) where the ... are the expressions you want to insert into the string. With this approach, you leave the curly brackets empty:

```
"{}, {}" .format(a, b)
```

The notation with a dot and then a command to do something is called *calling a method*, and the action we want Python to take is called a *method*. We get to methods in Chapter 11. What you put inside the parentheses in the method call are called arguments; here the arguments are the two variables a and b. The arguments do not have to be variables; expressions work just as well:

```
"{}, {}" .format("hello", "world!")
```

The placeholders are filled by the arguments' values in the order they appear between the parentheses. This will flip hello and world because we insert "world!" at the first location and "hello" at the second:

"{}, {}" .format("world!", "hello")

It is possible to name the placeholders if you also name the arguments. The syntax looks like this:

"{x}, {y}" .format(x = "hello", y = "world!")

If you do this, you do not need to give the arguments in the same order as the placeholders. The values that are inserted into the string will match the names you use for the arguments. This expression

"{x}, {y}" .format(y = "world!", x = "hello")

will give us the same result as the preceding one.

If you want to extract a substring from a string, you can use *subscripting*. Here, you use square brackets behind the string. For example,

"hello" [1]

will give you the string "e". The reason you get "e" and not "h" when you index with 1 is that Python starts indices at zero. This is commonly used in programming languages and has some benefits for algorithmic programming that we will not get into in this book; it won't matter for the algorithms we will see. You can use a negative number, but then we pick substrings from the end of the string:

"hello" [-1]

Here we get the last letter. You might wonder why we do not index from zero when we start at the end. That is because we do not have a negative zero; –0 is the same as 0, and zero gives us the first letter.

Exercise: Extract the "h" and the "o" from "hello".

If you write two numbers in the brackets, you get a so-called *slice* of the string. This will usually be a string longer than one letter, but it can also have length zero or one. To extract the two "l"'s, we would write

"hello" [2:4]

Although the string we want is from indexes 2 to 3 (remember that we start at zero), we use the range 2:4. This is because Python will include the first index in the range but not the second. There are also good reasons for this, but again, it is not crucial for this book. So to get indexes 2–3 from the string, we use a slice from 2 to 4; 2 and 3 are extracted but 4, the last index, is not.

Exercise: What happens if the first and last numbers in a slice are the same? What happens if the second is one larger than the first?

You can add a third number to the string. That is used as a step size, and the result is a substring, where you only take letters that are the step size apart. For example, to extract every second letter, we can write

```
"hello" [0:5:2]
```

If you want to know the length of a string, you can write

```
len("hello")
```

This syntax, where you have a command and arguments to it, but not the dot notation, is called a *function call* and len is a *function*. We get to functions in Chapter 6. Functions work just as methods in most cases.

Lists

Strings are sequences of characters, but you can have sequences containing any type of objects. A *list* is a structure that contains arbitrary values. Where you create strings by quoting a series of letters, you create a list by writing objects in square brackets:

```
alist = [1, 2, 3]
another_list = ["foo", 42, "bar"]
```

You can do the same slicing with lists as you can with strings. You can concatenate them using the addition operator. For example,

```
[1, 2] + [3, 4]
```

is the list [1, 2, 3, 4].

You can get a list's length using the len function, and you can get a list that repeats values several times using multiplication. With this operation

```
[1, 2] * 3
```

we get the list [1, 2, 1, 2, 1, 2].

Unlike strings that cannot be modified once created, you can update a list. You can assign a value to an index in a list. If you do this

```
x = [1, 2, 3]
x[1] = 42
```

then the list that x refers to will be [1, 42, 3]. With mutable structures, such as lists, it is important that you remember that variables are merely labels we use to refer to an object. They do not contain the object itself. If you do this

```
x = [1, 2, 3]
y = x
z = [1, 2, 3]
```

then x, y, and z all hold references to a list with the value [1, 2, 3]. The list that x and y point to is the same, while z points to a different list. We created two lists when we put values in square brackets, but when we assigned y = x, we merely gave the first list a second label. If we update the list that x refers to

```
x[1] = 42
```

then we see the change in both x and y. After all, it is the same list the two variables point to so if we modify it through one variable, we will see the change through all other variables pointing to the same list. We will not have updated the list that z refers to since this is an entirely different list.

If you use the multiplication operator to make a list, be careful how you do it. You might think that this would give you an $n \times m$ table:

```
T = [[0] * m] * n
```

In one way, it does. You can get index i, j as T[i][j]. But if you update one row, you will update them all. The inner multiplication, [0] * m, makes m copies of zero, but this is not dangerous. Zero is not an object with a state we can change, and if we assigned to an index into the list, we would replace zero with something else. There is no problem there. But the

27

outer multiplication, [...] * n, makes *n* copies of the list on the left-hand side. This list contains a *reference* to the list of zeros, and it is the reference we duplicate *n* times. Each row is a reference to the same list, so if you modify one row, you will modify them all.

There are, of course, ways to build a table that doesn't have this problem. One piece of magic that will do it is this:

```
T = [[0] * m for _ in range(n)]
```

I explain how it works in the following in the "Loops (for and while)" section.

The range function in the expression also makes a sequence, but not a list. It will create a sequence that you can iterate through, see in the following, but not one you can modify. You can create a list from one, though, if you write

```
list(range(n))
```

If you call range with one parameter, as I did in the preceding, you will get a sequence of numbers from zero to (but not including) *n*. The function works similar to slicing. If you give range two arguments, it will provide you with a range of numbers that starts at the first parameter and ends at the last parameter. If you give it through arguments, it will consider the last a step size.

You can add and remove elements to and from a list. With the insert method, you add an element at an index of your choice. If you insert a value at index idx, then the new value will be at that position, and the rest of the original list will come after it.

If we do this

```
x = [1, 2, 3]
value = 12
idx = 1
x.insert(idx, value)
```

the x list will have the value [1, 12, 2, 3].

You can remove the value at an index i using

```
x.pop(i)
```

It will move all the elements after index i up by one position.

An alternative syntax for deleting an element at a given index doesn't look like anything else we have seen so far, but it looks like this:

```
del x[1]
```

After doing this, x is back to [1, 2, 3]. The `del` command is not a function nor is it a method, but you can use it to delete any object. You do not use it much in Python programs. I don't think that I have ever used it. But it is how you delete an element from a list by index.

There is a method, `remove`, that also removes objects from a list, but with `remove` you use the value you want to remove, not an index.

If you do this

```
x = [1, 2, 3]
x.remove(2)
```

then the x list will contain [1, 3].

The method only removes the first occurrence, so if you do this

```
x = [1, 2, 3, 2]
x.remove(2)
```

you get the list [1, 3, 2]. In the following, in the "Loops (`for` and `while`)" section, I will show you how to remove all occurrences.

For reasons that shall remain a mystery until a later chapter, inserting and removing are slow operations unless you add to the end of a list or remove the last element in a list. You add using the `append` method. After this

```
x = [1, 2, 3]
x.append(4)
```

the x list is [1, 2, 3, 4]. The `pop` method removes the last element in a list and returns the value. If you do this with the x from the preceding

```
y = x.pop()
```

then x will be the list [1, 2, 3] again and y will be 4.

If you want a subsequence of a list, say all the elements from index i up to (but not including) index j, you can write x[i:j]. For example, if x is [0, 1, 2, 3, 4, 5], then x[1:4] is [1, 2, 3] (indexes 1–4, but not including 4). If you leave out the first index, it is implicitly 0, so x[:4] is [0, 1, 2, 3]. If you leave out the last, it is implicitly the length of the list, so x[1:] is [1, 2, 3, 4, 5]. If you write x[:], you get all the values from index 0 to the length of x, so you get a copy of x.

You can add a third number, and that will be interpreted as the step size. If you write x[1:4:2], you are asking for the indices from 1 to 4, but only every second, so the result is [1,3]. The step size can be negative, in which case you run in the opposite direction. If you write x[4:1:-2], you are asking for the values at index 4 (included because it is the first index) to index 1 (excluded because it is the second index), in step size of –2, so you get the list [4, 2]. You can use this notation to get a reversed copy of a list: x[::-1]. It takes the entire list because we use the implicit values for the first two numbers, and we get it reversed because the step size is –1.

Tuples

Tuples are another type of sequence, and you can think about them as lists that you cannot modify. You create them the same way that you create lists except that you use normal parentheses instead of square brackets:

```
tup = (1, 2, 3)
```

You can index and slice tuples the same way as you can with lists, but you cannot update them. You cannot assign to an index or a slice, and you cannot insert, remove, or append to a tuple. Tuples are convenient for keeping related values together, but you cannot use them if you need to update said values. Then you need to use a list.

Sets and Dictionaries

There are two more types in Python that you frequently use, sets and dictionaries (or tables). You can create a set by putting elements between curly brackets:

```
s = { 1, 2, 3 }
```

You cannot make an empty set as {}; this creates an empty dictionary. That this is a dictionary rather than a set is for historical reasons. If you need an empty set, you should write set().

You can check if an element is in a set using

```
1 in s
4 in s
```

and you can add and remove an element with

```
s.add(4)
s.remove(1)
```

You can do many more things with sets; you can get a list of the methods sets have with

```
dir(s)
```

and read what they do with, for example,

```
help(s.union)
```

In general, you can use `dir()` and `help()` to learn what you can do with every value in Python, so if you want to know what you can do with strings, you can use `dir("")` or what you can do with lists with `dir([])`.

A dictionary is a table that maps keys to values, and you create them using curly brackets, but this time with keys followed by colons and then values:

```
d = { "one": 1, "two": 2, "three": 3 }
```

You can check if a key is in a dictionary similar to how you test if an element is in a set:

```
"two" in d
```

You can look up the value associated with a key using subscripting

```
d["one"]
```

and you can update the value a key refers to by assigning to a subscript:

```
d["one"] = 12
```

If you need to delete a key, you use

```
del d["one"]
```

Input and Output

If we cannot get data into Python to analyze it in a program or we cannot get the results out again, then our programs are mostly useless. We can run Python in the terminal and interact with it there, but executing programs like that substantially limits how we can organize our code. We would need the user to assign data to a variable and call relevant functions themselves and then read the result on the terminal. We need our programs to interact with the outside world without using the Python terminal.

The simplest form of input/output (IO) is interacting with the user through text. This is almost like the terminal, but it is your program that decides when to ask for data and when to return results. If you want to ask the user for data, you can use the function input. You call it with a string that becomes the prompt shown to the user. Try writing this:

```python
input("$ ")
```

When the user presses Enter, input returns the text they wrote to the prompt. The result of calling input is a string, also if you write a number at the prompt.

If you need the input to be an integer or a float, you must explicitly convert it—you can use the functions int and float for this.

```python
int(input("give me an integer: "))
float(input("give me a float: "))
```

These functions will give you an error if the strings they get are not integers or floats. It is possible to catch these errors and validate a program's input—and in a real program that others will use, you have to do this—but it is beyond this book. We will always assume that the input we get for an algorithm is valid input.

For you to get information back to the user, an obvious way is to print a string to them. For this, you can use the function print:

```python
print("hello, world!")
```

You can give print more than one argument. The arguments you provide the function will all be printed with a space between them. Try this:

```python
print("There are", 9e6, "bicycles in Beijing")
```

While input is useful for interacting with a user, it does not scale to large data. We need to handle files if we are to write useful programs.

If you have a file, `file.txt`, and you want to read its content, then you first have to open it:

```
f = open("file.txt", "r")
```

The second argument, `"r"`, tells open that it is a file you want to read from. If you're going to write to a file, then use `"w"`. Do not open a file with `"w"` if you want to keep its content; you will delete it when you open it for writing.[2] The result you get from calling open is a file object; here, `f` refers to that object. To read the entire content of the file, you can use the method read:

```
f.read()
```

If you do, you get the entire content of `file.txt` as a string. You can also get the content of `f` as a list of lines if you use

```
f.readlines()
```

One thing you should be aware of when reading from a file is that what you have already read will not be read again. If you call `f.read()` twice, you only get the file content the first time. When you call it the second time, you get an empty string. In general, when reading from a file, you will always read from the last place you read before. If you try the method `readline` (note, not `readlines`), you will get one line from the file. Every time you call `readline`, you will get the next line. The file object remembers where it got too with the earlier reads. To go back to the beginning to read from there again, you can reopen the file by calling open again.[3]

You can use the `print` function to print to files as well as to the terminal. You just need to tell `print` that an argument is a file. If you open a file `f`, you can write to it like this:

```
f = open("output.txt", "w")
print("hello, world!", file = f)
```

---

[2]It is possible to open a file for both reading and writing and to open a file for writing without deleting its content, but we won't need this in this book.

[3]There are more ways to deal with files and to place the point where the next read will start, but for our purposes, it suffices to read one or all lines from a file and to reopen it if we need to start from the beginning again.

Similarly to how reading from a file updates a pointer to where we finished reading, so the next read continues from that point, when we write to a file, then the file object will remember how far it got into the file. If you print to a file several times, you will concatenate the results.

The syntax `name = value` used in the `print` call is called a "keyword argument." You can use keyword arguments for all functions—if you know the names of their arguments. For `print` it is how you can tell it to print to a file.

Conditional Statements (**if** Statements)

We do not always want to execute exactly the same commands independently of what our data looks like. Quite often, we want to do one thing if the data satisfies some property and do another thing if it does not.

To conditionally execute some code, you use `if` statements. The simplest case is when you want to execute code if a given predicate is true and otherwise not execute it. There, the syntax is this:

```
print("before if")
if x < y:
    print("x is smaller than y")
print("after if")
```

The `print("x is smaller than y")` statement is only executed if x is indeed smaller than y. If so, the output will be this:

```
before if
x is smaller than y
after if
```

If y is smaller than x or if they are equal, then you get

```
before if
after if
```

If you want to do one thing when the predicate is true and another when it is false (and not just continue to the next statement when it is false, as in the preceding), then you add an else statement:

```
print("before if")
if x < y:
    print("x is smaller than y")
else:
    print("y is smaller than or equal to x")
print("after if")
```

Now, if x < y, we get

```
before if
x is smaller than y
after if
```

and if y <= x we get

```
before if
y is smaller than or equal to x
after if
```

If you want to test more than one property, you could, for example, only want to do something if either x < y or y < x but not when they are equal; then you can add more tests using an elif statement:

```
print("before if")
if x < y:
    print("x is smaller than y")
elif y < x:
    print("y is smaller than x")
print("after if")
```

You can add as many elif as you want, and you can finish with an else. The first predicate that is true picks which code to run, and if none of the predicates are true, you run the code in the else part if any:

```
print("before if")
if x < y:
```

```
    print("x is smaller than y")
elif y < x:
    print("y is smaller than x")
else:
    print("x == y")
print("after  if")
```

Since Python will only execute the first code where a predicate is true, using elif is different than a sequence of if statements. For example, with this code

```
x, y = 4, 12
if x < y:
    print("x is smaller than y")
elif x < 5:
    print("x is smaller than 5")
else:
    print("y <= x")
```

you will print x is smaller than y and only that.

With this code

```
if x < y:
    print("x is smaller than y")
if x < 5:
    print("x is smaller than 5")
else:
    print("y <= x")
```

you will print both x is smaller than y and x is smaller than 5. Both predicates x < y and x < 5 are true, and if you have two separate if statements, you will execute the code for both predicates. With elif you only execute the first block with a true predicate.

Loops (`for` and `while`)

In most programs, you want to do the same thing many times, for example, you might want to do something for each element in a list or for each line in a file. What you want to do is *loop* over the items. There are two constructions for looping in Python, `for` and `while` statements.

The `for` construction is the one you will use the most. It is used to run through each element of a sequence. If you work with lists and want to do something to each item, then `for` is the way to go.

To iterate through numbers from zero to (and including) nine, you can use this:

```python
for x in range(10):
    print(x)
```

As you recall, `range(10)` is not a list, but it can be iterated through to give you all the numbers in a range. The variable x is set to the number we have gotten to in the iteration each time the loop progresses to the next element.

If you want to iterate over every line in a file, you can do this:

```python
for line in open("some-file.txt"):
    print(line)
```

Because an open file can also be used as a sequence, you can iterate over.

Many things look like sequences in Python, and you can add new sequence objects as well, but we will only use lists and `range` objects.

If you have a set, s, you can iterate over its elements using a `for` loop:

```python
for item in s:
    print(item)
```

For dictionaries, you can iterate over the keys, the values (what the keys point to), and both keys and values using

```python
for key in d:
    print(key)
for value in d.values():
    print(value)
for key, value in d.items():
    print(key, value)
```

If you want to build a new list from an old one by applying some operation to each element, there is a concise syntax that does the same as a loop. This statement

```
x = [2 * i for i in range(5)]
```

does the same as this loop

```
x = []
for i in range(5):
    x.append(2 * i)
```

The alternative syntax is called *list comprehensions.*

You can combine it with an `if` statement to only include some elements in the output:

```
x = [2 * i for i in range(5) if i % 2 == 0]

x = []
for i in range(5):
    if i % 2 == 0:
        x.append(2 * i)
```

It was the list comprehension syntax I used when I created the table in the "Lists" section:

```
T = [[0] * m for _ in range(n)]
```

I used the variable _ because I didn't need the variable. This is a convention in Python, but you can use any variable name.

The list comprehension syntax packs more code into a single statement, and this can make it harder to read if you are not familiar with the syntax, but it is also apparent that you are building a list from some other sequence, so once you *are* familiar with the syntax, it can make your code easier to read. It is mostly a matter of taste which you use, though.

The other loop construction, `while`, is used when you do not have a sequence to iterate over, but you want to iterate as long as some predicate is true.

If you did not have the range `range(10)`, you could print the numbers from zero to ten using this code:

```
x = 0
while x < 10:
    print(x)
    x += 1
```

The `while` loop will run as long as x < 10 is true. Inside the loop body, the print and the addition statements, you need to update the program's state so you will eventually terminate the loop. Of course, this particular example is not something we would use `while`. It is much easier to iterate through a fixed number of elements using `for`. But consider deleting all elements in a list. We can implement this as

```
x = [1, 2, 3, 2]
while 2 in x:
    x.remove(2)
```

We keep removing 2 until it is no longer in the list.

This is not an efficient algorithm, but modifying a list will always be slow. I will explain why in a later chapter. A faster solution is to use list comprehension:

```
x = [a for a in x if a != 2]
```

This creates a new list, however, so you cannot use it if other variables refer to the old list and you want them to see the changes.

Using Modules

Modules contain reusable code and are essential for building even moderately sized Python programs. But since the focus in this book is not on software engineering but on thinking about and implementing algorithms, we will not get into how you build your own modules, nor will we explore existing modules. We will use a few modules in some chapters, though, so we need to know the syntax for working with them at least.

If you want to use variables or functions from a module, say `random` (a module for getting random numbers), then you need to import the module. The syntax for this is

```
import random
```

You can get a list of all variables in the module using

```
dir(random)
```

If you want to access a variable from the module, you must prefix it with the module name and then dot, for example, to call `randint` (that gives you a random integer), you use

```
random.randint(0, 10)
```

This gives you a random number between zero and ten.

You can make some or all of the variables in a module work as variables in your own program in two different ways.

```
from random import randint
```

gives you the `randint` function as a variable where you do not need to prefix it with the module:

```
randint(0, 10)
```

You can add as many variables after the `import` as you want:

```
from random import randint, sample
```

If you want to import everything a module holds, you can use * instead of the names:

```
from random import *
```

This is usually a bad idea since you don't have much control over what you get, so avoid this unless you use most of the functionality in a module.

There might be variables you want in a module that clash with variables you have used in your own program. And you might have used those variables a lot, so rewriting the program to fix this issue is not an attractive prospect. If you want to import a variable but give it a different name, you can use the `as` syntax that looks like this:

```
from random import randint as ri, sample as sa
```

Here, the two functions `randint` and `sample` are imported but under the names `ri` and `sa`, respectively.

You can also import a module under a new name like this:

```
import random as ran
```

CHAPTER 3

Introduction to Algorithms

We briefly discussed what we mean by *algorithms* in Chapter 1, but perhaps it bears repeating; algorithms are recipes for solving a specific computational problem. They describe the steps you (or more usually your computer) must take to get from input to output and should guarantee you that if you follow the instructions exactly, you will (1) finish after a finite number of steps and (2) your output will be a solution to the problem they should solve, given the input you had.

If you think I'm being pedantic with (1), consider this program:

```
x = 0
while True:
    x += 1
```

It computes the largest possible integer—or rather, it would if it ever finished computing and if such an integer existed. It runs forever, however, increasing x by one in each iteration of the loop, but, of course, it will never finish. Theoretically, at least, eventually the computer executing the program will break down and stop running, but if the computer never breaks, it will keep running this program forever. This is not an algorithm because it takes an infinite number of steps to finish.

When we design an algorithm, the first goal is to make sure that we actually develop a proper *algorithm*. That means that steps we describe in solving a problem must be finite and actually solve the problem. We say that an algorithm *terminates* if it finishes computing in a finite number of steps (and it isn't a proper algorithm if it doesn't). If it also computes the right answer, we say that it is *correct*. When we design an algorithm, we must ensure both properties, which usually means proving them mathematically. With experience, you can get a little lax in formally proving this for simple algorithms, but as soon as your algorithm gets sufficiently complicated, you will revert to formal proofs, and as a beginner, it is useful to do this for simple algorithms as well.

41

© Thomas Mailund 2021
T. Mailund, *Introduction to Computational Thinking*, https://doi.org/10.1007/978-1-4842-7077-6_3

We could describe this as the algorithm for checking an algorithm:

1. Check if it terminates.

2. If so, check if it is correct.

This, funny enough, is not an algorithm, even if I have seen it described as such a few places. Of course, there aren't sufficient details to see how we would execute either step, but the first step cannot be solved by any algorithms at all. It is beyond this book to show you why, but there are problems that cannot be solved on any computer ever constructed, in the past or in the future, because it is mathematically impossible to do so. Checking if a given program, however you choose to encode it as input to the computer, will terminate on any specific input is one such problem. It is known as the *halting problem*, since we also use the term *halt* for *terminate* when we consider more fundamental aspects of computation. Checking if a generic program satisfies a specific problem is also undecidable. Both properties that algorithms must satisfy are in the category of problems that we cannot check automatically. We must always prove them for the specific instances.

It is impossible to write a computer program—or generally design an algorithm—that can check these two properties of a suggested algorithm, but nevertheless, it is what you must do to show that your proposed solution to a problem is actually an algorithm. We cannot put up a formula for doing this, for very fundamental reasons, but some general techniques might help you with proving the properties. These techniques are useful when you already have proposed an algorithm, but they can often also guide you in coming up with this proposal in the first place. The first part of this chapter focuses on these techniques and how they can guide you in designing an algorithm, proving that it terminates, and proving that it is correct.

Once we have an actual algorithm, we know how to solve the computational problem at hand. You can compute a solution to your problem in a finite number of steps. That number, however, can be enormous. In practice, there is little difference between a program that never finishes and one that will finish in a billion years. Knowing that we can solve a problem in a finite number of steps is good, but we usually need more than that. We want to solve the problem in a reasonable time, where "reasonable" can depend on the problem at hand.

We have ways of reasoning about the computational complexity of both problems and algorithms that abstract away details about the actual software and hardware the algorithm will be implemented in and run on. Those techniques are the topic for Chapter 4. These techniques let us compare different algorithms and decide which is best independently on how different low-level operations will be carried out on any particular computer and also give us some rough ideas about whether an algorithm will run in a reasonable time on any computer system you have available.

When we compare algorithms this way, we will say we compare their *efficiency*, and we generally go for efficient algorithms over inefficient algorithms, naturally, at least as long as we can implement either with roughly the same effort. We use algorithmic efficiency to determine how fast a given problem can be solved by a given algorithm.

We can also compare problems this way, and when we do, we say that we compare the problems' *complexity*. Some problems are intrinsically harder to solve than others. The halting problem, determining if a given algorithm will ever terminate on any given input, is *undecidable*, meaning that no algorithm can solve it in general. That is a tough problem indeed. Other problems are known to be solvable, but, as far as we know, any solution will take an unacceptably long time to do it. We call such problems *intractable*, and unfortunately, many of the problems we are interested in, in various disciplines, are in this category. Very many optimization problems fall into this category. I did say "as far as we know" because for many of these problems, we do not *know* if it is impossible to derive efficient solutions, and this is one of the most significant open questions in theoretical computer science, known as the *P vs. NP problem*.

Figuring out how difficult different problems are is a discipline of theoretical computer science known as *complexity theory*, and the topic is beyond this book. For this book, it is sufficient to know that it is possible to show that some problems need a certain number of steps to be solved. Where it is relevant, I will mention those bounds.

For designing algorithms, we do not necessarily care so much about a problem's complexity except for two reasons: On one hand, we do not want to spend time attempting to find an efficient solution to a problem that does not have any efficient solutions. If we have a problem that is known to be intractable, we cannot solve it efficiently—or if we can, we have just solved the N vs. NP problem and should bask in the glory and fame rather than worry about the problem that led us there in the first place. Or you could start a lucrative life of crime, since most Internet trade is based on cryptographic protocols that rely on certain problems being intractable to solve, and you just found a way to solve them, and thus break cryptography, efficiently.

If the problem is intractable as specified, we should try to rethink the problem instead. Figure out if a different problem would be equally interesting to solve. Surprisingly often, rephrasing a computational problem solves the underlying scientific problem equally well as the original phrasing, but changes the problem from being intractable to tractable. If we cannot do this, we can try to come up with algorithms that approximate a solution—they might not be the optimal solutions but can perhaps guarantee that they are within a certain fraction of optimal.

The other case where we care about complexity is when we have a tractable problem, that is, we know a lower bound of how fast it is possible to solve the problem, and it is not too terrible, and we want to design an algorithm that solves the problem within that bound. When we reason about algorithmic efficiency, we usually derive upper bounds for how fast (or slow) they will run, while when we reason about problem complexity, we derive lower bounds for how long all algorithms must run, at the very least, to solve the problem. If we can make these two ends meet, we have an optimal algorithm. We cannot make an even faster algorithm than what we already have. Not measured the way we measure efficiency and complexity, at least. In practice, theoretical running times can be misleading for actual running times, and often, a theoretically faster algorithm, but a more complex one, can be slower on typical input than a more straightforward but theoretically slower one. At the end of the day, the efficiency of programs is measured by how long they run on actual data, so some experimentation is needed when you start implementing algorithms.

Before we worry about algorithmic complexity and efficiency, however, we need to learn how to construct algorithms.

Designing Algorithms

When we set out to develop an algorithm, it is because we have some computational problem that we want to solve. That problem often starts out as somewhat vague. It could be a loose prose description or some property about a physical system that we want to explore; more often than not, it is not formal enough that we can reason about it formally. That is the first issue we must deal with. We need to find out *exactly* what it is we are trying to solve since otherwise, we don't know if we are solving it.

The next step is then usually to make a model of the system we want to compute on. The real world is very messy, and there will always be details that we do not care about. We want to abstract away aspects irrelevant to the problem we have defined in step 1 and then find a way to represent the relevant parts in a computer.

Imagine, as an example, that we have a map with some cities on it and we want to know the shortest distance between all pairs of cities. Maybe we are writing a navigation system or planning a trip; it doesn't matter. Let's just say that this is a problem that we want to solve.

Here, there is not much problem in defining what the problem is. We already know what we mean by distances, and we understand that by pairwise distances between cities, we want the distance we need to go, to come from one city to another, perhaps passing through some of the others.

What about the abstractions? Do we need to know the actual map to solve this problem? Is it relevant to know the exact locations of the cities? What information do we have to start from, and what do we strictly need to solve the problem?

Let's say that we know the length of all the roads on the map. We need to get distances from somewhere, and it is not unreasonable to think that we can get the length of individual roads. If we know which cities any given road connects, would that suffice?

It probably would, so we can start developing an algorithm that assumes this is the information that we have. That means that we have reduced the model of reality to just roads, where we know which cities each road connects and each road's length.

How do we represent cities? Do we need their names? Perhaps, perhaps not, but what we definitely want is a unique way of identifying cities (and city names are not unique), so it might not be the best way to go. Instead, let's require that each city is represented by a unique integer. To make things easier on ourselves, let's require that our cities are numbered from 0 up to $n - 1$, where n is the number of cities on the map.

We haven't made any progress on the algorithm yet, but now we know what the data we will manipulate will look like, and that is always the first step. It might turn out that we were wrong about the assumptions, and we would then have to go back to the modeling to fix this. This often happens, and you get used to that. Still, we need a starting point, a first attempt at the model, and for our problem, we say that the roads, with cities represented as integers, are our model.

If you also want to implement the algorithm, you need to decide how to represent this data in code. It is simple in this application, and we can use a tuple per road that specifies the two cities the road connects and the length of the road, something like this:

```
roads = [
    (0, 1, 0.4),
    (0, 2, 1.2),
    (1, 3, 0.1),
    (1, 4, 0.6),
    (2, 3, 0.5),
    (3, 4, 0.1)
]
```

Here, I use the first two elements in the tuples to represent the cities, and the last element is the road's length. We consider the order of cities irrelevant because all roads here are bidirectional (if that changes later, we might have to go back and update the entire algorithm,[1] but there will always be assumptions that might be wrong).

If you draw the map, using just this information, you could get something like Figure 3-1.

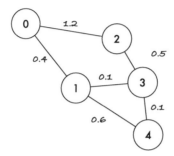

Figure 3-1. *Simplified map*

What do we then want to end up with once our algorithm is done? We want some sort of table that can give us the distance between all pairs of cities. One option could be to represent this as a list of lists. An index into the first list would give us a new list of distances. The first index picks one city and the index into the corresponding list the distance to the second city:

```
dist      # table of all pairwise distances
dist[i]   # list of all distances from i
dist[i][j] # distance from i to j
```

Let's decide that this is the form of the output that we want. Choosing what the output should look like is also often part of developing an algorithm.

Now we have everything we need, except the actual algorithm. We know what our input will look like and what our output should look like; we just haven't worked out yet how to get from one to the other. This is where most would say that the real algorithmic work is, but without the first steps that we just took, we wouldn't be able to do it at all. We always need to model and define the problem before we can solve it.

---

[1] I know where we end up, and we would have to change the algorithm, but only slightly, but I will leave it to you to figure out what you need to change if you are interested.

A Reductionist Approach to Designing Algorithms

The first and perhaps the most important lesson about designing algorithms is this: if you cannot see an immediate solution to your problem, try to break the problem into subproblems and see if you can solve these. This is generally a good recipe for solving any problems in life—and, incidentally, what recipes do. It might seem like an insurmountable task to cook a large dinner, but a dinner can be split into different dishes, and each dish is prepared in several smaller steps, and each of the smaller steps is manageable. When I write a book, I can't attack the writing as a single task. I break the book into chapters, then chapters into sections, sections into paragraphs, and paragraphs into sentences.

There must be some system to the madness of breaking down a problem into smaller steps. We should ensure that the smaller steps are easier to solve than it is to solve the full problem, and we should ensure that if we complete all the steps of the larger problem, we will have successfully solved the full problem. These two requirements are, not coincidentally, similar to the conditions we had for a recipe being an algorithm. When we break a problem into smaller steps, such that the smaller steps are more manageable, we are making a kind of progress. This progress should lead us to our goal; when we know that the steps, when all are completed, solve the original problem, we have a correct algorithm.

It is not always easy to get started even, but one approach that often works is to consider what we would do if we had empty input or only processed our input in the most trivial way, without solving the full problem. How would we then get something that looked like our desired output?

Let's try both. We want this `dist` table, so what if we had no roads whatsoever? What should the output look like? Well, we would always be able to get from a city to itself by traveling zero distance, but we could not get anywhere else. Could we represent the "could not get anywhere" somehow? How about saying that the distance would be infinite? Then, we could construct our table like this:

```
from math import inf
dist = [
    # 0,    1,    2,    3,    4
    [ 0,  inf, inf, inf, inf ], # city 0
    [inf,   0, inf, inf, inf ], # city 1
    [inf, inf,   0, inf, inf ], # city 2
```

```
    [inf, inf, inf,   0, inf ], # city 3
    [inf, inf, inf, inf,   0 ]  # city 4
]
```

The `inf` variable refers to infinity, and comparing numbers to it will treat it as infinity.

If we didn't have any roads, this would be a solution to the problem.

What if we add the roads? For example, we could say that we added distances between cities we can reach by taking just a single road. That would simply be adding the input directly to this table:

```
for i,j,d in roads:
    dist[i][j] = dist[j][i] = d
```

The roads are symmetric, so we need to assign to both `dist[i][j]` and `dist[j][i]`.

This gets us a little closer to the solution—it is not much, but it is a start. We now have a solution that tells us the distance between pairs of cities if we follow zero or one road. Alternatively phrased, we know the shortest distances from the departure point where we visit zero or one extra city.

When you have worked with programming and algorithms for a bit, you would have run into a rule of thumb that says "zero, one, many." It means that if you have a solution that handles zero cases and one case, then the next step will handle the rest. Zero and one are often special, but you rarely have to handle, for example, four or seven, as special cases. So having zero and one is a good start.

If we can handle trips that visit zero or one extra city and then work out how to get to distances with trips that visit up to two extra cities, we might just have a solution for any number of cities by iterating the last step. We don't know how yet; it might not be true, but it is generally speaking a good place to be.

You might think that we are still at the starting point because we haven't solved anything of the original problem. We have handled two special cases, sure, but we still need to handle "all trips," and talking about "zero, one, many" doesn't change that. This is, strictly speaking, true. We have no guarantee that handling trips visiting two cities will get us to any number of cities—but it is a rule of thumb because it is *usually* correct. So we might be in a situation where we just need to work out how to get the distances between cities if we go through zero, one, or two other cities. The last step might generalize.

The good news is that it might be a lot easier to work out how to add the second city than add any number of cities. Say that we know the distance from all pairs of cities a and b visiting zero or one extra city. The distance might be infinite if a and b are different and you can't get directly from one to the other, but that is okay. If we can get there with a shorter distance, by allowing one more city, that is, we can get there if we visit up to two extra cities, then it is because we go through another city, c, such that `dist[a][c]+dist[c][b] < dist[a][b]`, right? We can get from a to b by driving through c, taking the shortest way from a to c and then the shortest way from c to b. If that trip is shorter than the one we had, then that is the new one we want.

The route we had from a to c saw zero or one city, the same for the route from c to b, so the route from a to b *via* c might see one more city. If we explore all such triplets a, b, and c, we get all trips that visit zero, one, or two cities after departure.

If we do something like this

```
no_cities = 5
for i in range(no_cities):
    for j in range(i):
        d = inf
        for k in range(no_cities):
            d = min(d, dist[i][k] + dist[k][j])
        dist[i][j] = dist[j][i] = d
```

after we have initialized the `dist` table with all the roads in the input, we have the distances that include routes with up to two cities.

We actually have a little more because we could have updated the `dist` table to include a trip with two cities before we look up a distance in it. We might have distances with more than two cities, but that is not a problem for us. We want distances that include any number of cities in the end. The important part is that we have all distances that use up to two cities.

So we now have "zero, one, two," but do we have many? Another way of phrasing that question is: if we do what we just did to include trips with up to two cities, will we then get trips up to three cities? If we do it again, do we have trips with up to four? Can we simply repeat what we did until we have trips that include up to n, the number of cities? By then, we would know that we have all the shortest distances (because we cannot have a shortest distance that takes us to the same city twice, we could always drop the round trip and get a shorter route).

Let's work it out. Assume that we have trips visiting up to two cities in dist. If we pick a pair of cities *a* and *b* and check if we can get a shorter distance by going via *c*, would dist[a][c]+dist[c][b] be a candidate for a distance with up to three cities? Yes, we explore all trips between *a* and *b* where we can add the extra city *c*.

So let us just say that we repeat this procedure. After we have initialized the table, we have the smallest pairwise distances that will have considered all trips with zero or one city, counting from the departure (so not including the first city of the trip). After the first iteration, we have considered all trips that visit up to two cities. Maybe more, the algorithm can do a little better, but at least that. After the second iteration, we have considered all trips that visit up to three cities. After iteration *i*, we have considered all trips with up to $i+1$ cities. When can we stop? Any trip with more than $n-1$ extra cities cannot be shorter than one that visits fewer cities, so we can stop after iteration $n-1$:

```
# Iterate until we know we have all trips
for k in range(no_cities):
    # Inner loops updating dist table
    for i in range(no_cities):
        for j in range(i):
            d = inf
            for l in range(no_cities):
                d = min(d, dist[i][l] + dist[l][j])
            dist[i][j] = dist[j][i] = d
```

This is a variation of an algorithm known as Floyd-Warshall's algorithm.

Floyd-Warshall's algorithm can handle slightly more general problems than what we saw here, but we shall not consider those in this book. It is also more efficient, because we use four nested loops, and it uses three. Why this is more efficient is something we cover in the next chapter, but you can probably guess that if we loop more, we spend more time.

The core of Floyd-Warshall's algorithm looks like this:

```
for k in range(no_cities):
    for i in range(no_cities):
        for j in range(no_cities):
            dist[i][j] = dist[j][i] = \
                min(dist[i][j], dist[i][k] + dist[k][j])
```

Notice that we have three and not four loops.

Reasoning about it is slightly more complicated, though. Here we have to think of `dist` containing all trips that go through cities with index smaller than k, and we update the table by allowing more and more cities to be included in paths.

It is not much different from what we ended up with, though, and we might have ended up with this as well if we had just approached the updates slightly differently. There are always more than one way to solve a problem, and both ours and Floyd-Warshall's algorithm do that here. Their algorithm is better, because it is faster, but speed is something you worry about after you have something that works.

Assertions and Invariants

Once we have an algorithm sketched out at the overall level, it is time to flesh out exactly what each step can expect from the preceding steps and what it must guarantee for those steps that come after it. Such requirements and promises we usually call *assertions*; the claims we make for what should be true *before* a step are *preconditions*, and the claims that should be true *after* a step are *post-conditions*. Pre- and post-conditions should match up so that the post-conditions of one step imply the following step's preconditions; they need not be the same conditions, but the post-conditions of one step cannot be weaker than the preconditions of the next.

To ensure that the algorithm works according to plan, we need each step to guarantee its post-conditions, allowing each step to assume that its preconditions are met. If the final post-condition says that the problem is solved and the precondition is true for all input we apply the algorithm on, we know that we have a correct algorithm.

We used this already when we developed the preceding algorithm; we just weren't strict about it. This is not unusual; if we can solve a problem without throwing too much logic and mathematics at it, that is fine, but it can make it easier to both design algorithms and prove that they work as intended if we use these techniques.

In the pairwise distance algorithm, we iteratively updated the `dist` table by picking the smallest `dist[a][c]+dist[c][b]` (which included the original `dist[a][b]` because you can get this as `dist[a][a]+dist[a][b]`). We argued that this would update the table to include trips with one more city. For this to work, the table must already have distances for trips up to k cities when we started—that would be the precondition for the three inner loops. The updates should then ensure that `dist` contained the distances for trips with up to $k + 1$ cities. That would be the post-condition.

By having the pre- and post-conditions, we can separate the code before and after this update to the table from how we do the update itself. There isn't much in this algorithm, but that is not always the case. We can separate the code that way because it doesn't matter *how* the precondition is satisfied for the update to work; it only matters that it is. So the code before the update can be anything at all, as long as it gives us this guarantee. The same goes for the code after the update. The only thing it needs to function correctly is that the post-condition is satisfied. How our update is implemented and how we guarantee the post-condition doesn't matter for the following code.

When you formally prove that some algorithm does what it is supposed to do, you do not need to consider the entire algorithm at once. You can verify for smaller steps that if the precondition for that part is satisfied, the code will guarantee the post-condition.

When you design an algorithm, you can also use this way of thinking. Maybe you don't know how to solve a particular subproblem yet, but you can specify what you want it to do and then make the rest of the algorithm. You don't need to know how to solve the missing part yet; you can assume that it is done and continue with your algorithm. At some later point, of course, you need to solve the part, but you can then focus on that small issue and ignore the rest of the algorithm—by then, you just need to figure out a way to get from the pre- to the post-condition.

If you think of the entire algorithm as something with a pre- and a post-condition, you will also have a stringent way of ensuring that it is fit for purpose and proving that it does what it is supposed to do. If the input matches what the algorithm expects—the precondition is satisfied—and the post-condition is what you want the algorithm to do, then you have a correct algorithm.

When you have loops, you often have conditions that must be true both before and after executing the loop body. These are called *invariants* and are conditions that work both as pre- and post-conditions for the loop body, ensuring that if you start executing the loop in a consistent state, then you also finish in a consistent state.

Think of invariants as what you want your loop to do and how you ensure it. When you write a loop, you always have some invariant in mind; it is what you want to do in each iteration and why you believe that doing so will solve the problem the entire loop is for. You might not think about it formally, but it is what you always do.

When it is hard to get an algorithm right, when you need to do something in a loop, it pays to be more formal about the invariant, and we will see several examples in the book.

In the example algorithm we developed, our invariant was the update conditions we just discussed: that before and after the loop, the `dist` table should hold distances for trips up to some k cities. That k is the number of iterations we have run so far and is a part of the loop. It doesn't exist as something concrete inside the loop body (the three inner loops), but it is important for why the algorithm works and why we know that we can stop when we have iterated $n - 1$ times.

If we had ended up with Floyd-Warshall's algorithm instead, the invariant would be that `dist` contains all the distances where you are only allowed to visit cities with index smaller than k.

A common way to prove that an entire loop works as intended is to consider that the invariant and the termination condition for the loop must both be true when the loop stops. In the example, this means that `dist` must hold all the distances for trips up to k cities, the conditions for the inner loops, *and* that $k = n - 1$ because that is the condition at which the loop terminates. Those combined tell us that we know the distances for all trips with up to $n - 1$ cities, which gives us that the entire algorithm computes what it is supposed to.

With Floyd-Warshall's, the invariant was that we have the shortest distance on trips that can go through cities with index smaller than k, so when $k = n$ we know that we have considered all cities and thus all possible trips. Again we have that combining the invariant and the termination condition ensures us that the algorithm calculates the correct answer.

When you work with loops, you must always guarantee that the invariant is true before you enter the loop. Then the loop body must ensure that it is still true after you execute the body. When the invariant is true and the termination condition met, you must guarantee that the loop's post-condition is met. The last part is usually the easy part. If it seems abstract now, don't worry. We will see invariants in action in the coming chapters.

Breaking down the steps we need to take to solve a problem and then asserting what should hold true before and after any step is a potent approach both for designing algorithms and proving their correctness. It is not necessarily easy, however. It might look simple when following the steps taken when I have written them down, but you often have to work at getting just the right invariants. As with everything else in life, though, it gets easier with practice, so do not skip the exercises later in this chapter. In many of the algorithms, you need to come up with invariants to prove correctness, and in a few of the exercises, you also need to derive an algorithm from scratch.

Measuring Progress

When we loop, we do not necessarily know in advance how many steps we need for any given problem. When you use a for loop, you iterate over a number of elements in a sequence, and the length of that sequence often depends on the input.

Whenever we need an unknown number of steps to solve a problem, we have the issue of termination. To have a proper algorithm, we need to ensure that we only need a finite number of steps on any valid input. To ensure this, we want each step to take us closer to the final solution. If we can, somehow, associate a measure of progress toward the ultimate solution to each step, in such a way that we will always reach the solution and not merely move asymptotically toward it, then we can prove that our algorithm will eventually terminate.

We usually do not worry about capturing the progress we make toward our goal outside a loop. Computations we make outside any loop are only ever done once, so there is no concern about them preventing termination. We usually do not worry about for loops either, since in most cases they iterate over each element in a finite sequence. It is possible to create infinite sequences in Python, but we will not consider such constructions in this book, so all for loops we see are guaranteed to terminate. We might not know exactly how many times a loop body will be executed, but we know that it is finite as long as the sequence we iterate over is finite.

The real issue is when we have while loops. With those, we keep iterating until the loop condition evaluates to False, so we need to ensure that this will eventually happen.

Consider this problem: given two numbers, n and m, we want to compute how many times m divides n and what the remainder is. We can readily do this in Python using the (integer) division and modulus operator

```
n = 42
m = 11
print(n // m, n % m)
```

but assume, for the sake of the example, that we did not have those operators. A simple approach to solving the problem would then be to repeatedly remove m from n until we are left with a number less than m. In Python, this could look like this:

```
a = n ; p = 0
while a >= m:
```

```
    a -= m
    p += 1
print(p, a)
```

After running this algorithm, p will be n // m and a will be n % m. I will leave it to you to come up with a loop invariant that can be used to prove the correctness of this and focus on how we demonstrate that the computation terminates.

To ensure that the loop terminates, we must prove that eventually a >= m will be false, that is, eventually a will be less than m. It should be obvious that this happens with this simple algorithm, since we decrease a in each iteration and we never increase it, but to formalize this reasoning, we can say that we associate with the loop a *termination* function, *t*, that measures how close we are to the point where the loop condition is false. Thinking in terms of such a function will help us when the loops are more complicated than this one.

Such a termination function should have the following properties:

1.   The termination function maps the algorithm's state to a nonnegative integer.

2.   In each iteration, it is decreasing.

3.   The loop condition is False when the termination function reaches zero.

For the first point, we need to know what we mean when we say "the algorithm's state." This is just the value of all the variables we use in the algorithm. We want the termination function to be a map of the current value of the variable to a number that measures how far we are from completion. We don't need to use all the variables, but if it depends on none of them, then the value it gives us will never change, and we cannot ensure the other two points. In our simple algorithm, we have a loop condition that depends only on a and m; our termination function will also only depend on these. We define it to be

$$t(a, m) = a - m$$

Here, the termination function only depends on the variables used in the loop condition, but this need not always be the case. The condition variables might not capture all the information in the algorithm that is needed to measure progress. Then we have to make it depend on more variables.

The second and third conditions to the termination function should be more straightforward to interpret. If we can show that $t(a, m)$ decreases in each iteration and that $t(a, m) \leq 0$ implies that the loop condition is False, then we are guaranteed termination.

For our example algorithm, conditions 2 and 3 are easy to prove. In each iteration, we decrease a while m never changes, so the termination function must decrease by the same amount that a is decreased by. This guarantees the second condition. For the third condition, we simply observe that when $t(a, m) = m - a \leq 0$, the condition a >= m must be False.

Let us consider another example, equally simple. Say we want to print out the bits that the binary representation of a number is. We can use arithmetic where we can get the least significant bit by taking modulus 2 and then shift the remaining bits down by dividing by two:

```
reverse_bits = []
while n > 0:
    reverse_bits.append(n % 2)
    n //= 2
print(reverse_bits[::-1])
```

The expression reverse_bits[::-1] extracts the entire list reverse_bits[:], but with a step of –1, reverse_bits[::-1], so it will give us all the elements in the list but in reverse order.

The loop condition is n > 0, so a natural choice for the termination function is $t(n) = n$. Let us check if that works. Obviously, the function maps the algorithmic state to a number, the value of the variable n. This variable is decreased in each iteration when we set n to half its current value. When n is eventually at zero, the loop condition is false. So this would be a termination function that proves that this algorithm terminates.

Exercises for Sequential Algorithms

The following exercises test that you have understood algorithms and algorithmic design in sufficient detail to reason about termination and correctness and that you have enough experience with Python programming to implement simple sequential (also known as iterative) algorithms. Here, by sequential, I only mean that the algorithms iterate through one or more loops to achieve their goal.

Below or Above

Here's a game you can play with a friend: one of you think of a number between 1 and 20, both 1 and 20 included. The other has to figure out what that number is. They can guess at the number and after guessing will be told if the guess is correct, too high, or too low. Unless the guess is correct, the guesser must try again until the guess *is* correct.

The following program implements this game for the case where the computer picks the number and you have to guess it. Play with the computer as long as you like:

```python
# This is code for picking a number. You don't need
# to understand it but can just go to the loop below.
from numpy.random import randint
def input_integer(prompt):
    while True:
        try:
            inp = input(prompt)
            i = int(inp)
            return i
        except Exception:
            print(inp, "is not a valid integer.")

# When picking a random number, we specify the interval
# [low,high). Since high is not included in the interval,
# we need to use 1 to 21 to get a random number in the
# interval [1,20].
n = randint(1, 21, size = 1)
guess = input_integer("Make a guess> ")
while guess != n:
    if guess > n:
        print("Your guess is too high!")
    else:
        print("Your guess is too low!")
    guess = input_integer("Make a guess> ")
print("You got it!")
```

Here are three different strategies you could use to guess the number:

1. Start with one. If it isn't the right number, it has to be too low—there are no smaller numbers the right one could be. So if it isn't one, you guess it is two. If it isn't, you have once again guessed too low, so now you try three. You continue by incrementing your guess by one until you get the right answer.

2. Alternatively, you start at 20. If the correct number is 20, great, you got it in one guess, but if it is not, your guess must be too high—it cannot possibly be too small. So you try 19 instead, and this time you work your way down until you get the right answer.

3. Tired of trying all numbers from one end to the other, you can pick this strategy: you start by guessing 10. If this is correct, you are done; if it is too high, you know the real number must be in the interval [1, 9], and if the guess is too low, you know the right answer must be in the interval [11, 20]—so for your next guess, you pick the middle of the interval it must be. With each new guess, you update the range where the real number can hide and choose the middle of the previous range.

Exercise: Prove that all three strategies terminate and with the correct answer, that is, they are algorithms for solving this problem.

Exercise: Would you judge all three approaches to be equally efficient in finding the right number? If not, how would you order the three strategies such that the method most likely to get the correct number first is ranked highest and the algorithm most likely to get the right number last is rated lowest? Justify your answer.

If you do not lie to the computer when it asks you about your guess compared to the number you are thinking of, this program implements the first strategy:

```
# This is code for picking a choice. You don't need
# to understand it but can just go to the loop below.

def input_selection(prompt, options):
    """Get user input, restrict it to fixed options."""
    modified_prompt = "{} [{}]: ".format(
        prompt.strip(), ", ".join(options)
    )
```

```
    while True:
        inp = input(modified_prompt)
        if inp in options:
            return inp
        # nope, not a valid answer...
        print("Invalid choice! Must be in [{}]".format(
            ", ".join(options)
        ))

for guess in range(1,21):
    result = input_selection(
        "How is my guess {}?".format(guess),
        ["low", "hit", "high"]
    )
    if result == "hit":
        print("Wuhuu!")
        break
    else:
        print("I must have been too low, right?", result)
```

Exercise: Implement the other two strategies and test them.

When iterating from 20 and down, for the second strategy, you should always get the result "high" when you ask about your guess, so you can use a for loop and not worry about the actual result from input_selection. When you implement strategy number 3, however, you need to keep track of a candidate interval with a lower bound, initially 1, and an upper bound, initially 20. If you guess too high, you should lower your upper bound to the value you just guessed minus one (no need to include the guess we know is too high). If you guess too low, you must increase your lower bound to the number you just guessed plus one. In both cases, after updating the interval, you should guess for the middle point in the new range. When you compute the middle value in your interval, you can use

```
guess = (upper_bound + lower_bound) // 2
```

Exercises on Lists

Lists are representations of ordered sequences of elements. These exercises involve algorithms where we have to examine or manipulate lists to solve a problem.

Changing Numerical Base

When we write a number such as 123, we usually mean this to be in base 10, that is, we implicitly understand this to be the number $3 \times 10^0 + 2 \times 10^1 + 1 \times 10^2$. Starting from the right and moving toward the left, each digit represents an increasing power of tens. The number *could* also be in octal, although then we would usually write it like 123_8. If the number were in octal, each digit would represent a power of eight, and the number should be understood as $3 \times 8^0 + 2 \times 8^1 + 3 \times 8^2$.

Binary, octal, and hexadecimal numbers—notation where the bases are 2, 8, and 16, respectively—are frequently used in computer science as they capture the numbers you can put in 1, 3, and 4 bits. The computer works with bits, so it naturally speaks binary. For us humans, binary is a pain because it requires long sequences of ones and zeros for even relatively small numbers, and it is hard for us to readily see if we have five or six or so zeros or ones in a row.

Using octal and hexadecimal is more comfortable for humans than binary, and you can map the digits in octal and hexadecimal to 3- and 4-bit numbers, respectively. Modern computers are based on bytes (and multiples of bytes) where a byte is 8 bits. Since a hexadecimal number is 4 bits, you can write any number that fits into a byte using two hexadecimal digits rather than eight binary digits. Octal numbers are less useful on modern computers, since two octal digits, 6 bits, are too small for a byte, while three octal digits, 9 bits, are too large. Some older systems, however, were based on 12-bit numbers, and there you had four octal numbers. Now, octal numbers are merely used for historical reasons; on modern computers, hexadecimal numbers are better.

Leaving computer science, base 12, called duodecimal, has been proposed as a better choice than base 10 for doing arithmetic because 12 has more factors than 10 and this system would be simpler to do multiplication and division in. It is probably unlikely that this idea gets traction, but if it did, we would have to get used to converting old decimal numbers into duodecimal.

In this exercise, we do not want to do arithmetic in different bases but want to write a function that prints an integer in different bases.

When the base is higher than 10, we need a way to represent the digits from 10 and up. There are proposed special symbols for these, and these can be found in Unicode, but we will use letters, as is typically done for hexadecimal. We won't go above base 16, so we can use this table to map a number to a digit up to that base:

```
digits = {}

for i in range(0,10):
    digits[i] = str(i)

digits[10] = 'A'
digits[11] = 'B'
digits[12] = 'C'
digits[13] = 'D'
digits[14] = 'E'
digits[15] = 'F'
```

To get the last digit in a number, in base b, we can take the division rest, the modulus, and map that using the `digits` table:

```
digits[i % b]
```

Try it out.

You can extract the base b representation of a number by building a list of digits starting with the smallest. You can use `digits[i % b]` to get the last digit and remember that in a list. Then we need to move on to the next digit. Now, if the number we are processing is $n = b^0 \times a_0 + b^1 \times a_1 + b^2 \times a_2 + ... + b^m a_m$, then a_0 is the remainder in a division by b and the digit we just extracted. Additionally, if $//$ denotes integer division, $n//b = b^0 \times a_1 + b^1 \times a_2 + ...b^{m-1}a_m$. So we can get the next digit by first dividing n by b and then extract the smallest digit.

If you iteratively extract the lowest digit and put it in a list and then reduce the number by dividing it by b, you should eventually have a list with all the digits, although they will be in reverse order. If your list is named `lst`, you can reverse it using this expression `lst[::-1]`. The expression says that we want `lst` from the beginning to the end—the default values of a range when we do not provide anything—in steps of minus one.

Exercise: Flesh out an algorithm, based on the preceding observations, that can print any integer in any base $b \leq 16$. Show that your method terminates and outputs the correct string of digits.

The Sieve of Eratosthenes

Sift the Two's and Sift the Three's,

The Sieve of Eratosthenes.

When the multiples sublime,

The numbers that remain are Prime.

The Sieve of Eratosthenes is an early algorithm for computing all prime numbers less than some upper bound n. It works as follows: we start with a set of candidates for numbers that could be primes, and since we do not a priori know which numbers will be primes, we start with all the natural numbers from two and up to n:

```
candidates = list(range(2, n + 1))
```

We are going to figure out which are primes by elimination and put the primes in another list that is initially empty:

```
primes = []
```

The trick now is to remove from the candidates the numbers we know are not primes. We will require the following loop invariants:

1. All numbers in `primes` are primes.

2. No number in `candidates` can be divided by a number in `primes`.

3. The smallest number in `candidates` is a prime.

Exercise: Prove that the invariants are true with the initial lists defined as in the preceding.

We will now loop as long as there are candidates left. In the loop, we take the smallest number in the `candidates` list, which the invariant states must be a prime. Call it p. We then remove all candidates that are divisible by p and then add p to `primes`.

Exercise: Prove that the invariants are satisfied after these steps whenever they are satisfied before the steps.

Exercise: Prove that this algorithm terminates and is correct, that is, `primes` once the algorithm terminates contains all primes less than or equal to n. Correctness does not follow directly from the invariants, so you might have to extend them.

Exercise: Implement and test this algorithm.

Longest Increasing Substring

Assume you have a list of numbers, for example

```
x = [12, 45, 32, 65, 78, 23, 35, 45, 57]
```

Exercise: Design an algorithm that finds the longest subsequence x[i:j] such that consecutive numbers are increasing, that is, x[k] < x[k+1] for all k in range(i,j) (or one of the longest, if there are more than one with the same length).

Compute the Powerset of a Set

The *powerset* $P(S)$ of a set S is the set that contains all possible subsets of S. For example, if $S = \{a, b, c\}$, then

$$P(S) = \{\varnothing, \{a\}, \{b\}, \{c\}, \{a, b\}, \{a, c\}, \{b, c\}, \{a, b, c\}\}$$

Exercise: Assume that S is represented as a list. Design an algorithm that prints out all possible subsets of S. Prove that it terminates and is correct.

Hint   You can solve this problem by combining the numerical base algorithm with an observation about the binary representation of a number and a subset of S. We can represent any subset of S by the indices into the list representation of S. Given the indices, just pick out the elements at those indices. One way to represent a list of indices is as a binary sequence. The indices of the bits that are 1 should be included; the indices where the bits are 0 should not. If you can generate all the binary vectors of length k=len(S), then you have implicitly generated all subsets of S. You can get all these bit vectors by getting all the numbers from zero to 2^k and extracting the binary representation.

Longest Increasing Subsequence

Notice that this problem has a different name than "longest increasing *substring*; it is a slightly different problem. Assume, again, that you have a list of numbers. We want to find the longest subsequence of increasing numbers, but this time we are not looking for a slice of consecutive indices i:j, but a sequence of indices $i_0, i_1, ..., i_m$ such that $i_k < i_{k+1}$ and $x[i_k] < x[i_{k+1}]$.

Exercise Design an algorithm for computing the longest (or *a* longest) such sequence of indices $i_0, i_1, ..., i_m$.

Hint   This problem is harder than the previous one, but you can brute-force it by generating *all* subsequences and checking if the invariant is satisfied. This is a *very* inefficient approach, but in this chapter we do not worry about efficiency, but only correctness.

Merging

Assume you have two sorted lists, x and y, and you want to combine them into a new sequence, z, that contains all the elements from x and all the elements from y, in sorted order. You can create z by *merging* x and y as follows: have an index, i, into x and another index, j, into y—both initially zero—and compare x[i] to y[j]. If x[i] < y[j], then append x[i] to z and increment i by one. Otherwise, append y[j] to z and increment j. If either i reaches the length of x or j reaches the end of y, simply copy the remainder of the other list to z.

Exercise: Argue why this approach creates the correct z list and why it terminates.

CHAPTER 4

Algorithmic Efficiency

As a general rule, we want our algorithms to work as efficiently as possible, which usually means that we want them to quickly solve the problem they are designed for using as few resources, such as memory or disk space, as possible. This is just a rule of thumb, of course, since we also need to factor in programmer time. If you need a problem solved a month from now and you have an algorithm that can solve the problem in two weeks and takes one week to implement, that is preferable over an algorithm that can solve the problem in an hour but takes a month to implement.

It is notoriously hard to estimate how long it will take to implement a new algorithm, however, as this depends on the skills of the programmer, the chosen programming language, and which libraries are available; we will not attempt to do that here. With experience, you will get a feel for how hard it will be to implement any given algorithm, and while you are unlikely ever to be able to estimate precisely how much work goes into implementing one, you will be able to determine which of two choices is the more complex algorithm. Unless there are good reasons for wanting a more complicated but potentially more efficient algorithm, you should go for the most straightforward algorithm that can get the job done. Sometimes, the simplest algorithm *will* be too slow for your problem, and you have to replace it with a more complex one. Or sometimes you expect to run your algorithm many times on many data sets, and spending a little more programming time for faster execution down the line might pay off. But as a general rule, you do not want to spend more time programming than what is warranted for your problem. Programmer time is much more valuable than computer time, so simple algorithms that can be implemented quickly are generally preferable to more sophisticated algorithms that are hard to implement.

This chapter is not about the complexity of algorithms in the sense of how complicated they are to implement. Instead, it is about how efficiently algorithms solve a problem once implemented. That is, the chapter is about how fast you can expect an

65

© Thomas Mailund 2021
T. Mailund, *Introduction to Computational Thinking*, https://doi.org/10.1007/978-1-4842-7077-6_4

algorithm to complete its job on any given data. Whenever you have the choice between two algorithms that look roughly equally complicated to implement, you want to go with the one that is likely to be the more efficient of the two.

The best way to measure which of two algorithms is superior for solving a given problem is, of course, to program the best implementations of the two that you can manage and then measure how fast they are on your data. Whichever your stopwatch tells you is the best unquestionably is. That, of course, is not an option if your focus is on actually solving a problem rather than comparing two algorithms. To answer your question that way, you have to do twice the work. You need to implement both algorithms and then run both of them on your actual data. What we need is a way of reasoning about how likely it is that one algorithm is better than another without using a stopwatch.

The way we reason about algorithmic efficiency is similar to how we reason about the physical world when we do science: we use a model of a computer that is much simpler than the real thing, but one we can reason about without too many complications. We then work out how many primitive operations an algorithm needs to make on the input we give it. This is not an entirely accurate measurement of how long the actual algorithm will run on a real computer, but it is a reasonable estimate.

To make it even simpler to reason about efficiency, we often don't care about counting the number of primitive operations accurately either. We will only care about how the number of calculations depends on the input in an asymptotic sense that should be clear by the end of this chapter. This might sound a bit sloppy, but there is a mathematical underpinning that justifies this, and by using this approach, we can quickly determine which of two algorithms is likely to be faster than the other.

The RAM Model of a Computer and Its Primitive Operations

Any actual computer you will ever use is a very complex machine. At its core are a gazillion transistors, wired together to implement different logical operations in hardware. The hardware in your computer handles both simple computations, such as comparing numbers or doing arithmetic, and managing how data is moved around. Information is stored in different places in such a computer; you have persistent storage on disk that lives outside of running programs, and while programs run, you have data moving between different layers of memory hierarchies. At the core of the computer is one or more central processing units, or CPUs, that do actual computations.[1] Data needs to be moved to these CPUs for them to compute on it. They can hold some data themselves, in what are called *registers*, and they can do computations on such data very quickly. There are only a finite number of registers, though, so data needs to be moved to and from these registers. Below registers are several layers of memory called *caches*, and the closer caches are to the registers, the faster data can be moved between them. Below caches, you have *random-access memory*, or RAM, and below that are disks, which can be solid-state or actual rotating disks or some combination thereof.

The levels of the memory hierarchy are vital to the actual performance of an algorithm. Every time you move data from one level to the next, the time it takes to access it grows by orders of magnitude. Your CPUs can compute on data much faster than they can fetch it from memory and put it back. Moving data up and down the memory hierarchy, however, is handled automatically by the computer, so we don't have to deal with it explicitly. We can construct algorithms that ignore the memory hierarchy entirely and still get well-working programs. Considering the memory hierarchy can help us improve the running time of a program immensely, but doing this also hugely complicates our algorithms, and in many cases, solutions will depend on the actual hardware our software runs on.

I am mentioning all this to make it clear that considering any real computer dramatically complicates how we can reason about the actual performance of an algorithm. If we have to consider any actual computer, reasoning about running time becomes practically impossible. When we reason about algorithmic complexity, we use much simpler models of computers, and a traditional model is the so-called *RAM model*.

The critical property of the RAM model is that we assume that any data we need and know where to find, we can access in constant time. We understand that there is such a thing as a *computer word*, which you should think of as a number, a character, or a primitive piece of data like that. We cannot store arbitrarily large chunks of data in single computer words, but we assume that if the size of the input data for your algorithm is n, then our computer words can hold at least the number n. In other words, if your input data is of size n, then you can represent $\lceil \log_2 n \rceil$ bits in a single computer word. Any computer word in our input data, or any computer word we create in our algorithm, can be accessed in constant time. We ignore that some computer words can be located much

---

[1]There are also graphical processing units, GPUs. These are often used for running many simple calculations in parallel. For the purpose of this chapter, you can just consider them a different kind of CPU.

faster than others; they are all just accessible in constant time. We also assume that we can compare computer words in constant time and that any arithmetic operation we do on numbers that can be stored in a single computer word can be done in constant time.

The reason we have to be a little careful about what a computer word is is that we want to make the assumption about how fast we can perform calculations on it. We want our abstract computer words to roughly match what the actual computer can work on within its registers. In the hardware of a real computer, the different operations you can do on numbers and bit patterns are wired together, so the CPUs consider operating on words in registers as primitive operations. The time it takes actual hardware to do a primitive operation depends on what that operation is. The hardware for multiplication is more complicated than the hardware for simple comparison, but a lot of the computation involves parallel calculations, and at a rough approximation, all primitive operations take the same time. To actually compare two numbers that can be up to n large, we need to compare $\lceil \log_2 n \rceil$ bits, so it *isn't* constant time, but if a computer word has at least that many bits, then in a sense we can; then it is a single CPU operation.

As long as you do not work with numbers that are larger than the size of the input, the RAM model says that

1. You can compare numbers in constant time.

2. You can access any computer word in constant time.

3. You can do any arithmetic or bit-wise operation on computer words in constant time.

This is a considerable simplification of actual hardware. If we make these simple assumptions about how fast our model of a computer can do calculations and we assume that all such operations take the same amount of time, then we can just count how many of these primitive operations an algorithm will need on any given input to get an estimate of how fast it will run.

Let us try counting primitive operations in a small example. Let us assume that we have a list of numbers:

```
numbers = [1, 2, 3, 4, 5]
```

In this case, we have $n = 5$ numbers. We usually do not count the operations it takes to get our input. Sometimes, we need to read it in from disk, or in this example, we need to tell Python what the numbers are, and this will take around n operations to create this list. If the data is part of our input, however, we do not count those instructions. The reason for this is that there are many algorithms where we use less than *n* operations to answer questions about our data, and we do not want to have our analysis of the efficiency of these dominated by how long it takes to get the input. Such algorithms are used as building blocks for other algorithms that will be responsible for getting the input in the right form for what we need, and we consider that a cost of the other algorithm. If you need to create a list as part of your algorithm, the number of operations it takes has to be included in the accounting, but here we just assume that the input is present before we start counting.

Let us now consider the task of adding all these numbers up. We can do this using this algorithm:

```
accumulator = 0
for n in numbers:
    accumulator += n
```

First, we create a variable to store intermediate values, `accumulator`. Then we have a `for` loop that runs over our input, and for each input number add that number to `accumulator`. Initializing a variable with a number amounts to setting a computer word to a value, so it takes one operation in our RAM model. Adding two numbers is also a single operation, and on all modern computers, you can add a number to an existing computer word as a single operation, so we consider `accumulator += n` as a single operation—if you want to think about it as `accumulator = accumulator + n`, you can count it as two operations. If, however, we consider updating `accumulator` a single operation, we have $1 + n$ operations for initializing and updating `accumulator`. It is less straightforward to know how many operations we spend on the `for` loop, however. That depends on how Python handles `for` loop statements. The `for` loop construction is not as primitive as the RAM model. We can implement the same loop using a `while` loop, however, using only primitive operations:

```
accumulator = 0
length = len(numbers)
i = 0
while i < length:
    n = numbers[i]
    accumulator += n
    i += 1
```

Here, we have a more transparent view of the primitive operations a `for` loop likely implements. To iterate over a list, we need to know how long it is.[2] The statement

```
length = len(numbers)
```

isn't actually primitive either. It uses Python's `len` function to get the length of a sequence, and we don't know how many primitive operations *that* takes. If we assume, however, that lists store their lengths in a single computer word, which they really do, and that `len` simply gets that computer word, which is not far from the truth, we can consider this statement a single operation as well:[3]

```
accumulator = 0.        # one operation
length = len(numbers)   # one operation
```

We then initialize the variable `i` that we use to keep track of how many elements we have processed. That is also a single primitive operation.

The `while` loop construction does two things. It evaluates its condition, and if it is `True` it executes the code in the loop body; if it is `False`, it sends the program to the point right after the loop to start executing the statements there, if any are left. We call such an operation a *branching operation* because it sends the point of execution to one of two places, and such an operation is implemented as a single instruction in hardware. So we will count the decision of where to continue execution as a single operation. We need to evaluate the loop condition first, however, which is a single numeric comparison, so that takes another primitive operation. We evaluate the loop condition once for each element in `numbers`, that is, n times, so now we have

```
accumulator = 0         # one operation
length = len(numbers)   # one operation
i = 0                   # one operation
while i < length:       # 2n operations
    ...
```

---

[2]In Python, iterating over sequences doesn't actually require that we know how many elements we have, because the `for` loop construction is vastly more powerful than what we implement with this simple `while` loop, but using the length is the simplest we can do if we implement the `for` construction ourselves.

[3]Again we have an operation that Python provides for us, like the `for` loop construction, that is actually more powerful than we give it credit for when we count the number of primitive operations the operation takes. We have to limit the level of detail we consider, so this is as deep as I want to take us down this particular rabbit hole.

Each of the statements inside the loop body will be evaluated *n* times, so we just need to figure out how many operations are required for each of the statements there and multiply that with *n*. The last two statements are simple; they update a number by adding another number to it, and that is a single operation:

```
accumulator = 0          # one operation
length = len(numbers)    # one operation
i = 0                    # one operation
while i < length:        # 2n operations
    n = numbers[i]       # ? * n operations
    accumulator += n     # 2n operations
    i += 1               # 2n operations
```

The remaining question is how many operations it takes to handle the statement n = numbers[i]. Here, we need to understand what something like numbers[i] means. Once again, we use a Python construction that we do not necessarily know how many operations it takes to execute. To understand that, we need to know how Python represents lists in computer memory, and that is beyond the scope of this chapter. You will have to take my word on this, but it is possible to get the *i*th element in a list by adding two computer words and then reading one, so we count this as two operations and end up with

```
accumulator = 0          # one operation
length = len(numbers)    # one operation
i = 0                    # one operation
while i < length:        # 2n operations
    n = numbers[i]       # 2n operations
    accumulator += n     # n operations
    i += 1               # n operations
```

If we add it all up, we get that to compute the sum of *n* numbers this way, we need to use $3 + 6n$ primitive operations.

If we assume that all for loops are implemented by first capturing the length of the sequence, then setting a counter to zero, and then iterating through the sequence, comparing the counter with the length as the loop condition, incrementing the counter at the end of the loop body, and accessing elements in the sequence by indexing, that is, the for loop

```
for element in a_list:
    # do something
```

can be translated into this while loop

```
length = length(a_list)        # 1 operation
counter = 0                    # 1 operation
while counter < length:        # 2n operations
    element = a_list[counter]  # 2n operations
    # do something
    counter += 1               # n operations
```

we can say that a for loop iterating over a sequence of length n takes $5n + 2$ operations. If we go back to our original for loop adding algorithm, we then get

```
accumulator = 0          # 1 operation
for n in numbers:        # 5n + 2 operations
    accumulator += n     # n operations
```

which gives us the same $6n + 3$ operations as before.

If you feel a bit overwhelmed by how difficult it is to count the number of primitive operations in something as simple as this, I understand you and feel for you. If it is this hard to count operations in the abstract RAM model, where we even make some assumptions about how many operations Python needs to implement its operations, you will understand why we do not even attempt to accurately estimate how much time it will take to execute code on a real computer.

The good news is that we very rarely do count the number of operations an algorithm needs this carefully. Remember that I said, at the beginning of the chapter, that we generally consider functions such as $2x^2 + x$ and $100x^2 + 1000x$ the same. We will also consider $6n + 3$ operations the same as n number of operations, in a way I will explain a little later. First, however, you should try to count primitive operations in a few examples yourself.

Counting Primitive Operations Exercises

Exercise: Consider this way of computing the mean of a sequence of numbers:

```
accumulator = 0
for n in numbers:
    accumulator += n
mean = accumulator / len(numbers)
```

Count how many primitive operations it takes. To do it correctly, you need to distinguish between updating a variable and assigning a value to a new one. Updating the accumulator `accumulator += n` usually maps to a single operation on a CPU because it involves changing the value of a number that is most likely in a register. Assigning to a new variable, as in

```
mean = accumulator / len(numbers)
```

doesn't update `accumulator` with a new value; rather, it needs to compute a division, which is one operation (and it needs `len(numbers)` before it can do this, which is another operation), and then write the result in a new variable, which is an additional operation.

Exercise: Consider this alternative algorithm for computing the mean of a sequence of numbers:

```
accumulator = 0
length = 0
for n in numbers:
    accumulator += n
    length += 1
mean = accumulator / length
```

How many operations are needed here? Is it more or less efficient than the previous algorithm?

Types of Efficiency

When computing the sum of a sequence of numbers, the number of operations we need is independent of what the individual numbers are, so we could express the number of operations as a function of the input size, n. Things are not always that simple.

Consider this algorithm for determining if a number x is in the sequence of numbers `numbers`:

```
in_list = False
for n in numbers:
    if n == x:
        in_list = True
        break
```

73

Here, we assume that both `numbers` and `x` are initialized beforehand. The algorithm sets a variable, `in_list`, to `False`—one primitive operation—and then iterates through the numbers. This would usually cost us $5n + 2$ operations for the `for` loop, but notice that we `break` if we find the value in the list. We won't spend more than $5n + 2$ operations on the `for` loop, but we might spend considerably less. Let us say that we iterate m times, so the cost of the `for` loop is $5m + 2$ instead. Then we can count operations like this:

```
in_list = False           # 1 operation
for n in numbers:         # 5m + 2 operations
    if n == x:            # 2m operations
        in_list = True    # 1 operation
        break             # 1 operation
```

The `if` statement is a branching operation just like the `while` loop; we need to compare two numbers, which is one operation, and then decide whether we continue executing inside the `if` body or whether we continue after the `if` block, which is another operation. Inside the `if` block, we have two primitive operations. Setting the variable `in_list` is a primitive operation like before, and `break` is another branching operation that does not need a comparison first, but that simply moves us to the point in the code after the loop. These two operations are only executed once since they are only executed when the `n == x` expression evaluates to `True`, and we leave the loop right after that.

When we add up all the operations, we find that the algorithm takes $7m + 5$ operations in total, where m depends on the input. It is not unusual that the running time of an algorithm depends on the actual input, but taking that into account vastly complicates the analysis. The analysis is, in contrast, greatly simplified if we count the running time as a function of the size of the input, n, and do not have to consider the actual data in the input.

Best-Case, Worst-Case, and Average-Case (or Expected-Case) Complexity

For this simple search algorithm, we apparently cannot reduce the running time to a function of n, because it depends on how soon we see the value x in the sequence, if at all. To get out of the problem, we usually consider one of three cases: the *worst-case* complexity, the *best-case* complexity, or the *average-case* complexity of an algorithm.

To get the worst-case estimate of the number of operations the algorithm needs to take, we need to consider how the data can have a form where the algorithm needs to execute the maximum number of operations it can possibly do. In the search, if x is not found in the sequence, we will have to search the entire sequence, which is as bad as it gets, so the worst-case time usage is $7n + 5$. If the very first element in numbers is x, then $m = 1$, which is as good as it gets, so the best-case running time is 12 operations.

The average case is much harder to pin down. To know how well our algorithm will work on average, we need to consider our input as randomly sampled from some distribution—it does not make sense to think of averages over something that doesn't have an underlying distribution the data could come from because then we would have nothing to average over. Because of this, we will generally not consider average-case complexities in this book. Average-case complexity is an important part of so-called randomized algorithms, where randomness is explicitly used in algorithms and where we have some control over the data. To get a feeling for how we would reason about average-case complexity, imagine for a second that x is in the numbers list but at a random location. I realize that would make it very silly to run the algorithm in the first place, since the result will always be True, but indulge me for a second. If x is a random number from numbers, then the probability that it is at index j for any j in 1, ..., n is $1/n$. Since we stop when we find the item we are searching for, our variable m is j. The mean of m is therefore $\mathrm{E}[m] = \sum_{j=1}^{n} j/n$, which is $\dfrac{n+1}{2}$. Plugging that into $7m + 5$, we get the average-case time usage $7/2(n+1) + 5$.

Of the three cases, we are usually most concerned with the worst-case performance of an algorithm. The average case is of interest if we have to run the algorithm many times over data that is distributed in a way that matches the distributions we use for the analysis, but for any single input, it does not tell us much about how long the algorithm will actually run. The best case is only hit by luck, so relying on that in our analysis is often overly optimistic. The worst-case performance, however, gives us some guarantees about how fast the algorithm will be on any data, however pathological, we give it.

Exercise

Recall the guessing game from the previous chapter, where one player thinks a number between 1 and 20 and the other has to guess it. We had three strategies for the guesser:

1. Start with one. If it isn't the right number, it has to be too low—there are no smaller numbers the right one could be. So if it isn't one, you guess it is two. If it isn't, you have once again guessed too low, so now you try three. You continue by incrementing your guess by one until you get the right answer.

2. Alternatively, you start at 20. If the right number is 20, great, you got it in one guess, but if it is not, your guess must be too high—it cannot possibly be too small. So you try 19 instead, and this time you work your way down until you get the right answer.

3. The third strategy is this: you start by guessing ten. If this is correct, you are done; if it is too high, you know the real number must be in the range $[1, 9]$, and if the guess is too low, you know the right answer must be in the range $[11, 20]$—so for your next guess, you pick the middle of the range it must be. With each new guess, you update the interval where the real number can be hidden and pick the middle of the new range.

Exercise: Identify the best- and worst-case scenarios for each strategy and derive the best-case and worst-case time usage.

Amortized Complexity

There is yet another kind of complexity that we often use both for reasoning about algorithms and about the performance of the data structures we will see later in the book. This is *amortized* complexity. At first glance, it resembles average-case complexity. If performing some operation n times takes tn computational time, we can naturally say that each operation takes time t (whatever t is). It is the average time per operation that it took to perform the total of n operations. However, when we talk about the average time, we do so with some distribution in mind, or if an operation is sometimes fast and sometimes slow, the average is over sufficiently many operations that the statistical properties of the operation are relevant. That is not the case with an amortized complexity. There we say that for n operations, however few or many, we use tn time. If an operation is sometimes fast and sometimes slow, then we cannot perform an expensive operation taking time $s > t$ at the beginning of a sequence. If we did, then we could stop there, and the running time would be $sn > tn$ (with $n = 1$ here, of course). For every n, no matter how many and which operations are slow and which are fast, we must *always* have a time of tn.

An example is operations on Python's lists. Python puts the elements in a list in consecutive memory, which means that the elements in a list have to sit next to each other. When you assign into a list, `x[i] = y`, you spend some time on that, but you keep the elements next to each other; there is just a new one at index `i`. If you delete an element in the middle of a list, however, then Python will move all the data after the element one step forward. Let us say that each time you move one element, it takes time t. If there are m elements after the one you removed, it will take tm to move them. When you remove the *last* element in a list, though, you don't have to move any other elements. It still takes some time to remove the last element, of course, but let us for convenience ignore that.

Where it gets interesting is when you add elements. If you add an element in the middle of a list—not assign to an index but insert one that should be put between the first and last parts of the list—then Python also has to move the elements that follow the one we insert. If there are m of those, it takes time tm. But there is a further complication. Python allocates a block of memory to hold the list, and that block might be too small when you add elements. If it is, Python needs to get a new block of memory and move all the elements there. If the list is n long, we spend tn time on that.

This is generally the rule, but there is a special case. When you add an element at the end of a list, `x.append(y)`, we can analyze the complexity differently. When Python finds the space for a list, it gets more space than it needs. After the end of a list, there is space for more elements; see Figure 4-1. When we append, Python will put the new element in the free space it has available. If we say that it takes the same time as copying an element, that is t time. But if there is no more space available, because we have filled the entire list with n elements, Python needs to get more memory. This usually means that it needs to put all the elements in a new memory block, and that means that we need to copy all n elements, which takes tn time.

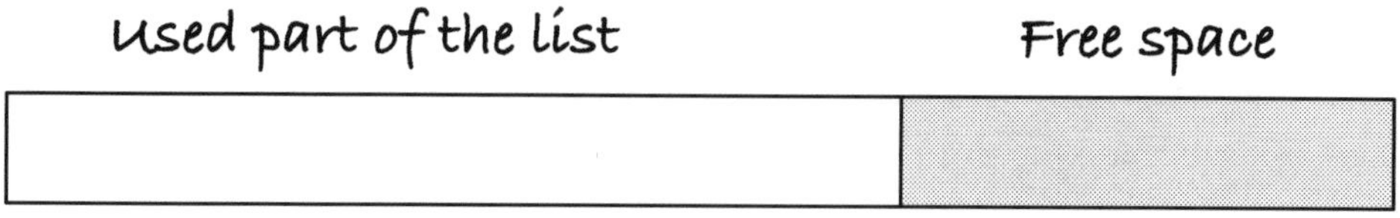

Figure 4-1. *Memory layout of a list*

And yet, we can safely assume that we only use about t time on each append because Python uses a trick, and an amortized analysis will show that it is a good trick. The trick is this: whenever Python needs a new memory block, it gets twice as much as it needs.[4] So if we need to fit n elements into a list, Python gets $2n$ places for them, half of them used and half free. That means that before Python needs to copy elements again, you need to insert another n elements. And when you get there, you have to insert $2n$ elements before Python goes and gets memory for $4n$ elements.

Obviously, some operations, appending when we don't have to copy, take t time, and some take tn time. Append is worst-case tn when there are n elements in a list, but we will now see that if we perform n append operations, for any n, we will only have used $3tn$ time. There are cheap operations that take time t and expensive operations that take time tn when we need to copy n elements. Still, if we pretend that the cheap operations really take time $3t$, then we can also pretend that the expensive operations take time $3t$.

There are generally two ways of doing an analysis like this, the *banker's method* and the *potential method*. In the first, you think like a banker and pretend that the cheap operations save up some computation in a bank that you can then use later. I find this the easiest to use, and I will use it for arguing that appending to a list is faster than the worst-case complexity indicates.

This is how we can use the banker's method to argue that appending "really" takes time $3t$, even when some operations are cheap and others are expensive.

---

[4]This is a white lie. Python doesn't double the length of lists each time it has to grow them, and there is more engineering involved in the actual implementation. The argument we use here is simpler because we double, but as long as you grow a list by an amount proportional to the current size, you get amortized constant-time append. Python's implementation is more complex, but the idea is the simple one we see here.

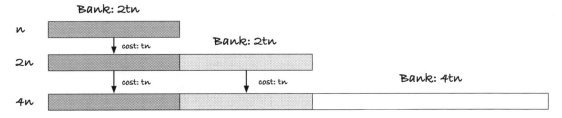

Figure 4-2. *Amortized (banker's method) analysis of appending to lists*

Pretend that each time you append an element, you use $3t$ operations. You only use t for appending when it is cheap, which leaves you $2t$ in the bank or $2tn$ when you have performed n cheap operations. So let us start with an empty list and assume that Python got n indices allocated. Before we run into an expensive operation, we must have inserted n elements, and by the preceding argument, it means that we have $2tn$ computations in the bank; see Figure 4-2. Then, in the next operation, we don't have enough memory in the list, so we must copy. We need to copy n elements, which takes tn time, but we have $2tn$ in the bank to spend on that. It leaves us tn, which I will gamble away since I don't need it for the rest of the analysis (I just needed it for a special case for the first "free" block of memory). So let us assume that I have gambled the money away and the bank is empty.

That is a problem if we need an expensive operation again now, but we don't. We have to append n more elements before we have filled the space for the new list. When we get there, we have saved up another $2tn$ computations, and that can pay for copying both the old and the new elements—there are n of each, so we copy $2n$ elements, and it costs us $2tn$, and that is what we have in the bank. Next time we need to copy items, by the same reasoning, we must have inserted $2n$ elements and therefore must have $4tn$ computations in the bank. That is also the number of objects we need to copy, so we can pay for the expensive operation. I believe you can see how this continues for longer and longer lists.

By this reasoning, we can say that for any n operations, we have spent $3tn$ time, even though the individual operations are faster or (much) slower. We always do cheap operations and save away computations first, so we have money in the bank when we need it.

The potential method works similarly. There, the idea is that there is a potential in your algorithm or data structure that you build up but cannot use up. You can always pretend that the money you put in the bank in the banker's method is a potential, but this is not where the potential method is most useful. With the banker's method, you can always see where you have saved resources for the expensive operations. Where the potential method shines is when that is not obvious, but where you can show that all expensive operations are bounded by a potential function that you can define and prove can't exceed a specific bound. At this point in the book, we haven't seen anything where the potential method would be useful, but we will see cases later.

Amortized analysis can be extremely useful. In most algorithms, you do not care how fast individual operations are, but only how fast it is to complete the entire algorithm. In such cases, it isn't the worst-case analysis but the amortized complexity that is important. In most cases, the bounds are the same, but there are many important cases where they are not. We will see amortized analysis in several places in the book.

Asymptotic Running Time and Big-Oh Notation

As we have seen, counting the actual number of primitive operations used by an algorithm quickly becomes very tedious. Considering that all operations are not actually equal and given that memory hierarchies make access to different data more or less expensive, it also seems to be a waste of time to be that precise in counting operations. If adding ten numbers can be much faster than multiplying three, why should we worry that the first involves nine operations and the second only two? In fact, we very rarely do count the actual operations, and when we do, it is for elementary but essential algorithms. What we really care about is how the running time (or memory or disk space usage or whatever critical resource our algorithm needs) grows as a function of the input size in some rough sense that we will now consider.

When we have a function of the input size, $f(n)$, we care about the *order* of f. We classify functions into classes and only care about which class of functions f belongs to, not what the actual function f is. Given a function f, we define its "order class" $O(f)$ as

$$O(f)=\left\{g(n): \exists c \in \mathbb{R}^+, n_0 \in \mathbb{N}: \forall n \in \mathbb{N}: n \geq n_0 : 0 \leq g(n) \leq c\, f(n)\right\}$$

Put into words, this means that the class of functions of order f are those functions $g(n)$ that, as n goes to infinity, will eventually be dominated by $f(n)$ times a positive constant c.

If g is in $O(f)$, we write $g \in O(f)$, as per usual mathematical notation, but you will often also see it written as $g = O(f)$. This is an abuse of notation, but you might run into it, so I should mention it, even if I will not use that notation myself.

Consider functions $f(n) = 10n + 100$ and $g(n) = 3n + 100,000$. We have $g \in O(f)$ because, eventually, a line with incline 10 will grow faster than one with incline 3, so eventually, regardless of where the lines intersect the y-axis, the former will be above the latter. We also have $f \in O(g)$ because we can simply multiply $g(n)$ by 10/3 and it is already above $f(n)$ because it intersects the y-axis at a higher value. This "big-Oh" notation is not symmetric, however. Consider the function $h(n) = n^2$. We have both $f \in O(h)$ and $g \in O(h)$ because, regardless of where a line intersects the y-axis, n^2 will eventually be larger than the line. We do *not* have $h \in O(f)$, however, for the same reason. There is no constant n_0 after which a line, regardless of what its intercept is, will always be larger than n^2.

When we write $f \in O(g)$, we provide an *upper bound* on f. We know that as n goes to infinity, $f(n)$ will be bounded by $cg(n)$ for some constant c. The upper bound need not be exact, however, as we saw with $h(n)$. We have a separate notation for that, the "big-Theta" notation:

$$\Theta(f) = \left\{ g(n) : \exists c_1, c_2 \in \mathbb{R}^+, n_0 \in \mathbb{N} : \forall n \in \mathbb{N} : n \geq n_0 : 0 \leq c_1 f(n) \leq g(n) \leq c_2 f(n) \right\}$$

The class of functions $\Theta(f)$ are those that, depending on which constant you multiply them with, can be both upper and lower bounds of $f(n)$ as n goes to infinity. This notation *is* symmetric: $g \in \Theta(f)$ if and only if $f \in \Theta(g)$. For our two lines, $f(n) = 10n + 100$ and $g(n) = 3n + 100,000$, we have $f \in \Theta(g)$ and $g \in \Theta(f)$, and we can in good conscience write $\Theta(f) = \Theta(g)$ as they are the same classes of functions. We can also write $O(f(n)) = O(g(n)) = O(n)$ since these are also the same classes, but $O(f) \neq O(h)$ because $O(h(n)) = O(n^2)$ is a larger class than $O(n)$. There are functions that are bounded, up to a constant, by n^2 that are not bounded by n, regardless of which constant we multiply to n.

The big-Oh notation can be thought of as saying something like "less than or equal to." When we say that $g \in O(f)$, we are saying that g doesn't grow faster than f, up to some constant and after a certain n_0. Because the notation is concerned with what happens as n goes to infinity, it captures *asymptotic behavior*. This is just a math term for saying that we concern ourselves with what a function does as it moves toward a limit, in this case infinity. When we analyze algorithms, we usually care more about how efficient they are on large input data compared to how they behave on small input data, so we care about their asymptotic efficiency more than we care about the details of how they behave for small n.

Consider algorithms that use n^2 vs. $10n + 100$ operations on input of size n. For small n, the n^2 algorithm will use fewer operations than the $10n + 100$ algorithm, but unless we expect that the input size will always be small, the $10n + 100$ algorithm is superior. As n grows, it will eventually be *much* faster than the n^2 algorithm.

When we have an algorithm that uses $f(n)$ operations for input of size n and we know $f \in O(g)$, then we know that g will eventually bound the running time for the algorithm. We will say that "the algorithm runs in time $O(g)$"—or usually qualify that we consider worst-case complexity, say, by saying that "the algorithm runs in worst-case time $O(g)$."

Consider the example from earlier where we added n numbers together. We counted that this involved $6n + 3$ primitive operations. If we pick any constant $c > 6$, then cn will eventually be larger than $6n + 3$, so we can say that the algorithm runs in time $O(n)$. The cost of each individual operation will vary according to the actual hardware you will execute the algorithm on, and it will not be the same cost for each operation; knowing that the running time is linear, that is, the algorithm runs in time $O(n)$, is much more important than to know what the exact number of operations is. Therefore, we usually do not care about the actual number of operations but only the big-Oh of them.

The big-Oh notation is the most used notation of the three. It is often easier to show that an algorithm does not do more than a certain number of operations, f(n), than to show that it doesn't do fewer. In many cases, we can show that an algorithm's running time is in big-Theta, $\Theta(f)$, which gives us more information about the actual running time, but it can sometimes be harder to get such an exact function of its running time. When we use big-Oh, it is not a problem to overcount how many operations we actually use; when we use big-Theta, we have to get it right.

Other Classes

In the vast majority of times when we use this asymptotic notation, we use big-Oh. We often do that even when we know an algorithm's complexity accurately and could use big-Theta. This is just because we usually care much more about bounding the running time of an algorithm than we care about getting the running time precisely right. For completeness, however, I will briefly define a few more classes, in case you run into these outside of this book.

The big-Oh class of a function is all functions that work as upper bounds of it. If $g \in O(f)$, then after some n_0 and for some constant c, $g(n) \leq cf(n)$. This is the sense in which big-Oh means less than or equal to. But there are cases where we want to say that one function grows strictly slower than another. That does not simply mean that we replace the less-than-or-equal-to sign with a less-than sign, which we could achieve in any case by multiplying by a larger c. We want to capture that regardless of what constant we multiply with, after some point, the function on the left, g, will grow slower than the function on the right, f. To capture that, we need the "little-oh" notation, defined as

$$o(f) = \left\{ g(n) : \forall c \in \mathbb{R}^+ : \exists n_0 \in \mathbb{N} : \forall n \in \mathbb{N} : n \geq n_0 : 0 \leq g(n) \leq cf(n) \right\}$$

The notation says exactly what we said in words in the preceding. For any constant you choose, there will be a point after which $g(n)$ is smaller than $cf(n)$.

If $g \in o(f)$, then we know that $g \in O(f)$ as well but also that $f \notin O(g)$. Asymptotically, f grows strictly faster than g.

We also have notation for lower bounds. Similar to big-Oh and little-oh, we have big-Omega and little-omega:

$$\Omega(f) = \left\{ g(n) : \exists c \in \mathbb{R}^+, n_0 \in \mathbb{N} : \forall n \in \mathbb{N} : n \geq n_0 : 0 \leq f(n) \leq cg(n) \right\}$$
$$\omega(f) = \left\{ g(n) : \forall c \in \mathbb{R}^+ : \exists n_0 \in \mathbb{N} : \forall n \in \mathbb{N} : n \geq n_0 : 0 \leq f(n) \leq cg(n) \right\}$$

These capture lower bounds, strict or otherwise. When $g \in \Theta(f)$, we have that, asymptotically, f can dominate g and g can dominate f; so saying $g \in \Theta(f)$ is equivalent to saying $g \in O(f)$ as well as $g \in \Omega(f)$.

When we reason about the efficiency of an algorithm, we care about upper bounds and use the big-Oh or little-oh notation; if we instead worry about how intrinsically complex problems are, we usually care about the lower bounds for any algorithm that solves them and use the omega notation. If we have a problem that we know requires $\Omega(f)$ to solve, but we also have an algorithm that solves it in $O(f)$, we have a tight bound of $\Theta(f)$. We do not concern ourselves much with the complexity of problems in this book, but it will come up from time to time, so keep this in mind.

Properties of Complexity Classes

These classes of functions have a few rules that are easy to derive that can help us reason about them in general. As long as we do not use the strict upper- and lower-bound classes, a function is going to be in its own class:

$$f \in \Theta(f)$$
$$f \in O(f)$$
$$f \in \Omega(f)$$

There is a symmetry between upper and lower bounds:

$$f \in O(g) \quad \text{if and only if} \quad g \in \Omega(f)$$
$$f \in o(g) \quad \text{if and only if} \quad g \in \omega(f)$$

Furthermore, there is transitivity in these senses:

$$f \in \Theta(g) \wedge g \in \Theta(h) \Rightarrow f \in \Theta(h)$$
$$f \in O(g) \wedge g \in O(h) \Rightarrow f \in O(h)$$
$$f \in \Omega(g) \wedge g \in \Omega(h) \Rightarrow f \in \Omega(h)$$
$$f \in o(g) \wedge g \in o(h) \Rightarrow f \in o(h)$$
$$f \in \omega(g) \wedge g \in \omega(h) \Rightarrow f \in \omega(h)$$

I have personally found very few opportunities where these rules have been useful, but if you can see why the rules must be correct, you have taken a significant step toward understanding this asymptotic function notation.

One rule that can be very useful is this: if $f \in \Theta(g)$, that is, there exists $c_1, c_2 \in \mathbb{R}^+$ such that $c_1 g(n) \le f(n) \le c_2 g(n)$ as n goes to infinity, then we also have

$$c_1 \le \frac{f(n)}{g(n)} \le c_2.$$

This means that if we believe that an algorithm runs in time $f \in \Theta g$, we can experimentally measure its running time and divide it by $g(n)$. If we are right about the theoretical running time, the measured ratio should eventually stay confined to the interval between these two constants. In other words, $f(n)/g(n)$ should flatten out as n goes to infinity, not entirely because it can fluctuate between c_1 and c_2, but it will eventually be bounded by these two constants. In practice, the ratio often does converge to a single constant nonzero. If we are wrong about the complexity, this doesn't happen. If $f \in o(g)$, then the ratio will converge to zero and not a positive constant, while if $f \in \omega(g)$, the ratio will grow unbounded.

Reasoning About Algorithmic Efficiency Using the Big-Oh Notation

Here is how we would reason about an algorithm when using big-Oh notation. Any sequence of primitive operations that we only do once is $O(1)$. Regardless of what the actual cost of an operation is, say c, it is still $O(1)$ because $O(1) = O(c)$ for all constants.

It also doesn't matter how many things we do, as long as we do each of them only once, since $O(1 + 1) = O(1)$. Whenever we loop over n elements, that loop costs us $O(n)$ operations. Any operation that happens inside the loop body can be multiplied by n to account for its cost. It doesn't matter if we actually *do* execute that operation for each iteration; the big-Oh notation gives us an upper bound for the running time, so if we count an operation more often than we really should, that is okay.

In the summation algorithm, we therefore have

```
accumulator = 0          # O(1)
for n in numbers:        # O(n)
    accumulator += n     # n * O(1)
```

where $n \times O(1)$ should be read as $O(n)$—we are really saying that we do something that has a constant cost, say c, but we do it n times, so we do something that costs cn, which is in $O(n)$.

With the search algorithm, we can reason similarly and get

```
in_list = False          # O(1)
for n in numbers:        # O(n)
    if n == x:           # n * O(1)
        in_list = True   # n * O(1)
        break            # n * O(1)
```

We know that we only ever execute the body of the if statement once, but it is easier just to multiply all the operations inside the loop by n, and since the big-Oh notation only tells us about upper bounds, it works out okay.[5]

To make the big-Oh reasoning about these algorithms even more relaxed, we will work out how to add big-Oh expressions together.

Doing Arithmetic in Big-Oh

When analyzing algorithms as we just did, we often end up with multiplying a function to a big-Oh class, as we did with $n \cdot O(1)$, and if we want to combine a number of calculations where we know their big-Oh class, we need to add them together, that is, we want to know how to interpret $O(f) + O(g)$.

---

[5]In this particular case, we could just as easily count the if body as constant time as well, but it doesn't matter for the big-Oh analysis. The entire algorithm runs in $\Theta(n)$.

First, we need to know how to do arithmetic on functions. If you have a function f and multiply it with a constant, c, you have cf, which is the function $h(n) = c \cdot f(n)$. Similarly, $f + c$ is the function $h(n) = f(n) + c$. If you have two functions, f and g, then $f \cdot g$ is the function $h(n) = f(n)g(n)$ and $f + g$ is the function $h(n) = f(n) + g(n)$. Do not confuse function multiplication, $f \cdot g$, with function composition, $f \circ g$. The former means that $(f \cdot g)(n) = f(n) \cdot g(n)$, while the latter means that $(f \circ g)(n) = f(g(n))$.

For the rules for doing arithmetic with big-Oh notation, let f, f_1, f_2, g, g_1, g_2 denote functions.

The first important rule is this:

$$f_1 \in O(g_1) \wedge f_2 \in O(g_2) \Rightarrow f_1 + f_2 \in O(g_1 + g_2)$$

We can also write this as

$$O(f) + O(g) = O(f + g).$$

Since $g + g$ is the same as $2g$, we furthermore have that

$$f_1 \in O(g) \wedge f_2 \in O(g) \Rightarrow f_1 + f_2 \in O(g)$$

This means that if we can bound two separate pieces of the running time of an algorithm by the same function, then the entire algorithm's running time is bounded by that. Because of the transitivity rules for big-Oh, this also means that if $f \in O(g)$ then $f + g \in O(g)$. So when we add together different parts of a runtime analysis, whenever one function dominates the other, we can simply discard the dominated part. Thus, if we add a constant number of operations, $O(1)$, to a linear number of operations, $O(n)$, as we have to in our examples, we end up with something that is still linear $O(n)$.

We also have a rule for multiplying functions:

$$f_1 \in O(g_1) \wedge f_2 \in O(g_2) \Rightarrow f_1 \cdot f_2 \in O(g_1 \cdot g_2)$$

or

$$O(f) \cdot O(g) = O(f \cdot g).$$

This rule is particularly useful when we reason about loops. The time it takes to execute a loop over n elements is $O(n)$ multiplied by the time it takes to execute the loop body, which could be some function $f(n)$, so the total running time for such a loop is $n \cdot f(n) \in O(nf(n))$.

We also have rules for multiplying into big-Oh classes:

$$f \cdot O(g) = O(f \cdot g)$$

We can use this in our examples where we have expressions such as $n \times O(1)$. This simply becomes $O(n)$. From this rule, it follows that when c is a nonzero constant, we have

$$c \cdot O(f) = O(f)$$

You can see this by merely considering c a constant function $c(n) = c$ and then apply the previous rule.

We can now apply these rules to get a final, big-Oh running time for our example algorithms. Consider first the summation:

```
accumulator = 0          # O(1)
for n in numbers:        # O(n)
    accumulator += n     # n * O(1)
```

We have to work out $O(1) + O(n) + n \cdot O(1)$. This is the same as $O(1) + O(n) + O(n)$ by the rule for how to multiply into a big-Oh class, and then, by the addition rule, we get $O(1 + n + n) = O(n)$.

For the search we have

```
in_list = False          # O(1)
for n in numbers:        # O(n)
    if n == x:           # n * O(1)
        in_list = True   # n * O(1)
        break            # n * O(1)
```

which breaks down to $O(1) + O(n) + 3 \times n \times O(1) = O(n)$.

Consider now a different algorithm:

```
for i in range(1,len(numbers)):
    x = numbers[i]
    j = i
    while j > 0 and numbers[j-1] > numbers[j]:
        numbers[j-1], numbers[j] = numbers[j], numbers[j-1]
        j -= 1
```

This is an algorithm called "insertion sort," and we return to it in the next chapter where we prove that it sorts numbers. Here, we will just consider its running time. The algorithm consists of two nested loops. So we reason as follows: The outer loop iterates over numbers, which gives us an $O(n)$ contribution. It doesn't include the first element in numbers, but that doesn't change anything since $O(n-1) = O(n)$. Inside the loop body, we have two constant-time contributions and an inner loop. The constant-time contributions give us $O(1)$, and the inner loop is bounded by $O(n)$ (j starts at a number less than n and is decreased by at least one in each iteration and leaves the loop if it reaches zero). Therefore, we have the running time

$$O(n) \times \left(O(1) + O(n) \right) = O\left(n^2 \right).$$

In other words, this sorting algorithm runs in quadratic time. Or rather, we should say that its *worst-case* running time is $O(n^2)$. In the analysis, we assumed that the inner loop could execute n iterations; if the list is already sorted, then numbers[j-1] > numbers[j] is always False, and the inner loop will actually take constant time; the *best-case* running time is only $O(n)$.

Now consider this algorithm, called *binary search*. This is another algorithm we return to in the next chapter. It searches for a number, *x*, in a sorted list of numbers using the third strategy from the guessing game we have seen a few times by now. It has a range in which to search, bracketed by low and high. If *x* is in the list, we know that it must be between these two indices. We pick the midpoint of the range and check if we have found *x*, in which case we terminate the search. If we haven't, we check if the midpoint number is smaller or larger than *x*. If it is smaller, we move low up to the midpoint plus one. If it is larger, we move high down to the midpoint. We do not move it to the midpoint minus one. If we did, it would be possible to miss the index where *x* is hiding; this can happen if the interval is of length one and low is the index where *x* resides, as we will see next chapter:

```
low, high = 0, len(numbers)
found = False
while low < high:
    mid = (low + high) // 2
    if numbers[mid] == x:
        found = True
        break
```

```
elif numbers[mid] < x:
    low = mid + 1
else:
    high = mid
```

We can analyze its complexity as follows: we have some constant-time operations at the beginning, $O(1)$, and then a loop. It is less obvious how many iterations the loop will make in this algorithm than in the previous ones we have looked at, but let us call that number m. Then the loop takes time $O(m)$ times the time it takes to execute the loop body. All the operations inside the loop are constant time, $O(1)$, so we have

$$O(1)+O(m)\times O(1)=O(m).$$

Of course, this isn't entirely satisfying. We don't know what m is, and we want the running time to be a function of n.

The interval we are searching in decreases in each iteration, so if we start with an interval of size n, we could, correctly, argue that the loop is bounded by n as well and derive a running time of $O(n)$. This is correct; $O(n)$ is an upper bound for the (worst-case) complexity. In fact, however, the algorithm is much faster than that. It really runs in $O(\log_2 n)$, where $\log_2$ is the base-two logarithm. To see this, consider how much we shrink the interval by in each iteration. When we update the interval, we always shrink the interval to half the size of the previous one. So we can ask ourselves, how many times can you halve n before you get below one? That is $\lceil \log_2 n \rceil$, so m is bounded by $O(\lceil \log_2 n \rceil)$. We typically do not include the rounding-up notation when we write this but consider it implicit, so we simply write $O(\log_2 n)$.

Important Complexity Classes

Some complexity classes pop up again and again in algorithms, so you should get familiar with them. From fastest to slowest, these are

- *Constant time*: $O(1)$. This is, obviously, the best you can achieve asymptotically, but since it does not depend on the input size, we very rarely see algorithms running in this time.

- *Logarithmic time*: $O(\log n)$. We saw that binary search was one such algorithm. Generally, we see this complexity when we can reduce the size of the input we look at by a fixed fraction in each iteration of a loop. Typically, we can cut the data in half, and we get a base-two logarithm, but since the difference between two different-based logarithms is a constant, $\log_a(x) = 1/\log_b(a) \cdot \log_b(x)$, we rarely write the base in big-Oh notation.

- *Linear time*: $O(n)$. We saw several examples of linear-time algorithms in this chapter. Whenever we do something where we have to, in the worst case, examine all our input, the complexity will be at least this.

- *Log-linear time*: $O(n \log n)$. We haven't seen examples of this class yet, but it will show up several times in Chapter 9.

- *Quadratic time*: $O(n^2)$. We saw a sorting algorithm with this complexity. This complexity often shows up when we have nested loops.

- *Cubic time*: $O(n^3)$. This is another class we haven't seen yet, but when we have three levels of nested loops, we see it. If you multiply two $n \times n$ algorithms the straightforward way,[6] $C = AB$, you have to compute $n \times n$ values in C, and for each compute $c_{ij} = \sum_k a_{ik} b_{kj}$ where you add n values, giving you a total running time of n^3.

- *Exponential time*: $O(2^n)$. You should avoid this complexity like the plague. Even for tiny n, this running time is practically forever. It does, unfortunately, pop up in many important optimization problems where we do not know of any faster algorithms. If you have a problem that can only be solved in this complexity, you should try to modify the problem to something you can solve more efficiently, or you should try to approximate the solution instead of getting the optimal solution. Algorithms that run in this complexity are rarely worth considering.

In Figure 4-3, I have plotted the growth of the different classes. As you can see in the upper-left frame, logarithmic growth is very slow compared to linear growth. On the upper right, you can see that log-linear growth is slower than linear, but compared to quadratic time, it is much faster. Cubic time, lower left, is much slower than quadratic time, and exponential time, lower right, just grows to infinity before you even get started.

---

[6]It is possible to multiply matrices faster than this, but that is beyond this book.

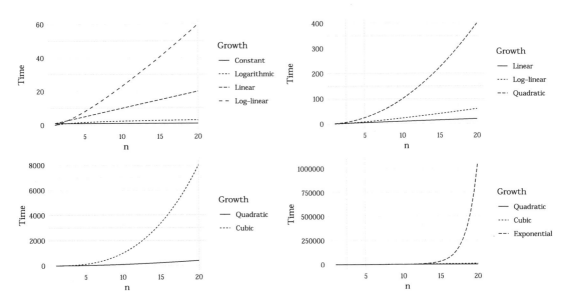

Figure 4-3. *Growth of different complexity classes*

The figure only shows one representative for each class, but of course, there are many that grow with different speeds; we just hide that in the notation. That also means that you must be a little careful when you work with big-Oh notation. An algorithm that runs in $O(n^2)$ with a very low constant might be faster than one that runs in $O(n)$ for all sizes of n that you are interested in. The notation tells us what happens as n goes to infinity, but not what happens in particular ranges of n that we might be more interested in. It is highly useful too, but it does have its limitations in some cases.

Asymptotic Complexity Exercises

In the following exercises, you can test your understanding of the big-Oh notation and in how you derive upper bounds for algorithms' running time.

Function Growth

Consider the classes

1. $O(\log n)$, $o(\log n)$, $\Omega(\log n)$, and $\omega(\log n)$

2. $O(n)$, $o(n)$, $\Omega(n)$, and $\omega(n)$

3. $O(n^2)$, $o(n^2)$, $\Omega(n^2)$, and $\omega(n^2)$

4. $O(2^n)$, $o(2^n)$, $\Omega(2^n)$, and $\omega(2^n)$

Exercise: For each of the following functions, determine which of the 16 classes it belongs in. Remember that the complexity classes overlap, so, for example, if $f \in o(g)$ then $f \in O(g)$ as well and if $f \in \Theta(g)$ then $f \in O(g)$ as well as $\Omega(g)$ (but $f \notin o(g)$ and $f \notin \omega(g)$):

1. $f(n) = 23n$

2. $f(n) = 42n^2 - 100n$

3. $f(n) = n/\log n$

4. $f(n) = \log(n)/n$

5. $f(n) = n^2/\log n$

6. $f(n) = \log n + \log(n)/n$

7. $f(n) = 5^n - n^3$

8. $f(n) = n!$

9. $f(n) = 2^n/n$

10. $f(n) = \log(\log n)$

Insertion Sort

Consider the insertion sort algorithm. We argued that the worst-case running time was $O(n^2)$ but the best-case running time was $O(n)$.

Exercise: Describe what the input data, numbers, should look like to actually achieve the worst- and best-case running times.

Binary Search

We argued that the worst-case running time for the binary search is $O(\log n)$.

Exercise: What is the best-case running time, and what would the input data look like to achieve it?

Sieve of Eratosthenes

Recall the Sieve of Eratosthenes from the previous chapter.

Exercise: Derive an upper bound for its running time.

Exercise: Is there a difference between its best-case and worst-case running times?

The Longest Increasing Substring

Recall the exercise from the previous chapter where you should design an algorithm that finds the longest subsequence x[i:j] such that consecutive numbers are increasing, that is, x[k] < x[k+1] for all k in range(i,j) (or one of the longest, if there are more than one with the same length).

Exercise: What is the time complexity of your solution?

Exercise: Can you construct a linear-time algorithm for solving this problem?

Hint   One way to approach this is to consider the longest sequence seen so far and the longest sequence up to a given index into x. From this, you can formalize invariants that should get you through.

Merging

Recall the *merging* algorithm from the previous chapter.

Exercise: Show that you can merge two sorted lists of sizes n and m, respectively, into one sorted list containing the elements from the two, in time $O(n + m)$.

Empirically Validating Algorithms' Running Time

It is not unheard of that programmers make mistakes. Theoretical computer scientists have been known to make mistakes also. So, once you have a derived asymptotic running time, you are usually best validating that the running time is what you expect. That means measuring its running time on actual data and comparing it with the expected running time. A good first approach is to measure the running time for variable-size data and then plot it. You can test statistically if the running time is correct, but eyeballing it works just as well. If you need a statistical model to check what you cannot see in a plot, then the difference between the theoretical running time and the empirical running time is so slight that it likely doesn't matter.

If you simply plot an algorithm's running time, it can be hard to see if it runs as expected. For positive n, the functions n^2 and n^3 look similar if you just eyeball them. One thing you can do, to make it easier to see if your running time matches the expected running time, is to plot the empirical running time divided by the expected running time. If your empirical running time fits your theoretical running time, this plot should approach a horizontal line as *n* goes to infinity. If your empirical running time divided by the theoretical running time does not converge to a horizontal line, then the two are not equal. If the plot grows as the input size goes to infinity, then the empirical running time is larger than the theoretical one. If the plot moves closer and closer to zero, your algorithm is faster than the asymptotic limit.

In the following I will give you code that lets you measure and plot running time. It will look like magic if this book is your first introduction to Python because it uses features that we haven't covered and some features we will not cover. You can read an introductory book on Python programming and one on Numpy/SciPy, and you will understand. This book is not about this but about algorithms and how to implement them, so you can just take this code, consider it a magic spell for plotting the running time of an algorithm, and then not worry about it any longer.

We need a way to measure running time. We can get a function for doing that like this:

```python
from timeit import default_timer as timer
```

With that spell in place, you can measure the running time of your algorithm thusly:

```python
then = timer()
# algorithm...
now = timer()
running_time = now - then
```

You want to measure the running time for a range of input sizes, and you can do this by creating a sequence of sizes that you want to use and then loop through them:

```python
import numpy as np # for np.log and np.linspace
from time import sleep # for faking a running time

ns = np.linspace(10, 100, 50)

ys = []
for n in ns:
    then = timer()

    # Fake algorithm
    sleep((0.03 * n * np.log(n + 2) + 10) / 10)
```

```
now = timer()
running_time = now - then

# adding 1e-10 so we don't divide by zero
ys.append(running_time / (n * np.log(n) + 1e-10))
```

The `sleep()` function here is only needed to fake a running time. You don't need it to test your real algorithm. In that case, you can remove

```
from time import sleep # for faking a running time
```

You will not have to change much in this template to measure your own algorithm. You need to change

```
ys.append(running_time / (n * np.log(n) + 1e-10))
```

so you use your own theoretical running time, and you need to change this line:

```
ns = np.linspace(10, 100, 50)
```

It says that our *ns* should go from 10 to 100 and that we want 50 points, equally spaced, in this range. Choose a range that is appropriate for your algorithm.

Once you have input sizes, `ns`, and empirical divided by theoretical running times, `ys`, you can plot the two like this:

```
import matplotlib.pyplot as plt # plotting functionality
plt.plot(ns, ys)
plt.xlabel("Input size")
plt.ylabel("T(n) / n log n")
plt.savefig("my-plot.pdf")
```

In all of the preceding, I have only measured the algorithm's running time once on each input size. This can be problematic. First, there might be measurement uncertainty and the running time on the same input can vary between executions of the algorithm, and second, running time might depend on the input data's details beyond just the size of it.

Let us handle the easy one first. Suppose there is variation in the measured running time, which is only caused by measurement uncertainty. In that case, you just run the algorithm multiple times on the same size and take the average. The law of large numbers tells you that you get closer to the real mean the more measurements you make. Better yet, if you plot the measurements, you include all your measurements or summarize as scatter or box plots or similar. Measurement uncertainty is easy to deal with.

It is harder to deal with algorithms whose running time depends not only on the size of the data but also on properties of the data. If we have derived the best-case and worst-case running times, we can measure the empirical running time for data that gives us the best-case and worst-case behavior. Suppose we have an average-case running time and we can sample from the distribution that provides us with that average-case time. In that case, we can sample and compare the empirical results with the theoretical results.

The challenging part is when the running time depends on the input data, but we do not know in which way. If we measure the running time on the same data for each data size, we will not see this variation; we will only see the measurement uncertainty. We would need to vary the data from run to run. Here, we could pick random data for each run. This is a good strategy if we know nothing about what real data looks like, but it can give very misleading results about the running time in practice. The data the algorithm will crunch in an actual application is typically not random. You could be lucky, and your target data usually hits a best-case scenario, or you could be unlucky, and it hits a worst-case scenario. If you can get small subsets of your real data to test the empirical running time on or if you can simulate data that resembles the actual data, then you want to do that. This will give you a better estimate of how the algorithm will perform when you let it out into the wild.

CHAPTER 5

Searching and Sorting

In this chapter, we will explore two fundamental problems that are the foundations of many other algorithms: sorting sequences and searching for an element in them. These are central problems used as building blocks for a variety of other algorithms, and Python already has built-in functionality for solving them. You should practically always use the existing implementations; they are well engineered and optimized, so you are not likely to implement faster solutions yourself. The exception is when you have some a priori knowledge about your data that Python does not have that you can then exploit, while Python must use a general algorithm. Different algorithms have different pros and cons, and we will briefly discuss these. You can choose the right algorithm for the job because you know more about the data than Python does. Optimizing the algorithm you use this way is rarely worthwhile, though, so you are usually better off just using what Python already has. Anyway, onward to the algorithms.

Searching

We first consider the simplest of the two problems: searching. Given a sequence of numbers,[1] numbers, and a value, x, we want to determine if x is in numbers.

---

[1] In this chapter, we assume we are working with numbers, but we can search for any type of data as long as we can compare two items to see if they are equal. With only this assumption, the linear search will get the job done. If we furthermore assume that our data has a total order, that is, for any two items we can decide if they are equal or if the first is smaller than or greater than the second, then the elements can be sorted and we can use binary search. These properties are satisfied by more than just numbers, and we briefly discuss what it takes to handle more general sequences at the end of the chapter.

© Thomas Mailund 2021
T. Mailund, *Introduction to Computational Thinking*, https://doi.org/10.1007/978-1-4842-7077-6_5

We consider two solutions to this problem. The first, *linear search*, assumes nothing about numbers except that it is a sequence we can loop through. The second, *binary search*, makes a few more assumptions: (1) numbers is a sorted sequence and (2) we can access any element in numbers by index, numbers[i] in constant time.[2]

The linear search algorithm runs in worst-case linear time. Binary search only takes logarithmic time. This makes the binary search algorithm the preferred choice whenever your data is sorted. If the data is not sorted to begin with, however, the cost of sorting the data before you can use binary search should also be considered. If you search for m elements in a sequence of n numbers, the linear search will take time $O(mn)$, while binary search will take time $O(S(n) + m \log n)$ where $S(n)$ is the cost of sorting n numbers.

How fast we can sort data depends on the assumptions we can make about our data items. If all we can do with data objects is to compare them to learn which is smaller, then it can be shown that the sorting problem cannot be solved faster than $\Omega(n \log n)$. Algorithms that only assume that we can compare objects are called *comparison-based* sorting algorithms. Not that inventive, I know. We shall see comparison-based algorithms that run in time $O(n \log n)$ in Chapter 9. In this chapter, we will only see comparison-based sorting algorithms that run in worst-case time $O(n^2)$. We will also see algorithms that run in linear time. This doesn't conflict with the lower bound of $\Omega(n \log n)$ for comparison-based algorithms because our linear-time algorithms will depend on more than simple comparison; with more assumptions about what we can do with our data, we have more to exploit when building algorithms to solve a problem.

Linear Search

Linear search is straightforward. We loop over all the elements in numbers and compare each in turn to x. If we see x, we break the search and report that we found it. If we reach the end of numbers without seeing x, we report that it wasn't found.

---

[2]If we have a list or a tuple of numbers, we can always get the element at any given index in constant time. This property is called *random access*, and data structures where we can get an element by index in constant time are called *random-access* data structures. It is necessary to have the distinction between random-access data and not because there are many data structures where we do not have constant-time random access. In Chapter 13, we shall see one common sequence structure, linked lists, that enables us to scan through its elements in linear time but not access items by index in constant time. There are many more.

```
found = False
for n in numbers:
    if x == n:
        found = True
        break
```

The built-in solution in Python for linear search uses the in keyword:[3]

```
x in numbers
```

That the linear search algorithm has a worst-case running time of $O(n)$ is also straightforward. The for loop has to run over all the n elements in numbers if it doesn't find x and breaks early. The best-case running time is obviously $O(1)$ because we could get lucky and find x in the very first iteration.

Binary Search

If we assume we have random-access sorted input, we can do better than a linear search—we can do a binary search. We already saw the binary search algorithm in the previous chapter. It looks like this:

```
low, high = 0, len(numbers)
found = None
while low < high:
    mid = (low + high) // 2
    if numbers[mid] == x:
        found = mid
        break
```

---

[3]Unless you have a good reason to, you should use the in operator to check membership of an item in a data structure. It will work for all sequences, using the linear search algorithm, but for data structures that allow for faster lookup, such as dictionaries or sets, the in operator will use the faster algorithms. The only case I can think of where you wouldn't necessarily use in is for sorted, random-access sequences. Python cannot know if a sequence is sorted or not so it will use linear search when you use the in operator on general sequences. Even for sorted sequences, I would probably use in unless the search is a bottleneck in my algorithm because of the simpler syntax and because it makes it easier to replace a sequence with another data structure that provides faster membership checks.

```
    elif numbers[mid] < x:
        low = mid + 1
    else:
        high = mid
```

The algorithm works by keeping track of an interval, [low,high). The algorithm makes sure that if x is found in numbers, then it is found in this range. In each iteration of the while loop, we look at the midpoint of the range (if the midpoint is not an integer, we round down when we do integer division). If the midpoint is equal to x, we are done. If it is less than x, we know that x must be found in the interval [mid+1,high). The elements are sorted, so if the midpoint is less than x, then all elements to the left of the midpoint are less than x as well. If the midpoint is greater than x, then we know that all elements to the right of the midpoint are greater than x, so if x is in the list, then it must be in the interval [*low*, *mid*). Notice the asymmetry in the updated intervals. When we increase low, we use mid+1, but when we decrease high, we use mid. This is a consequence of how we generally represent ranges in Python. We include the point at low in the range but exclude the point at high. So, when we decrease high to mid, we have already eliminated the point at mid from the search, just as when we increase low to mid + 1.

Exercise: Consider a modified solution where we set high to mid-1 instead of mid. Give an example where the algorithm would give you the wrong answer.

The built-in solution in Python is implemented in the module bisect and looks like this:

```
import bisect
print(bisect.bisect(numbers, x))
```

The bisect algorithm does something *slightly* different from our implementation. It returns an index where x is found, or if x is not in numbers, it returns the index at which it should be inserted if we wanted to do that. We just consider the simpler problem of determining if x is in the sequence or not.

The numbers sequence has to be sorted for the algorithm to work. It is this property that gives us information about where to continue the search if the midpoint of the interval is smaller or larger than x. If the list were not sorted, knowing whether the midpoint is smaller than or larger than x would give us no information about where x would be found if it were in the list.

To hone our skills at reasoning about algorithms, we will formally prove termination and correctness. We look at termination first. For our termination function, we take high-low. Clearly, if this function is at or below zero, the while loop condition is false. To see that it decreases in each iteration, we consider the two options for updating the interval. If we set low to mid + 1, we clearly reduce high-low. To see that we also decrease the size of the interval when we update high, we observe that mid < high when we use integer division for determining mid.

Exercise: If we updated low by setting it to mid instead of mid + 1, our reasoning about the termination function fails. Give an example where this would result in the loop never terminating.

To prove correctness, we specify the loop invariant: x is not in the interval [0,low) and not in the interval [high,n). This invariant guarantees us that if we reach the point where the [low,high) interval is empty, then x is not in numbers. Since we do not set found to true unless we actually see *x*, we also know that we do not report that *x is* in numbers unless it is.

We already discussed the algorithms' running time in the previous chapter, but recall, if we reduce the size of a problem from *n* to *n*/2 in each iteration and only use $O(1)$ per iteration, then the running time amounts to the number of times we can divide *n* by two until we reach one (or below). That is the base-two logarithm of *n*, so the worst-case running time of binary search is $O(\log n)$.

Sorting

The sorting problem is this: given a sequence of elements *x* of length *n*, create a new sequence *y* that contains the same elements as *x* but such that $y[i] \leq y[i+1]$ for $i = 0$, ..., $n - 1$. For this problem to even make sense, we must make clear what we mean by $y[i] \leq y[i+1]$. Not all data has a natural order on elements. For some data, there is no natural way to define an order at all. For other data, it is possible to have a *partial order*, which means that for *some* elements *a* and *b* we can determine if $a = b$, $a < b$, or $a > b$, but not all; some elements $a \neq b$ are *neither a < b* nor *a > b*. In such a case, we might require of *y* that $y[i] \not> y[i+1]$. This is known as *topological sorting*, but is beyond the scope of this book. In this chapter, we only consider data that has a total order.

We assume that our elements have a *total order*, which means that for any two elements, *a* and *b* (exactly), one of these three relations is true: $a < b$, $a = b$, or $a > b$. This is, for example, the case for numbers, with the usual order, but also for strings with the alphabetical order, also known as the *lexical* order.

Even if we have managed to define a total order on our data points, we are not out of the woods yet. The total order only means that we have well-defined comparison relations, $a = b$, $a < b$, and $b > a$, where for any given elements a and b precisely one is true. But what *exactly* can we assume about a and b when we write $a = b$? Using the relation "=" to mean (object) equality is simple. If $a = b$, then we know that a and b are the same object. This isn't the only way we use equality, though. Sometimes it is used to define an equivalence relation instead of actual equality. This happens when we sort elements according to some key or keys, and the order is defined by these keys. If the keys are only part of the data, we can have two elements that have the same values for all keys (so we would conclude $a = b$), but they are actually different objects with different non-key attributes.

If we sort a list of people by their last name, then we consider "John Doe" and "Jane Doe" as equal with relation to the order—after all "Doe" equals "Doe"—but that does not mean that "John" equals "Jane." We can resolve this by first sorting by the last name and then according to the first name, but this creates a new problem. If we first sort by the last name and then according to the first name, do we risk messing up the first order? If we sort

- "John Doe"

- "John Smith"

- "Jane Doe"

by the last name, we get the order

- "John Doe"

- "Jane Doe"

- "Joe Smith"

(Or maybe we get "Jane Doe," "John Doe," and "Joe Smith" since "Jane Doe" and "John Doe" are equal concerning last names.) If we then sort by the first name, we mess up the first sort because now we might get "Jane Doe," "Joe Smith," and "John Doe."

When we only sort elements based some subset of their attributes, what we call *keys*, an algorithm can be *stable* or *unstable*. If it is stable, it means that elements we consider equal end up in the same order as they appear in the input; if it is unstable, there is no such guarantee. To correctly sort names, first by family name and then according to first name, we can first sort by first name and then use a stable sort on the family name. If we sort our list with the first names as keys, we get

- "Jane Doe"

- "Joe Smith"

- "John Doe"

If we then sort with a stable sort, using the family names as the key, "Jane Doe" must appear before "John Doe" because that is the order they are in when we apply the stable sort.

We also classify sorting algorithms by whether they are *comparison based* or not. If all we can do, when we have two elements, is to test which of the relations, $a < b$, $a = b$, and $a > b$, is true, then we are doing what is called *comparison* sort. As I mentioned at the start of this chapter, no comparison-based algorithm can sort n elements faster than $\Omega(n \log n)$, and some algorithms do run in $\Theta(n \log n)$, although we won't see them in this chapter. Sorting algorithms do not have to be comparison based, though. We will see two such algorithms in this chapter that can sort in worst-case linear time, as long as we can reduce our keys to numbers bounded by n.

Another property we use to classify sorting algorithms is whether they sort the elements *in place* or not. If we sort in place, it means that we swap around the items in our input sequence to turn it into a sorted sequence without using any additional memory. In the previous chapter, we focused on running time complexity, but how much memory an algorithm needs can be equally important. An in-place algorithm has optimal memory usage, $O(1)$. (Some might also classify as in-place algorithms that use $O(\log n)$ extra memory. This is to explicitly allow for the number of bits it takes to represent numbers up to magnitude n. We will not get this technical here). Just as we didn't include the input size for the time usage of the binary search algorithm, we do not include the input size as part of a sorting algorithm's memory usage. When algorithms are not in place, that is, when they use more than constant memory, their memory consumption is sometimes equally important to their time usage.

For implementations of sorting algorithms, we also distinguish between them being *destructive* and *nondestructive*. If you modify the input sequence when you sort it, you destroy the original order you got the data in. Sometimes, this is what you want. You only care about the sorted version of your data, so the original order is irrelevant. Other times, you want to keep the original order around, for some reason or another, and just want a sorted copy around as well. This is not so much a property of algorithms as it is for implementations. You can copy the input data and then use a destructive algorithm to sort it, thus preserving the original sequence. The only consequence of making a nondestructive sort out of a destructive one is the memory usage. You can take the memory usage of any sorting algorithm, make it at least linear, and then sort nondestructively in that complexity. In-place algorithms use constant space but are innately destructive; if you first create a copy of the input and sort that destructively, you now have a linear space implementation.

There are more properties used to classify sorting algorithms than these, but those are the main ones. To summarize, the classifications we have seen are

- *Comparison based*: All we can do with our data items is to compare pairs (a, b) to determine whether $a < b$, $a = b$, or $a > b$.

- *Stable*: When we sort data items by some key, we do not change the order of the input items that have the same key.

- *In place*: When we only use constant extra memory to sort a sequence.

- *Destructive* (for implementations): Whether sorting a sequence modifies it or whether we create a copy of the data in sorted order.

In this chapter, we will see three algorithms that are comparison-based algorithms and two that are not, four that are stable and one that is not, and three that are in place and two that are not.

Algorithm	Comparison based	Stable	In place
Insertion	✓	✓	✓
Bubble	✓	✓	✓
Selection	✓		✓
Bucket		✓	
Radix		✓	

You can implement all of them both as destructive and nondestructive. For the in-place algorithms, this changes the memory complexity from constant to linear; for bucket and radix sorts, it does not alter the space complexity.

Built-In Sorting in Python

Python lists have a built-in sorting method

```
x.sort()
```

using an algorithm known as *Timsort* (named after Tim Peters who created it). This is a comparison-based stable sorting algorithm that runs in worst-case time $O(n \log n)$ and best-case time $O(n)$ with $O(n)$ memory usage.[4]

Calling x.sort() is destructive and modifies x so the object is in sorted order after the call. Python also provides a nondestructive way to get a sorted copy:

```
y = sorted(x)
```

This uses the same Timsort algorithm as x.sort(); it just doesn't modify x but creates a new copy.

Comparison Sorts

We've seen enough algorithm classification terms now to satisfy even the most pedantic programmer, so we now turn to actual algorithms. We first consider three comparison-based, in-place sorting algorithms. Two of them, *insertion sort* and *bubble sort*, are stable and have a best-case running time of $O(n)$. The third, *selection sort*, is not stable and has a best-case running time of $O(n^2)$.

Selection Sort

A straightforward comparison sort algorithm is *selection sort*. It works similar to how you might sort items manually. You keep a list of sorted items and a set of yet-to-be-sorted items. One by one, you pick the smallest of the unsorted elements and append it to the list of sorted elements. Selection sort follows this strategy but keeps the sorted and the unsorted elements in the same list as the input, making it an in-place algorithm.

---

[4]Timsort modifies the input list in place when it can get away with it but uses additional memory to speed up the computations when necessary.

It uses a variable, i, that iterates from zero to $n - 1$, where n is the length of the input list. The items before i are kept sorted and are less than or equal to the items following i. Formalized as a loop invariant, we can write this as

$$I_1 : \forall j \in [1,i) : x[j-1] \leq x[j]$$

and

$$I_2 : \forall j \in [0,i), \forall k \in [i,n) : x[j] \leq x[k]$$

where x is the sequence to be sorted.

If i iterates from 0 to $n - 1$, then in the last iteration, when i is incremented from $n - 1$ to n, invariant I_1 guarantees us that all elements in the range $[0, n)$ are sorted, so the loop invariant guarantees correctness. (We still have to guarantee that we satisfy the invariant in each iteration over variable i, of course). The algorithm will consist of two loops, one nested inside the other, but both will be for loops, iterating through finite-length sequences, so termination is also guaranteed.

In each iteration, we locate the index of the smallest element in the range $[i, n)$, call it j, and swap $x[i]$ and $x[j]$; see Figure 5-1. From invariant I_2 we know that the $x[j]$ we locate is greater than or equal to all elements in the range $[0, i)$, so when we put it at index i, the range $[0, i + 1)$ is sorted, satisfying I_1. Since $x[j]$ was the smallest element in the range $[i, n)$, we also know that for all $l \in [i, n) : x[j] \leq x[l]$, so after we swap $x[i]$ and $x[j]$—we can call the resulting list x'—we have $l \in [i + 1, n) : x'[i] = x[j] \leq x[l]$, satisfying I_2. Thus, swapping the smallest element in $[i, n)$ into position $x[i]$ and incrementing i each iteration satisfies the loop invariants, so the algorithm is correct.

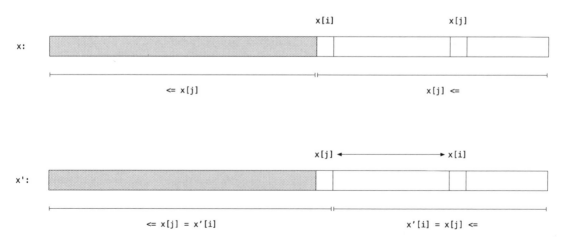

Figure 5-1. Swapping the jth and ith items in selection sort

Implemented in Python, the algorithm looks as follows:

```
for i in range(len(x)):
    # find index of smallest elm in x[i:]
    min_idx, min_val = i, x[i]
    for j in range(i, len(x)):
        if x[j] < min_val:
            min_idx, min_val = j, x[j]

    # swap x[i] and x[j] puts
    # x[j] at the right position
    x[i], x[min_idx] = min_val, x[i]
```

If we start with this input sequence

```
x = [1, 3, 2, 4, 5, 2, 3, 4, 1, 2, 3]
```

the states in the algorithm are given by these lists

```
[1] [3, 2, 4, 5, 2, 3, 4, 1, 2, 3]
[1, 1] [2, 4, 5, 2, 3, 4, 3, 2, 3]
[1, 1, 2] [4, 5, 2, 3, 4, 3, 2, 3]
[1, 1, 2, 2] [5, 4, 3, 4, 3, 2, 3]
[1, 1, 2, 2, 2] [4, 3, 4, 3, 5, 3]
[1, 1, 2, 2, 2, 3] [4, 4, 3, 5, 3]
[1, 1, 2, 2, 2, 3, 3] [4, 4, 5, 3]
[1, 1, 2, 2, 2, 3, 3, 3] [4, 5, 4]
[1, 1, 2, 2, 2, 3, 3, 3, 4] [5, 4]
[1, 1, 2, 2, 2, 3, 3, 3, 4, 4] [5]
[1, 1, 2, 2, 2, 3, 3, 3, 4, 4, 5] []
```

as they look at the end of each outer for loop body, where the first list shows the elements in the range $[0, i + 1)$ and the second list the elements in the range $[i + 1, n)$— before the loop body, we have $[0, i)$ sorted, but at the end of the body, we have $[0, i + 1)$ sorted, which is what I show here.

In each iteration, we locate the smallest element among those not yet sorted and append it to the sorted list. If we always picked the leftmost minimal value when there were ties, it seems like the algorithm should be stable, that is, the input order is preserved when elements have the same key. This reasoning is faulty, however, since it does not consider exactly *how* we append a minimal value to the sorted list. The swap we used to move the element at index j into index i also moves the element at index i over to index j. If there is another index, $k < j$, where the key of $x[k]$ is the same as the key of $x[i]$, then the swap of $x[i]$ and $x[j]$ has changed the order of $x[i]$ and $x[k]$ as well, which a stable algorithm shouldn't do.

Exercise: Give an example input where selection sort is not stable.

It *is* possible to make the algorithm stable, but not by swapping as we do here. For that, we need a data structure where we can move an element from one location to another in constant time. The linked lists we see in Chapter 13 permit this. With Python's built-in lists, we cannot do it.

To derive the running time of the algorithm, we see that the outer loop executes $n-1$ operations and the inner loop executes $n-i$ operations in iteration i of the outer loop, which gives us $n+(n-1)+(n-2)+\ldots+1=\sum_{i=1}^{n} i=\frac{1}{2}n(n+1)=\frac{1}{2}n^2+\frac{1}{2}n \in O(n^2)$. The running time does not depend on the actual input, only on the size, so this running time is also the best-case running time.

Insertion Sort

The *insertion sort* algorithm is superficially similar to selection sort. It is an in-place sorting algorithm where we keep the first part of the input array sorted. We iterate from the beginning of the input to the end, and in each iteration we move one element from the unsorted part to the sorted part. We can implement it as follows:

```
for i in range(1,len(x)):
    j = i
    while j > 0 and x[j-1] > x[j]:
        x[j-1], x[j] = x[j], x[j-1]
        j -= 1
```

Just as for selection sort, in iteration i, we have the loop invariant

$$I: \forall j \in [1,i): x[j-1] \leq x[j]$$

As we also observed for selection sort, this invariant guarantees us that when we reach $i = n$ and the algorithm terminates, all the elements in x are sorted. Unlike selection sort, however, we do not guarantee that the elements to the left of index i are smaller than or equal to the elements to the right of index i—the I_2 invariant for selection sort. And we do not search for the smallest element in the unsorted part of x in each iteration, but instead, we move $x[i]$ to the left until we find its proper location in the range $[0, i + 1)$.

When we consider $x[i]$ in iteration i, the elements to the left of i are sorted. This means that we can split this first part of x into three contiguous regions (all three can potentially be empty). The first region of x contains elements with keys less than $x[i]$, the second region contains elements with keys equal to $x[i]$, and the third region contains elements with keys larger than $x[i]$; see Figure 5-2. The inner loop in the insertion sort algorithm moves $x[i]$ to the left until it reaches the first index with a key that is equal to or less than $x[i]$. This move is made through swapping, so a side effect of moving $x[i]$ to the left is that all the elements in the sorted part of x that are larger than $x[i]$ will be moved one position to the right.

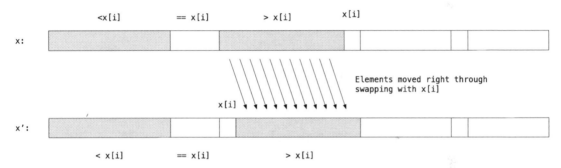

Figure 5-2. *Moving the ith element to its correct location by swapping it toward the left in insertion sort*

To see that the invariant I_1 is satisfied after each such move (if it was satisfied before the inner loop), consider the three blocks in Figure 5-2. The invariant guarantees us that the two gray segments of x are sorted, so when we extend the region where all keys are the same as $x[i]$'s by one, we still have a sorted list.

To see that the algorithm terminates, we first observe that the outer loop is a for loop through $n - 1$ elements, so this is guaranteed to terminate if the inner loop does. For the inner loop, we condition that $j > 0$, and we decrease j by one each iteration, so we can use j as a termination function. The inner loop might not actually reach $j = 0$ because we also condition on $x[j-1] > x[j]$, but using the termination function, we are guaranteed that the inner loop terminates.

For the running time, we can do an analysis similar to selection sort. We iterate $n - 1$ times in the outer loop, and the inner loop is bounded by i in iteration i, so we have the worst-case upper bound $1+2+3+\ldots+(n-2)+(n-1)=\frac{1}{2}(n-1)n \in O(n^2)$. In the best case, however, we only ever test the inner loop condition once, so the best-case time usage is only $O(n)$, unlike selection sort where the best case is also $O(n^2)$.

Exercise: Describe what the input list should look like to achieve best-case and worst-case time performance, respectively.

Now, since selection sort and insertion sort both have the same worst-case running time, but insertion sort has a better best-case running time—and would be expected to perform better every time we have runs of consecutive, nondecreasing elements in the input—we could argue that insertion sort is always the better choice. If the elements are as simple as single computer words, so swapping items costs no more than decreasing a counter, this would be true. The items in the input list *could*, however, be more complex, and swapping could, therefore, be a more expensive operation. If that is the case, we should also take into consideration the cost that swapping incurs; instead of merely counting operations, we should distinguish between comparison operations and swap operations.

Selection sort, as we have implemented it, swaps $O(n)$ elements on all input. We could avoid this by not moving the smallest item in the unsorted sequence to a temporary variable and only swapping $x[i]$ and $x[j]$ when $x[j] < x[j]$:

```
if x[i] > min_val:
    x[i], x[min_idx] = min_val, x[i]
```

In that case, selection sort will have a best-case swap count of zero, which happens when the input list is already sorted. So selection sort has a swap complexity of worst-case $O(n)$ and best-case $O(1)$.

The worst-case swap count for insertion sort is obviously $O(n^2)$. If we consider how elements are swapped more carefully, we will see that an element is first swapped down, when we insert it in the sorted part, and after that, it can only be swapped up again. It cannot move down after the first insertion. So each element can move down, at most n positions, and then up, again at most n positions, with a total of $O(n)$, or a total of $O(n^2)$ swaps for the entire algorithm. If the input list is already sorted, we swap zero elements. So insertion sort has a swap complexity of worst-case $O(n^2)$ and best-case $O(1)$.

The best-case scenario is better for insertion sort than selection sort since both algorithms would perform zero swaps, but selection sort will do $O(n^2)$ comparisons, while insertion sort will do only $O(n)$. The worst-case performance is better for selection sort. Selection sort will make $O(n^2)$ comparisons and $O(n)$ swaps, worst case, while insertion sort will do $O(n^2)$ comparisons and $O(n^2)$ swaps.

Algorithm	Comparisons worst case	Comparisons best case	Swaps worst case	Swaps best case
Selection	$O(n^2)$	$O(n^2)$	$O(n)$	$O(1)$
Insertion	$O(n^2)$	$O(n)$	$O(n^2)$	$O(1)$

Of course, if we need the sort to be stable, selection sort we have seen here cannot be used.

Bubble Sort

The *bubble sort* algorithm is a stable in-place algorithm that runs in the same complexity as insertion sort—worst-case $O(n^2)$ and best-case $O(n)$—and will always do the same number of swaps for any given input as insertion sort does. It usually requires more comparisons, though, so you should never prefer bubble sort over insertion sort. I present the algorithm here only because it is a classical algorithm and because it solves the sorting problem differently than the other two.[5] If the choice is between insertion sort and bubble sort, insertion sort is always better. This doesn't mean that we cannot learn something from considering the algorithm, to hone our computational thinking skills; figuring out *why* bubble sort is a worse choice than insertion sort will also teach us something.

Now, bubble sort is unlike the previous two algorithms in that it does not keep the first part of the input list sorted. Instead, it runs through the list repeatedly, swapping pairs that are in the wrong order, like this:

```
while True:
    swapped = False
    for i in range(1,len(x)):
        if x[i-1] > x[i]:
            x[i-1], x[i] = x[i], x[i-1]
            swapped = True
```

---

[5] "Seeing the wrong solution to a problem (and understanding why it is wrong) is often as informative as seeing the correct solution." —W. Richard Stevens

```
if not swapped:
    break
```

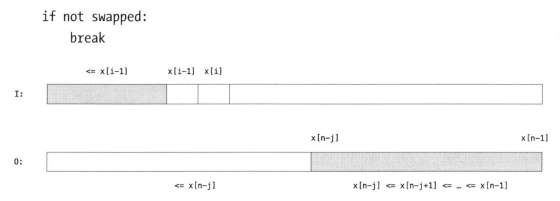

Figure 5-3. *Invariants for the inner and outer loops of bubble sort*

When no pairs are swapped, it is because the inner loop managed to get through the entire list without finding any out-of-order keys, so the list must be sorted. We keep track of when this happens using the variable swapped.

To prove that this algorithm is correct and terminates, we are going to add an imaginary variable, j. It doesn't appear in the algorithm, but we imagine that it starts at zero and gets incremented every time we finish the outer loop, so it counts how many times we have executed this loop. We need this variable for the termination function and the loop invariant. If you want to make it explicit, you can actually replace the outer loop with a for loop where j goes from zero to n, but we need to prove that the outer loop is not executed more than n times for us to be able to do this, so we stick with the while loop.

So we have indices i and j—with j imaginary—and we define the following invariants for the inner and outer loops, respectively (see Figure 5-3):

$$I : \forall k \in [0, i-1) : x[k] \leq x[i-1]$$
$$O_1 : \forall k \in [n-j, n-1) : x[k] \leq x[k+1]$$
$$O_2 : \forall k \in [0, n-j), x[k] \leq x[n-j]$$

Strictly speaking, predicate O_2 is only well defined when $j > 0$, but we are going to consider it true for all j—we could introduce another imaginary variable, $x[n] = \infty$, to make it factually true, but we might as well have the special case be $j = 0$. The invariants say the following in English: when we run the inner loop, then $x[i-1]$ is larger than all elements to the left of it in the list, and when we run the outer loop, then the last $n - j$ elements are sorted, and they are the largest in the list.

Invariant I is the easiest to prove. It is vacuously true when $i = 0$, and whenever we increase i we have first moved the smaller of $x[i-1]$ and $x[i]$ to $x[i-1]$ so the new $i-1$ satisfies the invariant. O_1 and O_2 are also vacuously true when $j = 0$ (or defined to be by setting the imaginary value $x[n]$ to infinity). Now, assume that the outer loop invariants are true when we begin iteration j. We need to show that it is true for $j + 1$ after we have executed the loop body. Consider now the inner loop. If the last j elements are already larger than those before them and already sorted, then the inner loop will not modify them. The interesting step in the inner loop happens when it reaches $n - j - 1$ and executes the inner body for this iteration, that is, when we update i to $n - j$. When it does, invariant I tells us that all $x[k]$ for $k \in [0, n-j)$ we have $x[k] \leq x[n-j-1]$. Combined with O_2, this tells us that the last $j + 1$ elements are now larger than the first $n - j - 1$ elements, giving us that O_2 is true at this point. Invariant O_1 combined with invariant I gives us that the range $[n-j, n)$ is sorted and $x[n-j-1]$ is less than or equal to all elements in the range $[n-j, n)$, so this means that the elements in the range $[n-j-1, n)$ are sorted, telling us that O_1 is also satisfied. Since the invariants are satisfied at the end of their respective loops, we have that the algorithm correctly sorts the input.

For termination, we observe that the invariants give us that the last j elements in x are sorted after iteration j, so when $j = n$, all the elements are sorted. A natural termination function would then be $n - j$. The pattern for how we think about termination functions isn't entirely satisfied, however. We used to require that the loop condition should be false when the termination function hits zero (or goes below zero), but True will never be false. We can rewrite the outer loop to

```
swapped = False
while not swapped:
    # the usual loop body
```

and observe that swapped is False when no elements are swapped, which happens when the inner loop finds no elements out of order—which it does when $j = n$.

Exercise: Since O_1 and O_2 tell us that the last j elements are already the largest numbers and are already sorted, we do not need to have the inner loop iterate through these last j elements. How would you exploit this to improve the running time of bubble sort? The worst-case behavior will not improve, but you can change the running time to about half of the one we have in the preceding. Show that this is the case.

If we consider the swaps executed by bubble sort more carefully, we will see, as for insertion sort, that the elements in the input sequence were either moved up or down to their correct position in the sorted list, but they never moved both up and down. So the swaps are only those necessary to move elements to their correct positions. Consequently, bubble sort must have the same swap complexity as insertion sort: the best-case number of swaps is zero, and the worst case is $O(n^2)$. For swapping, we also get the same complexity as insertion sort. The best-case number of comparisons happens when the elements are already sorted, in which case we never set swapped to True, and we perform $O(n)$ comparisons. In the worst case, when we have to execute the inner loop n times, we perform $O(n^2)$ comparisons.

Algorithm	Comparisons worst case	Comparisons best case	Swaps worst case	Swaps best case
Selection	$O(n^2)$	$O(n^2)$	$O(n)$	$O(1)$
Insertion	$O(n^2)$	$O(n)$	$O(n^2)$	$O(1)$
Bubble	$O(n^2)$	$O(n)$	$O(n^2)$	$O(1)$

The asymptotic complexity of insertion sort and bubble sort is the same. There is a difference in the actual number of comparisons hidden under the big-Oh, however.

For both algorithms, the number of comparisons is equal to the number of iterations we execute in the inner loop. In insertion sort, the inner loop iterates over the range $j \in (0, i]$ for each outer loop iteration $i = 1, ..., n$; bubble sort iterates over the entire range $i = 1, ..., n$ each time the outer loop is executed. Because insertion sort iterates over an interval that shrinks by one for every outer loop iteration, it performs $\frac{1}{2}(n-1)n$ comparisons. Bubble sort always iterates over the full range for each of the n outer loop iterations, so it performs n^2 comparisons—twice as many as insertion sort.

When bubble sort's inner loop encounters a key k, it moves that key to the right until it encounters a larger key. The largest key in the entire sequence is moved to the largest index in the very first iteration. The second time the inner loop is run, the second largest element is moved to the second largest index, and so on. In general, large values will move quickly to the right in the list; they "bubble up," which is where bubble sort gets its name.

Smaller values, however, are only moved one step to the left in each iteration of the inner loop. There is a variant of bubble sort that tries to move both large values quickly to the right but also small values quickly to the left. It essentially consists of two bubble sorts, one that bubbles left to right and one that bubbles right to left. It alternates between these two inner loops, and because it moves left and right in this motion, it is sometimes called the cocktail shaker algorithm, or simply cocktail sort. We can implement it like this:

```
while True:
    swapped = False
    for i in range(1, len(x)):
        if x[i-1] > x[i]:
            x[i-1], x[i] = x[i], x[i-1]
            swapped = True

    if not swapped:
        break

    for i in range(len(x)-1, 0, -1):
        if x[i-1] > x[i]:
            x[i-1], x[i] = x[i], x[i-1]
            swapped = True

    if not swapped:
        break
```

The analysis of this variant of bubble sort is not different from the one we did for bubble sort. Although the algorithm can run a bit faster than bubble sort in practice, the worst-case complexity is the same as bubble sort. It performs exactly as many swaps—because, again, elements are moved up or down using swaps until they find their final position—but it will usually make fewer comparisons when the list is close to sorted because it is faster in getting the elements to their right position.

Exercise: With cocktail sort, after running the outer loop j times, both the first j and the last j elements are in their final positions. Show that this is the case.

Exercise: Knowing that both the first and last j elements are already in their right position can be used to iterate over fewer elements in the inner loops. Modify the algorithm to exploit this. The worst-case complexity will still be $O(n^2)$, but you will make fewer comparisons. How much do you reduce the number of comparisons by?

In Figures 5-4 and 5-5, I have plotted the performance of selection sort, insertion sort, and the two variants of bubble sort, counting the number of comparisons and the number of swaps, respectively. I have generated data in four forms:

- Data that is already sorted—where insertion sort and the two bubble sorts run in $O(n)$, but selection sort runs in $O(n^2)$.

- Data where the elements are sorted in reverse order. Here, insertion sort and the two bubble sorts meet their worst-case setup, and we see that the bubble sorts use twice as many comparisons as insertion sort.

- Data where the elements are almost sorted. Here, I have generated a sorted list of the numbers 1 to n and swapped 20% of the elements to random positions. Here we get the performance where insertion sort and the two bubble sorts run in $O(n^2)$ but with fewer comparisons since the sorted elements are already in place and the inner loop in insertion sort iterates over fewer elements and the inner loop in bubble sort and cocktail sort is run fewer times. Cocktail sort performs fewer comparisons than bubble sort for the reasons we have already discussed.

- Finally, I have generated data that is random permutations of the elements from 1 to n. Here, the performance is close to the worst case for all algorithms in numbers of comparisons, but we do need fewer swaps in insertion sort and the bubble sorts than when the elements are sorted in reverse order. This is also to be expected since the reverse sorted case needs to swap elements the maximum possible number of times.

Exercise: Insertion sort runs in $O(n^2)$ when the input is sorted in the reverse order, but can process sorted sequences in $O(n)$. If we can recognize that the input is ordered in reverse, we could first reverse the sequence and then run insertion sort. Show that we can reverse a sequence, in place, in $O(n)$. Try to adapt insertion sort, so you first recognize consecutive runs of nonincreasing elements and then reverse these before you run insertion sort on the result. Show that the worst-case running time is still $O(n^2)$, but try to compare the modified algorithm with the traditional insertion sort to see if it works better in practice.

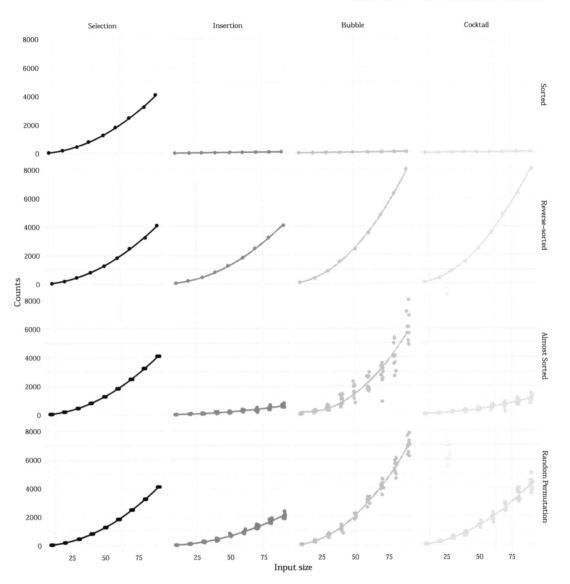

Figure 5-4. *Number of comparisons executed by the different quadratic-time sorting algorithms. Despite appearance, the insertion, bubble, and cocktail sorting algorithms do not run in constant time on sorted data. The lines are linear, but compared to quadratic growth, the linear number of comparisons is tiny. On sorted data, they all use exactly n − 1 comparisons*

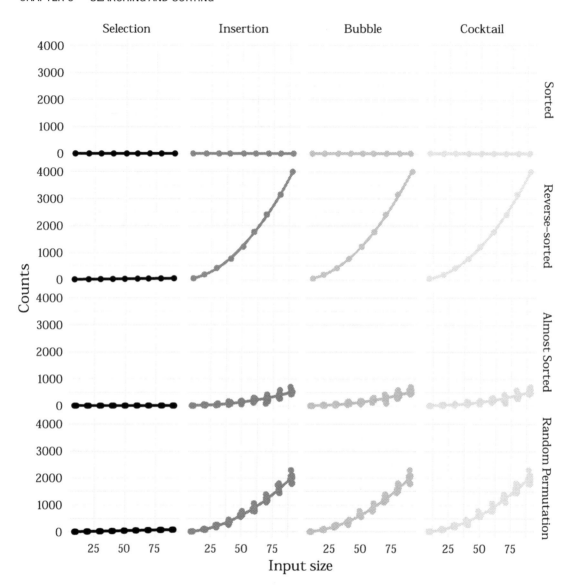

Figure 5-5. *Number of swaps executed by the different quadratic-time sorting algorithms*

Index-Based Sorting Algorithms

For much data that we can assign a total order to, all we can really do with it is determining if one object is smaller than, equal to, or greater than another. Sometimes, however, the data is in a form that we can exploit to build faster sorting algorithms. If our keys are small positive integers, we can use them as indices into lists. Let's call sorting algorithms that use this idea *index based*. (These algorithms are also known as *distribution sorting* algorithms, but I find it easier to remember "index based" than *distribution* since a critical property of these algorithms is to index into a list).

We can then exploit that we can create a list of length m in $O(m)$ and for a list x we can get index k, x[k], in constant time. We will also exploit that we can append elements to a list y, y.append(k), in constant time.[6] In this section, we will look at two algorithms that exploit this: *bucket sort* and its big brother *radix sort*.

Bucket sort assumes that we sort positive integer keys with a max value of m and runs in worst- and best-case $O(n + m)$. Radix sort relaxes the requirement that the keys should be less than m in magnitude but instead assumes that we can split keys into k subkeys that are bounded by m. It then uses bucket sort on these keys k times, achieving the best- and worst-case running time of $O(k(m + n))$.

The memory usage depends on whether we are only sorting keys—that is, the values we sort are identical to their keys—or whether our data items carry more information than their keys. This matters because we need to remember actual data values in the latter case but only a counter in the former. If we are merely sorting keys, then the memory usage for bucket sort is $O(m)$. If data items are more than their keys, bucket sort needs $O(n + m)$ memory. It is for this case that it is essential that we can add to a list in constant time; we use this to keep track of data items efficiently. Radix sort just runs bucket sort k times, without needing extra memory between runs, so its memory complexity is the same as bucket sort. Neither of these two algorithms is in place.

Bucket Sort

We first consider the case where our keys are positive integers bounded by some number m. The smaller, the better, but the important part is that they are bounded by a known value m. We can create a list of length m in time $O(m)$, and what we will do is,

---

[6]Strictly speaking, we are not guaranteed that appending to a list is always in constant time, but there is a guarantee that if we append to a list n times, then all n operations can be done in $O(n)$. So although some operations are not in $O(1)$, on average, they are. Using a different data structure, a so-called *doubly linked list* (see Chapter 13), we *can* achieve worst-case constant time for all append and prepend operations—at the cost of linear time to look up elements. If we use these, then we need a list x with constant-time lookup, as we have for Python list objects, and other lists, y, where prepend or append is in constant time, but where we do not need to access random indices. We consider linked lists later in the book; for the sorting algorithms we consider now, we can still use Python's list objects without affecting the worst-case running time.

for each key *k*, we put the element with that key at position *k* in this list. We call the list the *buckets*, and we just put our elements in different buckets based on their key. The algorithm is called *bucket sort*.

The simplest version of bucket is only sorting keys. We assume that our elements are equal to their keys, that is, we are sorting positive integers bounded by *m*. The algorithm then looks like this:

```
buckets = [0] * m
for key in x:
    buckets[key] += 1
result = []
for key in range(m):
    for i in range(buckets[key]):
        result.append(key)
```

Our input is the list x of length *n* and the bound on our keys, m. With this implementation, the bound *m* has to be strict. We create *m* buckets, but they are indexed with values from zero to *m* – 1. If the largest number in your keys is *m*, you need to allocate *m* + 1 buckets.

We first create a list of buckets of length *m* and set all buckets to zero—this takes time $O(m)$. Then we iterate over all the keys in x and increment the count in bucket[key]. After that, we simply collect the keys again in sorted order. We iterate through the buckets, and for each key, we output that key as many times as the bucket's counter— this is how many times that key was found in the input. We create a new list for the result and append to this list. Although we have two nested loops for collecting the results, the inner loop is only executed *n* times. The outer loop is executed *m* times and the inner loop, in total, *n* times. Since we can append to results in constant time, the running time for the entire algorithm is $O(n + m)$. The algorithm is not in place, and we use $O(n + m)$ extra memory, for the buckets list and the results list. If you want to avoid spending $O(n)$ memory on the results list, you can modify the input list instead:

```
buckets = [0] * m
for key in x:
    buckets[key] += 1
i = 0
```

```
for key in range(m):
    for j in range(buckets[key]):
        x[i] = key
        i += 1
```

This doesn't change the running time of the algorithm but reduces the memory usage to $O(m)$.

If $m \in O(n)$, this means we have a linear-time sorting algorithm. Since we cannot sort any list of n elements without at least looking at each key, this is an optimal algorithm—you cannot possibly sort n elements in time $o(n)$, and we sort them in $\Theta(n)$. This doesn't contradict that sorting n elements using comparisons takes time $\Omega(n \log n)$ because we do not rely on comparisons. The algorithm only works when our keys are positive integers bounded by $m \in O(n)$. Comparison sorting is more general than that and therefore a harder problem to solve.

Exercise: Argue why the inner loop in

```
result_keys, result_values = [], []
for key in range(m):
    for val in buckets[key]:
        result_keys.append(key)
        result_values.append(val)
```

only executes n times.

Exercise: Argue why bucket sort actually sorts the input.

This variant of bucket sort is also known as counting sort because we simply count how many times we see each key. This doesn't quite cut it if we need to sort elements where the keys are not the full information associated with them. If, for example, we have a list of values and another of keys and we need to sort the values according to the keys, then we need to remember which values are put in each bucket, not just how many there are in each bucket. We can do this by putting a list in each bucket and appending the values to their respective buckets:

```
buckets = [[] for bucket in range(m)]
for i in range(n):
    key = keys[i]
    val = values[i]
    buckets[key].append(val)
```

```
result_keys, result_values = [], []
for key in range(m):
    for val in buckets[key]:
        result_keys.append(key)
        result_values.append(val)
```

You cannot use

```
buckets = [] * m
```

It would just result in m concatenations of the empty list, which is still the empty list. Instead, we use the list comprehension expression

```
buckets = [[] for bucket in range(m)]
```

to create a new empty list for each bucket.

Other than that, the general bucket sort is not much different from counting sort. We append the values to the buckets instead of counting keys, and we collect the values from the buckets after that.

Because we need to store n elements in the buckets, the memory usage is now $O(n + m)$ rather than $O(m)$. We could still reuse the input lists when we collect the sorted elements, but it would not reduce the asymptotic memory usage.

Because we append values to the buckets and read them out later, in the order they were added, bucket sort is a stable algorithm. It wouldn't be if we prepended elements to the lists, but you shouldn't do this anyway with Python `list` objects. We can append to `list` objects in $O(1)$, but prepending takes time $O(l)$ if the list has length l.

Explicitly representing buckets as lists, the way we have done so far, makes it easy to see how bucket sort works, but people often take a different approach. We can compute how large each bucket should be in the same way as we did counting sort:

```
for key in keys:
    buckets[key] += 1
```

Then, we can translate this into the offset into the output that each bucket starts at—it is the accumulated sum of that:

```
k = 0
for i in range(1, m):
    buckets[i], k = k + buckets[i - 1], buckets[i]
```

Then, in a scan through the input, we can put the elements at the current head of its bucket in the output:

```
output = [None] * len(keys)
for i in range(len(keys)):
    output[buckets[keys[i]]] = values[i]
    buckets[keys[i]] += 1
```

It might be less obvious that we have buckets that we put our elements in when we use this version, but the approach has the benefit that it only uses simple lists on top of the input. In some programming languages, you don't have something like Python's `list` class, but you will always have data you can access by index.

If you read or write code in such a language, this is the version of bucket sort you will most likely meet. In Python, the first versions we write are fine and easier to follow.

Radix Sort

Bucket sort can sort n elements with keys bounded by m in time $O(n + m)$, which is excellent if m is small. As long as $m \in O(n)$, it is an optimal sorting algorithm. If m is much larger than n, however, handling m buckets slows down the algorithm. If, for example, all we knew about the keys were that they were 32-bit positive integers, we would need 2^{32} buckets, which is more than four billion buckets. Sorting 32-bit integer keys using bucket sort is clearly not a viable approach.

If, however, our keys can be broken down into d subkeys, each bounded by a reasonable m, we have an algorithm that will sort these in $O(d \cdot (n + m))$, by sorting for each subkey in turn, running d applications of bucket sort. For 32-bit integers, for example, we can split the keys into 4 bytes. Each byte can hold 2^8 different values, so $m = 256$ is an upper bound for these. You can, therefore, split a 32-bit integer into a tuple of four subkeys, each bounded by 256. You need some bit operations to do it, and it looks like this:

```
subkeys = (k          & 0xff
          ,(k >> 8)   & 0xff
          ,(k >> 16)  & 0xff
          ,(k >> 24)  & 0xff)
```

You do not need to know how this works to use the trick, but if you are interested, I explain in the last section of this chapter.

This algorithm for sorting *d* subkeys bounded by *m* is called *radix sort*, and that it runs *d* iterations of bucket sort tells you exactly how it works:

```
for j in range(d):
    key_buckets = [[] for bucket in range(m)]
    value_buckets = [[] for bucket in range(m)]
    for i in range(n):
        key = keys[i]
        subkey = key[j]
        val = values[i]
        key_buckets[subkey].append(key)
        value_buckets[subkey].append(val)

key_result, value_result = [], []
    for subkey in range(m):
        for key in key_buckets[subkey]:
            key_result.append(key)
        for val in value_buckets[subkey]:
            value_result.append(val)

keys = key_result
values = value_result
```

Here, *j* ranges over the *d* subkeys. In each bucket sort, we use *m* buckets. We need to keep track of both keys and values here because the subkeys do not contain the full information about the keys. We collect the results of the bucket sorts in two lists, key_result and value_result, and at the end of each outer loop, we update the keys and values lists to their sorted versions, so these are ready for the next iteration.

Radix sort only works because bucket sort is stable, and the order in which we sort the subkeys is critical. To see this, let us consider a simple case where we have two subkeys and we want to sort

```
keys = [(1,0), (2,1), (1,1), (0,1), (1,1)]
```

If we want to sort this into the usual tuple order, also called lexical order, we need first to sort the tuples by the first component and then by the second. So the list we want to end up with is this:

```
[(0, 1), (1, 0), (1, 1), (1, 1), (2, 1)]
```

If you set d to two and run radix sort, you will get the list sorted first by the second component and then by the first. We will get

`[(1, 0), (0, 1), (1, 1), (1, 1), (2, 1)]`

To see why, consider what happens in the two iterations of radix sort. In the first iteration, we do sort by the first tuple component. So we sort the list into this:

`[(0, 1), (1, 0), (1, 1), (1, 1), (2, 1)]`

If we only consider the first component, this list is sorted. Of course, we do not only consider the first component, so we execute a second bucket sort, this time on the second component, to get the result

`[(1, 0), (0, 1), (1, 1), (1, 1), (2, 1)]`

Since bucket sort is stable, we keep the order from the first sort within the buckets of the second sort. We keep the order of the tuples

`[(0, 1), (1, 1), (1, 1), (2, 1)]`

that all have the same value for the second subkey. Because the sort is stable and preserves the ordering for the first key, when we sort on the second key, we get a list that is sorted by both keys—in the opposite order from how we apply bucket sort, though. The second key we sort on becomes the major key and the first the minor key.

To sort the tuples in lexicographical order, we want to first sort by the second index in the tuples, to get all the tuples in the right order by that key. Then we apply the sort to the first index, which orders and groups the values for the first index by preserving the (sorted) order of the second key. We must sort with subkeys $k = d - 1, d - 2, ..., 1, 0$:

```
for j in range(d-1,-1,-1):
    # loop body same as before
```

Radix sort is a powerful algorithm for sorting positive integers that can fit into a constant number of computer words since these can generally be split into d bytes. For 32-bit integers, as we saw, we can split them into 4 bytes. For 64-bit words we need 8 bytes, and for 128-bit words we need 16 bytes, but in all cases, we can sort the integers in linear time because m is bounded by the constant 256.[7]

If we have both positive and negative integers, we cannot use radix sort out of the box. If we index into a list with a negative number, we just index from the back of the list, which is not what we want. If you actually break a negative number into 8-bit bytes and consider these as positive integers, you will get the wrong answer as well. This is a consequence of how negative integers are represented as bits in computer words. You do not necessarily need to know how negative integers are represented on your computer (but you are interested I will tell you at the end of the chapter). (Strictly speaking, how negative integers are represented is hardware dependent. The hardware can represent numbers in any way it wants. I know of no modern architecture that does not represent positive and negative integers as two's-complement numbers; see the last section in this chapter. The most significant byte might not be where you think it is, though, since the order of significance for bytes in a word does vary between architectures). Suffice to say that if you sort positive and negative numbers as bit patterns, you will not get the numbers sorted as integers.

There is a simple trick that usually works for sorting both positive and negative numbers, but emphasis on *usually*. If a is the smallest number in your input and it is negative, then add $-a$ to all the numbers. Now they are positive but in the same order as before. You can sort these and then subtract $-a$ again to get the original numbers back. This *only* works, however, if you can add $-a$ to all numbers without overflowing the size of the positive numbers. If you want to sort 32-bit integers, you might go beyond 32 bits if you add to the largest numbers in your input. If that is the case, you need to know about the representation of numbers to sort them correctly.

If you sort variable-length keys, for example, strings, you do not necessarily have a constant bound on how many subkeys you need. If $d \in O(n)$, you are back to having an $O(n^2)$ algorithm, and you can do better with an $O(n \log n)$ comparison sort.

---

[7]At this point, you are excused for getting the impression that we can always sort numbers in linear time using radix sort. It sounds like that is what I just wrote. This isn't true, however. I did write that we needed the numbers to fit into a constant number of computer words. This put a bound on how large the integers can be. If you want to be able to hold at least n distinct elements in your input, you need $O(\log n)$ bits. The time usage depends on the size of the integers, so they cannot grow arbitrarily larger. If you want to sort n distinct numbers, you need a logarithmic number of subkeys, and then you have the same runtime complexity as the fastest comparison sorting algorithms.

Exercise: In my implementation, I used a list to save the elements in each bucket. We saw in the previous section that this isn't necessary—we can compute the size of each bucket first and then scan through the input and put each element at the current front of each bucket in the output. Prove that this also works with the repeated bucket sorts we use in radix sort. Implement this version.

Generalizing Searching and Sorting

Before we leave sorting, there is one additional issue I want to mention. We have assumed that, for each item in the list we want to sort, we have an associated key (or keys) we use to define the ordering of the objects. We haven't discussed how we extract keys from the items we wish to sort or how we use them to compare objects.

If you only ever have to sort numbers, this isn't a concern. If you need to sort other types of objects and tailor your algorithm to the exact type of the objects, then you do not need to worry about it either. If, however, you want to implement a search or sort algorithm that works for different types of objects, it is a concern. You need to provide the user of your algorithm some handle by which to specify the order of objects. Since you are most likely to be the user at some point, you should make that handle easy to work with and yet flexible enough to handle all cases you will need.

The default approach Python has taken for its `sort` and `sorted` functions is this: For objects of simple types, like numbers and strings, Python already knows how to sort. Python can also sort composite types such as lists and tuples if they hold objects that Python can already sort. If you have more complicated objects or if you need to sort them according to some specialized ordering, then you need to provide a key function.

We haven't seen how to define our own functions yet (we will in Chapter 6), but we have used plenty, so you should be able to understand how this works with an example.

Consider a list of fruits:

```
fruit = [
    "apple",
    "orange",
    "banana",
    "kiwi"
]
```

If we sort these, we get their alphabetic (lexicographic) ordering:

```
>>> fruit = ["apple", "orange", "banana", "kiwi"]
>>> sorted(fruit)
['apple', 'banana', 'kiwi', 'orange']
```

If, for some reason, we want to sort the fruits by word length, we can do this:

```
>>> sorted(fruit, key = len)
['kiwi', 'apple', 'orange', 'banana']
```

The len function, which we have used several times already, gives us the length of a sequence—in this case, the length of a sequence of letters, so the length of a word. When we give this function to sorted, it becomes the key it sorts by. So when it looks at an object, it doesn't see the object itself, but rather the result of calling len on the object, so it sees word lengths rather than the actual strings.

An alternative approach is to specify a function for comparing two objects. A common approach is to require a function of two arguments, a and b, that determines if $a < b$ (or $a > b$; it doesn't matter which). Since we only aim for putting the objects in order, so no $x[i] > x[i + 1]$, we do not need any other information. If we want to search for an element, we also need to know how to test for equality, of course. To handle both, a common approach is to require that the function returns a negative number for $a < b$, zero for $a = b$, and a positive number for $a > b$.

In Python 2, it was a simple matter of providing an argument to the built-in sort and sorted functions to use a comparison function, but now, with Python 3, you need to do a little bit more. You still need to write a comparison function, but then you must use the cmp_to_key from the functools module to translate it into a different form that you can use as the key argument to sort.

Consider this, a bit longer, example:

```
x = "mississippi\x00"
n = len(x)
s = list(range(n))

def cmp(i,j):
    m = n - max(i, j)
    for k in range(m):
        if x[i + k] < x[j + k]: return -1
        if x[i + k] > x[j + k]: return +1
```

```
from functools import cmp_to_key
cmp = cmp_to_key(cmp)
s.sort(key = cmp)

for i in s:
    print(i, x[i:])
```

You haven't seen the function definition syntax—you will in the next chapter—so the cmp() code looks a little odd. You should be able to read the code indented under the def line, though, and see that we run through a for loop and compare characters in the string x. The return line, with –1 or +1, is what we use to determine if one key is smaller or greater than the other.

We have a string, x, that holds mississippi. The \x00 at the end is a so-called sentinel, a letter (here the letter with value zero) that doesn't appear elsewhere in the string, and has a value smaller than all the letters in the string. It is there to ensure that no suffix[8] of x is a prefix of another. Without it, the suffix "i" is a prefix of three other suffixes, "ississippi", "issippi", and "ippi". With the sentinel, since it is a unique letter, no suffix is a prefix of another. Since the sentinel letter is smaller than all the others, it means that if we compare two strings, say "i" and "ippi", we are really comparing "i\x00" and "ippi\x00", and these strings differ on the second letter, where "\x00" is smaller than "p". When you look up words in a dictionary, the shorter strings come before the longer strings when they share a prefix. For example, "a" comes before "and." When comparing strings, we want that behavior, but if we have a sentinel, we don't have to worry about one word being a prefix of another. If we compare strings, letter by letter, we are *guaranteed* to eventually find a point at which they differ, and if it is because one string is shorter than another, then the sentinel guarantees that the shorter string is considered smaller than the longer.

That is why I put that weird "\x00" at the end of x. It is a unique smallest character that I can use to guarantee that shorter strings will always sort as smaller than longer strings.

It is also why we don't handle the case where we have two identical strings in the cmp() function. There cannot be two identical suffixes of x when it has a sentinel at the end.

What the code does is sorting all suffixes of x, but in an indirect way. This is something that has applications in many string algorithms, but that is beyond the scope of this book.

---

[8]A suffix of a string is a substring that starts somewhere inside the string and continues to the end of the string. For x, any substring x[i:] is a suffix.

Instead of making a list of all suffixes of x, which would require us to copy a lot of substrings, we represent suffixes by their indices into x. So the suffix that starts at index i, the string x[i:], is represented simply by i, and we put all these suffixes in the list s.

To sort s, according to the suffixes the numbers represent, we need to compare suffixes and not the integers in s. We could extract the suffix strings from x with a key function

```
def suf(i):
    return x[i:]
s.sort(key = suf)
```

but that would copy the entire string x[i:] every time we need to look at it. For most comparisons, we can determine which suffix is smaller after one or two characters, so this is more work than we need. Instead, we use the cmp() function that directly compares the suffixes.

To use the cmp() function, we must transform it using cmp_to_key(), and after that, we can use it to sort.

For providing a handle into a search function, of the two approaches, providing a comparison function or a key function, I think the first is much simpler and more elegant, but your mileage may vary.

We can easily implement sorting algorithms that use a key_fun function. Selection sort will look like this:

```
for i in range(len(x)):
    # find index of smallest elm in x[i:]
    min_idx, min_val, min_key = i, None, x[i]
    for j in range(i, len(x)):
        if key_fun(x[j]) < min_key:
            min_idx, min_val, min_key = j, x[j], key_fun(x[j]) x[i],
    x[min_idx] = min_val, x[i]
```

Insertion sort looks like this:

```
for i in range(1,len(x)):
    j = i
    while j > 0 and key_fun(x[j-1]) > key_fun(x[j]):
        x[j-1], x[j] = x[j], x[j-1]
        j -= 1
```

Bucket sort requires that the key function maps to integers, and we need to find a number they are all smaller than, but other than that, it is simply this:

```
n = len(x)
m = max(key_fun(e) for e in x) + 1
buckets = [[] for bucket in range(m)]

y = []
for e in x:
    buckets[key_fun(e)].append(e)
for b in buckets:
    for e in b:
        y.append(e)
# Result is now in y
```

If we used a comparison function, we would only be able to write generic comparison algorithms. With a key function, we can also handle bucket sort, at least as long as the key function gives us a small integer. There is a bit more to do with radix sort, but you could imagine the key function returning a tuple of subkeys.

How Computers Represent Numbers

For most of what we have seen in this and the earlier chapters, we do not need to know how our computer actually represents numbers. A number is a number, and while we do have to differentiate between numbers that can fit into a computer word and numbers that cannot do so when we consider complexity in the RAM model, we do not worry about their representation beyond that. If we want to sort integers using radix sort, however, we do need to know a bit about how numbers are stored. I gave you a piece of code to extract bytes from a 32-bit integer:[9]

```
subkeys = (k          & 0xff
          ,(k >> 8)   & 0xff
          ,(k >> 16)  & 0xff
          ,(k >> 24)  & 0xff)
```

This extracts four 8-bit bytes from one 32-bit integer and gives us four subkeys. What I didn't tell you was that the order you should apply the bucket sort applications in radix sort to get the 32-bit integers sorted depends on your architecture. I explain why in the next subsection.

Manipulation of computer words with bit operations is very low-level programming and not something you usually worry about in day-to-day problem solving. If you are not interested in knowing the low-level details of how we do this, you can skip this section, but if you end up using radix sort on integers in the future, I recommend that you at least skim the next subsection.

In the last subsection, I explain how computers represent negative numbers. If you sort by adding a number to all your input to make them positive and then subtract it again when you are done, you do not need to know this, and I cannot think of any case where this is relevant for sorting. But if you are interested in knowing, then check out that section.

Layout of Bytes in a Word

For radix sorting integers, you do need to be able to split a computer word into bytes—or in general into $d \log_2 m$–bit subkeys—to get the $O(dm)$ running time. To extract the bytes for a computer word, we need two bit operations: right-shift and bit-AND. A right-shift

---

[9]It is somewhat arbitrary that I chose 32-bit integers here. Python's integers are not restricted to 32 bits and can be arbitrarily large. The underlying hardware, however, will work with fixed-sized integers, typically 32 or 64 bits, and this section is about the underlying hardware and not Python's integer representation.

simply moves the bits in a computer word to the right.[10] If we shift a word by 8 bits, we lose the eight lowest bits, the lowest byte, and we move the second byte down to replace the first (and the third to replace the second and the fourth to replace the third; for integers with more than 32 bits, this just goes on). If we shift by 16, we move the third byte down to the lowest byte, and if we shift by 24 bits, we move the highest byte down to the lowest (Figure 5-6). A bit-AND operation, the operator & in Python, takes as input two bit patterns and produces a bit pattern where each bit position only depends on the same positions in the two input words and each bit is set to one if both the input bits in the input are one, and otherwise it is set to zero. The hexadecimal numeric 0xff has the lowest bits set to one and all others to zero. If we AND a number with this number, we get the bits in the lowest byte only. AND'ing with a number like this is known as *masking*. When we mask one bit pattern with another, we extract parts of the bits and leave the others at zero.

When we do a computation such as

```
subkeys = (k          & 0xff
          ,(k >> 8)   & 0xff
          ,(k >> 16)  & 0xff
          ,(k >> 24)  & 0xff)
```

we create a tuple with four components that correspond to the 4 bytes in a 32-bit word; see Figure 5-6.

---

[10]What happens to the bits at the left end of a shifted word can vary from hardware to hardware and according to which type of shift we use. There are really two different versions of right-shift. One will always fill the bits on the left of the result with zeros. This is called a logical shift. Another shift, called arithmetic shift, will fill the bits with zeros or ones depending on whether the most significant bit is zero or one. It will fill the leftmost bits with the same value as the most significant bit in the input. The right-shift operator in Python, >>, does arithmetic shift. The reason that you might fill with ones if the top bit is one has to do with how negative numbers are represented.

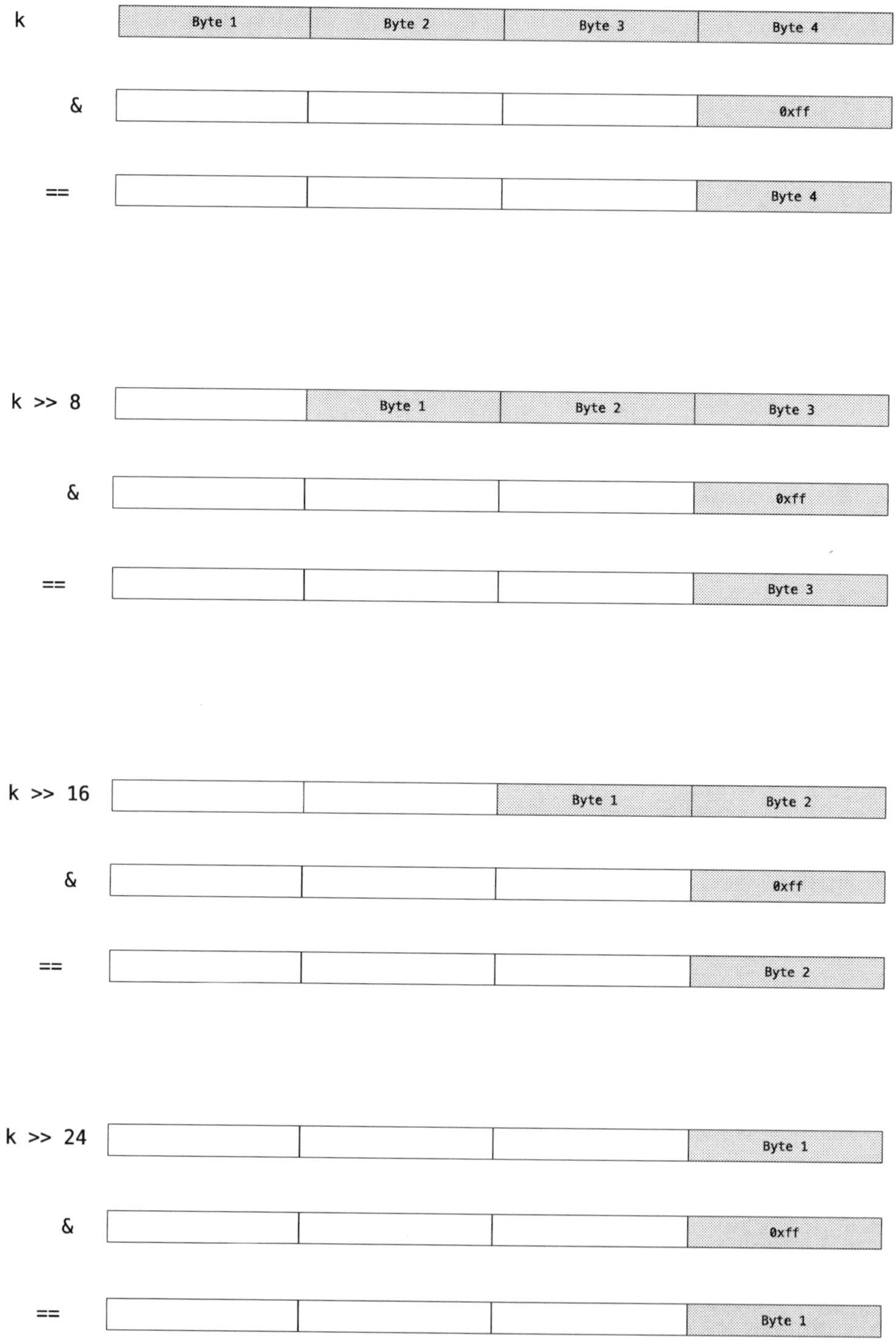

Figure 5-6. *Extracting 4 bytes from a 32-bit integer*

Integers in Python are not as simple as a fixed-sized bit pattern. They are represented such that they can grow to any size (but with a computational overhead that means that operations on them are not constant time as we assume in the RAM model, unless we keep them below a constant size). For this section, I want you to ignore that Python hides the truth from you; it means well, but a consequence is that integers in Python do not work as integers on the hardware. The Python integers cannot overflow, a common source of errors, but you the price you pay for it is a runtime penalty if you are not careful. I want you to imagine that our integers are always 32-bit computer words for the rest of this section. That means that an integer consists of 4 bytes.

Bytes, consisting of 8 bits, can represent numbers from zero to $2^8 - 1 = 255$. You can think of them as numbers in base 256. A 32-bit integer, considered as individual bytes b_1–b_4, would be $b_1 \times 256^0 + b_2 \times 256^1 + b_3 \times 256^2 + b_4 \times 256^3$ where b_1–b_4 are the 4 bytes in the word—just as a decimal number 123 is $3 \times 10^0 + 2 \times 10^1 + 3 \times 10^2$. This is what we exploit when we split a 32-bit integer into 4 bytes that we can then radix sort.

This sounds easy, and it is, and so of course hardware designers went and made it more complicated. Different hardware arranges the bytes in a computer word differently. Depending on your hardware, the number represented as a 32-bit integer can be both $b_1 \times 256^0 + b_2 \times 256^1 + b_3 \times 256^2 + b_4 \times 256^3$ and $b_4 \times 256^0 + b_3 \times 256^1 + b_2 \times 256^2 + b_1 \times 256^3$. Different hardware puts the most significant byte at the left or at the right. The different choices are called *endianness*. The name refers to Jonathan Swift's *Gulliver's Travels* where a civil war is fought over which end of an egg should be cracked when eating a soft-boiled egg. Fighting over which byte should be considered the most significant is equally silly, but you need to consider it when you manipulate bit patterns that represent integers. *Little-endian* computers put the least significant byte as the leftmost byte, and *big-endian* computers put the least significant byte as the rightmost byte. There is no *right* way to represent integers with respect to byte order, but people can get passionate about it.

If we pull out the bytes in an integer and sort using them, we can potentially get the order wrong. If we think that the numbers are little-endian, but they are big-endian, we are sorting the keys in the wrong order. With the bit-shifting in the preceding code, this isn't an issue, however. We are not extracting raw bytes from a computer word, but asking for bits, shifted and masked. The hardware might order the bytes in one order or the other, but it knows which bit is the most significant, the second most significant, and so on, and when we use shift operations, it will get the correct bits for us. The endianness matters if you look at the raw bits in memory, but the hardware that determines the endianness also implements the bit manipulation operations, and the two will match. So the code will give us the 4 bytes in a 32-bit integer, and if these are interpreted as nonnegative numbers, we can radix sort them with 256 buckets.

Two's-Complement Representation of Negative Numbers

The reason that we couldn't simply sort negative integers using radix sort is that bit patterns, interpreted as base-two numbers, do not match how the computer interprets the bit patterns for negative numbers. If you have only positive numbers, then you can sort these bit-wise. The negative numbers, however, will be considered *greater* than the positive numbers and will end up after the positive numbers in the sorted list.

On computers, we distinguish between *signed* and *unsigned* numbers. Unsigned numbers are always positive, and with n bits we can represent 2^n different numbers; zero is one of those numbers, so unsigned numbers can be any of 0, 1, ..., $2^n - 1$. With signed numbers, we can still represent 2^n numbers, but some will be negative, and some will be positive. A simple approach to represent negative numbers is to take one of the n bits and use it as the sign. This representation is known as *sign-and-magnitude* representation. If we do this, we get 2^{n-1} positive and 2^{n-1} negative numbers—we have $n - 1$ bits to represent the numbers when we use one bit for the sign—so we can represent the range $2^{n-1} - 1$, ..., 2^{n-1}. We end up having two zeros, though, one positive and one negative zero.

Another representation of negative numbers is *one's-complement* where a negative number is represented as the bit-wise negation of the corresponding positive number. What this means is that to change the sign of a number a, you negate all its bits, that is, you change all zeros to ones and vice versa. A 4-bit representation of 2 would be 0010, so the 4-bit representation for –2 would be 1101. We still get two different zeros, and we can represent that same range as when we use a sign bit. One's-complement is slightly easier to implement in hardware than sign-and-magnitude, and many older computers used this representation.

The representation that modern computers use is *two's-complement* and is even simpler for hardware to deal with, which is why it has won out as the dominant representation. I am not aware of any modern computers that do not use this representation. Arithmetic that mixes both positive and negative numbers can be done by only doing arithmetic on positive numbers. This means that there is less need for hardware circuits to deal with negative numbers.[11] For us humans, though, two's-complement can be a little harder to understand.

In two's-complement n-bit words, we can represent the integer range 2^{n-1} to $2^{n-1} - 1$. We have one more negative number than we have positive, and we have only one zero. To change a positive number a into $-a$, you first negate its bits (just as for one's-complement), but then you add one. For 4-bit numbers, 1 is 0001; negated, this is 1110. If we add one, we get 1111. This is -1 in two's-complement. To go from -1 to 1, we do the same. We negate the numbers for -1, 1111 to 0000, and add 1, 0001, and get 0001, which is 1. We do the same for 2, 0010. We negate it and get 1101 and then add one, 0001, and we get 1110. This is -2 in two's-complement. Going back, we do 1110 to 0001; add one, 0001; and get 0010, or 2 in decimal. For 3, 0011 in binary, we get $1100 + 0001 = 1101$ for -3.

In two's-complement, zero and all positive numbers have 0 at the most significant bit, and negative numbers have 1 at the most significant bit. This looks like a sign bit but isn't exactly. There is only one zero, the bit pattern with all bits set to zero. If only the most significant bit is set, this is not interpreted as negative zero, but rather the smallest negative number we can represent.

With 4 bits, the largest positive number we can represent is 0111, or 7 in decimal. We cannot represent 8; that would put 1 bit in the fourth position, and such a number we would consider negative. We can represent -8, however; it will be the bit pattern 1000. The positive number 8, if we did represent it in normal binary, would be 1000. The negation of this is 0111, and if we add one to it, we get 1000, which is -8 in two's-complement. We end up with the same bit pattern as the unsigned value for the positive number, but we interpret the bit pattern differently. In two's-complement 4-bit numbers, the bit pattern 1000 is always interpreted as -8 and never as $+8$.

What makes two's-complement particularly smart is that we can do arithmetic with both positive and negative numbers using only rules for positive numbers.

For example, to compute $a - b$, we can add the two's-complement representation of a and $-b$ in binary modulo 2^n, where n is the number of bits we have. Modulo 2^n in binary means using the n least significant bits, so any overflow of bits is ignored:

$$2_{10} - 1_{10} = 0010_2 - 0001_2 = 0010_2 + 1111_2 = 10001_2 = 0001_2 = 1_{10}$$
$$3_{10} - 4_{10} = 0011_2 - 0100_2 = 0011_2 + 1100_2 = 1111_2 = -1_{10}$$
$$5_{10} - 3_{10} = 0101_2 - 0011_2 = 0101_2 + 1101_2 = 10010_2 = 0010_2 = 2_{10}$$

---

[11]It is still necessary for division.

This means that we do not need separate hardware for addition and subtraction; we only need addition, which greatly simplifies the computer.

To see why we can replace subtraction with addition, we need a little algebra. The reason has to do with how we add modulo 2^n. In the ring of modulo 2^n, $-a$ is the same as $2^n - a$, so instead of subtracting a from a number, you can add $2^n - a$ to it. In two's-complement, $-a$ is the same as $2^n - a$ when n-bit words are considered unsigned. For example, in 4-bit words (where we do addition modulo $2^4 = 16$), -2 is 1110_2 (the negation of 2, 0010, is 1101, and you add one to that to get 1110). Unsigned, 1110_2 is 14_{10}, which is $(16 - 2)$ modulo 16. So if we want to compute $10 - 2 = 8$, we can do this as $10 + (16 - 2) = 10 + 14 = 24$, which is 8 modulo 16.

The way we shift bits is affected by the two's-complement representation of integers as well. If we shift a number k bits to the left, $n \ll k$, we always fill the rightmost bits with zeros, and this always amounts to multiplying m by 2^k (modulo 2^n):

$$3_{10} \ll 2 = 0011_2 \ll 2 = 1100_2 = 12_{10} = 3_{10} \times 2^2$$
$$-2_{10} \ll 2 = 1110_2 \ll 2 = 1000_2 = 8_{10} \bmod 16$$
$$-2_{10} \times 2^2 \bmod 16 = -8_{10} \bmod 16 = 8_{10} \bmod 16$$

Whether shifting to the right by k bits amounts to dividing by 2^k depends on whether we do logical or arithmetic shift. With logical shift, we fill the leftmost bits with zeros, and this amounts to dividing by 2^k for positive numbers but not negative numbers:

$$6_{10} \gg 1 = 0110_2 \gg 1 = 0011_2 = 3_{10} = 6_{10} / 2^1$$

but

$$-2_{10} \gg 1 = 1110_2 \gg 1 = 0011_2 = 3_{10} \bmod 16$$

where, of course, $-2/2^1 = -1 = 15 \bmod 16$.

With the arithmetic shift, we fill the leftmost bits with the value the leftmost bit has before we shift. For positive numbers, where the leftmost bit is zero, this doesn't change anything, but for negative numbers, where the leftmost bit is one, it ensures that shifting k bits to the right amounts to dividing by 2^k:

$$-2_{10} \gg 1 = 1110_2 \gg 1 = 1111_2 = 15_{10} \bmod 16 = -1 \bmod 16$$

In Python, shifting to the right is the arithmetic shift.

CHAPTER 6

Functions

So far, we have implemented algorithms where we have a reference to our input before we run our computations and where we print the algorithm's output when we are done. Our algorithm is the code between the input and the output. But what happens if, for example, we need to sort more than one list?

With the approach we have seen so far, we would need to copy the entire code for each time we need to run an algorithm. This will give us many copies of the same code, so what if there is an error in the code? We would need to fix the code each time we have a copy—and remember where each copy is in our program. This is not efficient, and writing large programs this way is infeasible.

Let's see an example. Consider a situation where we have two lists, we want to sort them separately, and then we want to merge the results into a single list with all the elements in sorted order. It sounds like a silly thing to do because we could just concatenate the two lists and sort them as one, but you have to trust me that this is something we need for an efficient sort algorithm we see in the next chapter.

Sorting the two lists looks like this:

```
x = [1, 2, 65, 8]
y = [9, 2, 4]

# Sort x
for i in range(1,len(x)):
    j = i
    while j > 0 and x[j-1] > x[j]:
        x[j-1], x[j] = x[j], x[j-1]
        j -= 1

# Sort y
for i in range(1,len(y)):
    j = i
```

© Thomas Mailund 2021
T. Mailund, *Introduction to Computational Thinking*, https://doi.org/10.1007/978-1-4842-7077-6_6

```
    while j > 0 and y[j-1] > y[j]:
        y[j-1], y[j] = y[j], y[j-1]
        j -= 1

# Merge sequences
result = []
i, j = 0, 0
while True:
    if i == len(x):
        # no more elements in x
        while j < len(y):
            result.append(y[j])
            j += 1
        break
    if j == len(y):
        # no more elements in y
        while i < len(x):
            result.append(x[i])
            i += 1
        break
    if x[i] < y[j]:
        result.append(x[i])
        i += 1
    else:
        result.append(y[j])
        j += 1
```

The merge algorithm doesn't do anything complicated, but it is rather long. It can, therefore, be hard to see, at a glance, what it is doing. It is simple enough, though: We move through x and y, using the indices i and j, pick the smallest of x[i] and y[j], and append that to our result. If we have made it to the end of either x or y, the first two if statements in the loop, we copy the remainder of the other list and then break out of the while True loop (it is the only way we can leave the loop, of course, since True is always true).

The key observation in the code is at the top. We need to sort both x and y, and we have to copy the insertion sort for each of the lists. We also have to, carefully, replace all references to x with references to y in the second copy; and it is easy to forget one of those references, which would mess up the entire algorithm.

We need a mechanism to implement an algorithm once and then reuse the implementation whenever we need to use that algorithm. Since the input and output of each use of the algorithm will vary each time we execute it, we need a mechanism for handling this as well.

One approach to reusing implementations is *functions*. A function is a piece of code that we can invoke from multiple places in a program. We can tell it what its input should be, so we can vary that from call to call of the function. Each time we invoke a function and complete its calculations, our program will continue from the place where we called the function.

I will show you the function versions of insertion sort and merging first and then explain how it works:

```python
def insertion_sort(x):
    for i in range(1,len(x)):
        j = i
        while j > 0 and x[j-1] > x[j]:
            x[j-1], x[j] = x[j], x[j-1]
            j -= 1
    return x

def merge(x, y):
    result = []
    i, j = 0, 0
    while True:
        if i == len(x):
            # no more elements in x
            while j < len(y):
                result.append(y[j])
                j += 1
            return result
    if j == len(y):
        # no more elements in y
        while i < len(x):
            result.append(x[i])
            i += 1
        return result
```

```
    if x[i] < y[j]:
        result.append(x[i])
        i += 1
    else:
        result.append(y[j])
        j += 1
```

To sort and merge the two sequences, you can now do this:

```
x = [1, 2, 65, 8]
y = [9, 2, 4]
z = merge(insertion_sort(x), insertion_sort(y))
```

So what is going on? The first part is where we define the functions. You do this using the keyword def, followed by the name you choose to give the function, and then in parentheses, you name the *parameters* of the function—you can use as many as you want and call them whatever you want as long as they are valid names for variables. After the parameters, you need to put a colon (:). The first function we defined we named insertion_sort(), and it takes one parameter that we called x. The second function, merge(), takes two parameters, and we called those x and y.

After the def line of the function definition, you put the code that the function should execute. We sometimes refer to this code as the *body* of the function. You need to indent this code, the same way as you indent the body of a for loop or an if statement.

When you define a function, you are really doing three separate things. You specify the parameters the function takes and the code it should run, but you also give it a name—the name you put after def and before the parentheses.

Giving a function a name is the same as assigning a value to a variable. There is no difference between a function name and any other variables, except for how you define the function. You can use values without assigning them to variables, but you must give a function a name, so you always assign a function to a variable.[1]

---

[1] Strictly speaking, it *is* possible in Python to create a function without a name, but only for very limited types of functions, and you don't have to worry about that—we won't use it in this book, and you rarely have to worry about it at all, since modern Python has better ways of solving problems where you would use this feature. It is a leftover from when Python didn't have list comprehension, and such anonymous functions were more useful then.

Consider this code:

```
def f(x):
    return x
g = f
f = 5
```

We define a function that takes one parameter and returns it unchanged, and we give it the name f. We then assign the value that f references to the variable g, so now both f and g refer to the same function object. In the final line, we change what f refers to, so it now points to the integer 5. I don't recommend that you write code like this; if you define a function and then change what its name refers to, it makes your code hard to read. However, there are cases where it is useful to assign a function to a variable, and we will see this later in the chapter. You should only do it in those limited cases.

When you *call* a function, when you want the function to do some computation for you, you use the function name, and in parentheses, you give it the values it should use as its parameters. In the example, we use insertion_sort(), twice. We call it with the list x and with the list y. Inside the function, we only refer to a list x, and we see how that works for both x and y shortly.

Inside the function body, you might have noticed the keyword return. This statement tells the function what to return to the caller, and the value you put after return is the result of the function. We will discuss it in more detail in the following.

But first, we see how variables and functions interact.

Parameters and Local and Global Variables

All programming languages have rules for something called *scope*. These are rules for determining what different variables refer to. Until this chapter, we have seen one type of scope, the *global scope*. The variables we have used are simple labels that let us use a name to refer to a value. All variables work that way, but the same label, say x, can refer to more than one value, depending on where you are in your program—if they are in different scopes.

Consider the simple global scope. We can tell Python to refer to the value 4 through the name x:

```
x = 4
print(x)
```

We can change the value that x refers to by assigning to it a different value, for example, a string:

```
x = "foo"
print(x)
```

The way we have written code so far, all variables are global (i.e., in the global scope), and while we can change which value they refer to, we cannot make them point to two different values at the same time. With functions, this changes.

Consider again the insertion_sort() function:

```
def insertion_sort(x):
    for i in range(1,len(x)):
        j = i
        while j > 0 and x[j-1] > x[j]:
            x[j-1], x[j] = x[j], x[j-1]
            j -= 1
    return x
```

The variable x is a parameter to the function. This means that *inside* the function, x refers to the value you gave the function when you called it. It is *not* the global variable x. This does not mean that it cannot refer to the same value. It depends on what we call the function with. When we call

```
insertion_sort(x)
```

we give insertion_sort() the value that the global x refers to as its parameter. Inside insertion_sort() we have a different x, but it is the same value the two variables refer to. There is nothing wrong with that, but it is sometimes a little confusing until you get used to how local variables work—and scopes in general. Just remember that when you are inside the function, x is the local variable, and when you are outside the function, x is the global variable. The distinction is clearer when we call

```
insertion_sort(y)
```

Then the global and local x point to different objects. Inside insertion_sort(), the local variable x refers to the object that the global variable y refers to. When we call the function, the parameter x is assigned the value that the parameter, y, is referencing.

Insertion sort uses two index variables, i and j. In this example, we didn't have global variables i and j, so there is no confusion about whether these two are global or local, but if you had global variables for i and j, the rule would be the same. The variables inside the function are independent of the variables outside the function. When you increment i and j, you do not change any global variable. When you assign to one, for example, in the line j = i, you only change the value that the j label refers to *inside* the function. You do not change or create a global variable when you do this.

I started by showing you two functions that can appear in real-life code because toy examples sometimes make it hard to see why something like functions are useful. But now that we have seen some real functions, we can safely look at simple examples that clarify global and local variables.

Take this code:

```
x = 5
def f():
    x = 25
    print(x)
print(x)
f()
print(x)
```

The function f() doesn't take any parameters, so we define and call it with empty parentheses. In the example, we have a global variable x and a local variable x. In the first print statement, we print the value that the global x refers to. When we call the function, it creates a local variable, x, that refers to 25 and prints that. After the function call, we print the global variable x again. It will still be 5 because the assignment inside the function was to the local x and not the global x.

If you wonder why f() didn't have a return, well spotted. You don't need to explicitly return from a function. I will get to the details of how a function call returns in the following, but the short explanation is that a function that doesn't explicitly return will implicitly return None. You can try to call

```
print(f())
```

to see what happens.

Inside the function call, f() will print 25, it will then return None, and that returned result is what print() will print.

There isn't much difference between function parameters and local variables, except for how you define them when you write your function. They are, in effect, both local variables and treated as such. Take this example:

```
def g(x):
    y = 5
    return x + y
g(3)
g(9)
```

The function g() takes one parameter, x, and creates a local variable with the statement y = 5. It then returns the sum of x and y. The difference between the two variables is that the function's caller can determine what value a function's parameter gets. In contrast, the local variable you assign to inside the function is something that the function decides.

You can use both global and local variables inside a function. Try this example:

```
y = 5
def h(x):
    return x + y
print(h(6))
y = 6
print(h(2))
```

First, it prints 11 (6 + 5), and then it prints 8 (2 + 6). When you call the function h(), you give it a value, and that value will get the label x. In the return statement, you add x and y, and y isn't a local variable—we didn't get it as a parameter, and we didn't assign to any y inside the function. What Python does, always, is that it first looks in the local scope. If it finds a variable there, it uses its value. If it doesn't find the variable, then it looks in the global scope.

The lookup rules are that you first look at local variables and only if you do not find it there you look at the global variables. If you have both a local variable and a global variable with the same name, those rules tell you that you can never see the global variable. With a global x and a local x, all references to x will be the local variable, because Python looks for local variables first. We say that the local variables *overshadow* the global variables. (There are ways around it, but they are tricky, and if you write code that jumps through hoops to do something like that, you are creating a headache for yourself if you need to change the code in the future.)

146

In the global scope, you cannot see local variables either. In these examples, this should be obvious. They don't exist before you call the function, and when the function returns you to the global code, the function call is gone, and so are the local variables. They are not always gone when a function returns, and we will see cases in the next chapter, but you still don't get to see them from the global scope. Not unless you write very advanced code, and you should probably never do that.

You can define a function that uses a global variable, even though that variable does not exist. It isn't until you call the function that it needs to look up the global variable. So, if we had written the function h() *before* we defined y

```
def h(x):
    return x + y
y = 5
```

then that would be fine. If you do not define y before you call h(), you will get an error, but as long as you do not call a function, it can refer to all the global variables you want.

The last thing I want to tell you about local variables is a little tricky, and I wouldn't tell you about it if it wasn't a common source of errors. It has to do with how Python decides if a variable is local or global and how that can lead to trouble if you want to use a global variable in a function.

Consider this function:

```
x = 5
def f():
    print(x)
    x = 6
    print(x)
f()
```

Try to run it. You will get an error that tells you that a local variable was referenced before assignment. In the function, you might naturally assume that you have the global variable, so when you print x in the first line of the function's body, you refer to that, since you are not creating a local variable until the next line. The last part is correct. You don't have the local variable until you assign to it, and that is what Python is complaining about. You are using a local variable that you haven't defined—you are *not* referring to the global x. Python still thinks that x is a local variable, because it will be later in the code, so that is what it is looking for, but you haven't assigned to it yet.

This is the rule that Python uses: If you assign to a variable anywhere inside a function, then that variable is a local variable. Since we assign to x in f(), we cannot use x to refer to the global variable, even though we don't assign to x until after the first print statement. This is not a universal rule. Some languages will allow you to access a global variable until you assign to a local variable with the same name, and some will not. This rule is just how Python does it, and when you program in Python, you must follow Python's rules.

It is generally considered bad practice to access global variables from inside functions because it can make it hard to follow a program's logic. It is better to use parameters to pass data around since then it is explicit what the function will work on when you call a function.

It *is* possible to assign to global variables from a Python function, but I will not tell you how. It is considered even worse practice, and I hope you will never do it. If you absolutely need to—and you should try every other solution first—then look up the keyword global.

Exercise: Write a function that takes three numbers as arguments and returns their product.

Exercise: Change the function, so it only takes one argument, gets another from the global scope, and assigns to a local variable for the last value.

Exercise: Write a function that takes two lists as input and returns the longest of the two.

Side Effects

Although you cannot assign to a global variable inside a function, you *can* modify a value that a global variable refers to, and we did that with insertion_sort(). The sorting we did was in place, meaning that we changed the list rather than created a new list. So we modify the list that the local variable x refers to. When we called the function with the lists x and y, it was the lists that these two global variables referred to that the function worked on. The function didn't refer to the global variables. It used the local variable, but the variables were referring to the same objects, first the list that the global x points to and second the list that the global variable y refers to.

There is a distinction between what are called *call by value* and *call by reference* in some languages. The former means that you, in effect, have a copy of a value inside the function. So if you call a function with a list and modify the list, those modifications only exist inside the function. A variable referring to the parameter, outside the function call, will point to an object that doesn't change. With *call by reference*, which Python has,[2] variables are just pointing to objects.

If you modify an object through one variable, other variables will still look at the same object and thus see the changes.

Take this function:

```
def f(x):
    x[0] = 15
y = [1, 2, 3]
f(y)
print(y) # prints [15, 2, 3]
```

The global variable y points to a list object. When we call f(), its local variable x points to the same list. It changes the list's first value to 15, and since y points to the same list, it will, of course, see the modified list.

With f() we used a parameter to get the list we modified, but it also works with a global variable:

```
def g():
    x[0] = 15
x = [1, 2, 3]
g()
print(x) # prints [15, 2, 3]
```

The function g() updates the list that the global variable x points at.

Notice that this is different from assigning to a global variable! You cannot assign to a global variable inside a function, but that is not what we are doing. We refer to a global variable, and we can always read its value (as long as we don't have a local variable that overshadows it). Once we have the value that a variable refers to, we can do with that value what we can with any other values. We use the global variable to get the list, and

---

[2]Some use the term *call by reference* to mean that you can modify variables you give a function as an argument. Python is not call by reference in this sense. Functions only get the values that you provide as arguments; in that sense, they are call by value, but the values are object references and you can modify those objects, so in that sense it is call by reference. Some call this *call by assignment*, but the important lesson for Python is that you can modify objects inside functions, and that is why I will simply call it *call by reference*. Function arguments are always references to objects, not copies of the caller's arguments.

then we modify the list. The scope rules tell us how we access variables, how we look up their values, and what it means to assign to a variable, but they have nothing to do with what we can do with a value once we get our hands on it.

With our insertion_sort() function, we modify our input and return the result:

```
def insertion_sort(x):
    for i in range(1,len(x)):
        j = i
        while j > 0 and x[j-1] > x[j]:
            x[j-1], x[j] = x[j], x[j-1]
            j -= 1
    return x
```

Try to run this code:

```
y = [9, 2, 4]
z = insertion_sort(y)
print(y)
print(z)
z[0] = 15
print(y)
```

You should get this output:

```
[2, 4, 9]
[2, 4, 9]
[15, 4, 9]
```

Insertion sort modifies the list that the local variable x points at, which is the same list that y points at, so y is sorted after we call the function. We assign the result of the call to z, and the function returns its input list, so after the call, z points at the same list as y. We can see that when we modify z's first value and print y.

We didn't have to return the input in insertion_sort(). It made this code easier to write in cases such as this

```
z = merge(insertion_sort(x), insertion_sort(y))
```

but we could just as well have written

```
insertion_sort(x)
```

150

```
insertion_sort(y)
z = merge(x, y)
```

For the `merge()` function, we had a local variable, `result`, that we updated to build the merged list. This is not a global variable, so we had to return it, so the caller could get the merged list.

Exercise: Write a version of `merge()` where you use a global variable to put the results in.

When you have done the exercise, there is something I want you to consider. What happens with the function if the global variable is not an empty list when you call the function? Who should be responsible for making it into an empty list? Should the function user (probably you, but anyone who writes code that calls the function) make sure that the variable always points to an empty list? What happens if they forget? Those complications are the reasons we should avoid writing functions that use global variables.

A function that modifies its input or objects referred to by global variables is said to have *side effects*, and side effects can make it hard to figure out what a function does. You need to know what it modifies and what the consequences of calling it are. A Python function does not work as a mathematical function, where you give it input and get output and nothing else changes because you invoke the function. It is possible to write your functions that way, though. Just don't modify your parameters—make copies if necessary—and use local variables instead of global variables. Some programming languages enforce this since it is easier to reason about code without side effects, but it comes at a runtime penalty. If we need to make a copy of a list each time we want to sort it, we are spending more time than strictly necessary. So, when you write programs in a language such as Python, which allows side effects, you often have to choose between efficiency and avoiding side effects. You can always avoid modifying data through global variables—use parameters and call the functions with global variables if you must. You cannot always write efficient code that doesn't modify the input, but when you can, you should. It is a rule of thumb, and with experience, you will learn how best to write your functions.

Returning from a Function

We have already seen the return statement several times by now, but it is time to dig into it a little deeper. From a programming perspective, returning from a function is relatively simple. Still, there are some interesting aspects to returning from functions, if we go into how function calls must be implemented.

When we write a function, we can return from it in two ways. We can run the code in its body until we get to the end of the function, and then the function will automatically return. The return value will be None. Alternatively, we can explicitly return from the function with a return statement. After the return keyword, you can put a value. If you do, then that will be the value that the function returns. If you do not, the function will return None. That is all you need to know to write a function.

But if you think a little deeper about function calls, there are things you need to know if you are ever implementing your own programming language or building your own hardware.

Consider this example:

```
insertion_sort(x)
insertion_sort(y)
```

We are calling insertion_sort() twice. We give it different parameters, so we are working with different lists. Nothing surprising here. But how does your program know what code to execute when you call a function? How does it know that you are in line 1 when you return from the first function call, while when you return from the second function call you are in line 2?

When your code runs, the computer has what is called an *instruction pointer*, and it points to the instruction you are currently executing. You can think of it as pointing to the line of code you are currently executing, although it is a little more complex as we shall see shortly. In the preceding code, we start with pointing at the first line of the code. Here, we call the function. When we call the function, we need to run the function body. There is a little setup that Python has to do before we get there, having to do with parameters and such, but think about it as moving the instruction pointer to the top of the function and then continuing executing statements down the function's body.

I said it was more complicated because there is more than one thing you can do in the same line of code. Consider this:

```
z = merge(insertion_sort(x), insertion_sort(y))
```

Here, we have two calls to insertion_sort(), one call to merge(), and then an assignment. There are multiple instructions, and the instruction pointer has to go through them one by one.

When you run a computer program, you practically never have a language where you execute the actual source code you write. It is first reduced to much simpler instructions that can be executed one by one. Python doesn't run the preceding line as it is. When you run a Python program, your program is first translated into a lower-level set of instructions.

You will be fine, though, if you just think of the instruction pointer going line by line. It is a fine conceptual model. When you write a program in a modern language, you never need to worry about instruction pointers. The language takes care of them. But the way a function call works is that you change the instruction pointer to the beginning of the function and start executing its body.

When we reach the end of the function body or we see a return statement, we need to get back to where we called the function from. So we need to set the instruction pointer to just after the function call. That is between the first and second lines for the first function call. When we call the function a second time, we again need the instruction pointer to go to the start of the function's body, execute the body, and then return. This time, the instruction pointer must return to just after line 2. How do you know when you should return to the first location and when you should return to the second? Or in general, how do you know where to return to if the same function is called many times all over the program?

A simple solution is to have a variable somewhere, where you store your current location every time you call a function. Before you call a function, you save the instruction pointer in this variable. You call the function and execute it, and when you return, you get the location from the variable and set the instruction pointer to the instruction right after where you made the call. Excellent.

But now consider this example:

```python
def f(x):
    return x
def g(y):
    return f(y)
def h(z):
    return g(z)
h(42)
```

The instruction pointer goes through the function definitions. Those are also code, and the instructions are executed one by one. That is not the exciting part, though. When we call h(), we save the instruction pointer and start running h()'s body. There, we need to call g(), so we save the instruction pointer, so we can return to the body of h() when g() returns. And then in g() we save the instruction pointer and call f(). From there, we return x, so we get the instruction pointer from the variable, and it tells us to go to g(), so that is what we do. When we left g() we were just about to return the result of f(y), so that is what we must now do. So we get the instruction pointer from the variable, *but this is the instruction pointer into g().* That is the last location we assigned to this variable. We cannot use a simple variable to store the instruction pointer if we permit one function to call another.

No problem. We can use a variable per function. Then, when we call h() we store the instruction pointer in its variable, when we call g() we store it in g()'s variable, and when g() calls f(), we store the instruction pointer in *its* variable. Now, when we return, we get the instruction pointers from different variables, and everything works.

This is how early programming languages solved the problem; they had one variable per function that kept track of where the instruction pointer should return to after a call. There is, however, a problem with this. Consider

```
def f(x):
    if x == 0:
        return 0
    else:
        return x + f(x - 1)
f(3)
```

I admit it looks a little complicated, but let us break it apart. We have the function f() that will return zero if its input is zero, and otherwise, it will call itself with x - 1 and return the result plus x. A function that calls itself is called a *recursive* function, and we cover this in great detail in Chapter 8. For now, let us just consider what happens when we call f(3).

We call f(), so we save the instruction pointer. In the first call, x is not zero, so we have to make a recursive call. Here, again, we need to save the instruction pointer—I think you can see where this is going—and because x is two and not zero, we have to call f() once more. Doing that, we overwrite the old instruction pointer in the function's instruction pointer variable. If you have a function that calls itself, you cannot do it with one variable per function.

It is not just functions that call themselves where this is a problem. They can call themselves indirectly. For example, we can rewrite f() from the preceding to use two functions:

```
def f(x):
    if x == 0:
        return 0
    else:
        return g(x)
def g(x):
    return x + f(x - 1)
```

Exercise: Work your way through how the instruction pointer should be set in this code; you will see that we also run into problems.

There is an elegant solution to this, and I will show it to you in Chapter 8. It is essential for recursive functions, but we do not need to worry about it for the rest of this chapter. It suffices to know that there is a solution, and you can write functions that call themselves, directly or indirectly.

One thing is the instruction pointer; another is the value a function returns. Consider again the sorting and merging example:

```
z = merge(insertion_sort(x), insertion_sort(y))
```

When merge() returns, Python puts the returned value in the variable z. That is probably straightforward. But what about the two calls to insertion_sort()? There, we don't have a variable to store the return values. Still, Python must remember them, so it can call merge(). We haven't talked about this earlier, but this is a general problem with expressions. If you write an expression such as

```
z = 2 * x + (y + 4) / x
```

there are many temporary results. For each operator, you get a result that you need to use with the other operators. The problem is the same for expressions and for function calls—operators are, in effect (and in many cases literally), function calls. They return a value, and you need to remember that value until you need it. You often need to calculate several sub-expressions to use in a function call, so you have many of these temporary values.

Here, however, there *is* a simple solution: use temporary variables to store the temporary values. A programming language will not make these variables available to a programmer. They are hidden, and rightly so because the programmers who make the language can optimize how they are used, so they can't be bound by what a user might think they can get away with. Still, the solution is to have local variables. When a function returns, its return value is put in the corresponding local variable.

Now, Python doesn't actually do this. It does something very similar, and very clever, called a *stack*, but we don't have the tools to see what it actually does yet. I will show you in Chapter 16. But that is Python. Many languages do use temporary variables, often combined with a stack, and you can safely think about those as the solution. Not that you ever have to worry about it when you write a program, but if you wonder how function calls are actually implemented, this is a safe mental model.

Higher-Order Functions

A function is an object like any others, and we can assign functions to variables and pass them on as parameters to function calls. The latter is a powerful tool in many applications.

Think back to when we discussed generalizing sorting in Chapter 5 and how we could use functions there. Imagine that we have different kinds of data and we want a sorting function that can sort all of them and in different ways. We do not want to write separate functions for each data type and each way we want to sort them, so we need a way to parameterize a single function to handle it. We could handle all the possible cases inside that function, but then we would need to update it any time there is a new type or new sorting approach, so we don't want that. Instead, we want to use parameters to handle such cases. And to parameterize behavior, functions are an excellent tool.

Consider insertion sort:

```python
def insertion_sort(x):
    for i in range(1,len(x)):
        j = i
        while j > 0 and x[j-1] > x[j]:
            x[j-1], x[j] = x[j], x[j-1]
            j -= 1
    return x
```

It sorts its input in increasing order. What if we want to sort in decreasing order as well? We can parameterize the comparison x[j-1] > x[j] and get what we want:

```
def insertion_sort(x, greater_than):
    for i in range(1,len(x)):
        j = i
        while j > 0 and greater_than(x[j-1], x[j]):
            x[j-1], x[j] = x[j], x[j-1]
            j -= 1
    return x

def greater(x, y):
    return x > y
insertion_sort(x, greater)

def smaller(x, y):
    return y > x
insertion_sort(x, smaller)
```

We use a function to compare two elements and have written two different functions for the comparison: one that says that x is greater than y, which means that we will sort in increasing order, and one that says that x is smaller than y, which means that we will sort the elements in decreasing order.

Exercise: Go through the code and make sure you understand why it sorts in increasing and decreasing order.

Or what about sorting tuples by different indices? We can do that as well:

```
x = [
    (1, "mark"),
    (6, "luke"),
    (2, "matthew"),
    (5, "gandalf"),
    (7, "john")
]

def first_greater(x, y):
    return x[0] > y[0]
def second_greater(x, y):
    return x[1] > y[1]
```

```
insertion_sort(x, first_greater)
insertion_sort(x, second_greater)
```

We call functions that either take functions as arguments or return them as their value *higher-order functions*. How well higher-order functions are supported by your programming language of choice varies, but I am not aware of any high-level language that doesn't support them to some degree. If you can generally treat functions like any other object type, we say they are *first-class objects*. It just means that we do not distinguish between functions and other types of data.

At the most primitive level, all objects we manipulate in a computer program are just binary numbers. In principle, you could point your instruction pointer anywhere and have the computer execute it as code. There is some hardware protection against this in practice since it is a security hole, but there isn't much difference between integers, strings, and functions at the lowest level of a computer.

Programming languages, however, must give you abstractions such as functions, lists, numbers, etc. Otherwise, it would be too cumbersome to write larger programs. Sometimes these abstractions mean that you cannot use functions as data, and sometimes they don't. In Python and many modern languages, functions are first-class objects, and using higher-order functions in your programs is common and recommended.

Consider another example. Say we have an application where we sometimes want to update a list by a function call on each element, that is, something like `x[i] = 2 * x[i]` or `x[i] = x[i] - 13`. Such a function could look like this:

```
def apply(x, f):
    for i in range(len(x)):
        x[i] = f(x[i])

def times_two(x):
    return 2 * x

def minus_13(x):
    return x - 13

x = [1, 2, 3]
apply(x, times_two)
```

```
print(x)
apply(x, minus_13)
print(x)
```

You should get

```
[2, 4, 6]
[-11, -9, -7]
```

Such an `apply()` function is standard in languages that frequently use functions as parameters, but traditionally, it creates a new list instead of changing its input.

In Python, a better way to do this is list comprehension

```
[f(x) for x in x]
```

Another common function is one that creates a list of only those elements that satisfy a predicate. It could look like this:

```
def filter(x, p):
    y = []
    for elm in x:
        if p(elm):
            y.append(elm)
    return y

def is_even(x):
    return x % 2 == 0

x = [1, 2, 3, 4]
print(filter(x, is_even))
```

Here, you should get the list [2, 4]. This is not a function you would normally use in Python because you can also do it with list comprehension:

```
[elm for elm in x if p(elm)]
```

The expression takes all the elements elm in the list x, if they satisfy the predicate p(elm).

List comprehension gives you both an "apply" and a "filter" function, and you should normally use that instead of writing functions for it. List comprehension does take functions as arguments, but they have a more straightforward syntax, which is why they are built into the language. However, they cannot do everything and certainly not everything where you might want to use function parameters. You can't, for example, use list comprehension to parameterize your sorting function.

As the last example, there is another classic function called reduce(). It takes a list and a function as input, and then it applies the function to the first and second elements in the list. It then takes the result and applies the function to that and the third element. It continues like that until it is through all the elements, and then it returns the final result:

$$f\left(f\left(f\left(\cdots f\left(x_0,x_1\right),x_2\right),x_3\right),\cdots,x_{n-1}\right)$$

If f() is addition, then reduce() will add the first two numbers and then add the result to the next, then the next, and so on, and the result is the sum of all the numbers. If f() is multiplication, you get the product. There are, of course, easier ways to add and multiply the numbers in a list, but I would like you to implement reduce() as an exercise.

Exercise: Implement the reduce() function and use it to compute the sum and product of a list of numbers. Add a third parameter to the function that gives you an initial value to use, so you compute

$$f\left(f\left(f\left(\cdots f\left(i,x_0\right),x_1\right),x_2\right),\cdots,x_{n-1}\right)$$

where i is the initial value. To compute the sum of all the elements, the natural initial value would be zero, and to compute the product, the natural initial value would be one.

Functions vs. Function Instances

Getting back to the recursive function we have seen before, there is a distinction between a function and a function *instance* that we need to be aware of.

Consider this code:

```
def f(x):
    if x == 0:
        return 0
```

```
    else:
        return x + f(x - 1)
x = 3
f(x)
```

When we call it with, say, f(x), where x is the global variable that refers to three, then the function parameter x gets the value 3, and because it isn't zero, we must evaluate the expression x + f(x - 1). That is a call to f(), so in that call, the local variable x gets the value 2. And here is the crucial part: those two local variables are not the same.

It is a little confusing when we talk about local variables in a function because we usually say that a *function* has local variables. But it is only partially true. When we define a function, we write the code in its body, and in that code, we use local variables. So in that way, we can talk about a function's local variables. However, when we write the code, it is only code, not the running program. There are no variables yet. We don't create them until we call the function; the instructions we put in the function's body tell Python to create local variables when the function is called, but we need to call the function before it does so.

When we call a function, we get a function *instance*. Consider Figure 6-1, which illustrates the instances in play when we call f(x) in the preceding code. On the left, we have the global scope and the code there. In the scope, we have two variables, f that points to a function object, I have written it as <function>, and the variable x that points to the integer 3. In the function call, f(x), we create a function instance that I have called <f(3)> in the figure. It also has a scope, where x points to 3, and it has the code from the function body. In that code, we call f(x- 1), which means that we call the function the variable f refers to, with the integer 2 as the argument. Notice that we are using two variables at this level, f and x, where f is a global variable and x is a local variable (which overshadows the global x).

In the second function call, we create another function instance, <f(2)>; it gets the local variable x that points to 2, and it has the function body as its code. This is another function instance, with another local variable, x. In this function instance, we can see this specific x, but not the global variable (it is overshadowed) and not the local variable in the other function instance.

I will let you continue working out the rest of the sequence.

Each of the function instances is independent. They are running the same code, and they all refer to the same global variable f, but otherwise, they do not interact. They all have their own local variable, and it is always the case that each function call has its own local variables.

However, as we can clearly see, the function instances do not *only* have their local variables. They do share the variables in the global scope. Suppose you modify values referenced by global variables in one function. In that case, the other instances will see the consequence, when they are called, if you update a value before you call them, or the calling function will see the changes after a function returns.

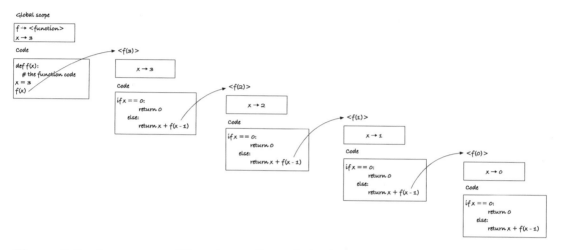

Figure 6-1. *A sequence of function calls and the function instances*

All functions can see their local scope and the global scope, but they generally cannot see the scope of the code that calls them and never the scope of the functions they call. In Chapter 7, we shall see that, if we define one function inside another, the scoping rules get a little more involved, but for now, your mental model of scopes should be that each function *instance* has its own local variables but can see (but not assign to) all the global variables.

Default Parameters and Keyword Arguments

It can sometimes be useful to specify default parameters for a function. Those are values that parameters will take if you do not provide values when you call the function. Default parameters are not possible in all programming languages, but many languages do provide them. They differ in how they work, though, so be careful to learn how any given programming language you use handles them. In this section, we only see how Python does it, though.

To give a parameter a default value, you assign to it in the list of parameters when you define the function, like this:

```
def add(a, b = 42):
    return a + b
```

This function will add two numbers, but if you only call it with one parameter, it will use the other's default and add 42 to the one parameter.

You must put the default parameters after the parameters you do not give default values. Here, you couldn't give a the default value and not b. It has to be the final variables that have default values. This is necessary because when you call a function, you must provide values for the parameters without defaults, so they must come first, or it would be difficult to work out which arguments you intended for which parameters.

With add() you can call it with one parameter; that parameter is the first argument, so it will be a. If you only use one parameter, b will be 42. If you call the function with two parameters, you give values to both a and b. When you call a function, you give values to the arguments in the order they are defined in the function. That is also what you do with a function that has default parameters, but if you call it with fewer arguments than parameters, then the remaining parameters take their default values.

Consider this function:

```
def f(a, b = 2, c = 0):
    return a + b ** c
```

We have one argument without a default value, so we must always call the function with at least one parameter (you can write functions where all arguments have default values if you want). We can also call the function with two or three arguments. If we call it as f(2), it will evaluate to 3 (because b ** c with b=2 and c=0 is the expression $2^0 = 1$). To set c to, for example, 2, you must call it as f(2, 2, 2) (and you will get the value 6).

If a function has many parameters with default values, having to specify all the values up until the last where you don't want the default, like specifying that b should still have the default value 2 here, can be a nuisance. There is another way around it. You can use so-called *keyword* arguments. Just call the function where you are explicit about which parameter you are giving another value. The syntax looks like this: f(2, c = 2). The arguments where we don't specify a parameter name are called *positional* and must come first, and those where we name the argument are called *keyword* arguments. In this call, we have one positional argument, and it will be the value for the first function parameter, a. We don't have any more positional arguments, so from here we only set parameters we explicitly name. Since we don't name b, it will get its default value. We specify c, so it will get a value—here 2.

You can use keyword arguments for any function parameter, not just those with default values, but any arguments you only provide positional must come first. So you cannot write f(c = 2, 2). Python doesn't infer that the second argument should probably be a (which is really the first parameter in the function) just because you have named the first parameter c. Positional arguments always come before keyword arguments. However, you can put keyword arguments in any order, so you could write f(c = 2, a = 2) if you wanted. Here you are explicit about which parameters you are providing values for, so Python doesn't have to infer anything.

Suppose you want to always make clear which parameters get which values. In that case, you can choose to use only keyword arguments in your code—it is a very explicit way to show how you call your functions—but we usually do not do that, unless you have functions with very many arguments. With default parameters, keyword arguments are the way to go if there are many of them, so you don't have to set many positional arguments to their default values in a function call.

When you use default parameters, it is important to know when the expressions you use when you define them are evaluated. This differs between programming languages, but usually, they are either evaluated when you create the function or call the function. There are two main reasons that this is important and why getting it wrong can lead to serious programming errors.

First, the scope when you define your function and when you call it might be different. Suppose your default arguments use an expression that references global variables, for example. In that case, you could get the value at the point where you define the function or call the function, and these variables can easily refer to different values at different times.

Second, when you evaluate the expressions, you get objects back, and it is important to know if all function instances get the same object—because the object was created when the function was defined—or if they all get separate objects—because the expressions are evaluated for the individual function instances.

As I said in the preceding, this varies between different programming languages, but for Python, the expressions are evaluated when you define the function, not when you call it.

With the two functions we have seen so far in this section, there wouldn't be any difference between evaluating the expressions when we define a function and when we call it. We have used integers as arguments, and although something like 2 is technically an expression that Python evaluates, there isn't much to it. You evaluate it, and you always get 2. But what if you do something like this?

```
def add(a, b = 2 * a):
    return a + b
```

You might expect that if you call it as add(2), b will have the value 2 * a, that is, 4. If Python evaluated the expression when we call add(), as some languages, then we would evaluate 2 * 2 and b would get the value 4.

It can get complicated if you have many default parameters with expressions that depend on each other, but those languages have ways of dealing with it. You need to check the documentation if you write code in one of those languages.

Since Python doesn't evaluate the default expression inside a function call, it won't know what value a will have when you call add(). Instead, it evaluates the expression when you define the function. If you are lucky, you will get an error when you define add() this way because Python doesn't know the variable a. If you are unlucky, you have a global variable named a, and that is the variable that Python would use. If you wanted b to have the value 2 * a, where a is the *parameter*, you would have a bug and one that is potentially hard to find.

If you want to have default values that depend on other parameters, you need to be more explicit about it. You can do something like this:

```
def add(a, b = None):
    if b is None:
        b = 2 * a
    return a + b
```

You still have a default parameter, so you don't need to specify b when you call add(), but b doesn't hold a value that you must evaluate before you call the function. If it is None, its default, then you explicitly get its value from the parameter a.

It can get even trickier if you have mutable data, that is, objects that you can modify. Consider this function that takes a list as its input, appends one to it, and returns it:

```
def append1(x = []):
    x.append(1)
    return x
```

Obviously, the default parameter says that if we call the function without a list, we should use the empty list. However, the default parameter, the empty list, is created when you define the function. That means that all function instances will refer to *the same* list. You don't get new empty lists each time you call the function! When you call it the first time without an argument, you get the list [1]. That is fine and what we expect. But if you call it a second time, you get the list [1, 1] because you appended one to the same list as in the first function call (and for the same reason you changed the list you got in the first call).

If you just remember that default parameters are evaluated when you *define* the function and not when you call it, you will be fine. But it is a common source of problems, so please always keep it in mind when you write a function and you want default values.

Generalizing Parameters

Positional and keyword parameters are all you use in everyday programming, but there are occasions where you want to write functions that can handle any number of parameters. Since you can write functions that take lists or sets or dictionaries as input, you can easily handle situations like that in day-to-day coding, but we sometimes write functions that manipulate other functions—we will see examples in the next chapter. Suppose the functions you manipulate don't take lists or dicts or such as input. In that case, you need a way to manipulate arguments as if they were sequences—for positional arguments— and dictionaries—for keyword arguments.

If you want to write a function that can take an arbitrary number of positional arguments, you give it one argument with an asterisk in front:

```
def sum(*args):
    result = 0
    for arg in args:
        result += arg
    return result
```

You can call using the normal syntax

```
sum(1, 2, 3)
```

but all the arguments go into `args`, which will be a tuple holding the function arguments. You can add explicit arguments in front of the * parameter, and you get the arguments passed there as normal:

```
def sum(x, y, *rest):
    result = x + y
    for arg in rest:
        result += arg
    return result
```

With this version, the function takes at least two arguments, x and y, and any following arguments go into `rest`.

With

```
sum(1, 2, 3, 4)
```

x will be 1, y will be 2, and `args` will be (3, 4). You have to put the positional arguments in front of the *args argument, since otherwise all positional arguments go into `args`, unless you give them as keyword arguments.

This would work

```
def sum(*rest, x, y):
    result = x + y
    for arg in rest:
        result += arg
    return result
```

```
sum(1, x = 2, y = 3)
```

but you will get an error if you call `sum(1, 2, 3)` because x and y will not hold values. The error will say that they are keyword-only arguments, but that just means that you have to explicitly give them as keyword arguments because `args` will take all the positional arguments. Don't do this; if you want explicit positional arguments, put them at the front of the argument list:

```
def sum(x, y, *rest):
    result = x + y
    for arg in rest:
        result += arg
    return result
```

If you have a list or tuple or any kind of object you can iterate through, then you can also call a function with that, and the elements in the iterator will be passed as positional arguments. If you want to do that, you have to put an asterisk in front of the iterator, like this:

```
sum(*[1, 2, 3])
```

You can combine positional arguments and this syntax, so you can, for example, write

```
print(sum(1, 2, 3, *[4, 5, 6]))
```

If you want default arguments, put them after *args:

```
def sum(*args, factor = 1):
    result = 0
    for arg in args:
        result += factor * arg
    return result

sum(1, 2, 3) # default factor
sum(1, 2, 3, factor = 2) # factor is two
```

When you declare the function, you *can* put the keyword arguments before the *args, as in

```
def sum(factor = 1, *args):
    # the sum function
```

unlike with positional arguments. You should generally avoid this, however.

You will assign to the keyword argument before *args, so

```
sum(2, 3, 4) # factor is 2, args is (3, 4)
```

doesn't use the default factor but the first argument. There is no easy way to set the factor as a named argument, because

```
sum(1, 2, 3, factor = 2) # error, multiple values for factor
```

will tell you that you have provided factor twice (once as a positional argument and once as a keyword argument), and

```
sum(factor = 2, 1, 2, 3) # error; named argument before positionals
```

168

is not valid syntax for calling a function. Just put the keyword arguments after the *args parameter.

You can also get keyword arguments in functions that work on arbitrary parameters, and here the syntax is two asterisks. This function goes through all positional arguments and treats them as keys to look up in a dictionary. The dictionary is kwargs, which will hold the keyword argument. The function looks up the keys and prints the values:

```
def call(*args, **kwargs):
    for arg in args:
        print(kwargs[arg])
```

How we treat the positional arguments with *args you already know, and the new thing is the keyword arguments. When we define the parameter **kwargs with two asterisks, it will take all the keyword arguments in a function call and put them in a dictionary that this parameter now holds.

So, if we call the function with

```
call("x", "y", "z", x = "foo", y = "bar", z = "baz")
```

the positional arguments are put into the tuple ("x","y","z") that the function gets in the args parameter, and the keyword arguments are put into a dictionary {"x": "foo", "y": "bar", "z": "baz"} that the variable kwargs will get.

Exercise: Work through the call, and convince yourself that you understand how the call and the two types of parameters work.

It might look a little complex, but to see what *args and **kwargs are when you call a function, try this:

```
def f(*args, **kwargs):
    print(args)
    print(kwargs)
f("x", "y", "z", x = "foo", y = "bar", z = "baz")
```

If you want to pass positional and keyword arguments to a function call using a sequence and a dictionary, the syntax looks like this:

```
args = ["x", "y", "z"]
d = {"x": "foo", "y": "bar", "z": "baz"}
call(*args, **d)
```

I will stress again that this is not something you will run into daily, but it certainly has its uses from time to time. You can write very general functions if you use these features correctly, and you can create functions from manipulating other functions with little knowledge about what those functions are and how they should be used. We will see a few examples in the next chapter.

Exceptions

There is an alternative mechanism for returning from functions called *exceptions*, because they usually handle exceptional cases. They are not exclusive to functions; you can use them anywhere in your code, but they are never *useful* outside of functions, which is why I haven't brought them up until now.

A typical use of exceptions is error handling. If something goes wrong when you call a function, for example, if it cannot handle the input you give it, then you need to provide the caller with this information. In some programming languages, you have to do this through a function's return value or through a parameter to the function, but this is an error-prone approach as it requires the user of your functions to always check for errors. Most modern languages have exceptions.

Let us, for example, assume we have a function that will multiply two numbers, but it is only safe to do so if the first number is positive. It is a toy example; it will probably never be useful, but it is so simple that we can focus on the exception mechanism instead of the main functionality of the function we write. One way to ensure that the function works is to test that we never call the function unless the first argument is positive:

```
def is_positive(x):
    return x > 0

def mult_positive(x, y):
    return x * y

    x, y = -1, 2
    if is_positive(x):
        print(mult_positive(x, y))
```

This is a dangerous approach, assuming that something can really go wrong if you call `mult_positive()` with a nonpositive number as its first argument (which of course isn't the case here, but imagine that it is). The user always has to test, and the one place in the code where you don't test, that is probably where something will go horribly wrong.

It is better if mult_positive() tests its input because then you will always be informed if you call it incorrectly. So we could write something like this:

```
def mult_positive(x, y):
    if not is_positive(x):
        print("Error")
    else:
        return x * y
```

This is better, since you won't get an incorrect result if you call it with incorrect data; whatever could go wrong if mult_positive() gets a nonpositive number won't happen, and instead your programming will probably crash because mult_positive() will return None (the default return value) instead of a number. To handle errors, you can call the function and test the type of what it returns. You need to test the return type everywhere, but it is better than risking a silent error if mult_positive() does something wrong if it doesn't get the input it expects. It is almost always better that your program crashes than if it gives you a wrong result, because then, at least, you know that something went wrong.

Testing the output is not a convenient approach to error handling, though. You need to know what return type or value indicates an error, and sometimes that isn't possible at all. Some functions are allowed to return *anything*. We could, for some bizarre reason, write a function that returns one of two values depending on a third that must be positive or negative; if it is zero, then we have an error:

```
def first_or_second(b, x, y):
    if b < 0:
        return x
    elif b > 0:
        return y
    else:
        print("Error")
```

If you call it with first_or_second(-1, None, 42), the correct return value is None, but you also get None if you call it with first_or_second(0, None, 42), which is an error. And in this case, it doesn't matter what type or value you choose to use as an error value because the function can return any type or value at all as a valid value.

Exceptions do not use the normal return syntax, so they cannot be confused for valid output of a function. There is a different syntax for returning an exception instead of a normal value and a different syntax for catching errors.

A variant of mult_positive() that uses an exception looks like this:

```
def mult_positive(x, y):
    if not is_positive(x):
        raise Exception()
    return x * y
```

It is the raise keyword you should focus on, and you can ignore the Exception() that follows it—we will get to that in the following. To return an exception, you use raise instead of return. To catch exceptions, you must use this syntax:

```
try:
    mult_positive(-1, 2)
    print("All is well")
except:
    print("Error")
```

You start with a try block, and you can put as much indented code after try as you please. If any exception is raised in this code, as it will be by the call to mult_positive() here, then the rest of the code in the try block will not be executed. Because mult_positive() will raise an exception here, you will never see "All is well" printed. Instead, Python jumps to the except block and executes the code there. You can write as much code as you like there as well.

You still have to handle errors; those do not magically go away because you have exceptions, but you are explicit about it, and you can never confuse an error with valid output from a function.

Exercise: A DNA string consists of A, C, G, and T letters. Write a function that counts how many times each of the letters occurs in a string, but raises an exception if there is a letter that isn't one of these four.

Of course, many things can go wrong if you call a function, and it is useful to provide further information that "something went wrong" when you raise an exception. The mechanism for this is to give raise a value, similar to how you give return a value. That value is the Exception() after raise we saw before.

The Exception() expression creates a type of object called Exception, but you can create your own types as well, as we shall see in Chapter 11. With an Exception, you can provide additional information, for example, a description of what went wrong:

```
def mult_positive(x, y):
    if not is_positive(x):
        raise Exception("x is not positive")
    return x * y

try:
    mult_positive(-1, 2)
    print("You will never get here")
except Exception as e:
    print(e.args[0])
```

The Exception() call creates an exception object that is then raised. The object you raise you can then catch in your except block. You can give the Exception() call any arguments you want; we just give it a string here. When we catch the exception, we need to specify that we want this particular kind of exception (Exception() is the most general, but there are others). When we write

```
except Exception as e:
```

we say that we can capture an exception of type Exception, and we give the exception the name e, so we can get to its values. The parameters you give Exception when you raise it are found in e.args. It is a list, and since we only used one argument when we raised the exception, we get e.args[0]. It is the string "x is not positive".

There is more to giving exceptions values, but we need to see so-called classes before we can go there, and we don't do that until Chapter 11, so until then, you have to use the Exception() call and the arguments you give it. Exceptions are widely used in Python, and all the errors you have seen while learning to program in Python were exceptions—syntax errors, type errors, index errors, and all exceptions that you can catch. It is not straightforward to handle them exclusively using the Exception type, however, but after Chapter 11 you will know all you need to know to capture your errors from inside a program.

Before we leave exceptions for now, however, you need to see what happens if a function calls another function that calls another and so on, for some nested level of function calls, and one of them raises an exception. Here, exceptions do not follow the normal return mechanism either.

If you want to catch an exception, you must have a `try`/`except` block. Otherwise, you won't get the exception. You won't even see that your function call returned at all. It is not just in a `try` block that Python won't continue executing code after an exception is raised. That is everywhere.

Try running this code in a file where you have defined `mult_positive()`:

```
print("Before call")
mult_positive(-1, 2)
print("After call")
```

Python will print "Before call" and call `mult_positive()`, which raises an exception, and then Python will terminate your program with an error. The second `print()` is never executed. If you raise an exception and don't catch it, your program crashes.

If you call a function that raises an exception, you do not need to catch the exception immediately, however. Exceptions propagate down through calling functions until you catch them (or your program crashes). Consider this simple example:

```
def compute(x, y):
    mult_positive(x, y)
    print("Fine")

try:
    compute(1, 2)
    compute(-1, 2)
    print("You do not get to here")
except:
    print("Error handling")
```

The function `compute()` calls `mult_positive()`, which will raise an exception if `x` is not positive. It doesn't catch any exceptions, however, so whoever calls `compute()`, directly or indirectly, must do so. We call it from the global level, first with valid and then with invalid input for `mult_positive()`. The first call to `compute()` makes a successful call to `mult_positive()`, so that function returns without errors, and `compute()` prints "Fine". The second time we call `compute()`, the `mult_positive()` call raises an exception. Because of this, the `print("Fine")` statement isn't executed—the rest of `compute()`'s body isn't executed because it comes after an exception that isn't caught. Instead, the exception propagates out to the top level, to the `try` block there. The rest of the `try` block isn't executed either, because of the exception, but we jump to the except block, where we print "Error handling". Since the exception is handled in the except block, it isn't propagated any longer, so the program doesn't crash this time.

You can handle exceptions at any level of function calls, and a raised exception will propagate down to the first function that has a try/except. This means that you can handle errors close to where they occur, and your global code doesn't have to know about everything that can go wrong. However, a function call close to an error might not be able to handle all exceptions. Sometimes, the error happened long before the function was called and just wasn't detected until later, and in that case, the exception should propagate further out the chain of function calls. Because of this, functions can capture exceptions and then reraise them if they cannot handle them.

Consider this example, which I admit is a little complicated, but I will explain it in the following:

```python
def raises_error(x):
    if x < 0:
        raise Exception("Negative", x)
    if x > 0:
        raise Exception("Positive", x)
    return 42

def f(x):
    return raises_error(x)

def g(x):
    try:
        print(f(x))
    except Exception as e:
        if e.args[0] == "Negative":
            print("g:", e.args[0])
            return f(0)
        else:
            raise
```

We have a function, raises_error(), that will raise an exception if its input is either negative or positive, but return 42 if its input is 0. The function f() just calls raises_error() and cannot handle any exceptions. So, if raises_error() throws an exception, then f() will simply propagate it to its caller. Function g() calls f(), but inside a try/

except. It will print the result of f(x) if f() returns normally, but if f() propagates an exception, we jump to g()'s except block. Here, we name the exception e, and we check if it was a "Negative" error we got. If so, we print a message and call f(0) and return the value (which will be 42). If e is a "Positive" error, we reraise the exception using raise with no argument.

Now, try running this code:

```
try:
    print(g(-1))
    print(g(1))
except Exception as e:
    print("Outer", e.args[0])
```

The first time we call g(), it will get an exception from raises_error() through f(). It can handle this exception, so it prints "g: Negative" and returns f(0), which is 42, and print(g(-1)) prints 42. The second time we call g(), raises_error() raises an exception again, but this time g() cannot handle it, so it propagates it to the global try/except, where the except block handles the exception and prints "Outer Positive".

Exercise: Go through this code carefully and make sure you understand what is happening. Make a drawing of the function calls for the two calls to g() and how exceptions propagate from raises_error().

We don't need to reraise an exception when we cannot handle it. We can raise a different exception instead. This is a way of changing low-level error handling, relevant to the gory details of an algorithm, into information that is relevant for the caller of an algorithm that doesn't necessarily know about the details of the algorithm. Think something like a numerical error, like division by zero, in linear algebra code. When you call a function that should handle some matrix algebra, you want to know that there is a problem with the data, for example, that you have a singular matrix when you shouldn't, but you don't care how the algorithm detects that. Functions deep into an implementation should know about low-level errors and handle those they can, but when they propagate exceptions, they should raise the abstraction level so the errors make sense to the user.

To change the exception you raise, you give raise an argument, they way you do when you first raise an exception. The exception you give it will be the new exception that will propagate up the function calls. For example, if we add an exception to g()

```
def g(x):
    try:
        print(f(x))
    except Exception as e:
    if e.args[0] == "Negative":
        print("g:", e.args[0])
        return f(0)
    else:
        raise Exception("Error in g")
```

the error you get at the global level will contain "Error in g" instead of "Positive".

How you structure your code to handle errors is a design issue, no different from how you design your code to implement algorithms and make them easier to use for other people. Both are complicated topics, far beyond what we can cover in this book, but it is something you will learn from experience, from reading other people's code, and from collaborating on projects.

Writing Your Own Python Modules

In the first chapter, we saw that you can import variables, such as functions, from modules. You can also write your own modules, and it is relatively easy. If you have written a set of useful functions and you want to put them in a module of your own, you only have to put them in a file. Let's say the file is called my_module.py. Put that file next to the code where you want to use the module, and you can import from it, just as from any other module.

Admittedly, if you want to use the same module in multiple projects, you don't want to copy the file into each directory you are using. There are several ways to do this and make Python packages you can automatically install (using, e.g., Anaconda or pip, which I mentioned in Chapter 1). However, I will refer to Python's documentation for this, so you can explore the different alternatives there.

If you are developing a large program, you will still want to split your code into modules, even though you will not reuse any of the code in other projects. It is easier to keep track of your code if you lump related functionality together, and an obvious way to do this is to put related functions into the same file, but keep unrelated code in separate files.

It also has the added benefit that you do not have to worry about name clashes between functions, that is, you don't need to worry that you have defined two different functions with the same name. If you import modules and use functions from them through the imported object

```
import my_module as my
my.f(1, 2, 3)
```

then you cannot use the same name twice in your module, but the same name in different modules will never be a problem.

And that brings me to an important point about scopes. We have talked about the global scope as the final destination when we search for variables, but I wasn't entirely honest when I said that, and I promised to get back to it.

The global scope is the file where you write your code. Two functions, in separate modules, have different global scopes. Global scope is really a module scope. If you think about it, you cannot see the functions in another module when you write your program, even if they are defined at the global level in their file, so they cannot be defined in the global scope you are currently working with. You have to explicitly import them, for example, via

```
from my_module import curry, switch_curry
```

When you import a module, the code in that file is evaluated, so global variables are created there (including function definitions, which is the same as declaring global variables that refer to functions). The code is evaluated in the global scope of the module. All the code inside the module can see this scope, but it is local to the file. When you import several modules, they are evaluated in different scopes.

## CHAPTER 7

Inner Functions

You don't have to define your functions at the outermost, global, level of your program. Anywhere you can have a statement such as `if` or `while` or a variable assignment, you can also define a function. A function definition is just another type of statement. This means that you can define a function inside the body of another function. This is a power tool; it enables you to write very flexible and elegant code, but as with all power tools, there is also a certain risk of self-harm. At least until you get comfortable with how scopes work when you do it.

With all the functions we have seen so far, we have defined them at the global level. We have seen that they can have local variables accessible in function instances (and that variables are independent between different instances). They have access to the global scope, where they can access global variables. Now I want you to think about scopes in a slightly different way. Not as two scopes, where you first look at the local level and then the global level, but a chain of scopes where you search for variables one scope after another. I want you to think that each scope has an *enclosing scope*—another scope it can refer to when it doesn't have a variable. In the interest of honesty, I will admit that this is not how Python implements scopes (but some languages, such as R, do it this way). However, as a conceptual model of how scopes work, I think it is better than what the actual implementation does.

When you search for a variable, you start at a function instance's local level. If you find the variable you want there, then you are done. If not, you look at its enclosing scope and check if the variable is there. If not, you need to search at the enclosing scope's enclosing scope and so on, until you run out of scopes.

Think of the global scope as the final scope. It isn't strictly true because of the module mechanism, but that will never make a difference for your programs. Inside Python modules, the outermost scope is the module. You can safely think of all chains of enclosing scopes as ending in the global scope for now.

© Thomas Mailund 2021
T. Mailund, *Introduction to Computational Thinking*, https://doi.org/10.1007/978-1-4842-7077-6_7

When you define a function, it remembers the scope in which it was defined. The enclosing scope of instances of that function will be the scope the function remembers, that is, the scope where you defined the function. So with all the functions we defined so far, that was the global scope.

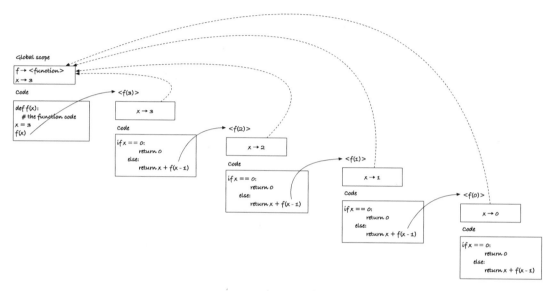

Figure 7-1. *Function instances with the enclosing graph*

If we look at the function from Chapter 6, defined in the global scope

```
def f(x):
    if x == 0:
        return 0
    else:
        return x + f(x - 1)
x = 3
f(x)
```

all the recursive instances will have the same enclosing scope—the global scope. I have added these enclosing scope references to the instance graph in Figure 7-1 as dashed lines.

All the function instances can find their own x and the global f because they can find x in their local scope and f in their enclosing scope. They don't directly "know" two different scopes that they look in, not in this conceptual model anyway; they just know that they should look in the local scope first and then move outward. They cannot see each other's local x variables because there is no enclosing scope pointer from one instance to another.

Do not confuse the sequence of functions calling functions, also a graph in the figure, with the enclosing scopes. They are two different things. One shows you which function calls which other function; the other tells you where functions find their variables. A function does *not* look for variables going back through the function calls. Some ancient languages did this, and that strategy is called *dynamic scope*. Not surprisingly, code that works that way can be very hard to work with, since you never know where a function will be called from when you write it. Modern languages use what is called *lexical scope*, and there you have the sequence of enclosing scopes based on how the static code looks. There, the enclosing scope of a function instance is always the scope where the function was defined.

Thinking about one scope's reference to an enclosing scope isn't easier than just thinking that we have a local and a global scope, but I want you to have this mental model when we now start adding more scopes.

A Comparison Function for a Search Algorithm

I want to go back to the case we had with sorting tuples based on different indices:

```
def first_greater(x, y):
    return x[0] > y[0]
def second_greater(x, y):
    return x[1] > y[1]

insertion_sort(x, first_greater)
insertion_sort(x, second_greater)
```

If we only ever sort based on the first or second index, there aren't any problems with writing two functions for it, but what if we have five, ten, or twenty indices and we have to use different ones at different points in the program? We *could* define a function for each, but it is cumbersome, and whenever there is a repetitive task, we usually want the computer to handle it rather than do it ourselves. This is how we can solve the problem with a single function:

```
def compare_index(i):
    def compare(x, y):
        return x[i] > y[i]
    return compare

insertion_sort(x, compare_index(0))
insertion_sort(x, compare_index(1))
```

The function `compare_index()` creates *another* function that it calls `compare()` and returns it. The `compare()` function compares based on the index i that `compare_index()` takes as an argument. When we sort, we use `compare_index(0)` and `compare_index(1)`, and these are comparison functions that compare based on the first and second indices.

We call a function that is defined inside another function an *inner function*, and sometimes you will see the term *closure*; that means the same thing (it is called a closure because it has a reference to an enclosed scope and the values assigned to variables in that scope).

Let us go through what happens here and use Figure 7-2 to follow along. We defined `insertion_sort()` and `compare_index()` in the global scope, and we must have a list x because we sort it. The figure shows what happens when we call `insertion_sort()` with `compare_index(0)`. When we call `compare_index(0)`, we create a function instance, `<compare_index(0)>`. It gets the local variable i as a parameter, and it creates the local variable compare that contains a function. It returns that function. Since the `compare()` function was defined inside the `<compare_index(0)>` function instance, it remembers that this is its scope. Inside the insertion sort instance, `<insertion_sort(x, index(0))>`, we have the list x, the two index variables i and j, and the function `greater_than` that we got as a parameter (and in this instance, it is the function we got when we called `compare_index(0)`). When `insertion_sort()` calls `greater_than()`, it calls the function we got from `compare_index(0)`, so we get an instance of that. That instance has the local variables x and y. Its code also references the variable i, but since that is not a parameter and the function never assigns to it, it is not a local variable, so it needs to get it elsewhere. That "elsewhere" always means a search through the enclosing scopes. The function was defined in the <compare_index(0)> instance, so the instance's enclosing scope is that instance. That is where it finds i. If the function needed something it couldn't find in its local scope nor its enclosing scope (it didn't, but if it did), it would continue the search through the enclosing scope of its enclosing scope. That scope is the enclosing scope of the <compare_index(0)> function instance, and since the compare_index() function was defined in the global scope, that is the instance's enclosing scope.

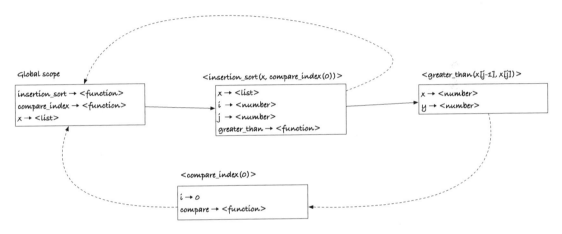

Figure 7-2. *Scopes with the compare inner function*

I realize that this can seem very complicated, but once again, I wanted to give you a complete example of something you will probably see in real-world code before I show you toy examples. If it is confusing now, read the following example and come back to it.

Before we get to the next examples, however, I want to give you another way of thinking about nested functions. I do this because it is a description you will most likely see in other books on Python programming. When you look at a function nested inside another—and these functions can be nested as deeply as you want—then to see what value a variable refers to, you just have to move outward, from the inner to the outer function. With

```
def compare_index(i):
    def compare(x, y):
        return x[i] > y[i]
    return compare
```

the nested function, compare(), has two local variables—the parameters. The i variable is not local—it is not assigned to, and it isn't a parameter—so we look outward to the function it is defined in. There we find it, so that is what i refers to. Consider this more contrived example:

```
w = 3
def f(z):
    def g(y):
        def h(x):
            return x + y + z + w
        return h
    return g
```

Never mind how we get h() out of calls to f()—you can work that out yourself, I am confident. Let's just focus on how we work out the variables in the return statement in h(). We can see that x is a parameter, so that is a local variable. Since the rest of the variables are not local, we look outward. The function that immediately encloses h() is g(), and that is where we find y—it is a local variable in g(). We need to go one step further out to get z, which we find as a local parameter of f. Finally, we have to go all the way out to the global scope to find w.

The technique of moving outward in your code to see where variables come from is fine—it is what you always do when you write your programs. The reason that I don't like this explanation for scopes is that it doesn't include function instances. It is *not* true that y sits in the function g(). That function doesn't have any local variable at all—only instances of g() will have a y. It is important to remember the distinction between functions and function instances. The function knows its code and the scope its instances should have as their enclosed scope (it is always the scope where the function is defined). The instances are the running execution of the code, and it is these that have variables. You can have many instances of g(), with different values for y, so it is not useful to think of y as something that sits in g(). Looking outward in the code is useful for figuring out where variables live, but you must always remember that they sit in function instances.

Exercise: Does it even make sense to talk about *the* function g() and *the* function h()? Consider where they are defined and whether more than one can be defined at the same time.

The reason that this "looking outward in the code, from inner to outer functions" works is that enclosing scopes are always where the function is *defined*, never where it is *called from*. This is the difference between *lexical scope* and *dynamic scope*—with lexical scope, you can see directly in the source code what enclosing scope a function will have. But in the running code, the enclosing scope is always a function instance and never the function itself. The inner functions do not exist before you call the outer functions—create instances for them—because it is when you execute the outer functions you define the inner ones. In the source code, you have written an inner function definition inside the outer function's body, but none of the code in the outer function is run before you call it—and the inner function doesn't exist before you create it. The inner function is created when you execute the outer function, in an instance of that function. Each time you call the outer function, you create a new inner function, as independent of other calls to the outer function as any other local variable you have in different instances of functions. Since Python has lexical scoping, you can see what the enclosing scopes will be in the source code. However, enclosing scopes of inner functions will always be function instances of the outer—the enclosing scope of a function instance is the scope in which the function is defined—that is not the outer function itself, but an instance.

Counter Function

But let us get to a simpler example:

```python
def counter():
    x = [0]
    def tick():
        x[0] += 1
        return x[0]
    return tick

c1 = counter()
c2 = counter()
print([c1(), c2(), c1(), c1(), c2()])
```

When you run the code, you should get

```
[1, 1, 2, 3, 2]
```

Here, the outer function, counter(), creates a list, x, with a single element, 0. Then it defines the function tick() and returns it. When we make two counters, c1 and c2, we have references to two tick() functions. When we call either of these functions, we run the code in tick(), which increments the value at x[0] and returns the new value. The result of calling a counter is a count of how many times we have called it.

This is not just a toy function. I have found it useful in many algorithms where I have needed to count something and where using a single variable was cumbersome. But the example is sufficiently simple for us to examine while sufficiently complex that we will learn something from it.

Let us examine the scopes in detail for this example as well, so please follow along in Figure 7-3. When we create c1, we call counter(). This creates a function instance; in that instance's scope, we set x and define the function tick(), and we get the function back. When we set c2 we have another call to counter(), so we get another function instance, and we create another function, tick(). The two instances and the two functions are independent; they are different objects and are only related in the sense that they are the results of calls to the same counter() function. In the figure, I have shown both calls to c1() and c2(). This doesn't happen simultaneously, of course—we must call one after another—but it illustrates how the counters work. When we call c1(), we get a function instance (it is an instance of the function tick() defined in the first call to counter()). We get a local scope that is empty because the tick() function doesn't have any local variable. The local scope has the <counter()> instance as its enclosing scope, so tick() can access the variable x. When we call c2(), the same thing happens, but we are calling a different tick() function, with a different enclosing scope, so the x we increment and return is a different x than the one we have in c1().

If you wonder why I used a list for x, this is the reason: If I tried to update x inside tick(), I would have to assign to it, and that would make it a local variable—remember that the rule is that if you write to a variable, that variable is local. I cannot assign to x, but I can get the object the variable refers to and modify it, which we do when we update x[0]. Just as with global variables, there is a way to write to a variable in an enclosing scope from inside a function, and if you really want to do that, you can search for the nonlocal keyword. For something like this counter function, it would be reasonable to use it, but as a general rule, you shouldn't—and the x as a list trick works fine, and it won't tempt you to do crazy things once you know how to do it.

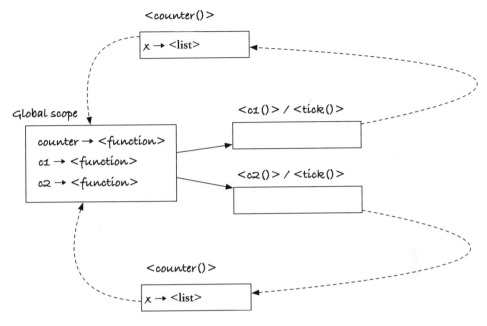

Figure 7-3. *Scopes for counters*

All functions always have their separate local scope, but they can share more than the global scope. If they are defined in the same scope, they have the same enclosing scope, which doesn't only happen in the global scope.

Consider the counter, and let's say that we want to query the counter without incrementing it. With the implementation we already have, we cannot do this; we can only get the new value when we increment. To get what we want, we can write two functions: one that increments and one that gives us the value. We don't want to work on a global variable because then we can only have one counter at a time. But we can create the two functions inside a function instance scope, and the functions can share the counter variable, without anyone else having access to it. This code does that:

```
def counter():
    x = [0]
    def tick():
```

```
        x[0] += 1
    def val():
        return x[0]
    return tick, val

tick, val = counter()
```

When we call `counter()`, we get a `<counter()>` instance, where we set x and define the two functions. We get the functions back (but not x). Since the two functions have the same enclosing scope, their instances will access the same x.

This is not the only way to share data between two or more functions, and it is not the preferred way because we could manage to split the two functions up and mix them with other function pairs. A better solution is to tie them more tightly together. So-called *object-oriented languages* have an elegant solution to this problem, and Python is such a langue. We leave it for Chapter 11, though.

Apply

So let us go to another example. We return to the `apply()` function from Chapter 6:

```
def apply(x, f):
    for i in range(len(x)):
        x[i] = f(x[i])

def times_two(x):
    return 2 * x

def minus_13(x):
    return x - 13
```

Here, we defined one function for multiplying by two and another for subtracting 13. We can make higher-order functions for the operations:

```
def times(x):
    def inner(y):
        return x * y
    return inner

def minus(x):
    def inner(y):
```

```
        return y - x
    return inner
times_two = times(2)
minus_13 = minus(13)
```

The `times()` and `minus()` functions take one parameter, the factor you should multiply with and the number you should subtract, and return functions that do that. Here, I defined `times_two()` and `minus_13()` using them, but of course, we don't have to name these two functions to apply them because we could also just do

```
apply(x, times(2))
apply(x, minus(13))
```

Exercise: What are the scopes when we call `apply()`?

Exercise: Write a function for addition and division.

Now for a slightly more complicated example. We can define functions for all the operators, for example

```
def add(x, y):
    return x + y
def sub(x, y):
    return x - y
def mul(x, y):
    return x * y
def gt(x, y):
    return x < y
```

and so on. We don't have to do this ourselves; you can get them from the module operator:

```
from operator import add, sub, mul, gt
```

It doesn't matter if you define them yourself or get them from `operator`; the point is that we can get them.

We can then rewrite our `times()` function like this:

```
def times(x):
    def inner(y):
        return mul(x, y)
    return inner
```

It doesn't change anything; we just use a function call instead of the * operator. But if we use a function, we can also use a parameter to get the function:

```
def bind1st(op, x):
    def inner(y):
        return op(x, y)
    return inner
```

It takes as arguments an operator and the first argument we want the operator to take, and then it returns a function that will give you the result of the operator when you call it with the second argument. I called it `bind1st()` because it binds the operator's first parameter to a value, so we only have to supply the second argument.

You can use it like this:

```
apply(x, bind1st(mul, 2))
```

I admit that this is less readable than having a times function, but it is something you can get used to, and if you need to use many operators with something like `apply()`, it can save some time when you write a program. Of course, with something as simple as `times()` and `minus()`, you don't gain much from this high-order function. I wouldn't use it for a simple thing such as this, but binding some arguments of a function can be useful in many more complicated contexts, and if you run into a case where it is useful, you now know the trick.

If you want to keep specialized functions for each operator, you can define them using `bind1st()`. It saves some coding, and you still get more readable code when you use them in apply:

```
def times(x):
    return bind1st(mul, x)
apply(x, times(2))
```

Exercise: Work out which functions are called when you do the `apply()` and what their enclosing environments are.

You are not saving much typing, I admit, but we are looking at simple code, so there weren't many lines to save to begin with.

For subtracting 13, we can't bind the first argument. We need to bind the second.

Exercise: Write a function `bind2nd()` that binds the second argument of a function. You should be able to use it in a call like this: `apply(x, bind2nd(sub, 13))`.

Currying Functions

A function like our `times()` splits one operation into two function calls. The first function gets the first argument to the multiplication operator, and it returns a second function. The returned function gets the second argument and gives us the operator's result, the two arguments' product. Splitting an operator of two arguments into a sequence of two function calls is called *currying* (after the mathematician Haskell Curry, after whom the programming language Haskell is named). In general, translating a function of any number of parameters into a sequence of function calls is called currying, but it is harder to implement a general function, so we will only look at functions with two arguments now.

We can write a function that curries any binary function like this:

```
def curry(op):
    def inner1(x):
        def inner2(y):
            return op(x, y)
        return inner2
    return inner1
```

We have three functions in play here. `curry()` gets the operator and returns the first function, `inner1()`. In the instance of the call to `curry()`, we have the variable op, so when we call `inner1()`, it can find it in its enclosing scope. When we call `inner1()`, we get a function instance that knows the local variable x, so the function that `inner1()` returns, `inner2()`, can get it from its enclosing scope (and get op from its enclosing scope's enclosing scope). When we then call `inner2()`, we have the final parameter, y, in its local scope; it can get the other two parameters from the enclosing scope chain to compute the final value.

Using `curry()`, we can define `times()` like this:

```
times = curry(mul)
```

Exercise: What happens if you evaluate `curry(mul)(2)(3)`? Explain why.

Exercise: Work your way through a call to `times()`, and identify all the called functions and their enclosing environments.

Exercise: Going the opposite direction, taking a chain of function calls and going back to one that takes all the arguments at once, is called *uncurrying*. Write a function take takes a curried function such as `times()` and translate it into one that takes two parameters and evaluate the chain of function calls in the curried function.

You now might be wondering if we can write a more general `curry()` function that can handle an arbitrary number of parameters. Yes, we can, and that is where we will go now. Feel free to skip to the next section if you are not interested—we won't see anything we will need in the following chapters. It is just an interesting exercise, and it might give you even more of an idea about what we can do with inner functions.

If we know how many arguments a function takes, we can construct functions that take one at a time. For functions that you define in Python, you can get that information. Getting information about objects such as functions from inside a program is called *reflection*, and in Python, we have the module `inspect` to do it. You can do a lot with reflection, but that is beyond the scope of this book. We will just use this function to get the number of arguments, and you will have to take on faith that this is what it does:

```
from inspect import signature
def number_of_arguments(f):
    return len(signature(f).parameters)
```

There are some caveats here. First, not all functions will work here. Some functions will not give us their "signature," from which we get the parameters. The `print()` function, for example, can't be curried (but since it takes an arbitrary number of arguments, we don't really want to curry it anyway). Second, if there are `*args` or `**kwargs` parameters, we cannot write a curried function—how would we know how many arguments to generate functions for? And in general, if there are keyword arguments, they can come in any order, and that would be impossible to handle if we curry the function. With `number_of_arguments()`, we get the positional parameters, and that is all we allow functions we curry to have.

Now, on to writing `curry()`. The trick I will use is to have a function that binds the arguments we have collected in calls so far. When I call it, I get a function back that remembers them. The function I get can be called with one argument, and if it is the last I am waiting for, then I call the original, uncurried function. Otherwise, it binds the argument it gets and returns a function that will handle the next argument. That solution looks like this:

```
def curry(f):
    no_args = number_of_arguments(f)
    def bind_args(args):
        def wrap(x):
            next_args = args + (x,)
```

```
            if len(next_args) == no_args:
                # we got the last arg
                return f(*next_args)
            else:
                return bind_args(next_args)
        return wrap
    return bind_args(args = ())
```

The `args` argument to `bind_args()` collects arguments each time we call it, and the wrapper we return from it thus knows its arguments. When we have enough, we call the function `f()` with all arguments, using the `f(*next_args)` syntax to give it a tuple of arguments that it will interpret as normal arguments.

Exercise: Why not have `next_args` as a list and `next_args.append(x)`? What could go wrong?

Exercise: Go through the steps and function calls if you run this code:

```
import operator
add = curry(operator.add)
add2 = add(2)
x = [1, 2, 3]
apply(x, add2)
```

We can also go in the other direction and translate a curried function into a non-curried version, but here we don't build a function that takes the right number of arguments exactly. It is impossible to determine how many times a function will return another function—not just hard, but impossible in the sense that you can never write an algorithm that can handle it for all functions. And even if we could, maybe the function we want to uncurry is *supposed* to return a curried function, so then we wouldn't want to call that function. No, instead we can write a function that takes a curried function and gives us a function that can take however many arguments we choose to give it and then keep applying the function for each of those:

```
def uncurry(f):
    def wrap(*args):
        next_call = f
```

```
        for arg in args[:-1]:
            next_call = next_call(arg)
        return next_call(args[-1])
    return wrap
```

Function Composition

We cannot directly use curry() for our minus() function because with minus() we need to reverse the order of the parameters. Not to worry, we can easily write a function that does that

```
def switch_params(op):
    def switch(x, y):
        return op(y, x)
    return switch
```

and use it to define minus():

```
minus = curry(switch_params(sub))
apply(x, minus(13))
```

We need to both switch and curry to get the function we want, so we call switch_params() to get the operator to curry().

If you have two functions, f and g, and you want to compute $f(g(x))$, you can *compose* them and get $(f \circ g)(x) = f(g(x))$. You should be familiar with this from mathematics (and if you are not, I think you can work out what is happening). A composed function applies one function first and then applies the second to the result of the first call. The mathematical notation, $f \circ g$, puts the first function you apply to the right of the second function, so it matches $f(g(x))$, so you have to read the function call order from right to left.

We know enough, now, to write a function that composes two functions:

```
def compose(f, g):
    def inner(x):
        return f(g(x))
    return inner
```

Exercise: Work out what this function does, what chain of function calls are involved when you use it, and how the scopes are connected.

Now we can do

```
from operator import mul, sub, add, truediv
switch_curry = compose(curry, switch_params)
add = curry(add)
times = curry(mul)
minus = switch_curry(sub)
divide_by = switch_curry(truediv)
```

to get curried versions of operators where we have switched the order of the parameters.

The truediv is the / operator. If you want integer division, you must use floordiv.

With the last few examples, I have dragged you away from the kind of code you would typically write in Python. There are programming languages where such constructions are typical, the Haskell language I mentioned in the preceding is one of them, and they are called *functional programming languages*. In Python, you tend to be more explicit with the functions you use. But high-level functions and inner functions are frequently used and when used carefully can significantly simplify your code. You might not ever use currying and function composition, but they illustrate what you can do with inner functions, and you can keep them in mind when you think you can benefit from nested functions.

Thunks and Lazy Evaluation

A function that doesn't take any arguments, (usually) has no side effects, and (usually) always returns the same value is called a *thunk*. The name comes from "something you have already thought about," but when you thought about it late at night, you "thunk" about it.

> In other words, it had "already been thought of"; thus it was
> christened a thunk, which is "the past tense of 'think' at two in the
> morning." —The Hacker's Dictionary

A function that doesn't take any input can still depend on variables outside its local scope and can affect data it can refer to through its enclosing scopes, so there is nothing odd about functions taking no input. But if a function doesn't take any parameters, doesn't affect anything via side effects, and gives you the same output every time you call it, it is essentially a constant—just a constant you need to call to get its underlying value. And perhaps that sounds like a silly thing to have. And yet, it has its usage.

The primary reason to use thunks is to wrap some computation that you may or may not want to be done later, so you don't spend time computing it yet. Consider a variant of our counter() function from a few sections ago. There, we wrote a function that returned a new value each time we called it, getting the value from its enclosing scope, but now we want one that gives us an infinite sequence, starting at a given index. A first attempt could be this:

```
def counter(i = 0):
    return i, counter(i + 1)
```

It returns its start count, followed by the count at the next position. It is what we want, but the first time we call it, it has to call itself, and then it has to call itself a second time, a third, and so on, forever. That clearly will not do. We try to evaluate the rest of the counts immediately, but we could instead delay that. We could write this function:

```
def counter(i = 0):
    def thunk():
        return counter(i + 1)
    return i, thunk
```

The thunk() inner function will evaluate the next counter when we call it, but when we define a function, we only define the code—we do not immediately call it. Of the pair that counter() returns, the first is the front of the current count, and the second is a function that we have to call to get the next value (and the thunk to continue from that point). We can use it in a pattern that looks like this:

```
i, next = counter()
i, next = next()
i, next = next()
```

When we evaluate expressions immediately as we encounter them, it is called *eager* evaluation. When we wrote counter(i + 1) in the first version, Python wants to evaluate the function call right away. Python always uses eager evaluation. Some other programming languages use *lazy* evaluation, where no expression is evaluated before we need it. To get lazy evaluation in Python, we must wrap expressions that we don't want to evaluate yet in thunks.

Delayed evaluation can be useful as function arguments. With eager evaluation, we have to evaluate all arguments before we can call a function, but the function might not need all its input. Depending on other arguments, it might only need the value of one or a few parameters.

Consider this example—we have some functions that potentially take a long time to run:

```
def f(i, j):
    # very long computation
    pass

def g(x):
    # also very long computation
    pass

def h(s, t, u, v):
    # maybe even longer computation
    pass
```

Somewhere in our code we have a function that compares two variables and returns one of three values, depending on whether the first variable is smaller than the second, they are equal, or the first is greater than the second:

```
def smaller_equal_greater(x, y, smaller, equal, greater):
    if x < y:
        return smaller
    if x == y:
        return equal
    if x > y:
        return greater
```

Now imagine that we want to execute this function call:

```
smaller_equal_greater(
    x, y,
    f(i, j),
    g(x),
    h(s, t, u, v)
)
```

This is not an unreasonable example—we could easily imagine that there is code like that—but to pick the right value of the three, we must evaluate all three functions. And they all take a long time to run, so we spend three times as long on the code as we strictly need.

We can delay the evaluation by providing the values to `smaller_equal_greater()` as thunks that we evaluate based on the comparison:

```python
def smaller_equal_greater(x, y, smaller, equal, greater):
    if x < y:
        return smaller()
    if x == y:
        return equal()
    if x > y:
        return greater()
```

Then we just need to wrap the function calls into thunks:

```python
def lazy(f, *args):
    def thunk():
        return f(*args)
    return thunk

smaller_equal_greater(
    x, y,
    lazy(f, i, j),
    lazy(g, x),
    lazy(h, s, t, u, v)
)
```

The `lazy()` function takes a function and its arguments, wrap the function call in a thunk, and returns the thunk. Using it, we don't have to write thunks for each of the three functions explicitly.

You don't often need lazy evaluation, so the default eager evaluation in Python suffices in almost all the code you will ever write. Still, when you do need to delay a computation, thunks are the way you achieve it. At the end of Chapter 8, you will see a construction that fundamentally relies on thunks.

Lambda Expressions

Python has a special keyword for creating simple closures called `lambda`. The name comes from the Greek letter and lambda calculus, a theoretical model for manipulating expressions and functions. You can create a closure with syntax such as this:

```
lambda x, y: f(x, y, z)
```

This creates a function that takes two arguments, x and y, and, when called, will evaluate f(x, y, z) in the current scope (where presumably it can find f and z). You put arguments for your closure between `lambda` and the colon, and to the right of the colon, you put the expression that the closure should evaluate.

Since lambda expressions can only have an expression to the right of the colon, they cannot do the same things as general functions can do. You can only evaluate an expression and not general code. They are typically used for cases where you want to wrap up a simple expression, and that is about all that they can do. They can be quite useful for arguments to higher-order functions, though.

You could use lambda expressions to create the thunks in the previous example in Python:

```
smaller_equal_greater(
    x, y,
    lambda: f(i, j),
    lambda: g(x),
    lambda: h(s, t, u, v)
)
```

The `lambda` expressions create small closures from the expression that follows the colon, which are the function calls we want to delay. We just wrap up the expression, as a thunk should, and we do not evaluate it yet. So, when we write `lambda: f(i,j)`, we get a function that will evaluate f(i,j) in the current closure when we call it. It is not *quite* the same as the thunks we made with the `lazy` function because we don't bind the parameters of f(i,j) to the current values of i and j, and if they change between when we create the thunk and when we evaluate it, `lazy` and `lambda` will behave differently. It won't happen in this code, however, because `smaller_equal_greater()` doesn't modify the current scope.

Decorators

If you have a function you have already defined and you want a curried version, then call `curry()` as we did in the preceding. If you're going to both define a function and then curry it, you would have to do this:

```
def mul2_add(x, y):
    return 2 * x + y
mul2_add = curry(mul2_add)
```

It is not that it requires a lot of typing to define a function this way, but it happens so often that Python has a special syntax for it, called *decorators*. If you put an `@curry` before the function definition

```
@curry
def mul2_add(x, y):
    return 2 * x + y
```

you get the same behavior. You get a function, `mul2_add()`, that is the curried version of the function you define below the `@curry` line.

This kind of function transformation is called a decorator because it is supposed to modify, decorate, its input function, giving you something that adds functionality to its input. Decorators don't have to, but they usually do.

Whenever you have a function, `decorator()`, and you want to define another function, `f()`, that you want to modify with `decorator()`

```
def decorator(f):
    def g():
        print("g")
        f()
    return g

def f():
    print("f")

f = decorator(f)
```

you can instead use

```
@decorator
def f():
    print("f")
```

It doesn't do *exactly* the same thing, but you will probably never notice. The difference between explicitly calling the decorator and using @decorator is that with @decorator you do not put the name of the first function into the namespace before assigning the modified function there. Compare this code

```
def decorator(f):
    def g():
        print("modified by first decorator")
        f()
    return g

@decorator
def decorator():
    print("second decorator")
```

with this:

```
def decorator(f):
    def g():
        print("modified by first decorator")
        f()
    return g

def decorator():
    print("second decorator")
decorator = decorator(decorator)
```

The first works and the second doesn't. In the second piece of code, we redefine decorator before calling it in the last line. In the last line, it is the *second* function we call, and that function doesn't take an argument. With the first code, we do not change what the decorator variable refers to before *after* we call decorator, so while the second function changes what decorator refers to, when we define it, the first is still in scope.

A decorator doesn't have to return a function, although it usually does. You can return any kind of object that you please, and in some cases returning other types of objects can be useful. Their input, however, has to be something you define using the def syntax. You cannot write

```
def f():
    print("f")
@decorator
f
```

The def function definition has to go after the decorator.

There is one slightly annoying issue with modifying a function via an inner function. The name the function will have is the name we give the inner function. If you decorate f

```
@decorator
def f():
    print("f")
```

and then ask for its name, which you can do with f.__name__, you get "g" because that is the name of the inner function in the decorator. This is very rarely something we worry about, but it is easy to fix, so our decorator should do this:

```
def decorator(f):
    def g():
        print("g")
        f()
    g.__name__ = f.__name__
    return g
```

You rarely care what a function thinks its name is, only the variable you use to refer to it, but you might as well set the new function's name in case someone, someday, will want to know.

Let's see another example of a decorator. This function wraps a function such that, whenever you call the function, it tells you that you called the function and it tells you when the function returned:

```
def logged(f):
    def inner(*args, **kwargs):
        print("calling", f.__name__)
        result = f(*args, **kwargs)
```

```
        print("returning from", f.__name__)
        return result
    inner.__name__ = f.__name__
    return inner
```

To use it, we use logged as a decorator:

```
@logged
def f(x, y):
    return x + y

print(f(2, 3))
```

The logged() function has to work on all functions, so the inner() function takes arguments and keyword arguments using the * and ** syntax and calls f() with *args and **kwargs. This way, whatever the function f() can handle, inner() can as well. It gets the name of f() from f.__name__. Assigning a function to other variables does not change the name of the function—it keeps it from when it was defined—so f.__name__ is its original name and not f, which is just the variable we use to reference it.

You can add arguments to decorators, but then it gets slightly more complicated. To add something like a verbose level, we might want a parameter to determine how much we need to log. You cannot do this

```
def logged(f, verbose_level = 0):
    def inner(*args, **kwargs):
        if verbose_level > 0:
            print("calling", f.__name__)
        result = f(*args, **kwargs)
        if verbose_level > 1:
            print("returning from", f.__name__)
        return result
    inner.__name__ = f.__name__
    return inner
```

and give logged() a keyword argument like this:

```
@logged(verbose_level = 2)
def f(x, y):
    return x + y
```

However, this is interpreted as this code:

```python
def f(x, y):
    return x + y
f = logged(verbose_level = 2)(f)
```

Python will take all the code after @ and call it with the following function as its argument. We wanted to call `logged(f, verbose_level = 2)`, but that isn't what we got.

Luckily, we can recognize something like `g()(f)` as a curried function, and we know how to write those. When you call `logged(verbose_level = 2)`, you need to return something we can call with f, so add another nested function:

```python
def logged(verbose_level = 0):
    def outer(f):
        def inner(*args, **kwargs):
            if verbose_level > 0:
                print("calling", f.__name__)
            result = f(*args, **kwargs)
            if verbose_level > 1:
                print("returning from", f.__name__)
            return result
        inner.__name__ = f.__name__
        return inner
    return outer

@logged(verbose_level = 1)
def f(x, y):
    return x + y
```

It looks a bit like it is something we should be able to handle with our `curry()` function because it is essentially currying, but that function wasn't general enough. It cannot handle default parameters or keyword parameters. You *could* do

```python
@curry # <- notice decorator
def logged(verbose_level, f):
    def inner(*args, **kwargs):
        if verbose_level > 0:
            print("calling", f.__name__)
```

```
        result = f(*args, **kwargs)
        if verbose_level > 1:
            print("returning from", f.__name__)
        return result
    inner.__name__ = f.__name__
    return inner

@logged(1)
def f(x, y):
    return x + y
```

but for something like the `logged` decorator, we probably want a default parameter and be able to specify what the argument means with a keyword argument. Writing a `curry()` function that can handle keyword arguments is dead on arrival. We can call functions with keyword arguments in any order, so it will not be clear at all what the function should do. Let us not go there. For decorators with arguments, write your own curried function.

Efficiency

One last thing I want to mention about inner functions relates to efficiency. From a code structure point of view, you might want to put functions that are only used inside another as an inner function. That way, you don't have to put the inner function in a scope where you don't use it. Do not do this if you can avoid it. Defining a function means that Python has to analyze it and create the function object. This can be slow. If you have a function that you call often, you don't want to create a new inner function each time. If you have an algorithm where you need to sort something and only need to sort inside that algorithm, it makes logical sense to put the sorting function inside the algorithm function. But don't do it. Your rule of thumb should be that you use inner functions when nested scopes are useful and make your code simpler and more elegant. Otherwise, avoid them.

CHAPTER 8

Recursion

In this chapter, we consider an immensely powerful technique for solving problems: *recursion*. Recursion involves recognizing that a problem really consists of the same kind of problem, just on a smaller scale. For example, to sort n elements, we can first find the smallest, then sort all the others, and put them after the smallest. This is, in its essence, what selection sort does; we just didn't explain it in these terms. When we do describe the algorithm like this, the recursive part is that we sort all but the smallest object as part of sorting all the items. To sort n elements, we need to sort $n - 1$. This is what recursion is.

Recursion is both a way to write functions and a way to design algorithms. When used to develop new algorithms, it is also called *divide and conquer*, and we return to this in Chapter 9. In this chapter, we will focus on recursive functions.

Definitions of Recursion

Recursion means defining something in terms of itself, and you have no doubt seen recursive definitions before, even if they were not called that. A classical example is the factorial of a number $n!$. The factorial is usually defined as this:

$$n! = \begin{cases} 1 & n = 1 \\ n \times (n-1)! & otherwise \end{cases}$$

The *Fibonacci* numbers can be defined as this:

$$F(n) = \begin{cases} 0 & n = 0 \\ 1 & n = 1 \\ F(n-1) + F(n-2) & \text{otherwise} \end{cases}$$

The pattern we see for these definitions is that we define the value for a number, n, as either a fixed constant or some expression that involves the function we are defining itself, applied to some smaller number. The cases where we can get a result immediately

207

© Thomas Mailund 2021
T. Mailund, *Introduction to Computational Thinking*, https://doi.org/10.1007/978-1-4842-7077-6_8

from the definition are called *base cases*. For factorials, the base case is $n = 1$ where we directly get the value 1. For Fibonacci numbers, the base cases are $n = 0$ and $n = 1$, where we get the value 0 or 1 right away. The other cases are called the *recursive cases*.

One way of defining natural numbers is also recursive. A number n is a natural number if it is zero or if $n - 1$ is a natural number.

For a recursive definition to be well defined, the recursive cases must bring us closer to base cases in a similar way to how termination functions in algorithms should ensure that we always move to termination in a finite number of steps. It is the same issue, just in a different disguise. We cannot take an arbitrary recursive function and an input and determine if the function will evaluate to a function or go infinitely deep in recursions, just as we cannot take a general program and its input and decide if it halts. They are two sides of the same coin. We must take some care in defining recursive functions to avoid this, just as we must take care to ensure that our algorithms terminate. In the case of recursions, we have a natural termination function—how far a function call is from a base case. If we can show that each recursive call brings us closer to a base case, then we are in the clear.

Because recursion is self-referential—it solves a smaller instance of the problem it is solving—a comic definition of recursion is this:

> Recursion, *see Recursion*.

The more useful definition of recursion is a definition where we have one or more base cases and one or more formulae that cover all other cases with references to the definition itself.

Strictly speaking, this would be a definition of *recursive definitions*, but it works equally well when we consider computational problems. We have a recursive algorithm when we have some base cases that we can handle directly and some rules for solving all other cases by resolving the same problem on smaller parts of the input.

Recursive Functions

We used recursion several times in Chapter 5 even though we never called it that. Consider the linear search algorithm. When we search through a list x, if we have reached the end of the list without finding the element we are searching for, we are done and can report that the object is not in the list. That would be a base case. Otherwise, we look at the first item in the list, and if that is the item that we are looking for, we are done and can report that we found it. That is another base case. Otherwise, we do a linear search in the remainder of the list. That is the recursive case.

We can make the recursive nature of linear search more explicit by defining a *recursive function*:

```
def linear_search(x, e, i = 0):
    if i == len(x):
        return False
    if e == x[i]:
        return True
    else:
        return linear_search(x, e, i + 1)
```

This does exactly what we described in the preceding. There are two base cases and one recursive case. For the function, the recursive case is handled by the function calling itself.

This version of linear search is, unmistakably, much more complicated than the one we had before, and I do not recommend that you use it instead of iterating through x. You should, however, be able to convince yourself that it does the same thing.

The only difference between a recursive definition and a recursive function in Python is that the former defines something, while the latter actually computes something. There is no other difference. For example, we can write a function for computing—as opposed to defining—the factorial of a number like this:

```
def factorial(n):
    if n == 1:
        return 1
    else:
        return n * factorial(n - 1)
```

Exercise: Implement a recursive function that computes the *n*th Fibonacci number.

Binary search is another example of a recursive algorithm. In this algorithm, we either have an empty interval to search in, in which case we can report False. Or we have the object we are searching for right in the middle of the range we need to explore, in which case we can report True. If all else fails, we have the recursive case: we continue our search in either the lower or the higher half of the range.

Again, we can be more explicit in defining this as a recursive computation by implementing it as a recursive function:

```
def bsearch(x, e, low = 0, high = None):
    if high == None:
        high = len(x)
    if low >= high:
        return False
    mid = (low + high) // 2
    if x[mid] == e:
        return True
    elif x[mid] < e:
        return bsearch(x, e, mid + 1, high)
    else:
        return bsearch(x, e, low, mid)
```

You should convince yourself that this, indeed, does the same as the binary search we have seen earlier.

If you recall, we required of recursive definitions that the recursive cases must move us closer to base cases and observed that this was related to termination. If each recursive call moves us closer to a base case—whatever that means—then the computation will eventually terminate. If not, then there is no such guarantee. You should think about recursive functions as more general termination functions and prove that they reach a base case for all input.

For binary search, the termination function is high - low. This works equally well for the iterative version we have seen earlier as it does for the recursive function defined in the preceding. We didn't use a termination function for our earlier implementation of linear search; we didn't need one because we know that a for loop over a finite sequence will terminate. For the recursive case, we cannot make as simple an argument, but of course, the situation is the same. In each recursive call, the index i gets closer to the end of x. So we can use as a termination function len(x)-i.

Some people find recursion a challenging concept, primarily when we use recursion for computation. Most people do not have any problem with accepting recursive definitions, but when we solve a problem by solving the exact same problem, it feels like a circular definition. "For recursion, see recursion." It isn't, however, and the reason is that we never solve a problem by trying to solve exactly the same problem. We solve a problem that is closer to a base case; our termination function decreases with every recursive function call.

If you still find recursive functions hard to wrap your mind around, you might take comfort in knowing that many early computer scientists did as well. Early programming languages could not define recursive functions. It just didn't occur to people that this might be useful. This doesn't mean that they didn't solve problems recursively; they just didn't use recursive functions, just like we did the linear and the binary search without recursive functions before we reformulated the algorithms as recursive. Recursion is such a powerful technique, however, that all modern languages support it. Some even go so far that they have replaced loops with recursion entirely; they will not let you implement loops at all, only recursive functions.

Recursion Stacks

To understand how recursive functions work, we first need to understand a little deeper how function calls work. Ignore for now that we can have nested scopes with inner functions. With closures, things get complicated, and early programming languages didn't have them. What I will explain in this section is how function calls are usually implemented when we don't handle closures.

Most languages with closures still use this technique but have to add additional mechanisms that will only complicate the explanation, which goes beyond this book.

Without inner functions, we have two different kinds of variables in Python, global and local variables. Global variables are those we assign to at the outermost level in a Python program, while local variables are either function parameters or variables we assign to inside a function. For example, in this program

```
x = 2
def add_one(x):
    return x + 1
add_one(2 * x)
```

we have two global variables, x and add_one. The x variable is one we have defined by assigning two to it. The add_one variable is the result of a function definition. Inside the add_one function, we have another variable named x; we have created it by making a function parameter. This variable is distinct from the global variable x; they have the same name but can refer to two different objects. Inside add_one, x is a local variable;

outside add_one, x is a global variable. When we call add_one(2 * x), we first look up what the variable add_one refers to and finds the function. Before we can call the function, we must evaluate the expression that will be its argument, that is, we must evaluate 2 * x. Since we call add_one at the outermost level, the global scope, x is the global variable. It refers to the value two, so 2 * x is 4. We then call add_one, and the parameter, which is the local variable x, will then refer to 4. This does not change the global variable; that variable still refers to 2. When we return x + 1, we use the local variable, which refers to 4, so we return 5.

You should be comfortable with the difference between global and local variables by now, but what happens when a function calls itself, as we did with the factorial function?

```
def factorial(n):
    if n == 1:
        return 1
    else:
        return n * factorial(n - 1)
```

When we call

```
factorial(4)
```

the local variable, n, will be set to refer to four. There is no problem there. But then we call factorial with n - 1 to evaluate n * factorial(n - 1). This makes the local variable refer to three, but we still need it to refer to four when, after the recursive call, we multiply the result of factorial(n - 1) by n. We need the local variable to refer to both four and three in the recursive case. How is that achieved?

This is something early programming languages often couldn't handle. In these early languages, local variables were tied to functions—each function had memory locations reserved for their local variables. Those were modified when calling a function and by updating variables inside the function body. If you called the same function twice, you would overwrite the memory locations assigned to the local variables. This isn't a problem if you do not use recursion, but it apparently is if you do. You cannot use the same memory location to hold both $n = 4$ and $n = 3$.

The solution to this problem is beautiful in its simplicity: instead of reserving fixed memory locations for local variables for each function, you reserve memory for the local variables in each function *call*. The memory locations you need for local variables are not hardwired in the program but will be allocated when you call a function. This memory is allocated on a so-called *call stack,* and it works as follows. You have a piece of your computer's memory set aside for this stack. You keep track of the top of the stack, and the function call you are currently executing has access to the top of the stack and any global variables, but not the rest of the stack. When you call a function, you reserve memory for the variables used in the function at the top of the stack. The memory set aside in this way is known as a function's *call frame,* but it isn't that important what we call it; what is essential is that we have it.[1]

Consider the call

```
factorial(4)
```

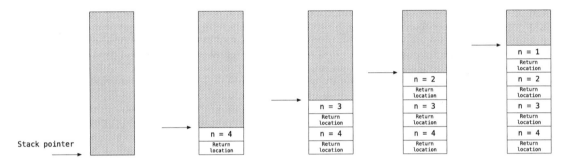

Figure 8-1. *Growing the call stack in recursive calls*

If we make this call at the outermost level, the call stack is empty. When we make the function call, Python puts two things on the call stack and increases the call stack pointer to point to the top of the stack. The function will know where to get to the local variables relative to the top of the stack. Not the direct memory addresses that hold them but where they can be found below the stack pointer. Knowing the absolute memory addresses is what early programming languages would do, and it fails if we need to have more instances of function calls at the same time. Knowing the offset below the stack pointer instead resolves this problem.

---

[1]The way Python handles global and local variables, and how it handles call frames, is a bit different from what I explain in the following. Python runs in a *virtual machine,* which is a program that understands Python better than the raw hardware does and that works as an intermediate between the two. The virtual machine runs as actual machine instructions on the CPU and Python runs on the virtual machine. My description of how calls work is almost correct, and all programming languages will do something similar to it, but the details can vary.

When we return from a function call, we also need to know where to return to. A function can be called from different places in your program, and we need some way of knowing where a function was called from, so we can return to that location in the program. We cannot use a fixed memory location to hold this information any more than we can use fixed locations for local variables, so we need to put this information on the stack as well.

When we call recursively, Python will put the information it needs for each function call—local variables and the return location—onto the stack and grow it as needed; see Figure 8-1.

When we reach $n = 1$, we hit a base case and immediately return one as the result. Now, Python needs to do two things. It needs to provide the return value of the function to its caller, and it needs to continue executing the program from the point where the function call was made. The caller location is found in the call stack, so we can always determine where the program needs to jump to. What about the return value, though?

We hadn't thought about where Python stores results of expressions before; we just assumed that it could remember them somehow. But of course, on a computer, you need to store intermediate results of expressions somewhere. Since results of (local) expressions are local to a function call, the only appropriate place is on the stack.[2]

When we return a value from a function, we need to put that value on the stack. We cannot make assumptions about where our function is called from, so we cannot use the caller's call frame. Instead, what is commonly done is to pop the current call frame off the stack, which means we decrease the stack pointer to where it was before the function call, and then put the result of the function call just one position above the new position of the stack pointer. To be able to do this, it needs to remember the return position if it overwrites that memory location, or it needs to allocate space on the stack for the return

---

[2]The way Python actually deals with local values and how it deals with the results of local expressions differ from the explanation I give here. Python does use a stack for this, it actually uses several, but that is beyond the scope of this chapter. We will see the real mechanism, although in a simple form, in Chapter 16. Programs that run on the raw hardware on your computer do not just use a stack. It is more efficient to put values in a CPU's registers than put them in memory, and that is what is usually done. Python has a layer between the raw hardware and your programs, the virtual machine. The virtual machine runs on the actual hardware, and it uses registers to hold temporary values and for passing values between functions. Your program, on the other hand, runs on the virtual machine, and this machine uses a different approach. If your Python programs actually ran on the real CPU, the description here wouldn't be far off of what would be happening with function calls.

value. Let us just assume that it can return and also put the function result value in its call frame.

Since we write the return value on the call frame of the function, we do not muck about in the caller's call frame, and the caller knows where to get the result. When we return from a recursion, we pop call frames from the stack, put the return values above the stack (overwriting the call frames), and keep doing this until we leave the recursion; see Figure 8-2.

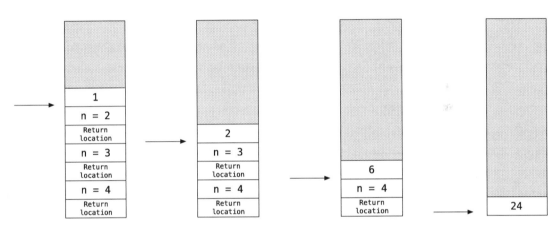

Figure 8-2. *Shrinking the call stack when returning from recursive calls*

If the calling function wants to remember the returned value, it needs to move it somewhere else before it can make further function calls. If it only calls a function for its side effects, it can ignore any value the called function might return, but if it needs to use the result, it must remember it. If it calls another function, the call frame of this function will be written on the stack, overwriting the returned value. We do not call other functions before we have used the result of the recursive call for factorial, but we do multiply a number with the result of a call. The simplest way to handle this is to save the result of the recursion and then handle the multiplication as we would handle any temporary result in an expression. With the factorial function, we can make the optimization where we use the returned value direction. We cannot always do this, however. For example, when computing Fibonacci numbers, we need to make two recursive calls and then add their returned values together. We need somewhere to store the result of the first recursive call, so we can add it to the result of the second call. In general, we might need to store the result of many function calls before we can use them in a local expression. Everything we need to save for later we need to move to a location in the current call frame before we call another function.

The call stack is not only used for recursion. It works the same way with all function calls. Consider this program:

```
def add_one(x):
    return x + 1

def add_two(x):
    return add_one(add_one(x))

add_two(1)
```

Figure 8-3 shows the call stack when evaluating this program. The call to add_two will put a return location and the local variable x on the stack. It also allocates space for the temporary value that it gets from the first call to add_one, so it can remember this for the second call. The add_two function then calls add_one. This call will put a return location and another x on the call stack. Once the call frame is set up, add_one will do its calculations, move the stack pointer down to where it was before the call—in effect popping the call frame from the stack—put the result of the function call just above the stack pointer, and then return to whence it was called.

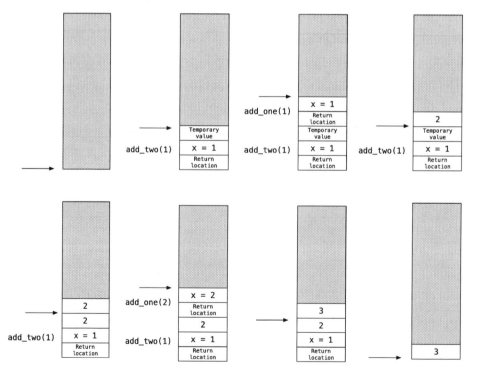

Figure 8-3. *Call stack when evaluating add_two(1)*

216

Now, the add_two function needs to call add_one once more. Since this call would overwrite the result of the first call, we need to save this value. We do this by moving the value from just above the stack pointer to the memory cell we allocated for this very purpose. We can then set up the call frame for the second call to add_one, make this call, and grab the result. This result is also the result of the add_two call, but we cannot simply use this result. We need to pop the call frame from the stack, which means we also need to move the add_one result down to where the caller of add_two expects to see it.

This example does not involve recursive calls, but the principle behind all function calls is the same. We might be able to optimize a specific combination of calls. For add_two we might manage to avoid moving the return value of the first call to add_one but simply putting it where it is needed for the second call; or we might be able to put the return value from the second call to add_one where it is needed when we return from add_two. Such optimization would only work for particular combinations of calls, however, while the operations we did in the example would work for all combinations of functions.

Exercise: Draw the call stack for computing the fourth Fibonacci number using the implementation you did in the previous exercise.

All this call stack business can look complicated, but the good news is that you never need to worry about it unless you implement recursion manually. The call stack is the reason why recursive function calls are possible, but you only need to know that Python can handle them.

Well, you *almost* never have to worry about the call stack. You might run into problems with a call stack if you fill it up. For example, what if you do something like this:

```
def f(x):
    return f(x + 1)
f(1)
```

This example results in an infinite recursion; the function doesn't even have a base case. You will not get an infinite recursion if you execute the code, however; instead, you will get an error that says "RecursionError: maximum recursion depth exceeded." This happens because the memory set aside for the call stack is limited and if the recursion gets too deep, there is no more stack available for more call frames.

For infinite recursions, we wouldn't expect something meaningful anyway, but there are many cases where there *is* a result of a recursion, but you do not have sufficient stack space. Linear and binary searches, if implemented recursively, could run into this problem if they are called on sufficiently many elements. We can alleviate the problem somewhat by telling Python that we want more stack space, using, for example

```
import sys
sys.setrecursionlimit(10_000)
```

to go from the default of one thousand calls to ten. But of course this doesn't solve the problem; it just pushes the limit a bit.

You will not run into this if you use iteration instead of recursion. It is certainly possible to write an infinite loop, but you will not run out of stack space as a result. Loops are also more efficient than recursive calls because the latter need to handle call frames, while the former do not. If you can implement an algorithm using iteration just as easily as you can do with recursion, you should always prefer the looping version. If you do need recursion, but the recursion is deeper than your call stack allows, you have no choice but to use a loop. There are general ways of handling recursion that avoid filling up the call stack (and we will return to this in Chapter 16), but for some recursive functions, it is particularly easy. These are *tail-recursive* functions. We get to those a little later in this chapter. First, though, we will consider the relationship between iteration and recursion in more detail in the next section.

However, to wrap up this section, let's just ask the question: "what about inner functions and scopes?" Obviously, if we use a stack frame to store local variables on and we remove the stack frame as soon as a function returns, we cannot refer to variables in enclosing scopes. No, that is true. As explained here, you cannot have closures with local variables sitting on the call stack. There are different solutions, but they all move some or all local variables off the stack when inner functions can refer to them. With few exceptions, though, languages that support closures still use a stack to manage function calls. You need the stack mechanism, or something like it, to handle function calls that move the point of execution elsewhere and return it again. You just cannot place local variables on a stack, if they should survive the lifetime of a function call. The details for how this issue is resolved vary between programming languages.

Recursion and Iteration

There is a close correspondence between recursion and iteration. You can always, directly, translate a loop into a recursive function; you cannot necessarily do the opposite. There are just more things you can easily do with a stack than you can with a loop. Obviously, you can implement the stack functionality yourself and then avoid recursive function calls, but this is just an implementation detail. Conceptually, you will still be using recursion and not a simple loop.

Just because you can implement all loops as recursive function calls doesn't mean that you should. Besides the problems with exceeding the stack limit, there is a substantial overhead in calling functions, so a recursive solution to a problem will always be slower than one that relies on loops. Programming languages that do not allow loops, but only recursive function calls, actually translate recursion into loops under the hood whenever possible. Python does not do such optimizations of recursive functions, so you should always prefer loops to recursions when you can. If you can solve a problem directly using loops, you should do that. Sometimes, however, it is easier first to derive a recursive solution to a problem and then translate it into a loop if possible. Divide and conquer algorithms (Chapter 9) are more naturally constructed in terms of recursion, but can still often be implemented using loops.

The purpose of this section is not to convince you that recursion is a better tool than iteration. If we can implement an algorithm using loops, then that is the better choice. When we cannot, then recursion is the only choice. We see examples of this when we discuss divide and conquer algorithms. The purpose of this section is to get you familiarized with the relationship between recursion and iteration. In the next section, we consider simple recursive functions that we can translate into loops. In this section, we will translate looping functions into recursive ones.

We will take a problem with an iterative solution and translate it into a recursive one. The result, I hope you will agree, is more straightforward than the iterative solution. This is why we usually prefer to develop an algorithm using recursion before we consider iteration. We do the translation in the opposite direction here. We start with loops, which you are already familiar, and show you how these loops can be simplified using recursion. The only reason for this is to get from something familiar, loops, and see how it relates to something new, recursion. As a side effect, I also hope to convince you that recursive solutions can be more straightforward than iterative ones.

The problem we will consider is that of merging two lists. This was an exercise in Chapter 4; if you haven't solved it already, give it a go before continuing.

The problem we need to solve is this: given two sorted lists, x and y, we want to create a list that contains the same elements as in x and y, combined, in sorted order.

The merge implementation from the previous chapter looked like this:

```python
def merge(x, y):
    result = []
    i, j = 0, 0
    while True:
        if i == len(x):
            # no more elements in x
            while j < len(y):
                result.append(y[j])
                j += 1
            return result
        if j == len(y):
            # no more elements in y
            while i < len(x):
                result.append(x[i])
                i += 1
            return result
        if x[i] < y[j]:
            result.append(x[i])
            i += 1
        else:
            result.append(y[j])
            j += 1
```

A much simpler implementation of the same idea is this:

```python
def merge(x, y):
    if len(x) == 0: return y
    if len(y) == 0: return x
```

```
        if x[0] < y[0]:
            return [x[0]] + merge(x[1:], y)
        else:
            return [y[0]] + merge(x, y[1:])
```

Here we can directly see the two base cases and the recursive case—the recursive case is one of two recursive calls, depending on which list has the smallest element. The most straightforward recursive solution is usually *much* simpler than an iterative solution. It is often also a lot less efficient, even if we ignore the function call overhead.

For reasons that I have not explained yet, slicing to get everything except the first element of a list, as we do when we call x[1:] and y[1:], is an expensive operation. It takes time proportional to the length of the lists (minus one). There is another implementation of lists than the one Python uses, linked lists that we will see in Chapter 13, where this would be a constant-time operation, but for Python list objects, it is not. Therefore, the recursive call takes time $O(n)$, where the lengths of x and y are in $O(n)$, plus how long it might take to compute the recursive function, and the result is an $O(n^2)$ running time all in all. I won't go into details about why we get this running time since we cover that in Chapter 9.

The iterative implementation runs in time $O(n)$—if you cannot see why immediately, try to work through the analysis. The recursive implementation runs in $O(n^2)$. This isn't a great advertisement for recursion. We generally do not want to trade efficiency for simplicity.

We can get rid of the expensive slicing of the first elements by reintroducing the index variables and get this implementation:

```
def merge(x, y, i = 0, j = 0):
    if i == len(x): return y[j:]
    if j == len(y): return x[i:]
    if x[i] < y[j]:
        return [x[i]] + merge(x, y, i + 1, j)
    else:
        return [y[j]] + merge(x, y, i, j + 1)
```

Unfortunately, this isn't much better. We avoid the slicing, but concatenating two lists, as we do in the recursive case, is also an $O(n)$ operation, so we end up with the same $O(n^2)$ running time.

To avoid both concatenation and slicing, we can do this:

```
def merge(x, y, i = 0, j = 0, result = None):
    result = result or []  # default empty list
    if i == len(x):
        # no more elements in x
        while j < len(y):
            result.append(y[j])
            j += 1
        return result
    if j == len(y):
        # no more elements in y
        while i < len(x):
            result.append(x[i])
            i += 1
        return result
    if x[i] < y[j]:
        result.append(x[i])
        return merge(x, y, i + 1, j, result)
    else:
        result.append(y[j])
        return merge(x, y, i, j + 1, result)
```

This leaves us pretty much back where we started. We now have a recursive solution to the problem, but it is just as complex as the iterative function we started with.

All is not lost, however. We can reconsider why we couldn't use the simpler recursive solutions. The main problem here was concatenation—we could avoid the slicing simply by using indices. Maybe we can avoid the concatenation in some other way? Indeed we can:

```
def merge_rec(x, y, i = 0, j = 0):
    if i == len(x): return y[j:]
    if j == len(y): return x[i:]
    if x[i] < y[j]:
        res = merge_rec(x, y, i + 1, j)
        res.append(x[i])
        return res
```

```
    else:
        res = merge_rec(x, y, i, j + 1)
        res.append(y[j])
        return res

def merge(x, y):
    return list(reversed(merge_rec(x, y)))
```

Since prepending one element to a list involves a concatenation operation, which is expensive, we replace it with an append operation, which is cheap. We construct the merged list in the reversed order, so we need to reverse it to get the right order once we are done with the merge. I have split this into two functions, one that recursively constructs the reversed result and one that reverses it to get the result in the right order. In the base cases, we still slice a list, but since this takes time proportional to the length of the list, it is not slower than the while loops we used earlier to do the same thing. In fact, it is likely to be faster since slicing is a built-in operation in Python and implemented very efficiently. The base cases, for example, would have been faster if we had used extend() on the result with sliced lists, instead of the loops we implemented explicitly.

Exercise: Implement the merge so you merge from the back instead of from the front. That way, you can extract and remove the last elements in constant time.

This solution is not quite as simple as the first recursive function, but we can make it almost so by moving the append operation to a function:

```
def app(lst, x):
    lst.append(x)
    return lst

def merge_rec(x, y, i = 0, j = 0):
    if i == len(x): return y[j:]
    if j == len(y): return x[i:]
    if x[i] < y[j]:
        return app(merge_rec(x, y, i + 1, j), x[i])
    else:
        return app(merge_rec(x, y, i, j + 1), y[j])
```

This solution is almost as simple as the first recursive function, and it runs in $O(n)$; we have replaced the expensive operations in the first recursive function with constant-time operations in this function. It is not as efficient as the iterative function. Function calls are constant-time operations but expensive ones, and we use those extensively here. We also need to reverse the result, which adds additional computations. The iterative solution avoids any function call beyond the call to the `merge` function and directly constructs the result list.

It is the simplicity of the recursive solution, compared to the iterative version, that makes it easier to construct recursive algorithms. Once we have a recursive solution, we usually then want to replace it with an iterative solution. In the next section, we will start with a recursive solution and use that to guide us to an iterative solution. Usually, we end up with an implementation very similar to what we would get if we set out to implement an iterative solution in the first place, but starting with a recursive solution and then modifying it, step by step, until we have an efficient iterative solution makes the programming task more manageable. As an added benefit, it also makes it easier to test our implementation; we can use the simplest solution to check the more complicated solutions against. As we, stepwise, transform a function to make it more efficient, we can test each rewrite. Since it is easier to get a simple solution correct and since it is easier to make incremental changes to a working implementation than it is to construct a function from scratch, implementing efficient solutions using this approach is a good strategy. Building an efficient function by a series of changes from a simple to an efficient one is more often than not the most effective way to get a fast and correct solution to a problem; aiming directly for a sophisticated, efficient solution is usually not a practical approach.

Before we get to translating recursive functions into iterative ones, however, you should do some exercises to test that you have understood recursion.

Exercise: To compute the sum of the elements in a list, we can obviously do this iteratively:

```
result = 0
for e in x:
  result += e
```

Implement a recursive function that computes the sum of the elements of a list.

Exercise: We can find the smallest element in a non-empty list, x, like this:

```
smallest = x[0]
for e in x:
    smallest = min(smallest, e)
```

Write a recursive function for finding the smallest element in a list. To avoid copying the list using slices, you will want to have the function take an index parameter as an argument.

Exercise: Modify your function, so it returns None if the list is empty. The easiest way to do this is probably to include the "smallest element seen so far" as a parameter to the function, with a default value of None. To compute the smallest value and still handle None, you can use this function:

```
def my_min(x, y):
    return y if x is None else min(x, y)
```

Exercise: Write a recursive function that reverses a list.

Exercise: Recall the exercise where you had to translate a base 10 number into some other base b (where we restricted the base to be less than 16). We can get the last digit of a number i, in base b, using this function

```
def get_last_digit(i, b):
    return digits[i % b]
```

where we defined the digits list as

```
digits = {}
```

```
for i in range(0,10):
    digits[i] = str(i)
```

```
digits[10] = 'A'
digits[11] = 'B'
digits[12] = 'C'
digits[13] = 'D'
digits[14] = 'E'
digits[15] = 'F'
```

We can then reduce the problem to the second-to-last digit by dividing i by b. Implement this idea using a recursive function.

Tail Calls

You can always translate an iterative algorithm into a recursive one, but since iterative algorithms are more efficient, you shouldn't do this. You are often interested in translating in the opposite direction, though. Recursive algorithms are often more straightforward to construct, so you will find yourself in the situation that you have an elegant recursive solution to a problem, and you want to translate it into a more efficient iterative solution. Translating a recursive function into an iterative one can always be done, but it can be trickier. This section is about how to do it for an especially easy class of functions.

Functions that are *tail recursive* can always be translated into loops. What characterizes a tail-recursive function is that the recursive case only consists of a recursive call, in the sense that the result from the recursive call is the return value of a recursive call, unchanged.

Consider the factorial function:

```python
def factorial(n):
    if n == 1:
        return 1
    else:
        return n * factorial(n - 1)
```

The recursive case involves a recursive call but not as the single result of the recursive case. We make a recursive call, and then we multiply the result with n. Because we have to multiply the result of the recursive call with n, the function is not tail recursive. We can translate it into a tail-recursive function by adding an accumulator to the function:

```python
def factorial(n, acc = 1):
    if n == 1:
        return acc
    else:
        return factorial(n - 1, n * acc)
```

Now, the result of the recursive case is the return value of another recursive call, unmodified. This makes the function tail recursive.

In many programming languages, tail-recursive functions are automatically translated into loops—this is called the *tail call optimization*—but Python is not one of them. Not to worry, though, the translation is so simple that you can always do it manually with minimal effort.

The accumulator handles the multiplication with n. We multiply the accumulator by n as we go down the recursion rather than multiply the result of the recursive call by n when we return from the recursion. Functions that only involve a single recursive call in the recursive case can always be translated into tail-recursive versions by adding an accumulator.

Exercise: Rewrite your recursive function for computing the sum of a list of numbers such that it becomes tail recursive.

Exercise: Rewrite your recursive function for finding the smallest element in a list to a version that is tail recursive.

With tail-recursive functions, we do not need to do anything with the result of the recursive call. Not doing anything with the result of a recursive call is just another way of saying that a function is tail recursive. The reason that this is important is that, when we do not need to do anything after the recursive call, then we can reuse the call frame for the recursive call. If we are not doing anything after the call, then we don't need any of the local variables after the call, and that means that we have no need for the call frame anymore, once we make the call. We can directly update the local variables to those we would use in the recursive call frame and go from there; we can replace a recursive call with a simple update of the function arguments or local variables.

When we call a function, we assign values to the function arguments. If we have a tail-recursive function, we can directly update the arguments we already have and then start executing the function body from the beginning again. We can wrap the function body in one big while True loop, and we can replace the recursive function call with an update to the function arguments and then continue the loop. If the recursive case is put at the end of the loop, we do not even need to continue; we are at the end of the loop, so we return to the beginning right after we update the variables.

For the factorial function, this transformation gives us

```python
def factorial(n):
    acc = 1
    while True:
        if n == 1:
            return acc
        n, acc = n - 1, n * acc
```

If you split the variable updates over multiple statements, you have to be careful about the order. When you update a variable, you affect expressions that depend on it. So you have to update the variables in the right order.

This will work:

```
def factorial(n):
    acc = 1
    while True:
        if n == 1:
            return acc
        acc = n * acc
        n = n - 1
```

This will not:

```
def factorial(n):
    acc = 1
    while True:
        if n == 1:
            return acc
        n = n - 1
        acc = n * acc
```

A parallel assignment, as we did for the first iterative implementation of the factorial function, will usually work. If we never do any operations with side effects, that is, whenever we need to update a data structure such as a list, we create a new one instead, then parallel assignment will work. If we actually modify a data structure, we cannot use parallel assignment, so we must be careful that we perform the update operations in the same order as they would have been performed in a function call.

Exercise: Do this transformation for your tail-recursive summation function.

Exercise: Do this transformation for your tail-recursive "find minimum" function.

Exercise: Consider our recursive implementation of binary search:

```
def bsearch(x, e, low = 0, high = len(x)):
    if low >= high:
        return False
    mid = (low + high) // 2
    if x[mid] == e:
```

```
        return True
    elif x[mid] < e:
        return bsearch(x, e, mid + 1, high)
    else:
        return bsearch(x, e, low, mid)
```

This function is tail recursive, so use the transformation to replace it with a loop. Compare it to the iterative solution we considered before this chapter.

To see a more complex case of using an accumulator in a tail-recursive function and then translate it into an iterative function, we can return to the problem of merging two lists. We left this problem with this recursive implementation:

```
def app(lst, x):
    lst.append(x)
    return lst

def merge_rec(x, y, i = 0, j = 0):
    if i == len(x): return y[j:]
    if j == len(y): return x[i:]
    if x[i] < y[j]:
        return app(merge_rec(x, y, i + 1, j), x[i])
    else:
        return app(merge_rec(x, y, i, j + 1), y[j])

def merge(x, y):
    return list(reversed(merge_rec(x, y)))
```

The reason we had to construct the merged list backward and then reverse it when we were done was because we didn't use an accumulator. If we add an accumulator, we can build the merged list in the right order:

```
def merge(x, y, i = 0, j = 0, acc = None):
    if acc is None: acc = []
    if i == len(x): return acc + y[j:]
    if j == len(y): return acc + x[i:]
    if x[i] < y[j]:
        return merge(x, y, i + 1, j, app(acc, x[i]))
    else:
        return merge(x, y, i, j + 1, app(acc, y[j]))
```

The way we handle the default value of the accumulator might look a bit weird, but it is crucial. If we set the default value of acc to an empty list, each call to merge that relies on the default parameter will get the *same* list. This means that if you call merge twice, the result of the first call will still be in the accumulator, and the new merge will be appended to it. This is not what we want, and it is because of this that we handle the default parameter the way we do.[3]

This function is tail recursive, so we can translate it into a looping version. The app function appends its second argument to its first, and it does this before the recursive call (because function arguments are evaluated before a function is called). Because of this, we can get rid of it and simply append instead. We have to be careful to append before we update the indices, though. The rewritten function looks like this:

```
def merge(x, y, i = 0, j = 0, acc = None):
    if acc is None:
        acc = []
    while True:
        if i == len(x): return acc + y[j:]
        if j == len(y): return acc + x[i:]
        if x[i] < y[j]:
            acc.append(x[i])
            i += 1
        else:
            acc.append(y[j])
            j += 1
```

If you want to avoid copying the accumulator in the base cases, you can use the extend method on the accumulator list. Using extend and a slice on one of the input lists is unlikely to be slower than a while loop where we move individual elements, since extend and slice are built-in operations and therefore highly optimized:

---

[3]A slightly more *Pythonic* way of writing the if statement would be to use the or operator instead. You could write ac = acc or []. Because or will return the second argument if the first is False and because None is interpreted as False in this context, you will get [] when acc is None. You will also get a new empty list if acc is an empty list because empty lists are also interpreted as False. We never recurse on an empty list, so that is not a problem.

```
def merge(x, y, i = 0, j = 0, acc = None):
    if acc is None:
        acc = []
    while True:
        if i == len(x):
            acc.extend(y[j:])
            return acc
        if j == len(y):
            acc.extend(x[i:])
            return acc
        if x[i] < y[j]:
            acc.append(x[i])
            i += 1
        else:
            acc.append(y[j])
            j += 1
```

If in the first iterative solution we used the extend method as well, we would have this solution. So we end up back where we started. Hopefully, we have learned something along the way.

Continuations

A final thing I want to show you is something you shouldn't actually use in Python because it is inefficient there. Python doesn't implement tail call optimizations, so the trick I will show you will involve calls that will fill your stack, and it will always be slower than an iterative solution. So don't use what I am about to show you directly in your Python code. In functional programming languages, where you don't have loops but only function calls, you can use the trick. I will show it to you here because it is a neat idea; it combines inner functions with recursion, it gives you a completely different way of looking at returning from functions, and it will blow your mind once you understand it. You can safely skip it, though, since I won't use it anywhere in the book. The idea is called *continuation-passing style* programming.

We will start by considering a function you will agree is elementary:

```
def fib(n):
    if n == 0 or n == 1:
        return 1
    else:
        return fib(n-1) + fib(n-2)
```

It is recursive, but it is not what I want to focus on right now. Rather, I will focus on what happens when we get in the else part of the function. There, we make two function calls and add the result of them. It looks like a single expression, of course, but we could rewrite the function to look like this:

```
def fib(n):
    if n == 0 or n == 1:
        return 1
    else:
        x = fib(n-1)
        y = fib(n-2)
        return x + y
```

We talked about how call stacks need to remember the code position to jump to when we return from a function, and we have two such points in fib():

```
def fib(n):
    if n == 0 or n == 1:
        return 1
    else:
        x = fib(n-1)
1>
        y = fib(n-2)
2>
        return x + y
```

When we return from the first (recursive) call, we go to position 1, then take the next statement in fib(), and call recursively again, and when we return from the second call, we go to position 2, and from there we execute the remaining part of the function.

You knew all that, of course, but now I will imagine a world where we don't have the return locations on our stack. If we want a function call to return to a specific code segment, we must explicitly tell it what code we want to be executed when the call is done. This means that we need one function for handling the first lines in fib(), then we need a function that handles when the first recursive call is done and calls the second recursion, and, finally, we need a function that handles the addition when both calls are done. The following code does this:

```
def fib(n, return_point):
    if n == 0 or n == 1:
        return_point(1)
    else:
        new_return_point = return_point_1(n, return_point)
        fib(n - 1, new_return_point)

def return_point_1(n, return_point):
    def code(x):
        new_return_point = return_point_2(x, return_point)
        fib(n - 2, new_return_point)
    return code

def return_point_2(x, return_point):
def code(y):
    return_point(x + y)
return code
```

The return_point_2() function handles the last part of the recursive fib() function. Think of it as encapsulating what we know just before the second recursive call, which would result from the first recursive call, x, and the point we should return to when we finish the calculation in fib(). It encapsulates this in a closure, the inner function code(), that we will pass along to the second recursive call. When the second recursive call "returns," it should call this code() function, providing it with the result of the second recursion, y. Once code() has that, it knows x and y and where the fib() function should return to, return_point(), so it returns by calling return_point(x + y). So, for the second recursive call to return, it must call the code() closure, and this closure will then combine the results of the two recursive calls and return from fib() by calling the closure's remembered return point.

Phrased in a slightly different way: the inner function code() handles "return x + y" in the original fib(), but the "return" keyword is replaced by a call to the return_point() function. It knows x from its closure, but it needs to get y from the second recursive call. It is the responsibility of the second recursive call to call code() with y.

The return_point_1() function handles the code between the two recursive calls. Again we have an inner and an outer function to capture that we know the n variable and the return_point function, and, again, the magic happens in the inner function. We call this inner function when the first recursion is done. That recursion will call the function with the result of the recursion, x. We need to call the second recursion, and that means that we need to tell that call where to return to. It should return to return_point_2(), so we create a version of this point that remembers x and return_point. It is this new return point function we give to the recursive call. When the recursion is done, the code jumps to the new return point we created, the code in return_point_2(). We don't lose the return point that *we* are supposed to return to because the second return point will call it.

Finally, in fib() we handle the base cases first. We don't return 1 when n is zero or one because we no longer return from functions. We call functions instead. So we call the return_point(), which is our new way of returning a value.

If we enter the recursive case, we create a new return point for the recursive call. When all the computation is done, we want to return to the point where fib() was called, so we give return_point to return_point_1(). As you remember, that function creates another return point function, and when we run the code, we make return point functions all the way down the recursion. Eventually, the return point will be called by the code in return_point_2(), and all the return point functions will be evaluated.

If we want to print the nth Fibonacci number (which is what we are computing), we can give the function a "return" point for that:

```
def outmost_return_point(x):
    print(x)
fib(n, outmost_return_point)
```

We usually don't throw return out the window just because we program in this way, so we could still write a function that returns a Fibonacci number. So we can still use return at the outermost level of the recursive function; we use the "return point functions" internally in the recursion only.

The nested functions in the example were only there to capture variables we needed to know in the return_point functions, and usually, it is easier to put the functions in the outer function to get the scope from there. We can rewrite the code like this:

```
def identity(x): return x
def fib(n, return_point = identity):
    if n == 0 or n == 1:
        return return_point(1)
    else:
        def first_point(x):
            def second_point(y):
                return return_point(x + y)
            return fib(n - 2, second_point)

        return fib(n - 1, first_point)
```

The return points are not really points in the code but rather the extra code we need to run after a function call and until the next call. There isn't any code to run after the outermost call to fib(), so we use an identity function that does not do further processing.

You should definitely think of these return_point functions as returning from a function, just not as a simple return statement; they combine returning a value with the code you want to run after the return.

You should also think of them as responsible for everything that happens when you return from a recursive call. In all recursive functions, we do some work before we call recursively, then handle the recursive calls, and then do some work after the calls.

We try to avoid doing extra computations after recursive calls when we can, since then, we can optimize tail calls. However, you can't always remove the work you need to do after a call, though. *Continuations*, which are what such return_point functions are called, make this post-recursion processing explicit but wrapping it in separate functions.

Looking at an even simpler example, the relationship between computing when we return from a recursion and computing when we call a continuation might be clearer. In the following, I have listed three different recursive functions for computing the sum of a list (very inefficient, but that is not the point right now):

```
def sum(x):
    if x == []:
        return 0
```

```
        else:
            return x[0] + sum(x[1:])

def sum_acc(x, acc = 0):
    if x == []:
        return acc
    else:
        return sum_acc(x[1:], acc + x[0])

def sum_cont(x, cont = identity):
    if x == []:
        return cont(0)
    else:
        def new_cont(y):
            return cont(x[0] + y)
        return sum_cont(x[1:], new_cont)
```

The first is the simplest solution. We take the first element of the list, compute the sum of the rest of the list, and then add the two. Going down the recursion, we split the list in the first and the rest of the elements, and returning from recursive calls, we add them together and propagate the sum up the recursion.

The second solution uses an accumulator, and here we do all the work going down the recursion—we split the list, *and* we add the numbers. If Python implemented tail call optimization, we wouldn't even return along a recursion stack because nothing is left to be done when we reach the function's base case.

The third solution uses a continuation and falls between the two. It only has a tail call and could be optimized if we so desired, but it doesn't do the work going down the recursion stack. It collects all the work it has to do in the continuation. At each level, a continuation will get a sum of the rest of the list as its input, add one element to it, and call the next continuation to continue the calculation. The continuations also have tail calls, though, and those could be optimized to an iteration as well if Python would bother to do it (but it is not as simple to do manually as it is to rewrite tail-recursive functions).

Exercise: Work your way through what happens when you call sum_cont() on a list. Capture which continuations are in play and which other continuations they wrap, and work out what happens when we reach the base case of the recursion.

Of the three solutions, sum_acc() is the fastest. If we ignore that slicing the list the way we do is an expensive operation, if we had tail call optimization, then the function would be as fast as a for loop. If we can implement a function using an accumulator, it will always be the best choice.

To reiterate, when we implement a Python function, there are points in the code where we should return to after a function call to continue executing the code. In the simple sum() function, slightly rewritten, it is after the recursive call:

```
def sum(x):
    if x == []:
        return 0
    else:
        y = sum(x[1:])
>
        return x[0] + y
```

If we want to implement function calls ourselves, we cannot easily handle these return points. We can't tell Python where it should continue the execution after a function call. What we can do is wrap up the code we want to be executed, here return x[0] + y, after the call. That is what we do with a continuation. We take the code between function calls (here there is only one chunk of code; with fib(), there were two) and put it in separate functions, and when we call a function, we tell it to call the function we give it, with the value it would otherwise return. When this continuation function is called, it executes the code up to the next function call, where it does the same thing again: wrap up the next chunk of code to execute after the call as a continuation function. So with sum(), the continuation needs to execute x[0] + y (where y is the return value from the sum(x[1:]) call and therefore will be the input to the continuation). It shouldn't return x[0] + y directly because there might be more code to run after the function call—the code we would execute when we return through several levels of the recursion—so instead, it must call the continuation. That is why we get the following version:

```
def sum_cont(x, cont = identity):
    if x == []:
        return cont(0)
```

```
    else:
        def new_cont(y):
            return cont(x[0] + y)
        return sum_cont(x[1:], new_cont)
```

The reason the translation for fib() is less straightforward is that we need to capture more than one return value in the second continuation. The return points are these

```
def fib(n):
    if n == 0 or n == 1:
        return 1
    else:
        x = fib(n-1)
1>
        y = fib(n-2)
2>
        return x + y
```

The first continuation should get x, the return value of the first call, and then execute the next statement, which is the fib(n - 2) call. So it should look like this:

```
def cont1(x):
    return fib(n - 2, cont2)
```

The second continuation should get the return value from fib(n - 2), y, and return x + y (and by return we mean call the continuation fib() got, cont). So it should look like this:

```
def cont2(y):
    return cont(x + y)
```

The problem with these two functions is that they don't know all the variables they need. In the normal code, the fib() function instance knows n, x, and y, but if we never return from a function and just call continuations, we can't assign to x and y like this. We can assign to a variable and then call the continuation, but the continuation cannot see the calling function variables.

If we put cont1() as an inner function in fib(), it will know n, and it will be called with x. The second continuation, if we define it in fib(), won't know x because it will only be cont1() that has it. It will know y, since the recursive call will give it y, but it won't know x. By nesting the two functions, so cont2() is defined inside cont1(), cont2() will have access to x from its enclosing scope. That is why we usually write nested continuations, although it can be harder to follow the code that way—at least until you get used to it.

The first version we wrote, here with renamed continuations, didn't have nested continuations but captured the scope of variables by generating the continuations in nested functions:

```
def first_recursive_cont(n, cont):
    def code(x):
        # x = fib(n - 1)
        return fib(n - 2, second_recursive_cont(x, cont))
    return code

def second_recursive_cont(x, cont):
    def code(y):
        # y = fib(n - 2)
        return cont(x + y)
    return code

def fib(n, cont = identity):
    if n == 0 or n == 1:
        return cont(1)
    else:
        return fib(n - 1, first_recursive_cont(n, cont))
```

The code does the same thing as the nested functions, and if you find it easier to read, this is a perfectly valid way to write continuations and continuation-passing style functions.

Continuations can appear as little more than a curiosity, as a different way of thinking about returning from functions, but otherwise not of much interest. However, if you have tail call optimization, they provide a way to *always* make tail call functions. We cannot translate the recursive fib() function into one that uses an accumulator because we need more than one recursive call. We could implement the tail call optimization for one but not both recursive calls. But as we just saw, if we add continuations to our repertoire, we can wrap all but the first call in a sequence of continuations.

Don't try to implement the tail call optimization from the previous section and combine it with continuations. First, the inner functions won't be independent between recursive "calls" because they sit in a loop and share the same scope. You could still fix that by explicitly wrapping the values you need to know in separate closures (as we did in our first implementation of fib()). That is fixable. The main problem is that you might be able to optimize the computation going *down* the recursion. Still, once you hit the base case, you have to evaluate all the continuations in turn, and you don't have a simple loop optimization of these. It is doable, of course, but it is more work than you might think.

But there is a way to get rid of the call stack if all your functions are tail calls, and that is by applying a so-called "trampoline."

Continuations, Thunks, and Trampolines

Our problem with the tail call optimization and continuations is that, even if we optimize the tail calls in the direct recursive calls, the continuations call each other, so we get a call stack as deep as we would get with the original recursions. Implementing a tail call optimization for functions we create on the fly is not trivial, not from inside the language itself anyway, so that is not the way to go. We need some way of using continuations that don't actually call each other. Not right away, in any case. We want them to remember what they should compute—just not compute it until we get to them—and they shouldn't call the next continuation until we are ready for that either.

We have the perfect tool for this already: *thunks*—functions that take no arguments, wrap a computation, and return the result when we call them (and obviously not before). We met them in Chapter 7 as a form of lazy or delayed evaluation, and that is exactly what we want now.

Consider the factorial() function

```
def factorial(n):
    if n <= 1:
        return 1
    else:
        x = factorial(n - 1)
        return n * x
```

and its continuation variant:

```
def factorial(n, cont = identity):
    if n <= 1:
        return cont(1)
    else:
        def new_cont(x):
            return cont(n * x)
        return factorial(n - 1, new_cont)
```

We will do this: we wrap each recursive call and each continuation call in a thunk. That means that every time we call a function, we do not make any additional calls; we get a thunk back that will execute the code up to the next function call, but not until we explicitly tell it to. And that thunk will give us a new function that we can call to take the next step and so on. The initial continuation shouldn't return a thunk, though. When we start the computation, we want a continuation that will give us a final value, but every single application of a continuation inside the function is wrapped in a thunk.

You can apply this idea brute-force by wrapping every function application after a return statement in a thunk, and for the factorial() function, it would look like this:

```
def identity(x):
    return x

def thunk(f, *args):
    def delayed():
        return f(*args)
    return delayed

def factorial_rec(n, cont = identity):
    if n <= 1:
        return thunk(cont, 1)
    else:
        def new_cont(x):
            return thunk(cont, n * x)
        return thunk(factorial_rec, n - 1, new_cont)
```

I renamed it factorial_rec() because I want to reserve the name factorial() for what comes next. The thunk in the base case doesn't give us anything—if cont() returns a thunk, we get a thunk, and if it returns a value, we get a value. Still, as we are not creating a new continuation, we are not in danger of creating multiple function calls if we just call cont() direction. You can put a thunk there or not; it doesn't matter for the result—you will just need one more application of a function if you include the thunk. I prefer not to:

```
def factorial_rec(n, cont = identity):
    if n <= 1:
        return cont(1)
    else:
        def new_cont(x):
            return thunk(cont, n * x)
        return thunk(factorial_rec, n - 1, new_cont)
```

Try to call factorial_rec() with 1. You will get 1 back because we enter the base case where cont() is identity(), so we get 1 back:

```
print(factorial_rec(1))        # cont(1)
```

If you call factorial_rec(2), you get the thunk wrapping factorial_rec(n - 1) back, and you need to apply it to make the actual factorial_rec() function call. When you do, you get an instance of new_cont() back because that is what the recursive call produces. You need to call that thunk before you get the final result:

```
print(factorial_rec(2))        # thunk(factorial_rec, ...)
print(factorial_rec(2)())      # thunk(cont, n * x)
print(factorial_rec(2)()())    # cont(1)
```

With factorial_rec(3) you need to go further down the recursion, for n equal to 2 and 1. Then you will call the continuation, which is a new_cont() instance. From that point, you are conceptually returning from the call stack by applying one continuation thunk after another until you get to the identity() function, and you get the final result.

```
print(factorial_rec(3))            # thunk(facto..., 2, ...)
print(factorial_rec(3)())          # thunk(facto..., 1, ...)
print(factorial_rec(3)()())        # new_cont() n = 1
print(factorial_rec(3)()()())      # new_cont() n = 2
print(factorial_rec(3)()()()())    # identity()
```

We don't call functions (except for thunk()) anywhere in the recursive function or the generated continuations, but we need to apply the result of a call to factorial_rec() a number of times until we get something that isn't a thunk. We can do that in a loop of repeated thunk calls:

```
def trampoline(f):
    while callable(f):
        f = f()
    return f

def factorial(n):
    return trampoline(factorial_rec(n))
```

This function is called trampoline(). The mental image is that thunks jump down on a trampoline. We apply one thunk, so it bounces up and comes down as another thunk, and thunks keep bouncing up and down until we are done. Don't blame me for the metaphor; I didn't invent it.

The function callable() is part of Python and determines if an object is something we can call, like a function. The trampoline() function keeps calling f as long as it is callable, and when it is not, it will return the value it holds.

This implementation cannot handle if the value you are computing is a function (or any callable object). We keep applying the function while it is callable, so we assume that whatever we are computing will always return a thunk if more work is to be done and something not callable when we are done. If you need a trampoline for a function that returns a callable value, you have to be more inventive. There are ways around this limitation, but I have never seen an application for a trampoline that creates a callable object, so I won't go through solutions to that.

Transforming the slightly more complicated fib() function into a trampolined version is just as mechanical as trampolining factorial(). You do the same thing with *every* continuation-passing style function to translate it into a trampolined version. This is the continuation version of the function:

```
def fib(n, cont = identity):
    if n == 0 or n == 1:
        return cont(1)
```

```
    else:
        def first_recursive_cont(x):
            def second_recursive_cont(y):
                return cont(x + y)
            return fib(n - 2, second_recursive_cont)
        return fib(n - 1, first_recursive_cont)
```

This is the trampolined version:

```
def fib_rec(n, cont = identity):
    if n == 0 or n == 1:
        return cont(1)
    else:
        def first_recursive_cont(x):
            def second_recursive_cont(y):
                return thunk(cont, x + y)
            return thunk(fib_rec, n - 2, second_recursive_cont)
        return thunk(fib_rec, n - 1, first_recursive_cont)
```

Once again, you can experiment with the thunks it gives you as you apply it a number of times:

```
print(fib_rec(2))         # thunk(fib_rec, n - 1, ...)
print(fib_rec(2)())       # thunk(fib_rec, n - 2, ...)
print(fib_rec(2)()())     # cont(1), cont = thunk(cont, x + y)
print(fib_rec(2)()()())   # x + y
```

Getting the fib() function we want, we use the trampoline() function:

```
def fib(n):
    return trampoline(fib_rec(n))
```

With continuations and either tail call optimizations or trampolines, we can get away with the call stack completely. But there is no free lunch. We didn't reduce the memory usage of function calls to a constant. The thunks that we create hold the same information as was previously on the stack; now, we have just moved the memory usage elsewhere. The call stack is usually more limited than the memory you have available for objects and functions, though, so the transformation is still useful.

If you explicitly create trampolined functions, you should first consider if they are really necessary. They are not hard to write; it is a mechanical transformation once you have transformed the function into one that uses continuations, but they are relatively slow. There is some overhead in creating thunks because Python analyzes and creates the functions each time you define one, which is not a fast operation. If you can translate your algorithm into one that you can directly implement as an iterative solution, that should always be your first choice. If you need recursion—or if it is simply much easier to implement than the iterative algorithm—try the direct approach first. You might not run into stack issues at all, and then there is no reason to write more complicated code to avoid it—you should always wait with solving a problem until it exists. If you really need recursion and stack overflow is an issue, trampolines can be the way to go. The solution is simple (once you understand it), and you can use it in every application you run into.

CHAPTER 9

Divide and Conquer and Dynamic Programming

Divide and conquer is the algorithmic version of recursion. The term comes from the political doctrine *divide et impera*, but for algorithms, a more correct description would be *divide and combine*. The key idea is to

1. Split a problem into subproblems of the same type.

2. Recursively solve these problems.

3. Combine the results of the recursive calls to a solution of the original problem.

Steps 1 and 3 can be trivial or complex, while step 2 is usually one or two recursive calls.

The binary search algorithm that we have seen several times by now is an example of a divide and conquer algorithm. Step 1 in the algorithm is identifying whether we should search to the left or to the right of the midpoint. The recursive step (step 2) is searching in one of these intervals. Step 3 is almost non-existing since we just return the result of the recursive solution.

The recursive steps in divide and conquer algorithms are often implemented as recursive function calls, but need not be. Conceptually, we recurse, but as we saw in binary search, we can replace recursive calls with loops. It is not necessary to use recursion in your implementation of a divide and conquer algorithm; the defining component of this class of algorithms is that we solve a subproblem of the same type as the original problem. Since we are using recursion, even if it is only conceptually, we need to have base cases and recursive cases. The base case in binary search is when we have an empty interval or when the midpoint is the element we are looking for. The recursive case handles everything else.

© Thomas Mailund 2021
T. Mailund, *Introduction to Computational Thinking*, https://doi.org/10.1007/978-1-4842-7077-6_9

Merge Sort

As another example of divide and conquer, we can consider a sorting algorithm known as *merge sort*. This algorithm works as follows:

1. Split the initial input into two pieces of half the size of the original problem: the first and the second half of the input list.

2. Sort these two smaller lists recursively.

3. Combine the two sorted lists using merge.

The algorithm involves two recursive subproblems, so it is not easy to implement it as an iterative solution. We will, therefore, deal with it recursively. The base cases for the recursion are when we have empty lists or lists of length one—these will be lists that are already sorted. The recursive case handles everything else.

A straightforward implementation of this could look as follows:

```
def merge_sort(x):
    if len(x) <= 1: return x
    mid = len(x) // 2
    return merge(merge_sort(x[:mid]), merge_sort(x[mid:]))
```

The function performs what we identified as the three steps of merge sort in the most straightforward manner, but you might be uncomfortable with the slicing we do to split the input x. For merge, as we saw in the previous chapter, using this form of slicing increased the running time from $O(n)$ to $O(n^2)$. It is not quite as bad in this algorithm since the linear-time slice operation is faster than the time it takes to sort the sublists—we discuss the running time shortly, but it will be $O(n \log n)$. Still, we could avoid it by using indices into x instead:

```
def merge_sort_rec(x, low, high):
    if high - low <= 1: return x[low:high]
    mid = (low + high) // 2
    return merge(merge_sort_rec(x, low, mid),
                merge_sort_rec(x, mid, high))

def merge_sort(x):
    return merge_sort_rec(x, 0, len(x))
```

I have implemented this using two separate functions, one that handles the actual sorting but takes indices as arguments and one that only takes x as its argument and calls the former. We cannot set low and high as default arguments, since high should be set to the length of x, and we do not know what x is until we call the function (recall that the default arguments of a function must be known when we *define* the function, not when we call it). We could use the trick of setting them to None and then checking if they are that, as we did merge, but then we would need to check the arguments in each recursive call. This wasn't a problem when we translated merge into an iterative algorithm, but we cannot do this with merge_sort since it is not tail recursive. Therefore, I prefer to split the algorithm into two functions.

Quick Sort

Consider another famous divide and conquer sorting algorithm: *quick sort*. This algorithm picks one of the elements in its input, called the *pivot*, and then it splits the data into three sets, those elements that are less than the pivot, those that are equal to the pivot, and those elements that are greater than the pivot. Naturally, the first set should go before the middle that should go before the last set in a sorted sequence, so if we sort the first set separately from the last set and then concatenate all three of them, then we have a sorted sequence.

The description is longer than a simple implementation:

```
def qsort(xs):
    if len(xs) < 2: return xs
    p = pick_pivot(xs)

    first = qsort_lc([x for x in xs if x < p])
    middle = [x for x in xs if x == p]
    last = qsort_lc([x for x in xs if x > p])
    return first + middle + last
```

Quick sort is called quick because picking the pivot and partitioning the data can be done, well, quickly. The preceding list comprehension version does follow the spirit of quick sort, but creating new lists and filtering them is not fast. And we haven't gotten to how to pick the pivot. For the latter, I will just pick the first element in the sequence we are to sort. This has some consequences for the expected running time, but we return to that in the next section.

We will not split the sequence into three sets but two. It is slightly harder to split it into those less than the pivot, those equal to the pivot, and those greater than the pivot, compared to splitting into less than or equal to the pivot and greater than the pivot, with the approach we take.

You have to be careful when you do as I just described. You could end up with an infinite recursion, if one of the two parts you create equals the original input.

Exercise: Show how this function could end up recursing forever:

```
def qsort(xs):
    if len(xs) < 2: return x
    p = pick_pivot(xs)
    return qsort([x for x in xs if x <= p]) +
           qsort([x for x in xs if x > p])
```

To avoid infinite recursion, we must make sure that at least one element is left out of the recursion in each step. We handle that by removing *one* element equal to the pivot instead of all of them.

We will use a function that satisfies this invariant:

```
def partition(x, i, j):
    """

    Let pivot = x[i]. This function will
    arrange x[i:j] into x'[i:k] + x'[k:j] such that
    x'[h] <= pivot for h = i ... k and
    x'[k] == pivot and
    x'[h] > pivot for h = k + 1 ... j
    and then returns this k
    """
```

...

Preferably one that is fast. With this function, quick sort is reduced to this:

```
def qsort_rec(x, i, j):
    if j - i <= 1: return
    k = partition(x, i, j)
    qsort_rec(x, i, k)
    qsort_rec(x, k + 1, j)
```

```
def qsort(x):
    qsort_rec(x, 0, len(x))
```

After partitioning, an element equal to the pivot is at index k, and all elements before index k should go before k in the sorted list, and all elements after index k should go after k. We leave out index k from the recursion—the first recursion is over $x[i:k]$ (i is included; k is not), and the second recursion is over $x[k+1:j]$. This means that we have to require of the `partition` function that `x[k]` is the pivot after calling the function.

The meat of the algorithm is in the `partition` function. The partition algorithm works as follows: We have an interval i–j of sequence x, i included and j not, and the pivot is at index i. We use two additional indices, k and h. We set k to $i+1$ and h to $j-1$. That is, k points one past the pivot, and h points to the last element in $x[i:j]$; see Figure 9-1.

We will have the invariant that all elements in $x[i:k]$ are less than or equal to the pivot and all elements in $x[h+1,j]$ are greater than the pivot (in both intervals, as always, we include the first index and exclude the second).

In each iteration, we look at $x[k]$ to check if it is greater than the pivot or not. If it is less than or equal to the pivot, we can increment k by one and still satisfy the invariant (Figure 9-2). If it is greater than the pivot, we cannot increment k, but we can move it to the end of the sequence where we keep those elements greater than the pivot. We swap it with $x[h]$ and decrement h by one (Figure 9-3).

The original $x[h]$ may or may not have been greater than the pivot; the invariant only tells us that elements in $x[h+1:j]$ are. This is irrelevant for the algorithm, however. If $x[h]$ was less than or equal to the pivot, then we would simply increment k in the next iteration. If it was greater than the pivot, then it would get swapped back in the next iteration. It might get swapped twice, but it is not worse than that. If swapping is costly, and you don't mind a slightly more complicated algorithm, you can decrease h until it points to an element that is not greater than the pivot after each swap. The extra loop is hardly worth it for avoiding one swap, but you can do it.

Figure 9-1. *Initial setup for "partition." We set k to point one after i and h to point one before j*

When h has moved past k, we have partitioned the sequence such that all elements in $x[i:k]$ are less than or equal to the pivot and all elements in $x[h+1, j]$ are greater than the pivot (Figure 9-4). The index we want the function to return is the last element in the part that is less than the pivot, not one past it, so we will return $k-1$ rather than k. Sorry for the confusion. For reasons explained in the preceding, we need the element at that position to be equal to the pivot. We know that $x[k-1]$ belongs in the first part, and it could be anywhere in there for all we care. The pivot at $x[i]$ also belongs in the first part, and since we want the pivot at index $k-1$, we just swap the two. Then all is well and we are done.

An implementation could look like this:

```python
def partition(x, i, j):
    pivot = x[i]
    k, h = i + 1, j - 1
    while k <= h:
        if x[k] <= pivot:
            k += 1
        elif x[k] > pivot:

            x[k], x[h] = x[h], x[k]
            h -= 1

x[i], x[k - 1] = x[k - 1], x[i]
return k - 1
```

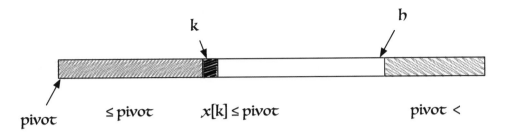

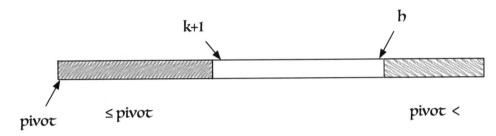

Figure 9-2. *If "x[k]" is less than the pivot, we can increase k and maintain the invariant*

All the operations in `partition` are simple comparisons and swaps, so it is fast—quick one might say—and it is that which makes quick sort a preferred algorithm in many cases.

Exercise: Prove that the partition algorithm is correct and that it runs in time $O(n)$.

Exercise: What is the best-case and the worst-case running time for quick sort?

Exercise: Is quick sort in place? Is it stable?

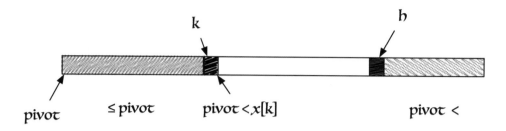

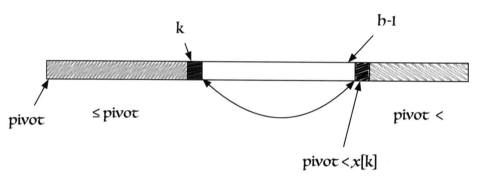

Figure 9-3. *If "x[k]" is greater than the pivot, we cannot increase k and maintain the invariant, but we can switch "x[k]" and "x[h-1]" and then decrease h. This will maintain the invariant*

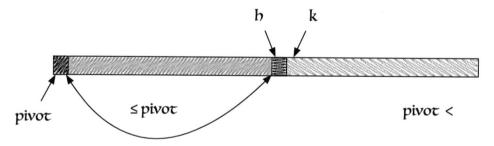

Figure 9-4. *When we are done with the partitioning, we need to put the pivot at the last position of the first part. We can do this simply by swapping the first and the kth element. We need to return the last position in the first part and that is k – 1*

If the data is almost random, then quick sort will spend linear time to split it in two almost equally sized parts and then recurse, giving us the following equation for the running time: $T(n) = 2 \cdot T(n/2) + O(n)$. It says that the time to handle input of size n is twice the time it takes to handle data of size $n/2$ plus some linear time. We will see more of such equations, called time recurrence equations, later in the chapter. We will also see why the solution to this one is $T(n) \in O(n \log n)$.

Of course, we might also be unlucky so the pivot we choose is the largest or smallest value in the range each time, which will partition the data into two parts where the first or last contains all the elements. We take care always to remove one element before we call the recursion, but we could recurse on $n - 1$ elements, giving us the equation $T(n) = T(n - 1) + O(n)$, which has the solution $T(n) \in O(n^2)$ as we shall also see later.

A common case for data we need to sort is that it is *almost* sorted to begin with. This happens, for example, when we are manipulating data that is sorted to begin with but only slightly sorted after our fiddling with it.

If we always pick the first element, then almost sorted data means that we partition the input very unevenly in each recursion. Quick sort will run in $O(n^2)$ (case 3 in the following) instead of $O(n \log n)$ (case 1 in the following). Insertion sort, on the other hand, will run in time $O(n)$ on almost sorted data (but $O(n^2)$ on random data). A strategy for a better sorting algorithm could be to let quick sort handle the data while it is far from sorted—assuming that it is random to begin with—but then switch to insertion sort once it is close to sorted. Once quick sort has reached some minimal sequence length, it can stop recursing. If all the recursions stop at that depth, then the sequence will consist of small segments of randomly ordered data, but each segment contains elements that are larger than the previous and smaller than the next. So the entire sequence is almost sorted. We can throw insertion sort at that sequence and expect the $O(n)$ best-case performance.

Exercise: Implement the following `qsort_rec` function to get the hybrid algorithm:

```
def qsort_rec(x, i, j, threshold):
    # Implement this

def qsort(x, threshold = 1):
    qsort_rec(x, 0, len(x), threshold)

def hybrid(x, threshold):
    qsort_rec(x, 0, len(x), threshold)
    insertion_sort(x)
```

Evaluate the hybrid algorithm empirically and compare it to basic quick sort and insertion sort algorithms. Explore how it performs for different choices of `threshold`.

An adaptive threshold would be better; if the data is already close to sorted at the beginning of the algorithm, we shouldn't wait until we are deep in the recursion before we switch to insertion sort.

Exercise: Consider ways to determine if a sequence is close to sorted—for some measure of "close"—and consider how you would use it to adaptively switch to insertion sort.

The motivation I gave for the hybrid algorithm was a little misleading. First, you sort for a bit with an $O(n \log n)$ algorithm, and then you switch to an $O(n)$ algorithm. This sounds like a reasonable idea, but it is a little misleading. If you evaluate the hybrid algorithm empirically, by running it and comparing it with quick sort and insertion sort, you will find that it is faster on random data, but the reason is slightly more complicated.

Let's say that we run the quick sort algorithm until we have split the input into segments of size m—there will be n/m such segments. If you start at length n and stop at length m, you need to do $\log(n/m) = \log(n) - \log(m)$ recursions, and at each recursion depth you do $O(n)$ work, so the quick sort part of the hybrid takes time $O(n(\log(n) - \log(m))$. After that, you need to sort n/m segments, each of which is random a sequence, with insertion sort, which takes time $O((n/m) \cdot m^2) = O(nm)$. So the worst-case running time for the hybrid is $O(n(\log(n) - \log(m) + m))$. This tells you that the optimal choice for m—the choice that minimizes the expression—is $m = 1$. That is the same as saying the optimal choice is only to use quick sort and not insertion sort at all.

If the theoretical analysis tells us not to bother with the hybrid approach, but the empirical measurements tell us that it is better, what is going on? We have run into one of the caveats in the sloppy analysis that big-Oh hides. When we analyze the two algorithms, we do not consider the overhead in the operations they perform. Quick sort is faster than merge sort, although both have the same big-Oh complexity because the operations it uses are faster. The operations that insertion sort uses, swapping two values, are faster than those quick sort uses, recursive function calls.

When we write down the running time for the hybrid algorithm, we could also write it as $\alpha \cdot n(\log(n) - \log(m)) + \beta \cdot m$, where α is the mean cost of an operation in quick sort and β is the cost of the operations in insertion sort.

The big-Oh analysis tells us that regardless of α and β, if we let n go toward infinity, then quick sort will be faster. But our empirical experiments tell us that there is a point, m, such that for input sizes smaller than m, insertion sort is better.

The reason the hybrid algorithm works better than quick sort is not that we somehow switch to a linear-time algorithm halfway through. The insertion sort algorithm runs in $O(nm)$ in the last part. But if we switch at the right threshold, we exploit that the overhead in insertion sort is less than that in quick sort. To understand why the hybrid algorithm works, we need to look a little beyond the big-Oh notation.

There are many cases where the big-Oh notation is not quite sufficient to get the best algorithm, and this is one of them. We will not explore it further, but it is something you ought to have in mind when you develop your own algorithms.

Divide and Conquer Running Times

Figuring out the running time for recursive functions—or algorithms that are recursive even if they are not implemented as recursive functions—means solving recurrence equations. If $T(n)$ denotes the running time on an input of size n, then a recurrence equation could look like this:

$$T(n) = 2 \cdot T(n/2) + O(n)$$

This is the recurrence equation for merge sort, and working it out will tell us what its worst-case time complexity is. To sort a list of length n, we solve two problems of half the size, $2T(n/2)$, and do some additional work in time $O(n)$. In the first version of merge sort, where we sliced the input, we used linear time both for the slicing and then for the merge; in the final version, we only spend linear time doing the merge. In either case, we spend linear time in addition to the recursive calls.

What characterizes recurrence equations is similar to what defines recursive solutions to problems. The equations refer to themselves. Strictly speaking, we need base cases for the recurrence equations to be well defined, so we would have

$$T(n) = \begin{cases} O(1) & n \leq 1 \\ 2 \cdot T(n/2) + O(n) & \text{otherwise} \end{cases}$$

but when we consider the running time of an algorithm, the base cases almost always involve constant time, so we often leave that out.

You can solve such recurrence equations by expanding them:

$$\begin{aligned} T(n) &= O(n) + 2 \cdot T(n/2) \\ &= O(n) + 2\left[O(n/2) + 2 \cdot T(n/4)\right] \\ &= O(n) + 2\left[O(n/2) + 2 \cdot \left[O(n/4) + T(n/8)\right]\right] \\ &= \cdots \end{aligned}$$

You have to be a little careful with the expansion and big-Oh notation, here. We see that we get an $O(n/2)$ in the first expansion, and normally, we would consider this equal to $O(n)$. It is, but as we keep expanding, we see the series $O(n) + O(n/2) + O(n/4) + \cdot +$ $O(n/n)$. If we pretend that all the $O(n/2^k)$ components are $O(n)$, this would give us $n \times$ $O(n) = O(n^2)$. This *is* an upper bound on the expression, but it is not tight. If you multiply into the parentheses in the equation, you will also get

$$2\left[O(n/2) + 2 \cdot T(n/4)\right] = 2O(n/2) + 4T(n/4) = O(n) + 4T(n/4)$$

which is actually okay, but if you translated $O(n/2)$ into $O(n)$, you would get

$$T(n) = 2O(n) + 4O(n) + 8O(n) + 16 \cdot T(n/8)$$

where each of the $O(n)$ components is multiplied by a number 2^k. You can consider that a constant in each step, but k depends on n, so it isn't really a constant. Neither is the number we divide n by inside the big-Oh.

The problem here is that we blindly translate the expanded numbers $2O(n/2)$ into $O(n)$ and do not consider that, as we continue the expansion, the number we multiply with and the number we divide by change for each expansion. They depend on n in how many times we do this and what the numbers are in each step. They are not constants. The arithmetic rules we have learned for the big-Oh notation are correct; the problem is not that. The problem is that we consider the numbers in the expansion as constants when they are not. This is usually not a trap you will fall into when reasoning about iterative algorithms as we have done earlier, but it is easy to fall into here.

When expanding a recurrence equation, it is easier to translate $O(n)$ into cn for some constant c. We know such a constant exists such that cn is an upper bound for whatever the $O(n)$ is capturing. Then we get an expansion like this:

$$
\begin{aligned}
T(n) &= cn + 2 \cdot T(n/2) \\
&= cn + 2\left[cn/2 + 2 \cdot T(n/4)\right] \\
&= cn + 2\left[cn/2 + 2\left[cn/4\right] + 2 \cdot T(n/8)\right] \\
&= \cdots
\end{aligned}
$$

If we take this expansion all the way down, we get

$$T(n) = \sum_{k=0}^{\log n} c \cdot 2^k n/2^k = \sum_{k=0}^{\log n} c \cdot n = c \cdot n \log n$$

where log n is the base-two logarithm, and we get that limit because $2^{\log n} = n$ is when we reach $n/n = 1$. This means that this recurrence is in $O(n \log n)$, so this is the big-Oh running time for merge sort.

We can conclude that the running time for merge sort is $O(n \log n)$.

What about quick sort? In the worst case, the recursive calls will go n deep; in each recursion, it can partition the sequence into one and the rest and thus recurse on $n - 1$ elements. The partitioning is fast compared to merging, but the asymptotic worst-case performance suffers from it. To get the same complexity as merge sort, we must have the recurrence $T(n) = 2T(n/2) + O(n)$. This happens when the partitioning gives us two parts that are roughly the same size. In the worst case, however, one has size $n - 1$ and the other is 1. We make sure to always reduce the sequence length by one by not including the pivot at index k, but we still might end up by a recursive call on a sequence of length $n - 1$. In that case, the depth of the call stack is linear, and since we do linear work at each level, we end up with a $O(n^2)$-time algorithm (see case 3 in the following).

If the sequence is random, then each element is expected to be roughly in the middle of the numbers, and then we expect that the partition will give us two equally sized parts. So the *average*-case running time is $O(n \log n)$—and it is fast when that happens. We cannot assume that we hit the average case, though, and with almost sorted data, picking the first element as the pivot is a particularly bad idea. There we will get the $O(n^2)$ running time. A hybrid algorithm, as in the earlier exercise, can give us the best of both worlds.

Frequently Occurring Recurrences and Their Running Times

There are common cases of recurrence equations that almost all divide and conquer algorithms match. If you memorize these, you will know the running time of most divide and conquer algorithms you run into. If that fails, you have to get to work and derive the running time yourself. This usually involves expanding the recurrence until you have a series you recognize, but quite often I find that a wisely chosen drawing works as well as the arithmetic. See the following for examples.

Case 1:

$$T(n) = 2 \cdot T(n/2) + O(n) \in O(n \log n)$$

Merge sort and quick sort are examples of this recurrence. Whenever you can break a problem into two subproblems of half the length as the original and you do not spend more than linear time splitting or combining, you get an $O(n \log n)$ algorithm. Merge sort can be shown to be optimal (in the sense of big-Oh) because all comparison-based sorting algorithms need to do $\Omega(n \log n)$ comparisons. Quick sort is only expected $O(n \log n)$ time.

When we were deriving the running time from the recurrence equation, we did a bit of arithmetic. Usually, you can solve recurrence equations just by expanding them and recognizing the form of the sum you get back from it. This often takes the form of a series, and if you know what it converges to, you are done. Doing it this way doesn't give you much intuition about why the running time is at it is, though, but a drawing of how it works can.

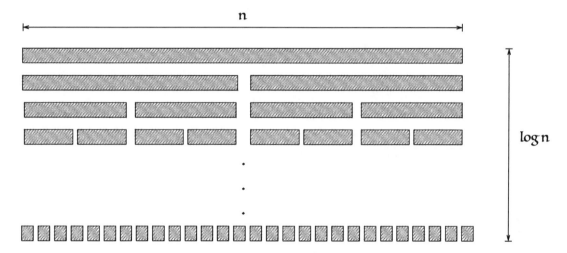

Figure 9-5. *Work when we recurse on twice the half size and do linear work at each step*

Consider the $T(n) = 2T(n/2) + O(n)$ recurrence and Figure 9-5. What the figure shows is that we do linear work first, shown as the gray bar. Then we recurse on two halves and do linear work there as well, but on half the size. In total, though, it is linear work; it is just split in two different calls. At the next time, we also do linear work, but now in four different calls. We continue like this until we hit base cases where the total work is linear again. The depth of the recursion, since we split the size of the data the recursive functions work on, is $O(\log n)$, so summing it all up gives us $O(n \log n)$. The drawing tells us the same as the arithmetic—which is reassuring—but I think the drawing is easier to follow and gives more intuition about why the recurrence gives us the time we got.

Case 2:

$$T(n) = T(n-1) + O(1) \in O(n)$$

If we, in constant time, remove one from the problem size, we have an algorithm that runs in linear time. If we consider linear search a recursive problem—the base case is when we find the element or we are at the end of the list, and the recursive case is doing a linear search on the rest of the input—then that would be an example of such an algorithm.

You can see a drawing that illustrates the running time in Figure 9-6, although drawing this is almost overkill. You can see that we read a linear call stack depth, and if each call costs us constant-time work, we must end up with $O(n)$. Another way to see this is to consider the workload at each level (the gray blocks in the figure). The running time will be the sum of all these. If we project all of them to the bottom of the figure, we see that we get n of them. That is certainly overkill for this recurrence, but it is at times a helpful way to reason about the running time.

Case 3:

$$T(n) = T(n-1) + O(n) \in O(n^2)$$

If we need linear time to reduce the problem size by one, then we get a quadratic-time algorithm. Selection sort, where we find the smallest element in the input, in linear time, swap it to the first element, and then recursively sort the rest of the list, is an example of this.

For a proof of the running time, consider Figure 9-7. If we have an $n{\times}n$ square, its area is n^2. If we do linear work per level and remove one "work block" at each level, we get the area in the figure. It is half the area of an $n{\times}n$ block, so it is $n^2/2 \in O(n^2)$. It is actually $n(n + 1)/2$ if you are more careful with the math—we cannot quite move down the diagonal, and there is a bit too much at each level. But $n(n + 1)/2$ is still in $O(n^2)$, so the figure is not lying.

Case 4:

$$T(n) = T(n/2) + O(1) \in O(\log n)$$

If you can reduce the problem to half its size in constant time, then you have a logarithmic-time algorithm. Binary search is an example of this.

Figure 9-8 is one way to illustrate why the running time is as it is. Here, again, I have shown the data and the work done in the recursive calls as white and gray bars, but I have drawn them along the x-axis and right to left. The rightmost chunk input has size n; to the immediate left of it, we have the recursive call with data of size $n/2$ and so forth until we have the base case, of size 1, at the leftmost position.

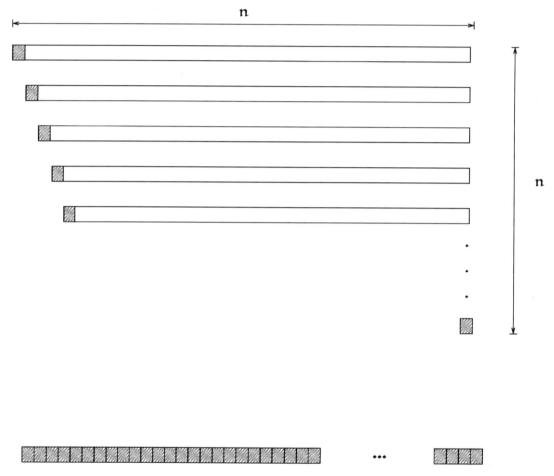

Figure 9-6. *The work done if we only do constant work per call but we recurse on data that is only one smaller than the original*

The reason I have drawn it this way is that I can now read it from left to right. Every time I reach a gray square, I put one above it such that the gray bars moving up along the y-axis are equidistant. Notice that each time I add a gray square, I have to move twice as long until I reach the next one than the length I had to move from the previous. Each time we double the size of the data on the x-axis, we add one to the y-axis. This is the log base-two function.

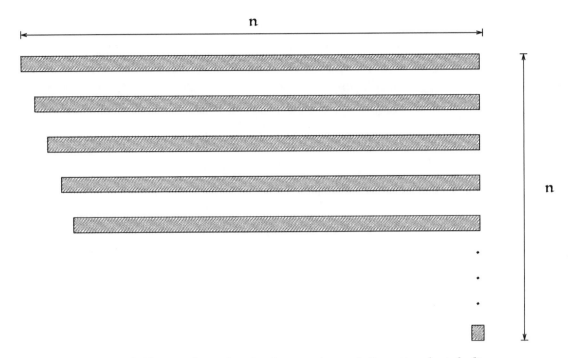

Figure 9-7. *Work if we reduce the size by one in each iteration but do linear work*

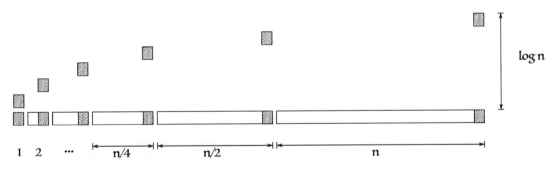

Figure 9-8. *Work if we cut the problem size in half at each level and do one piece of work*

Case 5:

$$T(n) = T(n/2) + O(n) \in O(n)$$

If you can reduce the problem to half its size in linear time, then you have a linear-time algorithm. Notice that this equation is different from the one we had for merge sort. In that recursion, we needed *two* recursive calls; in this, we only need one.

As an example of this running time, consider a function that adds a list of numbers by first adding them pairwise and then adding all the pairwise sums in a recursive call:

```
def binary_sum(x):
    if len(x) == 0: return 0
    if len(x) == 1: return x[0]

    # O(n) work
    y = []
    for i in range(1, len(x), 2):
        y.append(x[i - 1] + x[i])
    if i + 1 < len(x): # handle odd lengths
        y[0] += x[i + 1]

    return binary_sum(y) # recurse on n//2 size
```

This looks like just a complicated way of adding numbers—and in some ways it is—but it can be relevant if you need to compute the sum of floating-point numbers (see the last section of this chapter). When you add two floating-point numbers, you might not end up with their sum. If this surprises you, remember that a number must be represented in finite computer memory, but not all real numbers can. For example, the decimal representation of 1/3 requires infinitely many decimals, 0.333333... In your computer, you do not use decimal notation but binary, but the problem is the same. (You can, of course, represent rational numbers like 1/3 as two integers, and you can represent arbitrarily large integers, but floating-point numbers are much faster for the computer to work with.)

If you add two floating-point numbers, you will lose bits of information proportional to how many orders of magnitude the numbers are apart, so the greater the difference, the less precise your addition is. If you add the numbers in a long list, starting from the left and moving right, as we have done many times before, then this can become a problem. The accumulator will grow and grow as we add more and more numbers, and if the numbers in the list are of roughly the same order of magnitude, the accumulator might end up many orders of magnitude larger than the next number to be added. If the difference gets large enough, adding a number to the accumulator results in just the value of the accumulator.

If you start with numbers of the same order of magnitude, then adding them pairwise as in the preceding algorithm will keep them at roughly the same order of magnitude in the recursion, and this will alleviate the problem of losing precision in floating-point numbers.

A classical algorithm, *k-select*, is another algorithm that runs with this complexity. It is an adaption of quick sort that has this recurrence as an expected case running time. As input, it takes a sequence x and an index i, and it returns the value $x'[i]$ where x' is x sorted. If we sorted x, in $O(n \log n)$, and then returned $x'[i]$, in $O(1)$, we would have an $O(n \log n)$ algorithm. We can do better and get an $O(n)$ algorithm by not sorting x completely. We will partition the sequence exactly as we did in quick sort. This takes time $O(n)$. Then, if the partitioning index k is larger than i, we know that $x'[i]$ must be in the first part. If not, it must be in the second part. In the first case, we call recursively on the first part; in the second, we call recursively on the second part but adjust the index to reflect that we have eliminated $k + 1$ elements from the left part.

Exercise: Modify your quick sort implementation to implement k-select.

Figure 9-9 shows how you can think about the running time. At each level we do linear work, but we only take half the data with us in the recursion. The gray areas show the work we do at each level. I have put the recursion on the first half to the left at level 2. Then the quarter work is to the right of it, the eights to the right of that, and so on. If we take all the pieces except the first n down to the bottom of the figure and lay them next to each other, they add up to n. So the first n and the n from the rest of the calls sum to $2n \in O(n)$.

This analysis works for any fraction. If you can reduce the work you have to do in each recursion by a fixed fraction, then you get a linear-time algorithm. It requires just a bit of math to see that it will always work. Consider the sum $(1 - x)\sum_{i=0}^{n} x^i = \sum_{i=0}^{n} x^i - \sum_{i=0}^{n} x^{i+1}$.

We can rearrange the sum to $1 - \sum_{i=1}^{n}(x^i - x^i) - x^{n+1}$. When n goes to infinity, x^{n+1} goes to zero for all $|x| < 1$, and we get $\sum_{i=0}^{\infty} x^i = 1/(1 - x)$. For any fraction you want, plug it into x, and you get the constant that the series converges to. Here, we have the fraction 1/2, so we get $1/(1/2) = 2$, as we saw in the figure.

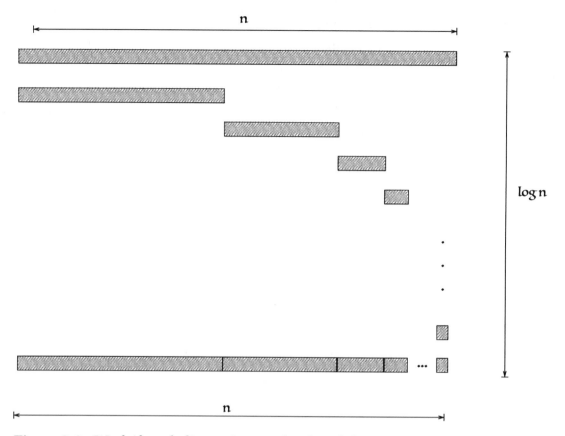

Figure 9-9. *Work if we do linear time per level and then only take half the problem size with us to the next level*

Case 6:

$$T(n) = 2 \cdot T(n/2) + O(1) \in O(n)$$

If we can split and combine in constant time, but require two recursive calls on half the size, we also get a linear-time algorithm. Again, notice that this is different from the recurrence equation for merge sort where we needed linear time to merge the results of the two recursive calls.

A simple example of an algorithm with this recurrence is another one that computes the sum of a list of values while trying to balance the magnitude of the numbers it adds. To get the sum of all values in a list x, get the sum of the first half and the second half with two recursive calls and then add the two:

```
def split_sum(x, i, j):
    if i >= j:      return 0
    if i + 1 == j: return x[i]
    mid = (i + j) // 2
    return split_sum(x, i, mid) + split_sum(x, mid + 1, j)
```

It should be obvious that the running time for this algorithm is the recurrence $T(n) = 2 \cdot T(n/2) + O(1) \in O(n)$.

It is a little harder to visualize why the running time is the way it is, but consider Figure 9-10. Here we show the work per level, but this time I don't want you to add the gray blocks. I just want you to read the figure from the bottom and up. At the bottom the work is n. At the second-to-last level, it is $n/2$. It continues that way until we get to the top level where the work is 1. That is *exactly* the setting we saw in case 5. The setup is different and so are the figures, but if you read this figure from the bottom and Figure 9-9 from the top, you will see that the work per level is exactly the same. If case 5 is $O(n)$, then case 6 must be as well.

Dynamic Programming

By now, we have seen how recursion is a powerful tool for both programming and algorithmic design, that is, divide and conquer. But you will not be surprised to learn that not all recursive programs are efficient. For some recursive functions, there is not much we can do about that, but for others, there is a trick that can take us from an intractable to an efficient algorithm. It simply involves placing previously computed values in a table, to avoid repeating the same computation multiple times.

Consider the recursive function for computing the nth Fibonacci number:

$$F(n) = \begin{cases} 1 & n = 1 \text{ or } n = 0 \\ F(n-1) + F(n-2) & n > 1 \end{cases}$$

Figure 9-10. *Work if we do constant work per recursion but do two recursive calls on half the data each*

To compute $F(5)$, you must compute $F(4)$ and $F(3)$. For $F(4)$ you must compute $F(3)$ and $F(2)$, for $F(3)$ you must compute $F(2)$ and $F(1)$, and so on; see Figure 9-11 where I have marked the base cases with checkmarks and the recursive cases with which recursive calls they make. The structure of the graph of recursive calls clearly leads to an explosion in the number of calls as n increases; see Figure 9-12. That makes this recursive calculation an unfeasible approach for computing $F(n)$ for large n.

If we could store the values of each function, illustrated in Figure 9-13, we would get a linear-time algorithm (Figure 9-14). You cannot determine that the algorithm's running time is linear just because the plot looks like a line, but I leave it to you to prove it, or you can take my word for it. To go from an exponential to a linear algorithm like this only requires a table to store results in and to look up values in:

```
tbl = {}
def fib(n):
    if n <= 1:
```

```
        return 1
    else:
        if n not in tbl:
            tbl[n] = fib(n - 1) + fib(n - 2)
        return tbl[n]
```

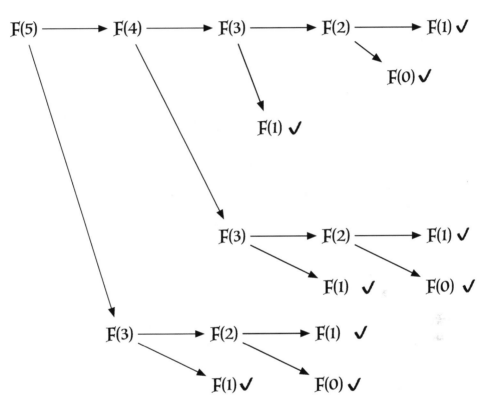

Figure 9-11. *The graph of recursions necessary to compute the fifth Fibonacci number*

This trick, of using a table to remember previously calculated values, is widely used, and in the functools module, there are decorators you can use to automatically translate a function into one that uses a table:

```
from functools import cache
```

```
@cache
def fib(n):
    if n <= 1: return 1
    else: return fib(n - 1) + fib(n - 2)
```

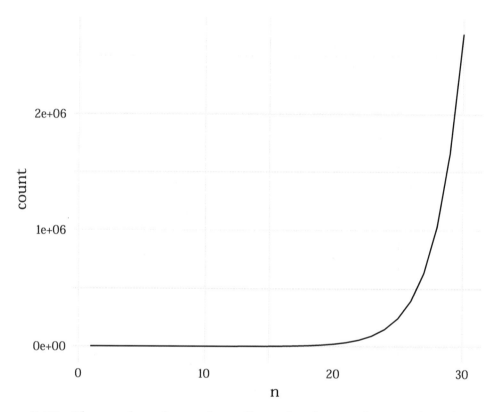

Figure 9-12. *The number of recursive calls made when evaluating the Fibonacci function*

The table will grow without bounds if you keep calling the function with new arguments, obviously since it needs to remember the result for each, but the module also has the decorator lru_cache where you can put an upper limit on how many values it should remember. It will then remember the most recently used values and forget others. You can read the documentation for details.

The $F(n)$ function is simple; we always know precisely which recursions we need and the sequence of recursions we need. This lets us turn the calculations around and start at the base cases and build $F(i) = F(i-1) + F(i-2)$ from 2 and up to n; see Figure 9-15.

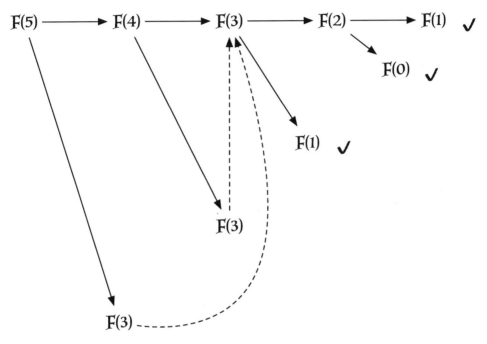

Figure 9-13. *The recursion graph for computing the fifth Fibonacci number if we remember the problems we have already solved*

We could build a table mapping the numbers $\{0, 1, 2, \ldots, n\}$ to the corresponding Fibonacci number and then fill the table starting from the smallest numbers and moving up. That way, whenever we need to compute $F(i)$ for some i, the values $F(i-1)$ and $F(i-2)$ are already in the table. This leads us to this algorithm that fills up a table and computes the Fibonacci numbers up to the one we want:

```
def fib(n):
    if n <= 1:
        return 1
```

```
    tbl = [1] * n
    for i in range(2, n + 1):

    tbl[i] = tbl[i - 1] + tbl[i - 2]
return tbl[n]
```

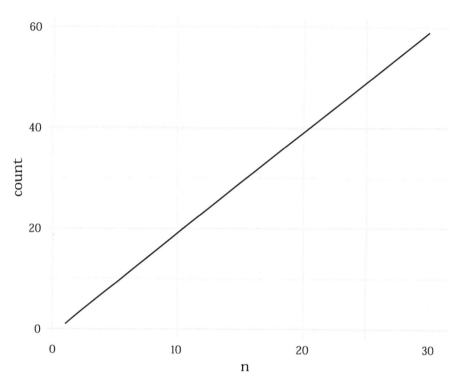

Figure 9-14. *Number of recursions for increasing n*

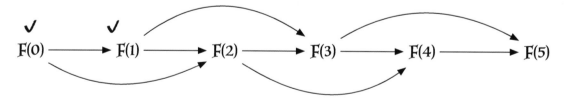

Figure 9-15. *The graph for computing the fifth Fibonacci number iteratively*

Of course, we only need the values $F(i-1)$ and $F(i-2)$; we do not need the full table when we compute $F(i)$, so we can save a bit of memory by only remembering the last two values. With two variables, representing $F(i-2)$ and $F(i-1)$, the iterative solution looks like this:

```
def fib(n):
    if n <= 1:
        return 1
    fi1, fi2 = 1, 1
    for i in range(n - 1):
        fi1, fi2 = fi1 + fi2, fi1
    return fi1
```

Dynamic programming is the straightforward idea that you should only calculate each value once. When we compute a value recursively and store results in a table, then we call it *memoization* (like memorization but without the "r"[1]) or *top-down* dynamic programming. When we build our way up from base cases to the one we want, we call it *bottom-up* dynamic programming. I personally think that the term memoization is more informative about what an implementation actually does, so I will use memoization rather than top-down dynamic programming. I will refer to bottom-up dynamic programming as dynamic programming.

For dynamic programming and memoization to work, you need a problem that you can split into subproblems that you can then solve independently. In that way, it matches the requirements for divide and conquer algorithms. For dynamic programming to give you any speedup, you also need the recursions to overlap, that is, during the computation, your algorithm should solve the same instance of a subproblem multiple times. With dynamic programming, we make sure to only solve each instance of a subproblem once—after that, we can look it up in a table when we need it. If all subproblems are unique, then we do not gain anything from dynamic programming. If the subproblems are only solved once, we are in the domain of divide and conquer (notice that in the divide and conquer algorithms earlier in the chapter, we only solved each subproblem once). Frequently dynamic programming algorithms are recursive problems that would take exponential time if we implemented them naïvely but where we have a polynomial solution using dynamic programming or memoization.

---

[1]The two words are cognates; they both derive from the Latin memorandum (to be remembered), but the version without the r, memoization, is the technical term used in computer science.

Engineering a Dynamic Programming Algorithm

To construct a divide and conquer algorithm, you first have to ask yourself if one is even possible. Does tabulating the results you get from recursive calls speed up your algorithm? If all function calls you do in your algorithm are unique, that is, you never call a function with the same arguments twice, then tabulating the results is pointless. If you do have several calls with the same arguments, then you can always store the results. You will in essence trade running time for memory usage. You cannot save the result of a recursive call more often than you make the call, though, so you can never use more memory than you must spend on time. (This is a general property of algorithms. Every piece of memory you use you must devote time to access.)

Now, it is worth considering if memoization will gain you anything and is even worthwhile. If the number of times you call the same function with the same parameters is bounded by a constant, then your memoization algorithm will still be in the same asymptotic class. On the other hand, you could have a situation similar to the Fibonacci numbers. Here, the number of calls you need as you move from $F(n)$ down to the base cases grows exponentially, but almost all calls are identical to other calls. In such scenarios, you will often be able to move from an exponential running time to a polynomial-time algorithm (and therefore also a polynomial space algorithm).

If you now have a memoization algorithm, the next step is to see if you can translate it into a dynamic programming algorithm. In the memoization algorithm, you need a table lookup in each recursive call to see if you have already called the function with the arguments you call it with right now. If you have a table where you can look up a value in constant time, then dynamic programming algorithms will never be asymptotically faster than memoization. However, there is overhead in table lookups, so if we can tabulate results without too much complexity, that is what we will want to do. That is the step where we move from memoization to dynamic programming.

You would use dynamic programming instead of memoization if (1) you know precisely which recursions you need to tabulate and (2) you know the order of recursions you will see in your algorithm.

Take the Fibonacci example once more. We can use dynamic programming because we know that $F(i - 1)$ and $F(i - 2)$ will be called by $F(i)$ for all i, so we know that we will use all $F(j), j = 0, \dots, n$ to compute $F(n)$. There are no $F(j), j > n$ called in the algorithm, and there are no $F(i)$ left out for $i = 0, \dots, n$. If we do not know which calls will be made, then we might build too large a table. With memoization, you store exactly the number of recursive calls your program makes. It is an optimal strategy for tabulating the necessary results. With dynamic programming, you can only get this if you know which calls will be made and which will not.

The reason that you need to know the order in which the results of recursions are required is that you need to tabulate the results of all recursions before they are made. If you do not do this correctly, then your algorithm will look up a value in a table that hasn't been stored there yet. That rarely goes well. If you have to check if a result is in the table, then you have simply taken the long way around to memoization.

Now, if you have made it to a full-fledged dynamic programming algorithm, you can potentially reduce the memory further by once again examining the dependency graph of recursive calls. In the Fibonacci example, we know that to compute $F(i)$ we only need to know $F(i-1)$ and $F(i-2)$. This means that we do not need to remember $F(j)$ for $j < i-2$; we have already used them to compute $F(i-1)$ and $F(i-2)$, but we no longer need them. The final algorithm that we derived in the preceding remembers two values in each iteration, and it does so because we can work out from the recursion dependency graph that this is all we need.

Edit Distance

The *edit distance* between two strings, x and y, is the minimal number of operations you need to transform x into y, where operations are as follows:

1. Replace one character with another.

2. Delete a character from x.

3. Insert a character into x.

Recursion

We can consider the minimal number of edits to go from a prefix of x, $x[:i]$, to a prefix of y, $y[:j]$.

A recursive function for counting the necessary edits can look like this:

$$d(i,j) = \min \begin{cases} d(i-1,j-1) + 1\left(x[i-1] \neq y[j-1]\right) & \text{match / substitution} \\ d(i,j-1) + 1 & \text{deletion} \\ d(i-1,j) + 1 & \text{insertion} \end{cases}$$

The function $\mathbf{1}(x[i-1] \neq y[j-1])$ is 1 if $x[i-1] \neq y[j-1]$ and zero if $x[i-1] = y[j-1]$. The base cases for the recursion are $d(0, j) = j$ and $d(i, 0) = i$. The edit distance between x and y is $d(n, m)$ where n is the length of x and m is the length of y.

Notice that we find the final result in $d(n, m)$. This means that we have indices from zero to n and m where we usually would not include the last two. If you work out an example, you will notice that $i = 0$ and $j = 0$ represent prefixes matched against the empty prefixes of x and y, respectively. To match the first character in either string, we move into row 1 or column 1. So the pair (i, j) is the match of $x[: i]$ and $y[: j]$. That is why we want the value at $d(n, m)$.

Once we have a recursion, implementing it as a recursive Python function is straightforward:

```python
def edit_dist(x, y, i = None, j = None):
    if i is None: i = len(x)
    if j is None: j = len(y)
    if i == 0: return j
    if j == 0: return i
    return min(
        edit_dist(x, y, i - 1, j - 1) + (x[i - 1] != y[j - 1]),
        edit_dist(x, y, i, j - 1) + 1,
        edit_dist(x, y, i - 1, j) + 1,
    )
```

In this function, I have included the strings x and y as parameters. The function needs them to check if $x[i-1] \neq y[j-1]$. Unless the strings are global variables, the function needs them as parameters. The indices, i and j, need to be parameters in the recursion, but we will always use the length of the two strings. You could always call the function like this:

```python
edit_dist(x,y,len(x),len(y))
```

However, the redundancy in the initial call is best avoided, and that is what the None default parameters do.

Memoization

Until you hit a base case in the recursion, you have three directions to go in for each (i, j), so calculating the recursion as it stands gives you an exponential running time. With memoization, the running time is $O(nm)$. To see this, observe that to compute $d(n, m)$, we have to compute $d(i, j)$ for all $i = 0, \ldots, n$ and $j = 0, \ldots, m$ and only those values, and there are $(n + 1) \times (m + 1)$ such pairs. It takes constant time plus the time to make the recursive call for each pair, and if memoization makes the recursive calls constant time, using a table lookup, then that gives us the $O(nm)$ running time.

Implementing the memoization solution is straightforward. Generally, once we have a recursion and have convinced ourselves that there are sufficient identical recursive calls to save results, we simply add a table to the recursive function:

```
def edit_dist(x, y, i = None, j = None, tbl = None):
    if i is None: i = len(x)
    if j is None: j = len(y)
    if tbl is None: tbl = {}

    if i == 0:
        tbl[i,j] = j
    elif j == 0:
        tbl[i,j] = i
    else:
        tbl[i,j] = min(
            edit_dist(x, y, i - 1, j - 1, tbl) +
                    (x[i - 1] != y[j - 1]),
            edit_dist(x, y, i, j - 1, tbl) + 1,
            edit_dist(x, y, i - 1, j, tbl) + 1,
    )
    return tbl[i,j]
```

Dynamic Programming

To move from memoization to dynamic programming, first, we need to introduce an $(n + 1) \times (m + 1)$ table D to hold all $d(i, j)$ values.

Second, we need to figure out in which order we need to fill the table. From the recursion, we can see that we loop at one row above and one column to the left in the recursion. So, if we fill out the table left to right and row by row, then the algorithm will work. We can also fill the table column by column and up to down.

To build a two-dimensional table in Python, you *can* use lists, constructed with the incantation we have seen before:

```
D = [ [0] * m for _ in range(n) ]
```

Then you need to index using D[i][j] instead of the D[i,j] notation that I will use in the following.

In general, however, when you need a table, you are better off by using the numpy package. By convention, you import it and give it the name np like this:

```
import numpy as np
```

You can build tables for any number of dimensions. For a two-dimensional table, with $n + 1$ rows and $m + 1$ columns, initialized as all zeros, you can use

```
np.zeros((n + 1, m + 1))
```

Back to the edit distance and dynamic programming. My implementation of the dynamic programming version of the edit distance looks like this:

```
def build_edit_table(x, y):
    n, m = len(x), len(y)
    D = np.zeros((n + 1, m + 1))

    # base cases
    for i in range(n + 1):
        D[i,0] = i
    for j in range(m + 1):
        D[0,j] = j

    # recursion
    for i in range(1, n + 1):
        for j in range(1, m + 1):
            D[i,j] = min(
                D[i - 1, j - 1] + (x[i - 1] != y[j - 1]),
                D[i, j - 1] + 1,
                D[i - 1, j] + 1
            )

    return D
```

```
def edit_dist(x, y):
    D = build_edit_table(x, y)
    n, m = len(x), len(y)
    return D[n,m]
```

Exercise: Since we only need to look one row up and one column left, we can reduce the memory usage to $O(n)$ or $O(m)$ depending on whether we remember two rows or two columns. Show how to do this.

Backtracking

Filling the table will get us the cost of the shortest edit distance between two strings, but if we also want to know what the edits are, we need to backtrack the modifications that lead to the cheapest edit. For this backtracking, we need, for each cell in the table, to figure out which of the (up to) three cells we got the optimal path from. We check the three cells in the recursion—up, diagonal, or left—for the value they contributed, remember what the step was, and then continue from the cell we found to be where our path came from. My implementation looks like this:

```
 1  def backtrack_(D, x, y, i, j, path):
 2      if i == 0:
 3          path.extend('D' * j)
 4          return
 5      if j == 0:
 6          path.extend('I' * i)
 7          return
 8
 9      left = D[i, j - 1] + 1
10      diag = D[i - 1, j - 1] + (x[i - 1] != y[j - 1])
11      up = D[i - 1, j] + 1
12
13      dist = left
14      op = 'D'
15      if diag < dist:
16          op = 'X' if x[i - 1] != y[j - 1] else '='
17          dist = diag
18      if up < dist:
```

```
19                op = 'I'
20
21       if op == 'D':
22            backtrack_(D, x, y, i, j - 1, path)
23       if op in ('=','X'):
24            backtrack_(D, x, y, i - 1, j - 1, path)
25       if op == 'I':
26            backtrack_(D, x, y, i - 1, j, path)
27       path.append(op)
```

Lines 2–7 handle the base cases where either i or j is zero. Then, on lines 9–11, we compute the values for the three cells our current value could have come from. We figure out which operation gave us the value in the (i, j) cell, lines 13–19. I have chosen to encode insertions as I, matches as =, substitutions as X, and deletions as D.

We call the function recursive according to the operation we identified, lines 21–26, and finally we add the operation to the backtracking path. We do this after the recursive calls, to get the path in the right order. If we added the operation here, before the recursion, we would get the operations in reverse.

The preceding function was just the recursive backtracking. To give backtracking a better interface, I call it from this function:

```
def backtrack(D, x, y):
    n, m = len(x), len(y)
    path = []
    backtrack_(D, x, y, n, m, path)
    return ''.join(path)
```

It sets n and m to the lengths of the strings. These are the indices, from which we must start the recursion and the path. We call backtrack_ to compute the path. Finally, it transforms the list into a string—just to make the result easier to read.

Exercise: Describe how you would use the table from memoization to implement backtracking.

Exercise: Can you also backtrack if you reduce space usage to $O(n)$ by only looking at two rows at a time?

Partitioning

Consider this problem: You have to analyze some sequence of data, and you can parallelize the computation such that it can run on multiple CPUs. The computations will be faster on contiguous substrings. You want to make the slowest computation as swift as possible. This problem is called the *partitioning problem*, and it takes as input a list, x, of length N, and you have to partition it into K contiguous parts such that the cost of the most expensive part is as small as possible. A part is a contiguous block, so the elements of x from some index i to another $j \geq i$. The cost of the block is the sum of the elements:

$$S(i,j) = \sum_{m=i}^{j-1} x[m]$$

If x is held in a global variable, x, then this function will compute $S(i,j)$:

```
def S(i, j):
    return sum(x[i:j])
```

Computing $S(i, j)$ as a sum takes time $O(j - i)$, but we can bring it down to constant time. If we preprocess our data by computing the cumulative sum

$$CS[i] = \sum_{j=0}^{i-1} x[j]$$

then we can compute $S(i, j) = CS[j] - CS[i]$.

Exercise: Show that you can compute the CS array in linear time. The following code does that:

```
import numpy as np
CS = np.zeros(N+1)
CS[1:] = np.cumsum(x)
```

Back to the partitioning problem. The cost of a given partitioning is the cost of the most expensive segment. We are looking for the partitioning with the smallest cost, that is, the partitioning where the largest cost is as small as possible. For example, if x is the list

```
x = [2, 5, 3, 7, 5]
```

we can split it into two partitions in the following ways:

```
[] [2, 5, 3, 7, 5]
[2] [5, 3, 7, 5]
[2, 5] [3, 7, 5]
[2, 5, 3] [7, 5]
[2, 5, 3, 7] [5]
[2, 5, 3, 7, 5] []
```

The cost of the first partition is 22, the second 20, the third 15, the fourth 12, the fifth 17, and the sixth 22. The best of these is the fourth with score 12.

If x has length n, then there are $n + 1$ ways to partition it into two (and $n - 1$ to partition x into $K = 2$ non-empty parts[2]). If we want $K = 3$ non-empty and distinct, that is, no two parts are identical, then we have $(n - 1)(n - 2)/2$ possibilities. We have $n - 1$ positions to put the first split in and then $n - 2$ positions for the next split. For $K = 3$ the number of partitions is $(n - 1)(n - 2)(n - 3)/6$. For general K the number of partitions is $\dfrac{(n-1)!}{(n-K-1)!K!}$. This is super-exponential, so clearly exhaustively trying out all partitions is not a feasible strategy.

Exercise: Prove that the number of partitions is $\dfrac{(n-1)!}{(n-K-1)!K!}$

Recursion

To derive a dynamic programming solution, we first derive a recursive solution to the problem. We can consider where to put the separator between the last partition and the previous partition. At some index i into x, we have the start index of the last partition. The cost of the last index is $S(i, N)$. The cost of this partitioning must be

$$\max\left[P(i,K-1),\ S(i,N) \right]$$

where $P(i, K-1)$ is the best partitioning of the array $x[0 : i]$ into $K - 1$ partitions. The best partitioning of x into K partitions is found by picking the optimal index i:

$$P(N,K) = \min_{N}^{i=0}\left\{\max\left[P(i,K-1), S(i,N) \right]\right\}$$

---

[2]In the optimization problem, we do not require that the partitioning has non-empty parts, but any partitioning with empty parts can split the partition with the greatest cost and thus reduce the cost. An optimal partitioning will, therefore, not contain empty parts.

Notice that the maximization is over two values, $P(i, K-1)$ and $S(i, N)$ while the minimization is over all indices in x. We can handle the first in constant time and the latter in linear time if we can look up all $P(i, K-1)$ in a table.

The base cases of the recursion are single partitions, where we have no choice but to put all elements in the same partition, $P(n, 1) = S(0, n)$ for all n, and the empty prefix of x where the cost of any number of partitions is zero, $P(0, k) = 0$, for all k.

In summary, we have

$$P(i,k) = \begin{cases} S(0,n) & k = 1 \\ 0 & i = 0 \\ \min_{j=0}^{i} \left\{ \max\left[P(j,K-1), S(j,N) \right] \right\} & \text{otherwise} \end{cases} \tag{9.1}$$

We can already look up $S(i, N)$ for all i (and N), but for $P(i, K-1)$ we need to compute recursively.

Exercise: Implement a recursive function that computes $P(n, k)$ for all $0 \le n \le N$ and $k \ge 0$, that is, implement Eq. 9.1 as a Python function.

Exercise: Implement memoization in the recursive function. You can simply check if you already have a value for the recursive call—identified by i and $K-1$—and compute it if you do not, and in either case return it. You can use a `dict` for the table.

Exercise: Instead of using a `dict` in the previous exercise, how would you use an $N \times K$ numpy table? You will need a way to indicate that a value has not been computed yet.

Dynamic Programming

Once we have our recursion, we can always build a memoization algorithm, but we need to examine it carefully to see if we can build it bottom up and get a dynamic programming algorithm as well. First, do we use all the values, and second, can we compute them such that we can guarantee that a result is available when we need it?

We can see directly from the recursion that to compute $P(i, k)$ we look at $P(j, k-1)$ for each $0 \le j < i$. The recursion on k will go down to the base case for k, so we will use all values of j and k, and we will use them one k at a time. If we know all $P(j, k-1), j < i$

when we compute $P(i, k)$, then we have all the values we need. By these observations, we know we can build a table, PT, and fill it up either by row or by column:

```
def P(M, K):
    PT = np.zeros((N+1,K+1))
    # Base cases
    for i in range(N+1):
        PT[i,1] = S(0,i)
    for j in range(2,K+1):
        PT[0,j] = 0

    # Recursive case
    for i in range(1,N+1):
        for j in range(2,K+1):
            PT[i,j] = min(max(PT[m,j-1], S(m,i))
                          for m in range(i))
    return PT[N, K]
```

Exercise: What is the running time of the dynamic programming solution? What about the memoization solution?

Exercise: Reduce the space complexity to $O(n)$ by only storing the previous row or column in the P table.

Exercise: Since we want to know the optimal partition and not just the cost of the optimal partition, we need to backtrack to get it. Show how this can be done and implement your solution.

Representing Floating-Point Numbers

Floating-point numbers, the computer analogue to real numbers, can be represented in different ways, but they are all variations of the informal presentation I give in this section. If you are not particularly interested in how these numbers are represented, you can safely skip this section. You can already return to it if you think you are getting weird behavior when working with floating-point numbers.

The representation used by modern computers is standardized as IEEE 754. It fundamentally represents numbers as explained in the following, but with some tweaks that let you represent plus and minus infinity and "not a number" (NaN), with higher precision for numbers close to zero than the presentation here would allow. It also uses a sign bit for the coefficient, while it represents the exponent as a signed integer with a slightly different encoding than what we saw for integers in Chapter 5, for reasons lost deep in numerical analysis. All that you need to know is that floating-point numbers work roughly as I have explained here, but with lots of technical complications. If you find yourself a heavy user of floating-point numbers, you will need to study numerical analysis beyond what we can cover in this book, and you can worry about the details of number representations there.

Floating-point numbers are similar to the *scientific notation* for base b numbers, where numbers are represented as

$$x = \pm a \times b^{\pm q}$$

where $a = a_1.a_2a_3 \ldots a_n$, $a_i \in \{0, 1, \ldots, b - 1\}$ is the *coefficient* and $q = q_1q_2q_3 \ldots q_m$, $q_i \in \{0, 1, \ldots, b - 1\}$ is the *exponent* of the number. To get a binary notation, replace b by 2. For non-zero numbers, a_1 must be 1, so we do not represent it explicitly, which gives us one more bit to work with. Not all real numbers can be represented with this notation if we require that both a and q are finite sequences,[3] but if we allow them to be infinite, we can. We can approximate any number arbitrarily close by using sufficiently long sequences of digits, n for the coefficient and m for the exponent. We usually assume that if $x \neq 0$ then $a_1 \neq 0$ since, if $a_1 = 0$, we can update a to $a_2.a_3 \ldots a_n$ and decrease q by one if positive or increase it by one of negative.

Where floating-point numbers differ from the real numbers is that we have a fixed limit on how many digits we have available for the coefficient and the exponent. To represent any real number, we can choose sufficiently high values for n and m, but with floating-point numbers, there is a fixed number of digits for a and b. You cannot approximate all numbers arbitrarily close. For example, with $b = 2$ and $n = m = 1$, we have $\pm a \in \{-1, 0, 1\}$, $\pm q \in \{-1, 0, 1\}$, so we can only represent the numbers $\{-1, -1/2, 0, 1/2, 1\}$: $\pm 1/2 = \pm 1 \times 2^{-1}$, $\pm 0 = \pm 0 \times 2^q$, and $\pm 1 = \pm 1 \times 2^{\pm 0}$ (where ± 0 might be represented as two different numbers, signed and unsigned zero, or as a single unsigned zero, depending on the details of the representation). If we use two bits for the exponent, we get the number line shown in Figure 9-16.

---

[3]Which real numbers are representable using a finite number of digits depends on the base, b. You cannot represent 1/3 using a finite decimal ($b = 10$) notation, but in base $b = 3$ it is simply 1×3^{-1}. Likewise, you cannot represent 1/10 in binary in a finite number of digits, where you trivially can in base 10.

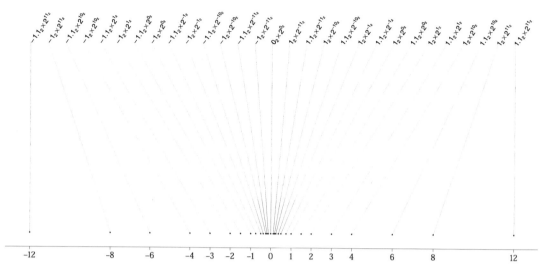

Figure 9-16. *Number line when we have one bit for the coefficient and two bits for the exponent and a single sign bit for the coefficient*

As a rule of thumb, floating-point numbers have the property that is illustrated in Figure 9-16. The numbers are closer together when you get closer to zero and further apart when their magnitude increases. There is a positive and a negative minimal number; you cannot get closer than those to zero except by being zero. If you need to represent a non-zero number of magnitude less than this, we say that you have an *underflow* error. There are also the smallest and the largest number (the positive and negative numbers furthest from zero). If you need to represent numbers of magnitude larger than these, we say you have an *overflow* error.

There isn't really much you can do about underflow and overflow problems except to try to avoid them. Translating numbers into their logarithm is often a viable approach if you only multiply numbers, but can be tricky if you also need to add them.

In the binary sum example from earlier, the problem is not underflow or overflow, but rather losing significant bits when adding numbers. The problem there is the fixed number of bits set aside for the coefficient. If you want to add two numbers of different magnitudes, that is, their exponents are different, then you first have to make the exponents equal, which you can do by moving the decimal point. Consider 1.01101×2^3 to 1.11010×2^0—where we have 5 bits for the coefficients (plus one that is always 1, i.e., $n = 6$). If you want to add 1.01101×2^3 to 1.11010×2^0, you have to move the decimal point in one of them. With the representation we have for the coefficients, $a = a_1 .a_2 \dots a_n$, we can only have one digit before the decimal point, so we cannot translate 1.01101×2^3 into 1011.01×2^0, but we have to translate 1.11010×2^0 into 0.00111010×2^3. We want the most significant bit to be one, of course, but we make this representation for the purpose of addition; once we have added the numbers, we put it in a form where the most significant bit in the coefficient is one. The problem with addition is that we cannot represent 0.00111010×2^3 if we only have 5 bits in the coefficient. We have 5 bits because our numbers are 6 bits long and the first one must always be 1. So we have to round the number off and get 0.00111×2^3. The difference in the sum is $2^{-4} = 0.0625$, so not a large difference in the final result, but we have lost 3 bits of accuracy from the smaller number.

Without limiting the number of bits, we have this calculation:

$$1.01101 \times 2^3 + 1.11010 \times 2^0 = \tag{9.2}$$
$$1.01101 \times 2^3 + 0.00111010 \times 2^3 = \tag{9.3}$$
$$1.01101 \times 2^3 + 0.00111010 \times 2^3 = 1.10100010 \times 2^3 \tag{9.4}$$
$$\tag{9.5}$$

If we cannot go beyond 5 bits, translating 1.11010 into 0.00111010×2^3 will get us 0.00111×2^3, and using that we get

$$1.01101 \times 2^3 + 0.00111 \times 2^3 = 1.10100 \times 2^3$$

This is clearly different from the calculation where we use more bits.

In general, you expect to lose bits equal to the difference in the exponents of the numbers. The actual loss depends on the details of the representation, but as a rule of thumb, this is what you will lose.

Assume we have one informative bit for the coefficient ($n = 2$) and two for the exponent, ($m = 2$), and we wanted to add six ones together, $6 \times 1.0_2 \times 2^0 = 1.1_2 \times 2^2$. Adding the numbers one at a time, we get

$$1.0 \times 2^0 + 1.0 \times 2^0 = 1.0 \times 2^1 \tag{9.6}$$
$$1.0 \times 2^1 + 0.1 \times 2^1 = 1.1 \times 2^1 \tag{9.7}$$
$$1.1 \times 2^1 + 0.1 \times 2^1 = 1.0 \times 2^2 \tag{9.8}$$
$$1.0 \times 2^2 + 0.01 \times 2^2 = 1.01 \times 2^2 = 1.0 \times 2^2 \tag{9.9}$$
$$\tag{9.10}$$

which is off by 0.1×2^2. If we add the numbers as we did with our `binary_sum` function, we instead have

$$1.0 \times 2^0 + 1.0 \times 2^0 = 1.0 \times 2^1 \; (\times 3) \tag{9.11}$$

$$1.0 \times 2^1 + 1.0 \times 2^1 = 1.0 \times 2^2 \tag{9.12}$$

$$1.0 \times 2^2 + 1.0 \times 2^2 = 1.1 \times 2^2 \tag{9.13}$$

which is correct.

Obviously, the floating-point numbers you use in Python have a much higher precision than 1 bit per coefficient and 2 per exponent, so you will not run into problems with accuracy as fast as in this example. The principle is the same, however. If you add enough numbers, you risk that the accumulator becomes too large for the addition with the next number to have an effect. If you run into this, then adding the numbers pairwise as in `binary_sum` can alleviate this.

CHAPTER 10

Hidden Markov Models

In this chapter, we consider an application of dynamic programming in the setting of statistical sequence analysis. We will explore *hidden Markov models* (HMMs) and two algorithms where dynamic programming is essential. Before we can start, however, we need a quick introduction to probability theory. If you are already familiar with probabilities, then you can safely skip the next two sections.

Probabilities

I will present a simplified definition of probability, where we only consider events that can have a finite number of outcomes. Generalizing to countable numbers is trivial, but we have to be more careful with more general types of outcomes. Since we will only need finite outcomes for hidden Markov models, I will not bother with that. I will also present some properties of probabilities without proof. They are not hard to prove, but we need to be slightly more formal to do that. You can pick up any textbook and find proofs on the first handful of pages if you feel you need it. Or you can trust me. You do trust me, right?

Probability theory is the mathematics we use for reasoning about "random" outcomes. These can be truly random or simply so complex that we do not attempt to model them in sufficient detail. Quantum mechanical effects are an example of the former since as far as we know, there is no underlying deterministic system that explains why they behave randomly. Tossing a coin is an example of the latter. When you flip a coin, classical physics take over, and the result is deterministic. However, it is sufficiently challenging to compute the outcome because it is sensitive to very subtle variations in how the coin is tossed, so it is easier to consider coin tosses random. When we assign probabilities to outcomes of some events, we give each outcome a nonnegative number, which we call the *probability* of that outcome. For example, with a coin, we could say that the probability of a head is 1/2 and the probability of a tail is also 1/2. With that probability assignment, we say that each outcome is equally likely. We require that if we

© Thomas Mailund 2021
T. Mailund, *Introduction to Computational Thinking*, https://doi.org/10.1007/978-1-4842-7077-6_10

sum the probability of all possible events, we get 1. This is a normalization that makes it easier to compare probabilities, but even without it, most of the theory works the same.

There are different ways of interpreting the numbers, but the simplest is to think of the probability of a given outcome as the fraction of how often that particular outcome happens if you repeat the experiment many times—ideally an infinite number of times. For the coin toss, if we give both head and tail the probability 1/2, we are saying that if we toss enough coins, then half of them should come up head and half should be tail. Here, it sounds like we can arbitrarily assign probabilities to events, and we can, but the field of statistics is concerned with estimating probabilities or underlying parameters of a system based on observations. There, you need to work out the probability of head vs. tail from a number of coin tosses. We will not concern ourselves with that, but it is an exciting field that I hope you will look at someday.

We have probabilities for each possible outcome of an event, but often we lump several events together. If you want the probability that an event is one of a set of outcomes, you add each outcome's probability in the set. For example, if the event is the roll of a six-sided die and you assign probability 1/6 to each side, you can take all the even numbers as your set: 2, 4, 6. Each has a probability of 1/6, and if you add them together, you get probability 3/6=1/2 (so, as your intuition would tell you, you are equally likely to see an even and an odd number when you roll a die).

We simplify this lumping further by talking about *stochastic (or random) variables*. These are functions that extract some measurement out of an outcome. When you consider rolling a die, the entire physical system is rather complex. If we only consider the number of eyes on the result, we have already reduced the complexity by only considering a summary of the full events.

The stochastic variable gives us the number of eyes from the more complex outcome. We use these stochastic variables to model the information we are interested in rather than consider the full complex system. We can define several stochastic variables to extract different information from the same event. We could, for example, let X be the stochastic variable that tells us the number of eyes we see on the die and the variable Y the stochastic variable that tells us if that number is even or odd. Here, the output we get from X tells us everything we need to determine Y, but this isn't always the case. Imagine, for example, rolling two dice. The variable X could give us the number of eyes on the first dice and Y the number of the second. We use the notation $P(X = n)$ to indicate the probability that X equals n, but we are a little lazy, so sometimes we simply write $P(X)$, with an implicit understanding that we either implicitly know the value of n

or we are talking about something that is true for all outcomes. When we have more than one stochastic variable, we use notation like this $P(X = n, Y = m)$ that you should read as the probability that X is n and at the same time $Y = m$.

This notation generalizes to any number of variables and to sets as well as single values. So to say that X has a value in set A and Y takes a value in set B, we write $P(X \in A, Y \in B)$. You get the value for this probability by summing over the elements in the set $A \times B$ the way you get the probability of a set for a single variable, so $P(X \in A, Y \in B) = \sum_{a \in A} \sum_{b \in B} P(X = a, Y = b)$. If you let either A or B be all possible values that the variable can take, X or Y, respectively, then you get $P(X) = \sum_Y P(Y)$ and $P(Y) = \sum_X P(X, Y)$ (here we use the sloppy notation where we sum over an implicit set, in this case, all possible values). This property follows from the observation that if we sum over all possible values of one of the variables, we are saying that this is the probability that one of the variables takes a specific value while the other can take any value whatsoever. This is the same as just saying that the first variable takes the specific value.

The process of summing over all outcomes of a stochastic variable is called *marginalization*, and it might look like a useless exercise, but appearances can be deceiving. It is one of the most useful operations in statistical modeling. Often, it is easier to model something if we can add "hidden" variables that we do not observe, but we include in the model nevertheless. When we want to know what the probability of some outcome is, where we only see some of the variables, we must marginalize over all the possible and unobserved values of the hidden variables.

We build models with many variables, and the models give us a joint probability of them all. We only care about some of them once we analyze data. The other variables are only there to make the modeling easier. Then, we marginalize them away as soon as we can to get information about the data we actually observe and not the variables we cannot observe. Because we get rid of the hidden variables when we can, we also call them *nuisance variables* (or sometimes *nuisance parameters*). I will call them hidden variables since we will talk about hidden Markov models, where the "hidden" in the name comes from such variables.

Let's assume that X and Y give us the outcome of two individual die tosses; X is the result of the first and Y the result of the second. What is the probability that X is two and Y is four, $P(X = 2, Y = 4)$? If the dice are tossed independently of each other, we do not expect the value of Y to depend in any way on the value of X. The probability that $P(Y = 4) = 1/6$ shouldn't change just because $X = 2$. The same goes for X; its value should not depend on the value of $Y = 4$.

Say we roll the first die, and we get 2 with the probability of 1/6. We have reduced the number of possible outcomes to one-sixth by this roll of the first die. Then we roll the second, and each outcome is equally likely, 1/6 for each possible value, and $P(Y = 4) = 1/6$. But the joint probability is not 1/6, far from it. We are getting one-sixth of the outcomes for Y *within* the space of outcomes where $X = 2$, which is only 1/6 of the total number of events. One-sixth of one-sixth of the possible outcomes, when all outcomes are equally likely, is $1/6 \cdot 1/6$. In other words, $P(X = 2, Y = 4) = P(X = 2)P(Y = 4)$. This is true for all the values the dice can take, so we can also write it as $P(X, Y) = P(X)P(Y)$.

This, however, is not always the case for other systems with two variables. When $P(X, Y) = P(X)P(Y)$, we say that the stochastic variables are *independent*, and it was the independence we used to reason our way to this result. There is an intuition to what we mean by independence here, related to how much we can learn about one variable by observing another, but I will get to that in a bit. That the joint probability equals the product of the marginal probabilities is how we *define* independence.

In general, you can think of the joint probability of two or more stochastic variables as a table, where you can look up the probabilities. For the preceding example, we have a two-dimensional table with six rows and six columns. Let's say that X indexes into the rows and Y into the columns. We can make one for the independent dice using numpy and get $P(X = 2, Y = 4)$:

```
import numpy as np
joint_XY = np.full((6,6), 1/6 * 1/6)
print(joint_XY[1,3])
```

We index into [1,3] because we index from zero in tables while we count from 1 for the dice, so index 1 is two eyes and index 3 is four eyes. You can get the marginal probabilities by summing over all the probabilities of one variable, and with a Numpy table, you can do it like this:

```
marginal_Y = joint_XY.sum(axis = 0)
marginal_X = joint_XY.sum(axis = 1)
```

Let us change the situation a little, so the dice are not entirely independent. We throw the first die and look at its value. Depending on the value, we pick one of two loaded dice for Y. If the first value is one, two, or three, we pick a die that gives a slightly smaller probability to one, two, and three for the second die, but if the first value is four, five, or six, we make those values more likely:

```
epsilon = 1/100
low_Y = [1/6*1/6 - epsilon] * 3 + \
        [1/6*1/6 + epsilon] * 3
high_Y = list(reversed(low_Y))
joint_XY = np.array(3 * [low_Y] + 3 * [high_Y])
```

We can compute the marginal probabilities once more, and we will find that they are uniform, that is, they give a probability of 1/6 for each outcome:

```
marginal_Y = joint_XY.sum(axis = 0)
marginal_X = joint_XY.sum(axis = 1)
```

```
>>> marginal_X
[0.16666667 0.16666667 0.16666667 0.16666667
 0.16666667 0.16666667]
>>> marginal_Y
[0.16666667 0.16666667 0.16666667 0.16666667
 0.16666667 0.16666667]
```

The floating-point numbers here are not exactly one-sixth because binary floating-point numbers cannot represent it, but it is as close as you get.

If the marginal probabilities are uniform, then the product of them must be as well. However, the entries in the joint probability table are not uniform. Some are smaller than others. So we do not have that $P(X, Y) = P(X)P(Y)$. The two stochastic variables are not independent—which, again, shouldn't surprise us as we explicitly made the second result depend on the first. As soon as you move away from the simplest textbook statistics, your stochastic variables are unlikely to be independent. This is not just because there are few truly independent events in the world, but because we build our models, so they do not contain completely independent aspects of what we model. If we wanted that, we could make our lives easier by making two separate models.

This does not mean that we never model independent variables. We often assume independence of some observable variables when we can't model the full complexity of what we want to analyze. We often start out with a model with independent variables, but once we start adding to the model, independence is lost. By lucky coincidence, or design, we sometimes get independence back when we marginalize over hidden variables later. Never assume that variables are independent, though; you have to show that they are before you start multiplying marginal probabilities to get joint probabilities.

If you have variables X and Y, with marginal probabilities $P(X)$ and $P(Y)$ and joint probability $P(X, Y)$, we define the *conditional* probabilities $P(Y|X)$ and $P(X|Y)$ as the functions that give us the equations

$$P(X,Y) = P(Y|X)P(X)$$

and

$$P(X,Y) = P(X|Y)P(Y)$$

The conditional probabilities are what we *really* have to multiply to a marginal probability to get the joint probability. You can think of $P(Y|X)$ as the probability that Y takes a specific value when you already know the value that X has. It is how the probability for outcomes of Y changes when you observe X; if you see X, you go from $P(Y)$ to $P(Y|X)$. If the variables are independent, so $P(X, Y) = P(Y)P(X) = P(Y|X)P(X)$, we see that $P(Y) = P(Y|X)$ (and symmetrical for $P(X) = P(X|Y)P(Y)$). You can read this as the probability of Y taking any given value is not changed when we observe X that it remains Y. This matches very well with our intuition about independence; knowing something about the first roll of a die does not affect where the second will land (unless we pick a different die for the second roll based on the outcome of the first, of course). You can rearrange the equations, when the marginal probability is not zero, to

$$\frac{P(X,Y)}{P(X)} = P(Y|X)$$

If you look at it this way, think about the result of X reducing the space of possible outcomes to some subset that happens with probability $P(X)$. It is inside this subspace that Y must fall. The intersection of X's and Y's subspace is $P(X, Y)$. We know which subspace we are in after observing X, and the fraction of that subspace is $P(X, Y)/P(X)$.

You can repeat this process to get conditional probabilities over many variables. If you have the joint probability $P(X, Y, Z)$, you can write it as $P(X)P(Y|X)P(Z|X, Y)$ or any other permutation of the three variables. The only thing you must keep in mind when doing this is that as you continue the process, all the variables you have had as a marginal or conditional probability must be included as variables you condition *on* later in the product. If you write $P(X, Y, Z) = P(X)P(Y|X)P(Z|Y)$, you are assuming independence, that is, knowing Y tells you everything you need to know about Z, independent of X, and you are saying that $P(Z|X, Y) = P(Z|Y)$. This is sometimes true, and the Markov and hidden Markov models we construct later have this property, but this is by construction. We build the models that way. It is not, in general, the case. But no matter what the model looks like, you will always have $P(X, Y, Z) = P(X)P(Y|X)P(Z|X, Y)$.

Every time you condition on one or more variables, you get a new probability function, and conditional probabilities work the same as other probabilities. If you have $P(Y|X)P(Z|X) = P(Y, Z|X)$, you have *conditional independence*. It is independence for the two probability functions $P(Y|X)$ and $P(Z|X)$. It does not imply independence, $P(Y, Z) = P(Y)P(Z)$, as $P(Y|X)$ and $P(Z|X)$ are different functions from $P(Y)$ and $P(Z)$. Nor does independence imply conditional independence.

To see that Y and Z can be independent, conditional on X, but not when we do not know X, consider this experiment. We toss a coin; the outcome is X. If we get heads, we pick one loaded die and roll it twice to get Y and Z. If we get tails, we pick another die and do the same thing. Now, if we know X, we know that Y and Z are independent rolls with the same loaded die, so they are independent outcomes. However, if we just observe Y, without knowing X, we get information about Z. They are rolls from the same die, so they have the same distribution, and therefore knowing about the outcome of one gives us information about the other. (There was information before as well, but only the information we already had by knowing X, which we already conditioned on, so there is no *new* information.) If there is information about Z in observing Y, they are not independent.

To see that we can have independence without conditional independence, let X and Y be independent dice rolls, and let $Z = X + Y$. With independent die rolls, X and Y are independent. But if we observe Z, we constrain what X and Y can be. Since $Y = Z - X$, observing X tells us everything about Y, so X and Y cannot be independent conditional on Z.

Most statistical modeling involves constructing a joint probability by combining conditional probabilities. We do not typically start with specifying a joint probability over many variables; rather, we introduce variables with conditional dependencies on each other. From that, we get the joint probability, and from the joint probability, we marginalize over hidden variables to get information about observable variables.

Conditional Probabilities and Dependency Graphs

As I mentioned in the previous section, the typical approach to construct statistical models is to start with some marginal probabilities and then build up the model with additional variables, where we specify conditional probabilities for each new variable. To make modeling easier, we often use a graphical notation when doing this. We draw the model with nodes for the variables and arrows when we want a conditional dependency. If there is no arrow, then the variables are conditionally independent.

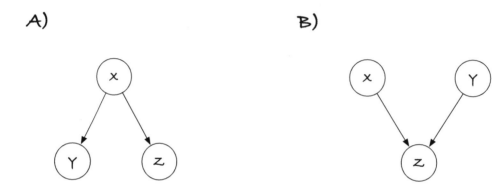

Figure 10-1. *Examples of simple dependency graphs*

Take the two examples I described in the previous section, where we defined conditional independence. In the first experiment (see Figure 10-1 (A)), we first toss a coin, X. This coin toss does not depend on anything else; we just pick up the coin and toss it. Then, however, we pick a loaded die dependent on the coin toss and roll the die twice for Y and Z. Since the choice of die depends on X, Y and Z depend on X, but they do not depend on each other. Where we would normally write $P(X, Y, Z) = P(X)P(Y|X)P(Z|Y, X)$ because we always have to condition on all the variables we have seen earlier in the equation, we can simplify it with $P(Z|Y, X) = P(Z|X)$ because the graph tells us so: if we know X, then Z does not depend on Y.

In (B), we have the example with $Z = X + Y$. We roll two dice independently of each other for X and Y, and since this is the first thing that we do, they do not depend on anything else, and since the rolls are independent, they do not depend on each other either. The variable Z, however, depends on both of them. It is the sum of their outcomes, after all, so we have arrows from both X and Y to Z.

The general procedure for translating a graph into a joint probability through several conditional probabilities is to start with all the nodes that do not have in-arrows and add their marginal probabilities. Then continue from them, and for each variable W, and each input arrow to it, $U_1, U_2, \ldots, U_n$, add $P(W|U_1, U_2, \ldots, U_n)$ to the equation. We need a place to start, so there must be nodes without in-arrows, and we cannot make a variable indirectly depend on itself, so there can be no cycles (paths leading from one node back to itself).

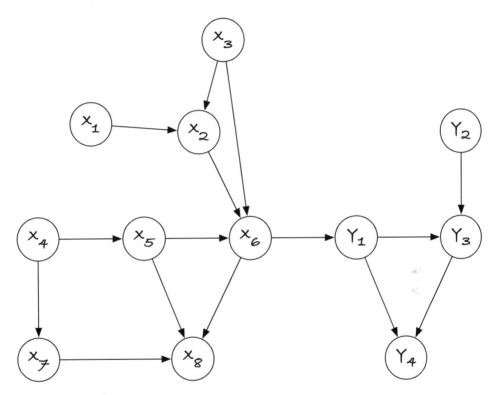

Figure 10-2. *A complex dependency graph*

Figure 10-2 shows a complex dependency graph. More complex than you would probably ever see in practice, but it will be informative for you to explore how you get the joint probability out of it.

Exercise: Write the joint probability, as a sequence of marginal and conditional probabilities, for the graph in Figure 10-2.

Markov Models

Markov models are designed to model sequential data. Think strings, for example, $X = X_1 X_2 \ldots X_N$, where one letter follows another. The simplest way to construct a statistical model of strings is to assume that each letter is independent of all the others, so the probability of the string would be the product of the probabilities of the letters, $P(X) = P(X_1)P(X_2) \ldots P(X_N)$. This, however, is usually too simplistic. If you read an English word, or a word in any language, you will have a good idea about the next letter once you are a few letters in. There is a lot of information in the prefix of a word about the next letter. There is a reason that we consider the observations as a sequence rather than just a lump of observations. A more detailed model of a sequence needs some level of dependency between the observations.

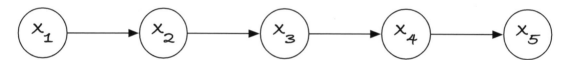

Figure 10-3. *Dependency graph for a Markov model*

The simplest, but still, nontrivial model is the *Markov model*. Here, we assume that each letter's probability depends on the previous one, but not earlier ones. It is still too trivial for words; if you see an "a" and an "n," you probably think that a "d" is likely to follow, which you wouldn't if you just saw an "n" at the beginning of a word. But we are talking simple models here.

The probability of the full sequence is then the marginal probability for the first letter and then conditional probabilities where letter X_i only depends on letter X_{i-1}: $P(X) = P(X_1)P(X_2|X_1) \cdot P(X_N|X_{N-1})$. The dependency graph in Figure 10-3 is such a Markov model. There are many processes where the state of affairs today holds all the information about what the states will be tomorrow, and knowing the state yesterday will not change our prediction. This doesn't mean that yesterday doesn't matter for the future; it just affects the future through the state we are in today. The past created the present, and the present will create the future. When we model the future, we think the same way: tomorrow depends on today, but whatever state we move to tomorrow, that state is all that will affect the day after tomorrow. We create tomorrow from the situation today, but we only affect the day after tomorrow through how we affect tomorrow. In any situation where you need to model a system that has this behavior, it is a Markov model you want.

It sounds straightforward unless you think of the present moment as encoding everything that went before it—that the current state somehow encapsulates all that came before us. If you add the memory of what we learned through history as part of today's current state, then it is likely a true model of affairs. However, that would be an incredibly difficult system to model, states would become insanely complicated, and we never do this. We consider simple systems such as this exactly to discard history, to get a simple model of states' progression.

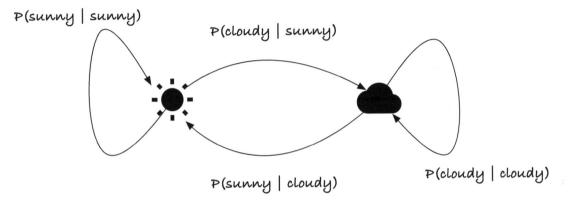

Figure 10-4. *Markov model state graph*

For example, consider the weather and pretend that we have no other available information except that it is sunny or cloudy on any given day. The probability of sun and rain varies over the seasons, of course, but on a sufficiently short time period, we could attempt to predict the weather for the next week as a Markov model. We have two outcomes per day, and when we talk about Markov models, we call these *states* as I did in the preceding. The states are "sunny" and "cloudy," for example. To specify the Markov model, we must first set the probability that we start with either a "sunny" or "cloudy" day. Then we specify the probability that one day is "sunny" and the next one is as well, that it is "sunny" and the next day is "cloudy," that a day is "cloudy" and the next day is as well, or that one day is "cloudy" and the next is "sunny." After that, we can write down the probability of every sequence of days.

We call conditional probabilities $P(Y|X)$ *transition probabilities* when we work with Markov models since they give us the probability that we transition from one state at index (day) i to another at index $i + 1$. The marginal probabilities we call *start states* because they are used at the start of the sequence. We represent the states and transitions in a graphical notation as well, but do not confuse this type of graphs with the dependency graphs.

They are related, but they are not the same thing. When we represent a Markov model as a graph, we have a node per possible state, not per observation in the sequence as in Figure 10-3. We have arrows between nodes X and Y whenever $P(Y|X)$ is not zero, and we often annotate the arrows with the probability for that transition. The sunny/cloudy Markov model would look like the graph in Figure 10-4.

Implementing a Markov model is as simple as drawing one. Build a table for the initial and transition probabilities, and follow the rule for translating dependency graphs into probabilities—particularly easy with a Markov model. For the sunny/cloudy model, an implementation can look like this:

```
import numpy as np

SUNNY = 0
CLOUDY = 1

start_probs = [0.1, 0.9] # it is almost always cloudy
transitions_from_SUNNY = [0.3, 0.7]
transitions_from_CLOUDY = [0.4, 0.6]
transition_probs = np.array([transitions_from_SUNNY,
                             transitions_from_CLOUDY])

print(transition_probs)

def joint_prob(X):
    result = start_probs[X[0]]
    for i in range(1, len(X)):
        from_state = X[i - 1]
        to_state = X[i]
        result *= transition_probs[from_state, to_state]
    return result

X = [SUNNY, SUNNY, CLOUDY, SUNNY]
print(joint_prob(X))
```

Arbitrarily, I have specified that you have only a 10% chance of starting with a sunny day. If today is sunny, tomorrow it is only sunny with a 30% probability, whereas if it is cloudy, you have 40%. Not realistic, I know, but it is the computations rather than the statistical accuracy you should focus on.

Exercise: Compute the joint probability for longer sequences. You will discover that the result gets smaller the longer the sequence—not surprisingly since we are multiplying numbers numerically smaller than one. This is a problem when computers only have a finite resolution because they store them as floating-point numbers. You can, however, compute the log of the probability instead. Implement that.

The initial state and transition probabilities are what we call *parameters* of the model. They are not stochastic, but the input we need to compute the probabilities. Because the probabilities depend on the parameters, call them θ, we can include parameters in the notation as $P(X|\theta)$, $P(X; \theta)$, or $P_{\theta}(X)$. The first notation is the same as for conditional probabilities. In some cases, in so-called *Bayesian statistics*, parameters are stochastic, and the two things are the same. However, in many cases, parameters are distinct from stochastic variables, and I prefer not to use that notation here. It is common enough, however, that you are likely to see it if you do any statistical model in your life. I will use the second notation, $P(X; \theta)$, when I want to make the parameters explicit. However, most of the time, I will leave them out when we implicitly know what they are.

With our Markov model, the parameters are the initial state probabilities and the transitions, so we can write $\theta = (\pi, T)$, where π are the start probabilities and T the transition probabilities. Using the parameters, we get this formula for the probability $P(X)$:

$$P(X) = \pi(X_1) \prod_{i=2}^{N} T[X_{i-1}, X_i]$$

Exercise: Write a function that computes this: given the two parameters, compute the probability of a sequence of observations.

Parameters must be inferred from data, and a common approach is *maximum-likelihood* estimates. There, you pick the parameters, θ, that maximize $P(X; \theta)$. You can see $P(X; \theta)$ both as a function of X that gives you the probability of observation X with the parameters fixed and as a function of the parameters that then gives you what we call the likelihood of the parameters θ given fixed observations X. When we consider it a function of X with fixed parameters, we call it the *probability* of X; when we consider it a function of the parameters, with a fixed X, we call it the *likelihood* of θ. The likelihood and the probability are the same formula; we just keep different things fixed. If you can compute $P(X; \theta)$, you can optimize it with respect to θ, and that will typically give you a good set of parameters you can use in the future. Because we use $P(X; \theta)$ both as the probability of X and the likelihood of θ, we call it both the probability and likelihood, depending on how we use it.

If you observe a set of sequences

$$\{X_1, X_2, \ldots, X_M\}, X_i = X_{i1}X_{i2}\cdots X_{Ni}$$

and you want to fit the parameters of a Markov model $\theta = (\pi, T)$, you can set the

probability of each start state as the frequency of start states, $\pi[k] = \sum_{i=1}^{M} 1(X_{i1} = k)/M$,

where $1(X_{i1} = k)$ is a function that is 1 if state X_{i1} is k and zero otherwise. Such a function
is called an *indicator function*. It is just a statistician's way of writing that you should
count how many times a sequence starts in state k. The transition probabilities you can

set to $T[k,h] = \sum_{i=1}^{M} \sum_{j=2}^{Ni} 1\left(X_{i(j-1)} = k, X_{ij} = h\right) / \sum_{i=1}^{M} (N_i - 1)$, where the indicator function tests if

we move from state k to state h. It is the number of times you see a transition from states
k to h in all the sequences, divided by the number of transitions you have. This gives you
the maximum-likelihood parameters, that is, $\text{argmax}_\theta P(X|\theta)$.

Exercise: If I flip a coin n times, with a parameter θ that tells me the probability of
seeing heads, what is the probability that I see k heads?

For physical reasons, it is close to impossible to create a loaded coin, so θ will be
1/2, but bear with me. There are many systems where you get a binary outcome and the
probabilities are not 50-50. A sequence of n tosses, $X = (X_1, X_2, \ldots, X_n)$, has probability

$\prod_{i=1}^{n} P(X_i) = \prod_{i=1}^{n} \theta^{X_i} (1-\theta)^{1-X_i}$ if we encode heads as 1 and tails as zero (we have probability

θ for head and $1 - \theta$ for tail; we can multiply the probabilities because the tosses are
independent). We can simplify this to $P(X) = \theta^k (1 - \theta)^{n-k}$ if there are k heads in the
sequence. That is the probability for this specific sequence, but if we want to know what
the probability is for a single toss, we don't want the order of events to matter. We want
to know what the probability of seeing k heads in n tosses is, since then we can set n to
one, and we have the probability we want: of seeing one head in one toss. If we want
the probability of k heads, we must sum together all the probabilities of sequences
with k heads. For this model, since each sequence with k heads and $n - k$ tails has the
same probability, we can simply multiply with how many sequences will have k out of

n heads, which is $\binom{n}{k}$, known as the *binomial coefficient*. So given θ, the probability of

seeing k heads out of n tosses is $P(k; n, \theta) = \binom{n}{k} \theta^k (1-\theta)^{n-k}$. The n goes as a parameter

in the probability because we fix the number of tosses to n and do not consider it a random variable. To find the maximum-likelihood estimate for θ, you must maximize $\binom{n}{k}\theta^k(1-\theta)^{n-k}$ with respect to θ. When we consider the probability a likelihood, we have fixed both n and k, so consider them constants, take the derivative with respect to θ, and set the result to zero.

Exercise: Show that this gives you $\theta = k/n$ as the maximum-likelihood parameter. If you see k heads out of n tails, the most likely probability for getting head in a single toss is k/n.

The probability distribution that tells you the probability of k heads out of n tosses, $P(k; n, \theta) = \binom{n}{k}\theta^k(1-\theta)^{n-k}$, is called the *binomial distribution*. If you have more than a binary outcome, say you roll dice instead of toss coins, the mathematics is very similar, and the distribution is called a *multinomial distribution*. If you see n_i outcomes of state i, in n experiments, then the maximum-likelihood parameter for the probability of seeing result i in a single experiment is n_i/n. You have a multinomial distribution for the starting probabilities in a Markov model, π. If you see n runs of the Markov model and n_i of the start in state i, then the maximum-likelihood parameter for π has $\pi[i] = n_i/n$.

At first glance, the transition probabilities look different because we have two variables in play. The transition parameter, T, is not a multinomial distribution. That is because it is a set of conditional probabilities: row k is the conditional probability $P(X_i|X_{i-1} = k)$. Each of the rows is a multinomial distribution, and you can estimate the parameters as such. Take one row at a time, say $T[k, -]$, then look at all the transitions out of k—those are the states you are conditioning on—and count how many times you move to each possible state. If you move from k to h n_{kh} times and you move out of a k state n_k times, then $T[k, h] = n_{kh}/n_k$.

Exercise: Write a program that estimates the parameters for a Markov model given a set of sequences.

As presented here, states in a Markov model only depend on the one before them, and the transition probabilities are the same for each position in the sequence. You can loosen these restrictions without much additional complexity. If states depend on a fixed number of previous states, say k, we call them k-order Markov chains. If you use different transition distributions at different indices in the sequence, you get an inhomogeneous Markov chain. The mathematics and the computational aspects remain much the same, however.

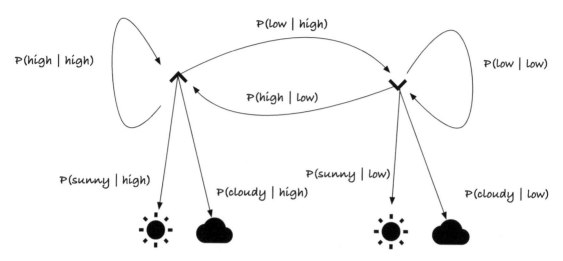

Figure 10-5. *States for a hidden Markov model of weather*

Hidden Markov Models

If you can directly observe the sequences you are interested in, Markov models should be your first choice. They are simple, they are computationally efficient to work with, and they often capture most of the behavior you want to study. However, there are cases where you suspect that there is some underlying sequence of events that create an observable effect, but you do not see the sequence itself.

Consider this example: We observe sunny and cloudy days, but we know that the sun and clouds are explained by some underlying weather state, like high pressure and low pressure. Assume now that we do not have access to a barometer—because otherwise, the example doesn't work. We cannot *observe* the high-/low-pressure states, only the weather, the sunny/cloudy states. If sunny and cloudy weather is determined by the underlying high-and low-pressure states, we shouldn't model a direct dependency between our observations from one day to another. We should model the weather as dependent sequences of the hidden states and let the observable states depend on those. We can draw a setting like that as in Figure 10-5. We have a Markov model of air pressure, and for each state there, we can observe both sunny and cloudy days, presumably with different probabilities. Our observations depend on the hidden states, but otherwise, they do not depend on each other. Each hidden state, however, depends on the hidden state before it.

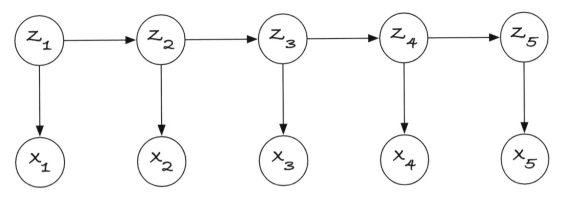

Figure 10-6. *The dependency graph for a hidden Markov model*

Let $Z = Z_1 Z_2 \ldots Z_N$ be a sequence of hidden states and $X = X_1 X_2 \ldots X_N$ a sequence of observable states. A hidden Markov model says that Z is a Markov model and the observable states are conditionally independent. The probability of a hidden state X_i conditional on all the remaining variables is the same as the probability only conditioned on Z_i:

$$P\left(X_i \middle| Z, X_1, \ldots, X_{i-1}, X_{i+1}, \ldots, X_N\right) = P\left(X_i \middle| Z_i\right)$$

In other words, if you know the outcome of the hidden state Z_i, then you have all the information about the observable state X_i that is in the system. Figure 10-6 shows the dependency graph for a hidden Markov model for a sequence of five hidden and observable states.

Exercise: Using the rules for extracting a joint probability from a dependency graph, write down the probability $P(X, Z)$ from the dependency graph.

Exercise: Implement a function that takes X and Z as input and computes $P(X, Z)$. The numbers will get too small for even relatively short sequences, so implement a function that computes $\log P(X, Z)$ as well. Obviously, you cannot just calculate $P(X, Z)$ first and then take the logarithm—you would still get a number underflow, and taking the log at the end doesn't help you. You need to take the log of each individual term and then add these log values together (remember that when you take the log of a product, you need to get the sum of the log of the terms).

Here is a quick warning: the observable states are independent if you know the hidden states, but they are not unconditionally independent. If you know some of the observable states, you have information about the other observable states; that is why we can reason about a hidden state that we cannot observe and that yet affects the observable states.

Assume that if we see the sun, we are more likely to be on a high-pressure day, and assume that high-pressure days are usually followed by another high-pressure day. Then, observing a sunny day today makes it more likely that we have high pressure. This then makes it likely that tomorrow will have high pressure as well and, therefore, likely to be sunny. The weather today informs me about the weather tomorrow, so the observable states cannot be independent. But all the information we have about tomorrow from today goes through the hidden states. If I already know that the air pressure is high today, then regardless of the current weather, it is likely that it will be high pressure tomorrow and thus sunny. We only have conditional independence, which is good, since otherwise, we couldn't say much about the hidden states.

A hidden Markov model has three parameters, two of which you are familiar with from Markov models. We have a start probability, π, we have transition probabilities, T—giving us the probability of moving from one hidden state to another—and we have *emission* probabilities, E, that for each hidden state give us the probability of emitting any given observable state. That is, $E[h, k] = P(X_i = k | Z_i = h)$. You already know how to estimate π and T from a set of hidden sequences, and the emission probabilities you can estimate similarly.

Exercise: Given a set of HMM runs, (X_i, Z_i), how do you estimate the probabilities $E[h, k]$?

Exercise: Write a program that, given a list of (X, Z) pairs, estimates the parameters for a hidden Markov model.

We can rearrange the joint probability for a hidden Markov model, $P(X, Z)$, as $P(Z)P(X|Z)$, where the $P(Z)$ term is the probability for a Markov model and the $P(X|Z)$ term is a product of conditionally independent $P(X_i|Z_i)$ terms. Suppose we want to know the margin probability for a sequence of hidden states in a hidden Markov model. In that case, we can approach this as we can with any other joint probability and sum over all possible outcomes of observable sequences, $P'(Z) = \sum_X P(Z, X)$. Here, I used $P'(Z)$ to distinguish from the $P(Z)$ probability for Z as a Markov model in the preceding. However, $P'(Z) = \sum_X P(Z, X) = P(Z) \sum_X P(X|Z)$. A conditional probability is still a probability, and those sum to one, which means that $\sum_X P(X|Z) = 1$ and that $P'(Z) = P(Z)$.

To get the probability of a hidden sequence, you should treat the hidden Markov model as a Markov model and ignore all the equation's observable states.

Exercise: If you have already observed the hidden sequence, Z, and you want to compute $P(X|Z)$ (but not marginalize over it), you can also exploit the rearranged formula. Take out the part that involves observable states and multiply the probabilities there. Write down the formula for this, and write a function that computes $P(X|Z)$ when it gets input X and Z. To prevent underflow, implement the function, so it gives you log P $(X|Z)$ instead of $P(X|Z)$.

If you only observe X and want to know $P(X)$, you cannot as easily compute $P(X) = \sum_Z P(X, Z)$. In the model, the formula for the probability has X depend on Z but not the other way; we cannot sum over some $P(Z/X)$ because we do not have an expression for that. It is no more readily available than $P(X)$ is. There are no tricks and no avoidance from summing over all the possible hidden paths. However, there is a dynamic programming algorithm for doing it, and that is what we get to now.

Forward Algorithm

Suppose we want to compute the probability of seeing a given observable sequence, regardless of what hidden sequences lie behind it. In that case, we are looking for the marginal probability $P(X) = \sum_Z P(X, Z)$. If you write down the expression for $P(X, Z)$, as you should have done in one of the exercises in the previous section, then you will see that there is no easy way to rearrange it to get a conditional probability, $P(Z|X)$, that sums to one. (You can, however, easily get $P(Z|X)$ from the joint and marginal probability, $P(Z|X) = P(X|Z)/P(X)$, but for that, we still need $P(X)$). You cannot brute-force sum over all possible hidden paths. If there are K hidden states and the sequence is N long, you have K^N such sequences. Going through all of them is impossible for even moderately long sequences. We need a smarter approach, and there is a dynamic programming algorithm, the *forward algorithm*, that does it. There is also a backward algorithm, in case you are wondering, and it does something similar; we won't see it here, though.

Before we get a dynamic programming algorithm, we need a recursive one. We focus on the last state in the sequence, Z_N. If we can get $P(Z_N, X)$ for all the K states that Z_N can be in, then we can compute $P(X) = \sum_k P(Z_N = k, X)$. We can write this probability as

$$P(Z_N, X) = \sum_{Z_{N-1}} P(X_1, \ldots, X_{N-1}, Z_{N-1}) P(Z_N | Z_{N-1}) P(X_N | Z_N).$$

This is a recursion for computing the probability of ending up in a specific hidden state, Z_N; after observing $X_1 X_2 \ldots X_N$, notice that the first term $P(X_1, \ldots, X_{N-1}, Z_{N-1})$ is the same as the one we are trying to compute for Z_N, so we are getting somewhere.

If we actually computed the value using this recursion, we would end up with the $O(K^N)$ running time because we would make K recursive calls that all would take $K(N-1)$ time, but we have dynamic programming to get us out of this trap: if we have a table with all $P(Z_{N-1} = k, X_1, ..., X_{N-1})$, let's call it $F[k, N-1]$, then we can get

$F[k', N] = \sum_k F[k, N-1] P(Z_N = k'|Z_{N-1} = k) P(X_N|Z_n = k')$ in time $O(K)$, and we can compute the entire column $F[-, N]$ in time $O(K^2)$ (for each k', of which there are K, we compute the value by summing over all the rows k in the previous column, $N-1$). This table, the *forward table*, is what we will compute.

What are the base cases? In the first column, $F[k, 1]$ is the probability that we saw X_1 while the first hidden state was $Z_1 = k$, or $F[k, 1] = \pi[k] \cdot E[k, X_1]$. We started in state $Z_1 = k$, and we emitted the first observable state. The recursive case is the one from the preceding, where we can use the HMM parameters in the formula:

$F[k', N] = \sum_k F[k, N-1] \cdot T[k, k'] \cdot E[k', Z_N]$.

Exercise: Implement the forward algorithm. In Python, we index from zero, and I have used one-indexed sequences, so you must correct for that. It shouldn't be that hard. You can use this template to get started:

```
def forward(X, pi, T, E):
    N = len(X)
    K = T.shape[0]
    F = np.zeros((K,N))
    F[:,0] = pi * E[:,X[0]]
    # Put the forward algorithm here
    return F
```

The line

```
F[:,0] = pi * E[:,X[0]]
```

is a very succinct way of doing

```
for k in range(K):
    F[k,0] = pi[k] * E[k,X[0]]
```

With Numpy tables, you can get entire rows or columns out of a matrix using the : operator. When we write `E[:,X[0]]`, we get the column that emits the observable state `X[0]`; the : tells Numpy that we want all the rows, and the `X[0]` picks the relevant column. When we multiply this column with `pi`, we get a table that has `pi[k] * E[k,X[0]]` at each index k. That is what we want as the first column in the F table.

If you are more comfortable with computing the column using an explicit loop, there is nothing wrong with that. It is slightly less effective, but it will not make a huge difference. Writing more explicit code has its benefits, and if that is what you are comfortable with, then that is what you should do. However, using abstractions rather than many lines of code also has its merits. If you are familiar with the abstractions, then using them makes the code clearer, and there is less code to inspect to see what an algorithm is doing. Using succinct expressions for sum, products, extracting rows and columns, etc. is part of the abstractions that Numpy provides, and if you have to write nontrivial programs using Numpy, it is worthwhile learning how to use them.

The initialization code assumes that your tables are Numpy tables, but X can be any sequence. You can try it out with

```
X = (0, 0, 1, 0)
pi = [0.5,0.4]
T = np.array((
    [0.1, 0.9],
    [0.2, 0.8]
))
E = np.array([
    [0.4, 0.4, 0.2],
    [0.2, 0.2, 0.6]
])

print(forward(X, pi, T, E))
```

If you have the forward table, you can get the likelihood like this:

```
def likelihood(X, pi, T, E):
    F = forward(X, pi, T, E)
    return sum(F[:,len(X) - 1])
```

The return statement's expression is a concise way to tell Python and Numpy to add all the values, :, in the last column, $len(X)-1$. An explicit loop would also work here.

The F table must have size $K \times N$ if there are K different hidden states and the sequence is N long. The forward algorithm uses constant space in addition to the table, so the space complexity is $O(KN)$. The running time is $O(K^2N)$ because it takes time $O(K)$ to fill in each of the $K \times N$ cells in the table. Once you have computed the F table, the likelihood for the parameters given the observed states, which is the same as the marginal probability of the observed states given the parameters, is $P(X;\theta) = \sum_k F[k, N]$.

What do we want to do with this likelihood? In itself, we do not use it for much. We rarely care what the probability of observations we have already made is or whether they are likely or unlikely. The common usage of a likelihood function is parameter estimation. If we have observations X and a likelihood function $P(X; \theta)$, then we can estimate parameters for our model by finding the θ that maximizes the likelihood. Once we have the parameters, we can, for example, use the model to predict future events.

In the previous section, we estimated the parameters of an HMM by counting how many times we see a state as the first in the hidden sequence, how often we see a transition from one state to another, and how often a given state emits a given observable. That is the best approach if we have observed both X and Z. You can get training data in some applications where you have both sequences, but in many applications, you can only get X. If so, you cannot count the transitions because you do not know what they are. In that case, one option is to maximize $P(X; \theta)$. I have written several papers based on hidden Markov models where I have maximized the likelihood, computed this way, for my parameters. All it took was the forward algorithm and a module for optimizing multivariate functions.

That being said, however, there are more efficient ways to estimate parameters if they can vary freely in the matrices (which they couldn't for the models in my research). These methods, however, also rely on the forward algorithm, and it is an essential algorithm when working with hidden Markov models. We won't explore parameter estimation more here, though.

With the forward algorithm, as with computing the likelihood if we know both observable and hidden sequences, we have a problem with numerical underflow. We are multiplying many numbers numerically smaller than one, so we get tiny numbers to insert in the table. At some point, the computer cannot distinguish them from zero.

When computing the likelihood for a Markov model, we can take the logarithm of all the probabilities and add them together. This, however, is only possible because those likelihoods consist entirely of the product of probabilities. With the forward algorithm, we also do addition. That $\log(a \cdot b) = \log(a) + \log(b)$ helps us with products, but there is no easy way to compute $\log(a + b)$ without computing the sum first and then applying the logarithm. Some implementations of hidden Markov models handle this using table lookups or other mathematical tricks, but the easiest solution, in my opinion, is to do without logarithms and instead *rescale* the numbers in each column of the forward table.

Each time that we have computed the values in a column, we add them together to get a scaling factor, and then we rescale them all by dividing them by this factor:

```python
def scale_forward(X, pi, T, E):
    N = len(X)
    K = T.shape[0]
    F = np.zeros((K,N))
    scales = np.zeros(N)

    F[:,0] = pi * E[:,X[0]]
    scales[0] = sum(F[:,0])
    F[:,0] /= scales[0]

    for i in range(1, N):
        # Compute column i here
        scales[i] = sum(F[:,i])
        F[:,i] /= scales[i]

    return F, scales
```

Each column is rescaled, so the column sums to one. You can get the original column back by multiplying the entries with the scale factor. That doesn't give you the corresponding column in the (unscaled) forward table because rescaling a single column doesn't change that the values there were based on the previous column that was also rescaled. You need to account for all the scaling factors to the left of a column to get the original F table back.

Let s_i be the scaling factor for column i. For the first column, the relationship between the scaled forward table, F', and the unscaled forward table, F', is $F'[k,1] = \dfrac{1}{s_1} F[k,1]$. For the second column, the forward recursion gives us that

$$F'[k,2] = \frac{1}{s_2} E[k,X[2]] \sum_{k'} T[k',k] \cdot F'[k',1]$$

which, because $F'[k',1] = \dfrac{1}{s_1} F[k',1]$, means

$$F'[k,2] = \frac{1}{s_2}\frac{1}{s_1} E[k,X[2]] \sum_{k'} T[k',k] \cdot F[k',1] = \frac{1}{s_2}\frac{1}{s_1} F[k',2]$$

311

If you continue expanding for other columns, you will find that

$$F'[k,i] = \frac{1}{\prod_{j=1}^{i} s_j} F[k,i]$$

or

$$F[k,i] = \prod_{j=1}^{i} s_j F'[k,i]$$

So, if you compute a list of the accumulated product of the scaling factors, you can multiply these to each column and get the original table back.

Not that you want to do that, of course. If you could represent the numbers in the original table without underflow, then there would be no need for scaling in the first place. However, since $F[k,N] = \prod_{j=1}^{N} s_j F'[k,N]$, the likelihood we want, $\sum_k F[k, N]$, is $\prod_{j=1}^{N} s_j \sum_k F'[k,N]$ and because of rescaling $\sum_k F'[k, N] = 1$. Thus, if we want the likelihood $P(X; \pi, T, E)$, then we can multiply all the scale factors together, $P(X; \pi\, T, E) = \prod_{j=1}^{N} s_j$. This is a pure product, so we can get the log-likelihood by summing the log of the factors, $\log P(X; \pi, T, E) = \sum_{j=1}^{N} \log(s_j)$, which greatly alleviates the underflow problem.

You can implement it like this:

```
def scale_log_likelihood(X, pi, T, E):
    _, scales = scale_forward(X, pi, T, E)
    return sum(np.log(scales))
```

The np.log() function is Numpy's logarithm function. Unlike the log() function from the math module, you can use it to take the log element-wise in a Numpy table, which is what scales is here.

Viterbi Algorithm

If you have a hidden Markov model, $\theta = (\pi, T, E)$, and you have somehow trained the parameters, a common usage is to predict the most likely hidden states given the observables. For example, you have a few weeks of weather data, collected as sunny or cloudy days, and you want to know which days are most likely high-pressure and most likely low-pressure days. Such a problem is called a *decoding* problem, and how do we figure that out?

One approach is to infer the most probable hidden sequence, conditional on the observed sequence, $Z' = \text{argmax}_Z P(Z|X)$. I have left out the HMM parameters $\theta = (\pi, T, E)$ here since we are assuming they are fixed. We don't have a direct expression for $P(Z|X)$ other than $P(Z|X) = P(X, Z)/P(Z)$, but since we do not vary X for this problem, we can optimize $P(X, Z)$ instead; we will get the same maximum sequence whether we divide by the then constant $P(X)$ or not. So the problem we want to solve is finding the sequence Z' that maximizes $P(X, Z)$. This is what the *Viterbi* algorithm does.

The Viterbi algorithm uses dynamic programming to compute the recursive function $V(k, i)$ that holds the probability of the most probable path $Z_1 \ldots Z_i$ that emitted $X_1 \ldots X_i$ and where we require that the last state is k: $Z_i = k$. In other words, $V(k, i) = \text{max}_{Z_1 \ldots Z_{i-1}} P(X_1 \ldots X_i, Z_1 \ldots Z_{i-1}, Z_i = k)$. Notice that we maximize over all the *previous* hidden states but not the *last* state; we get the probability of the most probable path conditional on it finishing in state k.

The base case, $V(k, 1)$, is trivial: $V(k, 1) = \pi[k] \cdot E[k, X[1]]$. The probability of the most probable path that begins and ends in state k is the probability of starting there. For the recursive case, we consider the previous state; call it k'. If the last step we took was from state k' to state k, then that cost us $T[k', k]$. The best possible path we can get from there is the best possible path that took us to k' in the previous column, so the best way to get to state k *through k'* has probability $T[k', k] \cdot V(k', i - 1)$. If we want to know the probability of the best path that ends in state k, regardless of which previous state we went through, we find the best of the previous states to go through to maximize over the previous states k'. We always have to pay for emissions as well, so that is also part of the recursion, and it looks like this:

$$V(k,i) = E\big[k, X[i]\big] \max_{k'} T\big[k', k\big] \cdot V\big(k', i-1\big)$$

With both the base cases and the recursion in place, translating it into a dynamic programming algorithms is straightforward: build a $K \times N$ table, V, fill in the first column using the base cases rule, and then iterate through the columns where you use the recursive case.

Exercise: Flesh out the dynamic programming algorithm.

Exercise: Implement the Viterbi algorithm.

When we have filled the V table, we are not quite done. We want the most probable sequence, Z', but what we get is a table where each column tells us, for each state, the most likely path that ends there.

That is not exactly what we want, but we can get Z' by backtracking through the table. We can find the most probable last state; it is $\mathrm{argmax}_k V(k, N)$. That is the last state in the most likely hidden path, $Z'_N = \mathrm{argmax}_k V(k, N)$. We cannot do the same for the second-to-last state, however. In column $N-1$, we know what the probability is for the most probable path through the first $N-1$ steps that ends in any given state, but the most probable end state here isn't necessarily the one that led us to the best state in column N. Instead, we must work out which state we actually went through, when going through column $N-1$, to end up in the best state in column N.

If $Z'_N = k$, then we got to k through a previous state, k', where $V(k, N) = E[k', X[N]] \cdot T[k', k] \cdot V(k', N-1)$. There might be more than one of these, but any of them was good enough to give us the best hidden path, so pick one of them. That state will be Z'_{N-1}. Now repeat the process back to the first column, and you have the path (or one of the paths) that maximizes $P(Z|X)$.

The running time for the Viterbi algorithm is $O(K^2 N)$ with $O(KN)$ space complexity. The V table is $K \times N$, and for each entry, we use $O(K)$ to find the maximum value. You need to consider K states in each column for backtracking, and the complexity is $O(KN)$.

What then about underflow? For the Viterbi, this is easier to deal with than for the forward algorithm. The log function is monotone in the sense that if $f(x) > f(y)$ then $\log(f(x)) > \log(f(y))$, so we can take the logarithm both inside and outside the maximization: $\log(\max(a, b)) = \max(\log a, \log b)$. That means that we can use a similar table, V', where

$$V'(k,1) = \log\left(E\left[k, X[1]\right]\right) + \log \pi[k]$$

and

$$V'(k, i) = \log\left(E\left[k, X[i]\right]\right) + \max_{k'}\left[\log\left(T[k', k]\right) + V'(k', i-1)\right]$$

and backtrack in this table to get the most probable path.

Exercise: Implement the Viterbi algorithm, with backtracking, using the logarithmic-transformed equations.

The Viterbi algorithm with backtracking gives us the most probable hidden path that explains an observed sequence, but it is not the only way to decode a hidden Markov model. You could, for example, be interested in knowing the most probable hidden state at index i: $\text{argmax}_k P(Z_i = k | X)$. If you get this value for all indices, it is called the *posterior decoding*, and it is different from the Viterbi decoding. With Viterbi decoding, you get the overall most likely sequence of hidden states. Still, the state that the most likely sequence has at index i is not necessarily the overall most likely state at index i. There are many possible paths (as we have argued, there are K^N differed paths), and of these, K^{N-1}, will have the state k and index i. If you add all of them together, k might be the most probable state at this index, even if the most likely complete path has a different state there, $Z'_k \neq k$. The Viterbi algorithm gives you a decoding informative about the entire sequence; the posterior decoding gives you information about a specific index. They both have their usage in different settings.

To compute the posterior decoding, you also use dynamic programming. In fact, you use the forward algorithm and the corresponding backward algorithm that we haven't covered here. We won't go into the details here, but it is a problem that you solve with essentially the same methods we have already seen.

There are more ways to decode, and there are more algorithms for estimating parameters, but the purpose of this chapter is not a thorough introduction to hidden Markov models. I wanted you to see a concrete example of an application, in this case a statistical model, that relies fundamentally on dynamic programming, and the two algorithms we have seen should do that. It is time to move on to the next topic.

## CHAPTER 11

Data Structures, Objects, and Classes

Until now, we have used basic Python data structures, such as dictionaries, tuples, and lists. These are excellent ways of representing data, but they are also primitive, and it can get challenging to rely on only these if you need to work with complex data—or even with not so complex data.

Let's say we have some medical data we need to work on, where for each patient, we have several measurements. For this example, we make it simple and say that we have a name, a height, and a weight for each of them. For this, we can use a list of tuples:

```
patients = [
    ("Henry", 173, 72),
    ("George", 166, 89),
    ("Edward", 181, 79)
]
```

Height is in cm, and weight is in kg, so from the data, you can probably guess that height is the second index and weight is the third. To get George's weight, we can look it up like this:

```
patients[1][2]
```

You could argue, correctly, that a map might be a better data structure than a list if we plan to look up people by name, but with such data, it is common to look up by all measurements and, for example, extract everyone within a certain weight range. There isn't necessarily anything wrong with putting the patients in a list.

What I do have an issue with, in this example, is how we extract names and measurements. We need to remember everywhere we access the data in our code, which index corresponds to which measurement. And when we read the code, we also have to

317

© Thomas Mailund 2021
T. Mailund, *Introduction to Computational Thinking*, https://doi.org/10.1007/978-1-4842-7077-6_11

remember that `patients[1][2]` is weight and not height. The data structure for a patient is a tuple, and a tuple knows nothing about patients and measurements, so it cannot help us here. We only have the option of looking up by indices.

We can, naturally, define variables that hold the indices

```
name = 0
height = 1
weight = 2
```

and write `patients[1][weight]` instead, and that alleviates the problem. But there is a better way.

Classes

All programming languages you are likely to use will have a mechanism for creating new data types. Python's mechanism is *classes*. It is a concept used in so-called *object-oriented languages*, and classes can do much more than we will use them for in this book. If you get into serious Python programming, you absolutely need to know about what classes can do. Still, I will refer to Python's documentation or books specifically aimed at Python programming for that. We will only use classes to define simple data types.

You can think of a class as a kind of function that gives you objects of a certain type and, at the same time, define what you can do with those types of objects. If we define a class for patients, then we can use it to create patient objects. You define a class with a syntax that resembles the one you used to define a function. For our Patient class, we can do this:

```
class Patient(object):
    pass
```

Instead of `def`, you use `class`. Then you have the class's name. By convention, function names start with a lowercase letter, but classes start with an uppercase letter. Python doesn't enforce it, but it is a convention that most programmers expect, so stick to it unless you have good reasons not to. The `(object)` isn't a parameter like for functions. It is part of a feature of classes called inheritance, and we won't use it yet, so ignore it for now.

After the first line, we indent and have the class body, similar to a function body. It doesn't work the same way as a function body does, you should not confuse the two, but it is where you define what objects of this class look like and behave like. I have put a single line in the body, pass, which means that I haven't defined anything at all for how patients should look or behave.

To create an object with the Patient type, you use the same syntax as you do for a function:

```
george = Patient()
```

Now george is an object of the type Patient. If you print it, you will get some gibberish like

```
print(george)
<__main__.Patient object at 0x10fbd62d0>
```

It says that we have an object of type Patient in the __main__ module (which is where you are when you evaluate a file; otherwise, it would be the name of the module you are in). The at 0x10fbd62d0 is where in memory the object sits. We cannot use it for anything except that it will be a unique ID for the object.

So far, so useless.

However, objects have their own *namespace*. This is another word for scope, except that they do not have nested scopes as functions do. We can assign to variables in them:

```
george.name = "George"
george.height = 166
george.weight = 89
```

We can make our list of patients like this, now:

```
henry = Patient()
henry.name = "Henry"
henry.height = 173
henry.weight = 72

george = Patient()
george.name = "George"
george.height = 166
george.weight = 89
```

```
edward = Patient()
edward.name = "Edward"
edward.height = 181
edward.weight = 79

patients = [
    henry,
    george,
    edward
]
```

And now you can get George's weight like this:

```
patients[1].weight
```

Variables we put in an object's namespace are called *attributes*.

We got rid of using indices to access our measurements, but it came at a hefty price. It is harder to create the patients now than it was when they were tuples. Naturally, there is a better way, or no one would use classes.

We can add something called a *constructor* to a class. It is a function that is responsible for initializing new objects. We will write one that sets the three values for a patient. We have to write it in the class body, and we have to call it __init__() since that is the name that Python looks for when it wants a constructor. The constructor can take as many arguments as you want, as long as there is at least one, and the first argument must be the object you will initialize.

For patients, we update the class

```
class Patient(object):
    def __init__(self, name, height, weight):
        self.name = name
        self.height = height
        self.weight = weight
```

and now we can initialize our list in the same way as we could with tuples, except that we make calls to Patient() for each element:

```
patients = [s
    Patient("Henry", 173, 72),
    Patient("George", 166, 89),
    Patient("Edward", 181, 79)
]
```

The self argument to the constructor is not one you supply when you create an object. You don't have it yet; after all, you want to create it. When you create the object, Python first creates it and then call the constructor to initialize it. The first argument will always be the object. The convention is that you should call it self. Every other programmer will expect that functions we define inside a class definition have, as their first argument, a parameter called self. Such functions will always be called with an object of the class' type, and it will always be the first argument—you are not in control of this. You can call the argument anything you want, but people expect it to be self.

Admittedly, we still haven't got that far from tuples. But we now have a way to access measurements without remembering indices, and we have a separate type for patients. If you have an object, you can get its type, and in the case of patients, that will be Patient:

```
print(type(george))
<class '__main__.Patient'>
```

You can use this to check if an object has the right type, but this isn't used much, and there are often better ways to write your code, so you don't need to test for types. But you can if you need to. If you use tuples for all your data, you do not have that option. You don't have any easy way to check if one tuple is a patient while another is a car.

When we print a patient object, we get a gibberish text, as we have seen. We can fix that by telling Python how to represent objects textually. For this, we need another function in the class body, this one called __repr__(). It takes the object as its only input—remember that we always call this object self—and then it should return the text we want. A good rule of thumb is to return the text you would use to create the object; in this case, we want something that looks like a call to the Patient() class:

```
class Patient(object):
    def __init__(self, name, height, weight):
        self.name = name
        self.height = height
        self.weight = weight
```

```
    def __repr__(self):
        return "Patient('{}', {}, {})".format(
            self.name, self.height, self.weight
)
```

Now, we get a nicer output for patients:

```
print(george)
Patient('George', 166, 89)
```

There are actually two different ways to get a better textual representation of an object. The __repr__() function should give you a "machine-readable" representation, which means that if you paste the output into your Python console, it should recreate the object. You can try to paste the output of george into your console, and you should get a patient named George, who is 166 cm tall and weighs 89 kg. For debugging purposes, this is very useful.

The other representation—and you implement it using a function called __str__()—should give you a "human-readable" representation. That one should be easier to read for yourself. When you print() an object, *that* is the function that Python will call. The reason that we got the preceding __repr__() string is that it will call __repr__() when you haven't implemented __str__(). If we implement __str__(), you will see a different result of printing:

```
class Patient(object):
    def __init__(self, name, height, weight):
        self.name = name
        self.height = height
        self.weight = weight

    def __repr__(self):
        return "Patient('{}', {}, {})".format(
            self.name, self.height, self.weight
        )

    def __str__(self):
        return "Patient {} is {} cm tall and weighs {} kg".format(
            self.name, self.height, self.weight
        )
```

```
george = Patient('George', 166, 89)
print(george)
```

Now the output is "Patient George is 166 cm tall and weighs 89 kg".

If you just write an object on the command prompt in Python, you get the __repr__()
representation, and if you print(), you get the __str__() representation. You can
explicitly ask for one or the other using the function repr() or str(), respectively. You can
see the difference if you evaluate this code:

```
print(str(george))
print(repr(george))
```

For simple data structures, like the Patient class we just implemented, I suggest that
you implement __repr__() and let Python use that for printing as well. From the output,
you can easily see the structure of an object, and if you want to, you can recreate it. For
complex data, where outputting code that might reconstruct it can be very verbose, you
probably want to implement __str__(), if not both functions.

Having separate types for different kinds of data, and using attributes to access the
data associated with an object, is a powerful tool for writing software. It is much easier to
follow the logic in your code if you do it, rather than rely on primitive types such as lists
or tuples, and if your code is easier to read, it is also easier to extend, maintain, and fix
when something goes wrong. All languages have some mechanism for defining new data
types for this very reason.

Exceptions and Classes

We introduced exceptions in Chapter 6, where we could raise an object of type
Exception, and I promised to return to them in this chapter. That is where we are now.
Exceptions are objects, and objects have types, and those types are classes. We can make
our own exceptions by making our own classes.

Consider this example from Chapter 6 that I have slightly simplified:

```
def raises_error(x):
    if x < 0:
        raise Exception("Negative", x)
    if x > 0:
        raise Exception("Positive", x)
    return 42
```

```python
def g(x):
    try:
        return raises_error(x)
    except Exception as e:
        if e.args[0] == "Negative":
            print("g:", e.args[0])
            return raises_error(0)
        else:
            raise

try:
    print(g(-1))
    print(g(1))
except Exception as e:
    print("Outer")
```

We have a function that raises exceptions for two kinds of errors: if it gets a negative and if it gets a positive number. The function g() handles cases with negative numbers, and we handle errors caused by positive numbers at the global level.

Since we are dealing with two kinds of errors, it is better to have two kinds of exceptions instead of using an attribute in an exception's class. We can define a negative and a positive error class like this:

```python
class NegativeError(Exception):
    pass

class PositiveError(Exception):
    pass
```

These are just like other class definitions, but we have to put Exception between the parentheses instead of object. The parenthesis syntax for class definitions means that the type you define is also of the type you put in the parentheses. When we use object, we say that our class objects are "objects"; it is the most basic type, and everything in Python is an object, so that isn't saying much. If you want to use a class as an exception, you must define it as such by saying that it is a kind of Exception, and that is what we do here. It is part of what is called *inheritance* in object-oriented programming languages, and you could fill entire books (and people have) on this topic. We will only briefly cover it in the next chapter. For now, all you need to know is that you should use Exception if you are defining an exception and object otherwise.

If we update the code to use our new types of exceptions, it looks like this:

```python
def raises_error(x):
    if x < 0:
        raise NegativeError()
    if x > 0:
        raise PositiveError()
    return 42

def g(x):
    try:
        return raises_error(x)
    except NegativeError:
        print("g: Negative")
        return raises_error(0)

try:
    print(g(-1))
    print(g(1))
except Exception as e:
    print("Outer")
```

It is much the same, but in g(), we no longer test the exception's content, and we no longer reraise an exception. When we write except NegativeError, we tell Python that we *only* want to catch exceptions of this type, so we know that we only get to the except block if this is the error we have.

Python checks which exceptions we can handle, and if it sees that we cannot handle PositiveError, it doesn't enter the except block but keeps propagating the exception. In the global code, the first call to g() will raise a NegativeError, which g() will handle, and the second call will raise a PositiveError, which g() will not handle, and Python will execute the except block instead. Why does it do that if we expect an Exception here and not a PositiveException?

That is because we defined PositiveException as a kind of Exception. All PositiveException objects are also Exception objects, but not all Exception objects are PositiveException objects. The Exception type is more general and the PositiveException type more specific.

You can make full hierarchies of exceptions—and classes in general—and this is frequently used to capture whole classes of errors.

Consider now this code that looks deceptively simple but shows you two new Python features:

```python
class ErrorOne(Exception):
    pass

class ErrorTwo(Exception):
    pass

class ErrorThree(Exception):
    pass

errors = [ErrorOne, ErrorTwo, ErrorThree]
for error in errors:
    try:
        raise error()
    except ErrorOne:
        print("ErrorOne")
    except ErrorTwo:
        print("ErrorTwo")
    except ErrorThree:
        print("ErrorThree")
```

We define three types of exceptions, and we make a list of them. This is the first feature we haven't seen before. Recall that, although functions have a special syntax when defining them, they are just objects that we assign to variables during the definition. We can assign functions to other variables, we can pass them as arguments to other functions, and we can put them in lists if we want.

It is the same with classes. Classes are objects, although objects we use to create other kinds of objects. Everything in Python is objects, including classes, so you can assign them to variables and put them in lists, and as long as you have a reference to them, you can access and use them the same way as if you used their original name. This also means that if you have a variable that refers to a class, you can use the function call syntax on that variable to create an object.

Here, we put them in a list, `errors`, and iterate through them. In each iteration, `error` refers to one of the three. They are exceptions, so `error` refers to an exception, and thus we can raise that exception. That is what we do in the `try` block. If it looks odd to you that we raise an exception directly in the try block, I agree with you. It isn't something we would normally do. But we can raise exceptions anywhere, and for the sake of an example, we do it here.

Now we get to the second new thing. Notice that we have more than one `except` block after the `try` block. If you have a sequence of `except` blocks, Python will check them one by one to find an exception type that matches the exception raised. It will then execute the corresponding block (and only that block). If it doesn't find a matching type, Python will propagate the exception further out the call chain or terminate if you do not catch the exception before you reach the outermost level.

If you run the code, you will see which block is executed for each of the exception types, and it should be what you expect.

Methods

All programming languages have some mechanism for defining new types of data structures. However, with languages such as Python, you can do more with your own data types than simply give them a name. You can add functionality to them, so you keep your data and the functions that operate on them closely together. You do this through *methods*.

I called `__init__()`, `__repr__()`, and `__str__()` "functions" in the previous section, but that is technically incorrect. They are *methods* of the class. There isn't much difference between functions and methods, except for how you call them, and for these three functions, we don't call them explicitly. So there was no reason to worry about terminology. Still, a function defined inside a class definition is called a method, and when we define our own and when we invoke them, we use a different syntax. And methods are what we will explore now.

Imagine that we wish to compute the BMI of our patients. That is the weight in kg divided by the square of the height in meters. We have used cm for our patients, so we need to multiply the height by 100 to get there. We can calculate BMI with this function

```
def bmi(patient):
    return patient.weight / (patient.height * 100)**2
```

and we can get George's BMI:

```
bmi(george)
```

You will find that he is obese, if that wasn't clear from his height and weight already.

To write a *method* instead of a function, all we have to do is move the function definition into the class body. Of course, we should use self as the parameter for the object then, but otherwise, we do not need to change the code:

```
class Patient(object):
    # __init__() and __repr__() code still
    # goes here

    def bmi(self):
        return self.weight / (self.height / 100)**2
```

The only difference we see between a method and a function is in how we call the thing. With bmi(george) we called the function. To call the method, you need to write

```
george.bmi()
```

Notice that we do not provide an argument to the method call, even though the method takes one. The first argument to a method is always the object, and Python knows which object you want because that is what you put before the dot in the call. So these three calls are equivalent

```
bmi(george)
Patient.bmi(george)
george.bmi()
```

except that the first calls the function and the second and third the method, with Patient.bmi(george) explicitly getting the method from the class and george.bmi() implicitly getting the method from the object george.

So when should you use methods, and when should you use functions? Generally, this is a matter of taste, although there are some cases where it is much easier to use methods, and we get to why in the next section. As a rule of thumb, I would say you should always use methods when you extract information about an object's attributes or when you modify the object. When I do more complex calculations on an object, I typically use functions. But it is a matter of taste, and as long as you are consistent in what you do, it doesn't matter.

You have used several methods already during the book. From Chapter 1, we saw methods for modifying a list

```
x.append(42)
x.insert(0, 13)
x.remove(2)
```

and such. These are methods on lists. The first argument the methods get is the x list before the dot. They modify the list, so it is natural that they are methods. Now you know why they look different from functions and how to write your own.

Let's see another example of a class. If you recall back when we discussed nested functions, we made a counter function:

```
def counter():
    x = [0]
    def tick():
        x[0] += 1
        return x[0]
    return tick
c1 = counter()
c2 = counter()
print(c1(), c2(), c1(), c1(), c2())
```

This is a good solution for what it does; it increments a counter every time we call it, but we also made a version where we got two functions, one for incrementing and one for getting the current value:

```
def counter():
    x = [0]
    def tick():
        x[0] += 1
    def val():
        return x[0]
    return tick, val

tick, val = counter()
```

A more natural way to implement this is to have a counter type, where we have methods for incrementing and getting the counter value:

```python
class Counter(object):
    def __init__(self):
        self.counter = 0
    def tick(self):
        self.counter += 1
    def value(self):
        return self.counter
    def __repr__(self):
        return "Counter({})".format(self.counter)

c = Counter()
c.tick()
c.tick()
print(c.value())
```

Strictly speaking, we don't need the value() method here. We can get the counter through c.counter. That was not an option for the function solution—we cannot get to the enclosing scope of those functions without calling them—but it would be an acceptable solution here.

However, there are schools of thoughts that say that you should never access attributes directly but always through methods. The reason for this is that you can hide the actual data an object contains from a user of the object, which allows you to change how the data is represented without breaking any existing code that uses the object.

With methods, you can always make sure that the data is consistent, and you can change the underlying representation at any time. If you access attributes directly, a user can leave the object in an inconsistent state, and if you change the representation, then all users need to update their code. This isn't a major issue with Python, which has a mechanism for changing an attribute into a method without changing the interface to an object that a user can access. I would recommend that you always use the attributes directly when you can for this reason; if the class changes later, there are other mechanisms for preserving the interface. If you need to replace such access to an object with methods, look up *properties* in the Python documentation.

Consider another example, a bank account. It has a balance, and you can insert and withdraw amounts of money. A class for that could look like this:

```python
class Account(object):
    def __init__(self, initial_balance):
        self.balance = initial_balance

    def insert(self, amount):
        self.balance += amount

    def withdraw(self, amount):
        if self.balance - amount < 0:
            raise Exception("Insufficient funds")
        self.balance -= amount

    def __repr__(self):
        return "Account({})".format(self.balance)
```

There is no overdrawing here—we raise an exception if there are insufficient funds.

Exercise: Make objects of the Account type and explore what happens when you insert and withdraw.

Yet another example is an object you can use to log events:

```python
from datetime import datetime

class Log(object):
    def __init__(self):
        self.log = []

    def add_entry(self, entry):
        now = datetime.now()
        self.log.append("{}: {}".format(now, entry))

    def print_entries(self):
        for entry in self.log:
            print(entry)
```

You can create an object, add entries to it (they will be tagged with the time you log them), and print all the entries.

Exercise: Write a program that adds log entries to a log and prints the log before you finish the program.

Exercise: Add a method that clears the log, that is, removes all entries.

Exercise: I didn't write a __repr__() method this time because there isn't any way to reconstruct the object from a list of log entries. If you add a parameter to the constructor, perhaps with a default parameter, you could do that. Try to extend the constructor and then write a __repr__() method that can reconstruct a Log object.

Polymorphism

Polymorphism, or "having many forms," is a simple idea, although not always simple to implement. Luckily, we don't need to worry about how to implement it; Python already has an implementation for us. The idea is this: we should be able to write code that will work on many different data types. We have already done so. We wrote sorting functions that will work on any type where we can test if one value is larger than another. That works for floating-point numbers, integers, strings, and many more types because we can compare these types the same way.

When we write a function, the operations we do on the objects it manipulates define what objects the function can handle. Some programming languages are very strict about what types a function can accept, and you might have to jump through many hoops to write a polymorphic function, but with Python, it is simple. You can write a function, and it will work on all objects where the operations you apply make sense.

Let's take an example, where we can use our own classes to get polymorphism. Imagine that we have a list of shapes and we want to compute the sum of their areas. Easy enough, if we have a method per shape for that:

```
def sum_of_areas(shapes):
    result = 0
    for shape in shapes:
        result += shape.area()
    return result
```

This function will work for all objects that have an area() method. So we need to define area methods for our shape types. For a rectangle, this could be the class

```python
class Rectangle(object):
    def __init__(self, width, height):
        self.width = width
        self.height = height
    def area(self):
        return self.width * self.height
```

while for a circle, this could be the class

```python
import math
class Circle(object):
    def __init__(self, radius):
        self.radius = radius
    def area(self):
        return math.pi * self.radius**2
```

The sum_of_areas() function works because we can define area methods for the different kinds of shapes we have. It doesn't have to know about which shapes we might have defined types for; it only needs to know that it can call shape.area(). The methods enable us to write a polymorphic function.

If we didn't have methods, we would need to handle different shape types separately. We might have to write something like this:

```python
def sum_of_areas(shapes):
    result = 0
    for shape in shapes:
        if type(shape) == Circle:
            result += math.pi * shape.radius**2
        if type(shape) == Rectangle:
            result += shape.width * shape.height
    return result
```

If we have many functions that need to compute the area of a shape, we shouldn't do that, but instead move the code to a function, and it would look similar:

```python
def area(shape):
    if type(shape) == Circle:
        return math.pi * shape.radius**2
```

```python
    if type(shape) == Rectangle:
        return shape.width * shape.height

def sum_of_areas(shapes):
    result = 0
    for shape in shapes:
        result += area(shape)
    return result
```

It works. sum_of_areas() looks almost the same, but there might be more functions like area() that need to handle different shapes. And if we introduce a new type of shape in the future, we need to find *all* such functions and make them handle a new kind.

With methods, we can put type-specific code in a class, and all other functions can use the operations we define there. It doesn't matter how often we add new types of shapes, the polymorphic functions will work the same as always, and we never need to update functions that test for types because those aren't necessary now.

A set of methods that you need for a function to manipulate objects is sometimes called an *interface*, and some programming languages are very strict about defining and using interfaces. Python is not—if you define the methods you need, then that is all that is required. It puts more responsibility on you because you have to make sure that you have implemented all the methods you need, and Python won't check this for you before your code runs and your program potentially crashes. But the flexibility makes it easy and fast to write code, as long as you are careful.

For a similar example, we might work with different kinds of animals, and we want to hear what they say. If we give them all a method for that, we do not need to test their types in any code; we just call that method:

```python
class Duck(object):
    def say(self):
        print("Quack!")

class Dog(object):
    def say(self):
        print("Wuff!")

class Worm(object):
    def say(self):
        print("...")
```

```
animals = [
    Duck(),
    Dog(),
    Worm()
]
for animal in animals:
    animal.say()
```

If you add a new kind of animal, you need to give it a say() method, but other than that, all existing code will function as before.

I didn't write __init__() methods for these classes because we don't need to initialize them with any data. You don't need to implement constructors if they do not do anything anyway.

Abstract Data Structures

Abstract data structures are an older concept than classes and polymorphism and stem back to early algorithmic design. The terms essentially mean the same thing, though. You will just be more likely to hear the term "abstract data structure" when you read about algorithms, while you are more likely to hear about interfaces and polymorphism when you read about software design.

Concrete data structures are representations of data combined with operations that we can use to query and modify said data. Lists, tuples, sets, and dictionaries are all data structures, and so are the classes we define ourselves. An *abstract* data structure is a definition of operations we want a type to have, but not an implementation of them. Think of them as a description of the methods that an object must have, for our polymorphic functions to work. It is a description of an interface and nothing more.

When we use abstract data structures together with algorithms, we do so because an algorithm might need to represent data in some unspecified way that doesn't matter, as long as the algorithm can perform certain operations on the data. Concrete implementations might vary in both practical and asymptotic complexity. Still, the algorithm's correctness is guaranteed as long as the concrete implementation satisfies the requirements we put on the abstract data structure.

Abstract data structures relate to polymorphism, although as a concept, they are much older. They define an interface, and any implementation that satisfies this interface can be used by the algorithm. You can plug in any implementation, depending on performance requirements, for example. Without polymorphism, you might still have to modify some of your code if you want to try another implementation of an abstract data structure, but with polymorphism, you can literally replace one implementation with another with no effort.

In later chapters, we will see different abstract data structures and how to implement them.

Magical Methods

By now we have seen three methods that start and end with double underscores, __init__(), __repr__(), and __str__(). You need __init__() if you want to initialize an object you make from a class. That is the method you use to do that, and it will automatically be called when you construct the object. If you want a textual representation of an object, __repr__() and __str__() are two different ways, for different purposes, to do this. But there are many more of these double underscore methods, and they tell Python how it should use your objects in various syntactic constructions. If you want to write a class where Python can test if it contains an element

```
if x in obj:
    pass
```

or if you want to iterate over an object

```
for element in obj:
    pass
```

you use double underscore methods. The same if you want to subscript an object

```
obj[i]
obj[j] = k
```

or apply arithmetic operations on objects:

```
obj1 + obj2
obj1 * obj2
```

You don't have to use any of these magical methods if you do not want to, but they tie in with Python's syntax, and in many cases, they will make it easier to use your classes. Don't give a class an addition method just because you can, but if your objects are something you could reasonably add together, your code will be easier to understand with the `obj1 + obj2` syntax rather than with `obj1.add(obj2)`.

I will not list all the special methods you can implement to fit your classes to Python's syntax. There are too many, and you will forget most of them anyway; I know I do. You can look them up in the Python documentation when you feel you need to use one. But practically everything that Python's built-in types can do, you can make your objects do as well.

Don't overdo it. Your choice of methods and how Python's syntax should work with your objects affect how readable your code is; use it when it helps readability, and leave it alone when it doesn't.

As a short example, we can implement a class for manipulating polynomials. I have implemented a version where you can evaluate a polynomial at a point and add two polynomials:

```python
import itertools
class Polynomial(object):
    def __init__(self, coefficients):
        self.coefficients = coefficients

    def __repr__(self):
        return 'Polynomial({})'.format(self.coefficients)

    def __str__(self):
        terms = []
        for pow, coef in enumerate(self.coefficients):
            terms.append("{}*x^{}".format(coef, pow))
        return ' + '.join(terms)

    def __call__(self, x):
        res = 0
        for pow, coef in enumerate(self.coefficients):
            res += coef * x**pow
            return res
```

```
def __add__(self, other):
    coefficients_pairs = \
        itertools.zip_longest(self.coefficients,
                              other.coefficients,
                              fillvalue = 0)
    new_coefficients = [a + b for a,b in coefficients_pairs]
    return Polynomial(new_coefficients)
```

We represent polynomials as lists of coefficients, and from the __str__() method, you should be able to work out how that works. Print an object, and it should be clear. It gets a little bit ugly with negative coefficients, because we write plus between them, and then a minus, but if you are interested, you can fix it:

Exercise: Make a prettier __str__() method that doesn't put a plus in front of a negative coefficient.

The __call__() method tells Python how to evaluate an object as if it was a function. Because we define __call__() here, we can evaluate a polynomial as poly(x). The __add__() method implements addition. Adding two polynomials, represented by lists of coefficients, means we must add them component-wise. If one list is longer than the other, we need to add zero to the longer list components. The function itertools.zip_longest() will give us a pair of elements, matching the indices in the two input lists, and use the fillvalue parameter for the shorter list when we run past its last element.

Try it out:

```
poly1 = Polynomial([1, 2])
poly2 = Polynomial([0, 1, 2])
poly3 = poly1 + poly2
```

Exercise: Subtracting a polynomial from another is as easy as adding them. Implement this in the __sub__() method. Be careful that you do not modify any of the two original polynomials.

Exercise: Multiplying two polynomials is more complicated, but try to implement the __mult__() method for the class. If it is difficult, then restrict your implementation to multiplying with a constant.

Exercise: Guess what I want you to do with division now? Find out which magical method you need to implement and then do it.

We will use selected magical methods in the following chapters, where they make sense for what we aim to do. Keep them in mind when you think that your classes should support syntax you are familiar with for other data types in Python.

Class Variables

We put attributes into an object whenever we write something like `obj.attribute = value`, so when we wrote

```python
class Patient(object):
    def __init__(self, name, height, weight):
        self.name = name
        self.height = height
        self.weight = weight
```

we defined a constructor that would initialize new objects with a name, a height, and a weight. While less used, you can also add attributes to a class itself. Classes also have their own namespace, and you can put variables there. If you assign to a variable inside the class definition body, it will sit in the class namespace, for example:

```python
class Patient(object):
    all_patients = []
    def __init__(self, name, height, weight):
        self.name = name
        self.height = height
        self.weight = weight
        self.all_patients.append(self)
```

Here, we have added a list to the class, but not the class's individual objects. We can see class variables through an object, so we can get the list using `self.all_patients`, but the list doesn't live in the object; it lives in the class. You can get hold of it using the class' name or through an object of the class:

```python
george = Patient("George", 166, 89)
edward = Patient("Edward", 181, 79)
print(Patient.all_patients)
print(george.all_patients)
```

You use class variables when you want to share something between objects of a class or when you want to define constants or similar that you don't want to put in the global scope.

I bring them up to explore in more detail what happens when you define a class. Just like when you define functions, you create an object and assign it a name in one statement. You can assign both classes and functions to different variables if you want, and you can pass them to function and method calls as you please.

With functions, Python doesn't evaluate the body when you define the function. That doesn't happen until you call the function. With classes, though, Python does exactly that: it runs the code inside the class body. Every variable you define there becomes a class variable. That includes variables you assign to and methods you define. A method definition is just a combination of creating a method object and giving it a name. Everything you define in a class lives in that class, but you can also access them through an object. It doesn't work the other way around, though. Values you put into an object are only held in that object, and they are not shared between all other objects of the class. When we call, for example, __init__() and it writes to self.x, for any attribute x, we access the object and not the class.

Consider this:

```
class MyClass(object):
    a = "A"
    def __init__(self):
        self.b = "B"
        self.__class__.c = "C"
        d = "D"
```

Here, we define a class global variable a, and only when we create an object do we give it the object-specific value self.b in __init__(). If we want to write to a class variable through an object, we cannot do so directly. If you write to obj.x = y, you write to the object obj. But we can get the object's class, obj.__class__, and write to that. That is what we do with c. If we just write to a variable in a method, we have a local variable, d in this example, just as with functions.

The variables you put into an object, like with self.b = "B", will go into a dictionary, and you can get the dictionary for an object obj through obj.__dict__:

```
obj = MyClass("foo")
obj.__dict__
```

In this case, it will be {'x': 'foo'}. It only holds x because we didn't put the other variables in the object but the class or the method's local environment.

A class is also an object, and it also has a dictionary that you can get it with:

```
MyClass.__dict__
```

There are many more variables in this dictionary because classes are more complex objects than our own, but it will contain the class variables and methods we assigned to or defined in the class body. They go into this dictionary.

Each object has its own dictionary, and each class—because these are just objects—has its own dictionary as well. Objects share the class variables because there is just one class object for them, the one we got when we defined the class. Those class variables do not sit in the objects' dictionaries as copies but sit in the class' dictionary. The objects have their separate dictionaries, where the other variables sit, and these are not shared because each distinct object has a distinct dictionary. You can get both object and class variables with the same syntax, obj.x, however, because this syntax does more than look in the dictionaries. We return to this later in the chapter.

When you define a class, you evaluate the class body's code, and everything you define there goes into the class' dictionary. You do not call any of the methods—you only define them. That works the same as with functions. When you create an object, you evaluate __init__() with an object of the class, and there you can set object attributes.

Methods are essentially just functions defined inside a class. You use the same syntax as when you define a function, although you should always have one argument and call it self. Calling it self isn't a hard rule, and you don't have to do it, but you always need a first argument that will be the object itself. You define them and give them a name at the same time. Because you give them a name, that name ends up in the class namespace, and you can get your methods from objects.

You can also simply put functions into a class if you want to:

```
def print_func(x, y):
    print(x.x + y)

class MyClass(object):
    def __init__(self, x):
        self.x = x
    def method(self, y):
        print(self.x + y)
    function = print_func
```

Here, we have a global function `print_func()`, and in objects of class `MyClass` we have class variables `method` and `function`. The first we have defined inside the class body, and the second we have just assigned to. They work the same way, though. If we have an object of type `MyClass`, then we can get both `method` and `function`, and we can call them:

```
obj = MyClass("foo")
print_func(obj, "bar")
MyClass.method(obj, "bar")
MyClass.function(obj, "bar")
obj.method("bar")
obj.function("bar")
```

All five calls will print "foobar." The only difference between the calls is where we put the `obj` argument. When you call a function, `print_func(obj, "bar")`, you need to give it two arguments, and the first should be an object from where we can get the attribute x. You can get both method and function from the class (and there is really no need to distinguish between functions and methods, so let's just call them methods). When you get them from the class' namespace, `MyClass.method`, you get functions/methods that take two arguments, just like the `print_func` (one of them is the same function, after all).

However, when you get the methods from the object, in the two last calls, something different happens. When you write `obj.method` or `obj.function`, you get an object that you can call, but it takes one less argument than the function from the global namespace or the functions we got from the class. When we get the methods from the *object*, we *bind* the first argument, so `self` will be `obj` when we call the methods. It is very similar to the `bind1st()` function we saw in Chapter 7. Because we always bind the first argument to the object itself, when we get the function from it, we call the first parameter `self`. That is all there is to it. You can see that it works just as well for a function we have defined outside the class.

It is when you get the method from an object that you bind the first argument. You don't need to call it before that happens. So you can extract a method with two arguments, where the first is `self`, and now you have a function that takes one argument because the first is already bound:

```
f = obj.function
f("bar")
```

If you get a method through the class and not indirectly through an object, you don't bind the first argument, and then you need to explicitly pass an object to it as the first argument:

```
MyClass.method(obj, "bar")
MyClass.function(obj, "bar")
```

But this isn't the whole story. The rules I wrote about classes—you define variables there, and if they hold objects that you can call, then something like obj.method will bind the first argument—are true. But it is true for *class variables*, not object attributes. If you put a function into an object

```
def f(x,y):
    return x + y

class MyClass(object):
    def __init__(self):
        self.f = f

obj = MyClass()
obj.f(1, 2)
```

then that function is just a function when you extract it with obj.f. *That* variable doesn't sit in the *class*, but in the *object*, and you always get attributes from objects without modifying them.

Well, Python is flexible enough that you can change that rule, but by default, you get exactly what you put in the object's dictionary, but variables you get from a class' dictionary can behave differently. The exact way that attributes work is complicated, but I will describe the way they typically work in the next section and give you the full explanation in the sections after that.

Anyway, if you want a method that always binds self, define it inside the class definition, or write a function that takes the object as its first argument and assign it to a class variable. If you want a function that you can get without binding the first argument, then put it in the object and not the class, or get the function directly from the class and not through an object.

If your head is spinning now and you find it all too complex, I will ask you to take a deep breath and calm down. You very rarely put functions in class variables, and if you only write methods (and remember that they need the self argument), then there is nothing to worry about. Just use class variables and methods when you want those, and put attributes in objects when they shouldn't be shared between objects.

Attributes (The Simple Story)

The full mechanism behind something as simple as getting an object attribute, `obj.attribute`, is very flexible and rather complex. If you understand it, you will have a solid grounding in how the object-oriented philosophy behind objects and classes works, and you will understand how attributes can behave differently when you get them from objects of different classes and when you access class vs. object attributes.

The whole mechanism can be rather abstract, however, and you certainly do not need to know about it to implement your own data types. In day-to-day programming, you rarely consider it at all. This section will describe how accessing attributes typically works, which is how your own classes and objects will behave unless you tap into the deeper magic in the following three sections.

The default behavior is what you will use in 95% of your code unless you are developing complex frameworks. Of the remaining 5%, 4.9% uses so-called *descriptors,* and you can safely jump to the section with that title after reading this one. These descriptors exploit the magic in the next three sections, but you can use them without understanding how they work. I include the next three sections in the book because they give you some hint of the power and flexibility in object-oriented programming that we do not otherwise cover, but you can skip them if you want to and still follow the rest of the book.

Let's build a class and create an object to see how looking up an attribute works:

```python
class MyClass(object):
    x, y = "foo", "bar"
    def m(self):
        pass

    def __init__(self):
        self.x = "qux"
        self.z = "qax"

        def f(x): pass
        self.f = f

obj = MyClass()
```

If you examine the dictionaries in the object and the class

```python
print(obj.__dict__)
print(MyClass.__dict__)
```

you see that the object has values for x, z, and f, while the class, among other things, has x, y, and m.

When you assign to an attribute

```
obj.foo = "bar"
MyClass.baz = "foo"
```

the default is always to put the value into the appropriate dictionary, the object dictionary or the class dictionary.

When you ask for an existing attribute, however, you might do more:

1. If you ask for obj.attribute and attribute is in obj. dict, you get the value in the dictionary. You get it exactly the way it is, and you don't modify it.

    This means that obj.x, obj.z, and obj.f get you the three values in obj.__dict__ and obj.f is the function and not a bound method. There is an x in both obj.__dict__ and MyClass.__dict__, but you get the one in the object because the lookup will always look in the object's dictionary first. It doesn't look anywhere else if it finds what it is looking for there.

    It is the same rule for a class. If you ask for MyClass.x, MyClass.y, or MyClass.m, you get the value from MyClass' dictionary, and MyClass.m is the value in the dictionary; it is not modified into a bound method.

2. If you ask for obj.attribute and attribute is *not* in obj.__dict__, you will instead look in obj.__class__.__dict__, so the class' dictionary. If you find what you are looking for here, you get it back, but if it is a function or method, you bind the first argument to obj before you get it.

    This means that if we ask for obj.y, we get the same value as if we had asked for MyClass.y because we find y in the same dictionary. However, if we ask for obj.m, which is a method, we get the *bound* method back, which we didn't when we asked for m directly from the class with MyClass.m.

There is a modification to the second rule when you access a descriptor, and you can read about that in the "Descriptors" section. There is another rule that says that if you cannot find it in the class' dictionary, you search through so-called superclasses, and we cover those in the next chapter. If you don't find `attribute` in any of the dictionaries, you will, by default, get an exception.

These rules are the standard behavior, and they are the ones you use in almost all code you write. But you can change the rules, and on very rare occasions, that can be a powerful tool. If you find that you need to do something like that, you will get an idea about how in the next three sections. If you just want to get on with programming and algorithms, you can now skip to the "Descriptors" section.

Objects, Classes, and Meta-classes

The rules for how you get an attribute are Python specific, although there are other languages with similar rules. The conceptual model underlying it is the ultimate model for object-oriented languages with classes; many languages approximate it, and few, like Python, implement it completely. It isn't something you *need* to know to write Python code—you can live a happy life without ever thinking about it, but some Python features can look like magic if you don't have the mental model to reason about it. You can safely skip this section if you are willing to accept that something magical happens from time to time, but you will see an elegant way to think about objects and classes if you continue reading.

The rules for how objects and classes work are both simple and complex. Simple because there really only is one rule, but complex because the rule is used to implement complex behavior. The rule is this: everything is an object, and all objects have classes that define how objects behave.

That also means that classes are objects and they have classes (called *meta-classes* because they are classes' classes). Just like a class defines how objects behave, a meta-class defines how a class behaves. Every operation we can do with an object is defined in the object's class; every operation we can do with a class is defined in the class' meta-class.

When you ask for an object's attribute, `obj.attribute`, the object's class defines what this operation means (and we get to how in the next section). This is not different from how a class defines what it means to add two objects, `x + y`, or print an object, `print(x)`, and is done with magical methods. Likewise, if you ask for an attribute in a class, `MyClass.attribute`, it is `MyClass`' meta-class that defines what that means.

A meta-class is also an object—because everything is an object—so it will also have a class that defines *its* behavior. This potentially leads to an infinite sequence of classes' classes, but the language solves it by having an ultimate meta-class that is its own class. We don't define that or anything; it is part of the language and not something we can do anything about.

So we define a class, and Python gives it a meta-class that determines how it works. You can give it different meta-classes, and you can define your own (because you can define classes), but that goes far beyond what we will cover in this book.

You extremely rarely need to write meta-classes. They are used in some frameworks, where redefining how classes behave greatly simplifies the code you have to write when using the frameworks, but there is little use for them outside of that. Outside of playing with the language, I think I have written one or two meta-classes in my life, and I am not even sure it was the right solution. But they are there; they define how a class behaves, and all the classes we have defined use the default one, called `type`. We get that when we write `object` in the parentheses in the `class` declaration. We will also get it if we use a superclass that inherits from `object`, but more about inheritance in the next chapter. The class of `type`, its meta-class, is `type` itself, so already here, we get to the loop that prevents us from looking at classes' meta-classes forever.

Try to evaluate this:

```
class MyClass(object):
    pass
print(type(MyClass))
obj = MyClass()
print(type(obj))
```

The first print statement gives you `<class 'type'>` and the second `<class '__main__.MyClass'>` (where `__main__` might be different depending on which file you evaluate the code in). This means that the type of `MyClass`—its class—is `type` and that the class of the instance, `obj`, is `MyClass`. With everything you try to do to the instance, `obj`, Python will ask `MyClass` how to handle it. You get some functionality for free from including `object` in the class definition, so your objects can do more than what you explicitly define in `MyClass`, but the combined functionality in `MyClass` and `object` determines how objects with class `MyClass` behave. In Figure 11-1 you can see how `obj`, `MyClass`, and `type` are connected as objects and classes.

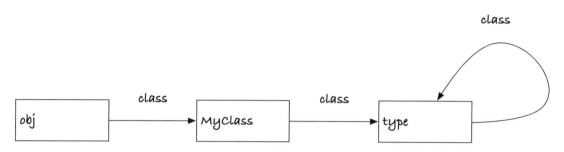

Figure 11-1. *Classes and meta-classes for an object of type MyClass*

When you create an object, its class decides how to do that. By default, as we have seen before, it will do some magic to create the object and then call __init__() so you can do your own setup. Then the object is created, and you can get it.

Similarly, if you define a class, then you are creating an object. The syntax is different for defining classes, but you *are* creating an object. The meta-class decides how to create the actual class object (it uses magical methods for this, just as we use __init__() for objects).

Once you have a class, the operations you do on it, like accessing an attribute, invoke magical methods in the meta-class—just like operations on an object invoke magical methods in the object's class. Objects/classes and classes/meta-classes are the same relationships.

We are not going to exploit meta-classes in this book—they are much too advanced for what we need—but I mention them to explain that you can get different behavior for something as simple as getting an attribute for different objects.

Getting Attributes

What about getting and setting attributes, then? And why does it work differently when you get methods (and different depending on whether it sits in a class or an object and whether you get it through an object or a class)?

The simple answer is that getting an attribute involves invoking a magical method; it is called __getattribute__(), and methods can do whatever they want. Different classes can implement different versions—the default behavior we saw earlier is one we get because we write (object) in our class definition—and classes can behave different from objects because their meta-classes can implement different __getattribute__() methods.

Try implementing this class

```
class MyClass(object):
    foo = "bar"
    def __getattribute__(self, name):
        print(self, "wants", name)
        return 42
```

and then run this:

```
obj = MyClass()
print(obj.foo)
print(obj.bar)
print(MyClass.foo)
```

You will see that accessing obj.foo and obj.bar will invoke __getattribute__() with the name foo and bar, respectively, and you will get 42 back. It doesn't matter that we do not have any foo or bar in the object's dictionary because our implementation of __getattribute__() doesn't look in the dictionary. It doesn't have to; that is just what the default implementation does.

When we access MyClass.foo, we get the default behavior. We have added __getattribute__() to the class, and that changes how obj.attribute behaves, but the class itself still uses its meta-class implementation.

If you want to change the behavior when you ask a class for an attribute, you have to change the __getattribute__() in the meta-class. The following code does that:

```
class Meta(type):
    def __getattribute__(self, name):
        print("Your class", self, "is trying to get", name)
        return 13
```

```
class MyClass(object, metaclass = Meta):
    def __getattribute__(self, name):
        print(self, "wants", name)
        return 42

obj = MyClass()
print(obj.foo)
print(obj.bar)
print(MyClass.foo)
```

As our MyClass is a kind of object, Meta is a kind of type, which is the kind of objects we use for meta-classes. We specify that it should be the meta-class for MyClass with the metaclass = Meta option to the class definition. I will not go more into how meta-classes behave.

With this code, the last line, print(MyClass.foo), invokes the __getattribute__() method in Meta.

Considering the default behavior of __getattribute__(), where we first look in the object's dictionary and then in the class' dictionary, we could ask ourselves if the second step would be asking the class for an attribute, thus invoking its __getattribute__().

Run this code and find out:

```
class Meta(type):
    def __getattribute__(self, name):
        print("Your class", self, "is trying to get", name)
        return 13

class MyClass(object, metaclass = Meta):
    foo = "bar"

obj = MyClass()
print(obj.foo)
```

You will find that when we ask for obj.foo, we get the class variable foo, but we did *not* invoke Meta's __getattribute__(). Whatever the default implementation is doing, it doesn't ask the meta-class for help in this way. Not that it had to, of course, but it could have; it didn't.

To invoke the meta-class __getattribute__(), we need to ask for the attribute in the class, and we didn't since the method wasn't run. The default lookup implementation gets access to the class dictionary without invoking __getattribute__() at all (so it can't even be doing self.__class__.__dict__ as that would be asking for the attribute __dict__).[1]

That leads me to a problem with writing your own __getattribute__(): you invoke it *every* time you try to get an attribute. If you tried to implement something akin to the default behavior like this

```
class MyClass(object):
    foo = "bar"
    def __getattribute__(self, name):
        if name in self.__dict__:
            return self.__dict__[name]
        else:
            return self.__class__.__dict__[name]

obj = MyClass()
print(obj.foo)
```

you would get an infinite recursion. When we try to look up self.__dict__, we invoke __getattribute__(), which will then try to get self.__dict__, which invokes __getattribute__() and so on.

You can get around it by using the default implementation that cheats its way around this problem:

```
class MyClass(object):
    foo = "bar"
    def __getattribute__(self, name):
        d = super().__getattribute__("__dict__")
        cls_d = super().__getattribute__("__class__").__dict__
        return d[name] if name in d else cls_d[name]

obj = MyClass()
print(obj.foo)
```

---

[1] The default attribute lookup is implemented in C for higher performance and doesn't quite play by the rules you and I have to follow, so it can cheat here and there, and it does.

The super().__getattribute__() is part of how inheritance works (see the next chapter) and tells Python to use the method we get from writing (object) in the class definition instead of the one we implemented ourselves. It uses the "superclass implementation." It allows us to access attributes without invoking our own method for it, thus avoiding infinite recursion.

If we did implement our own attribute lookup this way, we still wouldn't get the full default behavior, of course. We could get variables in both the object's and the class' dictionary, but we wouldn't bind methods. Try this for comparison:

```python
class MyClass(object):
    def m(self): pass

    def __getattribute__(self, name):
        d = super().__getattribute__("__class__").__dict__
        res = super().__getattribute__(name)
        return d[name], res

obj = MyClass()
print(obj.m)
```

Here, we get two values back from obj.m, the object we find in the class' dictionary and the object we would get if we used the default __getattribute__(). The second is a bound method; the first is just the function MyClass.m.

There is another way to tap into attribute lookups that doesn't replace the default __getattribute__() method but lets us capture when the lookup method fails. If the attribute lookup cannot find the attribute in the object, the class, or superclasses when we have inheritance, then it will normally raise an exception, but if we have defined the magical method __getattr__(), it will call it instead.

Try running this code:

```python
class MyClass(object):
    foo = "foo"
    def __init__(self):
        self.bar = "bar"
    def __getattr__(self, name):
        print("You tried to get", name)
```

```
obj = MyClass()
obj.foo
obj.bar
obj.baz
```

We haven't implemented a __getattribute__() method, so we get the default behavior. When we ask for obj.foo, we get the class variable; when we ask for obj.bar, we get the object variable, and when we ask for obj.baz, we would normally get an exception, but instead, Python invokes the __getattr__() method.

In the rare cases where you might want to change how attribute access works, you can generally handle it with __getattr__(). It is not enough if you want to modify the behavior *before* the usual lookup—there you do need __getattribute__()—but __getattr__() is almost always the best choice between the two. That being said, it is exceedingly rare that you need either.

You should now have some idea about why we can get different behavior depending on whether we get variables from classes or objects. We don't *actually* get different behavior; we call different methods. Different classes can implement them differently. The methods can return modified objects depending on what they find and where they find them.

Setting Attributes

For setting attributes, we can also redefine what should happen. We don't have two separate methods for it, like with __getattribute__() and __getattr__(), because it doesn't make sense to have a general method and one we use when we don't have the attribute stored in our dictionary. We also don't have the recursion issue when setting attributes, as it is usually easy to avoid a recursive write.

Don't do this; it will give you an infinite recursion:

```
def __setattr__(self, name, value):
    print("You tried to set", name, "to", "value")
    self.do_not_do_this = 42
```

However, you can use the object's dictionary because self.__dict__ is reading an attribute and not assigning to one, so you can do this:

```
class MyClass(object):
    def __init__(self):
        self.foo = 42

    def __getattr__(self, name):
        print("You tried to get", name)
        return "no such luck!"

    def __setattr__(self, name, value):
        print("You told me to set", name, "to", value,
              "(but got 'foo')")
        self.__dict__[name] = 'foo'

obj = MyClass()
print(obj.foo)
print(obj.bar)
obj.bar = 42
print(obj.bar)
```

When we create obj, we assign to self.foo, which calls __setattr__(). It does put a "foo" into the dictionary, but it cheats and ignores the actual value. We get "foo" instead of 42. When we get the attribute, __getattribute__() picks it from the dictionary (and we get "foo"), but it doesn't call __getattr__(). It does call __getattr__() when we access obj.bar (and the call returns None). Then we assign to obj.bar and __setattr__() maps "bar" to "foo" in the dictionary, and that is what we get out (without calling __getattr__()).

Exercise: Sit down and go through this code, drawing how the attribute access and assignment work and when the functions are called. I just described it, but it is a good exercise to go through it in small steps to make sure you really get it.

Properties

Now you know how you can change the way an object accesses attributes, but rewriting how all attribute access is handled with __getattribute__() and __setattr__() is usually overkill. Usually, we want to modify how individual attributes are handled instead, leaving all other attributes unaffected. The protocol for doing that is the topic for the next section. In this, I will simply give you a motivating example to get something we call *properties*.

Imagine, if you will, that we have an application where we manipulate geometric objects, and one type of objects is circles. For those, we need to know their radius and area for whatever reason. A fine implementation could look like this:

```
import math
class Circle(object):
    def __init__(self, radius):
        self.radius = radius
        self.area = math.pi * radius**2
```

We have the two properties as attributes, and we set them in the constructor. If we never modify them, that is a fine design (and if we never change the radius, we might as well compute the area once and for all, so it is a good design even).

But now imagine that we, months or years later, do need to change radii. Now we have a potential problem. If we do this

```
circ = Circle(2)
print(circ.radius, circ.area)
circ.radius = 4
print(circ.radius, circ.area)
```

we will, of course, see that we have changed the radius but not the area. When we set the new radius attribute, we do not automatically update area.

We could decide that the class users had to remember to update both attributes whenever they changed the radius, but that is an unsafe approach. It is easy to forget and hard to debug when someone fails. It is better to update the class so we always keep the two attributes consistent.

One way is to always recompute the area when we ask for it, and we could implement this with a method:

```
class Circle(object):
    def __init__(self, radius):
        self.radius = radius
    def get_area(self):
        return math.pi * self.radius**2
```

Another approach, if you need the area far more often than you update the radius and want to save a little computation time, is to update the area every time you set the radius:

```
class Circle(object):
    def set_radius(self, radius):
        self.radius = radius
        self.area = math.pi * radius**2
    def __init__(self, radius):
        self.set_radius(radius)
```

Both are fine choices, but now the user has to call get_area() instead of using the area attribute for the first class and has to call circ.set_radius(value) rather than writing circ.radius = value for the second solution. With the first solution, the user will get an error with circ.area because there isn't an area attribute anymore; with the second solution, circ.radius = value will now raise an exception, but it will mess up the object's consistency. Regardless of which version you use, however, you need to go back to all your existing code and update it to the new interface. That is annoying.

There are schools of programming that advocate that you should always use methods to access attributes and never allow users to see them directly, precisely to avoid problems such as this. If you always use methods, even if they only return an attribute, you can always change the implementation of the methods and keep the interface. Python doesn't take that approach because we can instead change how accessing an attribute works, so we can keep the interface where we can ask for circ.radius and circ.area, and update a radius with circ.radius = value, but run code to ensure the object's consistency when we do so.

If we want to change circ.area, so we always compute the area from the radius, we can tap into __getattr__():

```
class Circle(object):
    def __init__(self, radius):
        self.radius = radius
    def __getattr__(self, name):
        if name == 'area':
            return math.pi * self.radius**2
        else:
            return super().__getattribute__(name)
```

Here, we compute the area when we call `circ.area`, as long as `area` is not in the object's dictionary. If you want to make sure that the user never sets the `area` manually, you can update `__setattr__()` to prevent it:

```python
class Circle(object):
    def __init__(self, radius):
        self.radius = radius

    def __setattr__(self, name, value):
        if name == 'area':
            print("no way!")
        else:
            super().__setattr__(name, value)

    def __getattr__(self, name):
        if name == 'area':
            return math.pi * self.radius**2
        else:
            return super().__getattribute__(name)
```

Now it is impossible[2] to explicitly set the area, but you can ask for it as an object attribute, `circ.area`, and you will get the computed value in return.

If we want to take the other approach and tap into what happens when we try to update the radius, we can write

```python
class Circle(object):
    def __setattr__(self, name, value):
        if name == 'radius':
            self.__dict__['radius'] = value
            self.__dict__['area'] = math.pi * value**2
        elif name == 'area':
            print("no way!")
        else:
            super().__setattr__(name, value)

    def __init__(self, radius):
        self.radius = radius
```

---

[2]Well, not *impossible*. You can still put area in the object's `__dict__`. It is hard to make something *impossible*. But you cannot set the area by mistake; you have to work for it.

With this class, we can set the radius, and this will trigger the computation of the area. The class will have both a radius and an area attribute that we can access as normal attributes, but we cannot change them in any other way than setting the radius.

Complicated as this seems, having attributes where you tap into reading and writing is quite common. You often find yourself writing code where what was earlier a simple data object now has to execute some code when you read from it or write to it (which is why there is that school of thought that says that you should never access attributes directly in the first place). We can always define what reading and writing attributes should do by defining __getattr__() and __setattr__(), but it will always get as complicated as what we just saw. Worse, even, because if you have more than one or two attributes, you want to give special behavior, and you have to add all of it to these two methods. It can quickly become a big mess.

If this is something that we often do, you can safely bet that it isn't as complicated to do as the preceding examples suggest. There is a way to take a specific attribute and specify what reading and writing should do, independently of all other attributes and without touching __getattr__() and __setattr__(). I will show you the full and complicated rules for how it works in the next section and how you use it as a programmer now.

This is how we would normally implement the class where we always compute the area:

```python
import math
class Circle(object):
    def __init__(self, radius):
        self.radius = radius

    def get_area(self):
        return math.pi * self.radius**2

    # this is the magic
    area = property(get_area)
```

The magic happens in the line that has property(). Here, we say that the attribute area (it is a class variable, but don't worry about that) is an object we create with the call property(get_area). The property() is a class, but we don't need to examine it in detail just yet. It just gives us an object that we store as area in the Circle class. When we access the attribute

```
circ = Circle(2)
print(circ.radius, circ.area)
```

the circ.area will call the method we gave property, the method get_area(). So, by creating a property object and putting it in our class, we have told Python to call our method when we try to get the attribute. If you try to write to area, circ.area = 42, you will get an error. The property object we created lets us read the value, by calling our method, but not write to it. We can't write to it, because we didn't tell it how to do that. If we want to write as well, we need a second method:

```
import math
class Circle(object):
    def __init__(self, radius):
        self.radius = radius

    def get_radius(self):
        return self._radius
    def set_radius(self, value):
        self._radius = value
        self.area = math.pi * self._radius**2

    # this is the magic
    radius = property(get_radius, set_radius)
```

Here, we changed the radius attribute instead. Now it is a property, and because we gave it two methods, the first will be called when we try to read the radius and the second when we write to it. In the methods, we use self._radius, notice the underscore, to store the actual value. We cannot use self.radius because that will call one of the methods, and we would get an infinite recursion. The typical solution is to store a value, if you want to, in an attribute that starts with an underscore.

The property class actually allows up to three methods. The first is the method we want to call when we read an attribute, the second is the method we want to call when we write to an attribute, and the third is a method we want to call when we try to delete an attribute (e.g., if we write del circ.radius). If you don't provide a method or use None, it will be an error to attempt the corresponding operation. So, for example, if we allow a user to write to `radius` but not to read from it (for whatever bizarre reason that would be), we could change the class to

```
import math
class Circle(object):
    def __init__(self, radius):
        self.radius = radius

    def set_radius(self, value):
        self._radius = value
        self.area = math.pi * self._radius**2

    # this is the magic
    radius = property(None, set_radius)
```

With properties, you can define an attribute with one to three methods that you want Python to call when you read from, write to, or delete the attribute. You do not need to modify the magical methods for attributes to do so, and you can handle each attribute independently of all others.

The way properties work is through another set of rules for how Python accesses attributes with its default methods. That is the topic for the next section.

Descriptors

There is one more type of objects, besides functions and methods, that objects and classes treat differently when you ask for them as attributes. Objects of classes that define one of `__get__()`, `__set__()`, or `__delete__()` are called *descriptors* or *data objects* or are said to implement the *data model*, and they are treated differently, depending on what you try to do with them. The `__get__()` method is used when you get an attribute `obj.attribute`. When you write `obj.attribute`, you implicitly call `obj.attribute.__get__()`. The `__set__()` method is called when you assign to an attribute, `obj.attribute = value` works as `obj.attribute.__set__(value)`, and the `__delete__()` method is there to handle when you explicitly delete an attribute `del obj.attribute`.

If you use the default methods for getting attributes, this will happen: If you access an object through a class (see Figure 11-2 (A)), you use its meta-class methods. Then

- `cls.attribute` will find out that the attribute has a `__get__()` method, call it, and return the value.

- `cls.attribute = value` will change the attribute variable in the class—it will not call `__set__()`.

- `del cls.attribute` will delete the attribute from the class. It will not call `__delete__()`.

If you go through an object (a normal object and not its class, Figure 11-2 (B)), then if the attribute is in the object itself

- `obj.attribute` will give you the object, but not call get ().

- `obj.attribute = value` will write `value` to the attribute and not call `__set__()`.

- `del obj.attribute` will delete the attribute and not call `__delete__()`.

Finally (Figure 11-2 (C)), if you go through an object and the attribute is in its class

- `obj.attribute` will call `__get__()` and give you the value.

- `obj.attribute = value` will call the object's `__set__()` method.

- `del obj.attribute` will call the object's `__delete__()` method.

Notice the different behavior depending on which class an object or class has (whether it is the class or the meta-class) and where you find the attribute. Of course, all of this behavior can change by changing the various methods for getting and setting attributes we saw in the preceding. The protocol using `__get__()`, `__set__()`, and `__delete__()` is there, so you can change the behavior of getting attributes without writing new methods for your classes.

Return of the Decorator

Recall from Chapter 7 that if you have a function `f()` and write

```
def g():
    pass
g = f(g)
```

then Python gives you the shorthand

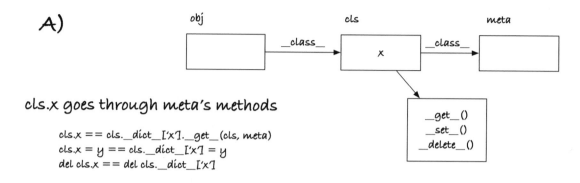

A)

cls.x goes through meta's methods

cls.x == cls.__dict__['x'].__get__(cls, meta)
cls.x = y == cls.__dict__['x'] = y
del cls.x == del cls.__dict__['x']

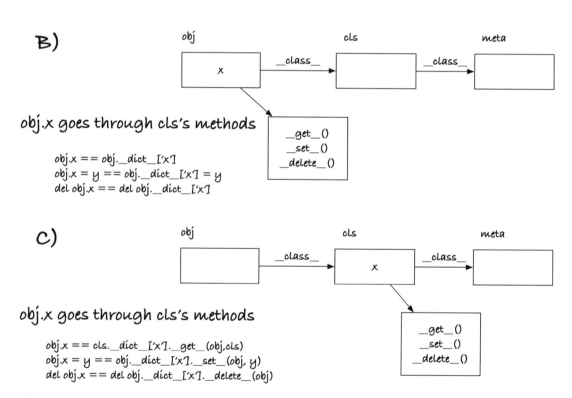

B)

obj.x goes through cls's methods

obj.x == obj.__dict__['x']
obj.x = y == obj.__dict__['x'] = y
del obj.x == del obj.__dict__['x']

C)

obj.x goes through cls's methods

obj.x == cls.__dict__['x'].__get__(obj,cls)
obj.x = y == obj.__dict__['x'].__set__(obj, y)
del obj.x == del obj.__dict__['x'].__delete__(obj)

Figure 11-2. *Accessing descriptors*

```
@f
def g():
    pass
```

that means (practically) the same thing. This syntax for decorating functions works just as well for methods. We could write a decorator that logs each method call like this:

```
from datetime import datetime
def logged(method):
    def other_method(*args, **kwargs):
        now = datetime.now()
        print("{}: calling {}".format(now, method.__name__))
        return method(*args, **kwargs)
    return other_method
```

and use it like this:

```
class Foo(object):
    @logged
    def say_hi(self):
        print("hi")
```

When we use the decorator inside a class definition, we call it with a method, but there is no practical difference. We return a function from logged(), but we write that result into say_hi in the class, and once a function is put in a class, it is for all intents and purposes a method. The difference between the two types of callable objects is so tiny that you never need to care.

A decorator doesn't have to be a function. You can call classes with the same syntax you use for functions, and since the @decorator notation is just shorthand for calling a function and assigning the result to a variable, if the call notation is the same, then decorators will work. So we can also write a class decorator. The result of using the decorator is an object, where the constructor got the function or method as its input. We can rewrite the logger decorator, so we can collect log entries in a list and print it later:

```
from datetime import datetime
class logged(object):
    log = []
    def __init__(self, f):
        self.f = f
```

```
    def __call__(self, *args, **kwargs):
        now = datetime.now()
        self.log.append(f"{now}: calling {self.f.__name__}")
        return self.f(*args, **kwargs)
@logged
def foo():
    print("hi")
foo()
print(logged.log)
```

The __call__() magic method handles when we call an object such as foo(). Because foo was the result of applying the decorator, it is an object of type logged; it is not a function. It doesn't matter as long as it implements __call__() because then we can still call it.

In this class, I made the log list part of the class rather than an instance variable, so I can get it as logged.log. You could just as well have made it an instance variable. With the current solution, one log is shared between all decorated functions; if you made the log an instance variable, by setting it to self.log in __init__(), you would have separate logs for each function you decorated.

Now you might think that since we can use decorators both for functions and for methods and since we can return both functions and objects, we should be able to use the new logger() decorator for methods as well. Not so fast, I am afraid. Recall that functions and methods, when they sit in a class and we access them through an object of the class, get their first argument bound. Other kinds of objects will not be bound this way. The logger we defined is a class; when we use it for our decorator, we get an object of that class, but not a function or method. So we don't automatically bind it. If you try this, you get an error:

```
class Foo(object):
    @logged
    def say_hi(self):
        print("hi")

foo = Foo()
foo.say_hi()
```

We need to tell Python that this kind of objects should be bound. For that, we can use the descriptor rules. We need to define a method called __get__() that will be called when we access logger objects. When you have an object, x, in a class and you write obj.x, Python will first check if x implements __get__(). If so, it returns the result of a call to that method. Only if it doesn't have __get__() will it return the object itself. We can add a __get__() so we can bind the object when we call the logged method:

```
class logged(object):
    def __init__(self, f):
        self.log = []
        self.f = f

    def __call__(self, *args, **kwargs):
        now = datetime.now()
        self.log.append("{}: calling {}".format(now, self.f.__name__))
        return self.f(*args, **kwargs)

    def __get__(self, obj, cls):
        def bound(*args, **kwargs):
            return self(obj, *args, **kwargs)
        return bound
```

Here, I put the log object in the instance to try something new. You can put it back as a class variable if you like. The __call__() method hasn't changed; it worked fine the way it did, and the __get__() method wraps a call to the object itself, thus binding self.

This suffices for a decorator that works with both functions and methods, but one issue with __get__() is that the result of the method is always what you get when you access the decorated object. You now can't get the object itself by conventional means. If you write

```
foo = Foo()
foo.say_hi
```

then foo.say_hi is a bound method. It is not the logged object.

You can still get to the object, for example, by going through the class' __dict__

```
Foo.__dict__['say_hi'].log
```

circumventing the descriptor rules, but you can no longer directly get the attribute. We can get a nicer way to get the log, however, by exploiting one other feature of the protocol. If we access the attribute through the class, we still call the __get__() method, but the obj parameter will be None. So, from that, we can tell if we are accessing the logged method through an object or through a class, so we can return a bound method in the first case or the log in the second:

```python
from datetime import datetime

class logged(object):
    def __init__(self, f):
        self.log = []
        self.f = f

    def __call__(self, *args, **kwargs):
        now = datetime.now()
        self.log.append(f"{now}: calling {self.f.__name__}")
        return self.f(*args, **kwargs)

    def __get__(self, obj, cls):
        if obj is None: # we accessed through the class
            return self.log

        # If we are here, obj is not None, so return
        # a bound method.
        def bound(*args, **kwargs):
            return self(obj, *args, **kwargs)
        return bound

class Foo(object):
    @logged
    def say_hi(self):
        print("hi")

x = Foo()
x.say_hi() # get and call the bound method
print(Foo.say_hi) # get the list of logged items
```

The Python standard library has a large collection of decorators for modifying both methods and classes. Many of them exploit the descriptor rules to implement useful abstractions for your code. We won't go through most of them in this book, but we will use a few here and there. You will learn about more of them as you gain more Python experience.

CHAPTER 12

Class Hierarchies and Inheritance

Methods and polymorphism using them are a key idea in object-oriented programming, and you have much more to learn about them as you progress in your programming career. But in object orientation, there is an additional feature for inheriting implementations from one class into another. You can build hierarchies of types, where some types can reuse code from other types. It is essential in the software engineering underlying many systems, and we get a little taste of what it means in this chapter.

We have seen two different names we can put in the parentheses after a class name, object and Exception, so it is time to look at what they do:

```python
class Patient(object):
    pass

class NegativeError(Exception):
    pass
```

They actually do a lot, as in a *lot* lot, and I can only give you a taste of it here—there are entire books longer than this just on that topic. The mechanism, known as *inheritance*, is key in many object-oriented languages. If you read that a language is object-oriented, it will have some feature that looks like it.

The two main purposes of inheritance are specifying hierarchies of types and reusing code. The former isn't that important in Python because Python is happy to implement polymorphism without knowing about the type an object has. The only thing that is important is which methods you can call on an object. Other languages can be very strict about the type an object has; typically, a function can only be called on specific types of

369

© Thomas Mailund 2021
T. Mailund, *Introduction to Computational Thinking*, https://doi.org/10.1007/978-1-4842-7077-6_12

objects. Since this isn't the case with Python, we will not explore this fully in this book, but this is how that works. You can define a type your function should work on, say fruits:

```python
class Fruit(object):
    pass
```

All the different fruits your program needs should have this type, and you define them by putting Fruit in the parentheses when you define their classes

```python
class Apple(Fruit):
    pass
class Orange(Fruit):
    pass
class Pear(Fruit):
    pass
class Lemon(Fruit):
    pass
```

and so on. You should read it as "the class Apple *is a* Fruit," "the class Orange *is a* Fruit," and so on. By the same rule, you can say that "the class Fruit is an object." The four types of fruits are different, but they are all a kind of the type Fruit.

Don't check if they are exactly the type Fruit, though:

```python
if type(fruit) == Fruit:
    # do something
```

They don't have the type in that sense; they will only be objects of type Fruit if you created them as fruit = Fruit(). But the four classes *inherit* from Fruit, or you could say that they *specialize* Fruit by adding something more to fruit. You can check if an object inherits a type using isinstance():

```python
apple = Apple()
print(type(apple) == Fruit)
print(isinstance(apple, Fruit))
```

In this code, the first test is False, and the second is True. The apple is an object of type Apple, not Fruit, but it is an instance of Fruit because Apple is a subtype (or subclass) of Fruit. You can check the relationship between types using issubclass:

```python
print(issubclass(Apple, Fruit))
print(issubclass(Fruit, Apple))
```

Here, the first test is `True` because `Apple` *is a* `Fruit`, but the second isn't because a `Fruit` isn't necessarily an `Apple`. `Fruit` is a more general class, so it can be many different types of fruits and not just apples.

You can continue specializing types if you want. For example, you can say that a golden delicious is a kind of apple:

```
class GoldenDelicious(Apple):
    pass
```

If a golden delicious is an apple, then it is also a fruit. The relationships are transitive: a golden delicious is an apple, and an apple is a fruit; therefore, a golden delicious is a fruit.

You can make type hierarchies as complex as you want, but I won't recommend building them too large. You can't avoid it in some languages because of how strict they are about types, but in Python, you can, and complex hierarchies are as bad as complex code—very hard to maintain and troublesome to extend. The computer can handle it, but our brains are very poor at managing complexity.

If this all sounds confusing, you can safely forget about it all right now. You very rarely need to check what type an object has—there are usually better solutions through polymorphism—and Python isn't strict about types in the first place. I have managed to program in Python for more than 20 years and only worried about class hierarchies for types a handful of times. Some textbooks, especially if they use a language that is strict about types, will make a big deal out of type hierarchies. I personally think you can live a long and happy life as a programmer without thinking much about them.

That being said, it can be very useful to *design* your software with hierarchies of types in mind. It makes sense to write code that should work on some abstract concept of fruit and have expectations about what you can do with fruits. All your concrete fruits have to provide the right interface, which means the right methods, so conceptually you have a fruit type in the form of an interface to fruit objects. But you don't have to make this explicit in your code through class inheritance. You can if you want to and if you think it makes the code easier to follow, but you don't have to. I rarely bother.

Let me give you a slightly larger example, but one that is more likely to be useful in a computer program: arithmetic expressions. For those, you have constants, maybe you have variables, you might have unary operators (like "-"), and you definitely have binary operators like +, -, *, and /. We can express this relationship between expressions in code like the following classes (but as I will mention in the following, we shouldn't always go this close to the conceptual hierarchy):

```python
class Expression(object):
    def evaluate(self):
        raise NotImplementedError()

class Constant(Expression):
    def __init__(self, value):
        self.value = value
    def evaluate(self):
        return self.value
    def __repr__(self):
        return "Constant(" + repr(self.value) + ")"
    def __str__(self):
        return str(self.value)

class UnaryOp(Expression):
    pass

class Minus(UnaryOp):
    def __init__(self, expr):
        self.expr = expr
    def evaluate(self):
        return - self.expr.evaluate()
    def __repr__(self):
        return "Minus(" + repr(self.expr) + ")"
    def __str__(self):
        return "-" + str(self.expr)

import math
class Exp(UnaryOp):
    def __init__(self, expr):
        self.expr = expr
    def evaluate(self):
        return math.exp(self.expr.evaluate())
    def __repr__(self):
        return "Exp(" + repr(self.expr) + ")"
```

```
    def __str__(self):
        return "exp(" + str(self.expr) + ")"

class BinaryOp(Expression):
    pass

class Add(BinaryOp):
    def __init__(self, left, right):
        self.left, self.right = left, right
    def evaluate(self):
        return self.left.evaluate() + self.right.evaluate()
    def __repr__(self):
        return "Add(" + repr(self.left) + ", " + repr(self.right) + ")"
    def __str__(self):
        return "(" + str(self.left) + " + " + str(self.right) + ")"

class Sub(BinaryOp):
    def __init__(self, left, right):
        self.left, self.right = left, right
    def evaluate(self):
        return self.left.evaluate() - self.right.evaluate()
    def __repr__(self):
        return "Sub(" + repr(self.left) + ", " + repr(self.right) + ")"
    def __str__(self):
        return "(" + str(self.left) + " - " + str(self.right) + ")"
```

We have a general class for expressions, and it has the method evaluate(). If you call it, you will get an error because the abstract class doesn't *implement* any evaluation. The NotImplementedError is an exception that Python has defined.

Then we have constants that hold a value, and they will evaluate to that. I have added code for printing constants in both machine-readable and human-readable forms. After that, we define an abstract unary operator class and two operators. Then we define an abstract binary operator class and two binary operators.

Exercise: Implement the log unary operator and the multiplication and division binary operators.

The types match our conceptual hierarchy. Minus is a unary operator, and unary operators are expressions. Add is a binary operator, and binary operators are also expressions. But the abstract classes do not bring anything to the table. We don't do anything at all in UnaryOp and BinaryOp. The only thing Expression gives us is a method that raises an exception if we haven't implemented it in our subclasses (and if we haven't implemented the method there, we will get an error anyway when we try to call it). The expression code would work just as well if we got rid of the abstract classes and only implemented the concrete ones, Constant, Minus, Add, and Sub. It is fine to think in terms of a hierarchy of classes the way we do here, but usually, if you have classes that do not do anything, it is better to leave them out. Our UnaryOp and BinaryOp, for example, bring nothing to the table here, and in a real application, we wouldn't include them.

I don't want to discard abstract classes entirely. They have their use, and you can tell Python that it is not allowed to make objects of a subclass that doesn't define a required method. If we want to tell Python that it *cannot* make an instance of an expression unless its class has redefined evaluate(), you can write this:

```
from abc import ABC, abstractmethod
class Expression(ABC):
@abstractmethod
def evaluate(self):
    raise NotImplementedError()
```

The ABC superclass does some magic that will prevent you from creating objects from a class that contains so-called "abstract methods." The @abstractmethod decorator creates such objects. So, here, we define an Expression class with an abstract method called evaluate(), and because it inherits from ABC, we cannot create instances of it or any subclasses of it that still have the abstract evaluate(). If we implement a new evaluate() in a subclass, however, that class will have a normal method instead of the abstract one, and then we can instantiate it. So, if we define Minus, for example

```
class Minus(UnaryOp):
    def __init__(self, expr):
        self.expr = expr
    def __repr__(self):
        return "Minus(" + repr(self.expr) + ")"
    def __str__(self):
        return "-" + str(self.expr)
```

```
# Here, we override Expression's evaluate, so
# in this class, it is no longer an abstractmethod
def evaluate(self):
    return - self.expr.evaluate()
```

then, when we redefine `evaluate()`, we give the class a normal method, so the `Minus` class doesn't have an abstract method anymore, and therefore we can initiate it.

Having an abstract method moves the error you get if you haven't implemented the method to the point where you create an object instead of where the method might be called. You are more likely to call a method deep inside complicated code than you are to create an object, so it can make it easier to debug.

Still, I would never use the abstract classes for something like these expressions, just because they do not add anything useful to the code. Conceptually, yes, that is the hierarchy of how expressions are, but it is a waste of keystrokes to implement the concepts explicitly.

Exercise: This exercise is not particularly aimed at class hierarchies but might give you more of a feeling for the expressions we just implemented. Add *variables* as a type of expression. They have to have a name, and that should be simple enough, but how are you going to evaluate them? You need a table that maps variables to values. You can't hardwire the variables to values; that would make them constants, so how do you provide a table to expressions when you evaluate them? There are several options. For example, you could use a class variable that holds a table, but that would share variables with all expressions, and that might not be what we want. Another solution could be to provide a table to each call to `evaluate()`. Consider the pros and cons, implement different solutions, and experiment with them.

Exercise: This is another exercise that tests your understanding of the `Expression` hierarchy more than class hierarchies in general. If we have simple arithmetic expressions, we know how to compute derivatives. The derivative of a constant is zero; the derivative of a variable, with respect to itself, is one $\frac{d}{dx}x = 1$; the derivative of a sum is the sum of the derivatives; the derivative of a product is $f(x)g(x) = f'(x)g(x) + f(x)g'(x)$; for function calls, you use the chain rule; and so on. For each specific class of expressions, you can write a method that computes the expression for the derivative and *use* calls to the same method on the sub-expression where needed. This way, you should be able to compute the derivative of an entire expression. Try to implement this. The result should be a new expression.

Inheritance and Code Reuse

When it comes to the second part that inheritance gives you, code reuse, there really is something to gain, even if you use a language as relaxed about types as Python. Here, inheriting from superclasses really shines, and code reuse through inheritance is not only powerful but it is also simple. If you inherit from a class, all the methods it defines are available to you, as if they were defined in your subclass.

Consider this somewhat artificial example where we have library items that you can borrow and return, and such items can be books (that you can read) or DVDs (that you can watch):

```python
class LibraryItem(object):
    def __init__(self, name):
        self.name = name

    def loan(self):
        print(f"Loaning {self.name}")

    def ret(self):
        print(f"Returning {self.name}")

class Book(LibraryItem):
    def read(self):
        print(f"Reading {self.name}")

class DVD(LibraryItem):
    def watch(self):
        print(f"Watching {self.name}")

book = Book("John Dies at the End")
book.loan() # The LibraryItem method
book.read()
book.ret() # The LibraryItem method

dvd = DVD("The Princess Bride")
dvd.loan() # The LibraryItem method
dvd.watch()
dvd.ret() # The LibraryItem method
```

The general class, `LibraryItem`, defines the methods that both books and DVDs should have, and the subclasses then define the methods that only they should have. When you call a method from the general class on an object of a subclass, you get the superclass' method. We say that the subclasses inherit them from the superclasses.

This inheritance—that subclasses have at least the same methods as superclasses—ties back to thinking about them as types. A superclass represents a more general concept than its subclass, so anything a more abstract concept can do, the more specific objects should also be able to do. A car is a vehicle, and vehicles can drive, so a car must be able to drive. A car might also be able to honk or run out of petrol, something not all vehicles can, but at the very least, a car must be able to do what all vehicles can.

A subclass doesn't have to accept the superclass' methods unchanged. If you reimplement a method in the subclass, then that is the one Python will run when you call the method with that name:

```
class Underwear(LibraryItem):
    def ret(self):
        print("Please don't return used underwear")
```

If you want *both* the code from the superclass and some additional code in a new method, then you can use the `super()` function:

```
class Underwear(LibraryItem):
    def ret(self):
        super().ret()
        print("Please don't return used underwear")
```

Here, we first execute `LibraryItem.ret()` and then print "Please don't return used underwear".

For a more practical example, let's go back to the expressions from the previous section. We had an entire class hierarchy of them, with some classes adding no value whatsoever to the code beyond giving us a conceptual type hierarchy. We can get rid of those easily, but you will notice a lot of similar code if you look at the two unary and the two binary operators. We don't want similar, or worse repeated, code in our programs because it leaves unnecessary many places for bugs to hide, and if we have to fix a bug, we need to find all the places where we have copied the code, so we can fix it there as well. It makes sense to take the code shared between the operators, move it to a superclass, and then specialize what we cannot share in subclasses.

We can't do much about constants. We can define them without the `Expression` superclass, but the code for constants doesn't change:

```
class Constant(object):
    def __init__(self, value):
        self.value = value
    def evaluate(self):
        return self.value
    def __repr__(self):
        return "Constant(" + repr(self.value) + ")"
    def __str__(self):
        return str(self.value)
```

We keep the `UnaryOp` class (but we don't need to make it a subclass of `Expression`). In the class, we put most of the code we had in the `Minus` and `Exp` classes before:

```
from abc import ABC, abstractmethod

class UnaryOp(ABC):
    def __init__(self, format_string, expr):
        self.format_string = format_string
        self.expr = expr

    def evaluate(self):
        return self.apply(self.expr.evaluate())
    @abstractmethod
    def apply(self, value):
        pass # subclasses must provide this one
def __repr__(self):
    name = self.__class__.__name__
    return name + "(" + repr(self.expr) + ")"
def __str__(self):
    return self.format_string.format(str(self.expr))
```

We have added a constructor, where we set the value, but we also want a string to help us format the operator when we translate it into a string with __str__(). That string is responsible for displaying the operator, and we use it with the string's `format()` method (see in the following). When we `evaluate()`, we get the evaluated value from `self.expr`, and we call a method `apply()` on it. We haven't implemented this method—it will be the responsibility of the subclass. The subclass knows how a concrete unary operator should evaluate a value, so `apply()` must be defined there. For `__repr__()`, we exploit that classes remember their name when we define them (I haven't told you that, but they do). We get the class of the object using `self.__class__`. When we call the function, it is through a subclass object, so it is the subclass we get. Then we take its name from its `__name__` attribute, and we use that for the text representation.

Now we can implement the concrete unary operators like this:

```
class Minus(UnaryOp):
    def __init__(self, expr):
        super().__init__("-{}", expr)
    def apply(self, value):
        return - value

import math
class Exp(UnaryOp):
    def __init__(self, expr):
        super().__init__("exp({})", expr)
    def apply(self, value):
        return math.exp(value)
```

The constructors call the superclass constructor with a format string and the value we create the unary operator objects with. For `Minus`, the format string is `"-{}"`. When we call that string with `"-{}".format(value)`, the text representation of `value` is put where the curly braces are. For `Exp`, the format string is `exp({})`. The `apply()` methods return minus the value for `Minus`. For `Exp`, `apply()` gives us `math.exp(value)`.

The code for `BinaryOp` is similar. We have a format string for the `__str__` method, we use the subclass' name for `__repr__`, and for `apply()`, we get the values for both the left and right expressions before we call the subclass method:

```
class BinaryOp(ABC):
    def __init__(self, format_string, left, right):
        self.format_string = format_string
    self.left, self.right = left, right
```

```
    def evaluate(self):
        return self.apply(self.left.evaluate(),
                          self.right.evaluate())
    @abstractmethod
    def apply(self, left, right)
        pass

    def __repr__(self):
        name = self.__class__.__name__
        return name + "(" + repr(self.left) + ", " \
                          + repr(self.right) + ")"
    def __str__(self):
        return self.format_string.format(str(self.left), str(self.right))
class Add(BinaryOp):
    def __init__(self, left, right):
        super().__init__("({} + {})", left, right)
    def apply(self, left, right):
        return left + right

class Sub(BinaryOp):
    def __init__(self, left, right):
        super().__init__("({} + {})", left, right)
    def apply(self, left, right):
        return left - right
```

We can simplify it even further. The abstract operators' constructors are there to get the underlying value(s) and the format string, but we don't set individual format strings for different objects. We can put these strings in the subclasses as class variables, and then the abstract classes can get them from there:

```
class UnaryOp(ABC):
    def __init__(self, expr):
        self.expr = expr

    def evaluate(self):
        return self.apply(self.expr.evaluate())
    @abstractmethod
```

```
    def apply(self, value):
        pass

    def __repr__(self):
        name = self.__class__.__name__
        return name + "(" + repr(self.expr) + ")"
    def __str__(self):
        format_string = self.format_string
        return self.format_string.format(str(self.expr))
class BinaryOp(ABC):
    def __init__(self, left, right):
        self.left, self.right = left, right

    def evaluate(self):
        return self.apply(self.left.evaluate(),
                          self.right.evaluate())
    @abstractmethod
    def apply(self, left, right):
        pass

    def __repr__(self):
        name = self.__class__.__name__
        return name + "(" + repr(self.left) + ", " \
                          + repr(self.right) + ")"
    def __str__(self):
        op = self.op
        return "(" + str(self.left) + op + str(self.right) + ")"
```

If we do this, we don't need constructors in the subclasses because we can use the ones we inherit. The superclasses' constructors take one or two expressions as arguments, which is what the subclass constructors did before. We only needed the subclass constructors to add the format string to the superclass constructors. Now the subclasses are as simple as this:

```
class Minus(UnaryOp):
    format_string = "-{}"
    def apply(self, value):
        return - value
```

```
import math
class Exp(UnaryOp):
    format_string = "exp({})"
    def apply(self, value):
        return math.exp(value)

class Add(BinaryOp):
    op = "+"
    def apply(self, left, right):
        return left + right

class Sub(BinaryOp):
    op = "-"
    def apply(self, left, right):
        return left - right
```

The superclasses look complicated now, but there are only two of them, and it is trivial to add new concrete expressions because you only need to set one class variable and define one method.

Reusing code is essential for all effective software development. We write functions, so we can reuse code through function calls. For classes, we use inheritance of methods to reuse entire interfaces. The process we just went through with the small expression example is something you will go through many times. You will develop functionality in classes to solve a problem, and then you will likely identify that you have some duplicated functionality. If you abstract that code slightly and extract the pieces you need to specialize—like the apply() method in our example—you can move code to a superclass and reuse it in subclasses.

Multiple Inheritance

Not everything fits neatly into a hierarchy where one type is an instance of one more general type. Sometimes, things belong to more than one category. A lion is an animal, and a tiger is an animal that fits the "is a" relationship between those two animals and the abstract concept of animals:

```
class Animal(object):
    pass
class Lion(Animal):
    pass
class Tiger(Animal):
    pass
```

But a *liger* is a hybrid between lions and tigers—it is the offspring of a male lion and a female tiger. We could say it is an animal and forget that it is a type of lions and tigers

```
class Liger(Animal):
    class
```

which wouldn't be entirely wrong, since it is a hybrid and separate from lions and tigers. On the other hand, it is also a kind of both of those animals.

We could say it is a kind of lion, or we could say that it is a type of tiger

```
class Liger(Lion):
    pass
```

or

```
class Liger(Tiger):
    pass
```

but that does not represent that it is a hybrid at all. What we might really want is to say that it is a kind of both animals, and we can do it like this:

```
class Liger(Lion, Tiger):
    pass
```

There isn't anything wrong with any of the choices. A liger is an animal, and you don't necessarily need to think about it as either a lion or a tiger. It is okay to think of it as either a lion or a tiger, and if you want, you can think of it as both. It is entirely up to what your conceptual model of these kinds of animals is. The point of the example was only to show you that it is possible to have more than one superclass. You just list more than one type in the parentheses after the class name. When you do, we call it *multiple inheritance*.

Multiple inheritance comes naturally when we try to fit every kind of object into neat categories. A zombie is a human, and a zombie is also a dead thing, so naturally

```
class Zombie(Human, DeadThings):
    pass
```

Keep in mind, though, when you think about types, that the way we use classes and inheritance when we program with them is that we write functions that manipulate abstractions of objects to get polymorphism. The concrete classes must provide the methods that give us the correct polymorphic behavior.

If we say that a zombie is both dead and human, all zombies must be able to do what both humans and dead things can do, that is, they must implement the methods that functions expect from both types. That is what we get from method inheritance, and it is what we must have in mind when we design our class hierarchies. If you choose to inherit from more than one class, you are in effect saying that your new class can do everything that all of its superclasses can do—and maybe more (like eat brains).

You don't always get this because sometimes you want to inherit from one or more classes to get their functionality while not supporting *all* they can do. If that is the case, submit to pragmatism. Support what methods you can, and be careful not to use your new class with methods that require more than you deliver. Pragmatism is more important than strict adherence to ideal rules. That goes for both single and multiple inheritance.

Many programming languages will not allow multiple inheritance, or only allow very restricted multiple inheritance, and there are good reasons for that.

Multiple inheritance is a rich source of confusion. Not when you write small hierarchies of classes with few methods, but as complexity grows, so does the potential for errors. And the problem mainly boils down to which implementation of a method will be executed when you call a method.

Consider

```
class Person(object):
    def __init__(self, name):
        print("Creating", name)
        self.name = name
    def hi(self):
        print("Hi from", self.name)
```

```
class Robot(object):
    def hi(self):
        print("0110001010")

class Cyborg(Robot, Person):
    pass
```

This looks sensible, even if you could consider it a little silly. A person has a name and can say hi. A robot doesn't have a name, but it can also say hi. There isn't any meaningful way we should connect Person and Robot because one is not a more abstract concept than the other (even though a Person can do the same as a robot and then a little more). When we define a Cyborg, which is half human and half machine, we get a class that belongs to both categories, which seems sensible. However, what happens when we execute this code?

```
robocop = Cyborg("Alex Murphy")
robocop.hi()
```

When we construct robocop, we must call a constructor. We haven't defined one in Cyborg, so Python must find one in the superclasses. If you run the code, you will see that it calls the one in Person. Since Robot doesn't implement __init__(), that probably makes sense. But what about when we call hi()? It will call Robot's hi() method, but why does it choose that method over Person's? And what would happen if we *did* implement __init__() in Robot?

```
class Robot(object):
    def __init__(self):
        print("rebooting...")
    def hi(self):
        print("0110001010")
```

If you try that implementation, you will get an error when you construct robocop, and the error complains that you gave the constructor one too many arguments.

Python searches for the first method with the right name, and then it picks that one to execute. We don't implement any of the methods in Cyborg, so it must search in the superclasses. There, it will search from left to right, so in the first implementation, it checked for __init__() in Robot, didn't find it, and then found it in Person. When it searched for hi(), it found one in Robot and didn't continue until Person. So while we intended to say that a cyborg is both a robot and a person, the order we specified the classes in gave Robot preferential treatment. In the second implementation, we got an error because Python found __init__() in Robot and called that implementation—and that implementation doesn't take name as an argument. If we gave it one, though, we would still be in trouble:

```python
class Person(object):
    def __init__(self, name):
        print("Creating", name)
        self.name = name
    def hi(self):
        print("Hi from", self.name)
    def my_name(self):
        return self.name

class Robot(object):
    def __init__(self, name):
        print("rebooting...")
    def hi(self):
        print("0110001010")

class Cyborg(Robot, Person):
    pass

robocop = Cyborg("Alex Murphy")
robocop.hi()
print(robocop.my_name())
```

Just because we can create an object doesn't mean that we have initialized the attributes that our superclasses rely on. In the case here, we initiate the Robot part of a Cyborg because it is that __init__() we execute, but we do not initialize the Person part because *that* method is *not* called.

Will this help?

```python
class Cyborg(Robot, Person):
    def __init__(self, name):
        super().__init__(name)
```

Try it. It does not help. We now tell Cyborg to use its superclass' constructor, but that is what already happened. It is just that the constructor that Python found was the one in Robot. To initialize *both* parts of a cyborg, we need to change the superclasses—we cannot do it from the subclass alone:

```python
class Person(object):
    def __init__(self, name):
        print("Creating", name)
        self.name = name
    def hi(self):
        print("Hi from", self.name)
    def my_name(self):
        return self.name

class Robot(object):
    def __init__(self, name):
        print("rebooting...")
        super().__init__(name)
    def hi(self):
        print("0110001010")

class Cyborg(Robot, Person):
    def __init__(self, name):
        super().__init__(name)
```

With this implementation, Cyborg's constructor calls Robot's constructor, and its constructor will call Person. Why Person? It is not a superclass of Robot, after all! No, but super() doesn't actually do what I have told you it does when multiple inheritance is involved.

When you have multiple inheritance, super() tells Python to go on searching for the next method in the class hierarchy. So, after calling Cyborg.__init__(), we get Robot.__init__() and then Person.__init__(). And just to scare you a little bit more, notice that we didn't have super().__init__(name) in Person. If you add it *there*, the code breaks again because we don't have an initializer that takes one argument from that point in the hierarchy. It looks like the entire hierarchy needs to know in which order a subclass wants to include superclasses.

And we didn't even get to what happens if the superclasses have superclasses. Trust me it doesn't get simpler if we add larger class hierarchies. Python will search in superclasses in an order called C3 linearization, and you can get the order for a given class with the `mro()` class method:

```
Cyborg.mro()
```

For `Cyborg` you will get

```
(<class '__main__.Cyborg'>, <class '__main__.Robot'>, <class '__main__.
Person'>,
```

and you can try moving classes around, adding superclasses to the hierarchy and such, to see what happens. Then keep in mind that this is a very simple example.

And here, I must warn you that it gets even worse if you also program in other languages that support multiple inheritance. Different languages have different rules for how they figure out which method you call in a complex hierarchy. Multiple inheritance is truly messy.

I realize that I haven't taught you anything useful in this section, besides showing that multiple inheritance is complex, but teaching you how to use multiple inheritance wasn't my intention. Scaring you was. Avoid multiple inheritance like the plague unless you have truly exceptional reasons to use it.

It is not as chaotic as I have made it look, but multiple inheritance is complicated. With single inheritance, you always know where Python will find a method. You know how you must initialize objects and other classes that inherit from them. You know that they can safely call methods through `super()` because you are not passing calls to someplace else in the class hierarchy. Such calls will only ever go upward to more abstract classes.

There is a reason for avoiding multiple inheritance, as many languages do, and you have gotten a little taste of what those reasons are. This, however, doesn't mean that you should avoid multiple inheritance entirely. There are safe ways to use it, and all it boils down to is how you implement the classes that you allow to be used in multiple inheritance. And that is the topic of the next section.

Mixins

A *mixin* is a class that adds methods to subclasses, and you use it to extend an interface or adapt one interface to another. They are intended for multiple inheritance, they don't hold any attributes, they don't have superclasses (except for `object`), and they usually only implement a few methods. You never use mixins on their own; they only live to serve other classes.

As a simple example, consider minimizing a function. The go-to method for minimizing functions over many parameters, such as neural networks, is called *gradient descent*. It works as follows: You start your search for the minimum at some arbitrary point. At that point, you compute the gradient of the function, the vector of first-order derivatives (the derivative with respect to each of the parameters). This gradient vector points in the direction where the function grows the most. So to minimize, you take a small step in the opposite direction. You let the step size depend on how long the gradient vector is, so you take smaller steps when the function is growing little compared to when it is growing fast. In the new point you reach, you iterate the process, and you keep moving until the change in the function value, or equivalently the size of the gradient vector, is small enough for your liking. The procedure won't necessarily find you a global minimum, but it will find a local minimum near where you started the search.

I don't want to spend space on a full implementation, so I will just show what it looks like in one dimension:

```
def gradient_descent(f, x0,
                     step_rate = 0.01,
                     tolerance = 1e-9,
                     max_steps = 10000):
    x = x0
    for _ in range(max_steps):
        step = step_rate * f.derivative(x)
        x = x - step
        if abs(step) <= tolerance:
            break
    return x, f(x)
```

The two required arguments are the function, f, and the starting point, x0. The step_rate is a parameter we use to determine how fast we move, and the tolerance and max_steps determine how long we search. We get the derivative in a point by calling the method f.derivative(). When we return from the search, we return the minimum point we found, x, and the function's value in that point, f(x).

If we look at this function and think of polymorphism, what do we require of the function? One, it has to have a method derivative(), and we must be able to evaluate it because we call f(x).

There are many statistical models where we have complicated, often dynamic programming–based, algorithms for computing the likelihood of observed data, and we often want to maximize the likelihood. If we take minus the likelihood and minimize that, we also get the maximum likelihood, so it looks like this is something we can use. However, in many of these models, we can evaluate the likelihood at a point; we just don't have an analytical solution to the derivative. It isn't necessarily easy to take the derivative of a dynamic programming table. But we can approximate the derivative by computing the change in the y value when we vary x an ε to either side of its current point. We can write a general method that does that:

```
class Derivative(object):
    def derivative(self, x, epsilon = 0.001):
        y1 = self(x - epsilon)
        y2 = self(x + epsilon)
        return (y2 - y1) / (2 * epsilon)
```

Here, the derivative() method approximates the derivative when called with an x value. It uses self() to get the value for x - epsilon and x + epsilon, so whatever class self has, it must implement __call__().

This class, Derivative, adds a numerical derivative function to the table, but it only works if a subclass that inherits it implements __call__(). If it does, then we can compute the derivative. The Derivative class doesn't do anything else. It only brings this little feature to the table.

If we now have a class that implements __call__(), we can inherit from that class *and* Derivative, and we get a class we can use with gradient_descent():

```
class Poly(Polynomial, Derivative):
    pass

print(gradient_descent(Poly([0, 0, 1]), 1))
```

For the example, I used `Polynomial` from the previous chapter. I realize that we can compute a polynomial derivative analytically, but I didn't want to add more complicated code just to show you that there are cases where you cannot.

Exercise: Write a method, `derivative()`, that uses the analytical solution to get the derivative of a `Polynomial`. Try it out with `gradient_descent()`.

The `Derivative` class is an example of a mixin. You can use it to pull in some minimal functionality, provided you implement the methods it needs in its subclass or that you inherit it from somewhere. It doesn't have any superclasses to confuse the search for methods, and it is unlikely to overshadow any other methods you need from your class hierarchy.

You will use mixins when there is functionality that you might want to add to several class hierarchies that are otherwise not related and thus should not share a common superclass. Keep them simple, but use them to adapt a class hierarchy to polymorphic code you need to use. You can include as many as you like when you mix them into another class hierarchy.

If you stick to mixins, then there is at most a single complicated hierarchy in place for each method call, and you avoid the problems you otherwise would have with multiple inheritance. You are not likely to have many name clashes if your mixins only define a few methods, but if you do, then remember that Python will search for methods from left to right in the classes you inherit. If you want mixins to overwrite methods from your class hierarchy, put the "real" superclass at the rightmost end and mixins to the left of it. If you want the inherited methods to overrule what the mixins bring, then put it at the left.

CHAPTER 13

Sequences

The first abstract data structure we will implement is *sequences*. We already know this data type because we have it built into Python as lists, but we will make our own implementations now. You are unlikely to need your own implementations of sequences, although there are alternative implementations where there are different trade-offs to the operations. Python's implementation is efficient and easy to use, and there is no need to implement something you already have readily available. There is, however, good reason to learn how to construct your own types for simple structures like these, so you are equipped to construct more complex data structures when you need to in the future.

We first specify the abstract data structure, that is, the operations that we want a sequence to provide. We will keep it simple and only require a few operations, even though Python's implementations provide many more.

Sequences

You can do a lot with Python's lists, but we will define the interface for a sequence, the abstract data structure, as something where we can append an element, get the first index where we can find a given element, and get and set elements by index.

Using Python's built-in list type, we can implement this interface like this:

```python
class ListSequence(object):
    def __init__(self):
        self.sequence = []
    def append(self, element):
        self.sequence.append(element)
    def get_at_index(self, index):
        return self.sequence[index]
```

© Thomas Mailund 2021
T. Mailund, *Introduction to Computational Thinking*, https://doi.org/10.1007/978-1-4842-7077-6_13

```
    def set_at_index(self, index, value):
        self.sequence[index] = value
    def __repr__(self):
        return repr(self.sequence)
```

The __repr__() function isn't part of the abstract data structure interface. Still, when possible, you should write the method since it makes it easier to explore your code interactively and to debug your data structures when something goes wrong.

There is more to an abstract data structure than just the methods. They need to do the same thing for all implementations. We have defined what that is informally, and that suffices in most cases, and I have rarely seen a case where more rigorous definitions are needed. So I will assume that we agree on what the methods should do when exploring an alternative implementation.

Implementations can differ in the operations' efficiency, but they must agree on the methods' behavior. This, however, also includes error handling. The append() method doesn't raise any exceptions in this implementation, but the other three operations do if an element isn't in the list or if we try to access an index out of bounds. All implementations should use the same exceptions if we want to be able to exchange one implementation for another, so we need to specify what those should be. We also need to consider special cases and make sure that all implementations handle them the same.

With a list, for example, you can use negative indices. This is easy to implement with the data structure that uses Python's lists, but it isn't always easy. Should we require that all implementations handle negative indices with the same behavior, regardless of how hard it would be to implement? Or should we make it an error, even if you have a list?

Those are design decisions, and you are free to choose what you find most appropriate. I will choose, for our implementations, that negative indices are not allowed; they should raise an exception.

Exercise: Create an instance of a ListSequence and call get_at_index() and set_at_index() with invalid input to see which exceptions you get.

The two functions will give you IndexError. That sounds like a reasonable error, so for my error handling, I will choose that all implementations should raise the same exceptions as the list implementation does. For negative indices, I will raise IndexError explicitly, since lists do not do this for us:

```
class ListSequence(object):
    def __init__(self):
        self.sequence = []
```

```
def append(self, element):
    self.sequence.append(element)
def get_at_index(self, index):
    if index < 0:
        raise IndexError("Negative index")
    return self.sequence[index]
def set_at_index(self, index, value):
    if index < 0:
        raise IndexError("Negative index")
    self.sequence[index] = value
def __repr__(self):
    return repr(self.sequence)
```

There, we now have a definition of an abstract data structure, and we have a concrete implementation using Python's lists.

Linked Lists Sequences

Now we will try to implement the sequence interface without using Python's built-in lists. One of the most straightforward structures that we can use is the *linked list*. A linked list, as the name suggests, is a sequence of *links*. A link is something that holds a value and a reference to the next link in the sequence. You can say that a linked list is a link that holds an element and another linked list or None. This is a recursive definition. A linked list is the first element and then another list, and data structures with this property are called *recursive data structures*. There isn't any more subtlety to recursive data structures; they are just recursively defined, and now that you are familiar with recursion, you can see why and why there is nothing fancy in that name.

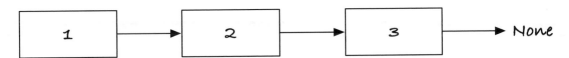

Figure 13-1. *A link listed containing the sequence 1, 2, and 3*

We can define a link like this:

```
class Link(object):
    def __init__(self, element, next):
        self.element = element
        self.next = next
    def __repr__(self):
        return 'Link({}, {})'.format(
            repr(self.element),
            repr(self.next)
        )
```

The only important part is the __init__() method. We set the first element of the list and the next link that contains the remaining list. The __repr__() method is just there for debugging purposes.

We will use None to represent an empty list. A list goes from a link until next is None. Then we have seen the last element. Graphically, we draw linked lists like in Figure 13-1. We put the elements in boxes and have arrows for the next attribute.

Links do not provide the interface we want for a sequence, and I will not give them these operations. We could, but it is easier to wrap a linked list in another class that provides the interface for our sequence data structure. We want to treat the links as very simple data structures, without methods themselves, since we always work on them collectively. To provide the sequence interface, we build a data structure that holds a linked list by a reference to the first link in the list.

With a recursive data structure, recursive implementations of our operations are usually the easiest, and that is also the case here. For append(), we say that the base case is the empty list, None. To append to an empty list, we must make a single link, with the value we want to append, and None as the next link. We return a new linked list for the recursive case by making a link that holds the value in the first link of the input list and whose next is the result of appending to the original list's next:

```
def append(link, element):
    if link is None:
        return Link(element, None)
    else:
        return Link(link.element,
                    append(link.next, element))
```

This append() doesn't implement the operation for our abstract data structure. It returns an updated list, while the abstract data structure operation changes an existing list. That is okay; we handle that in the wrapper class.

For get_at_index() and set_at_index(), we use index as an accumulator that we count down each time we move to the next link. This way, it captures how many indices we are from the one we want, and if we reach index zero, then we have the right link:

```
def get_at_index(link, index):
    if link is None:
        raise IndexError("Index out of bounds")
    if index == 0:
        return link.element
    return get_at_index(link.next, index - 1)

def set_at_index(link, index, value):
    if link is None:
        raise IndexError("Index out of bounds")
    if index == 0:
        link.element = value
    else:
        set_at_index(link.next, index - 1, value)
```

We don't check if the index is negative here; we leave that up to the wrapper. That wrapper can look like this:

```
class LinkedListSequence(object):
    def __init__(self):
        self.links = None

    def append(self, element):
        self.links = append(self.links, element)

    def get_at_index(self, index):
        if index < 0:
            raise IndexError("Negative index")
        return get_at_index(self.links, index)
```

```
    def set_at_index(self, index, value):
        if index < 0:
            raise IndexError("Negative index")
        set_at_index(self.links, index, value)
def __repr__(self):
    return repr(self.links)
```

The methods call the global functions with the same name. The names do not clash because you need to write "self." before the methods—they are in the object's own namespace—so you get the global functions when you just write the function names.

Exercise: To get a feeling for how you would write recursive functions on a list, try implementing a function, drop(), that removes k elements from a list, that is, a function that returns a new list that contains all of the elements from the input list except the first k.

Exercise: Write a function, take(), that creates a list of only the first k elements of a list.

Exercise: Write a function, reverse(), that reverses a linked list. The easiest way to do this is to add an accumulator to your function that constructs the new list. For each link you recurse on, you can prepend to that accumulator. When you reach the end of the list, you can return the accumulated list.

Iterative Solutions

As a rule of thumb, it is easier to write recursive functions for recursive data structures, but we do not have to. In many cases, we can get an iterative solution with minimal extra effort. Those solutions are often more efficient, and we avoid potential problems with deep recursions—and this could be a problem with long sequences.

If we take the iterative approach, we don't need extra functions. We are not recursing, so we can manipulate the list in LinkedListSequence directly. To iterate through a linked list, we use a variable, link, that points to the current link. When we want to move to the next link, we update the variable link = link.next. That will be the pattern for all our methods. For get_at_index() and set_at_index(), the implementations are relatively straightforward:

```
def get_at_index(self, index):
    if index < 0:
        raise IndexError("Negative index")
```

```
        link = self.links
        while link is not None:
            if index == 0:
                return link.element
            link = link.next
            index -= 1
        raise IndexError("Index out of bounds")
def set_at_index(self, index, value):
        if index < 0:
            raise IndexError("Negative index")
        link = self.links
        while link is not None:
            if index == 0:
                link.element = value
                return
            link = link.next
                index -= 1
        raise IndexError("Index out of bounds")
```

We decrement the index, so we know we have the correct index when we reach zero. You could also use a second variable and increment it until it reaches the index, but what we do is just as easy. When we reach the end of the `while` loops, we have gone past the end of the list without finding what we were looking for, so we raise exceptions there. Both the methods will return before this point if they find what we are searching for.

For `append()`, we have a special case that we need to handle. We cannot run along the list until we reach the end because we need to update the second-to-last link. When we enter the loop, we need to have a non-empty list, and we will continue until its `next` reference is `None`. Then we can append a new link to it. This means that we can't enter the loop if the initial list is empty, so we need to handle that case separately:

```
def append(self, element):
    if self.links is None:
        self.links = Link(element, None)
        return
```

```
link = self.links
while link.next is not None:
    link = link.next
link.next = Link(element, None)
```

We have to search through the list for the index functions to find what we are searching for, but perhaps we can do a little better for append(). We cannot directly append to a list because we need to find the last link first. But what if we keep a reference to the end of the list as well as the first? Then we can get the last link in constant time, set its next reference to a new link, and point the last reference to the new link as well:

```
class LinkedListSequence(object):
    def __init__(self):
        self.links = None
        self.last = None

    def append(self, element):
        if self.links is None:
            self.links = Link(element, None)
            self.last = self.links
            return
        self.last.next = Link(element, None)
        self.last = self.last.next

    # The other methods here
```

Adding a Dummy Element

Once again, we have a special case when the list is empty. Sometimes special cases are unavoidable, but because they require extra code, which is often error-prone, we should aim to reduce the number of such cases. For linked lists, there is a simple fix. We can use a "dummy" link at the front of our list. Then, there will always be a first and a last element. For append, you now only need the two assignments, but for all the other methods, you must start your search with the next reference in the dummy:

```
class LinkedListSequence(object):
    def __init__(self):
        self.dummy = Link(None, None)
        self.last = self.dummy
```

```
    def append(self, element):
        self.last.next = Link(element, None)
        self.last = self.last.next

    def get_at_index(self, index):
        if index < 0:
            raise IndexError("Negative index")
        link = self.dummy.next
        while link is not None:
            if index == 0:
                return link.element
            link = link.next
                index -= 1
            raise IndexError("Index out of bounds")

    def set_at_index(self, index, value):
        if index < 0:
            raise IndexError("Negative index")
        link = self.dummy.next
        while link is not None:
            if index == 0:
                link.element = value
                return
            link = link.next
            index -= 1
        raise IndexError("Index out of bounds")

    def __repr__(self):
        return repr(self.dummy.next)
```

The dummy element is a link with the value None, but it doesn't matter what value we put in the link—we never look at it. The dummy is only there to make append() simpler, and in all searches, we skip past it. Except for the negative indices that we have to handle explicitly, we do not have any special cases in this implementation.

If there is only a single place where we need to handle a special case, as in the previous implementation, I normally wouldn't bother to find a way around it. But if you find yourself with many methods where you have to handle special cases, such as handling empty lists, it is worthwhile to find a way to eliminate them. Dummy elements, like the link we just added, often solve the problem.

Analysis

Now, for the complexity of the operations. Append is a constant-time operation for both implementations, although the list implementation has an amortized constant-time complexity, while for the linked list, all append operations take constant time. For the get_at_index() and set_at_index(), the list operation takes constant time, while the linked list implementation takes linear time.

Concatenating

Based on just these three operations, the Python list is a better choice. It is never slower and sometimes faster. There are operations, however, where linked lists outperform Python's lists. One such operation is list concatenation. Python's lists have an extend() method that adds elements from one list to another. We can add that to our abstract data structure, and for the list version, we can implement it by a call to extend() on the underlying list:

```
def extend(self, other):
    self.sequence.extend(other.sequence)
```

The other argument should be a ListSequence and not a list, so we get its underlying list using other.sequence.

With Python's lists, you need to copy at least all the elements in other, and if they do not fit into the memory allocated for self.sequence, the elements from there must be copied as well. The operation takes time $O(n)$.

With the linked list, all we need to extend a list is to point the last link's next to the head of the other sequence:

```
def extend(self, other):
    self.last.next = other.dummy.next
    if other.last != other.dummy:
        self.last = other.last
```

We need to go past the dummy element for other because we don't want that, and we need to point self.last to the last link in other. However, we don't want last to point to the other sequence's dummy element, so we only move last for a non-empty sequence. So, if other.last is other.dummy, we leave self.last where it is. It is a special case, but we will get rid of it in the next section. The running time is $O(1)$ because we only update two references.

Now, admittedly, the two implementations do not behave exactly the same way, but the difference is subtle. With the list implementation, we copy all the elements in other's list, so if we modify other afterward, it does not affect the list we added other to. With linked lists, the two sequences share links after the concatenation; see Figure 13-2 (where the gray boxes are the dummy elements). If we concatenate Sequence 1 and Sequence 2, the last two elements of Sequence 1 will now be the same as the two elements in Sequence 2. If you modify the elements through either sequence, you will also change the other.

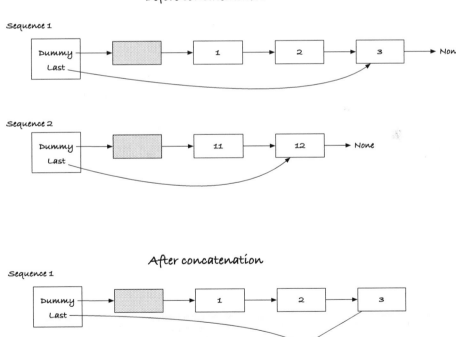

Figure 13-2. *Concatenating linked lists*

Generally, with linked lists, you can have many lists that refer to the same links. Occasionally, this is useful because it saves memory. Still, I don't recommend that you exploit this unless it is essential for your program because of side effects when you modify them.

If you want constant-time concatenation, then you pay for it by allowing one sequence to implicitly modify another. You cannot get the same behavior in your list implementation because the two sequences are entirely independent after the concatenation. The only way you can get the same behavior with the two implementations is by copying links in the linked list implementation.

Exercise: Write a function or method that makes a copy of a linked list.

There are many algorithms where constant-time concatenation is essential for the running time, and these usually do not update a list after you concatenate it with another. Technically, they do not provide you with the same interface, but they give you exactly the same behavior within the context of such algorithms. In that case, you have a trade-off to which sequence data structure you want. Is constant-time access to elements by index more important than constant-time concatenation? That depends on what you need the data structures for. You will almost always have different possibilities for concrete implementations of abstract data structures that differ in their operations' performance. You should choose, depending on what you need them for.

Adding an Operation for Removing the First Element

Another operation we could add to sequences is one for deleting the first element; let us call it remove_first(). For the linked list solution, we can implement it like this:

```
def remove_first(self):
    self.sequence.pop(0)
```

It copies everything except the first element, and that is necessary to keep elements in contiguous memory. Consequently, we have an $O(n)$ operation.

For the linked lists, we need to move the dummy link's next pointer to the next element in the list; that way, we skip past the first element, and we have in effect deleted it. An implementation can look like this:

```
def remove_first(self):
    if self.dummy.next is None:
        raise IndexError("Empty sequence")
    self.dummy.next = self.dummy.next.next
        if self.dummy.next is None:
            self.last = self.dummy
```

The first test, for an empty sequence, is necessary. We could just attempt to update the dummy.next link, but if it is None, we would get an exception we would have to catch anyway to translate it into an IndexError, so it is easier to explicitly test.

The next statement updates the next reference, so we skip the first element. The last statement deals with a special case. If the sequence contains a single element, then self.last points to the element we are deleting. Nothing good will come from leaving it pointing there, so if that is the case, we make self.last point to the dummy. It is annoying to have another special case, just as we got rid of the first one with a dummy object, but we cannot get rid of it with our current implementation. I will show one way to fix it in the next section.

The list solution runs in linear time because we need to copy the sequence's elements, while the linked list operation is constant time.

If we can remove the first element in a sequence, what about prepending an element as well? With the list implementation, we can do it like this:

```
def prepend(self, element):
    self.sequence.insert(0, element)
```

We need to copy all the old elements because the elements need to sit in adjacent memory, so this operation copies all the existing elements before putting the new at the beginning. Consequently, the operation takes time $O(n)$.

For the linked list solution, we need to make a new link, the link's next pointer should be the previous link, and dummy.next should point to the new link:

```
def prepend(self, element):
    new_link = Link(element, self.dummy.next)
    if self.last == self.dummy:
        self.last = new_link
    self.dummy.next = new_link
```

We have a special case again when we prepend to an empty list, but we will get rid of it in the next section. The issue is when we prepend, and the last reference points to the dummy. Then it should be updated to point to the new link. If it already points to a non-dummy link, it should keep pointing to that link.

This method only updates references, so it runs in constant time.

Remove the Last Element

What about an operation for removing the last element in a sequence? With Python lists, you can do this using the method pop(), so let us implement a remove_last() method for lists:

```
def remove_last(self):
    self.sequence.pop()
```

The method removes the last element in the sequence, as long as it is not empty, and if it is empty, it raises an IndexError exception. The pop() method takes constant time—generally, as long as you only modify the end of a Python list, an operation takes constant time.

We can't remove the last element using the self.last reference for the linked list solution. It is the link *before* the last link that we have to modify. Our only option is to run through the linked list until we find the second-to-last link—we can recognize it because its next reference is the last link, self.last. Once we find it, we set its next reference to the empty list, deleting the last element by doing that, and we move self.last to point to the new last element:

```
def remove_last(self):
    if self.dummy.next is None:
        raise IndexError("Empty sequence")
    link = self.dummy
    while link.next != self.last:
        link = link.next
    link.next = None
    self.last = link
```

Since we need to scan through the entire list, the running time is $O(n)$.

The problem with modifying the end of the list is that we cannot see what is the one before the last element. Our links only point to the next link, not the previous one. In the next section, we will change that to get *doubly linked lists*.

Before we start with that, let's summarize the complete implementations of what we have so far since the new methods were scattered throughout the text:

```python
class ListSequence(object):
    def __init__(self):
        self.sequence = []

    def append(self, element):
        self.sequence.append(element)

    def prepend(self, element):
        self.sequence.insert(0, element)

    def get_at_index(self, index):
        if index < 0:
            raise IndexError("Negative index")
        return self.sequence[index]

    def set_at_index(self, index, value):
        if index < 0:
            raise IndexError("Negative index")
        self.sequence[index] = value

    def extend(self, other):
        self.sequence.extend(other.sequence)

    def remove_last(self):
        self.sequence.pop()

    def remove_first(self):
        self.sequence.pop(0)

    def __repr__(self):
        return repr(self.sequence)
```

```python
class Link(object):
    def __init__(self, element, next):
        self.element = element
        self.next = next
    def __repr__(self):
        return 'Link({}, {})'.format(
            repr(self.element),
            repr(self.next)
        )

class LinkedListSequence(object):
    def __init__(self):
        self.dummy = Link(None, None)
        self.last = self.dummy

    def append(self, element):
        self.last.next = Link(element, None)
        self.last = self.last.next

    def prepend(self, element):
        new_link = Link(element, self.dummy.next)
        if self.last == self.dummy:
            self.last = new_link
        self.dummy.next = new_link

    def get_at_index(self, index):
        if index < 0:
            raise IndexError("Negative index")
        link = self.dummy.next
        while link is not None:
            if index == 0:
                return link.element
            link = link.next
            index -= 1
        raise IndexError("Index out of bounds")
```

```python
def set_at_index(self, index, value):
    if index < 0:
        raise IndexError("Negative index")
    link = self.dummy.next
    while link is not None:
        if index == 0:
            link.element = value
            return
        link = link.next
        index -= 1
    raise IndexError("Index out of bounds")

def extend(self, other):
    self.last.next = other.dummy.next
    if other.last != other.dummy:
        self.last = other.last

def remove_first(self):
    if self.dummy.next is None:
        raise IndexError("Empty sequence")
    self.dummy.next = self.dummy.next.next
    if self.dummy.next is None:
        self.last = self.dummy

def remove_last(self):
    if self.dummy.next is None:
        raise IndexError("Empty sequence")
    link = self.dummy
    while link.next != self.last:
        link = link.next
    link.next = None
    self.last = link

def __repr__(self):
    return repr(self.dummy.next)
```

Doubly Linked Lists

To delete the last element in a list in constant time, the `last` reference must access the link before it. A natural approach, then, is to add a reference to our links, so they can access the previous link in the list as well as the next:

```
class DoublyLink(object):
    def __init__(self, element, previous, next):
        self.element = element
        self.previous = previous
        self.next = next
    def __repr__(self):
        return 'DoublyLink({}, {})'.format(
            repr(self.element),
            repr(self.next)
        )
```

In `__repr__()`, I only print the `next` of the link. Trying to get both the previous and the next will give us an infinite recursion, since if we try to print the next and that one tries to print its previous reference, then we are back where we started.

When we construct a sequence, we create a dummy doubly link instead of a single link, but otherwise, nothing changes:

```
class DoublyLinkedListSequence(object):
    def __init__(self):
        self.dummy = DoublyLink(None, None, None)
        self.last = self.dummy
```

Updating `append()` is also straightforward. We create a new link with the new element and give it the last link as its `previous` pointer. Then we move `last` to the new link:

```
def append(self, element):
    self.last.next = DoublyLink(element, self.last, None)
    self.last = self.last.next
```

When prepending, we must make a link with the dummy link as the previous link and the link that `dummy` points to as its next link. Then `dummy` must point to the new link since that should now be the list's first link. Finally, we need to set the new link's next link's `previous` link to point to the new link (it is quite a mouthful, but see Figure 13-3,

where the dashed edges show old pointers and solid edges the current/new pointers).
However, when the list is empty, we have a special case, that is, when dummy's next link
is None; see Figure 13-4. We can't make None point back to the new link, so there is no
pointer to update there, and since last points to the dummy link when the list is empty,
we have to move it, so it points to the new link:

```
def prepend(self, element):
    new_link = DoublyLink(element,
                          self.dummy,
                          self.dummy.next)
    self.dummy.next = new_link
    if new_link.next is not None:
        new_link.next.previous = new_link
    if self.last == self.dummy:
        self.last = new_link
```

We do not need to change anything for get_at_index() and set_at_index(). They
follow links using the next reference, and we can still do that with doubly linked lists:

```
def get_at_index(self, index):
    if index < 0:
        raise IndexError("Negative index")
    link = self.dummy.next
    while link is not None:
        if index == 0:
            return link.element
        link = link.next
        index -= 1
    raise IndexError("Index out of bounds")

def set_at_index(self, index, value):
```

```
    if index < 0:
        raise IndexError("Negative index")
    link = self.dummy.next
    while link is not None:
        if index == 0:
            link.element = value
            return
        link = link.next
        index -= 1
    raise IndexError("Index out of bounds")
```

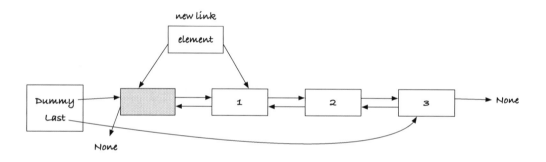

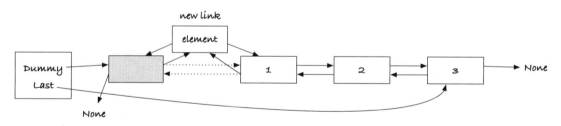

Figure 13-3. *The general case for prepending to a doubly linked list*

To remove the first element in a list, we must move dummy's next reference to point to the second link in the list. There will always be at least one link in the list because we explicitly test for empty lists, so it is safe to do dummy.next.next to get the second link. Then we need to update the second link's previous pointer, so it points at dummy; see the general case at the top of Figure 13-5. If there is only one link in the list, we have another special case. We cannot update previous on the second link—it is not there since that link is None. We also need to move last to point to dummy because the list will be empty after the removal:

```
def remove_first(self):
    if self.dummy.next is None:
        raise IndexError("Empty sequence")
    self.dummy.next = self.dummy.next.next
    if self.dummy.next is not None:
        self.dummy.next.previous = self.dummy
    if self.dummy.next is None:
        self.last = self.dummy
```

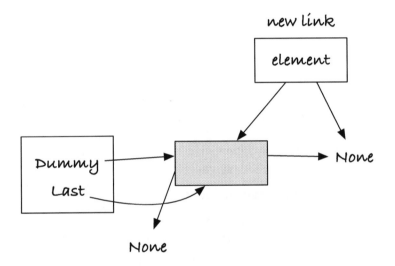

Figure 13-4. *Special case for prepending to a doubly linked list*

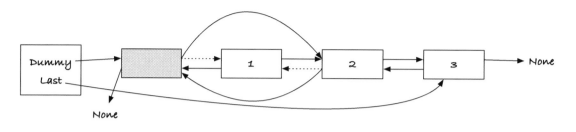

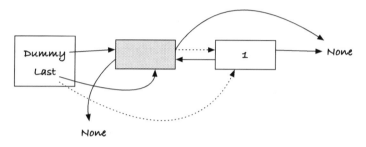

Figure 13-5. *Removing the first element in a doubly linked list*

The special cases are beginning to accumulate, and it will get worse before it gets better. But it will get better.

For removing the last element, surprisingly, we do not have a special case; see Figure 13-6. We need to take last's previous and point it at None, and then we need to move last, so it points to the new last link. If there is only a single element in the list, we can do the same. In that case, last.previous is the dummy link, but that doesn't change anything:

```
def remove_last(self):
    if self.dummy.next is None:
        raise IndexError("Empty sequence")
    self.last.previous.next = None
    self.last = self.last.previous
```

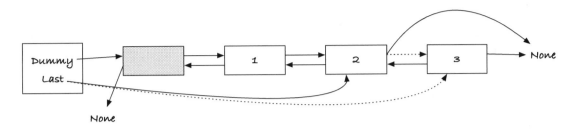

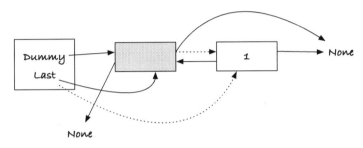

Figure 13-6. *Remove the last element in a doubly linked list*

For extend() we need to point the last link's next pointer to the first link in the second list, point that link's previous pointer to the last element in the first list, and move last, so it points at the last link in the second list; see Figure 13-7. It doesn't work, however, if the other list is empty. Then we make the last pointer point to a dummy element, which we don't want to do. However, if the second list is empty, we can extend without doing anything, so it is easy to handle the special case:

```
def extend(self, other):
    if other.last != other.dummy:
        # if other isn't empty
        self.last.next = other.dummy.next

        other.dummy.next.previous = self.last
        self.last = other.last
```

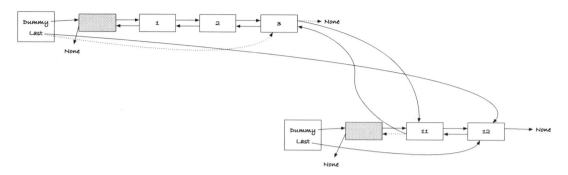

Figure 13-7. *Extending a doubly linked list*

This extend() diverges even more from the list implementation. The first implementation created lists that shared links, so changes to one would change the other. This implementation *destroys* the second list. When we change the previous pointer in its first link, we break the sequence, and many of the operations we implemented for it will no longer work. If this is acceptable, you have an O(1) extend operation, but you need to copy the second sequence in linear time if it isn't.

Adding a Last Dummy

We have several methods now where we need to handle special cases. Earlier, we introduced a dummy link at the beginning of the list to avoid just a single special case. That might be overkill, but it is worth it to eliminate at least some of them with these many cases. I suggested earlier that if you need to eliminate special cases, then dummy objects often help you. That is also the case now. We have a dummy link at the beginning of the sequence, and if we also add one at the end, see Figure 13-8, we greatly simplify our implementation. With the two dummies, call them first and last since there is more than one now, all proper links will have links both to the left and right. We do not have to worry about None neighbors, and we don't need to test for that anyway.

When we create a list with two dummy elements, we connect them, so the first dummy points to the last and the last points to the first. I have included a __repr__() method here for debugging purposes:

```
class DoublyLinkedListSequence(object):
    def __init__(self):
        self.first = DoublyLink(None, None, None)
        self.last = DoublyLink(None, None, None)
```

```
        self.first.next = self.last
        self.last.previous = self.first

    def __repr__(self):
        return repr(self.first.next)
```

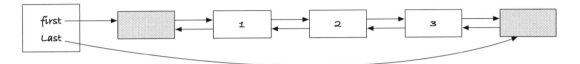

Figure 13-8. *Linked list with both an initial and a terminal dummy link*

The __repr__() method also prints the dummy at the end of the list. It is easier to do this than to try to fix it, and it doesn't make a difference for debugging purposes.

The two methods that iterate through the list mostly stay the way they are. We need to iterate until we see the last dummy instead of None, but that is the only change:

```
def get_at_index(self, index):
    if index < 0:
        raise IndexError("Negative index")
    link = self.first.next
    while link is not self.last:
        if index == 0:
            return link.element
        link = link.next
        index -= 1
    raise IndexError("Index out of bounds")

def set_at_index(self, index, value):
    if index < 0:
        raise IndexError("Negative index")
    link = self.first.next
```

```
    while link is not self.last:
        if index == 0:
            link.element = value
                return
        link = link.next
        index -= 1
    raise IndexError("Index out of bounds")
```

We don't need to treat insertion differently between inserting at the beginning and the end of a list. We can write a function that can insert an element anywhere after a link, as long as it has another link following it. We create a new link. Its previous reference is the link we insert it after, link, and its next reference is link.next. After that, we just have to update the new link's previous.next and next.previous pointers so both point to the new link:

```
def insert_after(link, element):
    new_link = DoublyLink(element, link, link.next)
    new_link.previous.next = new_link
    new_link.next.previous = new_link
```

Exercise: Draw a list and an insertion and convince yourself that this will work.

We can then implement the append() and prepend() methods using insert_after().

To append, we need to insert after self.last.previous, and to prepend, we need to insert after self.first:

```
def append(self, element):
    insert_after(self.last.previous, element)
```

```
def prepend(self, element):
    insert_after(self.first, element)
```

Similar to insert_after(), we can implement a function that removes a link. If you have a reference to a link and know that it has a previous and a next link, you can modify the link's two neighbors so their next and prev references, respectively, bypass it:

```
def remove_link(link):
    link.previous.next = link.next
    link.next.previous = link.previous
```

We can't call this function if a list is empty. Then we must either point to the first or last dummy, and they do not have links on both sides, but in remove_first() and remove_last(), we check if the sequence is empty anyway, so we can raise an exception. If the sequence is not empty, we can call remove_link(). To remove the first element, we call it with self.first.next, and to remove the last element, we call it with self.last. previous:

```
def remove_first(self):
    if self.first.next == self.last:
        raise IndexError("Empty sequence")
    remove_link(self.first.next)
```

```
def remove_last(self):
    if self.first.next == self.last:
        raise IndexError("Empty sequence")
    remove_link(self.last.previous)
```

If we can both prepend and append and remove the first and last elements, it seems a little silly that we cannot also *get* the value at both ends. Of course, we can always use get_at_index() for the first element, and if we can get the length of the sequence, we can get the last element, but if we have direct access to both ends, then it is easier just to implement methods that access them.

They are trivial to implement for the list sequence:

```
def get_first(self):
    return self.sequence[0]
```

```
def get_last(self):
    return self.sequence[-1]
```

These will throw an IndexError if the sequence is empty, so we should do the same for the linked list implementation. With the linked lists, we get the first value at first's next and the last at last's previous:

```
def get_first(self):
    if self.first.next == self.last:
        raise IndexError("Empty sequence")
    return self.first.next.element
```

```
def get_last(self):
    if self.first.next == self.last:
        raise IndexError("Empty sequence")
    return self.last.previous.element
```

For extend() you can connect the last real link, self.last.previous, to the first real link in other, other.first.next, and then move self.last, so it points to other.last. This removes the existing terminal dummy and replaces it with the other terminal dummy, but since the real links are still flanked by dummy links, this doesn't cause any trouble:

```
def extend(self, other):
    self.last.previous.next = other.first.next
    other.first.next.previous = self.last.previous
    self.last = other.last
```

Using two dummy elements, we have simplified most of our methods, and the remaining three have the same complexity as before. I'm sorry that I took you through all the code with special cases before we got to the elegant solution (that I could just have shown you). But I have bad experiences with teaching elegant solutions before showing why they are elegant in contrast to more straightforward implementations. I hope you now appreciate why adding dummy elements here is a good idea.

For an alternative implementation of extend(), we can write a more general function that lets us insert a list at any point inside another:

```
def insert_list_after(link, begin, end):
    end.next = link.next
    end.next.previous = end
    begin.previous = link
    begin.previous.next = begin
```

Here, with references to the beginning and end of any list (the real links and not terminal dummies), we can connect the list up to sit behind any link in our list. A singleton list is also a link, so we can reimplement insert_after() using this function:

```
def insert_after(link, element):
    new_link = DoublyLink(element, None, None)
    insert_list_after(link, new_link, new_link)
```

Then we can implement extend() as

```
def extend(self, other):
    insert_list_after(self.last.previous,
                      other.first.next,
                      other.last.previous)
```

This solution isn't simpler than the one we had before, but insert_list_after() is more general. We can use it, for example, for a method that lets us insert an entire sequence at a given index. An implementation for the ListSequence class could look like this:

```
def insert_sequence_at(self, index, other):
    if index >= len(self.sequence):
        raise IndexError("Index out of bounds")
    self.sequence[index:index] = other.sequence
```

With Python lists, you can assign to list slices, and if we assign to an empty one (which is what we get if the start and end of the slice, index:index, are the same), we insert a list at that position. Python copies both lists to make this insertion, so the operation runs in $O(n)$.

To insert at an index with our linked lists, we first need to get the link at that index. We can write a function for that, and since this is what get_at_index() and set_at_index() do as well, we can simplify those in the process:

```
def get_link(self, index):
    if index < 0:
        raise IndexError("Negative index")
    link = self.first.next
    while link is not self.last:
        if index == 0:
            return link
        link = link.next
        index -= 1
    raise IndexError("Index out of bounds")
```

```
def get_at_index(self, index):
    return self.get_link(index).element

def set_at_index(self, index, value):
    self.get_link(index).element = value
```

Once we have a link, we can use `insert_list_after()` to insert a sequence there. We just need to get the endpoints, and we get those at `other.first.next` and `other.last.previous`. So we can implement `insert_sequence_at()` for the linked lists like this:

```
def insert_sequence_at(self, index, other):
    link = self.get_link(index)
    insert_list_after(link,
                      other.first.next,
                      other.last.previous)
```

Splicing in the new sequence is a constant-time operation, but searching for the link takes linear time, so this is also an $O(n)$ operation. However, there are applications where we can keep links around in an algorithm and where it is useful that we can remove and insert sequences in constant time. We won't see them here, and for the sequence abstract data structures we implement in this chapter, we will pay a linear-time cost every time we access a linked list through an index.

Where we end up with our implementations, we have constant time for `append()` in both implementations. For `prepend()`, we have a linear cost for the list implementation and a constant-time cost for the linked list implementation. We have constant-time `get_at_index()` and `set_at_index()` for the `list` implementation and linear time for the linked list implementation. Removing the first element is constant time for linked lists and linear time for the `list` implementation, while for removing the last element, both implementations take constant time. Extending a list is linear time for the `list` implementation and constant time for the linked lists, and as we just saw, inserting a list at an index is linear time for both implementations.

Which implementation you should prefer depends on which of the operations you need to be fast. That depends on the algorithm you are implementing, and while there is always a trade-off, it can sometimes be obvious what is best—if you need to update by index many times, you should not choose the linked lists. Other times, you need to analyze the algorithm in more detail, or you have to measure the performance before you can make the right choice.

Summing up our doubly linked list implementation, we end up with this class:

```
def insert_list_after(link, begin, end):
    end.next = link.next
    end.next.previous = end
    begin.previous = link
    link.next = begin

def insert_after(link, element):
    new_link = DoublyLink(element, None, None)
    insert_list_after(link, new_link, new_link)

def remove_link(link):
    link.previous.next = link.next
    link.next.previous = link.previous

class DoublyLinkedListSequence(object):
    def __init__(self):
        self.first = DoublyLink(None, None, None)
        self.last = DoublyLink(None, None, None)
        self.first.next = self.last
        self.last.previous = self.first

    def append(self, element):
        insert_after(self.last.previous, element)

    def prepend(self, element):
        insert_after(self.first, element)

    def get_at_index(self, index):
        return self.get_link(index).element

    def set_at_index(self, index, value):
        self.get_link(index).element = value

    def extend(self, other):
        insert_list_after(self.last.previous,
                          other.first.next,
                          other.last.previous)
```

```
def insert_sequence_at(self, index, other):
    link = self.get_link(index)
    insert_list_after(link,
                      other.first.next,
                      other.last.previous)

def remove_first(self):
    if self.first.next == self.last:
        raise IndexError("Empty sequence")
    remove_link(self.first.next)

def remove_last(self):
    if self.first.next == self.last:
        raise IndexError("Empty sequence")
    remove_link(self.last.previous)

def __repr__(self):
    return repr(self.first.next)
```

Exercise: We have a first and a last dummy element now, but we never have anything before the first dummy or after the last dummy, so we could combine the two dummies into one. The real elements start at the next reference of the dummy and end when the next reference is the dummy again. Such a structure is called a *circular* list, and it has even fewer special cases. Change the implementation to use a circular list (you need to change *very* little).

A Word on Garbage Collection

We haven't talked about this before, and while it isn't related to sequences as such, we have to talk about it now because we have just run into a potential problem with our doubly linked lists. And what we have to talk about is *garbage collection*.

In Python and most modern programming languages, you generally do not have to worry about this. Still, if you ever find yourself programming in an older language, it is very much an issue and one you have to be careful about. The issue is this: when you create an object, that object might hold resources it gets from Python or the operating system, and it needs to give back those resources when it is no longer in use. Otherwise, your computer runs out of resources, which is a bad thing. Such resources can be files you have opened, network connections you've made, and, at the very least, the memory an object fills.

If you open a file, for example, which you do with the function open(), you get a resource from the operating system, and to give back that resource, you need to close the file again. This is a bad idea

```
for line in open("my-file.txt"):
    print(line.rstrip())
```

because we don't close the file. A better solution is closing the file after use:

```
f = open("my-file.txt")
for line in f:
    print(line.rstrip())
f.close()
```

This frees the resource immediately after you are done using it.

Python has a special syntax that makes it easier to handle resources and not forget to free them, called a *context manager*, and the syntax looks like this:

```
with open('my-file.txt') as f
    for line in f:
        print(line.rstrip())
```

When opening the file, the resource gets a name, f, and it exists inside the with block. Once you leave this block, f disappears, and Python takes back the resource it had.

Various resources that you can allocate implement the context manager interface, and you can write your own classes that implement it as well. You need to implement an __enter__() method for allocating resources and an __exit__() method for freeing them again and then use them in with blocks, as with the preceding file.

We won't worry about these kinds of resources in this book—but use the with syntax when you work with files. I encourage you to check the documentation when you use other kinds of objects that could hold resources, though, but most likely, you will mainly use files where this is something you should get used to doing.

We will, however, look at the memory resources that objects hold and how Python frees them. We don't explicitly free resources, as some older languages do, but use a so-called *garbage collector* that handles it for us. The garbage collector will also free the file resources for us if we don't use `with`, so don't get too scared about forgetting it, but it might do it later than when you are done with the file. Using `with` is better because you free resources as soon as you are done with them. This is the purpose of `with`.

But we don't use `with` blocks for each object we create, so do we allocate more and more memory to hold our objects as our program runs? No, with objects, we do rely on the garbage collector.

With the standard implementation of Python, CPython, you have two different garbage collectors. One uses an approach called *reference counting*, which is the most efficient version of garbage collectors and used in many languages, but also one with a serious flaw. It works like this: Python keeps track of how many references (variables or attributes) refer to any given object. If you have zero references to an object, your program can never get to the object, so clearly, it isn't necessary to keep it around. So as you add references to an object, by assigning to variables, passing objects to functions, or adding objects to objects or classes, the reference count goes up. When references go out of scope or other objects that reference an object are no longer around, then the reference count goes down. When it reaches zero, Python frees all resources and get rid of the object.

Until now, well, until we implemented doubly linked lists, that strategy worked perfectly. But with our doubly linked lists, we have links that refer to both the previous and the next link. If you have a reference to the previous link and it has a link to you, then your reference count is always at least one, even if no other objects reference these links. You might not have any variable through which you can get hold of the link, but it doesn't get collected because the reference count is not zero.

With the preceding file, you don't have such circular references, so the file will get garbage collected when `f` goes out of scope—which is why I said that you shouldn't worry too much about it. But with doubly linked lists, we do have references that prevent garbage collection, so we never free the links. If we build very long lists, even if we delete them afterward, the link resources remain in use, and in a long program, that could fill the entire memory of your computer.

When I say that the objects are *never* freed, I am exaggerating. Python has another garbage collection algorithm that might catch them, and if all else fails, you will free the resources when your program terminates. If you rely on this, and there is nothing wrong with that, you can explicitly trigger the garbage collection through the `gc` module:

```
import gc
gc.collect()
```

Because Python has this extra garbage collection strategy, you never need to worry about resources and freeing them unless you begin to see poor performance because of it.

If you want to trigger garbage collection when your doubly linked list is deleted, you can catch that it is about to be deleted by writing a method called __del__(). That method will be called before the object is deleted. Do not confuse __del__() for the __delete__() method you might recall from Chapter 11. That method handles when you try to delete an attribute from a class; __del__() gives you a handle for dealing with objects that are about to be deleted.

When you remove the last reference to our sequence, you can use it to trigger a garbage collection. The links are still around at this point because you still have references to the first and last dummy links, but if you remove those links, all the remaining links are in limbo. They should be deleted, but the circular reference structure prevents it. If you call gc.collect(), you get rid of them:

```
def __del__(self):
    self.first = None
    self.last = None
    gc.collect()
```

If you don't explicitly trigger garbage collection, your objects will eventually be freed, but not right away. You can hold on to resources long past when you don't need them, and that can affect your code's performance.

There is a better way to deal with circular references that uses the reference counting algorithm and frees objects as soon as you don't need them any longer. We need to make some of the references *weak*, which means that they are proper references to an object, but they don't add to the reference count. You have to be careful with these because if all your references to an object are weak, then the object is gone. If you need an object, keep at least one true reference to it.

If we use either previous or next (but not both) as a weak reference, then we do not get into trouble. A link that we use will have both references, except for the first dummy that doesn't have a previous and the last dummy that doesn't have a next reference. Still, we hold references in our sequence object for those two links, so we won't lose those until we garbage collect the sequence.

We can't allow other objects to directly access the previous attribute of an object now because we need to ensure that we only have weak references (and the various manipulations we make with links do not guarantee that). Furthermore, weak references do not work exactly like other references. You need to wrap references to use them, and you need to use the __call__() (function call) interface to get the underlying object. So we must implement methods for both getting and setting the previous attribute:

```
import weakref
class DoublyLink(object):
    def __init__(self, element, previous, next):
        self.element = element
        self.set_previous(previous)
        self.next = next

    def get_previous(self):
        if self._previous is None:
            return None
        else:
            return self._previous()

    def set_previous(self, ref):
        if ref is None:
            self._previous = None
        else:
            self._previous = weakref.ref(ref)
```

We need to explicitly handle None because we cannot create weak references to it. That is just part of how Python handles None. And even if we could, None wouldn't allow us to use the function call syntax that we need with weak references in the getter.

This will work, but it isn't aesthetically pleasing that we treat next and previous different when we manipulate lists. There is a better way. We can implement setters and getters, so they look like accessing and assigning to attributes. If we do that, we can leave all our remaining code alone; they already use the correct syntax. There are various ways to do this, but the easiest is using Python's property class:

```
import weakref
class DoublyLink(object):
    def __init__(self, element, previous, next):
        self.element = element
        self.set_previous(previous)
        self.next = next
```

```
def get_previous(self):
    if self._previous is None:
        return None
    else:
        return self._previous()

def set_previous(self, ref):
    if ref is None:
        self._previous = None
    else:
        self._previous = weakref.ref(ref)

previous = property(get_previous, set_previous)


def __repr__(self):
    return 'DoubleLink({}, {})'.format(
        repr(self.element),
        repr(self.next)
    )
```

We briefly saw properties in Chapter 11. When we call property, we get an object that we can access and write to. It uses yet another magic method interface to do this—it is the descriptors we saw in Chapter 11—but we don't need to worry about it here. Just know that it gives us something that we can access through the same interfaces as we can access attributes. When we read a property, link.previous, we call the getter method get_previous(), and when we write to the property, link.previous = another_link, we call set_previous(). We assign the object to a class variable, so when we write obj. previous, we get the object, and the magic in a property takes over.

With modern languages, you generally do not have to worry about garbage collection and releasing resources. Garbage collectors handle it. The only reason I mention it here is that it is useful to know about the issue, and if you need to use a more low-level language, you will have to handle all resource management yourself. When Python uses reference counting, instead of its alternative garbage collector, you get more efficient code, as a rule of thumb. Some languages do not let you do this and leave all resource management to garbage collectors. Others only implement reference counting, and then weak references are essential when you have circular data structures.

Iterators

We have implemented sequences, but ironically we do not have a simple way to iterate through them. We can get elements by index, which is a linear-time operation each time we use a linked list, but we cannot just go element by element through the sequences. That is obviously something we should fix, but how do we make an interface for that?

One strategy is to make a so-called *iterator*. This is an object that can move us from element to element, hiding how the sequence is implemented, so we can use it polymorphic, and at each position, it can give us the current element. We can define the operations we want an iterator to have, similar to how we defined what a sequence should provide. Any object that satisfies the interface is an iterator, regardless of how it is implemented. For our sequence iterators, we could say that we want a function that tests if there are any more elements and another that gives us the current value and increment the iterator. For the list implementation, it can look like this:

```
class ListSequenceIterator(object):
    def __init__(self, seq):
        self.seq = seq
        self.index = 0

    def has_more(self):
        return self.index < len(self.seq.sequence)

    def next(self):
        self.index += 1
        return self.seq.sequence[self.index - 1]
```

We save the sequence we iterate over and the current index. We have more elements as long as the index hasn't reached the end of the list, and we increment the iterator by incrementing the index. Because we should return the current element and we also have to increment the index, we have to increment the index first. Therefore, we index into the underlying list at one minus the incremented index.

We can create a ListSequenceIterator ourselves, with a sequence as its constructor variable, but it is better to put a method for it in the sequence class. That way, there is flexibility for the designer of the class to replace the iterator at a later time, and you will always get the best iterator when you ask the sequence for one. So we can add this method to ListSequence:

```
def iterator(self):
    return ListSequenceIterator(self)
```

With the iterator, we can run through all of a sequence's elements with code such as this:

```
iter = seq.iterator()
while iter.has_more():
    print(iter.next())
```

The linked list implementation is similarly straightforward. For the iterator, we can save the current link, initially `first.next`, and the terminal dummy. Then we can test if the iteration is done by checking if the link points to the dummy. When we increment the iterator, we move the link to its `next` reference. Then the value we need to return is now at its `previous` link, so we return that:

```
class DoublyLinkedListSequenceIterator(object):
    def __init__(self, seq):
        self.last = seq.last
        self.link = seq.first.next

    def has_more(self):
        return self.link != self.last

    def next(self):
        self.link = self.link.next
        return self.link.previous.element
```

For the sequence class, we need to return this iterator, so its `iterator()` method looks like this:

```
def iterator(self):
    return DoublyLinkedListSequenceIterator(self)
```

Iterators are more general than just for running through this kind of sequence data structures. They can implement anything where you want a sequence of objects you can iterate through. They can even handle infinitely long sequences. We can, for example, take our counter example from Chapter 11 and from Chapter 6. Here, we had a function

431

or object that we could use to count how many times we have called a function or a method. Let us now write an iterator with the same functionality. It would look like this:

```python
class Counter(object):
    def __init__(self):
        self.counter = 0
    def has_more(self):
        return True
    def next(self):
        self.counter += 1
        return self.counter - 1
```

With the counter, there are *always* more elements, so has_more() always returns True. The next() method is simple since it just increments the counter and returns the previous value. It has to be the previous value because we must by necessity increment before we can return.

Anytime you have something that you want to treat as a sequence, you can use an iterator. Python uses iterators to give you access to data in various data structures like lists and dictionaries, but it also provides interfaces for manipulating iterators in various ways, creating new iterators from other iterators, similar to how we used higher-order functions to translate one or more functions into new functions. Let us now look at how Python implements iterators.

Python Iterators and Other Interfaces

The while loop for iterators is useable, but in Python, we expect to use a for loop to go through a sequence. But we don't have a way to make a for loop use our two iterator methods. In some programming languages, that would just be too bad, but Python treats most objects as potentially implementing an interface. We implement algorithms that work on abstract data structures, and all data structures that implement the right methods will do for the algorithm. Similarly, Python's language constructions can use objects if they just implement the right set of methods. A Python for loop will happily work with iterators (in fact, it only works with iterators), if you implement them with the right interface.

You need to implement two methods to make an iterator. Not the two we just did, though. For technical reasons that we will not go into here, an iterator must provide a way for translating itself into an iterator. If you have an iterator and need to create one, the easiest to do is just to return the iterator itself. That is usually what you do, but the mechanism is there to handle complex cases. Then, naturally, an iterator needs to be able to increment to the next value. Python does not use a function that tests if there are more elements but instead relies on an exception of the type StopIteration to indicate when there are no more elements.

If we rewrite the list sequence iterator to match Python's expectation of an iterator, it looks like this:

```
class ListSequenceIterator(object):
    def __init__(self, seq):
        self.seq = seq
        self.index = 0

    def __iter__(self):
        return self

    def __next__(self):
        if self.index >= len(self.seq.sequence):
            raise StopIteration()
        self.index += 1
        return self.seq.sequence[self.index - 1]
```

The __iter__() method tells Python how you can convert the iterator into an iterator, and it is the __next__() method that lets Python increment the iterator in the for loop.

Now, we can call iterator() on a sequence and use a for loop to go through the elements:

```
for x in seq.iterator():
    print(x)
```

Of course, we would expect that we can just iterate through the sequence, as we can with Python lists, so how do we get Python to accept this?

```
for x in seq:
    print(x)
```

Well, for a for loop, the object to the right of in doesn't have to be an iterator itself, but it must be convertible into an iterator. You can convert an object into an iterator if it has an __iter__() method that returns an iterator, so if we implement such a method for the sequence

```
def __iter__(self):
    return ListSequenceIterator(self)
```

then we can iterate through sequences in a for loop, similar to how we would iterate through a built-in list.

Of course, suppose we need to create an iterator over the elements of the sequence. In that case, we can also just get the iterator for the underlying list object—it will do exactly the same as our own iterator—so we might as well do this:

```
def __iter__(self):
    return iter(self.sequence)
```

The iter() function essentially does the same as calling __iter__() on its input. It is just slightly more robust to what input it can deal with. Use iter() when you want an iterator from an object because it is more flexible, but implement __iter__() when you want to tell Python how to iterate over an object. To tell Python that you can iterate over an object, you need to give it an iterator, and the __iter__() method is how you do that. An actual iterator must also implement __iter__() and in addition must have __next__() to increment.

A Python iterator for the linked list sequence that must implement __iter__() and __next__() would look like this:

```
class DoublyLinkedListSequenceIterator(object):
    def __init__(self, seq):
        self.last = seq.last
        self.link = seq.first.next

    def __iter__(self):
        return self

    def __next__(self):
        if self.link == self.last:
            raise StopIteration()
        self.link = self.link.next
        return self.link.previous.element
```

The linked list sequence must have an __iter__() method that looks like this:

```
def __iter__(self):
    return DoublyLinkedListSequenceIterator(self)
```

If you implement the right methods, you can use for loops for iterators, but you also get other language features for free. You can, for example, use in to check if an element is in your sequence:

```
if 2 in seq:
    print("Yup, two is in the sequence.")
```

If Python can see that the object to the right of in is something it can iterate through, then it can do that and check if the element to the left of in is in the sequence. There are faster ways to determine if they contain an element for many data structures, and we will see some in the next chapter. If that is the case, you can tell Python to use that method. Still, if all we can do is iterate through a sequence, we get a linear search for free through the in keyword if we implement an iterator.

Python has several data structures that you can initialize from an iterator. The list type is one of them, so we can now convert a sequence into a list like this:

```
print(list(seq))
```

Exercise: It is often helpful if you can initialize a new data structure with a sequence through an iterator. Can you modify the two sequence classes we have made so they do that? Modify __repr__() so it gives you a text that you can use to reconstruct a sequence.

Generally, you don't want to translate an iterator into a list because that means copying all the elements. The iterator runs through all elements, one at a time, and that is usually all you need.

Our sequence data types have finite length, so it might be useful to have a method that gives us the length. With all the built-in data structures, we use the function len() to get the length, so we want to do that as well. Unfortunately, with len(), we don't get a free implementation because we provide an iterator. Iterators do not necessarily terminate after a finite number of increments—we could implement them, so they never raise StopIteration—so Python won't use them with len(). But we can tell Python that we know how to get the length of our sequences by implementing the __len__() method.

For the list implementation, we can just return the length of the underlying list:

```
def __len__(self):
    return len(self.sequence)
```

For the linked list version, we run through the list and count how many links we have:

```
def __len__(self):
    length = 0
    link = self.first.next
    while link != self.last:
        length += 1
        link = link.next
    return length
```

Once we have these two methods, we can get the length of either type of sequence using len():

```
print(len(seq))
```

What then about setting and getting values at an index? In Python, we expect syntax such as this

```
x[idx] = value
print(x[idx])
```

but our classes use get_at_index() and set_at_index(). Again, there are magic methods that tell Python what to do if we try to use the subscript syntax. They are called __getitem__() and __setitem__(), and for both of our classes, we can use them to call get_at_index() and set_at_index():

```
def __getitem__(self, index):
    return self.get_at_index(index)
```

```
def __setitem__(self, index, element):
    self.set_at_index(index, element)
```

Python is pretty relaxed about the interfaces it needs for its language constructions. It will find ways to give you what you want, even if the types you use do not directly support it. We saw that with in that automatically does a linear search if you do not tell it that there is a better method. It is the same with iterators. Suppose you give a class a method to access elements by index, using __getitem__(). If you then want to iterate over objects of the class, Python will use __getitem__(), one index after another, until it gets an IndexError exception. So this code will give us 2 × *i* for *i* < 10:

```
class Foo(object):
    def __getitem__(self, i):
        if i < 10: return 2 * i
        raise IndexError()

foo = Foo()
for i in foo:
    print(i)
```

This will also work with a linear search through the elements we can iterate over in this way, so you can also write

```
2 in foo # True
3 in foo # False
```

and get a linear search that way.

It works, but it can come at a severe runtime penalty, as it will with our linked lists. Each time we get the value at an index, it is a linear-time operation, so iterating through the sequences would take $O(n^2)$ with this approach. If you have a better way to do something, tell Python so it doesn't use a brute-force approach. We want the linear-time iterator for linked lists, but we could use the automatic one for the list implementation.

Generators

Iterators are a general trick that you can use in most programming languages. How well they integrate with the language's syntactic constructions varies—you cannot always just implement the right interface, and then your data structures behave like built-in types. But in practice, you can always implement iterators. Python, however, and a few other high-level languages have built-in features that make it easier to implement iterators. In Python, it is a construction called *generators*.

A generator looks like a hybrid of a function and an iterator. You write a function with a special keyword, yield, and when you call the function, you get an iterator back. The iterator works as follows: Every time you call next on the iterator, for example, in a for loop, the code in the generator progresses to the next yield statement. The first time you increment, you evaluate code from the generator's beginning until the first yield—the second time the code from the first yield to the next and so forth. The yield statements work like return statements. You yield a value, and that is the next element in the iterator. When the generator runs out of code or if you return from it, the iterator stops.

Consider this generator:

```
def animals():
    yield "Baboon"
    yield "Zebra"
    yield "Panda"
```

You yield three values, so when you create an instance with animals(), you get an iterator that will give you three values before it reaches its end. Try it out:

```
for animal in animals():
    print(animal)
```

When you are testing a generator that gives you a finite sequence, you can translate it into a list object to print it. It can give you a nicer output. This is easy to do because you can initialize lists with iterators, and that is what generator instances are, so you can use

```
print(list(animals()))
```

You get

```
['Baboon', 'Zebra', 'Panda']
```

It is easier to see what the sequence is than if you iterate through it and print each element. You cannot print the generator object itself. Well, you can. You can write print(animals()), but the output will be something like

```
<generator object animals at 0x10833ee58>
```

which is sufficiently useless that it isn't worth doing.

The animals() generator has three yield statements and produces three animals, but when I said that each increment goes from one yield to the next, I wasn't entirely honest. It executes the code from one yield statement to the next, and they do not have

438

to be separate yield statements in the code. If you loop over a list, for example, and yield each element, the generator works the same way:

```
def animals():
    for x in ["Baboon", "Zebra", "Panda"]:
        yield x
print(list(animals()))
```

Each time you increment the iterator, you run the generator code from the point where you left it until it calls yield again.

You can yield from an iterator you run through in your generator, so you can do something like this:

```
def more_animals():
    for x in animals():
        yield x
    for x in animals():
        yield x
```

However, if you simply want to yield elements from another generator unchanged, there is syntax for that as well:

```
def more_animals():
    yield from animals()
    yield from animals()
```

The yield from command says that the iterator should now run through another iterator and yield all the elements from there.

You can generate an infinite sequence from a generator easily; just use an infinite loop. Here's a counter generator:

```
def counter():
    count = 0
    while True:
        yield count
        count += 1
```

We don't need to increment the counter before we yield, unlike with our iterator implementation. The generator will run the code after the yield next time it increments, so we can increment count there.

You cannot call `print(list(counter()))` now because you get an infinitely large `list` that way, but we can write another generator that *modifies* an iterator:

```
def take(iterator, n):
    remaining = n
    for x in iterator:
        if remaining == 0:
            return
        yield x
        remaining -= 1
```

This guy runs through its input iterator and yields elements from it, but it keeps a counter of how many elements it has taken so far. When it reaches its limit, it returns, and that terminates the iterator. With both `counter()` and `take()`, you can write

```
print(list(take(counter(), 10)))
```

Try it.

There is another syntax for generators that is sometimes useful, and it looks precisely like list comprehension, except that you use round parentheses, (), instead of square brackets.

This will create a list

```
[x**2 for x in take(counter(), 10)]
```

while this will create a generator:

```
(x**2 for x in take(counter(), 10))
```

There isn't much difference in these two cases, but when you iterate over the generator, you generate the results of the expression one by one, and you do not generate all the elements as you do with the list. That means that we can use them on infinite sequences:

```
def square(iterator):
    return (x**2 for x in iterator)
def even(iterator):
    return (x for x in iterator if x % 2 == 0)
```

These two functions can modify an infinite sequence, and this is possible because we only evaluate one element at a time. You can combine several iterator modifiers if you want:

```
square_counts = square(counter())
print(list(take(square_counts, 10)))

even_counts = even(counter())
print(list(take(even_counts, 10)))

even_square_counts = even(square(counter()))
print(list(take(even_square_counts, 10)))
```

You need to be careful about only one thing if you start using generators instead of lists: you can only iterate through a generator object once. If you use a for loop to run over a list twice, it works as you would expect, but if you try to do that with a generator object, it won't. Once you reach the end of an iteration, you are done.

If you try to iterate again, the iterator is already at the end, so the for loop will terminate immediately. You need to create a new generator object if you want to iterate through the sequence again. A similar thing happens if you terminate the iteration early, as we do when we call take() in the preceding code. If we try to iterate through an object that we have terminated early, it will continue where it left off (which is generally what we want for iterators, but something that can bite you if you are not careful). You can try it with the preceding code. If you use even(square_counts) in the second-to-last line, you will find that square_counts will continue from where you left it after the second line in the code, so you get a different result in the last line.

It isn't a major worry, but occasionally, you see people try to write code that expects generator objects to work like lists. You could, for example, try something like this:

```
def more_animals():
    x = animals()
    yield from x
    yield from x
```

It will give you the list of animals once and not twice. I have only seen bugs like that when you assign a generator object or generator expression (those that look like list comprehensions) to a variable. It doesn't happen when you call an iterator every time you need it. So be careful if you assign generator objects to variables. It is, of course, the same with iterators in general, but I have never seen bugs because of them. With iterators, you typically use an object directly with the for loop, and you don't save it. If you did, you would have the same problem. With generators, because of generator expressions, it happens. Be careful with those; remember to call the generator each time you need an iterator.

To wrap up the chapter, let's go back and rewrite the linked list iterator as a generator. It looks like this:

```
def __iter__(self):
    link = self.first.next
    while link != self.last:
        yield link.element
        link = link.next
```

When the for loop calls __iter__(), it calls a generator, so it gets an iterator—no need to wrap anything in classes and no need to move the link to its next reference before we return a value. The generator takes care of it all.

CHAPTER 14

Sets

Conceptually, sets are simpler than sequences. The reason we took sequences first, though, is that we can implement sets in different ways to make operations more efficient, and some of these implementations are more complicated than the linked list data structure we made in the previous chapter.

There are many operations we might want for a set, for example, computing the union or intersection of two sets, but we will stick to the minimal interface we would expect a set to have. We want to be able to add elements to a set, remove elements, and test if an element is already in the set. With Python's built-in set type, the operations would look like this:

```
s = { 1, 2, 3 }
s.add(42)
s.remove(1)
2 in s
```

We cannot implement our own sets to initialize the same way that we can initialize Python's sets, with expressions such as { 1, 2, 3 }. Python's own sets have a privileged position in the language. To add something similar to our own sets, we will require that we initialize them from a sequencer (basically, any iterator over a finite sequence will do). Python's sets can also handle that, and you could create the set with elements 1, 2, and 3 using

```
s = set([1, 2, 3])
```

Here, the sequence is a list, but any sequence will do, and that is what we want for our own sets as well.

© Thomas Mailund 2021
T. Mailund, *Introduction to Computational Thinking*, https://doi.org/10.1007/978-1-4842-7077-6_14

Finally, just because we have already learned how to make iterators, we want to make them for our sets as well, so we can iterate through a set's element like we can for a built-in set:

```
for x in s:
    print(x)
```

Before we start, however, there is an issue we need to address, and that is what it means for two objects to be the same. When we insert objects in the set, we don't want more than one copy of what we consider the same object. It works fine with the numbers we used in the preceding because Python knows that 2 equals 2 and is different from 3, but it is less straightforward if you want a set of data structures you have defined yourself. That is because there is a difference between object *identity* and *equality*.

Consider the Patient class we wrote in Chapter 11. I have listed it in the following but left out the __repr__() method for brevity:

```
class Patient(object):
    def __init__(self, name, height, weight):
        self.name = name
        self.height = height
        self.weight = weight
```

Now, try to run this code:

```
henry = Patient("Henry", 173, 72)
george = Patient("George", 166, 89)

print(henry == george) # False
print(henry == henry) # True

print(henry == Patient("Henry", 173, 72)) # False
```

The first two comparisons are probably what you would expect, but the last might be surprising. After all, we have defined henry to be exactly the patient with the properties we have on the equality test's right. But they are, in fact, two different objects. Each time we call the Patient() constructor, we get a new object, regardless of the parameters we give it. Just because they are the same for the two objects doesn't mean that we get the same object.

If you have two references to the same object and modify it through one variable, the other variable will see the changes. That is because it is the same object we are modifying, so it is what we would expect:

```
x = []
y = x
x.append(42)
print(y) # [42]
print(x == y) # True
```

But if we have references to two different objects and we modify one of them, we naturally don't see the other object change:

```
x = []
y = []
x.append(42)
print(y) # []
print(x == y) # False
```

We have seen that several times before, and it shouldn't come as a surprise.

You can test if two variables refer to the same object using is, and it will be true if and only if you have the same object.

Consider this example:

```
print([] is []) # False
print([] == []) # True
```

We create two separate list objects using [ ], and since they are different objects, [ ] is [ ] is False. The two empty lists are equivalent, though, so if we compare them with ==, we are not asking Python if they are the same object—which they aren't—we are asking if they hold the same elements. There is a huge difference between asking if x is y and if x == y.

Python is comparing your Patient objects by checking if they are the same object using the is operator by default. But it clearly isn't doing that when it compares [ ] == [ ], so there must be a way to tell Python how it should decide if one element equals another. And indeed there is: you need to implement the __eq__() method. For the Patient class, it can look like this:

445

```
class Patient(object):
    def __init__(self, name, height, weight):
        self.name = name
        self.height = height
        self.weight = weight

    def __eq__(self, other):
        return self.name == other.name and \
                self.height == other.height and \
                self.weight == other.weight
```

Now you will get that `henry` and `Patient("Henry", 173, 72)` are equal:

```
print(henry == Patient("Henry", 173, 72)) # True
```

For our sets, we will say that it is this type of equality that we need.

Depending on the underlying data structures we use to implement sets, there will be further requirements. The interface to the abstract data structure "set" is not entirely defined by the operations we implement. This is not ideal, but it is a price we must pay for efficiency. However, we will start with sets where equality is the only requirement for the objects (and where you can use the default behavior if you want equality to mean identical objects).

Sets with Built-In Lists

The built-in `list` already has the operations we need to construct our abstract data structure, and an implementation can look like this:

```
class ListSet(object):
    def __init__(self, seq = ()):
        self.data = list(seq)
    def add(self, element):
        self.data.append(element)
    def remove(self, element):
        self.data.remove(element)
    def __iter__(self):
        return iter(self.data)
```

```
def __contains__(self, element):
    return element in self.data
def __repr__(self):
    return 'ListSet(' + repr(self.data) + ')'
```

The add() implementation uses append() on the list, since the list doesn't have an add() method. It also doesn't quite do what it is supposed to. It adds an element regardless of whether that element was already in the list. For a set, this is not what we want (and not what Python's set does). We can avoid it with an explicit test before we append:

```
def add(self, element):
    if element not in self:
        self.data.append(element)
```

We have the same problem with __init__() if the sequence we get in the constructor contains duplicates. We also need to remove those. We can use add() for inserting them into the underlying list object to guarantee that we do not have duplications:

```
def __init__(self, seq = ()):
    self.data = []
    for element in seq:
        self.add(element)
```

This would give us a quadratic-time constructor—for each insertion, we need to search through the entire list. We can cheat using the set class, insert all the elements in it, and then build the list from the elements there, but if we are going to use the set class, there isn't any reason to use list, so I won't. The exercise here is to see different implementations with different complexities for the operations, and if we use a sequence like this, we do get a quadratic running time.

We didn't have to implement __contains__() for this class. It will use a linear search when we write element in self.data because that is how the underlying list object implements the in operator, that is, the __contains__() method. If we only implemented the iterator interface, we would get the same behavior.

The remove() operation raises an exception if we try to delete an element that isn't in the set, and for consistency between different set operations, we need to decide if this is the behavior we want and, if it is, what exception to raise, so they all raise the

447

same. Different implementations do not provide the same interface to users if they cast different exceptions. Then we cannot write code that captures the right exception to handle errors (or that ignores the case if that is what we want). If we catch the exception from one implementation, we will still crash our program if we use the other implementation. With abstract data structures and polymorphism in general, it isn't enough that two different implementations have the same methods. They should behave the same way, including the exceptions they can raise.

One option is to allow the removal of elements that aren't in the set and silently ignore the case. To achieve this, we can use contains() before we use remove() on the underlying implementation:

```
def remove(self, element):
    if element in self:
        self.data.remove(element)
```

Alternatively, you can catch exceptions and raise another, to give them the same interface. Python's built-in sets will raise the KeyError exception, so we will use the same. Then we update remove() to this:

```
def remove(self, element):
    try:
        self.data.remove(element)
    except ValueError:
        raise KeyError()
```

For different sets, the __repr__() methods will not do the same thing, but that is fine. We do not consider them part of the interface, as they are mainly here to make debugging and experimentation easier, and they are supposed to give us a string we can use to recreate the set object. That wouldn't be possible if two different classes gave us the same string representation. We don't want an algorithm to depend on them, and we probably do not want to print objects for a specific implementation inside any algorithm we write.

The class looks deceptively simple, but this is because we simply delegate the operations to the list class without giving much thought to how they are implemented there. If we consider that this class holds its elements as a contiguous sequence of memory cells, we can expand on the operations a little and better understand what is happening.

With a list, when we remove an element, we must copy the remaining elements because a list is stored as contiguous memory. One solution is to find the index of the element we should remove, then take the elements before that index and the elements after the index, and replace the data with the concatenation of these two. It is not quite as efficient as Python's implementation because we copy the entire remaining list, but see the following exercise. This implementation makes remove() a linear-time implementation, as should be obvious, and so is Python's.

To test if an element is in a list, we need to use a linear search. That is also what Python does when you write x in some_list. We can implement it explicitly in our ListSet class:

```python
class ListSet(object):
    def __init__(self, seq = ()):
        self.data = list(seq)

    def add(self, element):
        if element not in self:
            self.data.append(element)

    def remove(self, element):
        try:
            idx = self.data.index(element)
            self.data.pop(idx)
        except ValueError:
            raise KeyError()

    def __iter__(self):
        return iter(self.data)

    def __contains__(self, element):
        for x in self.data:
            if x == element:
                return True
        return False

    def __repr__(self):
        return 'ListSet(' + repr(self.data) + ')'
```

Exercise: What is the complexity of add() with this implementation?

Exercise: The __contains__() method is a linear-time operation for ListSet, but if we used a binary search instead, we could get a logarithmic-time operation. That requires, however, that we keep the list sorted when we insert. If you append an element to a sorted list and swap it down until you find its location, similar to how we swap elements down in insertion sort, then you can keep the list sorted with a linear-time insertion. Implement this. Does it change the complexity of add(), considering that you can only implement __contains__() if you keep the list sorted? Explain.

Linked Lists Sets

Can we implement a set with linked lists? Of course, we can. We have already seen that we can add elements to a linked list sequence and remove them again, and it isn't hard to see how we can do a linear search through them, so we can implement __contains__() that way. A linked list implementation could look like this:

```
class Link(object):
    def __init__(self, element, next):
        self.element = element
        self.next = next
    def __repr__(self):
        return 'Link({}, {})'.format(
            repr(self.element),
            repr(self.next)
        )

def contains(links, element):
    if links is None:
        return False
    if links.element == element:
        return True
    return contains(links.next, element)

def remove(links, element):
    if links is None:
        raise KeyError()
```

```
        if links.element == element:
            return links.next
        return Link(links.element, remove(links.next, element))

def link_iterator(links):
    link = links
    while link is not None:
        yield link.element
        link = link.next

class LinkedListSet(object):
    def __init__(self, seq = ()):
        self.links = None
        for element in seq:
            self.add(element)

    def add(self, element):
        if not element in self:
            self.links = Link(element, self.links)

    def remove(self, element):
        self.links = remove(self.links, element)

    def __iter__(self):
        return link_iterator(self.links)

    def __contains__(self, element):
        return contains(self.links, element)

    def __repr__(self):
        return 'LinkedListSet(link_iterator(' + repr(self.links) + '))'
```

I have pulled out the main functionality as functions because I wanted recursive functions on the recursive Link data structure. You can implement an iterative version and keep the functionality in methods, which you will need anyway if your set is large and the recursion depth gets too high, but I will leave that as an exercise.

Exercise: Implement iterative versions of contains and remove. The other functions are fine the way they are; add() simply prepends an element after using the __contains__() method, and __init__() is already iterative.

The link_iterator() function could be a generator in the __iter__() method, but I used a function, so I could generate an iterator from a linked list in the __repr__() method. Otherwise, I would need to translate the linked list structure into another kind of iterator to output it with __repr__() or just give up and accept that __repr__() doesn't give me a text representation that I can get a new object from.

Exercise: What is the complexity of the operations in this implementation?

Search Trees

The set-based set from two sections ago has constant-time operations, except for building it from an iterator or producing an iterator, both of which are linear-time operations. The list and linked list implementations' operations are all in linear time. We will see how to get to constant-time operations later in the chapter, in the section "Hash Table." First, we will explore a data structure with potentially logarithmic-time insertion, lookups, and removes: *search trees*.

Search trees require that the values we put into them are *ordered*, meaning that we can determine if one element is smaller than, equal to, or greater than another—the same requirements we put on sorting elements. We define them recursively by saying that a search tree is either empty, and we represent that by None, or it is a *node* that has a value and a left and a right search tree:

```
class Node(object):
    def __init__(self, value,
                 left = None,
                 right = None):
        self.value = value
        self.left = left
        self.right = right

    def __repr__(self):
        return 'Node({}, left = {}, right = {})'.format(
            repr(self.value),
            repr(self.left),
            repr(self.right)
        )
```

You can try to create a tree and examine its structure like this:

```
tree = \
    Node(3,
         left = Node(1),
         right = Node(6,
```

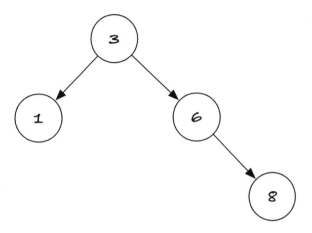

Figure 14-1. *Example search tree*

```
         left = None,
         right = Node(8))
    )
print(tree)
```

We will draw the tree like in Figure 14-1, where I only show references to non-None nodes to make it easier to read. In computer science, we draw trees with the root at the top. I don't know why; they did from before I was born, but that is how we do it.

We then require that all values in the left tree of a node be smaller than the node's value and that all values in the right tree must be greater. That means that we can search in the tree by going left every time the node's value is greater than the one we are looking for and going right if it is smaller. If it is equal to the value, then we have found the value, and if we reach an empty tree, then the element is not in the tree:

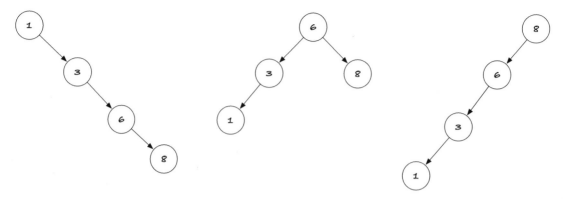

Figure 14-2. *Three alternative search trees for the numbers 1, 3, 6, and 8*

```
def contains(node, value):
    if node is None:
        return False
    if node.value == value:
        return True
    if node.value > value:
        return contains(node.left, value)
    if node.value < value:
        return contains(node.right, value)
```

A search tree over a set of elements is not unique. The requirement on how values relate to subtrees allows for many different tree topologies. In Figure 14-2 you can see three alternatives to the tree in Figure 14-1. All satisfy the requirement, and we can search in them equally well.

Inserting

To insert a value in a tree, we can also think recursively. Inserting into an empty tree means creating a new node with empty subtrees. If we are at a node that holds the value we must insert, we are done because the value is already there. Otherwise, we must insert the value in the left or right subtree, and we chose between left and right depending on how the new value compares to the one in the node—if the new value is smaller, it belongs in the left subtree, and if it is larger, it should go in the right tree:

```
def insert(node, value):
    if node is None:
        return Node(value)
    if node.value == value:
        return node
    elif node.value > value:
        return Node(node.value,
                    left = insert(node.left, value),
                    right = node.right)
    elif node.value < value:
        return Node(node.value,
                    left = node.left,
                    right = insert(node.right, value))
```

Removing

Removing an element is slightly more involved. It is simple if the node that contains the value has at least one empty subtree; see Figure 14-3. If the tree itself is empty, removing an element from it should give us an empty tree back. If the node that holds the value we wish to remove has one non-empty subtree, we can replace it with its subtree. If the entire tree satisfies the search tree invariant, then the subtree that holds the value we delete does as well. All the values in the subtree will be smaller than the value in the parent node—if it is a left subtree—or larger than the value in the parent—if it is a right subtree. That includes all the values in the one subtree that the node we are to delete has. Replacing the node that holds the value with its subtree will maintain the invariant. Figure 14-3 illustrates this when the node we delete sits in a left subtree; the case where it sits in a right subtree is analogous.

We can't always be this lucky, though, since nodes can have both a left and a right subtree. When that is the case, we do this: When we are in the node we have to delete, we will replace the value with one that will satisfy the invariant for values and subtrees. If we take one step to the left—and we know that there is a non-empty left subtree in this case—then we can run down the tree where we only follow right subtree references. When we cannot go any further, we have found the largest value in the left subtree. Every time we move right, we get a larger value, and all the values to the left of the path we explore are smaller, including the left subtree of the rightmost node in this subtree. We can take that value and put it in the first node; see Figure 14-4.

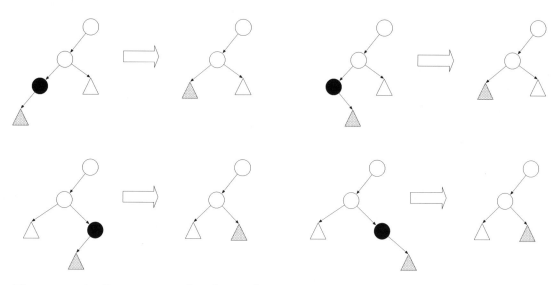

Figure 14-3. *Remove a node when it has at most one subtree*

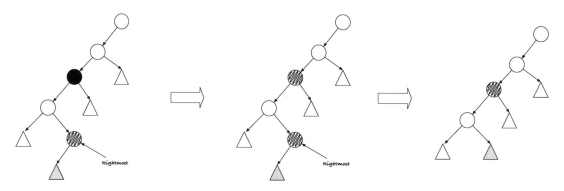

Figure 14-4. *The general case for removing a value in a search tree*

Now we are rid of the value we wanted to delete, and the search tree invariant is maintained. We have two copies of the leftmost value, though, so we need to delete one of them. The lowest one doesn't have a right subtree, by definition of being rightmost, so we can delete it from the left subtree using the rules from the preceding:

```
def remove(node, value):
    if node is None:
        return None
    if node.value > value:
```

```
        return Node(node.value,
                    left = remove(node.left, value),
                    right = node.right)
    if node.value < value:
        return Node(node.value,
                    left = node.left,
                    right = remove(node.right, value))

    # we have value == node.value
    if node.left is None:
        return node.right
    if node.right is None:
        return node.left

    replacement = rightmost_value(node.left)
    return Node(replacement,
                remove(node.left, replacement),
                node.right)
def rightmost_value(node):
    if node.right is None:
        return node.value
    else:
        return rightmost_value(node.right)
```

I didn't actually change the value in the node here, but created a new node instead. I will explain why a little later.

Iterator

Our set interface requires that we can iterate over a tree, and it might be less obvious how we would do that, but a generator and recursion will do it for us:

```
def tree_iter(node):
    if node is None: return # Done iterating
    yield from tree_iter(node.left)
    yield node.value
    yield from tree_iter(node.right)
```

We don't have to yield anything from an empty tree, so we stop the iteration there. Otherwise, we yield all the nodes in the left tree, using `yield from` to get and yield everything the recursive call gives us; then we yield this node's value and then all the nodes in the right subtree.

If we yield the values in this order, we get them in sorted order. So we immediately have a new sorting algorithm here, at least when there are no duplicated values: insert the elements you want to sort in a search tree, and then get them out in the right order. The reason we cannot handle duplicated values is that we enforce a set behavior in our implementation, but you could allow duplicated values in a search tree, and then the algorithm would work for general sorting.

The complexity is the time it takes to insert n elements plus the time it takes to get them out again. The recursive generator takes linear time to run, it is in effect constant work per node (plus the recursive calls), and if we have a search tree with n elements, we also have n nodes. The time to insert n elements is n times the time it takes to insert one element. The best we can hope for here is that the insertion operation takes logarithmic time. That would give us an $O(n \log n)$ comparison-based sort, and that is as good as it can possibly be. If we have that, we have done as well as it is humanly (and mathematically) possible. So let us examine the three operations we have implemented.

Analysis

All three operations, `contains()`, `insert()`, and `remove()`, involve a constant number of searches down the tree (with `remove()` you might need three, one to find the node, one to find the rightmost, and one to delete it, with the others only one). In each of the searches, we spend constant time per node. So the cost of the operations is proportional to the depth of the tree.

How deep is a tree? That depends on how balanced it is. If you have a tree that only has right subtrees or only has left subtrees, like the leftmost and rightmost trees in Figure 14-2, then you can go down n nodes from root to the deepest leaf. If you have a tree that looks like that, your search operations take time $O(n)$. Your sorting algorithm would then run in $O(n^2)$, and the set operations we are implementing would take linear time. If the tree is balanced, so there is roughly the same number of nodes to the left and to the right of each node, then the depth is logarithmic. The argument is the same as when we analyzed binary search; when you search down, you remove half of the problem in each recursive call, and you can't cut n in half more than $O(\log n)$ times before you reach a single element. If you have a balanced tree, all the operations run in $O(\log n)$, and using the search tree to sort gives you an $O(n \log n)$ algorithm.

Wrapping the Operations in a Set Class

We have all the operations we need for a set abstract data structure, but we have them as functions, so we should wrap them in a class. That is relatively easy:

```
class SearchTreeSet(object):
    def __init__(self, seq = ()):
        self.tree = None
        for value in seq:
            self.add(value)

    def add(self, element):
        self.tree = insert(self.tree, element)

    def remove(self, element):
        if element not in self:
            raise KeyError()
        self.tree = remove(self.tree, element)

    def __iter__(self):
        return tree_iter(self.tree)

    def __contains__(self, element):
        return contains(self.tree, element)

    def __repr__(self):
        return 'SearchTreeSet(tree_iter(' + repr(self.tree) + '))'
```

We don't need to check if an element is already in the set before we insert, since the insertion function doesn't add existing elements anyway. The remove() function ignores when an element is not in the set, but we require the interface that it should raise an exception, so we do this explicitly. That costs us an extra search, and we could remove it if we accepted a different interface to the class or if we made the function raise the exception for us.

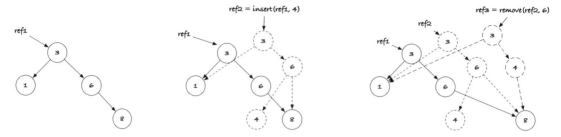

Figure 14-5. *Two persistent operations on a search tree*

Persistent and Ephemeral Data Structures

In none of the functions did I change any node, even though I explained the `remove()` algorithm as if I put the rightmost value in the node I wanted to delete. I didn't do it that way. In all the functions, I built new trees when returning from recursions. I did that partly because I avoid most special cases when dealing with empty nodes that I can't update, but mostly because I now want to tell you about two different kinds of data structures: *persistent* and *ephemeral*.

A persistent data structure is one that remains the same no matter how many operations we perform on it, while an ephemeral is one where each operation potentially changes the data structure. It might sound crazy that we would be interested in data structures that we can never modify, especially if we want to have something like sets, where in their nature we want to modify them if we add or remove elements. However, persistence doesn't mean exactly that. It means that if I have a reference to a data structure and you do an operation on it, my data structure doesn't change—yours will reflect the operation.

Consider Figure 14-5 where we start with a tree we have one reference to. We insert an element and save the result in another variable, but the tree hasn't changed from the first variable's perspective. It holds one tree, and the other holds another. Some parts of the trees are shared; here it is the nodes for 1 and 8, and in general, anything that isn't on the path we used in the recursion will be shared—after all, we only build a new tree when we return from the function calls, so we can only create new nodes there. After the insertion, we perform an operation on the second tree, we remove the number 6, and we end up with yet another tree. The first two trees are still there, though, and if we wanted to use them, we could.

This is what it means for a data structure to be persistent. When we do an operation, we get a new data structure, and we do not change anything that other variables are referring to.

The singly linked lists in Chapter 13 were almost a persistent data structure. If we implement them purely recursively, we can insert or remove a new link by constructing a new one that keeps the same list as the previous list:

```
def append(link, element):
    if link is None:
        return Link(element, None)
    else:
        return Link(link.element,
                    append(link.next, element))

def prepend(link, element):
    return Link(element, link)

def remove(link, element):
    if link is None:
        return None
    if link.element == element:
        return element.next
    else:
        return Link(link.element,
                    remove(link.next, element)
```

Exercise: Check that these functions build a new list but leave the previous one unaltered.

Exercise: Write a function that changes the value at an index, *without* modifying a link, and returns a new list.

With the doubly linked lists, we cannot make a persistent data structure in this way. We must update the previous link when we add or remove values, and that breaks the existing structure. If operations break the data structure, so other references see the changes, then we say that the data structure is *ephemeral*. The class we wrapped the search trees in is ephemeral, but only because we update its tree attribute with each operation. We could return new sets instead, and then it would be persistent again—it just wouldn't match the interface we agreed upon for sets.

Why do we care about the distinction between persistent and ephemeral data structures? We won't in this book, in all honesty, but there are applications where working with persistent structures is easier. Imagine, for example, that you have an algorithm with code that does multiple updates to a data structure, but where that code might raise an exception. If the exception is raised, you usually don't know if the data structure is in a consistent state; you don't know what the code has done to it before the exception. If you want to return to the point before you called the code that failed, it can get rather tricky. However, if you work with a persistent data structure, the structure before the call is readily available when the exception is raised because the code you ran only generated new data structures; it didn't change what you already had. Another case where persistent data structures shine is with concurrency, where multiple threads operate on the same data (which we will not consider in this book). There, if they work on a persistent data structure, the threads can share data and still only see their own changes. Persistent data structures are not only of academic interest; they are useful in practice. Just not with the topics we have room for in this book.

Naturally, you could always copy all elements in a data structure and create a new one, so in that sense, you can always make persistent structures. That, however, is usually as expensive as it sounds. When we care about persistent data structures, it is when we can create new copies much cheaper while preserving some of the original structure. If we have a balanced search tree and use the preceding implementation for the operations, we get a completely independent new set for each operation in logarithmic time.

As a rule of thumb, if you can implement operations on a data structure using recursion, where you build new nodes, links, whatever as you return from the recursion, then you can do it such that you have a persistent data structure. Often, you don't get a substantial time overhead by doing this, although iterative algorithms where you modify the same structure are faster in practice. You have logarithmic-time operations for search trees whether you make them ephemeral or not, so asymptotically, you don't lose much time to get a persistent structure. You cannot get persistence for some data structures because operations must destructively modify the underlying data—the hash tables that we see later work that way—and for some data structures, you can get faster destructive operations than you can get persistent operations.

An Iterative Solution

But now, we turn to an iterative implementation of search trees and one where we modify the nodes in the operations, giving us an ephemeral data structure. Iterative approaches are usually faster than recursive ones, which is why it is worth considering that approach as well. We also avoid problems with running out of stack space in recursive calls—although, if we can keep the trees balanced and never recurse deeper than $O(\log n)$, this is unlikely to be a problem. Nevertheless, we need to see an alternative solution.

All our three operations, contains(), insert(), and remove(), will use this function to get a node to operate on:

```python
def find_node(node, value):
    p, n = None, node
    while n:
        if n.value == value:
            return n
        elif n.value > value:
            # go left
            p, n = n, n.left
        elif n.value < value:
            # go right
            p, n = n, n.right
    return p
```

It finds the node where a value sits, if it is in the tree, and otherwise, it gives us the parent node where we should insert it if that is what we intend to do.

All it does is to run down the tree, going left or right depending on the value in a node and the value we search for, and then return the node if it contains the value and the node where we cannot continue further because we have to go to an empty tree. It does it in a while loop instead of a recursion, but it is the same search. We keep track of the parent of the current node in the variable p. We set it to None initially, but it will be updated every time we move down the tree. We consider it an error if n is None when we call the function, and in the first iteration, we will either return n (and not p), or we will set p to a valid node. When we go left or right, we set p to n, so we remember the parent of the new node that n now refers to. If n becomes None in the search, we return p.

The contains() function is trivial to implement once we have this function:

```python
def contains(node, value):
    return find_node(node, value).value == value
```

We get the node where the value should sit and test if it is there or if we only found the place where it *should* sit if it was in the tree.

Inserting isn't any harder. We get the node where the value should be, and if it is there, we are already done. Otherwise, we have to replace the empty subtree in that node with a new node that holds the value:

```
def insert(node, value):
    n = find_node(node, value)
    if n.value == value:
        return # already here
    elif n.value > value:
        n.left = Node(value)
    else:
        n.right = Node(value)
```

Now, for remove(), we have a problem. In the recursive solution, we returned a tree where the value was removed from the subtree, and returning from the recursion, we would insert this tree in the parent at the right location. If we find the node to delete using find_node(), we don't have a reference to the parent, so we cannot update it. The easiest way to get a parent from a node is to add a reference to parents to the nodes, so we do that:

```
class Node(object):
    def __init__(self, value,
                 parent = None,
                 left = None,
                 right = None):

        self.value = value
        self.parent = parent
        self.left = left
        self.right = right

        # guaranteeing consistency
        if self.left is not None:
            self.left.parent = self
        if self.right is not None:
            self.right.parent = self
```

```
def __repr__(self):
    return 'Node({}, left = {}, right = {})'.format(
        repr(self.value),
        repr(self.left),
        repr(self.right)
    )
```

This gives us a circular data structure; children point to parents that point back to children, affecting the efficiency of the garbage collection (recall the discussion we had in Chapter 13).

We won't have to worry about it for search trees when we explicitly delete nodes. Whenever we remove a node from a tree, we replace the parent's pointer to the node we delete when we insert a new subtree in the parent. That removes the circular structure, and the node we are deleting will be removed by the garbage collection. But if we delete the reference to the root of a tree while there are still subtrees around, then we still have a circular structure, and it might be something we should deal with. I will ignore it for now because nodes will be garbage collected eventually anyway, but I will return to the issue at the end of the section.

We need to set the parent references when we add nodes to the tree, so we modify insert() to do that:

```
def insert(node, value):
    n = find_node(node, value)
    if n.value == value:
    return # already here
elif n.value > value:
    n.left = Node(value, parent = n)
else:
    n.right = Node(value, parent = n)
```

Getting to removal, we need a function that gives us the rightmost node in a subtree, and we can easily do this iteratively by running down a tree until we get to a node that doesn't have a right subtree:

```
def get_rightmost(node):
    while node.right is not None:
        node = node.right
    return node
```

465

You could also get it using the get_node() function; if n is the node we want to delete, get_node(n.left, n.value) would search for a n.value that is larger than all the values in n.left (by the search tree invariant), and that will also give us the rightmost value in n.left.

We cannot call this function with an empty tree, but in the remove() function, we will never get the rightmost node if the original node doesn't have a left subtree.

Replacing one subtree with another, as we do when we remove a node (recall Figure 14-4), was easy with the recursive solution: if we called recursively to the left, we got the new left tree back, and if we recursed to the right, we got the new right tree back. With the solution we want now, we need to change a reference in a node's parent. There, we need to find out if we should replace the left or right tree. We use this tree for that:

```
def replace(child, new_child):
    if child.parent.left == child:
        child.parent.left = new_child
    else:
        child.parent.right = new_child
    if new_child is not None:
        new_child.parent = child.parent
```

It also sets the parent reference for the new node, provided it isn't an empty tree.

Finally, we get to remove(). There, we get the node that might hold the value. If it isn't there, I will raise an exception. It is what the set interface requires anyway, so we might as well do it in the function rather than explicitly doing a second search first to check if we have the value at all.

Otherwise, we check if the node has an empty left or right subtree and replace itself with the other tree if that is the case. Otherwise, get the rightmost node, replace rightmost with its left subtree in rightmost's parent (using replace()), and change the value in the node to the value in the rightmost node:

```
def remove(node, value):
    n = find_node(node, value)
    if n.value != value:
        return raise KeyError()

    if n.left is None:
        replace(n, n.right)
```

```
    elif n.right is None:
        replace(n, n.left)
    else:
        rightmost = get_rightmost(n.left)
        n.value = rightmost.value
        remove(n.left, rightmost.value)
```

We raise a KeyError error if we can't find the value. We have to handle missing values anyway, and this way, we don't need to explicitly test if the value is in the set before we remove it, which saves one search.

This function must be called with a non-None node, but it *also* requires that the node we find with find_node(), n, is not None—because we want to update subtrees of it! This means that all nodes in our tree must have a parent, whether it is empty or not. This calls for another special case, but we can get rid of it the way we got rid of special cases with linked lists: we can add a dummy node. If we put a dummy node in the set class and all the real elements in one of its subtrees, then all our nodes have a parent.

With the dummy node, the complete solution looks like this:

```
class SearchTreeSet(object):
    def __init__(self, seq = ()):
        self.tree = Node(None) # dummy node
        for value in seq:
            self.add(value)

    def add(self, element):
        if self.tree.left is None:
            self.tree.left = Node(element, parent = self.tree)
        else:
            insert(self.tree.left, element)

    def remove(self, element):
        if self.tree.left is None:
            raise KeyError()
        remove(self.tree.left, element)

    def __iter__(self):
        return tree_iter(self.tree.left)
```

467

```
    def __contains__(self, element):
        if self.tree.left is None:
            return False
        return contains(self.tree.left, element)

    def __repr__(self):
        return 'SearchTreeSet(tree_iter(' + repr(self.tree.left) + '))'
```

A Dummy Value for Removing Special Cases

Because we use find_node() and it cannot handle empty trees, we have to explicitly check for empty trees in add(), remove(), and __contains__(). The dummy element didn't help us get rid of those. The reason it didn't is that whatever element we put in it must be one we can compare to the values we will use the set for. We don't want it to look like a real value in the set, and if we ignore it, we certainly don't want to risk someone actually putting that value in the set.

If we had a "largest" or "smallest" number we never otherwise use, for example, minus or plus infinity, then we could use that—assuming that no one would want to put that value in the set. But that would only work if we always had sets of numbers. We would have to define the smallest or largest number for all possible types we would put in our set. We can do something smarter in Python, where we can define how values compare—we can create a class that is always greater than any value you compare it to:

```
class Greater(object):
    def __lt__(self, other):
        return False
    def __eq__(self, other):
        return False
    def __gt__(self, other):
        return True

class SearchTreeSet(object):
    def __init__(self, seq = ()):
        self.tree = Node(Greater()) # dummy node
        for value in seq:
            self.add(value)
```

```
def add(self, element):
    insert(self.tree, element)

def remove(self, element):
    remove(self.tree, element)

def __iter__(self):
    return tree_iter(self.tree.left)

def __contains__(self, element):
    return contains(self.tree, element)

def __repr__(self):
    return 'SearchTreeSet(tree_iter(' + repr(self.tree.left) + '))'

def __str__(self):
    return str(list(self))
```

The Greater class compares a Greater object on the left-hand side of <, >, and ==
comparisons. If we put it on the right-hand side of the comparison, Python will use the
special methods only if the left-hand side doesn't implement them, but otherwise, it will
use the methods the object on the left uses. So I have been careful to put all the nodes in
the tree on the left of the comparisons in the code. Otherwise, this trick wouldn't work,
and you would have to deal with special cases with empty trees.

Relying on something as subtle as on which side of comparisons you put the nodes
in a tree implementation is dangerous, to say the least. Still, the code is short and
simple—we only use this property in two functions, find_node() and insert()—so it is
something I would dare in this case. Still, we are jumping hard on thin ice here, and if the
code was only a little more complex, I would choose to handle the special cases instead
of risking subtle problems in comparisons.

If you find yourself with a language where you cannot define a class such as Greater,
you can always write your own comparison function, that is, one that tells you which of
two elements is smaller. You can most likely pick an element you cannot put in a search
tree anyway because you don't have an order it belongs to. For Python, that could be
None. Use that value in the dummy root and tell your comparison function to consider it
smaller or larger than all other values.

Restrictions to Your Own Classes

But `Greater` brings me to another and related point: what do you do with your own data structures if you want them in a search tree? You can only put them in a tree if you can order them, and if you can, you need to tell Python what the order is. If you want to insert objects from classes you have defined yourself, you need to implement the comparison operators.

This leads us to another issue. What happens if you modify an object you have put into a search tree? If it changes how your comparison operators put it in the order of objects, you have just broken the invariant in the tree. You cannot find it anymore because it isn't where it is supposed to be; searches down the tree that reach the object will not be able to determine which direction to continue the search. If you insert elements in a search tree, it is best not to change them afterward. If you absolutely want to, remove them from the set first, and then insert them after you have changed them. There are ways to enforce that your objects are immutable, that is, they cannot be modified, but doing so is a bit technical, and it will also prevent you from changing them outside the set. The best is just to keep it in mind when you decide to use a search tree. It is not an issue with the list-based sets, where we don't worry about order and where an element is still in the set if you have modified it.

Exercise: With a search tree, you can also find the minimal and the maximal element in a set in time proportional to the height of the tree. Write functions that do this.

Exercise: Implement the __len__() method for the search tree.

Either implementation of search trees, the persistent or the ephemeral, has the same asymptotic running time. All the operations run in time proportional to the tree depth. In the best case, the tree is balanced, and `insert()`, `contains()`, and `remove()` run in $O(\log n)$. Consequently, the constructor can build a set of n elements in $O(n \log n)$. Iterating over the elements, again in both cases, is $O(n)$, since it is a simple depth-first traversal of the tree. Worst case, `insert()`, `contains()`, and `remove()` run in linear time, so it takes $O(n^2)$ to construct a set, but still $O(n)$ for iteration since that algorithm doesn't depend on the structure of the tree.

If you have a random sequence or insert elements in a random order, you will likely get a balanced tree. Each value is equally likely to go left or right as we insert it in the tree. If you have that kind of data, there is no need to do anything more with search trees. They are already as good as they are going to get. If you cannot guarantee that your data behaves this way, if, for example, you could get it in sorted or reversed-sorted order, then you have to balance your trees explicitly to get logarithmic performance. There are many strategies for balancing trees, all involving modifying them when you insert or delete elements, and I will show you one approach in the next chapter.

Exercise: Why is sorted or reverse-sorted data the worst-case scenario when building a search tree?

Garbage Collection

Let us wrap up the section by talking about garbage collection. When we delete a set, we are leaving a tree behind with circular references, which prevents the reference count garbage collector from freeing the objects' resources. We can explicitly trigger the alternative garbage collector when we delete the `SearchTreeSet` object by removing the reference to the tree and calling `gc.collect()`. This is similar to what we did for doubly linked lists in Chapter 13. Or we can use weak references again. I will do the latter because I want to show you another trick.

I want to make the `parent` references weak, and I could write getter and setter methods for dealing with the weak references like I did with doubly linked lists and then wrap them in a `property` object. But I don't want to write getters and setters every time I want a weak reference. There must be a way to wrap references, so I can reuse getters and setters. And of course, there is.

To get there, we need to go back to what we learned about accessing attributes in objects in Chapter 11. We learned that if we put an object, which has methods __get__() and __set__(), in our class, then accessing the object will call __get__() when we write `obj.attribute` and call __set__() when we write `obj.attribute = value`. That is what we want. The `property` class is implemented the same way and will call the getters and setters we give it when we create the object. Our class will have its own that are specialized for handling weak references.

The class looks like this:

```
import weakref
class WeakRefProperty(object):
    def __get__(self, obj, cls):
        value = obj.__dict__[id(self)]
        if type(value) is weakref.ref:
            return value()
```

```
        else:
            return value

    def __set__(self, obj, value):
        try:
            value = weakref.ref(value)
        except TypeError:
            # can't make a weak ref
            pass
        obj.__dict__[id(self)] = value
```

There are a few things to unpack here. The parameters in __get__() are the WeakRefProperty object (self). It will be a class attribute and shared between all the objects of that class. Then there is the object that's part of the obj.attribute expression and the class the WeakRefProperty lives in.

Consider

```
class C(object):
    ref = WeakRefProperty()
obj = C()
obj.ref
```

In the attribute access obj.ref, the self argument is the object C.ref. There is one of those, and it sits in the class C. The obj argument is the object obj in obj.ref. There will be one for each instance of the class. The cls argument is the class C.

We don't care about the class argument here, so ignore it. When we want to get the value through a weak reference, we first need to get the reference. It doesn't sit in self because self will be an object that sits in the Node class, and we want a reference per object. So we need to get it from obj. We can put it in the dictionary where all obj's attributes sit through obj.__dict__.

But what key should the reference have? We can't really give it a fixed name because it might have more than one weak reference. But for each weak reference that an object should have, there must be a separate WeakRefProperty object in its class, and we can use its ID—which is unique between all objects in the entire program—as our key.

Of course, the key might not be in the dictionary, and then we get an error, but I don't care about that because the user is supposed to assign to the weak reference before they access it; I just need to add it to the dictionary in the setter. So we get the reference out.

It might not actually be a weak reference because not all objects can be wrapped in weak references, None among them (and we do assign None to values from time to time). So we explicitly test if we have a weak reference, and if we do, we return the wrapped object, and otherwise, we return the value itself.

For __set__(), we go the other way. We will insert the value in the object's dictionary with a key that is the WeakRefProperty's ID. We try to wrap it first, but that might fail—again because not all objects can be wrapped—but whether wrapped or not, we put it in the dictionary.

Adding it to the search tree is now a simple matter of adding an object to the class:

```
class Node(object):
    parent = WeakRefProperty()
    def __init__(self, value,
                 parent = None,
                 left = None,
                 right = None):
        self.value = value
        self.parent = parent
        self.left = left
        self.right = right

        # guaranteeing consistency
        if self.left is not None:
            self.left.parent = self
        if self.right is not None:
            self.right.parent = self

    def __repr__(self):
        return 'Node({}, left = {}, right = {})'.format(
            repr(self.value),
            repr(self.left),
            repr(self.right)
        )
```

It is only the single line parent = WeakRefProperty() that changes. All the remaining code remains precisely the same. The class variable changes how accessing the parent attribute behaves, but we use it in the code exactly the way we would for a normal object attribute.

Hash Table

The *hash table* data structure, the one underlying Python's set and dictionary implementations, has the fastest operations of the set implementations we will see in this chapter. On average, at least. It is similar to quick sort in that the analysis is based on probabilistic expectations. Its worst-case complexity is linear-time operations, but the expectation is constant time. The data structure is based on one simple idea: you have a way to map your data to an index into an array, so you can get to it in constant time. There are only two things you need to handle to make it work: you need to figure out how you map values to indices, and if you happen to map two different values to the same index, you need a way to deal with the collision. There are many variations for how to do both, and you could fill an entire book with just a few of them—I know because I wrote such a book—but we won't explore them.

Python already implements the mapping operation for basic types. For your own types, the default behavior uses object identity, but I will explain what you need to do to implement it for your own types if you have a different equality operator. There is an art to doing it, though, that we won't dwell deep into. For collision management, we will see one of the simplest approaches where we already have all the material we need. But first, let's explore the fundamental idea behind the data structure.

If we could assign to each object a unique index into a list, where we can access all indices in constant time, then putting an object into our set would be assigning it to the index. Testing if an element is in a set would be checking if it is at its index, and removing it would be removing it from its index—all constant-time operations.

There are two problems with the idea: First, how do we assign unique indices to all possible objects? Second, if we have to handle all possible objects, our list would have to be very long. Since we would have to initialize such a list, it would take an exorbitant amount of time to create an empty set. Still, that is unlikely to be a problem since the list wouldn't fit into memory anyway; it has to have an index for every possible object we could dream of inserting into the set, and that would be larger than the memory we have.

For the first problem, assigning indices to objects, we relax the requirement and do not require that all objects get a unique index. We want it to be unlikely that two objects get the same index, but as long as we can map objects to a number that we can treat as an index, we will be happy. This mapping is called a *hash function*.

For the second problem, we will use a small list with a length that adapts to the number of objects we put into our list and accepts that some objects end up at the same index. Since there can be more than one element for the same index, we now call the indices *bins*. To deal with collisions when they happen, we need a *collision strategy*.

Hash Functions

A hash function is a function that maps objects to numbers. We don't need to have a function that can map any object to a number, but for all objects we want to put into our hash table, there must be a hash function that gives us a number.

We use the hash function to pick the bin in the list where an object should be, so anytime we consider two objects equal, the function must map them to the same number. We also have to require that the same object will always map to the same hash value, no matter what we do with it. Otherwise, we could put it at an index based on the hash function at one point in time but not find it when we try to look for it later after modifying the object and changing its hash value.

We want the function to spread out the objects in the range of our list, so objects are unlikely to end up in the same bin. It takes time to deal with objects that sit in the same bin, so we want to minimize how often that happens. A function that spreads out objects uniformly over the range of indices is optimal, and the efficiency analysis of hash tables often assumes that this is the case. In the real world, of course, it is hard to achieve. The set of indices is smaller than the set of all possible objects, so if you pick a specific function, then some adversary can show up with the elements they want to put into your set, and they can pick them such that they all collide, that is, map to the same index.

There is a way to get around this problem, called *universal hashing*, where we pick hash functions at random and change them from time to time, so the average behavior will always be the same as if we assumed we had a function that mapped objects to random indices. We won't go there in this book. In practice, people write functions that seem to work well on the kind of data they need and then hope for the best. That is also what Python is doing.

I prefer to think of the hash function as two separate operations. One maps objects into some gigantic range of integers, and the second maps these numbers into the much smaller range of indices. If you look at it this way, I will use the "hashing function" to refer to the first step alone, and I will call the second *binning*. By separating the two steps, we can write a general function for hashing objects that is independent of the size of the list in the hash table and then let the hash table implementation worry about the binning.

The first step, hashing, is something Python already supports via the hash()
function. Try evaluating this code:

```
print(hash(42))
print(hash("foobar"))
print(hash(tuple()))
```

The first will give you 42 because Python hashes a number to itself. The other two
will give you some large positive or negative number.

You get numbers out of hashing the built-in data types, but not all of them. Hashing
a list, dictionary, or set will give you an error. Now, why is that? Remember that I said
that the hash function must always map the same object to the same hash value and
that if we consider two objects equal, they must have the same hash value? That isn't
necessarily true for all data structures in Python.

Types that cannot change are not a problem. We can construct a function that
traverses the data in a data structure and returns a value. If we never change the object,
we always hash it to the same value. But lists, sets, and dicts, for example, can change
over time. We could use their object identity, which never changes (an object is always
the same even if we modify its attributes). But then we cannot consider two different
sets containing the same values the same; they would have different hash values, and
different hash values have to mean different values.

Python doesn't implement hash() for its built-in mutable data structures for this
reason. The hash value cannot depend on the data because then it could change
between the point where we insert it into a bin and the point where we search for it later.
And if it doesn't depend on the data, how can we make sure that two objects with the
same attributes map to the same hash value? We can't, in general.

Remember the Patient we implemented an equality method for at the beginning of
the chapter. If we hadn't done that, we could hash it:

```
class Patient(object):
    def __init__(self, name, height, weight):
        self.name = name
        self.height = height
        self.weight = weight

hash(Patient("Henry", 173, 72))
```

but add __eq__() and we cannot

```
class Patient(object):
    def __init__(self, name, height, weight):
        self.name = name
        self.height = height
        self.weight = weight

    def __eq__(self, other):
        return self.name == other.name and \
                self.height == other.height and \
                self.weight == other.weight

hash(Patient("Henry", 173, 72)) # Error
```

By default, equality means object identity equality, so an object is only equal to itself. If that is the case, Python has a default hash function that only depends on object identity. There is no problem with putting such objects in a hash table—they never change identity, so they can't change hash values, and we never have to worry about considering two different objects the same in the sense we want for sets.

If you want an equality operator for your own data structures and want to be able to hash them, you must also implement a __hash__() method. The hash() function will call that method when it needs to hash an object. You should implement it, so it depends on the attributes you use for equality, since you never want two objects you consider equal to hash to different hash values. It is not a problem to hash unequal objects to the same hash value, though you should just try to avoid this for efficiency reasons. Never *ever* change the attributes you use in your __hash__() method if you want to find the object again in a set, though.

For the Patient class, we could implement the __hash__() method like this:

```
class Patient(object):
    def __init__(self, name, height, weight):
        self.name = name
        self.height = height
        self.weight = weight
```

```
def __eq__(self, other):
    return self.name == other.name and \
           self.height == other.height and \
           self.weight == other.weight

def __hash__(self):
    return hash(self.name) + \
           hash(self.height) + \
           hash(self.weight)
```

Okay, so now assume that we have a hash() function for the objects we want to put in a set. They give us large numbers, potentially at least, but we want to use them as indices in a much smaller list. This means that we need to project from the large space down to a smaller range, and if you have a large number n that you want to put in a smaller range of size m, you can do that by taking the division remainder n % m.

If the hash function is not uniform and there is some signal in it, choosing a prime number for m can spread out the indices somewhat, so a rule of thumb is that this is a good choice. It is not what I will do, though. Because it is easier to resize by powers of two (see resizing at the end of this section), my m is a power of two. Then, I can pick out the low bits from the hash value and map the large range to the smaller range that way. If I have randomly distributed numbers, then each bit is randomly zero or one, and then the lower bits are also randomly distributed. Powers of two are, of course, only prime if m=2, so the two rule ideas are not compatible. If you have an m that is a power of two and a prime $p \gg m$, you can map the hash values v to (v % p) % m and get the best of both worlds. It isn't necessary if you have a good hashing function, though.

Exercise: Convince yourself that if you pick out the lower bits of a number, you get the remainder of a power of 2. If you want to take the remainder with respect to m, then you can do it with the bit operations n & (m - 1). If m is a power of two, then it has a single bit set. In that case, m - 1 are all the bits below that one set and all else zero. Take the logical AND with n pulls out the lower bits. Bit operations are much faster than taking the remainder of a number, so you can use this to get a really fast index binning. It doesn't matter much in Python, though, since it doesn't give us that lightning-fast code where this would matter anyway. I will just take remainders in my code to keep it simple.

Collision strategy

Now we can map an object to a hash value and then to a bin in our list, but what do we do when there is more than one object that goes in the same bin? There are many strategies in the literature, but the simplest is the obvious one: putting a data structure in each bin that can hold the elements. A set there would be an obvious choice, but since we are implementing a set now, it feels circular to do that. I will use a Python list, but any structure would do. Linked lists are a common choice because they are simple and fast for the operations we need to do on them.

All the operations first get a bin via the hash value and the index mapping and then add, remove, or check if the element is in the bin. The totality of a hash table set can be implemented like this:

```python
class HashTableSet(object):
    def __init__(self, seq = ()):
        # Setting up the table
        self.size = 64
        self.array = [[] for _ in range(self.size)]

        # And insert the sequence items
        for value in seq:
            self.add(value)

    def get_bin(self, element):
        hash_val = hash(element)
        index = hash_val % self.size
        return self.array[index]

    def add(self, element):
        bin = self.get_bin(element)
        if element not in bin:
            bin.append(element)

    def remove(self, element):
        bin = self.get_bin(element)
        if element not in bin:
            raise KeyError()
        bin.remove(element)
```

```
def __iter__(self):
    for bin in self.array:
        yield from bin

def __contains__(self, element):
    bin = self.get_bin(element)
    return element in bin

def __repr__(self):
    return 'HashTableSet(' + repr(list(iter(self))) + ')'
```

The code

```
[[] for _ in range(self.size)]
```

creates `self.size` new lists. Don't write `[[]] * self.size`, as that would simply give you `self.size` references to the same list.

Its simplicity alone makes the data structure appealing, and it is efficient as well, as we shall see. However, the analysis depends on assumptions about how well the hash function works.

What is the complexity, then? All our operations involve one hash function evaluation and then the same operation on a bin. We cannot say anything about the hash functions here since they depend on the data and not the set implementation, but if you cannot implement an efficient hash function, then this data structure is not for you. Let us just assume that it is constant time, which it should be since the hash function certainly is not allowed to depend on how many elements we add to a table. It might be very slow, but it is constant time.

Then the complexity of all operations is the same as the operations on a list, and these are all linear. Yes, we can append to the list in `add()` in constant time, but we need to search the list first to avoid duplications when we insert, so even there, we pay a linear cost. Linear-time operations do not sound attractive, so why do I say it is an efficient data structure? Because we will grow the table such that we expect there to be only a constant number of elements in each bin.

Analysis

When analyzing hash tables, we usually use the term *load*, the number of elements in the table divided by its size, as a parameter of the analysis. For some conflict resolution strategies, performance degrades very poorly when the load increases, but our strategy degrades gracefully. This doesn't mean that it is the better strategy, others perform better at low load, but it does mean that we do not have to worry about a major runtime explosion if we put too many elements into a table.

If you put n elements into a table of size m and if the hash function and index mapping give us a uniform distribution in the range from zero to $m - 1$, then each bin is expected to have n/m elements (the load). It isn't constant time, but at least we have divided the linear-time operations by a factor m.

We get constant-time operations if we can keep n/m under a constant, and all it takes is to let m grow as n grows. We can choose any threshold, but if we, for example, say that we always want $n \leq m/2$, we expect less than one element per bin, and operations are expected to be in constant time then.

Resizing

It is simple enough to resize the table each time we add an element, but resizing is not cheap. We have to move *all* the objects since the mapped index they have might have changed. Their hash value is the same, but the mapping changes when we, for example, look at one more bit than before. So we have to resize, but not too often, to get constant-time operations.

The resize operation will take linear time because we have to move all the objects (and initialize a new list with the new size). So we cannot make an analysis that says that *all* operations take constant time. Instead, we can make an *amortized* analysis, which means that we put a limit on how much time we have spent whenever we have done n operations. The analysis closely resembles the one we had in Chapter 4 where we argued that we could append to lists in constant time.

Every time we insert an element, we have a constant-time operation, but we pretend that it was a little more expensive than it was. For example, we could say that we used one "computation" for the insertion, but we also put four in the bank, so the cost of the operation was "five" computations (which is still constant time). After $n/2$ operations, we have $2n$ in the bank to use for a resize. So, if we grow the table by a factor of two, taking $2n$ time, after we have inserted $n/2$ elements, we have only used $5n$ "computations," so the total is in $O(n)$. With n operations in $O(n)$, we have an amortized constant-time performance.

What about resizing when the number of elements shrinks? There isn't anything wrong with having a large table with few elements, except that it is wasteful in memory, but we might as well consider shrinking the table size as well, now that we are working with resizing. Here we have to be careful. If we grow the table each time we have $n = m/2$, we cannot shrink it when n is less than $m/2$. We risk alternating between growing and shrinking if we switch between adding and removing elements. We need a lower threshold than $m/2$ for shrinking.

If you have a number of operations where you end up with a table of size m, the minimum number of operations you made was $m/2$ insertions, but you just spent those on the resize. You have $n = m/2$ elements in the table, and your bank account is empty. You might have deleted elements along the way, and then there is a little more in the bank, but this is the worst case. If we say that we shrink when $n = m/4$, we might be able to save enough for that operation, which will cost us $m/2$ for building the new list for the table. The worst-case scenario is that you only make deletions. If we add insertions along the way, we can save more for the bank. So we will make at least $m/4$ deletions to go from $m/2$ to $m/4$, which cost $m/4$ in itself, and then save up for $m/2$. So save up two computations per deletion, and we once again have amortized constant time.

I have extended the hash table with resizing in the following:

```python
def next_power_of_two(n):
    # Not the most efficient solution
    # but probably the simplest
    power = 1
    while power < n:
        power *= 2
    return power

class HashTableSet(object):
    def __init__(self, seq = (), initial_size = 16):
        # we want len, which might exhaust an iterator
        seq = list(seq)
```

```
    # Make sure we don't resize while we insert the
    # initial sequence
    if 2 * len(seq) > initial_size:
        initial_size = next_power_of_two(2 * len(seq))

    # Setting up the table
    self.size = initial_size
    self.used = 0
    self.array = [[] for _ in range(initial_size)]

    # And insert the sequence items
    for value in seq:
        self.add(value)

def get_bin(self, element):
    hash_val = hash(element)
    index = hash_val % self.size
    return self.array[index]

def resize(self, new_size):
    old_array = self.array
    self.size = new_size
    self.used = 0
    self.array = [list() for _ in range(new_size)]
    for bin in old_array:
        for x in bin:
            self.add(x)

def add(self, element):
    bin = self.get_bin(element)
    if element not in bin:
        bin.append(element)
        self.used += 1
        if self.used > self.size / 2:
            self.resize(int(2 * self.size))
```

```
def remove(self, element):
    bin = self.get_bin(element)
    if element not in bin:
        raise KeyError()
    bin.remove(element)
    self.used -= 1
    if self.used < self.size / 4:
        self.resize(int(self.size / 2))

def __iter__(self):
    for bin in self.array:
        yield from bin

def __contains__(self, element):
    bin = self.get_bin(element)
    return element in bin

def __repr__(self):
    return 'HashTableSet(' + repr(list(iter(self))) + ')'
```

I wanted my size to be powers of two because it can be more efficient to extract lower bits than compute modulo. Still, in the implementation, I do use modulo, so it isn't strictly necessary to round up in the constructor. I do it anyway, in case I later decide to use the bit manipulation version for the mapping.

If we had gone for table sizes that were prime, we couldn't double and half the size in this way. That is not how prime numbers are distributed on the number axis. If you want to go that way, you can use a table of prime numbers roughly a factor two apart.

Exercise: Implement the __len__() method for the set.

Exercise: When we resize, we recompute the hash values for all objects. Computing the hash value might be an expensive operation, and the value never changes for an object, so it seems wasteful. Can you update the implementation to save the hash value together with the object and use it when you resize? You still need to do the bin mapping, of course, but reuse the hash value.

Dictionaries

Going from sets to dictionaries is not a tricky step. You can think of a dictionary as a set that holds pairs of keys and values. It isn't *quite* that because, for a set, we need to access elements by their entire data and not just a key, but the difference is negligible. In the following, I have implemented a dictionary based on our hash table set. I encourage you to try to implement a dictionary based on one of the other sets we have seen.

The Python syntax for a dictionary is

```
table[key] = val
print(table[key])
key in table
del key
```

for adding a key-value mapping, getting the value associated with a key, checking if a key is in the dictionary, and removing a key-value binding, respectively.

The magical methods we need to implement to get them are __setitem__(), __getitem__(), __contains__(), and __delitem__(). Setting a key-value binding corresponds to adding to a set. We don't have "getting a value" with sets, but we do have __contains__(). We used a method, remove(), to delete elements in our set, but now we will use Python's syntax.

Except that the bins contain key-value pairs and that we need to update a key-value pair instead of just deleting an element from a list, there aren't many changes to the previous hash table. I trust that you can decipher the code and follow how the hash dictionary works:

```
def next_power_of_two(n):
    # Not the most efficient solution
    # but probably the simplest
    power = 1
    while power < n:
        power *= 2
    return power

def get_bin_index(bin, key):
    for i, (k, v) in enumerate(bin):
        if k == key:
            return i
    return None
```

```python
class HashTableDict(object):
    def __init__(self, seq = (), initial_size = 16):
        # we want len, which might exhaust an iterator
        seq = list(seq)

        # Make sure we don't resize while we insert the
        # initial sequence
        if 2 * len(seq) > initial_size:
            initial_size = next_power_of_two(2 * len(seq))

        # Setting up the table
        self.size = initial_size
        self.used = 0
        self.array = [list() for _ in range(initial_size)]

        # And insert the sequence items
        for key, val in seq:
            self[key] = val

    def get_bin(self, key):
        hash_val = hash(key)
        index = hash_val % self.size
        return self.array[index]

    def resize(self, new_size):
        old_array = self.array
        self.size = new_size
        self.used = 0
        self.array = [list() for _ in range(new_size)]
        for bin in old_array:
            for key, val in bin:
                self[key] = val

    def __setitem__(self, key, value):
        bin = self.get_bin(key)
        idx = get_bin_index(bin, key)
        if idx is None:
            bin.append((key, value))
            self.used += 1
```

```
            if self.used > self.size / 2:
                self.resize(2 * self.size)
        else:
            bin[idx] = (key, value)

def __getitem__(self, key):
    bin = self.get_bin(key)
    idx = get_bin_index(bin, key)
    if idx is None:
        raise KeyError(key)
    else:
        k, v = bin[idx]
            return v

def __delitem__(self, key):
    bin = self.get_bin(key)
    idx = get_bin_index(bin, key)
    if idx is None:
        raise KeyError(key)
    else:
        bin.pop(idx)
        self.used -= 1
        if self.used < self.size / 4:
            self.resize(int(self.size / 2))

def __contains__(self, key):
    bin = self.get_bin(key)
    idx = get_bin_index(bin, key)
    return idx is not None

def __iter__(self):
    for bin in self.array:
        for k, v in bin:
            yield k

def __repr__(self):
    return 'HashTableDict(' + repr(list(iter(self))) + ')'
```

CHAPTER 15

Red-Black Search Trees

There are many strategies for balancing search trees to ensure logarithmic running time for their operations. All the approaches involve modifying them when you insert or delete elements and rebalancing them to minimize their height, and in this chapter, I will show you one technique: the *red-black search trees*. It is a search tree where we add one of two *colors* to each node, either *red* or *black*:

```
RED = 0
BLACK = 1

class Node(object):
    def __init__(self, value,
                 colour = RED,
                 left = None,
                 right = None):
        self.value = value
        self.colour = colour
        self.left = left
        self.right = right
```

We require two invariants of a red-black search tree:

- *Red invariant*: No red node can have a red parent.

- *Black invariant*: All paths from a node to any of its leaves must traverse the same number of black nodes.

These two invariants guarantee that the tree will be balanced. If we ignore the red nodes, the black invariant says that all paths from the root to a leaf have the same number of nodes, which means that the tree is perfectly balanced. The red invariant says that the longest path cannot get arbitrarily longer than the shortest path because it can have a maximum of twice as many nodes—the red nodes that we can legally add to a path of black nodes.

© Thomas Mailund 2021
T. Mailund, *Introduction to Computational Thinking*, https://doi.org/10.1007/978-1-4842-7077-6_15

For practical purposes, we will give all empty trees the same color. If we use None to indicate an empty tree, then we are forced to define a color for it, since we cannot add attributes to None, but even if we use our own class for empty trees, there are benefits to defining the color of an empty tree rather than having an explicit attribute. If we do this, then we have to define the color of empty trees to be black.

Exercise: Try drawing a search tree that holds two values, that is, has two non-empty trees, where one has two empty children and the other one empty child. Try coloring the empty trees red. Can you color the non-empty nodes so the tree satisfies the two color invariants? What if you color the empty trees black?

When we search in a red-black search tree, we use the functions we saw in the previous chapter. A red-black search tree is just a search tree unless we worry about balancing it. We only do that when we insert or delete elements, and this chapter is about how to ensure the invariants are upheld at the end of the two operations that modify the tree.

A Persistent Recursive Solution

Our first solution will be a persistent data structure, where we build new trees when we perform the operations. It will then, naturally, be based on recursive functions. We move down the tree to insert or delete as we did in the persistent solution for the plain search trees, but this time we will restructure the tree when we return from recursive calls. Whenever we recognize that the invariant is violated, we transform the current tree to satisfy the invariant.

Insertion

Insertion is the easiest, so let's handle that first. As earlier, we search down until we find the place where we should add the new node. The empty tree that it will replace is, by definition, black, and its children will also be black. If we color it black, its children will be one black node lower than the leaf we replaced, which breaks the invariant. So we color it red. Now the first invariant is satisfied, but we have violated the second if the new node's parent is red. As we return from the recursions, we will get rid of red nodes that are the parent of a red node by rearranging the tree. Unless we add extra red nodes when we return, which we won't, there will at most be one such case, so we only need to check for that. The transition rules in Figure 15-1 will restructure trees that violate the red invariant. If you have any of the trees around the edges, you need to translate it into the tree in the middle.

All the trees a, b, c, and d satisfy both the red and black invariants because the tree as a whole satisfies the black invariant, and the only violation of the red invariant is the two red nodes we see in the figure. When we transform the tree, the number of black nodes down to the leaves in a, b, c, and d remains the same. We remove one above them and replace it with another; we have two new black nodes, but not on the same path. It doesn't matter if any of a, b, c, and d have a red root because their root's parent is black in the transformed tree. I will leave it to you to check that the order of the trees is preserved. After the transformation, we have gotten rid of the two red nodes in a row, but we have created a tree with a red root, and if its parent is red, when we return from the recursive call, then we see one of the cases we must handle again. Not a problem, though; we do the transformation all the way up to the root. We might still have two red nodes in a row at the root—the transformations are only applied for trees with black roots. If we end up with two red nodes there, we need to fix it to still uphold the invariant. But that is easy: just color the root black every time you return from an insertion. Coloring a red root black adds one black node to all the paths, but since it is to *all* the paths, the invariant is satisfied.

The insertion code (except for the balancing) looks like this:

```
def insert_rec(node, value):
    if node is None:
        return Node(value, colour = RED)
```

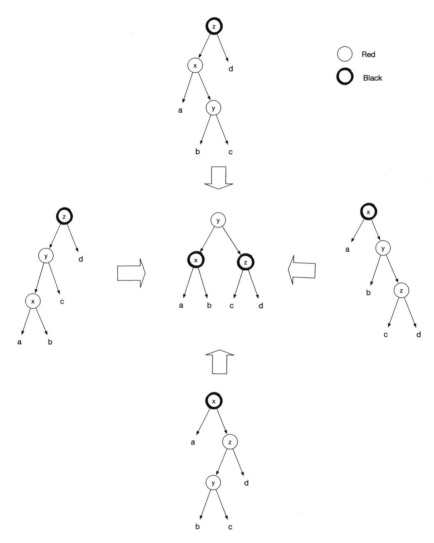

Figure 15-1. *Balancing rules for inserting in a red-black search tree*

```
if node.value == value:
    return node
elif node.value > value:
    new_tree = Node(node.value, node.colour,
                    left = insert_rec(node.left, value),
                    right = node.right)
    return balance(new_tree)
```

```
    else: # node.value < value:
        new_tree = Node(node.value, node.colour,
                        left = node.left,
                        right = insert_rec(node.right, value))
        return balance(new_tree)
def insert(node, value):
    new_tree = insert_rec(node, value)
    new_tree.colour = BLACK
    return new_tree
```

I have split the insertion function from the previous chapter into two to set the root's color to black at the end. We have an assignment to an attribute there, so it might look like we are modifying the data structure and not getting a persistent one, but it will be a new node that doesn't interfere with previous references to the set.

For balance(), you need to check if the tree it takes as input matches any of the four cases and then return the updated tree. Otherwise, it returns the input tree unchanged. The *checking* part, though, can be unpleasant to implement. You could check that "Is this node black, and does it have a left subtree with a red node, and does that subtree have a right subtree that is also red? And if so, extract x, y, z, and a, b, c, and d." And you have to do that for all four trees. Chances are that you will get at least one of the tests wrong or extract the wrong tree in one or two cases. I don't know about you, but I don't want to write code like that. I want to tell Python which tree should be translated to which tree and then have it figure out how to test if the tree matches the from topology and, if so, create a tree that matches the "to" topology. And because I want to solve the problem that way, you now have to learn about *domain-specific languages (DSLs)*.[1]

A Domain-Specific Language for Tree Transformations

A domain-specific language, or DSL, is a programming language that you build for a specific task. Python is *general purpose* because you can use it to write any kind of program, but domain-specific languages are usually much more restricted. In my

---

[1]What we use the domain-specific language for in this chapter is something that is making its way into the Python language, so by the time you read this, it might no longer be necessary to implement it. See the comment after we finish with persistent red-black search trees. I still think you should know about domain-specific languages, so even if this particular one isn't necessary soon, I urge you to read on.

opinion, they are underappreciated and should be used much more. You pay a small price upfront by implementing the code necessary to process it, but it pays off quickly when you avoid writing repetitive, tedious, and error-prone code. And I hope that the following two examples of how we can implement a DSL for our tree transformations will show you that it is not something to fear.

First, the language. We want to specify a "from" tree and a "to" tree, and we already have classes to specify nodes. Therefore, it will be natural to reuse those classes to specify transformation. This is how we could specify the leftmost tree in Figure 15-1

```
Node("z", BLACK,
    Node("x", RED,
        "a",
        Node("y", RED, "b", "c")),
    "d")
```

and this is what the middle tree would look like:

```
Node("y", RED,
    Node("x", BLACK, "a", "b"),
    Node("z", BLACK, "c", "d"))
```

We use exactly the same Node class, but we use strings for the values and the subtrees that aren't part of the pattern, that is, a, b, c, and d.

You might now object that this isn't much of a programming language, and you will be right, but that is often the case with a domain-specific language. They are small languages. However, as some people might claim, it is not the size that matters, but what you do with it. What we will do is to match the first tree specification against a real tree, and if we can and the colors match, we will extract the values and subtrees and put them in a table:

```
class MatchError(Exception):
    pass

def match(pattern, tree, table = None):
    if table is None:
        table = {}
```

```
    if type(pattern) is str:
        table[pattern] = tree
        return

    if tree is None:
        raise MatchError

    if pattern.colour != tree.colour:
        raise MatchError

    table[pattern.value] = tree.value
    match(pattern.left, tree.left, table)
    match(pattern.right, tree.right, table)
    return table
```

It is a recursion on both pattern and tree, where we extract a subtree if the pattern is a string—in our case, that would be when we have "a," "b," "c," or "d." If we hit a leaf, None, before we expect it, we can't match and throw an exception (that we have to catch in the balance() function). If the colors don't match, we also raise the exception. Otherwise, we get the value in the tree and continue matching recursively on both subtrees.

Building the tree from a pattern works similarly. Get values from the table when needed, and build the tree recursively from the pattern and the table:

```
def build_from_pattern(pattern, table):
    if type(pattern) is str:
        return table[pattern]
    val = table[pattern.value]
    col = pattern.colour
    return Node(val, col,
        left = build_from_pattern(pattern.left, table),
        right = build_from_pattern(pattern.right, table)
    )
```

Combine the two, and we have a transformation function:

```
def transform(from_pattern, to_pattern, tree):
    match_table = match(from_pattern, tree)
    return build_from_pattern(to_pattern, match_table)
```

Now we can run through the from patterns (the four trees along the edges in the figure) and try to transform them. If we manage a transformation, we return the result, but if we get through all the attempts, we return the original tree:

```
from_patterns = [
    Node("z", BLACK,
        Node("x", RED,
            "a",
            Node("y", RED, "b", "c")),
        "d"),
    Node("z", BLACK,
        Node("y", RED,
            Node("x", RED, "a", "b"),
                "c"),
        "d"),
    Node("x", BLACK,
        "a",
        Node("z", RED,
                Node("y", RED, "b", "c"),
                "d")),
    Node("x", BLACK,
        "a",
        Node("y", RED,
            "b",
            Node("z", RED, "c", "d")))
]
to_pattern = \
    Node("y", RED,
        Node("x", BLACK, "a", "b"),
        Node("z", BLACK, "c", "d"))

def balance(tree):
    for from_pattern in from_patterns:
        try:
            return transform(from_pattern, to_pattern, tree)
```

```
        except MatchError:
            pass
    # None of the patterns matched, so return the tree
    return tree
```

You might now think that this was more complicated than simply implementing the four transformations yourself, and perhaps it is. Still, it didn't take me much longer to write the automatic transformation than it would take me to implement one or two of them manually, and I only have one function to debug if something went wrong. And if you need more transformations—and you will—then the DSL pays off even more.

I am not quite satisfied with this solution, however, so I will show you another. The implementation we just made is something you can do in all programming languages; it doesn't involve particularly high-level features. However, we have to parse the DSL each time we try to match a tree, which takes time, and for an efficient implementation of a search tree that might make many insertions, we should want to save as much running time as we can. I also don't like that we have the patterns inside the balance() function. It makes the function look more complex than it really is. We could put them outside in a list, of course, but if we later add more from and to patterns, we must be careful to match them up correctly. So I want to do something else that is more to my liking.

The next solution, which is more efficient and more aesthetically pleasing, requires that we create functions on the fly. Some languages have better support for this than Python, and some have no support for it at all. There are always ways to do it, but it can be hard. It is not in Python, though.

We will create functions for matching a pattern and returning a transformed tree (or raise an exception if we can't). We generate the functions' source code from the "from" and "to" tree specification and ask Python to evaluate the source code and give us the function back, and that will work just as well as if we had written the functions ourselves.

For each transformation rule, we will generate a function that looks similar to this:

```
def rule(tree):
    try:
        z = tree
        if z.colour != BLACK: raise MatchError()
        x = z.left
        if x.colour != RED: raise MatchError()
        a = x.left
```

```
            y = x.right
            if y.colour != RED: raise MatchError()
            b = y.left
            c = y.right
            d = z.right
            return Node(y.value, RED,
                           Node(x.value, BLACK, a, b),
                           Node(z.value, BLACK, c, d))
        except AttributeError:
            raise MatchError()
```

This is the rule for the leftmost tree, and you can check it if you want. We don't explicitly check for whether a subtree exists; we just extract trees and hope for the best. In some languages, that could crash your program, but in Python, we will get an AttributeError if we try to get an attribute out of None, and then we just change it into a MatchError.

The function for creating rule functions look like this:

```
def transformation_rule(input, output):
    body_lines = collect_extraction(input, 'tree', [])
    body = "\n\t\t".join(body_lines)
    ret = "return {}".format(output_string(output))
    func = '\n'.join([
        "def rule(tree):",
        "\ttry:",
        '\t\t' + body,
        '\t\t' + ret,
        "\texcept AttributeError:",
        "\t\traise MatchError()"
    ])
    defs = {}
    exec(func, globals(), defs)
    return defs["rule"]
```

We have two helper functions, one for generating the lines inside the try block, collect_extraction(), and one for generating the output tree, output_string(). We get to them in the following. We wrap them in the function definition, func, that defines a function named rule, putting the subtrees and value extraction code in the try block followed by the returned tree, which is created if the extraction code doesn't fail, that is, if we match. The exec() function is where the magic happens. It will evaluate the code we give as the first argument in the namespace we give as the second argument. We give it globals(), which is the global scope. That is where it can find the Node() class that it needs for the return value. The last argument is a dictionary where it will put the variables we define. We define one, rule, that we extract and return.

The code for extracting information looks like this:

```
def collect_extraction(node, parent, code_lines):
    if type(node) is str:
        code_lines.append(
            "{} = {}".format(node, parent)
        )
        return code_lines

    code_lines.extend([
        '{} = {}'.format(node.value, parent),
        'if {}.colour != {}: raise MatchError()'.format(
            node.value, node.colour
        )
    ])
    collect_extraction(node.left,
                       node.value + ".left",
                       code_lines)
    collect_extraction(node.right,
                       node.value + ".right",
                       code_lines)
    return code_lines
```

We give it a node in the pattern structure as the first argument, a variable where we can extract values from, and the list it should put the code into. We return the list at the end to make it easier to get it in the transformation_rule() function. The idea is that we name all the subtrees of a node, so we can use the name to extract nested information. When we call it the first time, in the function we create, the node is tree, and we will assign tree to a variable that is the same as the value in the pattern. If that is all there is, we are done here. We have assigned to the variable the value we want it to have.

499

However, if it is a node, we recurse on the subtrees and tell them that they should get values from the left and right subtrees. When we have recursed, we change the variable to its value because it is the value we want in the output tree.

The return value should just be the tree. We can't use __repr__() from the Node class because it would write strings in "" quotes and it wouldn't handle trees that are just strings, but it is a simple recursion:

```
def output_string(output):
    if type(output) is str:
        return output

    value = output.value + ".value"

    return 'Node(' + value + ', ' \
                + str(output.colour) + ', ' \
                + output_string(output.left) + ', ' \
                + output_string(output.right) + ')'
```

Specifying the transformation rules is no prettier than before

```
from_patterns = [
    Node("z", BLACK,
        Node("x", RED,
            "a",
            Node("y", RED, "b", "c")),
        "d"),
    Node("z", BLACK,
        Node("y", RED,
            Node("x", RED, "a", "b"),
            "c"),
        "d"),
    Node("x", BLACK,
        "a",
        Node("z", RED,
            Node("y", RED, "b", "c"),
            "d")),
```

```
        Node("x", BLACK,
            "a",
            Node("y", RED,
                "b",
                Node("z", RED, "c", "d")))
    ]
to_pattern = \
    Node("y", RED,
        Node("x", BLACK, "a", "b"),
        Node("z", BLACK, "c", "d"))

transformations = [
    transformation_rule(from_pattern, to_pattern) for
    from_pattern in from_patterns
]
```

but still simpler than hand-coding the functions. The `balance()` function is cleaner, though:

```
def balance(tree):
    for rule in transformations:
        try:
            return rule(tree)
        except MatchError:
            pass
    # None of the patterns matched, so return the tree
    return tree
```

Adding more transformations later is also more straightforward now. We have to create a rule function for them, but our process for doing that can handle any transformation, so they are easy to add. We might have spent a little more time developing the DSL, but it will soon pay off because now we need to implement deletion, and there we have to add more rules.

There is another issue, though, that we might as well deal with. There are symmetries in the trees—the left and the right are simply mirrored vertically, as are the top and bottom trees (if you ignore the names we give the nodes and the subtrees). If we hand-code the pattern matching, we have to deal with all four cases, but with our DSL, we can write a function that mirrors the trees and use those. The fewer transitions we have to explicitly implement, the better, and that includes specifying them in the DSL. It is tedious, and it is error-prone, so writing symmetric cases is something we would like to avoid if we can, which of course we can. The computer is good at doing simple things like mirroring a tree—we just need to mirror a node's children and then switch left and right. For the transformations, we need to mirror the "to" tree as well for this strategy to work, since otherwise, we put the values and subtrees in the wrong order; I will leave it as an exercise for the eager student.

We can specify all four transformations like this:

```
top_case = \
    Node("z", BLACK,
        Node("x", RED,
            "a",
            Node("y", RED, "b", "c")),
        "d")
left_case = \
    Node("z", BLACK,
        Node("y", RED,
            Node("x", RED, "a", "b"),
            "c"),
        "d")
to_pattern = \
    Node("y", RED,
        Node("x", BLACK, "a", "b"),
        Node("z", BLACK, "c", "d"))

transformations = [
    transformation_rule(top_case, to_pattern),
    transformation_rule(mirror(top_case), mirror(to_pattern)),
    transformation_rule(left_case, to_pattern),
    transformation_rule(mirror(left_case), mirror(to_pattern))
]
```

Exercise: Convince yourself that you get the same transition for the right rule if you flip both left and middle trees and that you get the same rule for the bottom tree if you mirror the top tree and the middle tree.

Of course, it didn't save us any work this time because we had already implemented all four rules, so if this is all we had to do, there wouldn't be much point in coming up with the smarter solution now. That is something we should have thought about before, but now it is too late. If we need to add more transitions, however, it could come in handy.

Deletion

We take the same approach for red-black trees as with plain search trees when it comes to deleting elements. We locate the node we have to delete, we handle it immediately if it has at least one empty tree as a child, and, if not, we get the rightmost child in the left subtree and replace it with that. The issue for balancing is that we might break the black invariant and remove a black node from some paths. Consider Figure 15-2. The top three cases do not cause any problems. If the black invariant is satisfied before the deletion, then it is also satisfied after. But the bottom case is problematic. If we delete a black node that only has black leaves, we have a new leaf that is one closer to the root than all other leaves. We need it to have the same number of black nodes on the path, so we fake it by coloring it "double black." It carries one more black value than it should, and we will move it up the tree until we can get rid of the extra black color:

```
RED = 0
BLACK = 1
DOUBLE_BLACK = 2
```

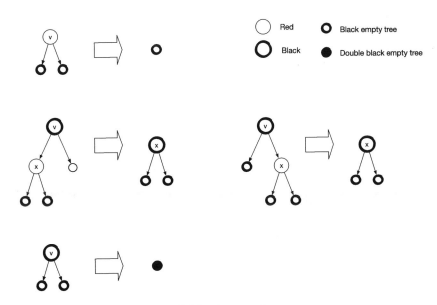

Figure 15-2. *Deleting leaves in red-black search trees*

We can now examine all possible inner node configurations, where a node has a double black child. There are many, so I will ignore nodes that are leaves and assume that *all* nodes have a left and a right subtree. Then, the full set of cases are those in Figure 15-3. If you look at it and think that it is not exhaustive because there are more color variations, remember that having two red nodes in these trees, when we know that one of the subtrees must be double black, is impossible. It would violate the red invariant, and it is satisfied in the tree before we do the removal. It must also be satisfied in the part of the tree that doesn't have the double black node because that subtree is the only one we changed when we did the removal.

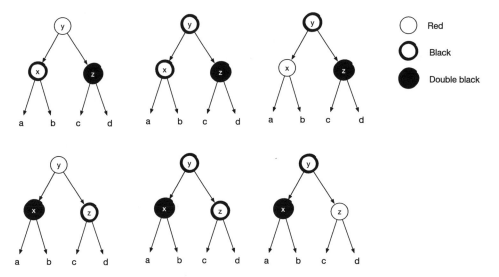

Figure 15-3. *Cases for parent nodes of double black nodes*

But can I ignore the empty subtree cases in my code? Yes, if I redefine what it means for a tree to be empty, I can. I will use actual nodes as empty trees and say that a tree is empty if both its subtrees are None. I won't allow a tree with one None tree and not the other, but there is nothing wrong with representing empty trees by special variants of nodes. It is merely another way to introduce a dummy element to simplify our code.

If I didn't do this trick and gave empty trees subtrees, none of the cases in Figure 15-3 could match the initial empty double black tree. With the trick, all such cases are captured.

I have to be careful in the transformations that I do not take a None subtree and put it somewhere with a non-None sibling, but we will see that this doesn't happen when we develop the rules:

```python
class Node(object):
    def __init__(self, value,
                       colour,
                       left,
                       right):
        self.value = value
        self.colour = colour
        self.left = left
        self.right = right

        if (self.left is None) != (self.right is None):
            raise TypeError("One child None, the other not.")

    def is_empty(self):
        return self.left is None

    def __repr__(self):
        return 'Node({}, {}, left = {}, right = {})'.format(
            repr(self.value),
            repr(self.colour),
            repr(self.left),
            repr(self.right)
        )
```

With this class, and by considering empty trees those with None subtrees, I can pattern match subtrees of an empty tree. As long as those subtrees go back into the same node, I can replace the color of a leaf during a pattern match transformation rule. I will get into trouble if I create a node that isn't empty but has a None child, but I check if that happens in the constructor and throw an exception if it does. None of the rules we will apply will do this. You could argue that since I only check the subtrees in the constructor, nothing prevents us from explicitly setting a subtree to None, and that is correct. In the persistent version of red-black search trees that we are currently implementing, that doesn't happen, though. We never change a node once it is created.

Just for convenience, I will define the two types of empty trees we will allow, so I don't have to type the full initialization of those each time I use them. It limits the risk of creating an empty tree incorrectly:

```
EmptyTree = Node(None, BLACK, None, None)

DoubleBlackEmptyTree = Node(None, DOUBLE_BLACK, None, None)
```

It would be great if we could use `EmptyTree` as default parameters for the `Node` constructor, but this isn't possible. We cannot create `EmptyTree` before we have defined `Node`, and by then, it is impossible to set the default parameters. (Well, there are hacks, trust me, but I don't want to go there.)

Now consider the cases in turn, starting with the two that have a red root. In these cases, we can move the black node to the top. We keep one of its children, whose subtree must satisfy the invariants as it hasn't changed in the removal (that change must have happened in the subtree with the double black node). We keep it under a black root, so we don't introduce a violation of the red rule, and since it has as many black nodes above it as before, the black invariant is also preserved. We put the other child under the red node. It doesn't add or remove any black nodes on the path to the root, so the black invariant is preserved. The red invariant might now be violated, so we need to balance the tree—we get there in a second. For the double black tree, we can change it to black. We have added a black node above it, and that compensates for the black node missing in a double black node. You can see the transformations at the top row of Figure 15-4. We keep the subtrees of the double black node in the same tree: a and b stay under x on the left; c and d stay under z on the right. That means that even if the black node was empty and those trees were `None`, we wouldn't risk moving `None` into a node higher in the tree. If the double black tree is empty, then the new black tree is empty as well, but we don't create a new tree that would invalidate our rule about `None` subtrees.

For the cases where there are two black nodes, we cannot get rid of the double black node, but we can move it upward in the tree—if we get it to the root, we can always get rid of it by setting the root to black. If we do that, all paths will have the same number of black nodes. So we move the double black node to the top, the subtree that was black we put beneath the original root, and we paint the original root red. See the second row in Figure 15-4. Since the root went under the double black node but got red, it has the same amount of black above it as before, and the black subtree has as well because we have moved the black node directly above it and put the extra black in the double black node in the new root. The y node may have a red child now, since c, on the left, or b, on the right, could have red roots. So, again, we have to balance the trees after the transformation. We keep the trees under the double black node as they were, so the observation about None subtrees from the preceding applies here.

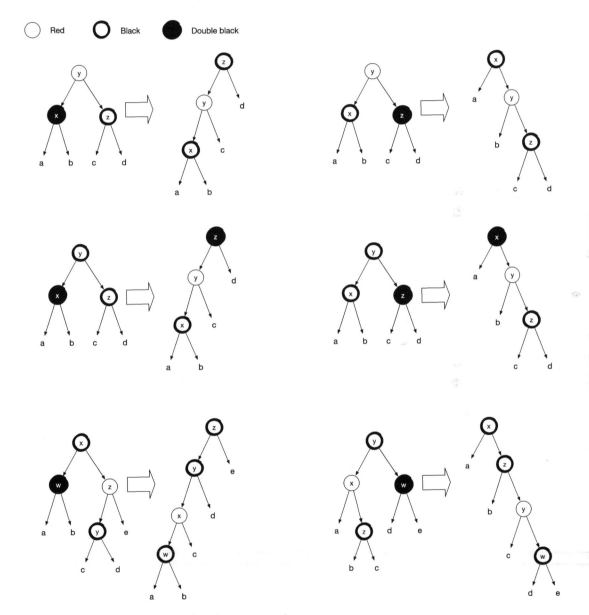

Figure 15-4. *Rotation rules for removal*

If we have a black root and a red subtree, we cannot transform the tree using just that. You can try out the different transformations, and you will find that they do not work. We can, however, look a little bit further down the red subtree. A red subtree will have black children because of the red invariant (and because empty trees are black or double black, so red trees must have subtrees). If we count the number of black nodes in these trees, we must also conclude that the children of the red node are not empty. There are at least three black nodes on the path from the root to the children of the double black node, one for the root and two for the double black. Therefore, there must also be at least three black nodes from the root, through the red node, down to the leaves. If any of the red nodes' children were empty, then there would only be two black nodes from the root to a leaf, so they cannot be. That means that it is safe to move the subtrees of the red node's children around. The double black tree might be empty, so its children might be None, but we keep them together in the transformation, so we won't have problems there either. To see that the transformation will preserve the black invariant, you simply have to count how many black nodes you get down to the subtrees a-e. I will leave that as an exercise for you. After we perform the transformation, we might have violated the red invariant. We put a red node about the c tree on the left, and c might have a red node as it had a black parent before. On the right, we put a red node above the c tree as well, and the same argument goes—we might have put a red node on top of a red node. Thus, again, we have to balance the tree afterward.

These transformations, which we will call *rotations*, eliminate the double black node or move it up toward the root where we can get rid of it. They all satisfy the black invariant, but all of them can violate the red invariant. The top row can be handled by the balancing rules we had for insertion. They handle all cases where we have a black root and two red nodes following it down a path. The rules cannot handle the second row. They do not know how to handle a double black root. No worries, there are two cases where we can have a double black root and two red nodes in a row, and we can rebalance them easily; see Figure 15-5.

For the last row, we can apply the insertion balancing rules again; we just need to do it for a subtree of the root, y on the left and z on the right. Those are the trees with a black root where there might be two red nodes on a row.

Now we are ready to implement the rotations and the new balancing rules. However, first, we look closely at the last row of the rotations and notice an issue.

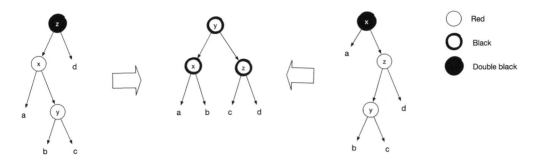

Figure 15-5. *Double black balancing rules*

There, we need to call `balance()` on a subtree of the transformation and not the full tree. We could implement the rotations using `transformation_rule()` as for the `balance()` function and then call `balance()` after rotation transformations, but that isn't good enough for the last two rules. There we need to call `balance()` as part of the transformation. And our DSL cannot handle that.

This happens all the time. You write a DSL or a function or a class that handles the cases you have seen so far, and then something appears that goes beyond the rules you thought were all there was to it. Not to worry, though, it is usually a simple matter of fixing it. Not always, sometimes your original thinking is fundamentally flawed, and this becomes apparent when you run into new cases, but *usually*, you can extend or generalize your code a little to handle new cases.

For our DSL, we need a way to specify that we call a function as part of the transformation, which means that in the `return` statement in the rules we generate, we must be able to add function calls on the tree we construct. This turns out to be simple. We create a call that wraps a function and use it to produce a function call string. We cannot use a function directly when specifying trees for the transformation because that would call it on the specification and not the result of the transformation, which would likely fail catastrophically. But we can wrap the information we need. I chose to implement this class to wrap a function:

```
class FunctionCall(object):
    def __init__(self, name, expr):
        self.name = name
        self.expr = expr
```

```
class Function(object):
    def __init__(self, name):
        self.name = name
    def __call__(self, dsl_expr):
        return FunctionCall(self.name, dsl_expr)
```

I can create it using a function name that I will insert in the string I create for the rule function. I then have a call () method to use in a call syntax. That way, it fits in nicely with the transformation rule syntax. I return a FunctionCall instance from call () because I want an object that I can get the function name and expression from once I have called it. I only need one function in these transformations, but the class would handle any function call should I need to add more in the future. I wrap the balance() function like this:

```
Balance = Function("balance")
```

It might be overkill to add two classes just to add balancing to transformation patterns, but it isn't complicated code, and it makes the expressions easy to read. So if I need to call functions in many patterns, the work will pay off quickly.

In the rule code generation, I add a case for the FunctionCall object:

```
def output_string(output):
    if type(output) is str:
        return output

    if type(output) is FunctionCall:
        return output.name + '(' + output_string(output.expr) + ')'

    return 'Node(' + output.value + ', ' \
                   + str(output.colour) + ', ' \
                   + output_string(output.left) + ', ' \
                   + output_string(output.right) + ')'
```

We also need to update mirror() if we want to be able to mirror patterns:

```
def mirror(tree):
    if type(tree) is str:
        return tree
```

```
elif type(tree) is FunctionCall:
    func = Function(tree.name)
    return func(mirror(tree.expr))
else:
    return Node(tree.value, tree.colour,
                mirror(tree.right),
                mirror(tree.left))
```

Here we create a new Function object with the function name from the tree
FunctionCall object and call it to build a new FunctionCall object. Don't modify tree.
expr, which would be the easy solution because the same object sitting in the un-
mirrored pattern would be affected.

For the rotation rules, I will put Balance() around the output specification for the
first two rows, so balance is called there, and for the last row, I will put Balance() on the
appropriate subtree.

But first, because it is the easiest, we add the new balancing rules. There is a
symmetry in the two cases—if we mirror the left tree and the middle tree, we get
the transformation from the right to the middle tree—so we exploit that in the
implementation:

```
from_double_black = \
    Node("z", DOUBLE_BLACK,
        Node("x", RED,
            "a",
            Node("y", RED, "b", "c")),
        "d")
to_double_black = \
Node("y", BLACK,
    Node("x", BLACK, "a", "b"),
    Node("z", BLACK, "c", "d"))

transformations.extend([
    transformation_rule(from_double_black, to_double_black),
    transformation_rule(mirror(from_double_black), mirror(to_double_black))
])
```

Then the rotation rules and balancing. Notice the symmetry between the two rules for each row. We can get the right rule by mirroring in the two trees on the left, so of course, we will use mirror() to do that:

```
first_row_from = \
    Node("y", RED,
        Node("x", DOUBLE_BLACK, "a", "b"),
        Node("z", BLACK, "c", "d"))
first_row_to = \
    Balance(
        Node("z", BLACK,
            Node("y", RED,
                Node("x", BLACK, "a", "b"),
                "c"),
            "d"))

second_row_from = \
    Node("y", BLACK,
        Node("x", DOUBLE_BLACK, "a", "b"),
        Node("z", BLACK, "c", "d"))
second_row_to = \
    Balance(Node("z", DOUBLE_BLACK,
                Node("y", RED,
                    Node("x", BLACK, "a", "b"),
                    "c"),
                "d"))

third_row_from = \
    Node("x", BLACK,
        Node("w", DOUBLE_BLACK, "a", "b"),
        Node("z", RED,
            Node("y", BLACK, "c", "d"),
            "e"))
third_row_to = \
    Node("z", BLACK,
        Balance(
            Node("y", BLACK,
```

```
                Node("x", RED,
                    Node("w", BLACK, "a", "b"),
                    "c"),
                "d")
        ),
        "e")

rotations = [
    # First row
    transformation_rule(
        first_row_from, first_row_to
    ),
    transformation_rule(
        mirror(first_row_from), mirror(first_row_to)
    ),

    # Second row
    transformation_rule(
        second_row_from, second_row_to
    ),
    transformation_rule(
        mirror(second_row_from), mirror(second_row_to)
    ),

    # Third row
    transformation_rule(
        third_row_from, third_row_to
    ),
    transformation_rule(
        mirror(third_row_from), mirror(third_row_to)
    )
]

def rotate_balance(tree):
    for rule in rotations:
        try:
            return rule(tree)
```

```
        except MatchError:
            pass
    # None of the patterns matched, so return the tree
    return tree
```

The complete implementation, with updated insertion code for dealing with the new definition of empty trees, is listed in the following:

```
RED = 0
BLACK = 1
DOUBLE_BLACK = 2

class Node(object):
    def __init__(self,
                    value,
                    colour,
                    left,
                    right):
        self.value = value
        self.colour = colour
        self.left = left
        self.right = right

        if (self.left is None) != (self.right is None):
            raise TypeError("Either both or neither subtree can be None")

    def is_empty(self):
        return self.left is None

    def __repr__(self):
        return 'Node({}, {}, left = {}, right = {})'.format(
            repr(self.value),
            repr(self.colour),
            repr(self.left),
            repr(self.right)
        )

EmptyTree = Node(None, BLACK, None, None)
DoubleBlackEmptyTree = Node(None, DOUBLE_BLACK, None, None)
```

```
def contains(node, value):
    if node.is_empty():
        return False
    if node.value == value:
        return True
    if node.value > value:
        return contains(node.left, value)
    if node.value < value:
        return contains(node.right, value)

def tree_iter(node):
    if node.is_empty():
        return
    yield from tree_iter(node.left)
    yield node.value
    yield from tree_iter(node.right)

class MatchError(Exception):
    pass

def collect_extraction(node, parent, code_lines):
    if type(node) is str:
        code_lines.append(
            "{} = {}".format(node, parent)
        )
        return code_lines

    code_lines.extend([
        '{} = {}'.format(node.value, parent),
        'if {}.colour != {}: raise MatchError()'.format(
            node.value, node.colour
        )
    ])
    collect_extraction(node.left,
                       node.value + ".left",
                       code_lines)
```

```
    collect_extraction(node.right,
                        node.value + ".right",
                        code_lines)
    code_lines.append(
        '{0} = {0}.value'.format(node.value)
    )
    return code_lines

class FunctionCall(object):
    def __init__(self, name, expr):
        self.name = name
        self.expr = expr

class Function(object):
    def __init__(self, name):
        self.name = name
    def __call__(self, dsl_expr):
        return FunctionCall(self.name, dsl_expr)

Balance = Function("balance")


def output_string(output):
    if type(output) is str:
        return output

    if type(output) is FunctionCall:
        return output.name + '(' + output_string(output.expr) + ')'

    return 'Node(' + output.value + ', ' \
                   + str(output.colour) + ', ' \
                   + output_string(output.left) + ', ' \
                   + output_string(output.right) + ')'

def transformation_rule(input, output):
    body_lines = collect_extraction(input, 'tree', [])
    body = "\n\t\t".join(body_lines)
    ret = "return {}".format(output_string(output))
```

```python
    func = '\n'.join([
        "def rule(tree):",
        "\ttry:",
        '\t\t' + body,
        '\t\t' + ret,
        "\texcept AttributeError:",
        "\t\traise MatchError()"
    ])
    defs = {}
    exec(func, globals(), defs)
    return defs["rule"]

def mirror(tree):
    if type(tree) is str:
        return tree
    elif type(tree) is FunctionCall:
        func = Function(tree.name)
        return func(mirror(tree.expr))
    else:
        return Node(tree.value, tree.colour,
                    mirror(tree.right),
                    mirror(tree.left))

top_case = \
    Node("z", BLACK,
        Node("x", RED,
            "a",
            Node("y", RED, "b", "c")),
        "d")
left_case = \
    Node("z", BLACK,
        Node("y", RED,
            Node("x", RED, "a", "b"),
            "c"),
        "d")
```

```
to_pattern = \
    Node("y", RED,
        Node("x", BLACK, "a", "b"),
        Node("z", BLACK, "c", "d"))

transformations = [
    transformation_rule(top_case, to_pattern),
    transformation_rule(mirror(top_case), mirror(to_pattern)),
    transformation_rule(left_case, to_pattern),
    transformation_rule(mirror(left_case), mirror(to_pattern))
]

from_double_black = \
    Node("z", DOUBLE_BLACK,
        Node("x", RED,
            "a",
            Node("y", RED, "b", "c")),
        "d")
to_double_black = \
    Node("y", BLACK,
        Node("x", BLACK, "a", "b"),
        Node("z", BLACK, "c", "d"))

transformations.extend([
    transformation_rule(from_double_black, to_double_black),
    transformation_rule(mirror(from_double_black), mirror(to_double_black))
])

    def balance(tree):
        for rule in transformations:
            try:
                return rule(tree)
            except MatchError:
                pass
        # None of the patterns matched, so return the tree
        return tree
```

```
def insert_rec(node, value):
    if node.is_empty():
        return Node(value, RED, EmptyTree, EmptyTree)

    if node.value == value:
        return node

    elif node.value > value:
        new_tree = Node(node.value, node.colour,
                        left = insert_rec(node.left, value),
                        right = node.right)
        return balance(new_tree)

    elif node.value < value:
        new_tree = Node(node.value, node.colour,
                        left = node.left,
                        right = insert_rec(node.right, value))
        return balance(new_tree)

def insert(node, value):
    new_tree = insert_rec(node, value)
    new_tree.colour = BLACK
    return new_tree

first_row_from = \
    Node("y", RED,
        Node("x", DOUBLE_BLACK, "a", "b"),
        Node("z", BLACK, "c", "d"))
first_row_to = \
    Balance(
        Node("z", BLACK,
            Node("y", RED,
                Node("x", BLACK, "a", "b"),
                "c"),
        "d"))
```

519

```
second_row_from = \
    Node("y", BLACK,
        Node("x", DOUBLE_BLACK, "a", "b"),
        Node("z", BLACK, "c", "d"))
second_row_to = \
    Balance(Node("z", DOUBLE_BLACK,
                Node("y", RED,
                    Node("x", BLACK, "a", "b"),
                "c"),
                "d"))

third_row_from = \
    Node("x", BLACK,
        Node("w", DOUBLE_BLACK, "a", "b"),
        Node("z", RED,
            Node("y", BLACK, "c", "d"),
            "e"))
third_row_to = \
    Node("z", BLACK,
        Balance(
            Node("y", BLACK,
                Node("x", RED,
                    Node("w", BLACK, "a", "b"),
                    "c"),
                "d")
        ),
        "e")

rotations = [
    # First row
    transformation_rule(
        first_row_from, first_row_to
    ),
    transformation_rule(
        mirror(first_row_from), mirror(first_row_to)
    ),
```

```python
        # Second row
        transformation_rule(
            second_row_from, second_row_to
        ),
        transformation_rule(
            mirror(second_row_from), mirror(second_row_to)
        ),

        # Third row
        transformation_rule(
            third_row_from, third_row_to
        ),
        transformation_rule(
            mirror(third_row_from), mirror(third_row_to)
        )
]

def rotate_balance(tree):
    for rule in rotations:
        try:
            return rule(tree)
        except MatchError:
            pass
    # None of the patterns matched, so return the tree
    return tree

def rightmost_value(node):
    if node.right.is_empty():
        return node.value
    else:
        return rightmost_value(node.right)

def remove_rec(node, value):
    if node.is_empty():
        # if we get to an empty tree, it means
        # that we couldn't find the value in the
        # tree
        raise KeyError()
```

```
if node.value > value:
    new_tree = Node(node.value,
                    node.colour,
                    left = remove_rec(node.left, value),
                    right = node.right)
    return rotate_balance(new_tree)

if node.value < value:
    new_tree = Node(node.value,
                    node.colour,
                    left = node.left,
                    right = remove_rec(node.right, value))
    return rotate_balance(new_tree)

# we have value == node.value
if node.left.is_empty() and node.right.is_empty():
    if node.colour is RED:
        return EmptyTree
    else:
        return DoubleBlackEmptyTree

if node.left.is_empty():
    return Node(node.right.value, BLACK,
                node.right.left, node.right.right)

if node.right.is_empty():
    return Node(node.left.value, BLACK,
                node.left.left, node.left.right)

# general case removal
replacement = rightmost_value(node.left)
new_tree = Node(replacement, node.colour,
                remove_rec(node.left, replacement),
                node.right)

    return rotate_balance(new_tree)
```

```
def remove(tree, value):
    new_tree = remove_rec(tree, value)
    new_tree.colour = BLACK
    return new_tree

class RedBlackSearchTreeSet(object):
    def __init__(self, seq = ()):
        self.tree = EmptyTree
        for value in seq:
            self.add(value)

    def add(self, element):
        self.tree = insert(self.tree, element)

    def remove(self, element):
        self.tree = remove(self.tree, element)

    def __iter__(self):
        return tree_iter(self.tree)

    def __contains__(self, element):
        return contains(self.tree, element)

    def __repr__(self):
        return 'RedBlackSearchTreeSet(tree_iter(' + repr(self.tree) + '))'
```

Pattern Matching in Python

The DSL we wrote for transforming trees is based on matching a pattern of trees
and then transforming the tree. This kind of pattern matching is built into some
programming languages, but at the time I am writing this, it isn't yet in Python. It is being
added, however, so by the time you read this, it might already be there. When it is already
in the language, we don't need to implement it ourselves.

I cannot promise that it will look exactly like the following code, but the current beta
releases of Python look like what I will show you. To match a pattern, you use the match
keyword, and after that you have a list of patterns to match.

For our trees, we cannot use simple integer variables like RED and BLACK for matching. Python will think that we are trying to assign variables to those. But we can wrap them up in a class and then "dot" our way to them to get pattern matching to work. You can define the colors like this:

```
from enum import Enum
class Colour(Enum):
    RED = 0
    BLACK = 1
```

Then, to pattern match a class, you must tell Python which variables the objects hold. You can do that with syntax that looks like this:

```
class Node(object):
    value: object
    colour: Colour
    left: Node
    right: Node
    __match_args__ = ("value", "colour", "left", "right")

    def __init__(self, value,
                    colour = Colour.RED,
                    left = None, right = None):
        self.value = value
        self.colour = colour
        self.left = left
        self.right = right
```

The top four lines in the class definition tell Python which variables we can match against and what type they have. The __match_args__ specifies the order the variables will come in. If you leave it out, you can still pattern match, but then you must use named variables in the matching.

With that definition of colors and nodes, the balancing function for dealing with double red violations will look like this:

```
def balance(tree):
    match tree:
        case Node(z, Colour.BLACK,
```

```
                Node(x, Colour.RED, a, Node(y, Colour.RED, b, c)),
                d):
        return Node(y, Colour.RED,
                    Node(x, Colour.BLACK, a, b),
                    Node(z, Colour.BLACK, c, d))

    case Node(z, Colour.BLACK,
                Node(y, Colour.RED, Node(x, Colour.RED, a, b), c),
                d):
        return Node(y, Colour.RED,
                    Node(x, Colour.BLACK, a, b),
                    Node(z, Colour.BLACK, c, d))

    case Node(x, Colour.BLACK,
                a,
                Node(z, Colour.RED, Node(y, Colour.RED, b, c), d)):
        return Node(y, Colour.RED,
                    Node(x, Colour.BLACK, a, b),
                    Node(z, Colour.BLACK, c, d))

    case Node(x, Colour.BLACK,
                a,
                Node(y, Colour.RED, b, Node(z, Colour.RED, c, d))):
        return Node(y, Colour.RED,
                    Node(x, Colour.BLACK, a, b),
                    Node(z, Colour.BLACK, c, d))

    case _:
        return tree
```

As you can see, it is close to the DSL we wrote (which isn't a coincidence), but now directly supported by the Python language.

Useful domain-specific languages often make their way into languages like this, and when you are reading this book, you might already have this kind of pattern matching in Python. It is still useful to know how to implement your own little languages, however. Not all such languages get promoted into the main language, and when you need one, you can't wait the years it takes before they do. So don't feel that you wasted your time on that part of this section.

An Iterative Solution

The persistent structure is sufficiently fast for most usage, and since we balance our trees to logarithmic height, we are unlikely to exhaust the call stack in the operations. However, we can get a little more speed with an iterative solution, where we save the overhead from function calls, and that solution also eliminates any call stack worries.

If the DSL, and the tree transformations with it, seemed overly complicated, then I have good news. The iterative and ephemeral solution is simpler if we implement it the right way, but we need to take a detour through more complicated rules. With the new solution, we will look upward in the tree instead of downward. It reduces the number of cases we need to consider substantially. A node only has one parent, one sibling, one grandparent, one uncle (parent's sibling), and such. In the previous section's insertion rules, we had four cases, but if we look from the perspective of the lower red node, we can match all of them simply by checking if it has a red parent. With the right abstractions added to nodes for examining the tree structure, we will eliminate all symmetric cases and simplify the pattern marching. We couldn't easily do the same thing with the persistent solution since we constructed new trees in recursion, but when we allow ourselves to move around a tree and modify it, we have more options.

For the transformations, we won't extract values and subtrees. We mostly leave the nodes as they are and rearrange them rather than build new nodes. We might change the color of a node, but never the value, and all transformations come in one of two forms: *left* and *right rotations* (see Figure 15-6). In the insertion rules from the preceding, we use a left or a right rotation depending on whether the two red nodes sit on the left or on the right. Left and right rotations are not symmetric, but we can make a *rotation* operation on the node we want to move up to the root and make it perform a right rotation on its parent if it is a left child and a left rotation on its parent if it is a right child. Then we would make the full insertion transformation rules for the left and right cases: "if the parent is red, rotate it, color this node and its new sibling black, and continue from the parent." For the top and bottom cases, we need an additional rotation around the parent of the bottom red node as well. We still have two cases, but the symmetric cases are implicitly handled by looking upward in the tree instead of downward. Plus, we don't have to access any values we are not directly modifying with rotations, so the transformations are much simpler (one or two rotations) than when we need to build new subtrees.

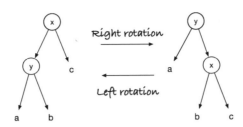

Figure 15-6. *Left and right rotations*

We won't use exactly the same transformation rules as with the persistent structure. There, we need to continue building a new tree all the way up from the recursion, but now we can restore the invariants early and terminate. Tweaking the rules a little, by examining slightly more of the tree, we finish processing with a constant number of tree rotations per insertion and deletion and an amortized constant number of color changes. But before we get to that, we must add the necessary functionality to nodes.

We first need to update our Node class. In the iterative solution, we need to run from leaves toward the root when we balance a tree, so we need to add a parent pointer. We will use the WeakRefProperty class from Chapter 10 for the parent reference, so the reference counter garbage collection will work. To ensure that children and parent pointers are always consistent, we can add getters and setters and put them in property classes. If we set a child of a node, we make sure that its parent is set accordingly. We will use a dummy class for empty trees, so we won't worry about not setting the parent of empty trees. We use the same object for all empty trees, so an empty tree's parent will be the most recent node we added it to, but we only use the parent reference of an empty tree in one place, which is when we delete, and there it will point to the correct node (because we set it to point there just before we use it). The other reason we use a dummy node for empty trees is that we want to be able to check the color of empty trees, find their siblings and similar, and check if in all ways they behave like trees, but just not hold any data or subtrees.

The node definition looks like this:

```
class Node(object):
    parent = WeakRefProperty()

    # Always update parent when left or right is set
    def get_left(self):
        return self._left
```

```
    def set_left(self, left):
        self._left = left
        left.parent = self
    left = property(get_left, set_left)

    def get_right(self):
        return self._right
    def set_right(self, right):
        self._right = right
        right.parent = self
    right = property(get_right, set_right)

    @property
    def is_red(self):
        return self.colour is RED
    @property
    def is_black(self):
        return self.colour is BLACK
```

Instead of putting a color in the empty tree, I chose to use is_red and is_black properties. I just find that this makes the code more readable, but it is a matter of taste. The @property decorator creates a property object (it calls the property constructor the way all decorators do). When used this way, we only give it a getter method—when we have used it earlier, we have called the constructor more explicitly and provided both a getter and a setter. When we use it as a decorator, we implicitly call the constructor with a single argument, the method we define following the decorator, so we give it a getter. For these properties, getters are all we need.

Instead of the domain-specific language, we will add properties to nodes that work just as well, and that lets us pattern match just as easy as we could with a DSL. To get there, we need the right properties to test the tree structure on. We will need to extract the parent, grandparent, sibling, and uncle of a node and check if it is an inner node (left child of a right child or right child of a left child) or whether it is an outer node. We will also need to get the inner or outer child of a node, defined analogously to what it means for a node to be inner or outer. These properties are straightforward to implement:

```
@property
def is_left(self):
    return self is self.parent.left
@property
def is_right(self):
    return not self.is_left

@property
def sibling(self):
    p = self.parent
    if p.left is self:
        return p.right
    else:
        return p.left
@property
def uncle(self):
    return self.parent.sibling
@property
def grandparent(self):
    return self.parent.parent

@property
def is_inner(self):
    return self.is_left and self.parent.is_right or\
        self.is_right and self.parent.is_left
@property
def is_outer(self):
    return not self.is_inner

@property
def inner_child(self):
    if self.is_left:
        return self.right
    else:
        return self.left
```

```python
@property
def outer_child(self):
    if self.is_left:
        return self.left
    else:
        return self.right
```

These properties give us a language to query a tree's structure, and you can consider it a new domain-specific language if you like. It has the qualities of one. We just usually do not call it that if we are simply using the features that Python readily provide us with.

Finally, we need methods that make it easy to transform trees, and that means a `rotate()` method to rotate a node one level up, through either a left or right rotation (depending on whether it is a left or right child):

```python
def replace_child(self, current, new):
    if current == self.left:
        self.left = new
    else:
        self.right = new

def rotate_left(self):
    self.parent.replace_child(self, self.right)
    b = self.right.left
    self.right.left = self
    self.right = b

def rotate_right(self):
    self.parent.replace_child(self, self.left)
    b = self.left.right
    self.left.right = self
    self.left = b

def rotate(self):
    if self.is_left:
        self.parent.rotate_right()
    else:
        self.parent.rotate_left()
```

There was no __init__() method in the Node definition, you might have noticed. That is because I want to use an empty tree as the default for subtrees, and at the same time, I want a dummy tree to be a node, so I can inherit all the functionality we will put into nodes. That creates a circular dependency that we have to break. Another issue is that I want a constructor that only takes subtrees as left and right trees (or at least something that behaves like them). That isn't possible for the empty tree—if it needed to hold other trees, it should be itself, or we would get infinite recursion. The only thing that prevents us from having an empty tree (without children) and default parameters for left and right is the constructor, so an easy solution is to use separate classes for empty and non-empty trees and put the constructors there:

```
class EmptyTree(Node):
    def __init__(self):
        self.colour = BLACK
EMPTY_TREE = EmptyTree()

class Tree(Node):
def __init__(self, value,
            colour = RED,
            left = EMPTY_TREE,
            right = EMPTY_TREE):
        self.value = value
        self.colour = colour
        self.parent = None
        self.left = left
        self.right = right
```

It is not pretty, but it gets the job done and allows us to make the basis of the recursive type definition an instance of the type itself.

Checking if a Value Is in the Search Tree

Unless we are adding or removing a node, we don't have to worry about balancing. If the red-black invariants are satisfied before a search, they are also satisfied after the search. So find_node() and contains() are the same as those we wrote in Chapter 14:

```
# Don't call with a None node
def find_node(tree, value):
    n = tree
    while True:
        if n.value == value:
            return n
        elif n.value > value:
            # go left
            if n.left is EMPTY_TREE:
                return n
            n = n.left
        else: # n.value < value:
            # go right
            if n.right is EMPTY_TREE:
                return n
            n = n.right

def contains(tree, value):
    return find_node(tree, value).value == value
```

Inserting

Most of the insertion operation also works as for general search trees: we search down the tree to find the node where we must insert a new value. We find a node with at most one subtree—because otherwise we could continue the search down one of them—and there we create a new node with empty subtrees. Because we have a red-black search tree and not a simple search tree, we have to give the new node a color, and we have to make sure that we satisfy the invariants after the insertion. We color it red because it implicitly has two black subtrees and it replaces a black empty tree. Because it is red, its subtrees are at the same black depth as the tree it replaced, and thus the black invariant is satisfied. However, its parent might also be red, so we need to fix the red invariant:

```
def insert(tree, value):
    n = find_node(tree, value)
    if n.value == value:
        return # already here
```

```
new_node = Tree(value)
if n.value > value:
    n.left = new_node
else:
    n.right = new_node
fix_red_red(new_node)
```

To fix the red invariant, we use these alternative rules that let us limit the modifications to the tree structure to a maximum of two and have all remaining updates simply change colors. Since modifying the tree structure is more expensive than changing colors—you have to update references to other nodes and not just a single value—there can be speedups in that. The rules are shown in Figure 15-7, except for symmetric cases. The arrow points to the node we are carrying in `fix_red_red()`. If you are in Case 3, you have restored the red invariant after the transformation. If you are in Case 2, you will be in Case 3 next, and only in Case 1 can you continue iterating; see Figure 15-8 where *Start* is where we consider which tree to transform, the arrows are how the transitions can be chained together, and *Done* is when we stop rebalancing the tree.

Case 2 and Case 3 change the tree structure, but you can only be in these cases twice per insertion (once for each). Case 1 only changes colors. With these rules, then, we always have a constant number of transformations. We shall see later that we also have an amortized constant number of color changes. Insertion still takes logarithmic time—finding where to insert a value costs a logarithmic-time search—but maintaining the balancing invariants is only constant time on top of that.

We can recognize Case 1 by testing if the node's uncle is red. We only run the fix if the node and its parent are red, and if the parent is red, we know that the grandparent is black, so it is only the uncle that determines which case we are in, and Case 1 is when it is red. In that case, we need to color the parent and uncle black and color the grandparent red. Case 2 differs from Case 3 by whether the relevant node is inner or outer. If it is inner, then we are in Case 2, and there we need to rotate it to do the transformation. If it is outer, we are in Case 3, and in that case, it is the parent we need to rotate. After that, we color the parent black and the (new) sibling red, and then we are done:

```
def fix_red_red(node):
    while node.parent.is_red:
        if node.uncle.is_red:
```

```
        # Case 1
        node.parent.colour = BLACK
        node.uncle.colour = BLACK
        node.grandparent.colour = RED
        node = node.grandparent
    elif node.is_inner:
        # Case 2
        old_parent = node.parent
        node.rotate()
        node = old_parent
    else:
        # Case 3
        node.parent.rotate()
        node.parent.colour = BLACK
        node.sibling.colour = RED
        return # Done with fixing
```

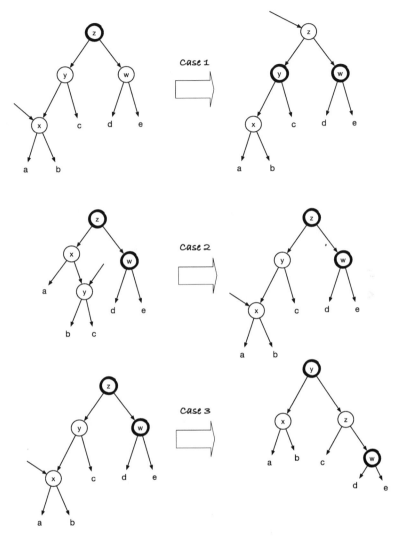

Figure 15-7. *Alternative rules for correcting the tree after inserting*

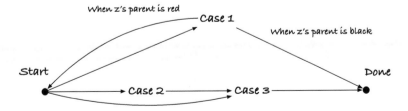

Figure 15-8. *Transitions between cases when inserting*

I think you will agree that even without a DSL, this version of the data structure is simpler to implement. Removing the symmetries by looking up in the tree dramatically simplifies things.

Deleting

The core idea for deletion is the same as always. Find the node to delete, and if it has two children, get the rightmost value in the left subtree, put it in the node, and delete the rightmost value from the left tree. If we need to delete a node with at most one subtree, then we get the non-empty subtree (or an empty one if they are both empty) and replace the node we delete with this subtree. If the node we delete is red, then we can't have violated any invariant. Both parent and child must be black, which means that we add a black node to a black node to not violate the red invariant. A red node doesn't count toward the black depth of paths, so removing it doesn't change anything, and thus the black invariant is satisfied. If the node we remove is black, however, we might be in trouble. The replacement might be red, in which case we risk invalidating the red invariant. That is an easy fix. We can color it black, and then the red invariant must be satisfied. If it was originally red, painting it black would satisfy the black invariant as well—we replaced its black parent with it, removing one black node from the paths, but then we added one back when we painted the replacement black. If it was already black and we paint it black again, we have painted it double black, and that is something we must fix.

The code, without the function for fixing double black nodes, looks like you would expect from the previous chapter:

```
def get_rightmost(node):
    while node.right is not EMPTY_TREE:
        node = node.right
    return node

def remove(tree, value):
    n = find_node(tree, value)
    if n.value != value:
        return # value wasn't in the tree
```

```
    if n.left is not EMPTY_TREE and n.right is not EMPTY_TREE:
        rightmost = get_rightmost(n.left)
        n.value = rightmost.value
        remove(n.left, rightmost.value)

    else:
        replacement = n.left \
                        if n.right is EMPTY_TREE \
                        else n.right
        n.parent.replace_child(n, replacement)
        if n.is_black:
            if replacement.is_red:
                replacement.colour = BLACK
        else:
            replacement.colour = BLACK
            fix_double_black(replacement)
```

We don't color any nodes extra black, but we use the color as a conceptual color representing an extra black node on paths down to leaves in a subtree as we did in the persistent solution. There, we needed the extra color for pattern matching, but now we will start each transformation with a reference to the one node that is double black, and that gives us all the information that we need about it.

There are many trees we could potentially have to match for transformations, depending on whether we have empty trees or such (although having dummy nodes for empty trees helps a lot). However, we can make an observation that limits the numbers somewhat. If we consider the double black node and its sibling, we will find that the sibling always has two non-empty trees. The path from the rule to a leaf in the subtree under the double black node is one black node short of the paths that go to leaves in the sibling's subtree, and the double black node is black. If the sibling is black, then black paths in the subtrees must count to the same as the subtree under the double black node, and it has at least a length of two (itself and its empty children, if they are empty). Therefore, the sibling's children must have (possibly empty) subtrees. If the sibling is red, you can run the same argument, except that the children must be larger still. This means that we can always assume that the sibling has non-empty children and consider trees consisting of the double back node, its parent, its sibling, and its sibling's children.

We consider all combinations of the double black node, its parent, its sibling, and the sibling's children for the new rules. That means all combinations of colors that satisfy the red invariant (i.e., if the parent is red, then the sibling cannot be red as well and such). I count the combinations to 18 (but I might be wrong, so you better check me). Luckily, we can cut it in half by considering symmetries, and it turns out that some of the rules are indifferent to some of the colors. You can see the new transformation rules in Figure 15-9 for the cases where the double black node is a left child. The four cases where it is a right tree are symmetric, and we can get them using the `mirror()` function.

Exercise: Convince yourself that these rules, combined with their mirrors, cover all combinations of a double black node, its parent, its sibling, and its sibling's children.

The gray nodes are either red or black, and except for Case 2, they retain their colors in the transformation. In Case 2, the root will be painted either black or double black by the transformation: black if y is originally red and double black otherwise (think of it as painting the node black, but when you paint a black node black, it becomes double black).

The rules are not always pushing the double black node up in the tree—something the previous rules did, and that obviously guaranteed some sort of progress when applying them. Now, only one of the rules potentially does that. One rule, Case 1, even pushes it down. So how can we see that the transformations will take us toward something that terminates? For that, we have to see which transformations each opens up for. Consider Case 1: After the transformation, the double black node has a red parent and a black sibling. That means that the next transformation is one of the other three. Case 2 will move the double black node upward or eliminate it entirely when the root is red (we will get to why). If we enter Case 2 from Case 1, the root is red, so we will terminate at this point. Case 3 will give the sibling a red right tree, which means that we can apply Case 4 to eliminate the black subtree. Figure 15-10 shows how the cases are connected. The only case you can cycle around is Case 2; all the others will lead to termination in a constant number of transitions—and in Case 2, we move the double black node upward, limiting how long we can continue. So eventually, applying these transformations will terminate.

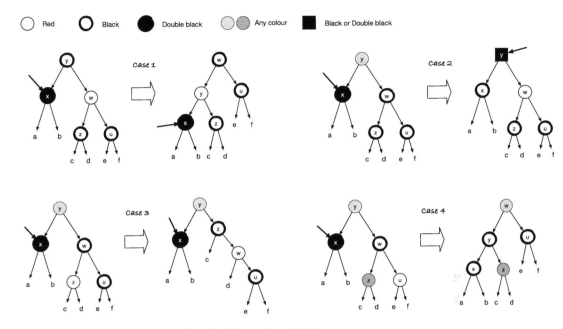

○ Red   ◯ Black   ● Double black   ◐ Any colour   ■ Black or Double black

Figure 15-9. *Rotation rules for iterative deletion*

Let us examine them in detail and check if they satisfy the invariant. First, the red invariant: For Case 1, we observe that there is only one red node, and it has black neighbors after the transformation. For Case 2, we introduce a red node with black children, and the parent will either be black or double black (which is also black). For Case 3, we have to examine node *w* and tree *d*, which is the only place we could invalidate the invariant. However, *d* sits under a red node before the transformation, so it cannot have a red root. In Case 4, the root's children are black and the same color as the root before the transformation, so it cannot violate the red invariant. Node *z* has the same color and children as before, so we cannot get into trouble there either.

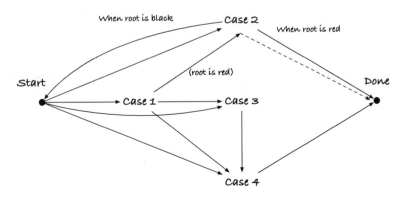

Figure 15-10. *Transitions between cases when deleting nodes*

Notice that since it is only possible to visit Case 2 more than once, we can't change the tree topology more than three times (the longest such path is Case 1 to Case 3 to Case 4), after which we only change the color of nodes. With a more elaborate DSL (as I hinted at when we discussed insertions), you can optimize the code and only update the attributes you strictly need. Since updating colors is faster than updating the references when you rotate the trees, it is worthwhile if you need a very fast search tree. Still, it is not necessary for our conceptual understanding, so I will not cover it here. As an exercise for developing a better DSL, however, I think you will find it interesting.

For the black invariant, consider the cases again, and count how many black nodes are above each terminal tree. They must be the same before and after the transformation. In Case 1, there is one black and one double black node above a and b and two black nodes above the others both before and after the transformation. In Case 2, it depends on what color the root on the left has. If it is red, we will color the root on the right black. That adds one black to the tree previously rooted by the double black node, but that simply means that we got our missing black node back, so we can change the double black node to simply black. For the remaining trees, we removed the black on node w but added it to the root, so we end up with the same number of black nodes. With this transformation, if the root on the left is red, we can terminate the fixing run because the double black node is gone. If the input root is black already, we paint the new root double black, leaving the same amount of black for a and b, but we have removed one black for the other trees, replacing it with a double black. This means that they have one black less than before (because double black means that we are lacking one black), but with the double black at the root, that matches the count. For Case 3, there is one double black above a and b before and after the transformation, one black above c and d before and after, and two black nodes above the remaining two trees, both before and after the transformation. Finally, for Case 4, we have a double black node above a and b. We change that to two black nodes, settling the accounting of the missing black. For the remaining trees, we have the same number of black nodes before and after the transformation.

We can implement the transitions like this:

```
def fix_double_black(node):
    # Only the *real* root doesn't have a
    # grandparent, and if we reach there we
    # are done.
    while node.grandparent:
```

```
if node.sibling.is_red:
    # Case 1 (sibling red means parent black)
    p = node.parent
    node.sibling.rotate()
    node.parent.colour = RED
    node.grandparent.colour = BLACK
    node.parent = p
    continue

# If we are here, we are in case 2, 3, or 4

if node.sibling.outer_child.is_red:
    # Case 4
    node.sibling.colour = node.parent.colour
    node.parent.colour = BLACK
    node.sibling.outer_child.colour = BLACK
    node.sibling.rotate()
    return # Done

# Now we know that the sibling's outer child
# is black, so we can check the inner to see if
# we are in case 3
if node.sibling.inner_child.is_red:
    # Case 3
    p = node.parent
    node.sibling.colour = RED
    node.sibling.inner_child.colour = BLACK
    node.sibling.inner_child.rotate()
    node.parent = p
    continue

# We must be in Case 2
node.sibling.colour = RED
if node.parent.is_red:
    node.parent.colour = BLACK
    return # Done
```

```
else:
    node.parent.colour = BLACK
    node = node.parent
    continue
```

I chose to match against the cases in a different order than in the figure since I found it easier to determine which case we are in using this order—where we can use the information we get from one test in the following—but otherwise, it is a simple translation of the transitions in the figure. However, there is one issue that the figure doesn't show but which we must handle in the implementation. The node we are working on can be the empty tree, and there is only one empty tree. That means that if a rotation involves an empty tree, then its parent will have changed. Therefore, I get the parent of the node before transitions and set it again after rotations, so we can continue the rebalancing after handling each case. You could get out of this problem by having separate empty trees every time you need one, but that would double the tree's space complexity.

Resetting the parent reference a few times in a single function is a small price to pay for not spending twice the memory we need.

That is all there was to removing elements.

The Final Set Class

Wrapping the chapter up, we will also wrap up the red-black search tree in a set class. It looks much like the search tree from the previous chapter. We use a dummy root for the tree to make sure that all real nodes have a parent, and we put a "greater than everything" value in it, which eliminates special cases in the operations. The real search tree will always sit in the left child of the dummy node (this, of course, violates the black invariant, since the right node will usually be much smaller than the left), but it is only a dummy node after all. Having the dummy also means that we always have a tree for our operations, although it could be empty, so in the operations where we might have to resolve invariants at the very root, we can always color the dummy's left tree black. There is a tree there; it is never None, and should it happen to be empty, we can still color it black without breaking anything:

```
def tree_iter(node):
    if node is EMPTY_TREE:
        return
    yield from tree_iter(node.left)
    yield node.value
    yield from tree_iter(node.right)

class Greater(object):
    def __lt__(self, other):
        return False
    def __eq__(self, other):
        return False
    def __gt__(self, other):
        return True

class RedBlackSearchTreeSet(object):
    def __init__(self, seq = ()):
        self.tree = Tree(Greater(), BLACK)
        for value in seq:
            self.add(value)

    def add(self, val):
        insert(self.tree, val)
        self.tree.left.colour = BLACK

    def remove(self, val):
        remove(self.tree, val)
        self.tree.left.colour = BLACK

    def __iter__(self):
        return tree_iter(self.tree.left)

    def __contains__(self, element):
        return contains(self.tree, element)

    def __repr__(self):
        return 'RedBlackSearchTreeSet(tree_iter(' + \
                repr(self.tree.left) + '))'
```

An Amortized Analysis

When we insert and delete, we spend $O(\log n)$ time, but we can split this time into the part that involves finding the location where we need to insert a node or delete it, which is the logarithmic-time search in the tree, and the time we spend on restoring the red-black invariants. If the tree is balanced, we cannot do better than logarithmic time for finding the location, but perhaps we spend less time than that on fixing the tree afterward. With a detailed analysis of the operations, we can show that we do indeed spend less time; we spend amortized constant time restoring the invariants, provided we use the rules in Figures 15-7 and 15-9.

The argument is slightly more involved than those we have seen earlier and requires a potential function. The idea here is to assign a potential to the current state of a tree so that the potential can never become negative. With each operation, we count how much the potential changes. If we cannot increase the potential by more than a fixed amount over all the operations we perform, then we cannot decrease it more than that either, since it cannot get negative, so once we have the function, the goal is to see that the increases are limited.

We will assign a potential to a black node: a black node with one red and one black child has a potential of 0, a black node with two black children has a potential of +1, and a black node with two red nodes has a potential of +2. All transformations we only perform once per operation can only add a constant amount of potential, limiting the increase of the potential to $O(n)$ from these operations. What we need to examine in detail are the transformations we can do more than once per insertion and deletion, and we need to show that for those, the potential decreases. Those transformations are Case 1 for insertions and Case 2 for deletions.

Consider Case 1 in the insertion transformations. The z node has a potential of +2 because it is black with two red children. Nodes y and w have a potential of 0 since they are red nodes. The children of w must be black since it is red, and we have to keep that in mind when we change it. We do not modify the other terminal nodes' colors, so we cannot change any potential there. When we color z red and its children back, we remove -2 potential. When we color w black, we add +1—it is red, so its children must be black—which gives us a total reduction of -1 when applying the case. When the potential is decreasing, we cannot run it more times than we have added potential, which is $O(n)$ for n operations, provided that the deletion case doesn't add potential.

Now consider Case 2 for deletions, and assume that y is black. If it isn't, we terminate the update, so that rule can only run once per deletion and thus can only add a constant amount of potential per deletion. We have a potential of +1 in y because it has two black rules, and we have a potential of +1 in w for the same reason. When we color w red, we remove -1 potential from y and -1 from w, so doing the transformation decreases the potential by -2.

We conclude that we have a constant number of tree transformations for both insertions and deletions, a maximum of two for insertions and three for deletion, and a number of color changes that are amortized constant. Rebalancing is thus fast; we do not pay much of an overhead compared to a normal search tree. We get a balanced tree that can at most have a factor two difference in paths to a leaf, so compared to perfectly balanced trees, with high $\log_2 n$, we can spend $2 \log_2 n$ on all operations where we need to search in the tree. So we can say that we get within a factor two of a perfect search tree for a constant amount of work.

CHAPTER 16

Stacks and Queues

This chapter will explore two additional abstract data structures, *stacks* and *queues*. We have already implemented them without our knowledge, so we won't spend much time on that but instead explore what we can do with them.

The operations we need from a stack are the following:

- You can *push* an element onto a stack.

- You can get the most recent element you pushed.

- You can *pop* an element from a stack, which means you remove the most recent element you pushed. Getting and removing the top element on the stack are often used together, so to make that usage pattern simpler, we want *pop* to return the element it deletes.

- You can check if the stack is empty.

For a queue

- You can *enqueue* an element.

- You can get the *front* element, which is the element that has been the longest in the queue.

- You can *dequeue* an element, meaning you remove the element that has been the longest in the queue. Getting and removing the front element in the queue are often used together, so to make that usage pattern simpler, we want *dequeue* to return the element it deletes.

- You can check if the queue is empty.

With the sequence data structures we developed in Chapter 13, we have all but one of the operations we want; we just need to rename them. We can do this by implementing mixin classes with the operations. Recall from Chapter 12 that mixins are superclasses that implement methods to extend another class but do not hold

547

© Thomas Mailund 2021
T. Mailund, *Introduction to Computational Thinking*, https://doi.org/10.1007/978-1-4842-7077-6_16

data themselves. To change one class' interface to another, we can often write mixins that translate between one abstract data structure and another. Using a mixin, we can implement the translation from a sequence to a stack or queue once and use it with any sequence class.

The final sequences we implemented gave us these operations that we can now exploit:

- Add an element to the front or back of a sequence.

- Get the element at the front or back of a sequence.

- Remove the element at the front or back of a sequence.

The two implementations we had didn't implement the operations with the same efficiency, but if we only care about the abstract data structures' interface, that doesn't matter. We can add the stack interface to a sequence like this:

```python
class EmptyStack(Exception):
    pass

class StackMixin(object):
    def push(self, x):
        self.append(x)

    def top(self):
        try:
            return self.get_last()
        except IndexError:
            raise EmptyStack()

    def pop(self):
        try:
            x = self.get_last()
            self.remove_last()
            return x
        except IndexError:
            raise EmptyStack()
```

I added a new exception for when the sequence is empty—we would get an IndexError otherwise, which is not informative about what went wrong with a stack operation. The mixin gives us most of the operations we need but not the test for whether the stack is empty. We didn't put that operation into the sequence, so we cannot use it in the mixin. Now, we could get the operation by accessing the last element and catching the IndexError if the sequence was empty, but using exceptions rather than explicit tests is less efficient and frankly less elegant. We could add the operation to the sequence interface. That might be the best solution since testing if a sequence is empty depends on the sequence's underlying implementation. Alternatively, we can add the operation when we combine the sequence operation and the mixin:

```
class Stack(StackMixin, DoublyLinkedListSequence):
    def is_empty(self):
        return self.first.next == self.last
```

or

```
class Stack(StackMixin, ListSequence):
    def is_empty(self):
        return len(self.sequence) == 0
```

Here, we take the operations from the mixin, get the sequence operations they need from the sequence implementations, and add the one implementation-dependent operation in the resulting classes. As a rule of thumb, if you need to work with details of an underlying implementation when you adapt it to another abstract data structure, you should prefer adding the operation to its interface. Otherwise, you are relying on the representation of a class that might change in the future. If that happens, all the operations in the class will be updated, but likely the programmer who updates the class won't know that you rely heavily on the existing implementation in another class that otherwise isn't closely related.

This, however, isn't always the most convenient approach. If you have many implementations of sequences, but you only want to use a few of them as stacks, maybe because only a few of them will give you efficient implementations of the operations, you don't want to go through all the implementations to add the one extra operation you need for your new abstract data structure. To this, I will add that if you only plan to use *one* of the other classes for your abstract data structure, there is no point in using a mixin either—just inherit from the class and add the extra operations. Should you later want to try different alternatives, you can always extract the operations and put them in a mixin at that point.

I didn't want to go back to my sequence code, all the way back in Chapter 13, and update the classes, so I just added the operations here. I will need the same operations for queues, and when you find yourself needing something more than one or two times, you always should consider if it is time to modify the existing code so you don't repeat yourself. I won't do that here either—but keep the option in mind.

A final comment on the `is_empty()` operation has nothing to do with the abstract data structure, but relates to how Python code usually looks. We will often write code where we pop from a stack until it is empty, and we can write a loop that does this like

```
while not stack.is_empty():
    ...
```

However, most of Python's data structures will treat an empty structure as `False` and a non-empty structure as `True`, so people might expect to be able to write

```
while stack:
    ...
```

We can tell Python how it should interpret objects as Booleans by defining the method `__bool__()`, and for our stacks (and queues) we could define

```
def __bool__(self):
    return not self.is_empty()
```

We didn't bother with the previous data structures because we typically do not use them with `while` loops like this, but for stacks and queues it is the typical usage pattern, so here it makes sense.

What about the complexity of the operations? Since we are working with the end of the sequence, both the doubly linked lists and the `list` implementation have constant-time operations. If we had used the beginning of the sequence, then the operations would still be constant time for the doubly linked lists, but we would have linear-time operations for pushing and popping with the `list` implementation.

For the queue abstract data structure, we can also write a mixin aimed at extending sequences:

```
class EmptyQueue(Exception):
    pass

class QueueMixin(object):
    def enqueue(self, x):
        self.prepend(x)
```

```
    def front(self):
        try:
            return self.get_last()
        except IndexError:
            raise EmptyQueue()

    def dequeue(self):
        try:
            x = self.get_last()
            self.remove_last()
            return x
        except IndexError:
            raise EmptyQueue()

    def __bool__(self):
        return not self.is_empty()

class Queue(QueueMixin, DoublyLinkedListSequence):
    def is_empty(self):
        return self.first.next == self.last
```

I only created a queue class from a doubly linked list since we get constant-time operations here, but linear-time enqueue() operations with the list implementation. Here, it would be easier to extend the DoublyLinkedSequence class to get a queue, but I showed you this solution to get symmetry between stacks and queues.

As you can see, the two data structures are very similar (which is why I cover them in the same chapter), and they only differ in the order in which you get elements out once you have inserted them into the structure. A queue gives you a first-in first-out (FIFO) order, and stacks give you a last-in first-out (LIFO) order. But, perhaps not surprisingly, it makes a huge difference for how we use them and in which applications we need one rather than the other.

Exercise: There is a generalized queue called *dequeue* for a double-ended queue. It allows you to add, inspect, and remove elements at both ends of a queue. Write a mixin that adds operations for accessing the most recently added element.

Building Stacks and Queues from Scratch

Of course, if you didn't have the sequences in your code already, implementing them just to get a stack or a queue is overkill. They are easy to implement from scratch, so before we move to applications, let us try that.

A list already has the operations we need for a stack; they just have the wrong names. If you use the end of a list, as we did with the preceding mixin, pushing is called append(), popping is called pop() (the method takes an argument that specifies which element to remove and return, but without an argument, it is the last element in the list), and we can test if the list is empty by checking if its length is zero. So a trivial stack implementation is

```python
class Stack(object):
    def __init__(self):
        self.stack = []

    def push(self, x):
        self.stack.append(x)

    def top(self):
        try:
            return self.stack[-1]
        except IndexError:
            raise EmptyStack()

    def pop(self):
        try:
            return self.stack.pop()
        except IndexError:
            raise EmptyStack()

    def is_empty(self):
        return len(self.stack) == 0

    def __bool__(self):
        return not self.is_empty()
```

Unless you want to explore more than one stack implementation in your program, the easiest is to use the list class operations directly and not worry about the names they have. In practice, that is what you would do in 99.99% of the cases where you need a stack. But with the preceding class, we have a proper stack interface.

The problem with implementing a queue from a list is that we only have constant-time operations at the end of the list and not the beginning. But there is a trick you can use to turn such a data structure into a queue. You can use the same trick if you only have singly linked lists where you have constant-time operations at the beginning of a list and not elsewhere. The trick is to have two lists, one you add to and one you remove from. When you enqueue, you add it to one of the lists at the end that is efficient to access. When you access the front of the list or you dequeue an element, you work on the other list, at the end, that is efficient there. The only thing you have to do to make this work is to move elements from the queuing list to the dequeuing list whenever the latter is empty. When that happens, you take all the elements in the first list, reverse them, and put them in the other list. You reverse them, so you can access them from the efficient end:

```
class Queue(object):
    def __init__(self):
        self.front = []
        self.back = []

    def is_empty(self):
        return len(self.front) == 0 and \
                len(self.back) == 0

    def __bool__(self):
        return not self.is_empty()

    def enqueue(self, x):
        self.back.append(x)

    def move_list(self):
        if len(self.front) == 0:
            self.front = self.back
            self.front.reverse()
            self.back = []
```

```
def front(self):
    if self.is_empty():
        raise EmptyQueue()
    self.move_list()
    return self.front[-1]

def dequeue(self):
    if self.is_empty():
        raise EmptyQueue()
    self.move_list()
    return self.front.pop()
```

Operations that do not involve moving elements from one list to the other are obviously constant time—we are explicitly working at the ends of the lists where we have constant-time operations. The problematic part is when we need to copy and reverse a list. That takes linear time. However, we can analyze the running time like this: Whenever we need to reverse a list and it has n elements, it takes n operations; however, there can only be n elements in the list if we have enqueued n elements. If we pretend that each enqueue operation costs two "computations," then we use one "computation" for the constant-time enqueuing and put another in the bank. When we have to copy n elements, we have n computations in the bank to pay for it. Each operation is not constant time, but every time we have done n operations, we haven't used more than $2n$ computations. So amortized over all n operations, each takes constant time.

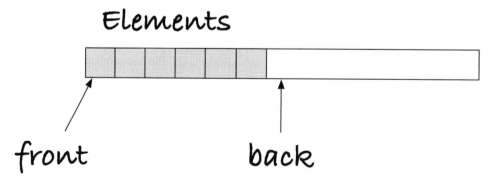

Figure 16-1. *Memory layout of a queue*

This isn't the only way to implement a queue, of course. It is just an elegant way, if all you have is a data structure that lets you access elements from one end only. Another way to do it, if you have something like a list with random access to elements (but where removing elements in the middle is costly), is to lay out the elements in contiguous memory like we do for lists and use two indices to identify the front and the back of the queue. It could look like the list in Figure 16-1. When you want to enqueue something, you put the element at index back and increment it. When you want the front element, it is at index front, and if you want to dequeue it, you increment that index.

A straightforward implementation could look like this:

```python
class Queue(object):
    def __init__(self, capacity = 10):
        self.data = [None] * capacity
        self.front_idx = 0
        self.back_idx = 0

    def is_empty(self):
        return self.front_idx == self.back_idx

    def __bool__(self):
        return not self.is_empty()

    def enqueue(self, x):
        self.data[self.back_idx] = x
        self.back_idx += 1

    def front(self):
        if self.is_empty(): raise EmptyQueue()
        return self.data[self.front_idx]

    def dequeue(self):
        val = self.front()
        self.front_idx += 1
        return val
```

The queue has a certain capacity that we set from the start, and that will of course be a problem. If we had infinite space to work with and never had to worry about wasting it, it would be a fine solution. But we don't. We will handle that in two steps.

First, let's consider what happens when the back of the queue reaches the end of the memory we have, but we dequeue elements, so there is free memory in the beginning of the list. We don't want to waste the memory at the front of the list; we can eventually run out of memory altogether if we do that. So we want to reuse it. There is a simple trick for that: when you update the indices, use modulo the size of the list. It works a bit like Pac-Man; when you reach the side of the screen, you continue from the left. When the back index reaches the size of the list, it doesn't get the size as its value; it gets zero, because *n*. We wrap the indices around, when we reach the end; see Figure 16-2. If you always wrap around when you reach the end, you can continue enqueuing elements as long as there is any free space to put them in.

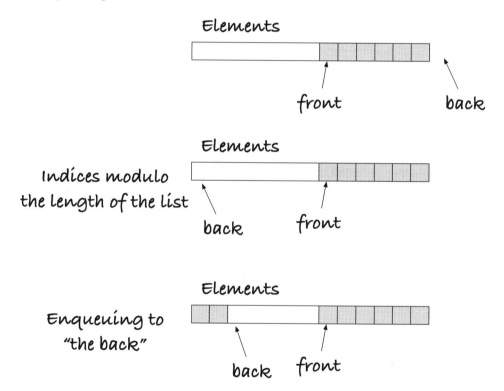

Figure 16-2. *Using index modulo the list size to wrap around*

To implement this, we only need a few changes to the implementation:

```python
class Queue(object):
    def __init__(self, capacity = 10):
        self.data = [None] * capacity
        self.used = 0
        self.front_idx = 0
```

```python
@property
def capacity(self):
    return len(self.data)

@property
def back_idx(self):
    return (self.front_idx + self.used) % self.capacity

def is_empty(self):
    return self.used == 0

def __bool__(self):
    return not self.is_empty()

def enqueue(self, x):
    self.data[self.back_idx] = x
    self.used += 1

def front(self):
    if self.is_empty(): raise EmptyQueue()
    return self.data[self.front_idx]

def dequeue(self):
    val = self.front()
    self.front_idx = (self.front_idx + 1) % self.capacity
    self.used -= 1
    return val
```

The main changes are the index updates, where we use % self.capacity to wrap them. I have used a property for the capacity, to make the code easier to read, but it is just the length of the underlying list. I have also added a self.used attribute to keep track of how many elements are in the list. When we wrap around like this, we cannot test if the list is empty by checking if the front and back point at the same element; that happens both when the list is empty and when it is filled to capacity. The self.used parameter helps us distinguish between the two cases.

Now that we have used, we can compute back_idx from it. We don't want to represent redundant information—we might update some information and forget the other—so instead of storing back_idx, we make it a computed property.

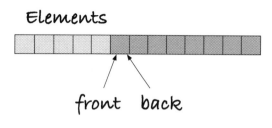

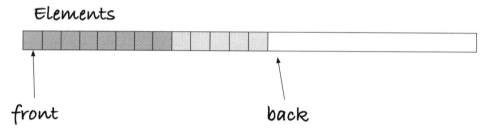

Figure 16-3. *Resizing a queue*

The self.used parameter will also help us with the last step of the solution. What happens when we want to enqueue to a list that is filled to capacity? Here, we must allocate a new list, just as when we append to a Python list that is filled to capacity. It is only slightly more complicated, because we need to keep the elements in order. But consider Figure 16-3. When we have filled the list, the elements at the front of the queue are those from the front index up to the end of the list, then wrapped around, and from the beginning of the list and up to the front index. We can copy them like that. Then we can use index zero as our updated front index and the number of elements as the updated back index and have space to the right of the back index for new elements. If we double the size every time we resize, the amortization argument we used for lists will work for our queue as well.

The full implementation looks like this:

```
class Queue(object):
    def __init__(self, capacity = 10):
        self.data = [None] * capacity
        self.used = 0
        self.front_idx = 0

    @property
    def capacity(self):
        return len(self.data)
```

```python
@property
def back_idx(self):
    return (self.front_idx + self.used) % self.capacity

def is_empty(self):
    return self.used == 0

def __bool__(self):
    return not self.is_empty()

def resize(self):
    self.data = self.data[self.front_idx:] + \
                self.data[:self.front_idx] + \
                [None] * self.used
    self.front_idx = 0

def enqueue(self, x):
    if self.used == self.capacity:
        self.resize()
    self.data[self.back_idx] = x
    self.used += 1

def front(self):
    if self.is_empty(): raise EmptyQueue()
    return self.data[self.front_idx]

def dequeue(self):
    val = self.front()
    self.front_idx = (self.front_idx + 1) % self.capacity
    self.used -= 1
    return val
```

Of course, you might also want to shrink the queue if there is too much free space. You can do that, for example, when it is only a quarter full. There is a bit more bookkeeping in copying the remaining elements, but it will be an interesting exercise for the eager student.

If you need to use a queue in your Python programs, you don't need to implement your own. In the module `collections`, the class `deque` gives you a double-ended queue. By definition of a deque, it is also a queue. Use the queue you get for free instead of building your own—but should you ever find yourself in a situation where you need a queue and don't have one, you now know how to implement one.

Expression Stacks and Stack Machines

When we develop algorithms, we think in terms of the RAM model, where our data is floating around in some memory space and where we can perform operations on it. This is a good mental model, but it is only valid as long as we don't think about where the low-level computations are done. Ignore memory hierarchies with several levels of caches and such; that is not where I am going. I mean, where are the really low-level computations done? Like adding two numbers? On a computer, it is in the CPUs (or in specialized cases GPUs) where this happens. When you want to add two numbers that you have in RAM, the computer first has to fetch them into the CPU, then it can do the computations, and, finally, it can put the result back to where you want it. It is the computations inside the CPU, at this low a level, that I am thinking of.

On all modern architectures, the CPU contains a number of so-called registers where you can store computer words and operate on them. To run a program, you need to specify in which registers your data go, which registers you use for input for your operations, and where the output goes. And not all registers are necessarily equal; some can be more efficient at some operations than others. It is a true nightmare, but programming languages abstract it away and deal with it for you. You are unlikely to ever need to manage this yourself, and if you end up needing it anyway, you need to read far beyond the topics of this book.

Registers and what a CPU does with them are not really what I want to talk about in this section either; rather, I want to talk about an alternative model for low-level computations called a *stack machine*. Here, all local memory is handled by a stack, and computations are done by popping operands off a stack and putting the result back. You can build stack machines in hardware, but people do not do it anymore; they did once, but no longer—register-based machines are faster. But stack machines are still very much alive, just implemented in software in *virtual machines*.

Many modern programming languages use a stack machine as their underlying computational model, including Python, if you use the CPython implementation (which you likely do as it is the default Python implementation). Naturally, software-based stack machines must run on register-based hardware, so in the end, everything runs on the register-based CPUs, but stack machines add a level of abstraction to a programming language. It is easier to translate high-level code down to a stack machine, and another program can then simulate the stack machine on hardware or translate the code the last step of the way.

There are several stacks in play in Python. We have already discussed the call stack for functions. The evaluation stack for low-level computations is another and separate one. And we will now build our own—for much simpler expressions than Python, admittedly. We will consider simple arithmetic expressions.

As I already mentioned, the idea behind a stack machine is that we push operands for an operation onto the stack and then evaluate the operation, which gets the operands from the stack and puts the result back on the stack. Take the expression 2 + 4 – 2. We have an addition, with operands 2 and 4, and then we subtract the result by 2 (we evaluate these operators left to right, so 2 + 4 – 2 always means (2 + 4) – 2, not that it matters in this case). To evaluate it on a stack, we would push 2 and then push 4, apply + that would pop 4 and 2, and put 2 + 4 back on the stack. Then we would push 2 onto the stack and apply –, which would take the two top elements and subtract one from the other. There is a notation for expressions that match the stack machine closely, called *postfix* or *reverse Polish* notation. In that notation, the same expression would be written 2 4 + 2 -. When you see a number, you push it on the stack; when you see an operator, you apply it to the stack's top elements. If you are old enough, you will remember that some calculators used this notation. The precursor for the PDF file format, PostScript, used this notation as well. They were stack machines, and reverse Polish notation is practically the programming language for stack machines.

In many ways, the notation is better than the arithmetic notation you are used to. It directly tells you how to calculate an expression without any confusion about operator precedence or the need for parentheses. The operator order gives you all the information you need. For example, the expression 2+5*6, which because of operator precedence we interpret as 2+(5*6), is 2 5 6 * + in reverse Polish notation. You explicitly multiply 5 and 6 before you add 2 to the result because * comes before +. If you want (2+5)*6, you write 2 5 + 6 *. The expression 1-2-3 is 1 2 - 3 -, while the expression 1-(2-3) is 1 2 3 - -. There is one thing that you cannot directly do with this notation, and that is to

use the same symbol, -, as both a unary and a binary operator. If you write 4 2 - ...,
does it mean that you want to do something with 4 -2 ..., or does it mean that you
want to do something with (4-2) ...? With this notation, you have to pick a symbol for
each version of -. I use ~ for unary minus and - for binary subtraction in my following
implementation.

I want us to write a function, calc(), that takes as input an expression in reverse
Polish notation and computes the result. To evaluate 1-2-3 we should call it with

calc(1, 2, '-', 3, '-')

For 1-(2-3) we should call it with

calc(1, 2, 3, '-', '-')

You can probably work out what you need to call it with for (2+5)*6. I will implement
it like this (where the ops table is explained in the following):

```python
class MalformedExpression(Exception):
    pass

def calc(*expressions):
    try:
        eval_stack = Stack()
        for expr in expressions:
            if expr in ops:
                ops[expr](eval_stack)
            else:
                eval_stack.push(expr)
        result = eval_stack.pop()
    except EmptyStack:
        raise MalformedExpression()

    if not eval_stack.is_empty():
        raise MalformedExpression()
    return result
```

The *expressions argument is there, so we can call calc() with expressions as in
the preceding. Otherwise, we would need to provide the expression as a list or tuple,
and this is (a little) easier. Once we have the expressions, we create a stack and run

through each expression in turn. I will make a table, ops, that contains the operators. If the expression is one of those, I get a function I have stored in the table and apply it. It will update the stack by popping its input and pushing its output. If it isn't an operator, I assume that it is a number, and I push it on the stack. Once I am through with the calculations, there should be one expression left on the stack—the result of evaluating the expression. If not, I throw an exception because something went wrong. If we unexpectedly hit an empty stack, I translate the EmptyStack exception into MalformedExpression, which is more relevant for evaluating expressions.

Exercise: Read the function carefully and make sure you understand what it is doing. The code is a little compact, but this is only because I have hidden some complexity in the functions I have in my ops table.

The functions we get from ops should handle both the stack—popping their input and pushing their output—and the arithmetic operations. We can implement some like this:

```python
def add(stack):
    b = stack.pop()
    a = stack.pop()
    stack.push(a + b)

def sub(stack):
    b = stack.pop()
    a = stack.pop()
    stack.push(a - b)

def mul(stack):
    b = stack.pop()
    a = stack.pop()
    stack.push(a * b)

def div(stack):
    b = stack.pop()
    a = stack.pop()
    stack.push(a / b)

def unary_minus(stack):
    a = stack.pop()
    stack.push(-a)
```

```
ops = {
    '+': add,
    '-': sub,
    '*': mul,
    '/': div,
    '~': unary_minus
}
```

Notice that, for the binary operators, we pop the second argument before the first. We push the first operand for an operation before we pop the second, so we need to get the numbers out in the opposite order.

Exercise: Try evaluating a few expressions in reverse Polish notation. For example, - ((2 + 3) * 2) in our traditional arithmetic notation translated into the stack machine operations would be calc(2, 3, '+', 2, '*', '~').

There is a lot of boilerplate code in these operations. If you only have to write a few functions with similar code, that is never a problem, but if you find yourself writing more of them, you enter the territory where you want to automate it. Even though it is a simple boilerplate code, you could make a mistake each time you write it. If all the operations work the same way, we should instead extract the code they share and write a more general function that we can parameterize with the code where they differ. That is not a problem; we know how to write a function that parameterizes a wrapper—we did it a lot in Chapter 7. We can write wrappers for binary and unary functions like this:

```
def binary_op(op):
    def wrap(stack):
        b = stack.pop()
        a = stack.pop()
        stack.push(op(a, b))
    return wrap

def unary_op(op):
    def wrap(stack):
        a = stack.pop()
        stack.push(op(a))
    return wrap
```

Then we can wrap our operators in one of these, explicitly

```
def add(a, b):
    return a + b
add = binary_op(add)
```

or using a decorator (which, as you recall, is just syntactic sugar for the same code as the explicit definition):

```
@binary_op
def sub(a, b):
    return a - b
```

Or, if we do not want to write functions for all the operators—since we already have them in the operator module as we saw in Chapter 7—we can write

```
import operator
mul = binary_op(operator.mul)
div = binary_op(operator.truediv)
unary_minus = unary_op(operator.neg)
```

This is where I would stop with generalizing the code. There is not much shared between the binary and unary operator wrappers, so although it isn't hard to write a function that handles an arbitrary number of arguments, we would probably end up with more code for the general solution than we have with two different wrappers. However— just for learning purposes—we could imagine that our stack machine allowed more complex operators with arbitrary numbers of arguments. Could we handle a general case like that? Of course, we can:

```
def operator(no_ops, func):
    def eval(stack):
        args = []
        for _ in range(no_ops):
            args.append(stack.pop())
        args.reverse()
        stack.push(func(*args))
    return eval
```

Exercise: Read this function just as carefully. It is not awfully complicated what it does, but it does it in few lines, and the result we get from calling it is an excellent abstraction from the raw functions we wrap.

Using operator we can try adding some list operations to our stack machine. We can add range() and make it a three-argument function. (The range() function isn't actually a list function but produces a range object that works as an iterator—not that it matters.) We cannot handle default arguments here, so we have to fix the number of parameters. If you call range() with three arguments, it is the from, to, and step size of the range. We can add list() as a unary operator to translate a range object into a list. And we can add a reversed operator that wraps the reversed() function. That function doesn't give us a reversed list—it gives us another object that works as an iterator—but we have the list operator to get a list back. Try running this code to see it in action:

```
ops['range'] = operator(3, range)
ops['list'] = operator(1, list)
ops['reversed'] = operator(1, reversed)

print(list(reversed(list(range(0, 10, 2)))))
print(calc(0, 10, 2, 'range', 'list', 'reversed', 'list'))
```

If we want to write our own functions as well, for example, to make list versions of range() and reversed(), we could do this:

```
def list_range(start, stop, step):
    return list(range(start, stop, step))
def list_reversed(x):
    return list(reversed(x))

ops['range'] = operator(3, list_range)
ops['reversed'] = operator(1, list_reversed)

print(calc(0, 10, 2, 'range', 'reversed'))
```

But here you might find that a decorator is a better solution. We cannot write decorators with two arguments; they are always called with the function we define below them, so we would need to write a curried version (see Chapter 7):

```
def operator(no_ops):
    def wrapper(func):
        def eval(stack):
```

```
            args = []
            for _ in range(no_ops):
                args.append(stack.pop())
            args.reverse()
            stack.push(func(*args))
        eval.__name__ = func.__name__
        return eval
    return wrapper

@operator(3)
def list_range(start, stop, step):
    return list(range(start, stop, step))
@operator(1)
def list_reversed(x):
    return list(reversed(x))
```

First, we tell the decorator how many arguments our operation needs; then we give it the function we wish to wrap. In the inner function, we give the inner-inner function the same name as the function we are wrapping to preserve the name we create using the decorator.

We can actually do a little better. We can get the number of arguments directly from the function, assuming that all arguments are positional and that we don't rely on default parameters (which our stack machine cannot handle anyway). We also saw how to do that in Chapter 7, and it is something we can extract from a function if we use the signature() function from the inspect module:

```
from inspect import signature
def number_of_arguments(f):
    return len(signature(f).parameters)

def operator(func):
    no_ops = number_of_arguments(func)
    def eval(stack):
        args = []
        for _ in range(no_ops):
            args.append(stack.pop())
        args.reverse()
```

```
        stack.push(func(*args))
    eval.__name__ = func.__name__
    return eval

@operator
def list_range(start, stop, step):
    return list(range(start, stop, step))

@operator
def list_reversed(x):
    return list(reversed(x))
```

But we are straying far from stack machines and into inner functions and decorators. Those are the Python features I would use to implement a stack machine, but you don't have to do it that way. All you need to know about stack machines is that we use a stack for computations; first, you push operands onto the stack, and then you apply an operator that gets them from there and pushes its result back to the stack. A program running on a stack machine is always in postfix or reverse Polish notation, so there is little to worry about in terms of syntax and language grammar. The program is executed one operation at a time, in a consistent manner.

So now you know how to write your own stack machine, and you can make it as simple or as complex as your heart desires. Every time you evaluate code in Python, a stack machine very similar to what we just implemented is doing the computations. The operators are often more complex, of course—there are operators for calling functions (using a separate stack) or creating classes—but the essentials are the same. And you can make your own stack machine as complicated as you want if you want.

Exercise: Write an operator, call, that calls a function. One approach could be to say that the top of the stack when you get the call operator must be a function, the next the number of arguments to call it with, and following that the arguments. It is not a trivial problem, but you should be able to implement this operator in fewer than ten lines of code once you have it figured out. After you have it, you should be able to evaluate expressions such as this:

```
def foo(x, y):
    return x - y

calc(5, 6, 2, foo, 'call')
```

Notice that this is different from the wrapper function we implemented earlier. There, we know at the time we make the operator how many parameters we need to call the wrapped function with. With the `call` operator, you need to get this information from the stack.

If you are curious about how Python uses an evaluation stack, you can get the stack code it uses to evaluate code from the `dis` module. If, for example, you run the code

```
def f(x, y):
    z = 3 * x + y
    return z / (x + y)

import dis
dis.dis(f)
```

you will see the code Python uses for the function `f()`. The code will print this list of instructions:

```
2        0 LOAD_CONST          1 (3)
         2 LOAD_FAST           0 (x)
         4 BINARY_MULTIPLY
         6 LOAD_FAST           1 (y)
         8 BINARY_ADD
        10 STORE_FAST          2 (z)

3       12 LOAD_FAST           2 (z)
        14 LOAD_FAST           0 (x)
        16 LOAD_FAST           1 (y)
        18 BINARY_ADD
        20 BINARY_TRUE_DIVIDE
        22 RETURN_VALUE
```

The LOAD_CONST operation pushes a constant on the stack. The LOAD_FAST pushes a local variable on the stack. So the first two operations push the constant 3 and the variable x on the stack. Then the operation BINARY_MULTIPLY multiplies them. That evaluates 3 * x. Then the code pushes y on the stack and adds the two top values, which gives us 3 * x + y on the top of the stack, which the STORE_FAST stores in the local variable z. That is the first statement in the function f().

Then we load z, x, and y onto the stack with the next three LOAD_FAST operations, add the two top values to give us x + y (so the stack now contains [z, x + y]), and then use BINARY_TRUE_DIV, which is the / operation. That leaves the stack as [z / (x + y)]. The RETURN_VALUE instruction returns the top of the stack.

To run a Python program, you need more complex operations than arithmetic, of course. There are operations for calling functions or creating functions and classes and such. But as you can probably see from this simple example, the underlying mechanism in Python is the same as what we just developed ourselves.

Quick Sort and the Call Stack

In Chapter 9 we implemented the *quick sort* algorithm, and the code looked like this:

```python
def partition(x, i, j):
    pivot = x[i]
    k, h = i + 1, j - 1
    while k <= h:
        if x[k] <= pivot:
            k += 1
        elif x[k] > pivot:
            x[k], x[h] = x[h], x[k]
            h -= 1
    x[i], x[k - 1] = x[k - 1], x[i]
    return k - 1

def qsort_rec(x, i, j):
    if j - i <= 1:
        return
    k = partition(x, i, j)
    qsort_rec(x, i, k)
    qsort_rec(x, k + 1, j)

def qsort(x):
    qsort_rec(x, 0, len(x))
```

I told you in Chapter 8 that function calls involve a stack, where we put local variables, and that recursion is only possible because of this stack. In this section, I want us to implement the quick sort algorithm using an explicit stack. We won't use a stack for calling the partition() function (and we won't use a stack for evaluating any of the arithmetic operations), but for all the recursive calls, we will push and pop function parameters.

Take a look at the recursive function qsort_rec(). It takes three parameters, x, i, and j, so those are the parameters we need to know when we handle a stack frame. Since x is constant, we can leave it out if we handle the algorithm in a function that already has a reference to it, and that is what we will do. That means that our stack will hold intervals represented as (i,j) pairs. In the first recursive call, in qsort(), we call qsort_rec() with i=0 and j=len(x), which means that the first stack frame we push is (0,len(x)). Then, each time we would have a recursive call, we instead get an interval from the stack, and if it isn't empty (in which case we wouldn't call recursively), we partition the interval and push the two smaller intervals onto the stack:

```
def qsort(x):
    stack = Stack()

    # qsort_rec(x, 0, len(x))
    stack.push((0, len(x)))

    while stack:
        # qsort_rec(i, j)
        i, j = stack.pop()

        if j - i <= 1:
            # leave loop body to go to the
            # next stack frame
            continue

        k = partition(x, i, j)
        # qsort_rec(x, i, k)
        stack.push((i, k))
        # qsort_rec(x, k + 1, j)
        stack.push((k + 1, j))
```

There you are, an almost trivial translation from a recursive function to an iterative function with an explicit stack. I don't want to leave you with the impression that replacing a call stack with an explicit stack is always this simple, and in the next two sections, we will see why. But usually, as long as you don't need the return value of a recursive call, translating a recursive solution to one with an explicit stack is relatively easy.

Writing an Iterator for a Search Tree

In Chapter 14 we defined search trees as nodes with a left and a right child:

```
class Node(object):
    def __init__(self, value,
                 left = None,
                 right = None):
        self.value = value
        self.left = left
        self.right = right

    def __repr__(self):
        return 'Node({}, left = {}, right = {})'.format(
            repr(self.value),
            repr(self.left),
            repr(self.right)
        )
```

For all nodes, we have the invariant that the left tree has smaller values than the one in the node and the right tree has larger values. We also wrote a generator for iterating through a tree, giving us the values in increasing order:

```
def tree_iter(node):
    if node is None: return
    yield from tree_iter(node.left)
    yield node.value
    yield from tree_iter(node.right)
```

Now, we will implement our own iterator class to do this. It is, of course, not as simple as a generator—there is a good reason why the language gives us generators—but with this approach, we avoid recursive calls. And if you find yourself someday in a language that doesn't have generators—most languages do not—then you can always use the new approach.

First, recall from Chapter 13 that a class implements Python's iterator interface if it defines the two methods __iter__() and __next__(), where __next__() must raise the exception StopIteration when there are no more elements to iterate through. Before we get to the good stuff, we can set up the boilerplate code for an iterator:

```
class TreeIterator(object):
    def __init__(self, tree):
        self.tree = tree
    def __iter__(self):
        return self
    def __next__(self):
        raise StopIteration()
```

The __iter__() method should return an iterator, and when we already have an iterator, that is practically always self. The __next__() method here says that we are already done.

A recursive generator doesn't work exactly like a recursive function, but we can attempt to translate the tree_iter() function into one with a stack the same way as we did for qsort(). The recursive calls mean pushing a frame on the stack, and we have a loop that takes the top stack frame and handles it. If we need to yield a value, we can return it because the stack remembers what we have to do the next time we call the method:

```
def __next__(self):
    while self.stack:
        node = self.stack.pop()
        if node is None:
            continue # return to next stack frame
        self.stack.push(node.left)
        return node.value
        self.stack.push(node.right)
    raise StopIteration()
```

This almost works, but if you run it, you will notice that right children are lost. If you study the method, you should see why: we return before we put the right child on the stack. Doing something after we `yield` works for generators because a generator continues from where you `yield`'ed, but it won't work when you `return`. The statements after `return` are never executed. We have to put the right child on the stack before we return:

```
def __next__(self):
    while self.stack:
        node = self.stack.pop()
        if node is None:
            continue # return to next stack frame
        self.stack.push(node.left)
        self.stack.push(node.right)
        return node.value
    raise StopIteration()
```

This doesn't work either. We get all the values, but we don't get them in the right order. We have to return the value in the node before we call recursively on the right node while also pushing the right child onto the stack before we return.

Okay, then what about this: We don't return the value in a node as soon as we see the node. We can push its left child on the stack, then its value, and then the right child. That way, the left child is handled first, then the value, and then the right child, which sounds like what we want. Since we assume that we get nodes from the stack and values aren't nodes, we need to distinguish between the two. Not to worry, we can check the type of the element we get from the stack. If it is a node, we treat it as such; otherwise, we consider it a value that we should return. You are not in danger of having nodes as values in any case because there is no order to nodes, so they cannot go into a search tree in the first place. The same goes for None that we use as leaves. Those cannot be values in a search tree either, since None is not ordered:

```
def __next__(self):
    while self.stack:
        x = self.stack.pop()
    if x is None:
        # if x is none, it is a leaf
        continue # return to next stack frame
```

```
    if type(x) is Node:
        self.stack.push(x.left)
        self.stack.push(x.value)
        self.stack.push(x.right)
    else:
        return x
raise StopIteration()
```

With high hopes, we run the iterator, and to our shock, we find that we now get the values in reverse order. Why are the gods punishing us? When we run the recursive function, we first call on the left—and here we push the left node—and then in the function, we *return from the left* before we take the next step. That is *not* what we are doing now. In recursive functions, when we call recursively, we always complete the recursive call before we call again, but with our stack, we push both recursive calls onto the stack. First, we push the left tree, then the value, and then the right tree. When we pop from the stack in the next iterator, we thus get the right tree first. Not to worry, we can just flip left and right:

```
def __next__(self):
    while self.stack:
        x = self.stack.pop()
        if x is None:
            continue # return to next stack frame
        if type(x) is Node:
            self.stack.push(x.right)
            self.stack.push(x.value)
            self.stack.push(x.left)
        else:
            return x
    raise StopIteration()
```

We had the same situation with qsort; we just didn't notice it there because the order in which we sort intervals doesn't matter. If the order of recursive calls does matter, a direct translation from recursive calls to a stack will give you the wrong order. You need to flip the calls to get the right push order.

Will this approach always work? Of course not. Programs and function calls are more complex, and there is one more thing that we haven't considered, and in the next section, we have to do that.

Merge Sort with an Explicit Stack

The *merge sort* algorithm, also from Chapter 9, splits a list into two halves, sorts them recursively, and then merges them:

```python
def merge(x, y):
    i, n = 0, len(x)
    j, m = 0, len(y)
    z = []
    while i < n and j < m:
        if x[i] <= y[j]:
            z.append(x[i])
            i += 1
        else:
            z.append(y[j])
            j += 1
    if i < n:
        assert j == m
        z.extend(x[i:])
    if j < m:
        assert i == n
        z.extend(y[j:])
    return z

def merge_sort_rec(x, low, high):
    if high - low <= 1: return x[low:high]
    mid = (low + high) // 2
    left = merge_sort_rec(x, low, mid)
    right = merge_sort_rec(x, mid, high)
    return merge(left, right)

def merge_sort(x):
    return merge_sort_rec(x, 0, len(x))
```

As for quick sort, the order of the recursive calls does not matter for merge sort, but we get values back from the recursive calls, and we need to merge those values. That is different from quick sort, where we were done as soon as we had made the recursive call.

Simply pushing and popping stack frames won't help us here; we need to deal with the return values of functions because we need those as input for other functions. We could put return values and function parameters on the stack, and that is what the underlying hardware does on your computer. Still, there is a lot of bookkeeping in managing where temporary variables and such go, so we don't want to go there. We already have an easier way to do it—the stack machine we saw earlier in the chapter. We can use one stack for function calls and one for computing (which, incidentally, is what Python does).

When we want to call a function, we put the function on the call stack and its arguments on the evaluation stack. When it is done, its return value will lie on the stack. Easy-peasy. Well, until you try it. It is not a bad idea at all, and as I said, Python does exactly this. Still, if we try to schedule both a left-hand- and a right-hand-side recursive call and a merge by pushing all three functions onto the stack, we will get the return value from the left call on the top of the stack when we call the right-hand side, which is not what we want. We really do need to finish the calculations on the left before we can call on the right. Somehow, we have to split the last three lines in merge_sort_rec() into separate operations that are evaluated in order, such that the first is done before we push the next onto the stack. On a real call stack, you need to have the return point into a function, so you can jump to the right place after a function call. We need the same thing here.

We cannot jump to arbitrary places in a function. With sufficiently many if statements, we could set it up, but such code is close to unreadable and would be a gigantic source of errors. Instead, we can split the function into different operations. We can write one function that handles the code up to the first recursive call, then another that handles the second recursive call, and, lastly, a function that handles the merge.

Since we have to push and pop multiple values when we have function calls, we will add two convenience functions for that:

```
def pop(stack, n):
    vals = []
    for _ in range(n):
        vals.append(stack.pop())
    vals.reverse()
    return vals
```

```
def push(stack, *args):
    for arg in args:
        stack.push(arg)
```

Merge is easy to implement with the stack machine. It takes two arguments, it doesn't call any functions, and it pushes a merged list:

```
def merge(eval_stack, call_stack):
    x, y = pop(eval_stack, 2)

    i, n = 0, len(x)
    j, m = 0, len(y)
    z = []
    while i < n and j < m:
        if x[i] <= y[j]:
            z.append(x[i])
            i += 1
        else:
            z.append(y[j])
            j += 1
    if i < n:
        assert j == m
        z.extend(x[i:])
    if j < m:
        assert i == n
        z.extend(y[j:])

    push(eval_stack, z)
```

The merge_sort() wrapper function is equally simple—it pushes the first arguments on the evaluation stack and pushes the recursive function on the call stack:

```
def merge_sort(x):
    eval_stack = Stack()
    call_stack = Stack()

    # First function call: merge_sort_rec(x, 0, len(x))
    push(eval_stack, x, 0, len(x))
    call_stack.push(merge_sort_rec)
```

```
    # Handle all function calls until we are done
    while call_stack:
        call = call_stack.pop()
        call(eval_stack, call_stack)
    return eval_stack.pop()
```

The recursive merge sort, split into two functions, will look like this:

```
def merge_sort_rec(eval_stack, call_stack):
    x, low, high = pop(eval_stack, 3)

    if high - low <= 1:
        eval_stack.push(x[low:high])
    else:
        mid = (low + high) // 2

        #right = merge_sort_rec(x, mid, high)
        push(eval_stack, x, mid, high)
        call_stack.push(merge_sort_right)

        #left = merge_sort_rec(x, low, mid)
        push(eval_stack, x, low, mid)
        call_stack.push(merge_sort_rec)

def merge_sort_right(eval_stack, call_stack):
    x, low, high, left = pop(eval_stack, 4)

    # save left for merge but call merge sort
    # with the interval
    push(eval_stack, left, x, low, high)

    # first call recursively, then merge
    call_stack.push(merge)
    call_stack.push(merge_sort_rec)
```

The first function handles the code down to the first recursive call in the original. It figures out the subintervals and finishes the recursion if it can; then if recursion is necessary, it pushes the arguments for both left and right calls onto the stack. It doesn't push the same function for left and right recursions, though. First, it pushes the right interval and the function that handles the last recursion, and then it pushes the left interval and itself for a recursive call. The recursive call is pushed last, so it is evaluated first. Once that left-hand side is handled, the resulting list is at the top of the evaluation stack, and the merge_sort_right() function is at the top of the call stack. When called, merge_sort_right() fetches the left-hand side's result and the arguments for the right recursive call. It pushes the result of the left sort to the stack to save it for the following merge and then pushes merge() on the stack because we want to call merge once the second recursive call is done. Finally, it pushes its interval onto the evaluation stack and calls merge_sort_rec() by pushing the function on the call stack.

This is very close to how an actual call stack works. The main difference is that we push a function on the stack that we want to call after a computation when we push merge_sort_right() in merge_sort_rec() and when we push merge() in merge_sort_right(). A function call always returns us to the place where we called a function when it returns with a real call stack. That is not something you will ever want to program yourself. You cannot do it without littering your code with if statements that check a return value if you want to do it in Python, and I am not aware of any high-level language that will support such behavior. You can, however, always take the approach of providing a function that handles the remaining computation of your code and splitting a function into multiple parts the way we split merge_sort_rec() into two. That "return" function would be a *continuation* (see Chapter 8), so we would, in effect, be indirectly implementing continuations. Depending on your preferences, you might find functional continuations easier or harder to read than a computation split over several functions you have to call back to, but the idea is the same. We don't need a stack when we use continuations, but we build up functions that serve the same purpose. In one case, we build up a collection of inner functions for handling returning; in the other, we do the same thing with a stack containing the functions. In practice, we are doing the same thing.

In any case, now you know how you can use an explicit stack (possibly with an evaluation stack as well) to implement your own call stack. This is very rarely necessary, but there are occasions where recursion depth is an issue, and in those cases, using an explicit stack will usually solve the problem. If you don't have generators—and in most languages, you don't—then the stack we used to build a tree iterator is the way to go.

Breadth-First Tree Traversal and Queues

Now queues are essential for many applications involving concurrent processes communicating or for handling interactive applications, neither of which we will examine in this book. Still, for algorithmic programming, you use them less than stacks, so I will only give you one example in this chapter. They do pop up again in Chapter 17, though.

A frequent use of queues is when you need to search a tree breadth first. The most frequent traversal of a tree is *depth first* or *post-order*, where you explore a node's children before you examine the node itself. If you first look at the node itself, then the left subtree, and then the right subtree, it is called *pre-order*. In the iterator we wrote for a search tree, we went *in-order*, which means that we first went down the left child, then handled the node, and then went down the right child. All three of these traversal orders are easily implemented with recursion or with an explicit stack. *Breadth-first order*, however, requires a queue.

A breadth-first order traversal first handles a node, then its children, then all its grandchildren, and so forth. You handle all nodes at the same distance from the root before you handle any of the nodes that are further down the tree. In Figure 16-4 I have illustrated in-order and breadth-first order. With in-order traversal, we first go all the way down to the leftmost child of the tree and report the value there. Then we go up to that child's parent, report its value, and then go down the parent's right-hand tree. As we continue traversing, we always handle all nodes in a left tree before we report the value in a node, and then we report all the values in the right tree. As an exercise, you can try to draw a post- and a pre-order traversal, that is, traversals where you always report the right or left subtree before you report the value in a node. On the right in Figure 16-4, I have illustrated the breadth-first order. First, we handle the root, then its immediate children, and after that the grandchildren, and we continue downward, but we never handle a node deeper in the tree than one we haven't handled yet.

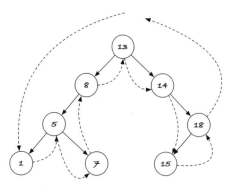
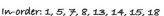
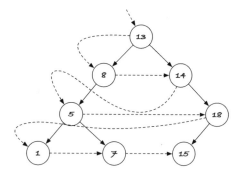

In-order: 1, 5, 7, 8, 13, 14, 15, 18   Breadth-first order: 13, 8, 14, 5, 18, 1, 7, 15

Figure 16-4. *In-order and breadth-first tree traversal*

We get this traversal order if we put the nodes in a queue, and each time we get a node from the queue and process it, we put its children at the end of the queue. If we start with the root, the queue order guarantees that the root's children will come before their children, and when the left child puts its children into the queue, the right child is in front of them. The right child will put its children into the queue as well and do this before the left child's children add their children. Using our queue, we can implement a breadth-first traversal as simple as this:

```
def breath_first(tree):
    queue = Queue()
    queue.enqueue(tree)
    while not queue.is_empty():
        node = queue.dequeue()
        if node is not None:
            print("handling node", node.value)
        queue.enqueue(node.left)
        queue.enqueue(node.right)
```

CHAPTER 17

Priority Queues

A *priority queue* is an abstract data structure that provides the following operations:

- You can add elements to it.

- We can test if it is empty.

- You can get the smallest element in the heap.

- You can remove the smallest element in the heap.

The operations are not hard to implement. Here is a version that uses Python's `list` class:

```python
class PriorityQueue(object):
    def __init__(self, seq = ()):
        self.list = list(seq)

    def is_empty(self):
        return len(self.list) == 0

    def __bool__(self):
        return not self.is_empty()

    def add(self, x):
        self.list.append(x)

    def get_min(self):
        return min(self.list)

    def delete_min(self):
        x = self.get_min()
        self.list.remove(x)
        return x
```

© Thomas Mailund 2021
T. Mailund, *Introduction to Computational Thinking*, https://doi.org/10.1007/978-1-4842-7077-6_17

As for sets, I have added a constructor to the interface that lets us create a priority queue from a sequence. With the `list` implementation, this is something that happens in linear time. The `is_empty()` and `add()` functions run in constant time, and `get_min()` and `delete_min()` run in linear time. This chapter aims to reduce the linear-time operations to logarithmic time (but it will increase the `add()` operation time to logarithmic as well).

Just as we can implement sets with search trees, there is a tree structure, called a *heap*, that we can use to implement priority queues. The *heap property* is an invariant on values in a tree's nodes, just like the search tree invariant that says that values to the left should be smaller than the value in a node and values to the right should be greater. For heaps, the property is that the value in a node should be smaller than the value in both of the node's children. We will use this property in different variations to implement the priority queue abstract data structure.

However, before we start with that, I want to show you yet another sorting algorithm, *heap sort*. The name refers to the heap data structure, but as you can see in the following, you can implement it with any priority queue data structure. If you have the operations in a priority queue and you want to sort a list, you can put all the elements into the heap and repeatedly remove the smallest and put it in the sorted list:

```
def heapsort(x):
    heap = PriorityQueue(x)
    out = []
    while heap:
        out.append(heap.delete_min())
    return out
```

The running time depends on how fast we can get the elements into the heap and how fast we can get the smallest element out again. For the `list` heap, the first is linear time, and the second is quadratic because we have to perform the linear-time `delete_min()` operation n times. If we can keep the heap construction time under $O(n \log n)$ and get logarithmic `delete_min()`, then we would have an optimal $O(n \log n)$ sorting algorithm. Since it is theoretically impossible for a comparison-based sort to run faster than $O(n \log n)$, the heap sort algorithm tells us something about the trade-offs we must necessarily consider when implementing a priority queue. If we can construct a priority queue in $O(n)$, we cannot also delete the smallest element in constant time—that would give us a comparison-based sorting algorithm that runs in linear time. If we can delete the minimal element in constant time, then the construction must take at least $O(n \log n)$ time. We will go for linear construction time and logarithmic deletion. Let's get to it!

Exercise: In a search tree, you can find the smallest element by searching leftward until you can go no further. Implement get_min() that way. This takes time in $O(\log n)$ if you keep the tree balanced. You can also delete elements in logarithmic time, so delete_min() will also run in $O(\log n)$. Implement that. We already have an insertion in logarithmic time, so add() is already there. If you remember the smallest value in the class that wraps the search tree, you can get get_min() down to constant time. Implement this.

Exercise: Unlike with sets, which is where we used our search trees, heaps can contain the same element twice. The code we wrote earlier for search trees assumes that each element is only found once in the tree, but you can handle multiple copies. When inserting, you can treat the same value as if it was smaller (or larger) and insert at that point as usual. When you delete, you can continue as usual—you find the first occurrence of the value when you search down, and then you delete it. If there are other occurrences of the same value, they remain in the tree. Modify your search tree to handle multiple copies of the same value.

Using a search tree, we get the operations in the running time we need for heap sort. The following sections' goal is to see other approaches to implementing heaps, some with the same asymptotic running time as with a search tree—but often faster or with additional operations—and one that improves asymptotically on the running time of insertions.

A Tree Representation for a Heap

As I briefly mentioned in the preceding, we can implement priority queues as trees with the so-called heap property. In the simplest form, we will represent heaps as binary trees, very similar to search trees:

```
class Node(object):
    def __init__(self, value, left = None, right = None):
        self.value = value
        self.left = left
        self.right = right
```

```
def __repr__(self):
    return 'Node({}, {}, {})'.format(
        repr(self.value),
        repr(self.left),
        repr(self.right)
    )
```

The invariant for these heap trees is different from search trees. For heaps, we do not require that the children in the left/right trees are smaller/larger than the value in the node itself. Instead, we require that the node's value is smaller than all the values in its two children. The tree in Figure 17-1 is an example of a tree in this "heap order."

Two of the operations are trivial from this representation. We can check is_empty() by checking if the root of the heap tree is None, and get_min() can return the value in the root (if it is not empty):

```
def is_empty(heap):
    return heap is None
```

```
def get_min(heap):
    return heap.value
```

The other two operations will be based on a fifth operation, merge(), that, as the name suggests, merges two heaps into one. If we can merge two heaps, we can handle insertion by creating a singleton heap for the first element and then merge it into the heap:

```
def add(heap, x):
    return merge(heap, Node(x))
```

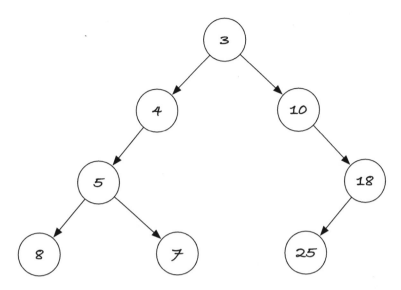

Figure 17-1. *A heap-ordered binary tree*

We can delete the smallest element by merging the two children of the root and leave out the root value in the result:

```
def delete_min(heap):
    return heap.value, merge(heap.left, heap.right)
```

This delete_min() function returns both the minimal values and the updated tree. In the class interface, we only returned the minimal value, but we can do that if we remember the updated heap in an object attribute. So, in a class that wraps functions that operate on trees, the way we have dealt with persistent data structures earlier, we could write

```
class Heap(object):
    # ... other methods ...
    def delete_min(self):
        res, self.heap = delete_min(self.heap)
        return res
```

See in the following.

These two operations obviously run in the same time as the merge() operation, whatever that may be. A straightforward merge is similar to how we merge lists. We look at the top of the two heaps, and if one is empty, we return the other. Otherwise, we want a heap that has the smallest element in its root, so we compare the roots of the two heaps—the smallest element in the two should be at the root, and we pick this value for our new root. The heap that doesn't have the smallest value can go into any subtree. Its values must all be smaller than the one in the new root. We merge into either of the children of the other. It doesn't matter which subtree since only the heap order matters:

```
def merge(x, y):
    if x is None: return y
    if y is None: return x
    if x.value < y.value:
        return Node(x.value, x.left, merge(x.right, y))
    else:
        return Node(y.value, y.left, merge(y.right, x))
```

What is the complexity of merge() (and add() and delete_min())? The way we have implemented it, the running time is proportional to the depth of the two heaps, and unless we do something to balance them, this can be $O(n)$. This is better than for a search tree heap, where merging means that we have to insert all elements from one tree into the other, which would take time $O(n \log n)$. If the heaps are balanced, on the other hand, the depth is $O(\log n)$, so we should balance them, and we will do this in the next section. Before we go there, though, let us, just for completeness, wrap our functions in a class that implements the heap interface:

```
def node_iter(node):
    if node is None:
        return
    yield node.value
    yield from node_iter(node.left)
    yield from node_iter(node.right)

class Heap(object):
    def __init__(self, seq = ()):
        self.heap = None
        for x in seq:
            self.add(x)

    def is_empty(self):
        return is_empty(self.heap)
```

```
def __bool__(self):
    return not self.is_empty()

def add(self, x):
    self.heap = add(self.heap, x)

def get_min(self):
    return get_min(self.heap)

def delete_min(self):
    res, self.heap = delete_min(self.heap)
    return res

def __repr__(self):
    return 'Heap(' + repr(list(node_iter(self.heap))) + ')'
```

Leftist Heaps

If we can balance the heap, then merge() will run in time $O(\log n)$, since that is the depth of a balanced tree. We cannot implement a faster merge() since we can both build a heap in time n times the time it takes to merge heaps—by repeatedly calling add() n times—and we can delete the smallest element in the same time by repeatedly calling delete_min(). That would give us a heapsort() faster than $O(n \log n)$, which we know to be impossible.

So how do we balance a heap? There are several approaches, and a particularly simple one is called *leftist heaps*. We define the *right spine* of a heap as the nodes we will see if we always follow the right subtree down to an empty node. If you recall the get_rightmost() function we implemented for search trees in Chapter 14, it would be the nodes it would traverse. We associate a *rank* for each node, which is the length of the right spine for that node. For a leftist heap, we require the invariant that the left sub-heap of a node always has a rank higher than or equal to the right sub-heap. This doesn't make the heap balanced as such—it will be "left-heavy" because there will potentially be more nodes in left trees than in right trees—but we will only operate on right trees when merging, so that is fine.

Consider now a heap with n elements and how many possible right steps we could take. We notice that if we move to the right subtree, we have eliminated at least half of them—the rank of the left sub-heap is larger than the rank of the right heap, so at least half of the possible right moves are in the left tree that we just avoided. If we can eliminate half of the possible right moves each time we move right—and the total possible number of right steps cannot be larger than n in a heap with n elements—then we cannot make more than $O(\log n)$ right steps in total. If we always merge into the right trees, we cannot go deeper than $O(\log n)$ nodes, and so the merge runs in $O(\log n)$. If we can uphold the leftist invariant while we merge, we have a logarithmic-time merge.

If we always merge down the right spine (as we did in the preceding), we can merge as usual without worrying about the leftist invariant as we go down the invariant. We might end up invalidating the invariant in the merge, but as we return from the recursion, we can flip left and right trees to restore it.

First, add the rank to nodes, so we have immediate access to it. If you want, you could also return it with each recursive call to merge, but it is easier to remember it in the nodes:

```
def rank(node):
    if node is None:
        return 0
    else:
        return node.rank
```

```
class Node(object):
    def __init__(self, value, left = None, right = None):
        self.value = value
        self.left = left
        self.right = right
        self.rank = rank(right) + 1
```

The merge function doesn't change much; we just add a call to restore() that is responsible for restoring the invariant:

```
def merge(x, y):
    if x is None: return y
    if y is None: return x
    if x.value < y.value:
        return restore(x.value, x.left, merge(x.right, y))
    else:
        return restore(y.value, y.left, merge(y.right, x))
```

The restore function flips the children if necessary:

```
def restore(value, left, right):
    if rank(left) < rank(right):
        left, right = right, left
    return Node(value, left, right)
```

The implementation gives you a persistent data structure. In the merge, we build new heaps rather than modifying existing nodes. This is, by far, the easiest way to merge heaps, and getting a persistent data structure is just icing on the cake.

With a logarithmic merge, we immediately can construct a heap in $O(n \log n)$ time, but I promised you that we could do it in linear time. How do we do that? The trick is mostly in the time analysis; the approach is this:

Start by creating singleton heaps (heaps with a single element) out of all your data values. Then you merge them together, but not by merging a singleton into an ever-growing heap. Rather, you merge heaps of similar size. First, you merge all the singletons by pairs, leaving half as many doubletons. Then you merge the doubletons into heaps with four elements. You continue this way until you have one single heap remaining, containing all your elements.

We need the queue data structure we built in Chapter 16 to merge heaps in order according to size. We put all the singletons into the queue, and then we iteratively dequeue two heaps and push the merged heap:

```
def build_heap(seq):
    queue = Queue()

    for x in seq:
        queue.enqueue(Node(x))

    while queue:
        first = queue.dequeue()
        if queue.is_empty():
            # done
            return first
        second = queue.dequeue()
        queue.enqueue(merge(first, second))

    # We can only get here if seq was empty; in that
    # case we want the empty heap, which is None
    return None
```

You can put it in the constructor of the Heap class:

```
class Heap(object):
    def __init__(self, seq = ()):
        self.heap = build_heap(seq)
```

So why does this run in $O(n)$? Consider the "levels" where we merge heaps. The first level is n heaps of size one. Then $n/2$ heaps of size 2, then $n/4$ of size 4, then $n/8$ of size 8, and so on. When we handle level i, we merge $n/2^i$ heaps of size 2^i—each in time $O(\log_2 2^i) = O(i)$. So the total work per level is $O(n \cdot i/2^i)$, and we must sum over all levels $O\left(n \cdot \sum_{i=1}^{\log n} i/2^i\right)$. The sum $\sum_{i=1}^{\infty} i \cdot 2^{-i}$ converges, leaving us the running time $O(n)$.

To see that the sum converges, we need a tiny bit of calculus. Let $f(x) = \sum_{i=0}^{\infty} x^i = 1/(1-x)$ for $|x| < 1$. (We saw why this equation holds in Chapter 9, and it is a matter of letting n go to infinity in the sum $(1-x)\sum_{i=0}^{n} x^i$). Now calculate the derivative of $f(x)$ both as $1/(1-x)$ and term by term in the sum: $f'(x) = 1/(1-x)^2 = \sum_{i=0}^{\infty} ix^{i-1}$. The first term of the sum is zero, so we can start at one, $\sum_{i=1}^{\infty} ix^{i-1}$, and let $j = i + 1$ to get $\sum_{j=0}^{\infty} (j+1)x^j$, which, since the name of a variable doesn't matter, is also $\sum_{i=0}^{\infty} (i+1)x^i$. We can rearrange this sum to get $\sum_{i=0}^{\infty} ix^i + \sum_{i=0}^{\infty} x^i = \sum_{i=0}^{\infty} ix^i + f(x)$. From this, we get that $\sum_{i=0}^{\infty} ix^i = f'(x) - f(x)$ (for $|x| < 1$). Insert $x = 1/2$, and we get $\sum_{i=0}^{\infty} \frac{i}{2^i} = \frac{1}{(1-1/2)^2} - \frac{1}{1-1/2} = 4 - 2 = 2$. The sum $\sum_{i=1}^{\infty} i \cdot 2^{-i}$ is therefore 2 (which we can agree is a constant).

Exercise: Decide on appropriate exceptions for the heap operations and add them to the leftist heap.

You can implement a lazy form of leftist queues with the same performance, although amortized, where you up front merge in constant time and thus insert in constant time as well. It is not a free lunch, though; you do the same work in the long run, but you delay the work you have to do for merging and inserting until you need to run get_min() or delete_min(). There you have to make up for your laziness.

The idea is this—when you merge two heaps, you create a dummy node that you mark as "dead" and put the two heaps as children for the node:

```
class Node(object):
    def __init__(self, value, left = None, right = None,
```

```
                dead = False):
        self.value = value
        self.left = left
        self.right = right
        self.rank = rank(right) + 1
        self.dead = dead

def lazy_merge(x, y):
    if x is None:
        return y
    if y is None:
        return x
    if rank(x) < rank(y):
        x, y = y, x
    return Node(None, x, y, dead = True)

def add(heap, x):
    return lazy_merge(heap, Node(x))
```

This leaves you some dead nodes proportional to how many nodes you have inserted, and when you need the smallest element in the heap, you might have a dead node at the top. At this point, you need to get rid of all the dead nodes, so you can run through the heap and get them. They are sitting at the top of the heap, so do a traversal of the tree and collect the trees that are not dead. Such a traversal takes time proportional to the tree, but since you only traverse dead nodes, that means it is linear in the number of insertions you have made:

```
def collect_real_heaps(heap, queue):
    if heap is None:
        return
    if not heap.dead:
        queue.enqueue(heap)
    else:
        collect_real_heaps(heap.left, queue)
        collect_real_heaps(heap.right, queue)
```

After you have collected them, build a new heap from them using the "non-lazy" merge():

```
def fix_dead_heaps(heap):
    queue = Queue()
    collect_real_heaps(heap, queue)
    while queue:
        first = queue.dequeue()
        if queue.is_empty():
            # done
            return first
        second = queue.dequeue()
        queue.enqueue(merge(first, second))
```

This looks much like the build_heap() function, but it doesn't run in the same complexity. We start with a collection of t trees that already contains nodes that can be proportional to n, and since we need to merge them, the time is $O(t \log n)$. This can be paid for by pretending that each insertion took a loan of $O(\log n)$ computations that we now have to pay back, so we end with the same complexity as before, only we always pay for deletions and never for insertions (where we just take a loan). When you build a heap from scratch, you should still use build_heap(). If you use lazy merging and pay for it when you access a minimal element, you end up with $O(n \log n)$.

We use fix_dead_heaps() in get_min() and delete_min():

```
def get_min(heap):
    heap = fix_dead_heaps(heap)
    return heap.min, heap
```

```
def delete_min(heap):
    heap = fix_dead_heaps(heap)
    min = heap.value
    return min, lazy_merge(heap.left, heap.right)
```

With repeated calls to get_min(), we only pay the high price the first time. Subsequently, the heap is already fixed. So we still have $O(1)$ complexity. With repeated calls to delete_min(), the fix is also almost done after the first call, but we do a lazy merge at the end of each deletion that we have to pay for at the next call, and since that involves fixing and (real) merging, we still pay a $O(\log n)$ time. (If we didn't, we would have a linear-time heap sort, which would tell us that we did something wrong somewhere.)

Binomial Heaps

Another heap structure that gives us logarithmic merge operations is the *binomial heap*. It is also known as the binomial queue, but it isn't a queue in the sense we defined it in Chapter 16, but rather a priority queue. The data structure is based on so-called *binomial trees* and a close correspondence between lists of these and the binary representation of integers. We will implement an ephemeral data structure—operations will modify the data structure rather than return a new and independent structure—but it is straightforward to change it into a persistent data structure. I have left those as exercises later in the section.

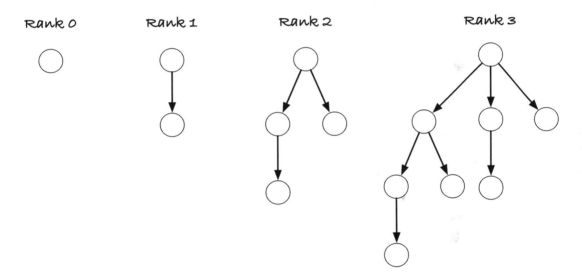

Figure 17-2. Binomial trees

A *binomial tree* is a tree that satisfies the heap property—that the value in a node is smaller than (or equal to) all values in its subtrees. For binomial trees, we do not restrict ourselves to binary trees—trees with two children—but we have a list of children. A binomial tree of rank 0 is a single node. A binomial tree of rank 1 is a node with a single rank 0 child. A rank 2 tree is a node with two children, one rank 1 child and one rank 0 child. In general, a rank r binomial tree has r children of rank 0 to $r - 1$; see Figure 17-2. The name *binomial tree* comes from the property that if you count the number of nodes at depth k from the root, there are $\binom{r}{k}$ of them, the binomial coefficient. I won't prove it since it isn't relevant for our usage here, but that is why they have the name.

We can represent a binomial tree like this:

```
class BT(object):
    def __init__(self, value, rank = 0,
                    sibling = None,
                    children = None):
        self.value = value
        self.rank = rank
        self.sibling = sibling
        self.children = children
```

This doesn't look exactly like the figures, but let me explain. Each node has a value and a rank, and those should be obvious. The `sibling` and `children` attributes are perhaps less straightforward. The idea with those is that we represent lists of trees similarly to how we represented linked lists, so `children` will be a reference to another BT object or None. If it is a BT object, then that is the head of the list of children. To get the remaining children, you run through `sibling` references, the way we used a next reference for linked lists.

We could represent the children of nodes as Python lists, but there is one operation that is much simpler to implement if we use linked lists, and we get an amortized complexity argument that we wouldn't get if we used Python's lists. Plus, of course, it is nice to see linked lists used in a nontrivial data structure.

A rank 0 tree contains one value. A rank 1 tree contains two, and a rank 2 tree contains four, and in general, a rank r tree will have 2^r nodes. It is obviously true for rank 0, so we can prove it by induction. Assume that it is true for all trees of rank less than r and consider a tree of rank r. It has one root node and then r children. Its children sum to $\sum_{i=0}^{r-1} 2^i$. Whatever this number is, it is a sequence of r 1 bits in the binary representation—the first bit in a binary number counts as 2^0, the second as 2^1, the third as 2^2, and so on, by the definition of binary numbers. If we add one to a string of all ones in a binary number, we set them all to zero and put a one at the position after the largest of the bits. With $\sum_{i=0}^{r-1} 2^i$ we have r 1 bits, at index zero up to $r - 1$. Adding one to that gives us the binary number with a one at index r and zero elsewhere, which is the binary representation for the number 2^r.

We can build a rank *r* tree from two rank *r*-1 trees by adding one of the trees to the children of the other:

```
def sib(x, y):
    # prepend x to y's sibling list (returns new node)
    return BT(x.value, x.rank, sibling = y, children = x.children)

def link(x, y):
    # link one tree as the first child of another
    assert x.rank == y.rank
    if x.value < y.value:
        return BT(x.value, x.rank + 1, children = sib(y, x.children))
    else:
        return BT(y.value, y.rank + 1, children = sib(x, y.children))
```

We have to add the tree with the largest root value to the one with the smallest to satisfy the heap property, so we compare the values before we link the trees. In this function, we create new nodes for the trees we would otherwise modify. We don't have to do this. We could simply update the attributes, but I will do this throughout to get us a persistent data structure.

Here, where we link one node under another, we only have access to the first child of a node. Later on, we want lists of trees to be sorted according to rank. We actually want them to be sorted in increasing order, but we also want to link in constant time, and when we link, the new child we add will have a rank that is one larger than the previous first child (because it has the same rank as the tree we modify, before we modify it). So what we will do is we keep children sorted with decreasing rank, so we can link in constant time, and when we need them to be sorted with increasing rank, we reverse them. The operation where we need this is expensive, so the reversal will not change the asymptotic running time.

If you think of rank *r* trees as corresponding to binary numbers where there is a 1 at the *r*th bit and zeros elsewhere, linking two *r*-1 trees this way corresponds to adding these two bits together, producing a number with one 1 bit at index *r*. Binary addition works like decimal addition, so adding these two numbers will add zeroes for the bits 0, ... , *r*-2, leaving those at zero, and then add 1 + 1 at index *r*-1. That gives us, in binary, a zero plus a bit we must carry over to index *r*. With these two numbers, that bit will be zero, so we put the carry bit there. The result is a number where index *r* is one and all other bits are zero, consistent with thinking about binomial trees at 1 bits in a binary number.

We cannot use binomial trees directly to implement a heap because they can only contain n values if n is a power of two. However, just as we can represent any number in binary, we can distribute n values into a list of some k binomial trees, $t_1, t_2, \ldots , t_k$, all with different ranks $r_1, r_2, \ldots , r_k$, so the bit each rank corresponds to matches the binary representation of $n : n = \sum_{i=1}^{k} 2^{r_i}$; see Figure 17-3.

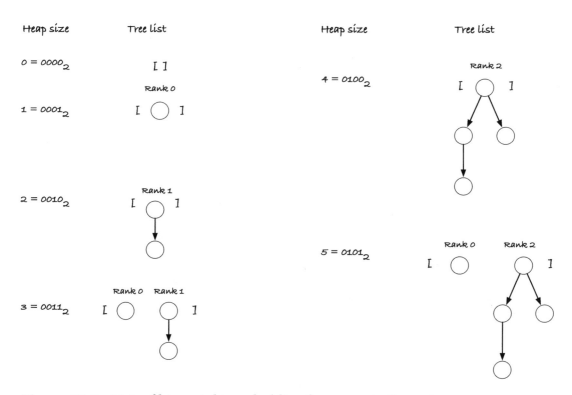

Figure 17-3. *Lists of binomial trees holding from zero to five values*

We will represent our heaps as lists of binomial trees sorted by rank (all with distinct ranks). Because of the relationship between binomial trees and the binary representation of a number, it should be clear that we can put n elements into the trees in the list such that the length of the list is $O(\log n)$—you only ever need $\lceil \log_2 n \rceil$ bits to represent the number n.

If we can implement all operations in time linear in the list of trees, then the operations run in $O(\log n)$ where n is the number of elements in the heap. It is trivial to check if a heap is empty—check if the list is empty—so we leave that for later when we wrap up lists in a Heap class. Of the other operations, adding a new value to a heap is the simplest. We will implement a more general function for inserting a tree into a heap. It will be useful later, and inserting a value only requires that we put it in a rank 0 tree and then insert the tree.

To see how we design the function, you must once again keep binary numbers in mind. If we are inserting a tree of rank r, we are adding a bit at index r to the number that the list represents. If there is a zero at that index, we can insert the tree, and we are done. If there is a one, we have to put a zero there and then carry a bit. When it comes to trees, carrying the bit means linking two trees and continuing with a rank $r + 1$ tree.

The function we write will not handle the insertion of any tree into a heap. The tree must have rank less than or equal to the smallest tree in the list. This can never be a problem for inserting a new value into the heap because we start with a rank 0 tree, and ranks don't go lower than that. When we use the function later for merging larger heaps, we will see that we also satisfy that property. This requirement is only there to make it easier to write the function, and if you want, you can extend it and skip past the lower-rank trees. We just don't need to handle it, so we don't bother. That means that we can start at the front of the list, check if the tree we insert has a lower rank, and, if so, return it and the list. Otherwise, we link the tree with the first in the list and continue inserting in the rest of the list:

```
def insert_tree(t, trees):
    # trees must be sorted in non-decreasing order.
    # t cannot have larger rank than trees.
    if trees is None: return t
    if t.rank < trees.rank:
        return sib(t, trees)
    else:
        return insert_tree(link(t, trees), trees.sibling)
```

The function clearly runs in linear time in the size of the list, so $O(\log n)$. Therefore, we can insert elements in logarithmic time.

This function, as you can see from the comment, requires that trees are sorted with increasing rank, so you cannot use it directly on the children of a tree—but then, you cannot add a single tree to the children of a binomial tree without violating the invariants of that tree anyway. It already has the number of children it is allowed to have. We use insert_tree() when we have a list of sorted trees; we do not use it to add trees as children to other trees. We only use link() for that.

We can also get the minimum element in $O(\log n)$. Here, we simply search through the list of binomial trees. They all satisfy the heap property, so the smallest value in each tree is in the root; thus, the smallest root value among the trees is the smallest value in the heap:

```
def get_smallest(trees):
    # trees must be non-empty
    x = trees
    y = trees.sibling
    while y is not None:
        if y.value < x.value:
            x = y
        y = y.sibling
    return x

def get_min(trees):
    return get_smallest(trees).value
```

This is a worse complexity than for leftist heaps, $O(\log n)$ vs. $O(1)$, but we will cache the smallest value in a Heap class later and get a constant-time operation.

We don't use merge() for insertion this time—we use insert_tree()—but we will still need the function for deletion and for constructing heaps in linear time.

We implement merge() like this:

```
def merge(x, y):
    # x and y must be sorted in non-decreasing rank.
    if x is None: return y
    if y is None: return x
    if x.rank < y.rank:
        return sib(x, merge(x.sibling, y))
    elif x.rank > y.rank:
        return sib(y, merge(x, y.sibling))
    else: # x.rank == y.rank:
        return insert_tree(link(x, y), merge(x.sibling, y.sibling))
```

This is a straightforward merge function where we put the smaller rank node in front of the larger rank node when they differ. When the rank is the same, however, we need to do a little more. There, we link the two nodes, creating a new node with a rank that is one larger than the two; then we merge the rest of the lists and insert the new node into it. Why this works, and what the running time is when we nest calls to merge() and insert_tree(), is not trivial, but this is where it helps to think about binary numbers.

Merging two lists of trees also corresponds to the manipulation of binary numbers; in this case, we are adding them. When you add two binary numbers, you start at the least significant bit and then, bit by bit, add your way up to the most significant bit. When you see 0 + 0, you get a 0 bit; when you see 0 + 1 or 1 + 0, you get a 1 bit; and when you see 1 + 1, you get a 0 bit, but you need to carry a bit to the next position. This is exactly how you were taught to add numbers in binary, except that there are only zero and one when we do it in binary.

When we merge trees, we only explicitly represent the 1 bit positions in the numbers we conceptually add, but we do the same thing. We scan from the lowest rank and upward. When we have two trees where one has a rank smaller than the other, we are adding a zero and a one (we don't see the zero plus zero positions because we do not represent them). For those 0+1 and 1+0, we have one 1 bit in the form of the tree with the smaller rank, and then we move onward. When we see two trees with the same rank, we have a 1 + 1 addition. We conceptually put a zero at the current rank by not putting any tree in the list here, and then we create a new tree that functions as the carry bit. It has a rank that is one larger, similar to how a carry moves one position up in the addition.

The way you were taught to add numbers, you probably added a carry immediately while adding the digits in the next position, but we don't have to do that. We can add numbers in any order, so you could simply handle the rest of the addition first and then apply the additional carry at the end. It is the latter we are doing here. It simplifies the function that we do not have to keep track of a "carry tree" as we merge, and we get the same result as long as we insert the carry tree when we are done with the merge.

Does this affect the running time? If you move along a number with carry bits as necessary, you clearly only spend time proportional to the number of bits in the number. With our function, we first compute the merge of the remainder of the lists, something that could take $O(\log n)$, and then we do another insert_tree() call, which could also take time $O(\log n)$. If we nest these calls many times, could we end up with something like $O(\log n \times \log n)$ time?

It is more efficient to carry the tree with you, so you don't need to modify the result of the merge afterward, but doing so requires much more bookkeeping. We would do it, if the asymptotic running time was worse, but it isn't. To see this, consider how far you can carry a bit. We have to carry a bit as long as the result of a single-bit addition is more than 1. When we insert the carry bit, we add one bit to the result of the merge, and we will keep carrying the bit as long as there is a 1 bit left from the merge. But if there was another position in the list where we introduced a "carry tree," then there would be no tree at that position; it is a 0 bit there. You cannot carry a bit any further than where the next carry started. The parts of the list we update with insert_tree() do not overlap, so the worst we can do with this merge() is to spend twice as long on updating the lists as we would if we carried the bit (and the simpler code where we do not handle carry bits is faster to run, so we don't even spend that much extra time).

This merge() implementation only runs in this time because we use linked lists. If we used Python's lists, then updating the result of merge() would not be proportional to the prefix we modify in the call to insert_tree(). If we had to copy suffixes of Python lists, the running time would be worse, and an implementation using Python lists is more complicated. You can still handle carry bits in a similar way, first identifying the positions where you need to carry a bit and then handling the addition without carry bits inside blocks, but it is more complicated.

To delete the smallest element, we find the tree that holds the element and remove it from the list. That removes more than the element in that tree's root, of course, so we need to get the other values back. To do that, we merge the children into the heap trees. The children of a node are sorted in decreasing rank, and to merge we need them in increasing rank, so we need to reverse them first. It is relatively straightforward to implement, however:

```python
def delete_tree(t, trees):
    if trees is None: return None
    if trees == t: return trees.sibling
    trees.sibling = delete_tree(t, trees.sibling)
    return trees

def reverse_trees(x):
    res = None
    while x:
        res = sib(x, res)
        x = x.sibling
    return res
```

```
def delete_min(trees):
    t = get_smallest(trees)
    trees = delete_tree(t, trees)
    return merge(reverse_trees(t.children), trees)
```

Reversing the children before we merge doesn't cost us more than the merge operation, so it doesn't affect the asymptotic running time.

Those were the operations. We can add elements, get the smallest value, and remove the smallest value (and we can always check if a list is empty). Now all that remains is wrapping the operations up in a class:

```
class Heap(object):
    def __init__(self, seq = ()):
        self.trees = None
        self.min = None
        for x in seq: # This is O(n), see below
            self.add(x)

    def is_empty(self):
        return self.trees is None

    def __bool__(self):
        return not self.is_empty()

    def get_min(self):
        return self.min

    def add(self, x):
        if self.min is None or x < self.min:
            self.min = x
        self.trees = insert_tree(BT(x), self.trees)

def delete_min(self):
    t = get_smallest(self.trees)
    min_val = t.value
    self.trees = delete_tree(t, self.trees)
    self.trees = merge(reverse_trees(t.children), self.trees)
```

```
# cache new min value
if not self.is_empty():
    t = get_smallest(self.trees)
    self.min = t.value
return min_val
```

The only new thing here is that we explicitly store the smallest value in the heap for constant-time get_min(). We need to get it in the constructor when we constructed the heap from a set of values; we might need to update it when we add an element, and we need to replace it with the next smallest value when we delete the smallest.

The binomial heap is more complex than the leftist heap, the operations run in the same worst-case time, and we even have to remember the minimal value to get constant-time get_min(), so why bother with this data structure at all? It has one redeeming property, and that is the insertion complexity. Both heap data structures insert in worst-case $O(\log n)$, but if you insert n elements, a leftist heap takes time $O(n \log n)$, while a binomial heap takes time $O(n)$ (which is why I didn't use the queue and merge trick in the preceding constructor).

The argument for this complexity is an amortization analysis. When we insert a new element, we start with a rank 0 tree, which we think of as a 1 bit at index zero in a binary number. We then link trees down the list until we find a place where we can put a new tree—corresponding to moving past a number of 1 bits until we find the first 0 bit. There, we insert the tree and conceptually set the 0 bit to 1. We flip a number of 1 bits to 0, up to $O(\log n)$ bits, and we set exactly one 0 bit to 1. Now imagine that every time we set a bit to 1, we pay a little more for doing that—enough to flip it back to 0 again. Then, when we move through a sequence of 1 bits when inserting and flip them to zero, we have already paid for that. Inserting n elements means that we set one 0 bit to 1 n times (while flipping some 1 bits to 0 as well). If flipping the 1 bits to 0 is paid for by flipping 0 bits to 1, then we spend in total $O(n)$ time. Each individual insertion can take time $O(\log n)$, but a sequence of n insertions doesn't take more than $O(n)$.

The argument does not hold if you interleave insertions and deletions. A deletion can introduce up to $\log n$ new 1 bits, and the following insertion could then be $\log n$. If you interleave insertions and deletions, both operations run in logarithmic time. So an operation of a insertions and b deletions will take $O(a + b \log n)$ if you insert all elements at the beginning, but if you interleave insertions and deletions, you will use $O((a + b) \log n)$.

The argument here is different from the constant-time insertion (merge) operations in a lazy leftist heap. There, we don't get constant-time operations; we borrow time that `get_min()` and `delete_min()` have to pay back later. With binomial heaps, you pay up front, and you have already saved up sufficiently to pay for an expensive operation when you get to one.

As implemented, the binomial heap we have here is a persistent data structure. We create new nodes every time we "update" a heap. The amortization argument, however, is only valid if you don't exploit this persistent nature. We can spend logarithmic time on an insertion, hold on to the previous version of the heap, and then insert an element again, taking logarithmic time. A sequence of insertions on progressive heaps will still take linear time, just not if you go back to previous instances and start again. Then the argument can fail.

If you don't mind having only an ephemeral binomial heap, you can get an amortized constant-time merge as well. The trick is to implement the operations lazy, so you don't keep the invariants at all time, but fix them when you need them. You keep the list of trees as a doubly linked list (which is why we don't get a persistent structure). When you insert, you don't bother with carrying the bit to update the trees, but you just put the new tree at the beginning of the list (or end; it doesn't matter). When you merge, you merge the two doubly linked lists in constant time. The problem is when you need to delete the minimal element. If you don't keep the trees sorted and have several trees with the same rank, this operation can take linear time. You need to fix the tree when you get to this operation.

First, you need to sort the trees in your list by rank and then fix adjacent trees with the same rank. The latter you can do similar to what we did in the preceding where there could be two of the same rank; there is a little more work to do, but it is not much. For sorting the trees by rank, observe that we have a bound on the rank, $\log n$, so we can do a bucket sort of the trees in $O(\log n + t)$ if there are t trees, and following that use $O(t)$ for linking trees with the same rank (there are t trees, and each can only be put in as a subtree in a link operation once). You can use the bins for this. As long as you have more than one tree in a bin, pick a pair, link them, and put the result in the next bin. Continue along with the bins like this. You can run out of bins if you need to carry a bit past the last one, but you can't get more than one tree in the overflow bin (think addition of binary numbers where you can't get a bit more than one above the largest in the input). Handle that as a special case. Running through the bins this way costs you $O(\log n)$, as there are $\log n$ of them, and that stays below the complexity of the sort.

Since t could be n—for example, if we start by inserting n trees before we do anything else—we can have n trees in the heap when we do our first delete_min(). But this is where an amortization argument comes into play. If we have t trees, then we must have inserted them. Let each insertion operation put one "computation" in the bank, and then we can pay for the cleanup when we do delete_min(), leaving the operation in $O(\log n)$. What about interleaving insertions and deletions? That is where the amortization argument for the (eager) heap fails. We clearly can insert again after a deletion in constant time, but we have spent our savings on the deletion, so could that be a problem? After a deletion, there are at most $2 \log n$ trees in the heap (there are at most $\log n$ in both the heap after we fix it and in the list of children in the heap we break up). Assume we insert s new trees after the deletion and before the next one. Then we have $t = s + O(2 \log n)$ trees when we delete again. That gives us the complexity $O(\log n + t) = O(\log n + 2 \log n + s) = O(\log n + s)$, so the analysis holds. After the deletion, we are back to $O(2 \log n)$ trees, so there was no trickery in a growing constant in front of the logarithm under the big-Oh. You always start with no more than $2 \log n$ trees after a deletion.

So if you want both fast insert and fast merge, then this lazy approach to binomial heaps gives you constant-time operations. The cost is that delete_min() goes from amortized logarithmic time instead of worst-case logarithmic time. For interactive programs, or programs that have to react in real time, this can be a problem, but for all others, it is the average time over many operations that matters, and there it is a small price to pay to move from worst-case to amortized running time.

Exercise: Implement a lazy binomial heap. You have to change the list representation with doubly linked lists to merge in constant time, and you need to change the deletion operation to sort and merge the trees in a list.

Exercise: Add exceptions for the binomial heap operations to match the leftist heap interface.

Binary Heaps

The way we implemented leftist heaps, we got a persistent data structure—except for when we wrapped it in a Heap class. However, that can easily be modified to make operations on that class persistent as well. We implemented binomial heaps with operations that mutated heaps, but you can turn it into a persistent data structure as an exercise. The next heap implementation we will see, *binary heaps*,[1] cannot easily be made persistent because of the way we represent the structure in a list of contiguous memory. We won't get a logarithmic-time merge() operation, but we will get $O(1)$ get_min() and is_empty() and $O(\log n)$ add() and delete_min(). We will still be able to construct a heap from n elements in $O(n)$, despite not having the merge() operation. The operations we need to implement are much simpler than those for the heaps we have already seen. Similar to how quick sort is generally faster than the other $O(n \log n)$ sorting algorithms because the operations it uses are simpler, this heap is also usually faster than those with more complex operations. If you do not need a persistent data structure or the constant-time insertions of binomial heaps, then this heap should probably be your first choice; it is simple and fast.

We still think of our heap as a tree, once again a binary tree, with the heap property, so each node has a value that is smaller or equal to all the values in its children. This time we will keep the tree as balanced as possible. This means that we fill up the tree level by level, or generation by generation if you prefer, so you don't add nodes at depth k from the root before you have added all possible nodes at depth k–1. You can't add grandchildren of the root before the root has both a left and a right child. You cannot add great-grandchildren before you have added all grandchildren and so on; see Figure 17-4. We won't explicitly represent the heap as a tree, only conceptually think about it as such. We can lay out the values in a list, in breadth-first order of the tree. You can always do that with a tree, but with a balanced tree like this, we can also use index arithmetic to determine where the children and parent of a node are. The parent of a child at index j is at $(j - 1)//2$, where the division is integer division. The left child of a node at index i is at $2i + 1$, and the right child is at $2i + 2$:

```
def parent(j):
    return (j - 1) // 2
def left(i):
```

---

[1]This is the heap that is implemented in Python's standard library heapq.

```
    return 2 * i + 1
def right(i):
    return 2 * i + 2
```

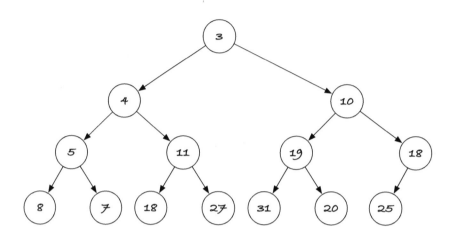

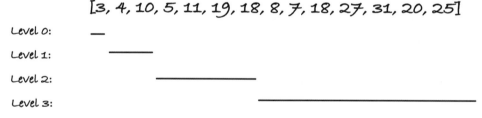

$$[3, 4, 10, 5, 11, 19, 18, 8, 7, 18, 27, 31, 20, 25]$$

Level 0:   —

Level 1:   ——

Level 2:   ————

Level 3:   ————————

Figure 17-4. *A binary heap and its list representation*

There is no need for a class to represent nodes; these three functions and a list contain all the information we would put in a Node class.

If we put our values in a list, we can add and remove values from the end of the list in constant time, so we will exploit that. When we add a value, we append it to the list. When we remove one, we swap the minimum element (the one at the first index in the list) with the one at the end of the element, and then we pop the last value. You can convince yourself that this keeps the right values in the list, but of course, these operations are likely to invalidate the heap property, so we need to restore it.

Consider insertion; see Figure 17-5. We append the value we add to the end of the list, which in the tree representation means that we add it to the right at the lowest layer or as the first node in the next layer if the lowest is full. In either case, we might now have a node with a value that is smaller than its parent. If that happens, we swap the values in the node and its parent. We don't break the heap invariant in the other child of the parent this way because all elements there are smaller than the parent and thus smaller than the new value we put there.

Now we have the new value one level higher in the tree, and there it could still be smaller than its parent. All the values in the subtree under our new value were smaller than the parent node before we inserted the new value, so they still are. Therefore, we can swap the new value with its parent without violating the heap property in that subtree. All the values in the other child of the parent are smaller than the parent, so swapping up the new value—smaller than the parent—won't violate the property there either. We can continue doing this, preserving the heap property everywhere except where the new value is until we either reach the root or find a smaller parent than the value. When we do that, we have restored the heap property. The time for this operation is obviously bounded by the height of the tree, which for a perfectly balanced binary tree is $O(\log n)$.

We can implement addition with these two methods (where self.nodes is the list that holds the values):

```
def fix_up(self, j):
    n = self.nodes # for shorter notation
    while j > 0:
        i = parent(j)
        if n[j] >= n[i]:
            # we satisfy the heap
```

```
        # property so we are done
        break
    # flip values
    n[i], n[j] = n[j], n[i]
    j = i # continue from parent
def add(self, x):
    self.nodes.append(x)
    self.fix_up(len(self.nodes) - 1)
```

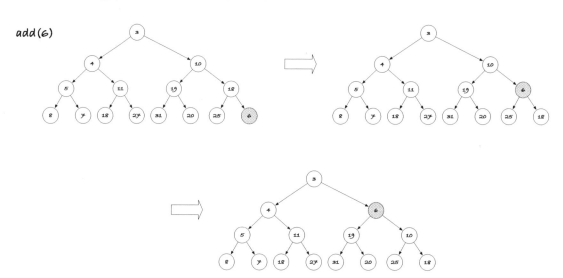

Figure 17-5. *Adding an element to a binary heap*

The fix_up() function is often called *swim* in the literature, but I think fix_up() is more informative about what it does.

For deleting the minimal value, we first swap the root with the rightmost value in the list and then pop away the minimal value; see Figure 17-6. Now we have a root that might be larger than its children. If we take its smallest child and swap with that, then the heap property is preserved for the other child—lowering the value of its parent doesn't change that all the values in the subtree are smaller. We might still violate the heap property in the new subtree we find ourselves in, but then we just continue with the same procedure. We continue until we find a place where we are larger than both children or until we reach the bottom layer. When we do, we have restored the heap property. Again, the running time is bounded by the height of the tree, so in $O(\log n)$. Asymptotically, the two operations take the same time, but when you move a value down, you have to compare it with both children, while when you move it up, you only have to compare the value with the parent, so insertion is actually twice as fast as deletion.

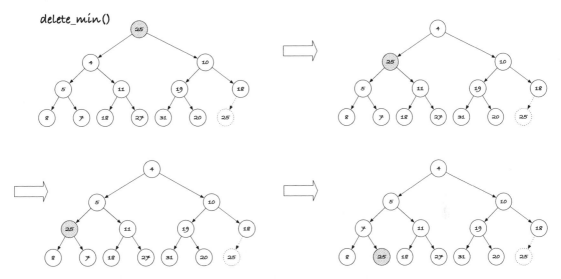

Figure 17-6. *Deleting an element in a binary heap*

We can implement deleting the minimal element like this:

```
def fix_down(self, i):
    n = self.nodes # for shorter notation
    while i < len(self.nodes):
        j, k = left(i), right(i)

        if j >= len(self.nodes):
            break # we don't have children, so done

        if k >= len(self.nodes):
            # we have a left child but not a right
            if n[i] > n[j]:
                n[i], n[j] = n[j], n[i]
            break # done

        if n[i] <= n[j] and n[i] <= n[k]:
            # children are larger, so we are done
            break
```

```
        # flip with the smallest
        if n[j] < n[k]:
            n[i], n[j] = n[j], n[i]
            i = j
        else:
            n[i], n[k] = n[k], n[i]
            i = k
def delete_min(self):
    m = self.nodes[0]
    self.nodes[0] = self.nodes.pop()
    self.fix_down(0)
    return m
```

The fix_down() function is called *sink* in the literature, but again I prefer the more informative name.

With a binary heap, we don't have an efficient merge. You can concatenate the two lists and create a new heap in time $O(n)$ (as I am about to show you), but you don't get a logarithmic-time merge. That also means that the queue plus merge approach to constructing a heap in linear time doesn't work. But there is another way, based on the same runtime analysis. We build the heap layer by layer, where each layer takes $n/2^i$ $\log_2(2^i)$ time. This is the same time as for the logarithmic merge, so obviously, we get the same result for this approach, namely, $O(n)$ construction time.

Start with the rightmost node and move leftward to progress through the levels from the bottom and upward to the root. At each node, fix values down:

```
def construct_heap(self):
    for i in reversed(range(len(self.nodes))):
        self.fix_down(i)
```

For each node you visit, you spend time logarithmic in its height, so you do $n/2^i$ $\log_2(2^i)$ work per level, giving us the linear running time.

The complete implementation looks like this:

```
def parent(j):
    return (j - 1) // 2
def left(i):
    return 2 * i + 1
```

```python
def right(i):
    return 2 * i + 2

class Heap(object):
    def construct_heap(self):
        for i in reversed(range(len(self.nodes))):
            self.fix_down(i)

    def __init__(self, seq = ()):
        self.nodes = list(seq)
        self.construct_heap()

    def is_empty(self):
        return len(self.nodes) == 0

    def get_min(self):
        return self.nodes[0]

    def fix_up(self, j):
        n = self.nodes # for shorter notation
        while j > 0:
            i = parent(j)
            if n[j] >= n[i]:
                # we satisfy the heap
                # property so we are done
                break
            # flip values
            n[i], n[j] = n[j], n[i]
            j = i # continue from parent

    def add(self, x):
        self.nodes.append(x)
        self.fix_up(len(self.nodes) - 1)

    def fix_down(self, i):
        n = self.nodes # for shorter notation
        while i < len(self.nodes):
            j, k = left(i), right(i)
```

```
        if j >= len(self.nodes):
            break # we don't have children, so done

        if k >= len(self.nodes):
            # we have a left child but not a right
            if n[i] > n[j]:
                n[i], n[j] = n[j], n[i]
            break # done

        if n[i] <= n[j] and n[i] <= n[k]:
            # children are larger, so we are done
            break

        # flip with the smallest
        if n[j] < n[k]:
            n[i], n[j] = n[j], n[i]
            i = j
        else:
            n[i], n[k] = n[k], n[i]
            i = k

    def delete_min(self):
        m = self.nodes[0]
        self.nodes[0] = self.nodes.pop()
        self.fix_down(0)
        return m

    def __repr__(self):
        return 'Heap(' + repr(self.nodes) + ')'
```

Exercise: We can modify this heap to give us an even smarter heap sort. We have implemented the heap, so it is the smallest element we have at the top, but you can naturally also put the largest element in each sub-heap at the root and have a delete_max() operation instead. If you take a list of values and want to sort them, you can first construct a heap of them, which means rearranging the values and nothing more. Then you iteratively delete the maximum, which includes putting it at the back of the list. Don't pop() the last element, but just keep an index that tells you where the current end of the nodes is. As you keep removing the elements, they are added to the end of the list in sorted order. When you have removed the last element, your list is sorted. This gives you a heap sort that doesn't use more space than the input itself. With merge sort, you use additional memory, and with quick sort, you only get an expected $O(n \log n)$ running time, but with this approach, you use $O(1)$ extra space and worst-case $O(n \log n)$ time. Implement this sorting algorithm.

The operations on a binary heap run in the same amortized complexity as a heap implemented as a search tree, except that we can build a heap from a sequence in linear time and need $O(n \log n)$ for the search tree, so merging heaps would be faster with a binary heap than with a search tree. Even if we don't need that, however, the heap is faster in practice—we don't have to spend time on restoring the balance after we modify the tree.

Adding Keys and Values

We use priority queues for more than heap sort, and in most applications, we need to add additional values to the queue. In such cases, what we have called the values so far are the *priority* we associate with each *value*. When we want the minimal element, it is the value associated with the minimum priority we want. We put values into the queue to get them out in order of priority, but the actual priority is often of lesser concern.

When we associate values with priorities, there are cases where we also want to manipulate the priority queue because of the values. In the following, I will distinguish between values we might put in the heap, keys we use to refer to them with, and priorities that determine which element is at the top of the heap. The keys must be unique in the priority queue since we will use them to index into it. We use all three when inserting data. We use keys to access the data from the heap. This is no different from a map (implemented as a dictionary in Python, and we saw how to build our own at the end of Chapter 14). We add operations to the heaps, however, that let us manipulate heaps using the keys. We will add an operation for deleting data based on a key—something we might do when we have scheduled an event or such in a priority queue, but we no longer want it. We will add another operation for changing the priority for a key, moving it closer to or further away from the top of the heap, an operation that is used in many algorithms. The updated interface for a heap will be this:

```
class Heap(object):
    def __init__(self, seq):
        # Build a heap where seq is (key, value,priority)
        # tuples
```

```
def is_empty(self):
    # Is the heap empty?

def __bool__(self):
    return not self.is_empty()

def add(self, key, value, priority):
    # Insert a value with a priority

def get_min(self):
    # Return the value with the lowest priority

def delete_min(self):
    # Delete the value with smallest priority and
    # return the value

def delete_key(self, key):
    # Remove the key,value,priority triplet
    # for the given key from the heap

def updated_priority(self, key, priority):
    # Change the priority for the value the
    # key refers to.
```

I will show you a complete implementation of the new interface using a binary heap, explain how you can do the operations with leftist and binomial heaps, and leave the implementation as exercises. I will leave it entirely as an exercise to modify a search tree to support the new operations.

Binary Heap

For jumping around the heap, we need these functions that we implemented earlier. They are not changed because we add new operations:

```
def parent(j):
    return (j - 1) // 2
def left(i):
    return 2 * i + 1
def right(i):
    return 2 * i + 2
```

To combine keys, values, and priorities in the heap, I will make a Node class. Using tuples or using a list for each of the three pieces of data is equally simple, but with a class, we are more explicit about how our data is tied together:

```
class Node(object):
    def __init__(self, key, value, priority):
        self.key = key
        self.value = value
        self.priority = priority
```

In the heap constructor, we add a dictionary, so we can map between keys and nodes. For the operations we do on nodes in an array, it is more convenient to have an index into the array rather than a reference to a node, so that is what we will store in the table. If we get a sequence as input, we iterate through it, create nodes, and append them to our underlying list, and we point the key to the index. Constructing the heap after that works as before:

```
class HeapMap(object):
    def __init__(self, seq = ()):
        self.key_map = {}
        self.nodes = []
        for i, (key, value, priority) in enumerate(seq):
            node = Node(key, value, priority)
            self.key_map[key] = i
            self.nodes.append(node)
        self.construct_heap()

def construct_heap(self):
    for i in reversed(range(len(self.nodes))):
        self.fix_down(i)
```

Nothing changes with is_empty(), but with get_min() we need to return the value of the node and not the node itself:

```
def is_empty(self):
    return len(self.nodes) == 0

def get_min(self):
    return self.nodes[0].value
```

Restoring the heap property when we have inserted or deleted relies on `fix_up()` and `fix_down()`. The only thing that changes there is that we need to look at nodes' priority instead of the nodes themselves, and we need to update the map from keys to indices when we swap two nodes:

```python
def swap(self, i, j):
    ni, nj = self.nodes[i], self.nodes[j]
    self.key_map[ni.key] = j
    self.key_map[nj.key] = i
    self.nodes[i], self.nodes[j] = nj, ni

def fix_up(self, j):
    while j > 0:
        i = parent(j)
        if self.nodes[j].priority >= \
                    self.nodes[i].priority:
            # we satisfy the heap
            # property so we are done
            break
        # flip values
        self.swap(i, j)
        j = i # continue from parent

def fix_down(self, i):
    while i < len(self.nodes):
        j, k = left(i), right(i)

        if j >= len(self.nodes):
            break # we don't have children, so done

        if k >= len(self.nodes):
            # we have a left child but not a right
            if self.nodes[i].priority > \
                    self.nodes[j].priority:
                self.swap(i, j)
            break # done
```

```
    if self.nodes[i].priority <= self.nodes[j].priority \
        and self.nodes[i].priority <= self.nodes[k].priority:
        # children are larger, so we are done
        break

    # flip with the smallest
    if self.nodes[j].priority < self.nodes[k].priority:
        self.swap(i, j)
        i = j
    else:
        self.swap(i, k)
        i = k
```

When we add data we have to wrap it up in a node, we have to update the map from keys to indices, but otherwise adding works as before:

```
def add(self, key, value, priority):
    n = len(self.nodes)
    node = Node(key, value, priority)
    self.key_map[key] = n
    self.nodes.append(node)
    self.fix_up(n)
```

Updating a priority can use the two fix methods directly. When we change the priority of a node, we fix up or down depending on how the priority changed:

```
def fix(self, i, previous_priority, new_priority):
    if previous_priority < new_priority:
        # we replaced with a larger value,
        # so we have to fix downwards
        self.fix_down(i)
    elif previous_priority > new_priority:
        # we replaced with a smaller value,
        # so we have to fix upwards
        self.fix_up(i)
```

```
def updated_priority(self, key, priority):
    i = self.key_map[key]
    node = self.nodes[i]
    old_priority = node.priority
    node.priority = priority
    self.fix(i, old_priority, priority)
```

The running time of update_priority() is clearly $O(\log n)$ since both fix_up() and fix_down() are in $O(\log n)$.

If we can delete a node at an arbitrary index, then we can either delete the minimal value (at index zero) or delete it by a key (by looking up the index in the keys table). Doing that is just a generalization of the delete_min() we had earlier. Get the node you want to delete, and move the rightmost node in the lowest layer to that position (and pop the old value). Then fix the heap starting at the index in question. The complexity is the same as the previous delete_min() because it uses only constant time moving a node and $O(\log n)$ on either fix_up() or fix_down(). Remember to delete the key from the key_map dictionary as well:

```
def delete_index(self, i):
    del self.key_map[self.nodes[i].key]
    old_priority = self.nodes[i].priority
    new_priority = self.nodes[-1].priority
    self.swap(i, -1)
    self.nodes.pop()
    self.fix(i, old_priority, new_priority)
```

The two delete operations from the interface are implemented in terms of the more general method:

```
def delete_min(self):
    min = self.nodes[0].value
    self.delete_index(0)
    return min

def delete_key(self, key):
    i = self.key_map[key]
    self.delete_index(i)
```

We end up with a heap where the complexity of all the previous operations remains the same and where the two new operations take logarithmic time.

Leftist Heaps

For leftist heaps, you get to implement most of the new functionality yourself, but I will give some hints first. The easiest way to add all three pieces of data to the heap is to put them in the heap nodes. To delete arbitrary nodes, as we will see, you will need to run upward in the heap, so you will need a parent pointer. I suggest that you use a weak reference, so the garbage collection will handle your heap efficiently. You can use the WeakRefProperty we implemented in Chapter 10 to assist the reference count garbage collection when we add parent pointers:

```python
def rank(node):
    if node is None:
        return 0
    else:
        return node.rank

class Node(object):
    parent = WeakRefProperty()

    def __init__(self, key, value, priority,
                 left = None, right = None):
        self.key = key
        self.value = value
        self.priority = priority
        self.left = left
        self.right = right
        self.rank = rank(right) + 1
        self.parent = None

        if left is not None:
            left.parent = self
        if right is not None:
            right.parent = self
```

Exercise: Update your implementation of a leftist heap, so you put keys, values, and priorities in nodes, update a map from keys to nodes, and make all the existing methods work by looking at nodes' priorities instead of values as they did before.

To keep the keymap up to date, I will recommend wrapping node construction in a method. If you only create nodes through the method, then it is easy to make sure that the table's key always points to the node where you used the key—it won't work, of course, if you have more than one node with the same key, but we didn't allow that anyway:

```
def make_node(self, key, value, priority,
              left = None, right = None):
    node = Node(key, value, priority, left, right)
    self.key_map[key] = node
    return node
```

You still need to remember to delete a key from the table when you delete the root node, but you can handle that explicitly there.

The changes to the heap don't affect the operations' running times. There is a constant-time table lookup (assuming that you use Python's `dict` class that is implemented as a hash table) and all the same operations.

After you have updated the entire heap, the remaining task is deleting and updating priorities. If we can delete efficiently, we can also update a priority efficiently—we delete the existing value and insert a new one:

```
def updated_priority(self, key, priority):
    value = self.key_map[key].value
    self.delete_key(key)
    self.add(key, value, priority)
```

That is what we will do here. If we tried to fix values up and down as we did for binary heaps, we wouldn't be able to control the running time. Leftist heaps are short on the right but can be arbitrarily long on other paths, so the best we could promise with that approach is $O(n)$ operations. We can, however, delete in logarithmic time.

If there is a node we want to delete, we can remove it and replace it with the merge of its two children. The heap property will be maintained because the root of the merged tree is less than its new parent, but the invariant on right paths can be violated and must be fixed. We don't know if the merged tree shrinks or grows; it can go either way depending on the merge, so there are many cases we need to consider when fixing the heap. We can get out of most of them by not putting in the merged tree until we fix it.

622

Consider Figure 17-7, where the gray node represents the node we want to delete. We will cut out the entire subtree, put its sibling as the parent's left tree, and set aside the subtrees a and b for later. We will fix the entire leftist invariant from here, and when we are done, we will merge the result with the merge of a and b. All three heaps will satisfy the leftist heap invariants at this point, so we can merge them in $O(\log n)$. If we can fix the tree in $O(\log n)$, then we can delete arbitrary nodes in logarithmic time.

Since we move the sibling of the deleted node to the left, if necessary, we can assume that the modified heap is always the right child as we move upward, applying the rules in Figure 17-8. In the figure, and in Figure 17-7, the arrow points to the node we have to process. The tree that we have already modified is always the right child of this node. In the top row, where the tree on the left has a larger rank than the one on the right (the rank of the tree we point to is one plus the rank of tree b), we have nothing left to fix. Here we don't end up with the modified tree on the right, but we will not continue processing either. In the next row, we violate the leftist property and must swap the pointed-to tree with its sibling. The tree is then on the right of the next node to process. In the last row, we are already in the right tree. We don't have to switch the trees because we already satisfy the leftist heap property here, but we have to continue processing because we might be violating it higher in the tree.

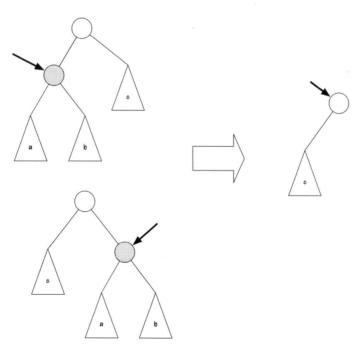

Figure 17-7. *Cutting out a subtree in a leftist heap*

We need a limit on how far we will process as we move up in the heap. The heap is not balanced, so we cannot simply rely on that to give us a logarithmic algorithm. However, when we stop fixing the heap, we do so because we have restored the leftist invariant. That means that the fixed heap's rightmost path cannot be longer than $O(\log n)$. And as you will notice from the figure, all the nodes we have processed must lie on that path. If all the nodes we touched lie on a path that is no longer than $O(\log n)$, we can't have done more than logarithmic work. Thus, we conclude that we can delete (and therefore also update the priority of a node) in $O(logn)$.

Exercise: Implement the deletion algorithm. Remember to update the keys table when you delete and remember to merge the deleted node children into the heap once you are done with fixing the heap.

If you go for a lazy implementation of the leftist heap, where you allow dead nodes in the heap and handle them when you merge in `delete_min()`, then you can delete much easier. Just tag the node as dead. You can do that in constant time, but you have to pay for it later. When you merge, you now need to handle dead nodes. You didn't need that earlier because we got rid of them when collecting the heaps to merge *before* we did the (eager) merge. If you merge now, you need to fix dead heaps as you meet them and continue the merge after they are fixed. In the merge, you pay $O(\log n)$ for each deletion you have done, so you pay the same price—but the implementation is substantially simpler.

Binomial Heaps

Exercise: Update the existing implementation with keys, values, and priorities. The complexity of all the operations remains the same because adding the data doesn't change the data structure's topology and thus any of the operations.

Changing the priority in a leftist heap is problematic but can be solved with a deletion and an insertion. For binomial trees, we need a different approach. Here, it turns out to be easy to decrease a node's priority, and the simplest implementation of delete is via decreasing a priority. For increasing a priority, we will delete and then reinsert, as we did for leftist heaps.

Without going through a decrease priority operation, it is not simple to delete a specific node. Binomial trees can only have a number of nodes that are a power of two, so we would have to fracture a tree completely and rebuild it to remove a node in the middle of one. However, if we can change the priority of a node to minus infinity, then we can use `delete_min()` to get rid of it, and that we know we can do in $O(\log n)$:

```
def delete_key(self, key):
    self.update_priority(key, float("-Inf"))
    self.delete_min()
```

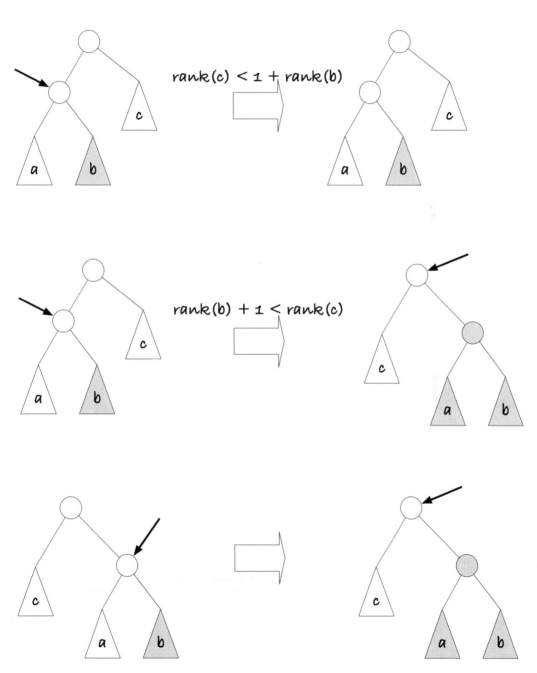

Figure 17-8. *Fixing the leftist property after cutting*

Here I used `float("-Inf")` for minus infinity. This will work for numbers but not other data types. You can implement a class that is smaller than all other classes, as we did for search trees in Chapter 14, if you want a general solution.

If we can update a priority in logarithmic time, then we also have deletion in logarithmic time. Decreasing a priority turns out to be similar to what we did with binary heaps: change the priority in a node and fix up. When you "fix up," you should swap the attributes of nodes rather than the nodes themselves. If you try to swap nodes, you need to update the list of children, which takes logarithmic time. If you have a pointer from a node to its parent and you swap the values in the nodes, you can swap them in constant time.

Exercise: Implement `fix_up()` for a binomial heap. For `fix_up()` you need a parent pointer.

For the complexity of `fix_up()`, notice that each time you move to the parent of a node, you find yourself in a tree with twice as many nodes. So each step up doubles the number of elements, and if you start with one node, you cannot double more than $O(\log n)$ times before you reach n nodes. This means that any path from a leaf to the root has at most $O(\log n)$ nodes, and consequently, we can run `fix_up()` in logarithmic time.

To increase a priority, we could use a `fix_down()` similar to the one from binary heaps. Obviously, like for `fix_up()`, also know that paths from the root to leaves are at most $O(\log n)$ long. Every time we move from parent to child, we have cut the number of nodes in the subtree we consider at least in half. But we need to search through up to $O(\log n)$ children in each node to find the minimal value, so you can swap with that. That takes time $O((\log n)\cdot(\log n))$ (which we usually write as $O(\log^2 n)$). We don't have to increase a priority this way, though; we can always change a priority by first deleting by key and then inserting with a new priority. We can already delete in $O(\log n)$ (by decreasing the priority to $-\infty$ and then `delete_min()`), and we know that we can insert in $O(\log n)$, so we can increase a priority with that approach instead.

Search Trees

If you do the following exercises, you will have adapted a search tree to the new priority queue interface.

Exercise: Add keys and values to a search tree and implement the bookkeeping needed to use them with the heap operations you already have.

Exercise: When deleting an arbitrary node, remember that you delete in a search tree based on the value in the node we sort by, which is the priority and not the key. Just using delete() from the search tree doesn't work. But if the map gives you the node for the key, you can delete the node as if you had searched for it. If you swap values between the node and the rightmost, you must also update the keymap. If you swap the nodes themselves, the keymap for the rightmost is still valid; the node just sits at another position in the tree. You still have to delete the original key from the map, though. Implement delete_key() for a search tree heap.

Exercise: In a search tree, the easiest approach is to delete and reinsert for update_priority() (since moving a node to a completely different part of the tree is hard). When deleting, remember that the key is not the priority, and the search tree delete operation needs the priority in the nodes. Implement update_priority().

Comparisons

With four heap implementations under our belt, we can compare their theoretical performance. The best choice will always depend on the given application, and the theoretical performance will help guide you to the best choice. Still, asymptotic complexity hides the exact cost of each operation, so you should also keep in mind that operations that have the same performance, in theory, can differ substantially in practice.

Search Tree

Assuming that the search tree is balanced, we get the following complexities:

- build_heap(): $O(n \log n)$ by building the heap element by element with insertions into the search tree.

- merge(): $O(n \log n)$ by adding the elements from one heap into the other element by element. It is possible to merge search trees faster if all elements in one are smaller than all elements in the other, but that is not the case here.

- add(): $O(\log n)$ using search tree insertion.

- get_min(): $O(\log n)$ if we search for the leftmost element and $O(1)$ if we cache the minimal element.

- delete_min(): $O(\log n)$ by finding the leftmost node and deleting it.

- delete_key(): $O(\log n)$ using search tree deletion.

- update_priority(): $O(\log n)$ by deleting the element and then inserting it again.

Leftist Heap

For the key operations, adding, getting, and deleting the minimum value, a leftist heap has the same complexity as a search tree, so if you don't need to efficiently build a heap from an existing set of elements or merge heaps together, there is not much benefit to this data structure. However, if you need merge, it is a simple data structure to get it, with a reasonable performance:

- build_heap(): $O(n)$ by merging sub-heaps in increasing order

- merge(): $O(\log n)$ by merging along right paths

- add(): $O(\log n)$ via merging

- get_min(): $O(1)$ since the minimal element is in the root of the heap

- delete_min(): $O(\log n)$ via merge

- delete_key(): $O(\log n)$ by deleting a tree, fixing the leftist property, and then inserting the children of the tree we deleted

- update_priority(): $O(\log n)$ via delete_key()

If you don't need delete_key() and update_priority(), the straightforward implementation gives you a persistent data structure.

Binomial Heap

A binomial heap improves the asymptotic complexity of add() (amortized), so if you need many additions, it is a better choice than the other two. It is often also faster than the leftist heap in practice, even though it looks like a more complex data structure with more expensive operations. They are only complex when we describe them; they are fast once implemented. If you implement the heap as a lazy data structure, you also get constant-time merge:

- build_heap(): $O(n)$ either by inserting element by element into the heap exploiting the constant-time insertion or by merging sub-heaps in increasing order.

- merge(): $O(\log n)$ by (eager) merging (similar to binary addition) or $O(1)$ amortized in a lazy implementation.

- add(): $O(1)$ amortized, as long as you do not interleave insertions and deletions. If you use the lazy implementation, you also get amortized constant time when you interleave insertions and deletions.

- get_min(): $O(\log n)$ if we search the roots of the heap's trees or $O(1)$ if we cache the minimal element.

- delete_min(): $O(\log n)$ via merging children.

- delete_key(): $O(\log n)$ if you decrease the priority to minus infinity and then use delete_min().

- update_priority(): $O(\log n)$ where you either use fix_up() when decreasing a priority or use delete_key() followed by add().

The binomial heap improves the theoretical performance compared to the other three heaps we have considered, but the relative performance in practice will depend on your application and your implementation of the heaps.

If you don't need delete_key() and update_priority() and you use linked lists instead of the mutable Python lists, a natural implementation gives you a persistent data structure (left as an exercise when we covered the data structure).

Binary Heap

If you don't need `build_heap()` and `merge()`—which are used less frequently than the other operations—this heap has the same complexity as the search tree, but without the overhead associated with balancing the search tree to keep the operations in logarithmic time. Because the heap is naturally balanced, the operations are faster in practice:

- `build_heap()`: $O(n)$ by building the heap from smaller to larger sub-heaps

- `merge()`: $O(n)$ if we take all the elements from the two heaps and rebuild a new heap from them

- `add()`: $O(n)$ by adding the value to the next available slot and fixing the heap property

- `get_min()`: $O(1)$ since the minimal element is at the top

- `delete_min()`: $O(\log n)$ by replacing the minimal element with the rightmost leaf at the bottom layer and then fixing the heap property

- `delete_key()`: $(\log n)$ similar to `delete_min()`

- `update_priority()`: $O(\log n)$ by changing the priority of a node and fixing the heap property with `fix_up()` or `fix_down()`

The nature of the binary heap precludes a persistent structure because we lay out the values in a list where we swap elements around.

Other Heaps

More complex heap data structures improve on the theoretical complexity. You can get constant time for all except the `delete_min()` operation. Usually amortized, but, for example, the *Brodal queue* gives you the operations in worst-case constant time. However, that data structure is only of theoretical interest as it is too complex to be efficient in practice. The *strict Fibonacci* heap also provides constant-time operations for all except `delete_min()`, and while you can use it in practice, it is generally considered slower than the *Fibonacci heap* it is based on, but that only provides amortized constant-time `update_priority()` and logarithmic `delete_min()`. A heap that gives us all operations in constant time is impossible—it would give us a linear-time heap sort—so heaps that give us constant-time operations for everything except `delete_min()` are theoretically optimal. In practice, the simpler heap data structures outcompete the more complex unless you have very large data sets because the hidden constant we ignore in the big-Oh notation is smaller.

Huffman Encoding

Many algorithms rely on priority queues, especially in more advanced searching techniques, but unfortunately, there wasn't room in this book to include them. Instead, I will show you a simple but useful data structure for encoding strings where we need a heap.

Huffman encoding is a method used to compress a string or to minimize bandwidth over a network (by compressing the data). The idea is this: you have some string, aabac, and you want to represent it with as few bits as possible. That means that you should use as few bits as possible for the most frequent letters in the string but at the cost of using more bits on infrequent letters. To achieve that, we construct a binary tree with the letters at the leaves. When we want to output the encoding for a letter, we follow the path down the tree, emitting a zero if we go left and a one if we go right. We can build a table that maps each letter to the string of bits/the path in the tree for encoding, and when we read the resulting bit string back, we can run down the tree until we reach a leaf, write the letter we find there, and then go back to the root to start decoding the next letter.

In the string aabac, the letter a is the most frequent—it appears three times—while b and c only appear once. We should therefore prefer to encode a with fewer bits. With three letters, we can encode them in 2 bits (because we can represent up to four letters with 2 bits), and we can encode a as 1 and use 2 bits for b and c, for example, 00 for c and 01 for b. The corresponding tree is shown in Figure 17-9. The optimal encoding is not unique; you can flip the bits and, in larger examples, have different encodings for letters deeper in the tree, but it will efficiently compress a string. It is optimal for encoding strings symbol by symbol, but better approaches exist if you compress larger strings as single symbols.

You can represent a Huffman tree like you would any binary tree, but add a letter to the leaves:

```
class HuffmanTree(object):
    def __init__(self,
                 left = None, right = None,
                 letter = None):
```

```
        self.left = left
        self.right = right
        self.letter = letter
```

Then you can create the tree in Figure 17-9 like this:

```
tree = HuffmanTree(
    HuffmanTree(
        HuffmanTree(letter = 'c'),
        HuffmanTree(letter = 'b')
    ),
    HuffmanTree(letter = 'a')
)
```

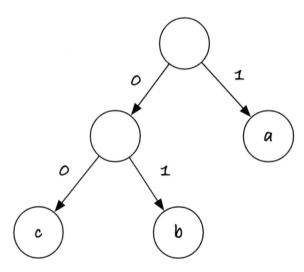

Figure 17-9. *Huffman encoding of "aabac"*

For encoding, we can build a table of letters to bit strings with a tree traversal

```
def build_table(tree, bits = None, table = None):
    # Create the table and bits unless we have them
    # already
    bits = bits if bits is not None else []
```

```
table = table if table is not None else {}

if tree.letter is not None:
    # We are in a leaf
    bit_encoding = ''.join(bits)
    table[tree.letter] = bit_encoding
    return table
else:
    bits.append('0')
    build_table(tree.left, bits, table)
    bits.pop()
    bits.append('1')
    build_table(tree.right, bits, table)
    bits.pop()
    return table
```

and encode strings letter by letter:

```
def encode(tree, string):
    table = build_table(tree)
    bits = [table[x] for x in string]
    return ''.join(bits)
```

To decode a string, move down the tree until you find a leaf (a node that contains a letter), emit it, and go back to the root:

```
def decode(tree, bit_string):
    node = tree
    string = []
    for bit in bit_string:
        if bit == '0':
            node = node.left
        if bit == '1':
            node = node.right
        if node.letter is not None:
            string.append(node.letter)
            node = tree
    return ''.join(string)
```

It is when we want to build the tree that a heap comes in handy. You can create an initial heap containing the count of occurrences for each letter combined with the leaf node containing the letter. The letters with the fewest occurrences will have the highest priority, but we are going to build the tree bottom-up, so that is what we want. Now you repeatedly pick out two trees and join them, giving the new tree the priority that is the sum of the occurrences in the child trees. It is because we need to use the sum of counts that we store the counts as well as the trees as values in the heap (if delete_min() gave us the priority as well as the value we store in the heap, then we could get it from there, but that is not how we implemented the heaps). As you build the Huffman tree this way, the less frequent letters go to the tree's bottom, while the more frequent letters end up closer to the root:

```
from collections import Counter
def build_huffman_tree(string):
    # Calculate the number of occurrences
    # of each letter
    counts = Counter(string)
    # Now build the priority queue
    # (just use the letter as the key)
    queue_input = []
    for letter, count in counts.items():
        queue_input.append((
            # Key (not used)
            letter,
            # Value -- (count, leaf tree)
            (count, HuffmanTree(letter = letter)),
            # Priority
            count
        ))
    heap = HeapMap(queue_input)
    # Construct the huffman tree from the heap

    while True: # We explicitly return from the loop
    left_count, left = heap.delete_min()
    if heap.is_empty():
        return left
```

```
right_count, right = heap.delete_min()
print(left, right)
heap.add(
    # Key -- we don't use it
    None,
    # Value
    (left_count + right_count,
    HuffmanTree(left, right)),
    # Priority
    left_count + right_count
)
```

CHAPTER 18

Conclusions

Well, that's it. You have reached the end of the book. But I hope you haven't reached the end of your programming and algorithmic career.

The techniques we have covered in this book should give you a better understanding of how a computer stores and manipulates data and how different choices in how you implement this will affect the performance of programs you write. We have used Python to implement the algorithms we have explored, but the techniques are general. Built-in data structures will vary between different programming languages, and different software libraries will provide alternative algorithms and data structures. Still, you should now be able to understand the trade-offs when choosing between alternatives.

Most commonly used algorithms and data structures will be available in any high-level programming language environment, so you will rarely need to implement them yourself. However, knowing the pros of cons of different choices is essential for using your programming environment effectively, and this knowledge is likely to be the most important lesson you can take from this book. When you cannot use algorithms and data structures readily available in your programming environment, you now also have the skills to adapt them to your needs and, when necessary, to implement alternatives that better suit your needs.

Python is a very high-level programming language, and it has many powerful features that make programming using it more effective. I have only used a few of those constructions in this book, where they are necessary to write code that a Python programmer would expect to read, so what you have learned here can most likely be directly translated to other programming languages, if needed. That being said, different programming languages have idiomatic ways of solving problems. If you learn a new programming language, it is worthwhile to learn these idioms. You shouldn't simply use the constructions from Python in a different language. If you simply use the language constructions you know from Python, you can write programs in other languages, but you will be using only the subset of constructions common to both Python and other languages, and that is not the most effective approach. It is always worthwhile to know

© Thomas Mailund 2021
T. Mailund, *Introduction to Computational Thinking*, https://doi.org/10.1007/978-1-4842-7077-6_18

the idioms in the language you are using. Since this book is primarily about computing and algorithmic thinking, I have used the simplest constructions in Python that will get the job done. Still, if you want to become an effective Python programmer, you should learn the more advanced features you have in the language. Likewise, if you want to be an effective R or Ruby programmer or a programmer in any other language, you should learn the idiomatic ways of solving problems in those languages. The computational issues you need to deal with, however, will be the same.

Python is not a particularly fast language, by which I mean that Python programs are likely to run slower than similar programs in more low-level languages. As a general rule of thumb, this is usually the case; programs written in a high-level language are likely to run slower than programs written in a low-level language. This isn't always the case and depends strongly on the interpreter or compiler you use, but it is usually the case. If you want complete control of how your programs are executed, so you can get the utmost performance out of your computer, you will need to program in a very low-level language—close to the iron, as we say. This, however, is usually not an effective way to solve problems. Programs written in a low-level language might run faster, but it comes at a cost in programmer time—programs written in a high-level language are much faster to write. There is always a trade-off between programmer efficiency and program efficiency, and optimizing at a low level is rarely worth the effort.

Occasionally, it is worthwhile to optimize key hotspots in a program by rewriting those parts in a lower-level language, but choosing the right algorithms and the right data structures is much more important. A low-level implementation of a slow algorithm will always be outperformed by a smarter algorithm implemented in a high-level language when you work with large data. You now have the skills to evaluate algorithms and to choose the best for your tasks. That is much more important than the skills to program in a low-level language.

Where to Go from Here

After reading this book, you should be familiar with basic programming and a few more advanced programming tricks; you should be able to construct and reason about algorithms and understand how a computer represents and manipulates data. These are the cornerstones of writing efficient programs and effectively analyzing data. There is much more to learn to use computers and Python optimally, however.

The next step you should take in becoming a better programmer or data scientist depends on what you wish to achieve in your future use of Python. If you have gotten a taste for programming and want to start developing software, you should pick up some books on Python programming. I have only covered the aspects of Python that I needed to teach you about algorithms and data structures. Python has many features to make your programming more effective or aimed at making your software more reusable. At the very least, you should learn more about object-oriented programming and how classes and objects can be used to develop software that can be extended to solve many more problems than it was originally developed for.

If your aim is to get into heavy-duty scientific programming, you will need to study some numerical analysis, so you understand the issues you might run into when working with floating-point numbers. You will also want to get familiar with working with linear algebra and possibly tensors. Your next step should almost certainly be to get familiar with numpy and scipy.

If you would rather learn more about data science in Python, your next step should be learning about the pandas package. This is a Python package for manipulating and analyzing structured data of the kind you will usually run into in data analysis projects.

If you want to get into machine learning, then scikit-learn and tensorflow are good places to start. After that, you might want to study the keras package, which is a very efficient implementation of *deep learning neural networks*, a technology used in many high-profile artificial intelligence projects.

If you are more interested in learning further about algorithms and computational complexity, you should instead find some textbooks on those topics. Many good ones cover topics beyond what we have covered in this book, but they are typically not based on Python. Most general algorithmic books are language agnostic and use pseudo-code instead of real programming languages.

There are many places to go from here, and those are some directions you might want to go in if you want to learn more about computing and Python.

I will just end the book by wishing you good luck, and if you have found the book useful, I would love to hear from you.

Index

A

© Thomas Mailund 2021
T. Mailund, *Introduction to Computational Thinking*, https://doi.org/10.1007/978-1-4842-7077-6

C

E

Printed in the United States
by Baker & Taylor Publisher Services